Dictionary of Literary Biography

Documentary Series

Yearbooks

1980 edited by Karen L. Rood, Jean W. Ross, and Richard Ziegfeld (1981)

1981 edited by Karen L. Rood, Jean W. Ross, and Richard Ziegfeld (1982)

1982 edited by Richard Ziegfeld; associate editors: Jean W. Ross and Lynne C. Zeigler (1983)

1983 edited by Mary Bruccoli and Jean W. Ross; associate editor: Richard Ziegfeld (1984)

1984 edited by Jean W. Ross (1985)

1985 edited by Jean W. Ross (1986)

1986 edited by J. M. Brook (1987)

1987 edited by J. M. Brook (1988)

1988 edited by J. M. Brook (1989)

1989 edited by J. M. Brook (1990)

1990 edited by James W. Hipp (1991)

1991 edited by James W. Hipp (1992)

1992 edited by James W. Hipp (1993)

1993 edited by James W. Hipp, contributing editor George Garrett (1994)

1994 edited by James W. Hipp, contributing editor George Garrett (1995)

1995 edited by James W. Hipp, contributing editor George Garrett (1996)

1996 edited by Samuel W. Bruce and L. Kay Webster, contributing editor George Garrett (1997)

1997 edited by Matthew J. Bruccoli and George Garrett, with the assistance of L. Kay Webster (1998)

1998 edited by Matthew J. Bruccoli, contributing editor George Garrett, with the assistance of Denis Thomas (1999)

Concise Series

Concise Dictionary of American Literary Biography, 6 volumes (1988-1989): *The New Consciousness, 1941-1968; Colonization to the American Renaissance, 1640-1865; Realism, Naturalism, and Local Color, 1865-1917; The Twenties, 1917-1929; The Age of Maturity, 1929-1941; Broadening Views, 1968-1988.*

Concise Dictionary of British Literary Biography, 8 volumes (1991-1992): *Writers of the Middle Ages and Renaissance Before 1660; Writers of the Restoration and Eighteenth Century, 1660-1789; Writers of the Romantic Period, 1789-1832; Victorian Writers, 1832-1890; Late-Victorian and Edwardian Writers, 1890-1914; Modern Writers, 1914-1945; Writers After World War II, 1945-1960; Contemporary Writers, 1960 to Present.*

Dictionary of Literary Biography® • Volume Two Hundred Eight

Literature of the French and Occitan Middle Ages: Eleventh to Fifteenth Centuries

Dictionary of Literary Biography® • Volume Two Hundred Eight

Literature of the French and Occitan Middle Ages: Eleventh to Fifteenth Centuries

Edited by
Deborah Sinnreich-Levi
Stevens Institute of Technology
and
Ian S. Laurie
Flinders University

A Bruccoli Clark Layman Book
The Gale Group
Detroit, Washington, D.C., London

Printed in the United States of America

The paper used in this publication meets the minimum requirements
of American National Standard for Information Sciences–Permanence
Paper for Printed Library Materials, ANSI Z39.48-1984. ∞™

Library of Congress Cataloging-in-Publication Data

Literature of the French and Occitan Middle Ages: eleventh to fifteenth centuries / edited by
Deborah Sinnreich-Levi and Ian S. Laurie.
p. cm.–(Dictionary of literary biography: v. 208)
"A Bruccoli Clark Layman book."
Includes bibliographical references and index.
ISBN 0-7876-3102-7 (alk. paper)
1. French literature–To 1500 Dictionaries. 2. French literature–To 1500–Bio-bibliography Dictionaries.
3. Authors, French–To 1500–Biography Dictionaries. 4. Provençal poetry Dictionaries. 5. Provençal
poetry–Bio-bibliography Dictionaries. 6. Troubadours–Biography Dictionaries. I. Sinnreich-Levi,
Deborah M. and Laurie, Ian S. II. Series.
DF221.C8L57 1999
840.9'001–dc21   99–24673
                                                                                                        CIP

10 9 8 7 6 5 4 3 2 1

"Il ne scet riens qui ne va hors."
—Eustache Deschamp
Ballade 1311

Contents

Plan of the Series

... Almost the most prodigious asset of a country, and perhaps its most precious possession, is its native literary product—when that product is fine and noble and enduring.

Mark Twain*

The advisory board, the editors, and the publisher of the *Dictionary of Literary Biography* are joined in endorsing Mark Twain's declaration. The literature of a nation provides an inexhaustible resource of permanent worth. We intend to make literature and its creators better understood and more accessible to students and the reading public, while satisfying the standards of teachers and scholars.

To meet these requirements, *literary biography* has been construed in terms of the author's achievement. The most important thing about a writer is his writing. Accordingly, the entries in *DLB* are career biographies, tracing the development of the author's canon and the evolution of his reputation.

The purpose of *DLB* is not only to provide reliable information in a convenient format but also to place the figures in the larger perspective of literary history and to offer appraisals of their accomplishments by qualified scholars.

The publication plan for *DLB* resulted from two years of preparation. The project was proposed to Bruccoli Clark by Frederick G. Ruffner, president of the Gale Research Company, in November 1975. After specimen entries were prepared and typeset, an advisory board was formed to refine the entry format and develop the series rationale. In meetings held during 1976, the publisher, series editors, and advisory board approved the scheme for a comprehensive biographical dictionary of persons who contributed to North American literature. Editorial work on the first volume began in January 1977, and it was published in 1978. In order to make *DLB* more than a reference tool and to compile volumes that individually have claim to status as literary history, it was decided to organize volumes by

From an unpublished section of Mark Twain's autobiography, copyright by the Mark Twain Company

topic, period, or genre. Each of these freestanding volumes provides a biographical-bibliographical guide and overview for a particular area of literature. We are convinced that this organization—as opposed to a single alphabet method—constitutes a valuable innovation in the presentation of reference material. The volume plan necessarily requires many decisions for the placement and treatment of authors who might properly be included in two or three volumes. In some instances a major figure will be included in separate volumes, but with different entries emphasizing the aspect of his career appropriate to each volume. Ernest Hemingway, for example, is represented in *American Writers in Paris, 1920–1939* by an entry focusing on his expatriate apprenticeship; he is also in *American Novelists, 1910–1945* with an entry surveying his entire career, as well as in *American Short-Story Writers, 1910–1945, Second Series* with an entry concentrating on his short stories. Each volume includes a cumulative index of the subject authors and articles. Comprehensive indexes to the entire series are planned.

Since 1981 the series has been further augmented by the *DLB Yearbooks*, which update published entries and add new entries to keep the *DLB* current with contemporary activity. There have also been *DLB Documentary Series* volumes which provide biographical and critical source materials for figures whose work is judged to have particular interest for students. One of these companion volumes is entirely devoted to Tennessee Williams.

We define literature as the *intellectual commerce of a nation:* not merely as belles lettres but as that ample and complex process by which ideas are generated, shaped, and transmitted. *DLB* entries are not limited to "creative writers" but extend to other figures who in their time and in their way influenced the mind of a people. Thus the series encompasses historians, journalists, publishers, book collectors, and screenwriters. By this means readers of *DLB* may be aided to perceive literature not as cult scripture in the keeping of intellectual high priests but firmly positioned at the center of a nation's life.

DLB includes the major writers appropriate to each volume and those standing in the ranks behind them. Scholarly and critical counsel has been sought in deciding which minor figures to include and how full their entries should be. Wherever possible, useful references are made to figures who do not warrant separate entries.

Each *DLB* volume has an expert volume editor responsible for planning the volume, selecting the figures for inclusion, and assigning the entries. Volume editors are also responsible for preparing, where appropriate, appendices surveying the major periodicals and literary and intellectual movements for their volumes, as well as lists of further readings. Work on the series as a whole is coordinated at the Bruccoli Clark Layman editorial center in Columbia, South Carolina, where the editorial staff is responsible for accuracy and utility of the published volumes.

One feature that distinguishes *DLB* is the illustration policy—its concern with the iconography of literature. Just as an author is influenced by his surroundings, so is the reader's understanding of the author enhanced by a knowledge of his environment. Therefore *DLB* volumes include not only drawings, paintings, and photographs of authors, often depicting them at various stages in their careers, but also illustrations of their families and places where they lived. Title pages are regularly reproduced in facsimile along with dust jackets for modern authors. The dust jackets are a special feature of *DLB* because they often document better than anything else the way in which an author's work was perceived in its own time. Specimens of the writers' manuscripts and letters are included when feasible.

Samuel Johnson rightly decreed that "The chief glory of every people arises from its authors." The purpose of the *Dictionary of Literary Biography* is to compile literary history in the surest way available to us—by accurate and comprehensive treatment of the lives and work of those who contributed to it.

The *DLB* Advisory Board

Introduction

The adjective *middle* in *Middle Ages* requires some comment at the outset. Sixteenth-century Renaissance authors used it as a way of dismissing the long period between the fall of the Roman Empire at the end of the fifth century A.D. and their own times as an unfortunate interruption in the history of Western civilization. Greco-Roman civilization constituted one side of the divide, the Renaissance the other, but there was nothing of any consequence to be found between the two. Even if no one accepts this view now, the term has become accepted and can only be given meaning if it is understood that France began life as a colony of the Roman Empire.

This judgment, which offers a truncated version of France's history, is admittedly unjust to the centuries of Celtic civilization that preceded the conquest by Julius Caesar in 51 B.C. of the province the Romans called Gaul as well as to the civilizations that flourished in France twenty thousand years and more before the arrival of the Celts; for example, the civilization that produced cave paintings in places such as Lascaux. Civilization does not spring fully grown from a void but develops organically over the centuries. The explanation for the Renaissance judgment, however, is that the Roman conquest involved a fundamental break with the past. The assimilation of the Celts (the Romans called them Gauls) into the Roman Empire was one of the most permanent successes of any empire in the whole of recorded history. Their leaders were given administrative posts and encouraged to learn Latin and to send their sons to Rome to receive an elegant education. Under Roman tuition the Gauls replaced their towns with Roman cities planned on the military-camp, geometric-grid system still visible in the ancient centers of some French cities; they built Roman roads, theaters, amphitheaters, aqueducts, and villas; they even copied Roman fashions in hairstyles. They were not, however, mere imitators, since they rapidly became significant contributors to the empire in most domains ranging from architecture, sculpture, and literature down to more practical matters such as commerce. They even invented the wine barrel for the empire, exported their own vintages in it, and alarmed the emperor in Rome as to whether Italian wine could stand up to the competition.

So far had the collective memory of the Celtic past disappeared that even the triumphal arches that the Romans constructed at the principal entrances to the cities in Gaul, situated to remind all who passed beneath them of the Roman yoke, became symbols of civic pride from that time forward. Most decisively of all, the Celtic language was progressively abandoned in favor of Latin. French and Occitan, like the other romance languages, such as Italian, Spanish, Portuguese, Catalan, Romanian, and Romansch, have their origins in the spoken Latin of Gaul.

A great part of this Roman heritage remained with the Gauls even after the collapse of the empire at the end of the fifth century and the coronation of Clovis, the chief of the Salian Franks, one of the Germanic tribes who had invaded Gaul. Clovis married a Catholic princess, Clotilda, in 493 and soon after, in 496, converted to Catholicism, so beginning the alliance of the French monarchy with the Catholic Church that lasted until the French Revolution of 1789. Clovis gave the name of his tribe to the country now called France as well as to the French language, although his kingdom was situated as much in the northern, Germanic-speaking lands from which he had come, where romanization had been less complete than in the south. The spoken Latin that was to become French survived, however, and eventually predominated, albeit influenced by some Germanic speech habits and vocabulary. The Latin of the educated classes also survived in modified forms, remaining the language of the Church and also the principal means of communication for all serious matters: politics, religion, philosophy, administration, theology, mathematics, science, medicine, and more. A separate volume in this series would be required to do justice to all the works written in medieval Latin in France during the Middle Ages, so this volume confines itself principally to authors who wrote in the dialects of French and Occitan. The term *Occitan* is modern, not medieval, and was designed to include all the dialects of the South of France, dispelling the illusion that the dialect Provençal was the only or the most important dialect used. These languages are distinguished by the words its speakers used for "yes": *oc* in the south is characteristic of Occitan, *oïl* or *oui* in the north of French. Both words are corruptions of the Latin *hoc; oïl* added the sound of the second person singular, masculine pronoun *il*. The languages of the south, the "languedoc," gave their name to that southern region by which it is still known today. All of these dialects, including Picard, Anglo-Norman, Rhodanien, and the eponymous Francien, are linguistically noteworthy, but for the student of literature it is sufficient to note that at least from the twelfth century onward, both in the south and in the north, writers attempted to avoid the more prominent features of their own dialects in favor of a kind of court language or koine that might have greater currency. In the north this language was Francien, the dialect of the Ile de France around Paris. Francien owed its prominence to its geographic centrality and courtly speakers. In the south the koine adopted was that of the western part of the region, a dialect sometimes called *Limousin* in the twelfth century. It might well have become as important as Francien except for the destructive influences of the Albigensian Crusade. Francien's dominance in the north was never seriously challenged except by Picard during a brief period at the end of the twelfth century and the beginning of the thirteenth.

Neither French nor Occitan has a literary history before the ninth century if one judges solely by what texts have survived. Linguistically, they must have had an existence as they gradually became distinguishable from the spoken Latin of Gaul. What can be known about the first authors who wrote in them? Up until the eleventh century at least, it is sometimes assumed that they must have been clerics of some kind: priests, monks or nuns. This is because the collapse of the empire in France at the end of the fifth century had also involved the collapse of the Gallo-Roman educational system, its schools and universities. The only organization capable of taking on this function was the church. Cathedral schools, monasteries, and convents provided the only systematic education available at least until the foundation of the first universities at the end of the twelfth century. The theory was that society fell into three classes: the clergy, who did the praying and the studying; the nobility, who did the fighting; and the peasants (90 percent of the population), who did the working. It would, however, be imprudent to infer that the only literate people in France until the eleventh century must have been practicing clergy. Those few, perhaps no more than 5 percent of the population, who had received a clerical education often worked in the service of the nobility rather than that of the church. At least some of them must have attempted to share their skills with their patrons. The most famous example is that of the emperor Charlemagne in the eighth century. His biographer, Eginhard, writing in Latin, records that he once heard his master weeping loudly late at night. Alarmed, Eginhard entered Charlemagne's bedroom to

find the great man vainly wrestling with a quill in an attempt to learn to write.

Perhaps appropriately, the earliest piece of French prose concerns a nonaggression pact made between two of Charlemagne's descendants, Louis the German and Charles the Bald in 842, a pact known as the Strasbourg Oaths. The writer, Nithard, born shortly before 800, was not an ecclesiastic, belonged to the nobility, and actually died in battle in 844. Nithard, a careful historian who wrote in Latin, may well not have been the author of the French translation, which he called the *romana lingua* (Roman language) version of the Strasbourg Oaths. Informal translations from Latin into the vernacular must already have been common at this period, at least for the homilies which followed the reading of the gospel in the Gallican rite of the Mass: such translation into the *rusticam romanam linguam* (Roman as spoken by the common people) was expressly demanded by the Carolingian Reform Synods of 813.

The first surviving poem in French, the *Cantilène de sainte Eulalie* (St. Eulalie's Canticle), dates from the end of the ninth century and was inspired by Latin models but is not a translation of any that have survived. The heroine, a woman of principle, defied the "pagan" authorities until they had no alternative other than to have her put to death. Given the fact that the work may have been sung in church, there is every reason to believe that the author was an ecclesiastic.

It was not until about the middle of the eleventh century, however, that it is possible to begin the study of French and Occitan literatures. The lives of the saints–hagiographies–appear first. Hagiography is a genre which had been common in Latin even before the collapse of the empire, but the fascinating biographies presented do not constitute reliable history; rather, they fill a sociodidactic purpose. In *La Vie de saint Alexis* (The Life of St. Alexis), probably written about the middle of the eleventh century, the misogynist hero flees from his new bride on their wedding night in order to escape sin and dies seventeen years later in Rome, rendered unrecognizable by fasting and disease, a beggar in his own parents' house. Nothing is known about the author of the didactic work, but it is again reasonable to suppose an ecclesiastical author.

The first real masterpiece of French literature is also the greatest epic poem or chanson de geste in the French language, *La Chanson de Roland* (The Song of Roland). The earliest extant manuscript, written in an Anglo-Norman dialect, may have been copied about 1100. It recounts the defeat of Charlemagne's rearguard by the Muslims at Roncevaux in the Pyrenees more than three hundred years earlier, in 778. The author may or may not have been Turoldus, who is named in the text but who was perhaps no more than the performer or the jongleur of the work, sung as it probably was in the dining halls of the nobility. It is possible that he (no one has suggested a she) was a cleric, but if so, it is curious that he had as keen an eye for the fine detail of hand-to-hand combat as some modern boxing commentators. Like Eulalia and Alexis, Roland sacrificed his life (not to mention the lives of all his thousands of men) to principle, and the author comes close to presenting him as a martyr for the Christian faith. Roland could, however, have summoned reinforcements but refused lest he gain a reputation for cowardice. The author is careful to distance himself from what might appear to us as self-indulgent decision-making and leaves the judgment to his audience. This gives the author a claim to be the very first in the long line of writers called *moralistes* by the French. This term is not adequately translated in English as "moralist," because these French writers frequently construct situations that have strong ethical implications but do not preach at their readers, preferring to allow them to judge the matter for themselves. Other epics in verse followed in the twelfth century, and there were also prose versions of them from the thirteenth century and later but nothing to equal the *Roland*. From this point on, it is possible to give an account only of the most representative authors who wrote in French or Occitan.

At about this same period, the end of the eleventh century, the south of France produced the first great literary movement in a romance language. Writing in Occitan, the southern French lyric poets, the troubadours, who produced their finest works in the twelfth century, started something not unlike a social as well as a literary revolution. Even if the greater part of this was safely confined to their verse, their message was explosive. The accepted medieval view of marriage was that it was an arranged business contract breakable only by the death of one of the partners. All sexual relations had to take place within that exclusive contract. The most common theme in the troubadours, responding to these somewhat emotionless views, was that true love, the most ennobling of all emotions, had to exist outside the bonds of matrimony. This theme eventually swept through most of Europe. The label "amour courtois" or "courtly love" was not a troubadour coinage: nineteenth-century scholars adopted Gaston Paris's 1883 neologism to denote the linguistically packed *fin'amors* (refined love) and perpetuated a limited definition heavily influenced by Italian poets of the thirteenth and fourteenth centuries, who often excluded the physical aspects of love in their poetry. The troubadours and their northern imitators, the trouvères, who adopted their themes and forms, are the first authors about whom anything is known. Many of them were of the

local nobility, men who seem to have preferred to exchange the swords of the northern French epic for the quill and for the pleasures of civilized living in the courts and towns. Some were women; some were clerics; and some were members of a new class, the bourgeoisie, which became more and more important with the revival of the towns and which was compelled to be literate if only to manage business. Such was the prestige of the troubadours that efforts were made to write their biographies a century and more after their deaths in the thirteenth-century *Lives of the Troubadours*. As is the case with the earlier saints' lives, however, most of these tell us rather more than can safely be accepted about their subjects.

Northern French literature was to be changed almost beyond recognition under the influence of the troubadours, not least when they and their patrons were massacred or driven out of the country in the thirteenth century as a result of the Albigensian Crusade, an infamous episode in which the south was invaded by armies from the north on the pretext of suppressing a rival religion, Catharism. These heresies, one needs to note, had nothing to do with troubadour poetry. It was not only that the northern French produced their own courtly poets, the trouvères, but also that the courtly vein found expression in different works, for example in the first and also the finest religious play of the French middle ages, *Le Jeu d'Adan* (The Play of Adam). The author, perhaps an Anglo-Norman, wrote the play between 1146 and 1174 for performance just outside a church entrance, probably linking it to the liturgy. The Devil, who tempts Eve to eat the apple in the Garden of Eden, speaks with all the charm of a troubadour lover.

There is similar language in much longer and more substantial works, notably the first French novels. The south had produced one great novel in verse, the *Flamenca,* but nothing to rival the fashion for this and other narrative genres in the north in the twelfth century. Greatest among these verse novelists of the entire Middle Ages in France was Chrétien de Troyes. He too was possibly a cleric who spent his career at the courts of Marie de Champagne, and later Philippe de Flandre, around 1160 to 1185. Chrétien situated his characters in a mythical Celtic past at the court of King Arthur. Magicians, giants, enchanted springs, and assorted otherworldly presences abound but turn out to be little more than exotic Celtic stage props. The real business of Chrétien's romances is much more quotidian. His favorite subjects are matrimonial: Should a husband view his wife as more or less important than his job? Should a wife venture to tell her husband the truth about his reputation? Chrétien draws heavily throughout on the southern French courtly tradition. The gain is in plausibility: there are even the beginnings of real analysis of the inner life of the characters. Chrétien was not the only French novelist of his century; there were others who dealt with very different themes, for example mythical versions of the heroes of classical antiquity, but he towers above all of these.

Another substantial narrative work that is at least the equal of any of Chrétien's novels is the anonymous *Aucassin et Nicolette,* probably written between the last quarter of the twelfth century and the first half of the thirteenth, surviving in a manuscript in the Picard dialect. It escapes all standard generic classification, calling itself a *chantefable,* or "song and story." It consists of verse passages with music to be sung and prose passages to be read or perhaps mimed. A love story in which the young protagonists are separated and then reunited after exotic adventures, it includes good-humored parody of most of the literary genres examined so far, especially the epic and the romance. Andreas Capellanus's *De Amore* (On Love), written about the end of the twelfth century, must be mentioned, in spite of the fact that it is in Latin, because of its influence on writers in the vernaculars, as demonstrated by the fact that it was soon translated into French, Italian, Catalan, and German. Nothing is known about the author except that he may have been a cleric in the service of the king of France or of the countess of Champagne. An ostensible self-help book on how to proposition women, complete with model conversations, it has been a favorite with students of the European Middle Ages, whatever their views on its outrageous sexism.

Narrative genres shorter than that of the novel are another twelfth- and also thirteenth-century specialty. Here the most considerable figure in the twelfth century was a woman: Marie de France, who probably spent some of her career in England at the court of Henry II (1133–1189). She produced moralizing fables, often based on similar tales drawn from classical antiquity, but her best works were her lays. These short narrative poems, inspired according to her by the Celtic narrative songs of Brittany, are remembered not so much for the stories told but for the disquieting circumstances in which her most memorable characters lived, caught in destructive relationships. As a good *moraliste,* Marie subjects the values of her time to scrutiny but leaves any judgment on them to her readers.

The story of Tristan and Iseut also belongs to a mythical version of the Celtic past. Marie de France treats part of it, but more substantial poetry and later prose on the theme exists, for example mid-twelfth-century versions in verse by Béroul, who may have been a Norman at the English court and also by Thomas d'Angleterre, who seems to have known London well and who may have been a cleric. The popularity of the story in medieval times was great, perhaps because it had a strong tendency to explode the conventions of feudal honor as well as those derived from the troubadours in favor of love as a destructive and fatal passion.

There is a very different spirit in another series of verse and later prose narratives that belong to an animal-epic genre, the *Roman de Renart* (Romance of Renart), which flourished from about 1170 to 1250. The genre has something in common with the fable as revived from antiquity by Marie de France, but the animals generally have no real moral lesson to teach but rather offer a cynical commentary on the corrupt ways of what is in reality the human world.

Toward the end of the twelfth century and for the rest of the Middle Ages in France, prose began to assume increasing importance. Geoffroi de Villehardouin, a nobleman born about 1150 near Troyes, rose to high office as maréchal de Champagne and, as such, played an important role in the Fourth Crusade, which was diverted from its ostensible goals to defeat the Muslims in the Middle East to the conquest of fellow Christians in Constantinople in 1204. The diversion may have required some form of justification, and this may explain why Villehardouin decided to record it in one of the first historical chronicles in French, *La Conqueste de Constantinople* (The Conquest of Constantinople). This official version of the events may be contrasted with that of a much less important knight on the same crusade, Robert de Clari, who probably lived from about 1170 to some time after 1216.

At the turn of the thirteenth century, cynicism was a hallmark of the work of Rutebeuf, about whom little is known but whose parodies and polemics draw readers' eyes back to a time when the crusades were a noble endeavor and clerics could be trusted. Rutebeuf died around 1235 but left poems voicing both traditional piety and ascerbic social commentary: the Holy Land should be liberated; the mendicant orders, eyed askance.

Also at this time and more so in the thirteenth century, short narratives became very popular in another genre, the fabliau. The first of these poems that have survived were written by Jean Bodel (1165?–1210) from Arras. Little is known about him except that he appears to have made his living as a poet in the service of the local municipal establishment. His fabliaux, like those of the thirteenth and early fourteenth centuries, are domestic comedies set in a world largely inhabited by deceivers and victims, often presented in situations that once would have been called obscene. Jean Bodel was also the author of more-considerable works than these—for example, a verse epic called *La Chanson des Saisnes* (Song of the Saxons, last third of the twelfth century) that combines the epic, the courtly, and the fabliau traditions. He also wrote a miracle play, *Le Jeu de Saint Nicolas* (The Play of St. Nicholas), probably about the year 1200. For modern readers, the best parts of this lively play may well be the tavern scenes in the author's native Arras. The works that reveal most about his personality are his *congés* (farewells) to society when he learned that he had contracted leprosy, which prevented him from carrying out a plan to go on the Fourth Crusade.

Arras appears to have had an intense literary life in the thirteenth century because it also produced one of the major poets and musical composers of the French Middle Ages, Adam de la Halle. He was probably born in Arras between 1240 and 1250 of a fairly wealthy bourgeois family, married about 1270, and may have died in Italy in 1288 but could still have been alive in 1306 at the English court in Westminster. Like Bodel, he also wrote a *congé* to Arras but of a very satirical kind. Perhaps his most interesting literary works are his plays. His *Jeu de la Feuillée* (Play Among the Leaves), which he may have had performed in Arras in 1276, is the first truly secular play in French literature. In it he brings to life what he claims are his own problems (should he abandon his wife and study in Paris?) as well as those of the people he knew in Arras, but there are also elements of fantasy and magic in it that would not be out of place in William Shakespeare's *A Midsummer Night's Dream* (1600). Another play, the *Jeu de Robin et Marion* (Play of Robin and Marion) was presented about 1284 in Naples, where he had followed his patron Robert of Artois. This play is a dramatized version of a pastourelle, a lyric genre that had already been popular in France in the twelfth century, in which a shepherdess is propositioned by a wandering knight. Since the dialogues in this play are set to music, it has, perhaps, a claim to be the first surviving comic opera in Europe. He was a very considerable musical composer, and since he was given the title of master of arts, a degree acquired perhaps in Paris at the Sorbonne, it is possible to claim that he was one of the very first creative writers in French to have had a university degree.

The intellectual life of thirteenth-century universities is reflected much more directly in *Le Roman de la Rose* (The Romance of the Rose), one of the most copied manuscripts of the Middle Ages and also a work much translated into other languages: Geoffrey Chaucer, for example, produced an English translation. The work has two parts: the first, often attributed to Guillaume de Lorris, about whom nothing is known and who may not even have existed, turns the troubadour tradition into a narrative allegory; the second, attributed to Jean de Meun, an author who had probably taken a university degree and who had died by 1305, brings the story to a conclusion in which the attempt to possess the lady's love is eventually successful but which also includes an extensive excursus into thirteenth-century academic knowledge. The most unpleasant feature of the second part is a contempt for women, an unhappy reflection of the misogyny that disfigured most European universities until at least the nineteenth century.

An unusual prose work, the life of a saint by one of his friends, was written by Jean de Joinville, who was born in 1225 and became seneschal of Champagne. He had been on crusade with Louis IX, St. Louis, and was eventually persuaded, after the king's death, to set down his memories of the king at some time soon after 1272. Joinville was not an uncritical observer of the saint and produced a biography of him, *Vie de saint Louis* (Life of St. Louis, 1309), which has a claim to be one of the best in French literature of any period.

The fourteenth century is marked in verse by the gradual adoption of fixed forms, of which the most common are the ballade, rondeau, chanson royale, virelay, and lay. No French poet was more instrumental in this change than the great poet and musical composer, Guillaume de Machaut, born about 1300 of a humble family, perhaps in the little town of Machault in Champagne. He died in 1377, the most famous poet and composer of his age. Machaut acquired a university education, became a cleric and worked in the service of kings and princes, and following them on journeys as far afield as eastern Europe. His most productive period was spent as canon at the cathedral of Rheims. As a French poet he drew his inspiration largely from the courtly tradition and was also the last French poet to insist that poetry and music were indivisible. His disciple and admirer, Eustache Deschamps, born around 1340 in Vertus in Champagne, did not agree with his master on this point, and in his *Art de dictier* (Art of Composing Poetry) separated them in a way that was to become definitive, partly because he believed that the music of words was superior to instrumental music, partly because he thought that the complications of musical accompaniments needlessly restricted the audience for verse. Unlike Machaut, Deschamps used his poetry to reflect the problems of his age, the Hundred Years' War with England, the Black Death, urban and peasant revolts, and even his own problems with toothache. At least in his interest in the events of his age (he was also a considerable traveler), he may be compared with the greatest prose writer of the fourteenth century, Jean Froissart. Froissart was born in Valenciennes about 1337 and died some time after 1404. Like Machaut, he was a cleric who traveled widely, spending much time in England. His monumental prose masterpiece, *Les Chroniques de France, d'Angleterre et des pais voisins* (The Chronicles of France, England, and Neighboring Countries), presents the events between the coronation of Edward III in 1327 and the death of Richard III in 1400.

The beginning of the fifteenth century is marked by the first recorded literary battle in French literature, the *Querelle de la Rose* (Quarrel over the *Roman de la Rose*). The popularity of the work had led to attacks on what were construed as the misogynist points of view of the second part, and these surfaced in a debate in 1402 between Jean de Montreuil and the greatest woman poet since Marie de France, Christine de Pizan. Christine, who attacked the misogyny of the work, had a supporter in no less a personage than Jean Gerson (1363–1429), a courageous theologian who was the chancellor of the University of Paris. Christine, born in Italy about 1364, came to France with her father about 1368, married there, was widowed when she was about twenty-five, and lived by her literary talents thereafter. Among her many works in verse and prose, it is that part in which she attempts to correct prejudices against women which gives her a claim to be the first explicitly feminist writer in French although this may be a little unjust to Marie de France and to certain women troubadours, the *trobairitz*.

The fifteenth century produced two of the greatest poets in French literature of any period, Charles d'Orléans and François Villon. Charles (1394–1465), who was the duke of Orléans, ranks as the only major poet in any French royal family from Clovis at the end of the fifth century to the abolition of the French monarchy in the nineteenth. The catastrophic event of his life was his capture by the victorious English at the Battle of Agincourt in 1415. Held for ransom by the English until 1440, he was left with little to do other than develop his creative gifts. His poetry, in the courtly tradition, offers a private world in which the various aspects of his personality assume an allegorical life of their own, disputing one with the other in situations in which the poet himself figures largely as a passive observer. François Villon was a poet of an entirely different kind. Born in Paris, probably in 1431 or 1432, and later entrusted by his mother to a learned cleric, Guillaume de Villon, whose name he adopted, he had taken his bachelor of arts at the University of Paris by 1449 and master of arts in 1452. These academic successes should have assured him of a comfortable position in life, but the main references to him in contemporary records are in the law courts. Robbery, violence, even murder were among the charges. He disappears from the records in 1463. His poetry is that of the city, with specific reference to crime, debauchery, violence, misfortune, poverty, despair, and death.

Urban life is also a common theme in a great theatrical genre of the fifteenth century, the farce. In theme, these short plays have something in common with the earlier fabliaux, but they are often more clearly localized. In the greatest surviving farce, *La Farce de Maistre Pierre Pathelin* (The Farce of Master Pierre Pathelin), probably written between 1456 and 1469, the complex confidence tricks played by Pathelin on an unscrupulous draper, matched by the even greater cunning of an illiterate shepherd, may well have been written for a Parisian audience, perhaps including university students, who were best placed to appreciate jokes about the law and the foreign languages spoken at the university. Other theatrical genres existed in the fifteenth century, notably morality plays and also mystery plays, which presented religious themes often drawn from the New Testament.

The fifteenth century also produced the first great French novel in prose, *Le Petit Jean de Saintré,* by Antoine de La Sale. The author was born in 1385 or 1386, the illegitimate son of a minor nobleman and a woman from somewhere near Arles. He entered the service of Louis of Anjou and followed him to Italy for a period. His best work is this novel, which is a sort of bildungsroman. In it, a young man learns whatever young men need to learn from an older woman. The extent to which French prose had developed since the thirteenth century is also evident in the work of Philippe de Commynes, certainly the greatest French historian of the fifteenth century. Born in 1447 near Aire of a family of prominent Burgundian bureaucrats, he entered the service of the duke of Burgundy, Charles the Bold, but betrayed him by transferring his allegiance to the duke's rival, the king of France, Louis XI. Eventually disgraced, Commynes used his retirement to complete his great work, *Memoires* (Memoirs), from 1489 to 1498. He died in 1511. Unlike Froissart in the fourteenth century, Commynes attempted to draw lessons from the historical events to which he had been witness. Like Macchiavelli after him, he may have had the ambition to provide guidance for those in high office. It is in his reflections on events, personalities, and systems of government that he deserves a place as an historian and not simply that of a chronicler, who might have been as much at home in modern times as in the fifteenth century.

The present volume cannot hope to present all French authors in the Middle Ages but only those who are of first importance, which entailed a difficult selection process, choosing only a few writers from some six hundred years of literary history first on the grounds of distinction but also insofar as they represent elements in the French tradition that continue to modern times. The primary objective of *Dictionary of Literary Biography 208: Literature of the French and Occitan Middle Ages, Eleventh to Fifteenth Centuries* is to impart a knowledge of at least part of an immense field; within the constraints of this volume, we have sought to demonstrate that French writers have been working within the longest continuous tradition in European literature.

This volume would not exist without the erudition and energy of the contributors. They deserve the special gratitude of the editors. They were asked to participate because of their distinction in their fields, which also means that they are all busy people. The scholarship they have brought to this task will be obvious from the following pages.

–Deborah Sinnreich-Levi and Ian S. Laurie

Acknowledgments

This book was produced by Bruccoli Clark Layman, Inc. Karen L. Rood is senior editor for the *Dictionary of Literary Biography* series. Jan Peter F. van Rosevelt was the in-house editor. He was assisted by Samuel W. Bruce, R. Bland Lawson, and James F. Tidd.

Production manager is Philip B. Dematteis.

Administrative support was provided by Ann M. Cheschi, Tenesha S. Lee, and Joann Whittaker.

Accountant is Sayra Frances Cox. Assistant accountant is Angi Pleasant.

Copyediting supervisor is Phyllis A. Avant. The copyediting staff includes Ronald D. Aiken II, Brenda Carol Blanton, Worthy Evans, Thom Harman, Melissa D. Hinton, William Tobias Mathes, Raegan E. Quinn, and Audra Rouse. Freelance copyeditors are Brenda Cabra, Rebecca Mayo, Nicole M. Nichols, and Jennie Williamson.

Layout and graphics supervisor is Janet E. Hill. Graphics staff includes John F. Henson.

Office manager is Kathy Lawler Merlette.

Photography editors are Margo Dowling, Charles Mims, Scott Nemzek, Alison Smith, and Paul Talbot. Digital photographic copy work was performed by Joseph M. Bruccoli.

SGML supervisor is Cory McNair. The SGML staff includes Tim Bedford, Linda Drake, Frank Graham, and Alex Snead.

Systems manager is Marie L. Parker.

Database manager is Javed Nurani. Kimberly Kelly performed data entry.

Typesetting supervisor is Kathleen M. Flanagan. The typesetting staff includes Karla Corley Brown, Mark J. McEwan, Patricia Flanagan Salisbury, and Kathy F. Wooldridge. Freelance typesetters include Deidre Murphy and Delores Plastow.

Walter W. Ross and Steven Gross did library research. They were assisted by the following librarians at the Thomas Cooper Library of the University of South Carolina: Linda Holderfield and the interlibrary-loan staff; reference-department head Virginia Weathers; reference librarians Marilee Birchfield, Stefanie Buck, Stefanie DuBose, Rebecca Feind, Karen Joseph, Donna Lehman, Charlene Loope, Anthony McKissick, Jean Rhyne, and Kwamine Simpson; circulation-department head Caroline Taylor; and acquisitions-searching supervisor David Haggard.

Literature of the French and Occitan Middle Ages: Eleventh to Fifteenth Centuries

Dictionary of Literary Biography

Peter Abelard
(circa 1079 – 21 April 1142?)

Joel N. Feimer
Mercy College

See also the Abelard entry in *DLB 115: Medieval Philosophers*.

WORKS: *Introductiones Parvulorum* (circa 1105)

Logica Ingredentibus (circa 1112–1130)

Standard edition: *Pietro Abelardo: Scritti di logica,* edited by Mario Dal Pra, Pubblicazioni della Facolta di lettere e filosofia dell'Universita di Milano, no. 34 (Florence: La nuova Italia, 1958).

Edition in English: "The Glosses of Peter Abailard on Porphyry (Introduction)," translated, with an introduction, by Richard McKeon, in his *Selections from Medieval Philosophers,* volume 1 (New York: Scribners, 1929), pp. 202–258.

Sic et Non (circa 1117–1128)

Standard edition: The prologue is in *Sic et Non: prologus,* edited by Blanche Boyer and Richard McKeon (Chicago: University of Chicago Press, 1976–1977).

Theologia Summi Boni (circa 1118–1120)

Standard editions: *Petri Abaeladi opera theologica,* 2 volumes, edited by Eligius M. Buytaert (Turnhout, Belgium: Brepols, 1969); *Theologia Summi Boni: tractatus de unitate et trinitate divina: Abhandlung über die göttliche Einheit und Dreieinigkeit,* edited, with an introduction and notes, by Ursula Niggli (Hamburg: F. Meiner, 1988).

Logica Nostrorum Petitioni Sociorum (circa 1122–1125)

Tractatus de Intellectibus (circa 1122–1125)

Hymnarius Paraclithensis (circa 1123–1140)

Standard edition: *Peter Abelard's "Hymnarius Paraclithensis,"* 2 volumes, edited by Josef Szoverffy, Medieval Classics: Texts and Studies, nos. 2–3 (Albany, N. Y. & Brookline, Mass.: Classical Folia Editions, 1975).

Edition in English: *The Hymns of Abelard in English Verse,* translated by Jane Patricia (Lanham, Md. & London: University Press of America, 1986).

Theologia Scholarium, also known as *Introductio ad Theologium* (circa 1125–1130)

Manuscript: Oxford, Balliol College Ms. 296, ff. 1r–60v includes the only copy of the final and longest version of this work.

Dialectica (circa 1130–1142)

Standard edition: *Petrus Abaelardus, Dialectica, First Complete Edition of the Parisian Manuscript,* edited by L. M. De Rijk (Assen, Netherlands: Van Gorcum, 1956; revised, 1970).

Expositio Symboli Apostolorum (circa 1132–1134)

Expositio Orationis Dominicae (circa 1132–1134)

Expositio Fidei Sancti Athanasii (circa 1132–1134)

Commentaria in Epistolam Pauli ad Romanos (circa 1133)

Manuscript: Oxford, Balliol College Ms. 296, ff. 80r–160v, dating from the mid fourteenth century.

Historia Calamitatum Meum (circa 1133)

Standard editions: *Historia Calamitatum,* edited, with an introduction, by J. Monfrin (Paris: Librairie Philosophique J. Vin, 1959). "Peter Abelard's *Historia calamitatum,*" edited by Joseph T. Muckle, *Medieval Studies,* 12 (1950): 163–213; republished with a preface by Etienne Gilson (Toronto: Pontifical Institute of Medieval Studies, 1954).

Editions in English: *The Letters of Abelard and Héloïse: With a Particular Account of Their Lives, Amours, and Misfortunes: To Which Are Added Poems by Pope, Madan, Cawthorne, etc.* (Chiswick, U.K.: Whittingham, 1824); *The Letters of Abelard and Héloïse Now First Translated from the Latin,* translated

Peter Abelard (drawing from a manuscript; Paris, Bibliothèque Sainte-Genevieve, Ms. 1108, fol. 56r)

by C. C. Scott-Montcrieff (London: Chapman, 1925); *Historia calamitatum: The Story of His Misfortunes and The Personal Letters,* translated, with an introduction and notes, by Betty Radice (London: Folio Society, 1977). *Historia calamitatum: The Story of My Misfortunes: An Autobiography by Peter Abelard,* translated by Henry Adams Bellows (St. Paul, Minn.: Boyd, 1922);

Problemata Heloissae cum Petri Abalaerdi solutionibus (circa 1134)

Standard edition: "Abelard's Rule for Religious Women," edited by T. P. McLaughlin, *Medieval Studies,* 18 (1956): 241–292.

Expositio in Hexameron (circa 1134–1136)

Dialogus Petri Abælardi, also known as *Dialogus Inter Philosophum, Iudaeum, et Christanum* (circa 1136)

Manuscript: Oxford, Balliol College Ms. 296,

ff. 161r–189v divided into two parts and titled *Collationes* (Collocations, or Dialogues).

Standard editions: *Dialogus inter philosophum, Iudeaum, et Christianum,* edited by Rudolf Thomas (Stuttgart-Bad Cannstatt: Fromann-Holzboog, 1970); *Dialogo tra un filosofo, un giudeo e un cristiano,* edited, and translated into Italian, by Cristina Trovbo (Milan: Rizzoli, 1992); *Gesparach eines Philosophen, eines Iudenund eines Christen,* edited, and translated into German, by Hans-Wolgang Krautz (Frankfurt am Main: Insel, 1995).

Editions in English: *Dialogue of a Philosopher with a Jew and a Christian,* translated by Pierre Payer (Toronto: Pontifical Institute of Medieval Studies, 1979); *Ethical Writings: His Ethics, Or "Know Yourself" and Dialogue Between a Philosopher, a Jew, and a Christian,* translated by Paul Vincent Spade, introduction by Marilyn McCord Adams (Indianapolis: Hackett, 1995).

Theologia Christiana (circa 1136–1140)

Standard edition: *Epitome theologiae christianae: ex codicibus Monasterii S. Emmeramni Ratisbonensis, in bibliotheca aulica Monacensi asservatis,* edited by F. H. Rheinwald (Berlin: F. A. Herbig, 1835).

Ethica, or *Scito te ipsum* (circa 1138–1142)

Manuscripts: There are five extant copies dating before 1500. Two from the twelfth century are in the Bayerische Staatsbibliothek in Munich: CLM 14160 includes the *Ethica* on ff. 39v–67r; it is by a single hand and is impressively illuminated. The title reads, *Incipt Liber Magistri Petri Abelardi Qui Dicitur Scito te Ipsum* (Here begins the Book of Master Peter Abelard which is Called Know Thyself). CLM 28363, ff. 103r–132v is essentially the same text as that of 14160 with some minor variant readings. This manuscript may have originated in France toward the close of the twelfth century. Oxford, Balliol College, Ms. 296 ff. 61r–79v has an ending to book one and a commencement of book two of Abelard's *Ethics* not found in CLM 14160. CLM 18597, ff. 4r–51v and Mainz, Stadtbibliothek, Ms. Lat. 76, ff. 292v–320v are both fifteenth century.

Standard edition with English edition: *Peter Abelard's Ethics,* edited and translated by D. E. Luscombe (Oxford: Oxford University Press, 1971).

Edition in English: *Abailard's Ethics,* translated, with an introduction, by J. Ramsay McCallum (Oxford: Blackwell, 1935).

Apologia Contra Bernardum (circa 1140)

Carmen Astrolabium Filium (circa 1140)

Standard edition: *Peter Abelard, "Carmen ad astralabium,"* edited by Josepha Marie Annais Rubingh-Bosscher (Groningen, Netherlands: J. M. A. Rubingh-Bosscher, 1987).

Senteniae Secundum Magistrum Petrum (date unknown)

Standard edition: *Sententie magistri Petri Abelardi (Sentientie Hermanni)* edited by Sandro Buzzetti, Pubblicazioni della Facolta di lettere e filosofia dell'Universita di Milano, no. 101 (Florence: La nuova Italia, 1983).

Collected editions: *Oeuvrages inédits d'Abelard,* edited by Victor Cousin (Paris: Imprimerie Royale, 1836); *Petri Abaelardi Opera,* 2 volumes, edited by Cousin (Paris: Imprimerie Royale, 1859; republished, Hildesheim, Germany: G. Olms, 1970); *Petri Abaelardi opera omnia* in *Patralogiae latina,* 221 volumes, edited by Jacques-Paul Migne (Paris: Migne, 1841–1879), CLXXVIII; *Peter Abelards philosophische Schriften,* 4 volumes, edited by Bernhard Geyer, Beitrage zur Geschichte der Philosophie und Theologie des Mittelalters no. 21 (Münster, Germany: Aschendorf, 1919–1933).

Standard collected editions: *Pietro Abelardi: Scritti filosofici,* edited by Mario Dal Pra (Milan: Fratelli Boca, 1954); *Abaelardiana inedita,* edited by Lorenzo Minio-Paluello (Rome: Edizioni di storia e letteretura, 1958).

Peter Abelard is one of the most famous and influential intellects and one of the most notorious figures of the twelfth century, an era designated one of the renaissances of human thought because of the intensity of its intellectual and literary activity. His birthplace in Brittany was the wellspring of Arthurian narrative and a cradle of *fin'amor* (fine or noble love); however, Abelard renounced his claim to his patrimony to enter the lists of intellectual debate. Abelard's cause was that of reason in the service of faith; his approach to authority was to apply the process of dialectic in a respectful questioning, the purpose of which was often misinterpreted by his opponents. His methods, which were so suspect and vilified during his lifetime, paved the way for the flowering of Scholasticism in the thirteenth century.

Abelard was born circa 1079 into a house of the minor nobility of Brittany, at Le Pallet, about twelve miles from Nantes. Of his childhood and early life, little is known other than what is revealed in his autobiography, the *Historia Calamitaum Meum* (Story of My Misfortunes, written circa 1133), and the few extant records. His father, Berengar, was a member of the lesser nobility who served the count of Brittany. His mother's name was Lucia, and according to existing records, his siblings may have numbered four: three younger brothers, Dagobert, Porcarius, and Radulphus, and a sister,

Denise (Dionisia). Berengar was a knight who valued learning and had his sons trained in its rudiments before they undertook their training as warriors. Abelard was so taken with the pursuit of knowledge that he renounced his claim to his father's title and estate and entered a career that took him across France as a *vagante,* one of the scholars wandering the highways of learning, "perambulans provinicias" (rambling through the provinces). In his own words, "Martis curie penitis abdicarem ut Minerve gremio educar; et quoniam dialecticarum rationem armaturam omnibus philosophie documentis pretuli, his armis alia commutavi et tropheis bellorum conflictus pretulis disputationum" (the court of Mars I abdicated completely to learn in the bosom of Minerva; since I preferred the armaments of dialectic to all the other teachings of philosophy, and with these other arms I exchanged the trophies of war for conflict of disputation).

Little more is known of Abelard's early wanderings. It is certain that he studied under the dialectician Roscelin of Compiègne, who was persecuted for applying dialectic to the study of the Trinity, as Abelard himself later did. Roscelin, who also espoused the potentially heretical principle of nominalism, taught at this time in the town of Loches near Vannes. Some time around 1100 Abelard had probably reached Paris, where his career began in earnest.

Soon after reaching Paris, Abelard studied briefly at the Cloister School of Notre Dame with the renowned William of Champaux, the archdeacon of Paris, who was a student of Anselm of Laon and a proponent of the realism of universals; however, Abelard soon repudiated William as teacher and lecturer, engaging and defeating him in public debate. Abelard's personal charisma, intellectual gifts, and haughty, pugnacious personality set the course for the intellectual and personal strife which was to plague him until his death.

By 1105 Abelard was lecturing in Paris and the neighboring towns of Melun and Corbeil. He eventually set up a school at Mont St. Geneviève, which drew many of William's former pupils and became the cornerstone of the University of Paris. His earliest work, *Introductiones Parvulorum* (Short Introductions, or The Lesser Glosses on Logic), may have been written during this time. Between 1108 and 1113 Abelard traveled to Brittany on two separate occasions to visit his parents, each of whom had entered the religious life. Upon his return to Paris sometime after 1113, Abelard found that William of Champaux had been elevated to the position of bishop of Chalôns-sur-Marne, leaving Abelard without a rival for master of the Cloister School of Notre Dame, the prestigious position formerly held by William; however, Abelard left Paris yet

Peter Abelard and his lover, Héloïse (miniature from a fourteenth-century French manuscript for Le Roman de la Rose; *Chantilly, Musée Conde, 482/665, fol. 60v)*

again. This time, he sojourned at Laon where he briefly studied theology under Anselm of Laon but soon fell out with him, earning in the process two enemies who would set up Abelard's first trial for heresy, Alberic of Rheims and Lothulf of Lombardy.

After training himself in the workings of dialectic as a process of rational enquiry, Abelard accepted a challenge to apply his method of critical reading using logic to an interpretation of a difficult passage from Ezekiel. The passage is not specified, but Abelard recounts that his lectures interpreting this bit of Scripture were hugely successful and many of Anselm's students attended. It was Abelard's first attempt to examine Scripture critically, and it was immediately perceived as a dangerous challenge to *auctoritas* (authority), the dogmatic foundation of the Christian faith. Abelard claimed that he never intended to challenge the cornerstones of belief, the Scriptures and the works of the church fathers, but it was his firm conviction that his method of inquiry would uphold authority by having reason serve the interests of belief. His contemporaries, however, mistrusted both the method and the man, and Abelard reports that Alberic and Lothulf convinced Anselm to put a stop to the lectures.

In 1116 Abelard returned to Paris to assume leadership of the Cloister School of Notre Dame and was elected a canon of the church. The death of Anselm of Laon in 1117 left Abelard seemingly without an intellec-

tual rival, at the peak of his intellectual powers and at the height of his fame. His personal reputation drew students from all over Europe to study with him at his school in Paris.

During 1118 Abelard received an invitation from Fulbert, a fellow canon of Notre Dame and a great admirer of Abelard, to live in his house and tutor his niece, Héloïse. Abelard was approaching forty, while Héloïse was probably between fifteen and eighteen years of age. She had already made great progress in learning and showed promise of becoming an accomplished scholar in her own right. The two began a sexual relationship that soon became the driving passion of Abelard's existence, and he neglected both scholarship and teaching, instead composing love songs (now lost) celebrating Héloïse, which he allowed to be publicly circulated and sung in the streets of Paris. Of Abelard's love songs, only the reputation remains, but George F. Whicher (following Philip Schuyler) proposes eight lyrics from the thirteenth-century song anthology *Carmina burana* as attributable to Abelard, among them the "Dum Diane vitrea" (While Diana's brilliant lamp), "Olim sudor Herculis" (Once sweat from Hercules), and "Si linguis angelicis" (If tongues of angels).

Growing suspicious of the couple, Fulbert banished Abelard from the household, but Abelard and Héloïse continued to meet until Fulbert finally surprised them while they were engaged in sexual intercourse. The situation was intensified when Héloïse became pregnant. Abelard spirited her away to a convent in Brittany where she gave birth to a son, whom she named Astrolabe or Astrolabius.

Despite Héloïse's objections, Abelard proposed, and the two were secretly married. Héloïse did not want to marry Abelard because she knew, as Abelard did not, that the marriage would not appease her outraged guardian, Fulbert, and she knew that it would hinder Abelard's career. Abelard expected to be able to have Héloïse as his wife and continue his career as scholar and teacher. Canon law did not forbid marriage to a member of the minor orders, as Abelard almost certainly was, but Héloïse understood that the exigencies of marriage and parenthood would be significant impediments to the scholarly life Abelard had pursued until then. Unsatisfied with a secret marriage as a solution to the public scandal he had endured, and believing Abelard intended to rid himself of Héloïse by forcing her to become a nun, Fulbert and his friends and relatives plotted revenge. Bribing one of Abelard's servants, they entered Abelard's lodgings at night and castrated him.

By 1119 both Héloïse and Abelard entered religious orders, she becoming a nun at St. Marie at Argenteuil and he becoming a monk in the Benedictine

Abbey of St. Denis in Paris. Abelard embraced the physical and psychological sufferings caused by his castration as a penance for his lustful pursuit of happiness with Héloïse. After entering St. Denis in 1119, Abelard returned to scholarship and public teaching, only to encounter vehement opposition from his old enemies, Alberic and Lothulf. Abelard was convinced that human reason, applying logic to the textual sources of dogma, could assist in clarifying the truths taught by the church fathers and the Bible, and steer the faithful from the paths of error. Alberic and Lothulf, however, saw in Abelard's method a challenge to authority which provided the very foundations of Christian faith. It was at their instigation that in April 1121 the Council of Soissons condemned and burned Abelard's *De unitate et trinitate divina* (On the Unity and Trinity of God)—as his *Theologia Summi Boni* was subtitled. Around the same time Abelard's reproaching the monks of the cloister in which he had taken refuge for their lack of morals and piety, and his demonstration that their monastery had not been founded by Dionysus the Aeropagite, as they had believed, soon wore out his welcome. He found himself homeless and eventually received permission to establish a hermitage near Troyes that he called the Paraclete (Comforter). Soon after his installation there, students began to seek him out, and debilitated by the effects of his wound and a lifelong condition Betty Radice has identified as Hodgkin's disease, he found himself forced to return to teaching in return for assistance in maintaining his hermitage.

In about 1123—only a few years after his condemnation at Soissons—Abelard probably completed revising his *Sic et Non* (Yes and No), which applies the principles of dialectic to the texts of the church fathers, canon law, and the Bible. *Sic et Non* presents objectively the difficulties with the authoritative texts that Abelard hoped his methods of textual criticism and rational inquiry could address. After a brief introduction in which he explains his purpose and method of textual examination, Abelard simply cites a number of texts taken from various sources revered as authorities of faith by his contemporaries: Scripture, canon law, Patrist texts, and even liturgy. The citations are so arranged that one excerpt contradicts another, forcing readers to examine them closely and apply their critical faculties to resolving the seeming self-contradictions. While his work was an exciting experiment to his students and in complete accord with the spirit of the twelfth-century renaissance, it made Abelard's former teachers and other reactionary minds extremely uncomfortable. Abelard's applications of reason to the sources of belief and his personality continued to earn him enemies who he felt were ever watchful of his intel-

lectual activities and ready to pounce with another charge of heresy.

In 1125 or 1126 the monks of St. Gildas de Rhuys in a remote corner of Brittany chose Abelard to be their abbot. This seeming refuge became a living nightmare for Abelard. His spiritual charges at St. Gildas proved to be even more dissolute than his companions at St. Denis had been. Abelard describes them as a ruthless and sin-riddled lot who repeatedly tried to murder him, once by poisoning the wine in his chalice as he conducted Mass.

In 1128, Héloïse, who had risen to the position of prioress perhaps as early as 1123, was expelled with her nuns from their convent at Argenteuil by Abbot Adam Suger, who had discovered documents which he claimed revealed that the property was owned by the abbey of St. Denis. Abelard was able to intervene on behalf of his former lover, now his sister in Christ, and had Héloïse and her charges granted permission to take up residence at the Paraclete.

Hymnarius Paraclithensis (Hymns for the Paraclete), of which 133 survive, were probably written between 1123 and 1140. Typical of these is the "O quanta qualia / sunt illa sabbata" (O how mighty / are the sabbaths), which describes the longing of the faithful, suffering soul for the peace that awaits in the heavenly Jerusalem. Abelard also composed six laments for biblical figures, one of the most beautiful being "Vel confossus pariter / morerer feliciter" (Indeed transfixed alike, happily in the grave), whose persona is David grieving for his beloved Jonathan. Abelard composed the Expositio in *Hexameron* (Commentary on the Six Days of Creation, written circa 1134–1136) at Héloïse's request for the edification of her charges at the Paraclete. It is an explication of the opening chapter of Genesis, the first six days of Creation.

In 1129 Abelard traveled to Troyes from Brittany to assist Héloïse in establishing her house there. Abelard's frequent and necessarily prolonged visits to the Paraclete in those early years of Héloïse's residence provoked a great deal of malicious gossip. His old hermitage was in terrible disrepair, and the nuns suffered great deprivations in those early years; however, by 1131 Pope Innocent II, while visiting Auxère, granted a charter to Abbess Héloïse confirming the foundation of her house and its possessions in perpetuity. In January of 1131, Abelard was present at a large gathering of religious at the abbey of Morigny near Etampes to seek assistance in the form of a papal legate from Innocent II in order to bring the unruly monks at St. Gildas under control. Two things occurred during this meeting: Abelard's request was denied and he met Bernard of Clairvaux for the first time.

The date of 1133 has been suggested for the composition of both *Commentaria in Epistolam Pauli ad Romanos* (Commentary on St. Paul's Epistle to the Romans) and *Historia Calamitatum Meum*. The former continues Abelard's application of critical reading to patristic texts, while the latter survives as one of Abelard's most famous and far-reaching works. As Collin Morris has noted, his candid self-revelations contributed to the twelfth century's development of the concept of the individual, and they provide an invaluable glimpse into the motivations of an extraordinary personality. In his *Historia* Abelard establishes criteria for confessional writing, against which all later examples may be measured, and his narrative recounts the history of one of the most remarkable loves ever experienced; recent scholarship on autobiography has identified Abelard's narrative of his misfortunes as a watershed work in this genre. Héloïse apparently received a copy of this work, in which she is portrayed in such intimate detail, purely by chance.

It is conjectured that Abelard composed and circulated his autobiography to gain sympathy for his plight at St. Gildas and support for his request to leave it and return to teaching. If so, Abelard's strategy was successful, for he was teaching again in Paris at Mont St. Geneviève by 1136. He had been released from his duties but retained the rank of abbot. John of Salisbury reveals that it was during this period that he heard Abelard lecture on dialectic at Paris. Abelard departed from Paris shortly after first encountering John. Where Abelard went, or what he did between 1136 and 1140 is unclear, but it is certain that he continued to write, teach, and to draw the unfavorable attention of his intellectual enemies.

Between 1132 and 1140 Abelard produced his most important, influential, and provocative writings. The dating of Abelard's works is extremely uncertain, however—for example, although the *Dialectica* is generally considered to have been written circa 1130–1142, Constant Mews presents evidence to support a much earlier date, sometime between 1117 and 1121. Abelard also continued teaching during this period, probably at Paris. Among the charges brought against him at Sens was that he corrupted the Christian youth and seduced them from the path of faith through his teachings.

About 1135, Abelard produced his *Ethica*, or *Scito te ipsum* (Ethics, or Know Yourself). In this work Abelard proposes that the virtuousness or viciousness of human actions depends on intention alone. It is a principle which he held in common with Héloïse. In Abelard's remarkable thesis, sin consists solely in the subject's contempt for God's will, and virtue resides in the intent to do God's bidding. Furthermore, according to Abelard, the pleasures attending intercourse in marriage or consuming a delicious meal are not equated with lust or gluttony as some of his contemporaries taught. Intent alone determines the sinfulness or virtue of any human act.

The unfinished *Dialogus Petri Abælardi* (Dialogues of Peter Abelard), also known as *Dialogus Inter Philosophum, Iudaeum, et Christanum* (Dialogue between a Philosopher, a Jew and a Christian), probably dates from 1136, although Lief Grane suggests that this work was written later, during Abelard's last days while he was living under the protection of Peter the Venerable. Abelard uses the concept of the three ages of human history—pagan, Jewish, and Christian—to discuss his program of applied dialectics. The pagan philosopher, aided by intellect alone, seeks salvation. He engages the Jew and the Christian in dialogue to test their beliefs against his natural human reason. The rule of reason unaided by faith, which the pagan philosopher espouses, is demonstrably efficacious in identifying and acknowledging the truths inherent in revelation.

Abelard's *Theologia Christiana* (Christian Theology) and *Theologia* (Theology) in three volumes must both be considered works in progress. Abelard revised them constantly from about 1132 until their condemnation at Sens in 1140. Abelard's contemporaries found this work disturbing because he dared to assume that logic could test and reinforce the truths of revelation. Abelard's subject in these works is the nature of the Trinity, the core of Christian belief. Abelard distinguished between the name of the Father as signifying power; that of the Son, wisdom; and that of the Holy Spirit, goodness. Abelard asserted that his approach could render the mysteries of faith, most significantly the relationship between the persons of the Trinity, intelligible. It was this assumption that William of St. Thierry and Bernard of Clairvaux found so threatening to their concept of true Christian dogma.

Dialectica (Dialectics, circa 1130–1142) was Abelard's final work and represents his most systematic working out of the issue of universals. In this treatise, Abelard was able to demonstrate his understanding of logic as a purely formal endeavor, free from the entanglements of metaphysics. Abelard insisted on applying logic to his investigation of concepts and propositions, the language in which human beings express their perceptions of reality.

Sometime during 1139 a copy of Abelard's three-volume work-in-progress *Theologia* fell into the hands of William of St. Thierry, the abbot of the Cistercian Monastery of Signy. William discovered in

Abelard and Héloïse (from the opening page of a thirteenth-century manuscript for Abelard's Historia Calamitatum, *which belonged to the Italian poet Petrarch after 1337; Bibliothèque Nationale de France, lat. 2923, fol. 1r)*

Theologia what he considered to be thirteen points of heresy. He forwarded his findings to Bernard of Clairvaux and Bishop Geoffrey of Chartres. Bernard met Abelard on two separate occasions for the purpose of persuading him to recant voluntarily, but Abelard remained firm in his convictions. Bernard sought Abelard's trial for heresy, which was held at Sens in 1140. Although Abelard wanted an open debate with Bernard, he was never granted an opportunity to present his case in a public forum. His opponents feared that his charisma and the force of his logical mind would have provided formidable and effective defenses to the charges against him. As it was, the trial was orchestrated by his accusers with the result that Abelard was condemned and forbidden to pursue his careers as writer and teacher without being given a chance to present his case. Abelard's career, intentions, and fate were so remarkably similar to that of Socrates almost fifteen

centuries earlier that Peter the Venerable makes note of it in his *Epitaph on Abelard* (circa 1142–1143) identifying Abelard as "Gallorum Socrates, Plato maximus Hesperiarum, Noster Aristoteles" (Socrates of the Gauls, Great Plato of the Western Lands, Our Aristotle).

Abelard was resolved to take his case to the Pope and began the arduous journey to Rome, but it was a mission he never accomplished. The stress of the condemnation at Sens had seriously damaged his already failing health. His progress to Rome brought him fortuitously to Cluny and the compassionate, reverential care of its abbot, Peter the Venerable. While at Cluny, Abelard heard of the Pope's decision to uphold the verdict of Sens against him. Abelard was forbidden to write or teach, and was to live behind monastic walls in perpetual silence, while his books were condemned to the flames. Peter interceded on Abelard's behalf and succeeded in having Cluny selected as the site of his punishment. Furthermore, through Peter's personal intervention, a reconciliation was effected between Abelard, Bernard, and the Pope, and ultimately the ban against Abelard was lifted. Peter the Venerable persuaded Abelard to remain at Cluny and in one of its subsidiary houses at St. Marcel, near Chalon-sur-Sâone.

Peter wrote an account of Abelard's last days in a series of letters of consolation to Héloïse after Abelard's death. According to Peter the Venerable, Abelard lived a model monastic life of fasting, prayer, and study, approaching every task with devotion and humility. He continued his studying to the end of his days, but except for informal lectures and sermons composed for the benefit of his brothers, it is unlikely that he continued his writing. Thus the fiery and inflammatory proponent of reason in the service of faith expired humbled in spirit and broken in body, probably on 21 April 1142. The ever compassionate Peter had Abelard's earthly remains transferred from their original resting place at St. Marcel to the Paraclete and the devoted care of Abbess Héloïse and her nuns, whose spiritual well-being Abelard took such pains to nurture. After Héloïse died in 1163 or 1164, she was interred with Abelard; moved several times over the years, their remains have been in the Père Lachaise Cemetery in Paris since the nineteenth century.

The new ground broken by Abelard's approach to ethics had its impact on the centuries that followed. Abelard's theory of intent placed the burden of salvation squarely on the shoulders of the individual. His understanding of the psyche and his insistence on inner penitence for sin and on self-examination of motives by the individual was part of a movement which eventually gave rise to the practice of individual confession as a means to expiation and salvation. Geoffrey Chaucer makes intent, an essential feature of Abelard's concept of virtue and vice, one of the primary considerations of his pilgrims and the subject of their various narratives in *The Canterbury Tales* (written circa 1375–1400).

Abelard's presence at Paris was one of the determining factors that led to the rise of the university at that city; his personal charisma, intellectual integrity, and the compelling nature of the method he employed earned him many followers during his lifetime and after. Thus he—not his opponents—was able to set the course that teaching and scholarship would follow well into the next century. Abelard was the first scholar to formulate a comprehensive, systematic program for rational inquiry into the issues of religious dogma. Peter Lombard was among Abelard's pupils, and Lombard's *Sententiarum libri IV* (commonly known as *Sentences,* written between 1148 and 1151), which became one of the staple texts of courses in theology at universities throughout Europe, was indebted to the lectures and writings of Abelard.

The *Historia Calamitatum Meum,* Abelard's narrative of personal tribulations, is one of the watershed works of autobiography. The correspondence with Héloïse that the publication of the autobiography prompted is remarkable for the frankness of self-revelation exhibited by both parties, and reveals that they lived the debates which became the focus of so many *questions d'amour* (questions concerning love) in the lays and romances of the third quarter of the twelfth century. The notoriety of the tragic passion shared by Abelard and Héloïse has inspired many references to and narratives of their love from the Middle Ages to the present. Most important, Abelard's approach to authority and his application of dialectic to the issues of faith became essential features of scholastic philosophy in the thirteenth century. In the writings of St. Thomas Aquinas, logic became the handmaid of belief, and reason was naturally, lawfully, and fruitfully applied to questions of theology, and what was heresy in one century became the dogma of the next.

Biographies:

Etienne Gilson, *Héloïse and Abélard,* translated by L. K. Shook (Chicago: Regnery, 1951);

Leif Grane, *Peter Abelard: Philosophy and Christianity in the Middle Ages,* translated by Frederick Crowley and Christine Crowley (London: Allen & Unwin, 1970).

References:

Janet Coleman, "Abelard," in her *Ancient and Medieval Memories: Studies in the Reconstruction of the Past* (Cambridge & New York: Cambridge University Press, 1992), pp. 233–273;

Charles Homer Haskins, *The Renaissance of the Twelfth Century* (Cambridge, Mass.: Harvard University Press, 1927);

Louis LeLoir, ed. *Bernard of Clairvaux: Studies Presented to Dom Jean Leclerq,* Cistercian Studies no. 23 (Washington, D.C.: Cistercian Studies, Consortium Press, 1973);

David E. Luscombe, *The School of Peter Abelard: The Influence of Abelard's Thought in the Early Scholastic Period* (London: Cambridge University Press, 1969);

Constant Mews, "On Dating the Works of Peter Abelard," *Archives d'histoire doctrinale et littéraire du moyen âge,* 52 (1985): 73–134;

Colin Morris, *The Discovery of the Individual: 1050–1200* (Toronto: University of Toronto Press, 1991);

Helen Waddell, *The Wandering Scholars,* seventh edition (London: Constable, 1934).

Alain de Lille
(Alanus de Insulis)
(circa 1116 – April 1202/1203)

William E. Burgwinkle
University of Hawaii

WORKS: *Vix nodosum* (1130s?)

First publication and standard edition: "The Poem *Vix Nodosum* by Alan of Lille," edited by Nikolaus M. Häring, in *Medioevo: Rivista de storia della filosofia medievale,* 3 (1978): 165–185.

Hierarchia (circa 1155–1165)

First publication and standard edition: In *Alain de Lille, textes inédits,* Etudes de Philosophe Médiévale no. 52, edited by Marie-Thérèse d'Alverney (Paris: J. Vrin, 1965), pp. 223–235.

Summa Quoniam homines (circa 1155–1165)

Manuscripts: This work survives in two manuscripts: London, British Library, Royal 9 E. xxii. ff. 168–210, from the first quarter of the thirteenth century, and Klosterneuberg, no. 322, only incomplete form; of the three parts announced in the Prologue, part 1 is extant while part 2 is incomplete and part 3 is missing and may never have been written.

First publication and standard edition: "La Somme *Quoniam homines* d'Alain de Lille," edited by Palémon Glorieux, *Archives,* 20 (1953): 113–359.

De virtutibus et de vitiis et de donis Spiritus Sancti (circa 1155–1165)

Manuscripts: This work is represented in a variety of manuscripts; some, such as Paris, Bibliothèque Nationale de France, Lat. 323f., are shorter versions; others, such as London, British Library, Royal 9 E XII. f. 158–167, are longer. It is unclear as to whether the shorter version is an abridgment of the longer version, or the longer an elaboration of the short work.

First publication: "Über die Verknüpfung des Poetischen mit dem Theologischen bei Alanus de Insulis," edited by Johannes Huizinga, in *Mededeelingen der Koniklijk. Akademie van Wetenchappen, Afdeeling Letterkunde 74B* (Amsterdam: Noord-Hollandsche, 1932), pp. 95–110.

Standard edition: "Le Traité d'Alain de Lille sur les vertus, les vices et les dons du Saint-Esprit," edited by Odon Lottin, in his *Psychologie et morale aux xiie et xiiie siè-*des, 6 volumes (Gembloux: Duculot, 1960), VI: 28–36.

De planctu naturae (circa 1160–1165)

Manuscripts: There are at least 111 extant manuscripts of *De planctu*. Of these, only 6 belong to thirteenth century, and 3 of them are in Italian collections.

First publication: In *Historia poetarum et poematum medii aevi,* edited by P. Leyser (Halle, 1721); republished in *Patrologiae latina,* 221 volumes, edited by Jacques-Paul Migne (Paris: Migne, 1841–1879), CCX: 431A–482C.

Standard edition: In *Studi medievali,* third series 19, no. 2 (1978), edited by Nikolaus M. Häring (797–879).

Edition in English: *Alain of Lille: The Plaint of Nature,* edited by James J. Sheridan, based on the text established by Häring, Medieval Sources in Translation no. 26 (Toronto: Pontifical Institute of Mediaeval Studies, 1980).

Regulae or Theologicae Regulae (circa 1160)

Manuscripts: There are fifty-one extant manuscripts.

First publication: In *Anecdotorum Fascilus,* edited by J. Mingarellius (Rome, 1756).

Standard edition: In *Patrologiae Latinae,* 221 volumes, edited by Jacques-Paul Migne (Paris: Migne, 1841–1879), CCX: 622–684.

Anticlaudianus de Antirufino (circa 1181–1184)

Manuscripts: There are 112 extant manuscripts, with either the complete text or fragments. Only 6 manuscripts possibly date from the late twelfth century; an additional 34 date from the thirteenth century. The oldest manuscript, used by R. Bossuat in his standard edition of the text, is Cambridge, Pembroke College, ms.119. ff. 1–78 v, which dates from the twelfth century. There are 35 British, 24 French, 14 Italian, 11 German or Austrian manuscripts, and the remainder are in Belgian, Spanish, Dutch, Scandinavian, Swiss, Czech, and Catalan collections.

First publications: *Anticlaudiani libri IX* (Venice: 1582); *Anticlaudianus* (Antwerp: 1611).

Alain de Lille wearing his doctoral cap and the robes of a secular clerk (from an illumination in a thirteenth-century manuscript, British Library, Add. 19767)

Standard editions: In *Patrologiae latinae,* 221 volumes, edited by Jacques-Paul Migne (Paris: Migne, 1841–1879), CCX: 488–574; *Alain de Lille Anticlaudianus,* Textes Philosophiques du Moyen Age no. 1, edited, with an introduction, by R. Bossuat (Paris: J. Vrin, 1955).

Edition in English: *Anticlaudianus or The Good and Perfect Man,* edited by James J. Sheridan, based on the text established by Bossuat (Toronto: Pontifical Institute of Mediaeval Studies, 1973).

De fide catholica contra haereticos (circa 1184–1195)

Manuscripts: There are twenty-nine extant manuscripts, half of which belong to French, German, or Austrian collections and twelve of which date from the twelfth and thirteenth centuries.

First publication: *Opus adversus haereticos et Valdenses . . . Nunc primum e bibliotheca Papirii Massoni . . .,* edited by J. Massoni (Paris, 1612).

Standard editions: In *Patrologiae Latinae,* 221 volumes, edited by Jacques-Paul Migne (Paris: Migne, 1841–1879), CCX: 307–430; "Il Contra Haereticus di Alano di Lilla," edited by Cesare Vasoli, in *Archivio-Muratoriano,* 75 (1963): 123–172.

Expositio cuiusdam super orationem Dominicam (1190s?)

First publication and standard edition: "A Commentary on the 'Our Father' by Alan of Lille," edited by Nikolaus M. Häring, in *Analecta Cisterciensia,* 31 (1975): 149–177.

Expositio super symbolum (1190s?)

First publication and standard edition: "A Commentary on the Creed of the Mass by Alan of Lille," edited by Nikolaus M. Häring, in *Analecta Cisterciensia,* 31 (1974): 281–303.

Super Symbolum apostolorum (1190s?)

First publication and standard edition: "A Commentary on the Apostles' Creed by Alain of Lille (O. Cist.)," edited by Nikolaus M. Häring, in *Analecta Cisterciensia,* 30 (1974): 7–45.

Super Symbolum Quicumque (1190s?)

First publication and standard edition: "A Poem by Alan of Lille on the Pseudo-Athanasian Creed," edited by Nikolaus M. Häring, in *Revue d'histoire des textes,* 4 (1974): 226–238.

De arte praedicatoria (before 1194)

Manuscripts: This text, also known as *Ars praedicandi,* includes forty-eight sermons and is preserved in ninety-four manuscripts, almost two-thirds of which are either French, German, or Austrian.

First publication and standard edition: In *Patrologiae Latina,* 221 volumes, edited by Jacques-Paul Migne (Paris: Migne, 1841–1879), CCX: 111–198.

Regulae Caelestis Iuris (before 1194)

First publication and standard edition: "Regulae Caelestis Iuris," edited by Nikolaus M. Häring, in *Archives d'Histoire Doctrinale et Littéraire du Moyen Age,* 48 (1981): 97–226.

Sermones (before 1194)

Manuscripts: There are thirty-one extant manuscripts with sermons by Alain de Lille, all but six of which belong to French or German collections. Twenty-seven sermons and *Ars praedicandi* are included in Paris, Bibliothèque Nationale de France,

nouv. acq. Lat. 335, a manuscript from the end of the twelfth century.

First publication: In *Patrologiae Latinae,* 221 volumes, edited by Jacques-Paul Migne (Paris: Migne, 1841–1879), CCX: 198–228.

Standard edition: In *Alain de Lille, textes inédits,* Etudes de Philosophie Médiévale no. 52, edited by Marie-Thérèse d'Alverney (Paris: J. Vrin, 1965), pp. 241–306.

Liber in distinctionibus dictionum theologicalium (circa 1195)

Manuscripts: Commonly known as the *Distinctiones,* this work is represented in forty-one extant manuscripts, with seventeen in Munich.

First publication and standard edition: In *Patrologiae Latinae,* 221 volumes, edited by Jacques-Paul Migne (Paris: Migne, 1841–1879), CCX: 686–1012.

Liber poenitentialis (circa 1199–1202)

Manuscripts: Twenty-seven extant manuscripts include this text, with twenty-five dating from the thirteenth century; eleven belong to the Bibliothèque Nationale in Paris.

First publication: *Liber de poenitentia* (Augsberg, 1518).

Standard editions: In *Patrologiae Latinae,* 221 volumes, edited by Jacques-Paul Migne (Paris: Migne, 1841–1879), CCX: 279–304; *Liber Poenitentialis,* 2 volumes, edited by Jean Longère, Analecta Mediaevalia Namurcensia, nos. 17–18 (Louvain: Nauwelaerts, 1965).

De sex alis cherubim (date unknown)

First publication: In *De modo audiendi confessiones,* edited by J. Gerson (Nuremberg, 1478).

Standard edition: In *Patrologiae Latinae,* 221 volumes, edited by Jacques-Paul Migne (Paris: Migne, 1841–1879), CCX: 270–280.

Elucidatio in Cantica canticorum (date unknown)

First publication: In *Compendiosa in Cantica Canticorum ad laudem Deiparae Virginus Mariae elucidatio* (Paris, 1540).

Standard edition: In *Patrologiae Latinae,* 221 volumes, edited by Jacques-Paul Migne (Paris: Migne, 1841–1879), CCX: 51–110.

Epistola Magistri Alani quod non est celebrandum bis in die (date unknown)

Manuscripts: The standard edition is based on two manuscripts: the first, Oxford, Bodleian Library, Canon. Misc. Lat. 95, f. 113–115, was copied in the first half of the thirteenth century, probably by an Italian scribe; the second manuscript, Vatican, Ottoboni lat. 130, f. 135–137v, comprises two distinct parts, that which includes *Epistola* dates from the end of the twelfth century and was copied in the south of France.

First publication and standard edition: In *Alain de*

Lille, textes inédits, Etudes de Philosophe Médiévale no. 52, edited by Marie-Thérèse d'Alverney (Paris: J. Vrin, 1965), pp. 151–152.

Expositio prosae de angelis (date unknown)

First publication and standard edition: In *Alain de Lille, textes inédits,* Etudes de Philosophie Médiévale no. 52, edited by Marie-Thérèse d'Alverney (Paris: J. Vrin, 1965), pp. 85–106.

Rhythmus de incarnatione Christi (date unknown)

Manuscripts: This poem survives in several manuscripts, including Paris, Bibliothèque Nationale de France, nouv. acq. Lat. 1544; Douai, Bibliothèque Municipale, ms. 385; and Florence, Biblioteca Laurenzia, Plut. xxix.

First publication: In *Gallo-Flandria,* edited by J. Buzelin (Douai: N. p., 1625).

Standard editions: In *Patrologiae Latinae,* 221 volumes, edited by Jacques-Paul Migne (Paris: Migne, 1841–1879), CCX: 577A–580A; in "Alain de Lille et la 'Theologia,'" edited by Marie-Thérèse d'Alverney, in *Mélanges H. de Lubac,* 20 volumes (Paris: Aubier, 1964), II: 126–128.

Rhythmus de natura hominis fluxa et caduca (date unknown)

First publication and standard edition: In *Patrologiae Latinae,* 221 volumes, edited by Jacques-Paul Migne (Paris: Migne, 1841–1879), CCX: 579A–580C.

Liber parabolarum (date unknown)

First publication and standard edition: In *Patrologiae Latinae,* 221 volumes, edited by Jacques-Paul Migne (Paris: Migne, 1841–1879), CCX: 582–594.

Sermo de sphaera intelligibili (date unknown)

First publication and standard edition: In *Alain de Lille, textes inédits,* Etudes de Philosophie Médiévale no. 52, edited by Marie-Thérèse d'Alverney (Paris: J. Vrin, 1965), pp. 295–306.

Tractatus Magistri Alani (date unknown)

First publication and standard edition: "Deux questions sur la foi inspirées d'Alain de Lille," edited by Guy Raynaud de Lage, *Archives,* 14 (1943): 323–336.

Little is known for certain about the life of Alain de Lille (also known as Alanus de Insulis) or the conditions under which he composed his many influential texts. He is mentioned on several occasions by contemporaries and is celebrated especially for his allegorical epic, *Anticlaudianus de Antirufino* (Against Claudian's Against Rufinus, written circa 1181–1184), which soon became an object of commentary and imitation.

According to James J. Sheridan in the revisionist chronology in his *Alan of Lille: The Plaint of Nature* (1980), it would appear that Alain de Lille was born in the town of Lille in Flanders (now part of Belgium) in 1116 or 1117

and came to Paris to pursue advanced studies in 1136. He probably spent time in the schools of Paris and Chartres before taking up teaching in some of the major intellectual centers of his time, including most importantly Paris and Montpellier. *Vix nodosum* (I Can Scarcely Undo the Knotty Knot), a goliardic poem that discusses in sexually frank and playful terms the relative merits of loving a virgin or married woman, is usually considered his earliest work, composed while Alain was still under the influence of a student milieu.

Alain seems to have studied with some of the major figures of his time, in particular Gilbert de la Porrée, and to have played a role, if only through commentary, in some of the most significant contemporary philosophical and theological debates. His insistence throughout his works on the value and status of the trivium and his championing of the *artes* (the seven liberal arts, trivium and quadrivium, which included the study of grammar, rhetoric, logic, geometry, music, astronomy, and arithmetic) suggest a deeply committed scholar and teacher with a progressive bent. This does not mean, however, that Alain was a revolutionary thinker or a complete convert to the budding Scholastic movement. Although his methods were often innovative, he was basically a traditionalist, a partisan of the ancients when it came to canon formation and pedagogy. He championed the utility of the *artes* in the study of theology and philosophy as a limited but effective way to sharpen men's abilities to conceive of the ineffable, but the type of training in the liberal arts that he advocated still involved extensive philological commentary and glossing of the traditional *auctores,* that is, the Latin writers and Church Fathers. By midlife he had already established a reputation as an eminent philosopher and theologian among his contemporaries. Several of them refer to him as an authority–John of Garland called him "Virgilio maior et Homero certior" (greater than Virgil, more reliable than Homer)–and the *Anticlaudianus,* in particular, attracted many imitators and was accorded special status as a contemporary classic.

In 1972 Palémon Glorieux advanced the theory that Alain de Lille was, at some point in the first half of his life, a Benedictine monk and that he acquired much of his prodigious learning in the well-stocked library of the monastery at Bec. If this is the case, it would also appear that he left or was expelled from the order and then went on to treat subjects that would have been off-limits to him as a monk, and in a manner inimical to an orthodox Benedictine scholar.

Alain wrote several relatively unknown theological tracts. Some are yet to be edited, and few are available in English. Dating from circa 1155–1165, his *Summa Quoniam homines* (Since men . . .) offers treatises on the nature of God, the Trinity, angels, and men. *De virtutibus et de vitiis et de donis Spiritus Sancti* (On the Virtues and the Vices and the

Alain in a white monastic robe (from the opening page of an early thirteenth-century manuscript for his
Liber in distinctionibus dictionum theologicalium*(Biblioteca Vaticana, Ross 393)*

Gifts of the Holy Spirit) seems to date from the same period; it discusses the natural and theological virtues and vices in a manner that seems to have been developed by Peter Lombard in his famous *Sentences* (1157). *Regulae caelestis iuris* (Rules of Heavenly Justice), date of composition unknown, offers commentaries on God, Man, the Incarnation, and the Sacraments.

Theologicae Regulae (Maxims of Theology), written about 1160, is strongly influenced by Boethius's *De trinitate* (On the Trinity) and *De hebdomadibus* (On the Seventh Day), written early in the sixth century, and is also marked by the teachings of Gilbert de la Porrée. It is in this work that Alain most distinctively links theology and the techniques of the liberal arts, especially through reference to the methodology of geometry.

De planctu naturae (On the Plaint of Nature), though barely mentioned by his contemporaries, is the work for which Alain is now best known. Sheridan, in the commentary to his translation of *De planctu,* dates this text to Alain's middle years, circa 1160–1165, a period during which Breton, Arthurian, and historical romance; speculative theology; and the courtly lyric came into popularity. It cannot be determined to what extent Alain was touched by the explosion of interest in vernacular literature that was occurring around him, but it does appear that he was at least periodically associated with the circle of intellectuals that developed around the Anglo-Norman Plantagenet court and with the court of William VIII of Montpellier, two of the major centers at which the troubadours were perfecting their craft.

De Planctu is a Menippean satire, a type of seriocomic text that discusses philosophical issues in a light or humor-

ous manner. Primarily a rhetorical showpiece in which Alain could put to use his convoluted stylistic flourishes and delight in wordplay and erudition, it is also distinctive for its alternation of verse and prose. It was Alain's taste for rhetorical extravagance that for many years dissuaded scholars from according the text the status that it was granted in the twentieth century, when it became the object of much commentary about the influence it exerted on writers of the later Middle Ages, and especially for its unusual and sustained conflation of grammatical and sexual metaphors.

Although not the first in his era to develop metaphors that are based on theories of grammar but express ethical concerns in a sexually charged register, Alain is remarkable in his sustaining such a technique throughout a long and highly literary text. Other scholars, notably Walter of Châtillon and Matthew of Vendôme, used grammatico-sexual metaphors in a serious context, and the comic possibilities inherent in juxtaposing grammatical terminology and Latin sexual vocabulary were exploited by many others as well. Terms referring to acts of conjunction and dependence such as *copula, conjugate,* and *predicate* were particularly susceptible to innuendo and were therefore frequently used to humorous effect.

Alain, however, was clearly more interested in defending the moral and ethical components of grammar and its status as natural law than in developing facetious metaphors. As a Menippean satire, *De planctu* owes an obvious debt to earlier authors such as Martianus Capella and Boethius. The influence of Plato's *Timaeus* is also evident, as are the teachings of the School of Chartres, especially Bernard Silvestris's *Cosmographia*. In turn, *De planctu* exerted enormous influence over at least some of the major thirteenth-century Parisian intellectuals, especially Jean de Meun, who cites Alain in his continuation of *Le Roman de la Rose* (circa 1269–1278).

The subject of the *Planctu* is the betrayal of Nature by man and her subsequent complaint before the mournful poet who has summoned her. Nature, echoing the poet's own concerns with unorthodox sexual practices, reveals that having once been charged with executing the divine plan in the sublunary sphere, she turned to Venus for assistance in ensuring man's continued interest in the propagation of his species. Venus was more than happy to comply, and with the active participation of her son, Desire (Cupid), the product of her liaison with Hymenaeus, she set about to pique mankind's desire and patrol his active participation in the procreative process. Alain makes it clear that the effects of desire on men are not altogether negative or positive. Coupled with moderation and reason, Desire is portrayed as performing a necessary and worthwhile function. Nature's harmonious partnership with Venus is interrupted, however, by another of Venus's sons, the illegitimate Jocus (Game), whose effects on mankind are clearly deleterious, at least from Nature's point of view. Born of an illicit affair with Antigenius or Anteganus (Antimarriage), he is said to be the source of a series of vices and perversions that are wreaking havoc with the divine plan and Nature's watchdog role.

Nature has meanwhile had a daughter named Truth with her legitimate consort, Genius. Genius, the agent of genitalia and procreation, is portrayed as a writer whose status and function are symbolized as the mark of pen on parchment and the blow of the hammer on the anvil. Acting to bolster the divine plan and Nature's role in the generation of the species, Genius dons the robes of authority to excommunicate those who perform sexual acts whose aims are other than procreative. Genius says that Nature supplements divine agency in the sublunary, material world and that those men who willfully ignore her purpose are also subverting the divine plan. They are disruptive and destructive, and their acts are figured as rips and tears in the elaborately described gown that Nature wears on her first appearance before the despondent poet. The association of gown or cloak with language and signifying systems is a topos of representation throughout the twelfth and thirteenth centuries. The tears in Nature's robe represent the violence that acts of sodomy perpetrate upon the "natural body," the person of Nature.

Genius's ranting against homosexuality echoes the opening meters of the poem, in which the narrator laments that man has abandoned Nature's precepts in favor of unreasoned and ungrammatical couplings. These opening meters stress especially transgressions of what the poet, here the spokesman for Nature's precepts, considers gender-appropriate behavior. The narrator seems to assume the existence of universally valid, natural, and intrinsic laws that find their expression in grammar. According to such rules, subjects (men) must act upon predicates (women), not upon themselves or their like; and man must serve as adjective to woman's noun. The disgrace of homosexuality is that, in Sheridan's translation, "he's" (*illos*) become "she's" (*illas*) when the "active sex . . . sees itself degenerate into the passive sex" (*Activi generis sexus, se turpiter horret / Sic in passivum degenerare genus*). The masculine is thus conceived of as a grammatical principle, a construct that can be taken up, and lost just as easily, through the improper conjunction of two unlike terms (known as "vice" in grammatical theory). Loss of manhood, equivalent to the adoption of the neutral gender in grammatical terms, is likened to a state of confusion. That a man would voluntarily take up the attributes of femininity, here seen principally as a state of passivity, is beyond shame. Paradoxically, if it is assumed that Alain's intent is a valorization of the masculine drive to procreate, it is the feminine principle that emerges as more substantial, and less prone to perversion, even given its passive state. Alain seems to limit his condemnation of sodomy to men (adjectival, or figured as subjects in grammatical terms) who veer from their divinely scripted roles, never suggesting that verbs (feminine) couple or that unmodified nouns, lacking adjectives, would be tempted simply to modify themselves.

His condemnation of sodomy does, however, extend beyond simple same-sex coupling to improper heterosexual positions for intercourse and, of course, to any sign of passivity within the active subject that is man. Alain implies that sodomy is rampant in his day, denouncing the unmentionable and monstrous deeds of contemporary lovers who show no interest in "the little cleft of Venus" (*Veneris rimula*) and actually sell their favors in defiance of Nature. Sodomy is allied with irrationality, illogic, solecism, adornment, emotion, and bestiality. Genius, in an official decree, excommunicates those who interfere with Nature's plan from her favor and from Venus's ranks. Such men are condemned to sterility, banishment, and castration.

Where parody begins and ends is difficult to say. The lengths to which Alain goes to connect grammar and sexuality could be taken as proof of a deep-rooted homophobia, but he is ambiguous enough on occasion to at least suggest an ironic intention. Sodomy and approved heterosexual acts share the same metaphor, that of the hammer and anvil. Vice is the result of any reversal or transposition of the terms. Grammatical modification, as in anvil and hammer, or cross-linking of the terms, as in hammer and hammer, is already associated with sin. Linked as it is with simple slips in syntax or gender agreement, not only is sodomy not rare, it is practically unavoidable. Alain's sometimes sardonic references to beavers who gnaw at their own genitals and bats as hermaphrodites at least suggest that he is being facetious.

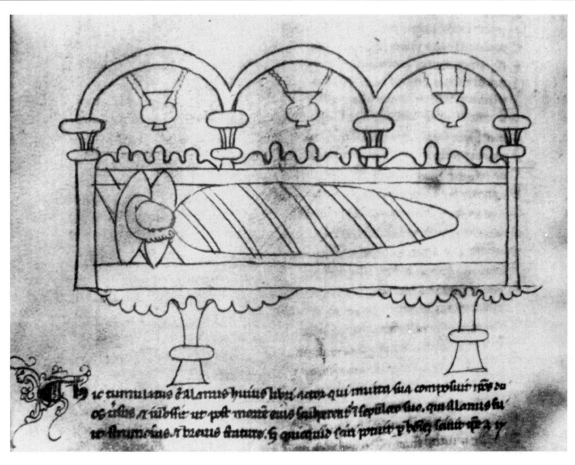

Alain depicted in his tomb at Cîteaux (sketch in a manuscript; Verona, Biblioteca Capitolina, CGLI)

It has been suggested that Alain was writing at a time when publicly orchestrated attacks upon sodomy in the monasteries were commonplace, and other contemporary texts implicate a widely tolerated homosexual subculture within the influential political circles surrounding the Plantagenet court. Was the *Planctu* part of a carefully orchestrated attack on influential public figures or a step toward the progressive institution of a more extensive and normalized disciplinary code on sexuality through which the Roman Catholic Church could extend its control over the private domain? It has, for instance, been suggested that in the *Planctu* Alain was launching a pointed, and politically motivated, attack on a contemporary figure, Roger of Pont-L'Evêque, archbishop of York, an avowed enemy of Thomas Becket. Regardless of whether *De planctu* was intended as an attack on a particular individual or group, it clearly participates in a wider social phenomenon in which sodomy is explicitly stigmatized as one of the major signs of societal degradation.

The full title of the most influential of Alain's literary texts in his own day is *Anticlaudianus de Antirufino* (Against Claudian's *Against Rufinus*). Another showpiece in which Alain displays the full gamut of his prodigious learning and rhetorical skill, the *Anticlaudianus* was probably composed about twenty years after the *Planctu* (circa 1182–1183). In terms of both ideas and presentation it is a more mature and balanced text, grounded in epic conventions. Written in dactylic hexameter, the meter of epic, Alain's text is a response to Claudian's fifth-century poem *In Rufinum,* which deals with the world's most wicked man, and is a sort of rival/companion to Walter of Châtillon's epic, the *Alexandreid* (1181). This Latin, although anti-Roman, epic was the most famous of the Middle Ages, celebrating Alexander as the perfect man, ruler, and conqueror. Instead of explicitly taking up an historical figure as Walter had, as a means of responding to the *In Rufinum,* Alain constructs his tale around Nature's resolve to create the perfect antidote to man's corruption in the person of a theoretically perfect man. This project allows Alain to return to his earlier creation, Lady Nature, and the main concerns of the *Planctu,* in what many have seen as a panegyric to the new king of France, the fourteen-year-old Philip Augustus.

In *Anticlaudianus* Nature is still hampered by her limitations and anxious to overcome them. Incapable of true originality, the exclusive province of God, she can only create through fostering procreation from within existing matter, or through replication of earlier models. Like any artist, she must therefore turn to another source of inspiration, here Neoplatonic and Christian, in terms largely defined by Thierry of Chartres and his influential school. At Nature's bidding, the Virtues arrive to help her in her quest to create the perfect man. Prudence and Reason, figures of human wisdom, join forces with the seven liberal arts to construct a vessel that will transport Prudence to the heavenly sphere. There she is to request, on Nature's behalf, a new model of the human soul. The chariot they construct is an encomium to the trivium and quadrivium, alone capable of providing man with the means to move beyond this material sphere. Reason is appointed the driver; the five senses, figured as horses, provide the pull. This chariot, however ideal, is nonetheless limited by the frailty of human reasoning and the senses. After having visited and commented on the successive regions of Air, Ether, and the Firmament, Prudence reaches the limits of the universe and is obliged to abandon her vessel and proceed on foot to the heavenly sphere.

At this crucial point she is joined by Theology, whose abode is located near the juncture of the material universe and the heavenly realm. Prudence, guided by Theology, must face the unfathomable, what no man has seen. Overcome with terror, her first reaction is to faint, but she is revived with the help of Faith. With the aid of a mirror, which allows her to see the brilliance of heaven without being blinded, she makes her way to the palace of God and enters into communication with the Divinity. He honors her request by ordering Noys to produce for her a new prototype of the human soul. When Prudence arrives on earth with the new soul, Nature again enlists the help of Concord, Arithmetic, and Music in order to construct a fitting vessel. She forges a body worthy to house the divine gift and calls the resulting creation "Novus Homo"–New Man. A celebration ensues, at which the Virtues and Arts offer their gifts in homage. Nobility, with her mother, Fortune, arrives to add the final and fitting touch, and with their contributions New Man is ready to confront the difficulties of human life. As Rumor spreads the news of the perfection that Nature has wrought, Novus Homo is attacked by Allecto and Vice. In a tribute to Prudentius, Alain orchestrates a battle to end all battles: Novus Homo, aided by Nature and the Virtues, confronts the Vices and vanquishes them. The new epic hero will rule earth with the aid of his allies, the Virtues and Arts, and the poem closes on a note of triumph.

Alain counsels the reader in the prologue to read his poem on three levels: the *sensus litteralis* (literal reading), on which level the text can be read as an adventure story for youths; the *moralis instructio* (the moral/instructive reading), which encourages a metaphorical reading for more educated students, including the adolescent king; and the *allegoria,* or allegorical level, which is destined to be studied and formally analyzed by fully educated men. Elsewhere in his works he suggests adding an anagogical reading as well, one that encourages mystical and exegetical interpretation. He thus resembles other literary figures of his time, such as Chrétien de Troyes and Marie de France, who openly advocate a multileveled reading of their works. The text is an introduction to, and expert defense of, the role of the liberal arts in the pursuit of human perfection and ultimate knowledge of God. Nature needs the arts in order to construct the vessel that serves as a link between human and divine creation. The arts are not antithetical to theological study; they are essential to it. Alain was attempting to bridge the gap between traditionalists and the advocates of Scholasticism by suggesting that the arts should be the handmaiden of theology and the tools that allow for the propagation of doctrine. New Man is the offspring of a creative impulse grounded in theology but fortified by traditional training in the trivium and quadrivium. The acclaim with which the text was received, and its many imitations, testify to its success.

De fide catholica contra haereticos (On the Catholic Faith, Against Heretics), dating from circa 1184–1195, is a four-volume study of heresies and their adherents, against which Alain had perhaps preached during his stay in the South of France. Along with sections on the Albigensian Cathars and the Waldensians, Alain also discusses Muslims and Jews, who were considered heretics by the medieval church. It is dedicated to William VIII of Montpellier (1172–1180), a prominent patron of the troubadours.

Alain also composed several biblical and liturgical commentaries. Many deal with theological issues that were much debated at the time (such as the Trinity and angelology) and provide evidence for his continued interest in reconciling theological study with the liberal arts. He is the author of several practical liturgical texts that were apparently much consulted and that served to ensure his continued fame. Works written sometime before 1194 include *Liber Sermonum* (Book of sermons), a collection of homilies that could be adopted for specific occasions, *Sermones diversi* (Diverse sermons), a book of eleven ready-made sermons, and *De arte praedicatoria,* also known as *Ars praedicandi* (On the Art of Preaching), which offers forty-eight complete sermons and ready-to-order scriptural citations that could be used in defense or condemnation of certain virtues or vices.

When he is mentioned near the end of his life in a 1194 chronicle by Otho of Sankt-Blasien, it is as one of the most eminent scholar/theologians of Paris rather than as a monk. In this same document special attention is called to a listing of the works for which he was already famous by that date, including the *Anticlaudianus, De fide catholica contra haereticos, De virtutibus et de vitiis et de donis Spiritus Sancti,* and *De arte praedicatoria.*

Liber poetentialis (Work on the Sacrament of Penance), written circa 1199–1202, is addressed to the clergy and offers a defense of frequent penance. It also contains a how-to manual on administering the sacrament and, in the longest version, a key containing suggested penalties to be administered by the priest after the penitent has confessed. These latter texts provide an added dimension that indicates Alain's interest in the pragmatic, as well as speculative and imaginative, uses of writing.

In 1200 Alain is mentioned as a witness to an agreement between the Knights Templar and the provost of Maguelone. At some point, probably in his later years, Alain joined the Cistercian order in the region of Montpellier, a customary choice for many high-ranking clergymen, intellectuals, and poets of the late twelfth century. He died sometime between April 1202 and April 1203 and was buried at the motherhouse of Cîteaux. When his tomb was excavated in 1960, a forensic scientist estimated his age at death as between eighty and ninety years. The inscription on his tomb testifies to the esteem in which he was held: "Alanum breuis hora breui tumulo sepeliuit / Qui duo, qui septem, qui totum scibile sciuit (Short life brought Alain to a little tomb. He knew the two [the testaments or philosophy and theology], the seven [the arts], he knew all that could be known.) Several anecdotes concerning him circulated among intellectuals in the years following his death that all share the view that he was a brilliant and dedicated scholar who preferred a life of poverty and intellectual pursuits to the glories of an ecclesiastical career or the piety of monasticism.

Alain's originality, his influence on his contemporaries, his prolific production, and the breadth of his interests are all indisputable; however, he is still something of an enigma to scholars. Attempts to link him too closely with any one school or master have generally been unsuccessful, and without further knowledge of the chronology of his works, his patrons, and monastic career, it is difficult to assess with any degree of surety his sympathies, political or intellectual. Alain's writings provide one of the most complete surveys of the philosophical, theological, and intellectual concerns that characterized the great courts whose patronage produced the literary innovations of the twelfth century and the schools and monastic centers which gave rise to the modern university. His position at the heart of the literary and ethical debates of his time, and his ability to integrate several fields of inquiry into the complex structure of his texts, ensure that his works will continue to interest scholars.

References:

Denise N. Baker, "The Priesthood of Genius: A Study of Medieval Tradition," *Speculum,* 51 (1976): 277–291;

J. F. Benton, ed., "*Mundus Deciduus,* Possibly by Alan of Lille," *Archives d'Histoire Doctrinale et Littéraire du Moyen Age,* 49 (1982): 292–295;

R. Bossuat, L. Pichard, G. Raynaud de Lage, G. Hasenohr, and M. Zink, *Dictionnaire des lettres françaises: Le Moyen Age* (Paris: Fayard, 1964; revised, 1994);

John Boswell, *Christianity, Social Tolerance, and Homosexuality: Gay People in Western Europe from the Beginning of the Christian Era to the Fourteenth Century* (Chicago: University of Chicago Press, 1980);

Jane Chance, "The Artist as Epic Hero in Alan of Lille's *Anticlaudianus,*" *Mittellateinisches Jahrbuch,* 18 (1983): 238–247;

Ernst Robert Curtius, *European Literature and the Latin Middle Ages,* translated by W. R. Trask (New York & Evanston, Ill.: Harper & Row, 1963);

Gillian R. Evans, *Alan of Lille: The Frontiers of Theology in the Later Twelfth Century* (Cambridge & New York: Cambridge University Press, 1983);

Palémon Glorieux, "Alain de Lille, le moine et l'abbaye du Bec," *Recherches de théologie ancienne et médiévale,* 39 (1972): 51–62;

Nikolaus M. Häring, ed., "Two Theological Poems Probably Composed by Alan of Lille," *Analecta Cisterciensia,* 32 (1976): 238–250;

Linda E. Marshall, "The Identity of the 'New Man' in *Anticlaudianus* of Alan of Lille," *Viator,* 10 (1979): 77–94;

Maureen Quilligan, "Allegory, Allegoresis, and the Deallegorization of Language: The *Roman de la Rose,* the *De planctu Naturae,* and the *Parlement of Foules,*" in *Allegory, Myth, and Symbol,* Harvard English Studies no. 9, edited by M. Bloomfield (Cambridge: Harvard University Press, 1981): 163–186;

G. Raynaud de Lage, *Alain de Lille: poète du XIIe siècle* (Paris: J. Vrin, 1951);

Jeffrey T. Schnapp, "Dante's Sexual Solecisms: Gender and Genre in the *Commedia,*" in *The New Medievalism,* edited by Marina S. Brownlee, Kevin Brownlee, Stephen G. Nichols (Baltimore & London: Johns Hopkins University Press, 1991), pp. 210–225;

James Simpson, *Sciences and the Self in Medieval Poetry: Alan of Lille's* Anticlaudianus *and John Gower's* Confessio Amantis (Cambridge: Cambridge University Press, 1995);

John M. Trout, *The Voyage of Prudence: The World View of Alan of Lille* (Washington, D.C.: University Press of America, 1979);

Winthrop Wetherbee, *Platonism and Poetry in the Twelfth Century* (Princeton: Princeton University Press, 1972);

Jan Ziolkowski, *Alan of Lille's Grammar of Sex: The Meaning of Grammar to a Twelfth-Century Intellectual,* Speculum Anniversary Monographs no. 10 (Cambridge, Mass.: Medieval Academy of America, 1985).

Andreas Capellanus

(flourished circa 1185)

Don A. Monson
College of William and Mary

WORK: *De amore* (circa 1185)

Manuscripts: The Latin text is extant in forty-one manuscripts, of which thirty are complete or nearly so. Three manuscripts date from the thirteenth century, seven from the fourteenth, and thirty-one from the fifteenth, including Milan, Biblioteca Ambrosiana, A 136 sup., and Wolfenbüttel, Herzog-August-Bibliothek, 83.18 Aug., on which the standard edition is based.

First publications: In *Tractatus amoris et de amoris remedio Andree Capellani pape Innocencij quarti ad Gualterum* (N.p., late fifteenth century); *Erotica. seu, Amatoria Andreae Capellani regii . . . ad venerandum suum amicum Guualterum scripta. Nunquam ante hac edita . . . in publicum emissa à Dethmaro Mulhero.* (Dortmund: Typis Westhovianis, 1610).

Standard edition: *Andreae capellani regü Francorum, De amore libri tres,* edited by E. Trojel (Copenhagen: Gad, 1892).

Editions in English: *The Art of Courtly Love,* translated by John Jay Parry, Records of Civilization: Sources and Studies no. 33 (New York: Columbia University Press, 1941);

Andreas Capellanus On Love, edited and translated with Latin text by P. G. Walsh (London: Duckworth, 1982).

Andreas Capellanus, or André le Chapelain, is known for a single work, *De amore* (On Love), but it is generally considered to be among the most important and influential documents of medieval civilization. Written about 1185, *De amore* is the earliest and doubtless the most successful attempt to analyze and systematize the new attitudes toward love between the sexes that pervaded all the medieval vernacular literatures of Western Europe. The influence of *De amore* in the late Middle Ages is attested by a rich manuscript tradition, by many quotations from it in medieval authors, and especially by translations or adaptations of it into several vernacular languages. In modern times it has become a central document in the ongoing controversy concerning the existence and nature of the phenomenon known as courtly love. This factor has combined with the ambiguity of *De amore* to make it one of the most discussed works of medieval literature.

Nothing is known about the life of the author except that which can be deduced from his work, and much of that is conjectural and controversial. The name Andreas appears as author in the rubrics of eleven manuscripts, ten of which add the title *Capellanus* (Chaplain), usually with some further qualification. One manuscript describes the author as chaplain of the king, and three others describe him as chaplain of the king of France or of the royal court of France. These rubrics may be derived, however, from a passage within the treatise that refers to Andreas the lover, chaplain of the royal court, which may actually refer to the court of the King of Love, as described in the Fifth Dialogue, thus depriving the rubrics of any biographical meaning.

The date of composition given to the work is largely conjectural. Andreas's Seventh Dialogue includes a letter attributed to Marie de Champagne that is dated 1 May 1174; although the letter itself is doubtless fictitious, its date is generally regarded as providing a reliable *terminus a quo,* or earliest possible date of composition. A *terminus ante quem,* or last possible date of composition, for *De amore* is provided by the fact that it was quoted in 1238 by Albertanus of Brescia in his *De amore et dilectione dei et proximi et aliarum rerum et de forma vita* (Concerning the Love and Cherishing of God and Those Near Him and Other Matters and the Shape of Life). The reference to Marie de Champagne, and similar references within the work, suggest a place of origin somewhere in northern France.

Attempts have been made to provide a more precise date for *De amore;* the one most widely recognized concerns a passage from the Fifth Dialogue in which a noblewoman states that she would prefer to live modestly in France rather than to be laden with Hungarian silver but subject to a foreign power. This passage is usually taken as an allusion to the marriage in 1186 of Princess Margaret, daughter of Louis VII of France, to

Bela III of Hungary. Such an allusion would have been topical shortly after the marriage took place or in 1184–1185, when it was being planned. This dating would place the composition of the treatise during the reign of Philip II Augustus, who ruled from 1180 to 1223, but no chaplain by the name of Andreas is mentioned in records of the royal chancellery during that period.

De amore is dedicated to a certain Gautier or Gualterus (Walter) who is addressed as *venerandus* (venerable), thus indicating a person of high rank. The only other information given about the addressee is that he is in love, but young and inexperienced, hence his need for instruction. A rubric from one late manuscript calls Gualterus *nepos* (nephew) of the king of France, and another refers to him as son of the king. The only Gautier in the royal family at the time was Gautier de Charros, grandson of Pierre de Courtenay and grand-nephew of Louis VII, but he was apparently too young to be Andreas's addressee. Outside the royal family the name Gautier was so common that most scholars have given up the search as futile. Many see in the addressee a fictitious character embodying the rhetorical topos of affected modesty, of which one variant consists in attributing a work's origin to the request of a patron or friend.

Among contemporary historical figures, the one most often cited in *De amore* is Countess Marie of Champagne. In addition to her letter in the Seventh Dialogue, she is asked to decide seven of the "Love Cases" of book 2, more than any other lady, and her opinion is quoted in several other passages of the treatise. This fact has led to the hypothesis that the work was written at the court of Champagne at Marie's behest. A chaplain named Andreas is referred to in nine charters from that court during the period from 1182 to 1186, and many scholars have identified this Andreas as the author of *De amore*. Since the countess was the half-sister of Philip Augustus, it is argued, relations would have been close between the courts of Champagne and France, so it would not be surprising for a chaplain employed in Troyes to continue his career in Paris, thus accounting for the rubrics associating Andreas with the royal court.

Marie de Champagne was a well-known patroness of writers such as Chrétien de Troyes, who dedicated to her his *Le Chevalier de la charrette, ou, Lancelot* (The Knight of the Cart, or, Lancelot), written circa 1179–1180. French scholar Gaston Paris saw in Chrétien's romance and Andreas's treatise a common attitude toward love, derived from the troubadours, for which he coined the expression *amour courtois,* or courtly love, in a widely influential 1883 essay. Marie and her mother, Eleanor of Aquitaine (granddaughter of the William of Poitiers, the first troubadour), are often cred-

ited with playing a key role in introducing this doctrine into the courts of northern France, with Chrétien and Andreas as their most illustrious disciples.

The association of *De amore* with the court of Champagne has been sharply criticized since the 1950s by scholars such as John F. Benton, D. W. Robertson Jr., and Alfred Karnein. They stress that the hypothesis is not supported by any of the manuscripts, some of which specifically associate Andreas with the royal court. The many mentions of Marie de Champagne within the treatise may be ironic gibes at an erstwhile political opponent of Philip Augustus, they argue. There is no evidence, according to Benton, that Marie could read Latin, and the treatise must have been addressed to a learned clerical audience, such as that of the royal chancellery.

The question has been substantially renewed thanks to a hypothesis advanced in 1985 by Alfred Karnein situating the work's origins firmly in the royal court. In addition to the three manuscript rubrics, Karnein cites the presence in the French chancellery in the mid 1180s of a young official, Gautier le Jeune, who would have been of an appropriate age to be the recipient of Andreas's advice. Moreover, there are several royal charters from 1190 to 1191 witnessed by a certain Andrew the Chamberlain (*Andreas cambellanus*), who could have written the treatise several years before, at an earlier stage of his career, when he was only a chaplain and not yet a chamberlain (Gautier le Jeune followed just such a career pattern). Finally, there are two inventories of royal charters from the mid fourteenth century that mention *De amore* among the documents dating from before the time of St. Louis; Karnein suggests that it might have been placed in the royal archives by Gualterus himself.

The archival evidence adduced by Karnein is impressive, and his hypothesis concerning Andreas's identity is perhaps the strongest that has been put forward. The matter is far from resolved because of the tenuous and problematic manuscript tradition supporting that identification; nevertheless, the Champagne hypothesis, despite its many partisans, appears even more conjectural. It is unlikely that it will ever be known with any certainty where Andreas lived and wrote.

Andreas's treatise on love is divided into three books. The first and longest, consisting of twelve chapters comprising about two-thirds of the entire treatise, is devoted primarily to how love is acquired. Book 2, broken into eight chapters, discusses how love may be retained, among other subjects. The final book, undivided and the shortest, is titled "The Rejection of Love."

Illumination for a French translation of De amore, *depicting Héloïse, lover of Peter Abelard, lecturing courtiers on Andreas Capellanus's teachings on love (British Library, Royal 16. F. 11, f. 137)*

After the preface addressed to Gualterus and a brief outline of the subjects to be examined, the first five chapters of book 1 offer a scholastic treatment of love strongly influenced by the medieval academic prologues (*accessus ad auctores*). Chapter 1 provides the cornerstone of this discussion with a definition of love that has become the subject of much controversy.

Andreas defines love as *passio quaedam innata* (a certain inborn suffering) arising from the sight of and excessive meditation upon the beauty of the opposite sex, whereby a person wishes above all else to enjoy the embraces of the other and by mutual consent to carry out all of Love's precepts. Sometimes viewed as an ironic allusion to Scripture in the patristic tradition or as a physiological description in the medical tradition, this is, in fact, a properly philosophic definition firmly rooted in the tradition of early medieval philosophy. The expression *Passio innata,* a variant of the more common *passio interior* (internal suffering) or *passio animae* (soul suffering), provides the genus of the phenomenon,

identifying love as an emotion, the remainder of the definition serving as *differentiae* (differences) to distinguish this particular emotion from all others. Moreover, the entire definition is couched in terms of Aristotelian causality, with the internal formal and material causes mentioned first, followed by the external efficient and final causes.

Chapters 2 through 5 expand upon various aspects of the definition using a technique of glossing key terms already established in the first chapter. Chapter 2, "Between What Persons Love May Exist," limits love to heterosexual relationships, thus elaborating on the definition's phrase of the "opposite sex." The third chapter completes the definition of the thing with a definition of the name, that is, an etymology. In chapter 4, "What Are the Effects of Love," the overriding desire for the embraces of the other is developed into the principle of chaste fidelity to one woman. This principle is further expanded in chapter 5, "What Persons Are Fit for Love," to exclude the excessively voluptuous who are unable to confine themselves to a single partner, and the blind are also excluded, owing to the fundamental role of sight in the origin of love.

Chapter 6 enumerates five means of acquiring love: physical beauty, excellence of character, eloquence, wealth, and the easy granting of the favors requested. The last two means are dismissed summarily as unworthy, and the superiority of character to beauty is argued at length. The role of eloquence, which is to create a presumption of excellence of character, is then illustrated in eight dialogues, comprising more than one-half of the treatise.

The dialogues are organized around the social class of the participants, according to the principle of the three levels of style, which medieval rhetoric associated with social class. They illustrate the arguments that, respectively, a man from the middle class, the nobility, or the higher nobility might use in wooing a woman from each of those classes, as well as the reasoning that she could invoke in rejecting his suit. The discussion is rational and logical in tone, employing all the techniques of Scholastic disputation in place of the emotional appeal that the subject might lead us to anticipate. In two of the dialogues the participants change status in mid conversation, going from an old man or woman to a young one, from a married man to a cleric, from a widow to a virgin, and so on, thus illustrating the function of the dialogues as a specialized *topica,* a repertory of all the possible arguments about love corresponding to a variety of rhetorical situations.

The single most important topic of discussion in the dialogues concerns the conflicting claims of nobility of birth and nobility of character. In the Third Dialogue the woman delivers a sermon on the duties of the would-be lover. The Fifth Dialogue includes the allegorical tale of the Purgatory of Cruel Beauties ending with a list of twelve Precepts of Love emanating from the King of Love. The Seventh Dialogue, on the question of love and marriage, ends with an exchange of letters with the countess of Champagne, who declares their incompatibility. The last and longest of the dialogues discusses such subjects as love and the clergy and the relative merits of pure and mixed love.

The last six chapters of book 1 provide supplementary discussion on various points relating to the acquiring of love. Chapters 7, 8, and 11 complete the sociological schema of the dialogues by extending the analysis to the clergy, to nuns, and to peasants, respectively. The other three chapters examine love bought with money, easily obtained, or conducted with prostitutes, thus elaborating on the summary condemnation at the beginning of chapter 6 of the two means of acquiring love that are deemed unworthy.

The first four chapters of book 2 examine, respectively, how love, once acquired, may be retained, increased, decreased, and ended. Chapter 5, titled "Indications That One's Love is Returned," is devoted primarily to the signs of infidelity in a partner. A long chapter on what to do if one of the lovers is unfaithful considers several such situations, rendering judgment according to the circumstances. This casuistic tendency is further developed in chapter 7, which consists of twenty-one "Love Cases" decided by noble ladies of the court, such as Marie of Champagne or Eleanor of Aquitaine. The final chapter relates an Arthurian tale concerning a British knight embarked upon a symbolic quest who receives a parchment listing thirty-one Rules of Love pronounced by the King of Love.

Book 3 begins with a disclaimer: Andreas has instructed Gualterus thoroughly in the art of love, he says, not so that his pupil may engage in this activity, but so that he may refrain from doing so, thereby earning a greater eternal reward. The rest of the book presents a long recitation of all the reasons why a wise man should avoid love altogether. Many of these arguments are theological—love offends God, leads to eternal punishment, and so on—but some are practical in nature, such as the contentions that love leads inevitably to poverty and to loss of worldly honor and that it debilitates mind and body. A central part of the discussion is devoted to a long anti-feminist diatribe claiming that all women are guilty of every vice and that they can therefore never reciprocate a man's love. Book 3 ends with an evocation of the two points of view presented in the treatise as a whole, exhorting Gualterus to eschew earlier teachings on the art of love in favor of the final salutary warnings against it.

Doubtless the most striking feature of *De amore* is its complexity, which is discernible at every level. On the surface it presents a bewildering combination of illustrative dialogues and letters, cases and codes, and Arthurian tales and mythological allegories, linked together by the authorial voice of the Chaplain. It draws its inspiration from a remarkably wide array of clerical and courtly sources, including the Bible and the church fathers, the pagan authors of classical antiquity, medieval love literature, and the beliefs and practices of contemporary feudal society. The work presents both a scientific treatise on a natural phenomenon, love, and a practical manual on the art of loving. Interwoven with these two generic vectors is a strong ethical strand, most evident in book 3 but also clearly present in the first two books, which condemns love between the sexes on the grounds of Christian morality.

Andreas's starting point seems to be the love writings of Ovid, who is, after the Bible, the authority most frequently cited in *De amore*. The influence of the *Ars amatoria* (Art of Loving) is manifest in the tripartite structure of the work and is reflected in book and chapter titles. Encompassing the form as well as the content, the Ovidian inspiration remains a constant throughout the treatise. *De amore* is not simply an imitation of Ovid, however, but a deliberate and conscious reworking and adaptation of the Ovidian material in terms of specifically medieval modes of thought and expression. As such it calls on several medieval models of discourse, Latin and vernacular, clerical and courtly, in reinterpreting Ovidian love lore for twelfth-century audiences.

Andreas's most significant innovation with respect to his Ovidian model is his application of the tools for medieval Scholasticism, especially the liberal arts of rhetoric and dialectic, to the subject of love. Most evident in the first five chapters of the treatise, the Chaplain's Scholastic method extends well beyond them to inform and permeate the entire work. Scholasticism is responsible for the systematic treatment afforded the subject, in contrast with the much looser organization of the *Arts amatoria*. Its most important manifestation is the systematic assembling and dialectical confrontation of conflicting authoritative opinions from a variety of traditions, according to the method made popular by Abelard in his *Sic et non* (Yes and No, circa 1117–1128). Most obvious in the dialogues, this tendency is apparent throughout the treatise. Indeed, dialectic provides an important key to understanding the problematic relationship of book 3 to the first two books.

Andreas makes a scarcely less important innovation with respect to the scholastic model that he has superimposed upon the Ovidian model; that is the extension of the notion of authority to include courtly vernacular sources in addition to the traditional clerical sources of classical and Christian authors writing in Latin. Thus, alongside quotations from the Bible or from Ovid are found explicit allusions to characters from medieval romances, as well as many commonplaces from courtly vernacular love poetry. Moreover, this expanded notion of authority is extended to nonliterary, social intertexts, most obviously in the use of prominent ladies of the court to decide disputed questions in the Love Cases of book 2, but also in the appeal to common proverbs and to public opinion. Several courtly vernacular poetic genres, including the love song, the *pastourelle* (literally, "shepherdess," but also the name for a type of poem in which a knight attempts to seduce a shepherdess), the debates between knights and clerics, and the *partimens* (dilemmatic debate poems), also provided models for the structuring of various parts of the treatise, entering into a dialectic of forms with respect to the overall Ovidian model.

The several themes developed in *De amore* can be grouped roughly into three main categories: first, psychological questions concerning the status of love as a natural phenomenon; second, social questions involving the relationship of love to feudal society; and third, moral problems regarding the implications of love for Christian ethics. Many of these themes are closely interrelated, and their discussion is interwoven throughout the treatise. Although the conclusions reached are often fragmentary, even contradictory, some fairly clear tendencies emerge.

Starting from an essentially psychological definition of love, Andreas develops the psychological ramifications of his definitions throughout the treatise. The aspects of the subject treated include the role of sight and meditation in the generation of love, the function of desire and will in its subsequent development, the physical and mental aptitudes required for loving, the dynamics that the process generally assumes once it is set in motion, and the pain and suffering, fear and jealousy, that are the habitual result of those dynamics. A synthesis is attempted between the love psychology of Ovid, that of the vernacular poetry, early Scholastic philosophy, medicine, and canon law. Despite some tensions and contradictions Andreas is consistent in stressing the central role of meditation and desire in the psychology of love, and also in expressing considerable pessimism concerning the possibility of establishing and maintaining reciprocal love relationships.

An important but neglected aspect of *De amore* concerns the relationship of love to feudal society. The initial focus appears to be the question of nobility and social class around which the dialogues are organized. From this starting point, other subjects are drawn into the discussion: deeds and service, wealth and generosity, courtesy and reputation. The conflict between nobility of birth and nobility of character provides the most important controversy relating to social matters. Otherwise the relative lack of controversy probably reflects relative homogeneity of the sources, which are primarily contemporary and courtly. The largely successful effort to compile and systematize the social themes of medieval vernacular love poetry constitutes one of the major achievements of *De amore*.

Doubtless the most important group of themes in *De amore* concerns the relationship of love to Christian ethics. Long before his rejection of love in book 3, Andreas had undertaken in the first two books a systematic effort to accommodate the secular love ethic of the troubadours with the dictates of Christian morality. Taking as his point of departure the idealizing tendencies in vernacular love poetry, Andreas attempts to establish love as a source of moral virtue while at the same time limiting sexual activity in terms both of fidelity to a single partner and of the restriction, or at least delay, of physical intimacy. By declaring the utter incompatibility of love and marriage, in exaggerated imitation of a common vernacular poetic theme, he apparently tries to protect the sacrament of holy matrimony from the moral contamination of love even as he seeks to regulate and moralize love by adapting to it various provisions of the canon law on marriage. Although there is no reason to doubt the sincerity of these efforts to moralize love, they meet with only limited success, which may help to account for the strong denunciation of love in book 3.

It is unknown how Andreas's immediate contemporaries received his work since the earliest extant reactions date from some fifty years later. From about the middle of the thirteenth century, however, *De amore* was the subject of a rich and varied reception extending throughout the late Middle Ages and into the early modern period. Rediscovered near the end of the nineteenth century after a long period of neglect, the treatise has been an important focus of medieval literary scholarship for more than one hundred years, exercising a fascination that remains unabated today.

Some parts of *De amore* appear to have been anthologized very early in the florilegia, which were responsible for the earliest reactions. Thus, Albertanus of Brescia, in the first extant reference to the treatise (in 1238), quoted the definition of love and the Rules of Love, and in the third quarter of the thirteenth century Jean de Meun translated Andreas's definition of love into Old French in *Le Roman de la Rose* (The Romance of the Rose). A more substantial reaction to Andreas is in the *Livre d'Enanchet* (Book of Enanchet), a didactic prose work written in Franco-Italian in northern Italy before 1252, that translates large sections of *De amore,* including five of the dialogues.

In 1277 Etienne Tempier, bishop of Paris, included *De amore* in a list of 219 books condemned for use at the University of Paris, along with works of magic or of Averroist philosophy. Confirming the work's popularity among students, this condemnation also seems to indicate that the bishop found it dangerous to faith and morals, despite the retraction in book 3.

During the Middle Ages *De amore* was translated into several vernacular languages. The oldest of these was a verse translation into Old French completed by Drouart la Vache in 1290. During the fourteenth century anonymous prose translations of the treatise were made into Catalan and, in two different versions, into Italian. In 1440 Johann Hartlieb translated Andreas into German. There are several vernacular translations of specific parts of the work, such as the Rules of Love and book 3, both of which also circulated separately in Latin.

The modern reception of *De amore* began with Gaston Paris's 1883 article in which he coined the term *amour courtois,* or courtly love. In this and most subsequent discussions of courtly love Andreas provides one of the three pillars on which the theory is based, along with the poetry of the troubadours and the romances of Chrétien de Troyes. The most explicit of these sources, the Chaplain's treatise, has always occupied a special place in the discussion, hence its frequent use as a key to understanding a wide variety of medieval works of literature, a practice that still continues despite the lack of agreement among modern scholars as to the meaning and intention of the work, and even as to the existence of courtly love.

The most persistent controversy surrounding the treatise concerns the difficult relationship of book 3 to the first two books. Earlier scholars were fairly unanimous in considering book 3 a hypocritical afterthought designed to appease ecclesiastical authorities who might have been offended by the tone of the two earlier books. More recently, other possible solutions have been proposed. One widely held view, first advanced by Robertson in the 1950s, sees in the first two books an ironic condemnation of sexual love, and thus an indirect confirmation of the message of Book Three. Another interpretation, first formulated by Betsy Bowden in 1979, regards the treatise as a kind of elaborate dirty joke, composed of a series of thinly veiled obscene images and puns. Neither of these theories has achieved general acceptance, and so, in the absence of a scholarly consensus, Andreas's authorial intentions remain problematic.

The wide diversity of the interpretations that *De amore* has elicited underscores the work's complexity. Perhaps the most obvious intention discernible in the treatise is that of assembling and synthesizing as wide a spectrum as possible of the medieval discourses on love. It may be that the ultimate impossibility of reconciling such divergent points of view as those of vernacular literature, Christianity, and Ovid accounts for Andreas's failure to communicate a clear and focused message. In any case, the intrinsic interest of the subject and the rich and varied approach that Andreas brings to it will doubtless assure a continuing readership for *De amore* among students of medieval literature and culture.

References:

John W. Baldwin, *The Language of Sex: Five Voices from Northern France around 1200* (Chicago & London: University of Chicago Press, 1994);

John F. Benton, "The Court of Champagne as a Literary Center," *Speculum,* 36 (1961): 551–591;

Benton, "The Evidence for Andreas Capellanus Re-examined Again," *Studies in Philology,* 59 (1962): 471–478;

Betsy Bowden, "The Art of Courtly Copulation," *Medievalia et Humanistica,* 9 (1979): 67–85;

Francis Cairns, "Andreas Capellanus, Ovid, and the Consistency of *De amore,*" *Res Publicum Litterarum,* 16 (1993): 101–117;

Paolo Cherchi, *Andrea Cappellano, i trovatori e altri temi romanzi* (Rome: Bulzoni, 1979);

Cherchi, *Andreas and the Ambiguity of Courtly Love* (Toronto: University of Toronto Press, 1994);

Michael D. Cherniss, "The Literary Comedy of Andreas Capellanus," *Modern Philology,* 71 (1974–1975): 223–237;

Peter Dronke, "Andreas Capellanus," *Journal of Medieval Latin,* 4 (1994): 51–63;

Tony Hunt, "Aristotle, Dialectic, and Courtly Literature," *Viator,* 10 (1979): 95–129;

William T. H. Jackson, "The *De amore* of Andreas Capellanus and the Practice of Love at Court," *Romanic Review,* 49 (1958): 243–251;

Alfred Karnein, *De amore in volkssprachlicher Literatur: Untersuchungen zur Andreas-Capellanus-Rezeption in Mittelalter und Renaissance* (Heidelberg: Winter, 1985);

Douglas Kelly, "Courtly Love in Perspective: The Hierarchy of Love in Andreas Capellanus," *Traditio,* 24 (1968): 119–147;

Ursula Liebertz-Grün, "Satire und Utopie in Andreas Capellanus,' Traktat *De amore,*" *Beiträge zur Geschichte der deutschen Sprache und Literatur,* 111, no. 2 (1989): 210–225;

Toril Moi, "Desire in Language: Andreas Capellanus and the Controversy of Courtly Love," in *Medieval Literature: Criticism, Ideology, and History,* edited by David Aers (New York: St. Martin's Press, 1986), pp. 11–33;

Don A. Monson, "Andreas Capellanus and the Problem of Irony," *Speculum,* 63 (1988): 539–572;

Monson, "Andreas Capellanus' Scholastic Definition of Love," *Viator,* 25 (1994): 197–214;

Gaston Paris, "Etudes sur les romans de la Table Ronde. Lancelot du Lac. II. Le *Conte de la Charrette,*" *Romania,* 12 (1883): 459–534;

D. W. Robertson Jr., "The Subject of the *De amore* of Andreas Capellanus," *Modern Philology,* 50 (1952–1953): 145–161;

Robertson, *A Preface to Chaucer* (Princeton, N. J.: Princeton University Press, 1963);

Bruno Roy, "A la recherche des lecteurs médiévaux du *De amore* d'André le Chapelain," *University of Ottawa Quarterly,* 55 (1985): 45–73;

Doris Ruhe, "Intertextuelle Spiele bei Andreas Capellanus," *Germanisch-Romanische Monatsschrift,* 37, new series no. 3 (1987): 264–279;

Ernstpeter Ruhe and Rudolf Beherns, eds., *Mittelalterbilder aus neuer Perspektive: Diskussionsanstöße zu amour courtois, Subjektivität in der Dichtung und Strategien des Erzählens* (Munich: Fink, 1985);

Felix Schlösser, *Andreas Capellanus: Seine Minnelehre und das christliche Weltbild um 1200* (Bonn: Bouvier, 1962);

Rüdiger Schnell, *Andreas Capellanus: Zur Rezeption des römischen und kanonischen Rechts in De amore* (Munich: Fink, 1982);

Irving Singer, "Andreas Capellanus: A Reading of the *Tractatus,*" *Modern Language Notes,* 88 (1973): 1288–1315;

Hermann John Weigand, *Three Chapters on Courtly Love in Arthurian France and Germany: Lancelot–Andreas Capellanus–Wolfram von Eschenbach's Parzival,* Studies in the Germanic Languages and Literatures no. 17 (Chapel Hill: University of North Carolina Press, 1956).

Bernard of Clairvaux

(1090 – 20 August 1153)

James Hala
Drew University

WORKS: *Apologia* (before 1125)

> **Manuscripts:** More than fifty manuscripts exist, including Paris, Bibliothèque Nationale de France, Lat. 2042, f. 150–153; Paris, Bibliothèque Mazarine 998, f. 120v–130v.

De gradibus humilitatis et superbiae (1124 or 1125)

> **Manuscripts:** There are seventy extant manuscripts, including Cambridge, Pembroke College, 118 (f 12–20); Dijon, 658 f. 73–86v; Douai, 372, I, f. 100–107; Munich, Lat. 18646, f. 40–57; Paris, Bibliothèque de l'Arsenal 323; Paris, Bibliothèque Nationale de France, Lat. 14877; Paris, Bibliothèque Nationale de France, Lat. 18099.

De in laudibus matris virginis (before 1125)

> **Manuscripts:** Nearly eighty manuscripts are extant, including: Dijon, 658, f. 25–40v; Douai 372, t. I, f. 114–122; Lambach, O. S. B., 42, f. 103–121; Oxford, Bodleian Library, Laud., Misc., 344, f. 68v–81v. Paris, Bibliothèque de l' Arsenal 323, f. 113–134v.

De diligendo Deo (circa 1126–1141)

> **Manuscripts:** This work is present in sixty extant manuscripts, including Douai, 372, I, f. 122–127v; Oxford, Bodleian Library, Laud. Misc. 344, f. 100–113v.

De gratia et libero arbitrio (circa 1126–1135)

> **Manuscripts:** Fifty-six extant manuscripts hold this work, including Douai, 372, I, f. 141v–148; Paris, Bibliothèque Nationale de France, Lat. 2883, f. 22–23.

De laude novae militiae (circa 1128–1135)

> **Manuscripts:** Thirty-three manuscripts are extant, including Berlin, Phillipps 1996, f. 243–252v; Ms. Dijon 658, f. 86v–93.

Sermones in canticum canticorum (circa 1136)

> **Manuscripts:** This work is represented in 122 extant manuscripts, including Paris, Bibliothèque Nationale de France, Lat. 14305.

Liber de praecepto et dispensatione (circa 1141–1144)

> **Manuscripts:** There are nearly sixty extant manuscripts, including Dijon 658, f. 54–66; Douai 372, I, f. 107–114; Oxford, Bodleian Library, Lat. th. f. 15, f. 1–133v; Paris, Bibliothèque Nationale de France, Lat. 2883, f. 34–50.

De consideratione (circa 1148–1153)

> **Manuscripts:** There are seventy-three extant manuscripts that contain this work, including Brussels, Bibliothèque Royale Koninklijke Bibliotheek, 1840–1848, f. 3–54; Douai, 372, I, f. 166–177v.

Vitae Sancti Malachiae (after 1148)

> **Manuscripts:** There are thirty-nine extant manuscripts, including Dijon, 658, f. 1–22v; Douai, 372, I, 177–188v.

> **Standard editions:** *Sancti Bernardi abbatis Primi Clarae-Valensis, opera omnia,* 6 volumes in 2, edited by Jean Mabillon (Paris: Sumptibus Petri Aubovyn, Petri Emery, Caroli Clouisier, 1690) republished in *Patrologia latina,* 221 volumes, edited by Jacques-Paul Migne (Paris: Migne, 1841–1879), CLXXXII–CLXXXIII; *Sancti Bernardi opera,* 8 volumes in 9, edited by Jean Leclercq, Henri Rochais, and Charles H. Talbot (Rome: Editiones Cisterciensis, 1957–1979).

Editions in English: *The Works of Bernard of Clairvaux,* Cistercian Fathers Series (Kalamazoo, Mich.: Cistercian Publications; Shannon: Irish University Press; London: Mowbrays, 1970–); *The Letters of Saint Bernard,* edited and translated by Bruno Scott James (London: Burns, Oates, 1953).

Bernard of Clairvaux is one of the most influential figures in the latter half of the Middle Ages, and one of the most paradoxical. Even Bernard thought of himself as "the chimera of his century." He was first and foremost a Cistercian monk burning with the zeal of reform. He was a severe critic of the Benedictine order, which he regarded as lax and undisciplined, and he made his opinions of the monastery at Cluny in particular publicly known, even as he became a friend and admirer of the abbot of Cluny, Peter the Venerable. At times his severe discipline estranged his followers; yet,

Bernard of Clairvaux, altar piece from the chapel of Pont-d'Aube (Hôtel de ville, Bar-sur-Aube, France)

in the development of mystical theology in the later Middle Ages and Renaissance.

As a writer Bernard is unequaled in his mastery of a rhetorically elaborate style of Latin. His ability to incorporate Scripture seamlessly into his writings and his capacity to evoke the ineffable through metaphor and analogy are remarkable. Often referred to as "the last of the Church fathers," Bernard of Clairvaux's influence extends from the theology, literature, and history of the twelfth century through to the present.

Bernard of Clairvaux was born in 1090 at the Château de Fontaines-les-Dijon in Burgundy into a noble family; his father, uncle, and older brothers distinguished themselves as knights, and Bernard may have derived the chivalric imagery that he was to employ so skillfully in his writings from his family's military and knightly orientation. He was the third of seven children born to Tescelin and his wife, Aleth. In the *Vita prima Bernardi,* a biography written by some of his contemporaries and translated in the twentieth century by Geoffrey Webb and Adrian Walker, William of St. Thierry tells the following story: while she was pregnant with Bernard, Aleth had a premonitory dream that she had within her "a barking dog, which had a white coat and a tawny back." (Cistercian robes are white, as opposed to the black robes of the Benedictines, hence the respective soubriquets of "the White Monks" and "the Black Monks.") The dream frightened Aleth, and she sought a holy man to explicate it for her.

> You are to be the mother of a wonderful dog who is to be the guardian of the Lord's house. You heard him barking, because very soon now he will rush out against the enemies of the faith. He is to be a marvelous preacher, and as a dog will lick its master's wounds clean of all that may poison them, so the words that his tongue speaks will heal and cure many of the evils that disease men's souls.

Putting questions of the veracity of hagiography aside, the story provides a vivid characterization of Bernard by a contemporary friend and admirer.

Bernard attended the school of the secular canons of St.-Vorles, where he probably studied grammar, dialectic, and rhetoric, the medieval trivium of liberal arts. The method of training would have been to study examples from pagan antiquity and the Christian era, memorizing them, reciting them, and ultimately imitating them. The education at St.-Vorles must have been good; in his life, Bernard proved himself a master of all three disciplines and displayed a remarkable capacity for citing religious and secular texts from memory.

Bernard's mother, Aleth, had a reputation for holiness and strict discipline, and her son is said to have been devoted to her. Their relationship has been com-

they still admired and were drawn toward his charismatic holiness. Responsible for establishing sixty-eight Cistercian foundations throughout continental Europe, Britain, and Ireland, Bernard nevertheless declined an invitation to establish the order in Jerusalem, nor did he want Cistercian foundations established beyond the Pyrenees. Bernard desired nothing so much as the quiet discipline of the cloister, but nevertheless became a major figure in the political and doctrinal fights of his day. He sang the praises of the Virgin Mother and was instrumental in the development of Marian devotion, the veneration of the Virgin Mary; yet, he scoffed at the idea of the Immaculate Conception. A man of peace whose best-known sermons preached the centrality of love, he also preached in favor of the Second Crusade. He could be the most excellent of friends, and a most dangerous enemy. In spite of having left no systematic exposition of his religious beliefs, he is a central figure pared to that of St. Augustine of Hippo and his mother, Monica. It is generally believed that Bernard's love for his mother was in part responsible for his later Marian devotion, and Aleth's death in 1107 was in all likelihood very difficult for Bernard. Little is known of Bernard's life until 1111, when he entered the abbey of Cîteaux, near Dijon. The Cistercians were the most reform-minded order of the time, believing in rigorous adhesion to monastic discipline, and this strictness appealed to the young man. Bernard was soon joined there by his brothers and other relatives; three years later, recognizing Bernard's devotion, Stephen Harding, the abbot of Cîteaux, appointed Bernard to found a new chapter house at Clairvaux.

Bernard brought four brothers, an uncle, two cousins, an architect, and two other monks with him to establish the new foundation at Clairvaux, where he served as abbot. They were soon joined by Bernard's father, Tescelin, who died shortly thereafter. Life in the early years of Clairvaux was extremely difficult, and the new foundation struggled for ten years before becoming self-sufficient. While the rigors of survival at Clairvaux were a great test of physical strength and stamina, Bernard added a fierce monastic discipline to the already harsh life. The account in the *Vita prima* indicates that Bernard's sermons at the time were beyond his auditors' comprehension and that monks who confessed carnal thoughts to their abbot were severely chastised.

The severity of Bernard's abbacy is reflected in an incident of 1119 or 1120. Bernard's own "nephew," as he called him—really his cousin—Robert of Châtillon, fled Clairvaux without permission. As a child Robert had been promised to the Benedictines of Cluny by his parents, but once old enough to speak for himself, he chose to go to Cîteaux and then followed his cousin to Clairvaux. At Clairvaux he found the austerities of monastic life harsh, especially when compared to his experience of Cluny, to which he returned. In a letter to Bernard, Robert charged that there was a degree of pride in the austerities practiced at Clairvaux and argued that he was still bound to Cluny by his parents' promise. The charges point to a clash between the abbot's zeal and his monks' human frailties. Bernard opposed on principle the practice of *transitus* (moving) from one order to another, but to move from what Bernard saw as the spiritual perfection of Clairvaux to the decadence of Cluny, and to do so without permission, was inconceivable to him.

Bernard's response in a letter was made public, and was the first angry note in the dispute that was to develop between Bernard's reformist Cistercians and the Benedictines of Cluny. Bernard condemns those who maintained that a strict poverty was not necessary, calling their arguments "sophistries" by which a credulous innocent was led astray so that a soul for whom Christ died was lost to Cluny. Bernard insists that a terrible judgment awaits Cluny for its misdeeds and laxity. Thus, the letter is at the same time both a critique of Cluny and a very personal appeal to Robert. First, Bernard pleads the injury done to him by Robert's desertion ("I must cast myself at the feet of him who should cast himself at mine"). Bernard then says "We will not let arguments about who is to blame delay correction of what is blameworthy" and goes on to exonerate Robert by admitting that he had been too hard on the boy and promises that he has changed. The blame is ultimately shifted to Cluny, however, because it has turned the boy's head with its decadence. Finally, Bernard exhorts him to take up the fight by returning to the austere discipline of Clairvaux: "Arise, soldier of Christ, I say arise." The letter is highly instructive of Bernard's affective, psychologically astute employment of rhetoric. The letter is at once shaming and ennobling, impassioned yet reasoned, and tenacious, never willing to allow Robert the option of remaining at Cluny.

Bernard's first known formal treatise is *De gradibus humilitatis et superbiae* (The Steps of Humility and Pride). Written in 1124 or 1125, the tract was composed for Godfrey of Langres, abbot of Fontenay, Clairvaux's second foundation. The "Retractio" with which *De gradibus* begins was added many years later. The "Retractio" is at once a defense against charges that the true subject of *De gradibus* was not humility but pride and a correction of errors made by the young Bernard with regard to Scripture—errors made, Bernard acknowledges, because he depended on his memory of the general sense of the Scriptures without referring to the Scriptures themselves. The text of *De gradibus* is an elaboration of what is often considered the most important chapter of the Rule of Saint Benedict, the seventh, in which the twelve steps of humility are outlined.

In the treatise Bernard delineates a threefold division of truth: truth in one's self, truth in one's neighbor, and truth in itself. The first is the perception of one's own sinful state, and the second is the recognition of the same state in others. Having discovered the wretched state of human existence, a monk is ready to contemplate truth directly by leaving human understanding behind. *De gradibus* is the first statement of Bernard's contemplative, mystic, and affective theology. Stylistically, the treatise clearly displays Bernard's gift for vivid metaphor, the skillful deployment of rhetorical devices, and a talent for description and characterization.

De gradibus provides an insight into the theological reasoning behind Bernard's strict discipline at Clairvaux. Bernard himself practiced what he preached; he imposed no hardship on those he called his sons that he

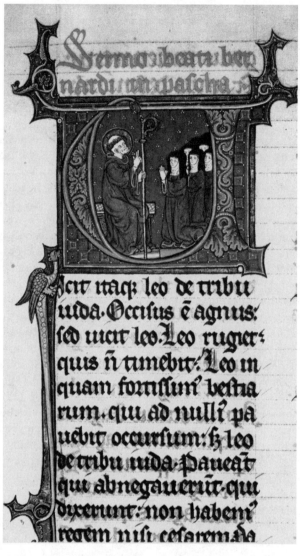

Bernard of Clairvaux preaching to a group of nuns (from an illuminated thirteenth-century manuscript for his Sermones; *Brussels, Bibliothèque Royale/Koninklijke Bibliotheek)*

did not impose upon himself. His relentless fasting and unremitting work schedule led to severe health problems, but the abbot would not give up his rigorous daily regimens until forced to do so by William of Champeaux, bishop of Châlons-sur-Marne. Bernard's strength returned despite the ministrations of a healer whom the patient, according to the *Vita prima,* referred to as "an irrational brute." He resumed his duties as abbot at the end of the year, but he would have problems with his health for the remainder of his life.

The one discipline Bernard was allowed to practice while under obedience to William of Chapeaux was writing. During his convalescence, Bernard wrote for a few hours before dawn each day. *De in laudibus matris virginis* (Sermons in Praise of the Virgin Mother),

written sometime before 1125, is the result. It is Bernard's first Marian writing, to be followed by Letter 174 to the canons of Lyon concerning the conception of Mary (written sometime after 1139), seven Assumption sermons, and scattered references throughout his works. There is little in Bernard's writing that is new in terms of Marian imagery. His meditations are firmly rooted in Scripture, especially Luke's story of the Annunciation. Bernard is, in fact, very conservative in Marian matters. He opposed the doctrine of the Immaculate Conception ("She does not need false claims," he wrote to the canons of Lyon), and he had little to say on the Assumption. Bernard sees himself as a knight errant serving the Mother of God, who is the object of a divine yet courtly love.

De in laudibus, however, is unusual in that it was not written at anyone's request, nor for any specific, extrinsic purpose. Thus, these sermons may reflect the young abbot writing for himself, expressing himself freely. Their elaborate stylistic embellishment along with their intense passion suggest a young man somewhat intemperate in his expression and offer an insight into the kind of forbidding zeal that his spiritual sons at Clairvaux must have known well.

Sometime before 1125 Bernard, at the request of Abbot William of St. Thierry, wrote what is known simply as the *Apologia.* The Cistercians had arisen in the late eleventh century considering themselves not so much reformers of the Benedictine Order but men with a vocation to begin monastic practice all over again with its original, ascetic austerity. This implied, of course, that the Benedictines were beyond reform, a notion to which the Black Monks naturally objected. The resultant quarrel between the two orders lasted throughout the twelfth century.

Bernard's *Apologia* is the most famous of the eleven or more tracts written in the dispute, and justly so, because in it Bernard manages to reconcile two seemingly contradictory objectives. William instructed Bernard to write a tract that criticized the Cistercians for their slandering of the Benedictines, even while criticizing the laxity of the Benedictines that had prompted the Cistercian reform in the first place. Bernard managed this assignment by employing a form that gave each side in turn its due. In the first half of the *Apologia,* Bernard sharply rebukes his fellow Cistercians for criticizing the Benedictines of Cluny. Then, having enlisted the Benedictines' sympathy for his writing, he comes around to rebuke them for their laxity and luxuriance. Both sides, then, are rebuked and justified in the same tract.

In 1128 Bernard was named secretary to the Council of Troyes, at which Hugh de Payens (a relative of Bernard) was granted ecclesiastic recognition of his order of monk-knights established in 1119, the Knights of the Temple. Bernard drew up the rule of the Templars, and then composed *De laude novae militiae* (In Praise of the New Knighthood) between 1128 and 1135 as an apologia for the order. The Knights Templar represented an entirely new idea: fighting men consecrated in a monastic discipline to Christ. Bernard praises the new order by contrasting them to the vanity and greed of worldly knights. The Templars were to be distinguished from worldly knights on the basis of their motives: the desire to defend Christianity. The principle functions of the Templars would be to keep safe Christian pilgrims on the way to and from the Holy Land and to guard Christianity's most sacred shrines. Bernard defends the Templars against the charge of incongruity between a monk's spiritual devotion and a knight's participation in acts of violence by suggesting that monks are like knights of the spirit. They defend the heavenly Jerusalem and, like a military order, need discipline, courage, and endurance to win the battle against the devil. The latter half of this short tract is given to meditations on the pilgrimage sites of the Holy Land.

In defining the Templars' mission in this way, Bernard harkens back to the "just war" doctrine of St. Augustine of Hippo's *De civitate Dei* (On the City of God, circa 413–426), asserting that if a knight engages in combat with pure motives for a just cause, the result can never be evil. The reasoning here is instructive as to why Bernard became the principal public advocate of the Second Crusade (1147–1149).

In 1130 Pope Honorius II died, and the double election of Innocent II and Anacletus II to the papacy led to schism. Bernard was firmly on the side of Innocent, as were most of those who favored reform monastic practices. The schism lasted for eight years, during which time Bernard untiringly traveled across Europe, negotiating on behalf of Innocent's cause with the most powerful men of England, Germany, France, Spain, and Sicily. Bernard was the only figure who commanded sufficient respect to make such delicate negotiations between so many secular and religious leaders possible. On 29 May 1138 at St. Peter's in Rome, the Antipope Anacletus II prostrated himself at the feet of Pope Innocent II and swore allegiance to him. Bernard's man had won.

At some time between 1126 and 1135, Bernard wrote *De gratia et libero arbitrio* (On Grace and Free Will). In this theological study Bernard describes free will as constituted first in freedom from necessity. All people are equally free to say "yes" or "no" to any idea. God created humanity in His own image, and the Fall has had no impact on that likeness to God. Before the Fall, however, humanity was like God in two other respects, as well: freedom from sin and freedom from misery. When humanity abused its freedom from necessity and said yes to evil, humanity lost its freedom from sin and misery, and thus became less like God. Only the grace of God through Christ can restore freedom from sin, and with freedom from sin will come freedom from misery. Thus, through Christ, humanity is restored to its full likeness unto God, which is necessary if one is to achieve ecstatic, mystical union with God.

Bernard's *Sermones in canticum canticorum* (Sermons on the Song of Songs), composed around 1136, is preeminent among his works, judging on the basis of later literary influence. These eighty-six sermons explicating the first two chapters of the Song of Songs comprise a kind of summa of Bernard's thought, weaving his mys-

Bernard (in white robe at left) praying as King Louis VII takes the cross of the Second Crusade (detail from an illumination in the manuscript for Les Passages faits Outremer, *ca. 1490; Bibliothèque Nationale de France, f. fr. 5594, f. 193)*

tical theology together with his affective call to his followers to know Christ personally. Bernard was not the first to allegorize the Song of Songs into an expression of the love between the Church and Christ or of the soul and the Word. Origen had done so in the third century, insisting that the literal, carnal sense of the Song of Songs must be cast aside. In the twelfth century, however, the trend was toward taking the literal sense of the Song of Songs back into account. The Song of Songs was believed to be an epithalamion for King Solomon and an Egyptian bride and consequently was considered part of the historical record for scholars such as Hugh of St. Victor and William of St. Thierry, Bernard's friend.

Bernard's particular contribution to this new trend lies in the extent to which he stresses a dynamic relation between the literal and figurative senses of the text, and in the extent to which he regards immersion in the literal sense as the necessary psychological starting point in bringing the soul to God. Ann Askell

argues that Bernard, rather than pushing aside or denying the erotic nature of the Song of Songs, seems at times to embellish it. In Sermon 40, Bernard expounds upon the verse "Thy cheeks are beautiful as turtle doves" (*Cant.* 1:9). Bernard writes of the bride's face,

> You must not give an earth-bound meaning to this coloring of the corruptible flesh, to this gathering of blood-red liquid that spreads evenly beneath the surface of her pearly skin, quietly mingling with it to enhance her physical beauty by the pink and white loveliness of her cheeks.

Bernard directly invokes the appeal of the Bride so as to create a desire for that which is feminine within his audience and so make them identify with the masculine desire of the Bridegroom, who is Christ in the spiritual sense. Bernard then redirects attention abruptly to this spiritual sense: "Try then as best you can to grasp the spiritual nature of this entity by means of a spiritual insight. . . . We may see in this flush on the cheek an unassuming disposition in which virtue and beauty thrive and grace increases." This spiritual insight is then ascribed to the soul. What begins as the concupiscent desire for the *signum* (sign) now becomes a desire for the spiritual *res* (thing). Thus, the desire for the letter comes to be understood as merely a sign for the desire within the soul for the Word.

Beginning with the Latin and vernacular lyrics of the High Middle Ages, Bernard's understanding of concupiscent desire as a token of divine love became part of a defining tension in secular love poetry right through the Renaissance, and part of the repertoire of the literature of the Christian mystics up to the present. Bernard enriched the poetry of *fin'amor* (refined or noble love) by providing a spiritual corollary to courtly love. Further, Bernard's emphasis on human experience as a means to God paved the way for the psychological depth of characterization that blossomed in the late Middle Ages in the writings of Giovanni Boccaccio, Petrarch, Geoffrey Chaucer, and others. It is Bernard who directs Dante's eyes toward the Queen of Heaven in canto 21 of Dante's *Paradiso* (circa 1308–1321).

De diligendo Deo (On Loving God), written between 1126 and 1141, is perhaps Bernard's finest display of biblical synthesis. It is addressed to Haimeric, who served as the Pope's chancellor from 1126 to his death in 1141. Bernard asserts that a human being loves God because God loved humanity first and because all of humanity's good qualities are gifts from God. Accordingly, one must never take pride in one's good qualities but should humbly thank God for them. All men should love God, including infidels, but Christians have a special obligation because of Christ's Passion. Taking his imagery from the Song of Songs, Bernard portrays the Church as the bride whose heart is pierced by the sword of love as she contemplates the Passion and Resurrection while reclining her head on Christ's left hand. Thus, Christ supports the weight of her flesh and its desires as her soul acknowledges that even its deepest love is too little in return for the love she receives. Bernard distinguishes four stages of love. One first loves oneself for natural reasons. Then, however, one becomes aware of a dependency on one's fellows and on God for sustenance, and so comes to love God for the good that one receives. When one accepts that God is the source of all good, one then comes to love God for what he is. Ultimately, one may momentarily achieve a transcendent state in which the soul fixes on nothing else but God and leaves the body and the world behind. Bernard then moves on to the imagery of food and sustenance. On earth, the just soul's food is comprised of the act of doing God's will. After death, the soul drinks wine mixed with milk, which betokens the soul's love of God even as it desires to be reunited with the body. Ultimately, the soul turns away from the body and begins to resemble God, at which point the soul receives the wine of wisdom and becomes intoxicated with the pure love of God.

In 1140, just two years after Innocent's victory over Anacletus, Bernard involved himself in another controversy. Hugh of St. Victor had already written with some alarm to Bernard in 1127 or 1128 to ask his opinions of Peter Abelard, the brilliant dialectician of Paris whose teachings had been condemned in 1121. Bernard's reply stuck to the doctrinal issues involved and the questions of how to proceed against Abelard. The points Bernard made were eventually incorporated into *De sacramentis* (On the Sacraments). It was, however, William of St. Thierry who roused "the dog who guards the Lord's house" by convincing Bernard that Abelard's teachings were not simply heterodox, but threatened the core doctrines of the Church. In Abelard's view, the real purpose of the Incarnation and Crucifixion was to demonstrate to humanity a perfected way of life. The redemption of humanity was a corollary benefit, one that did not require so great a sacrifice. If redemption were the point, Abelard argued, God could have effected that without the Crucifixion.

Few ideas could have been more offensive to Bernard, who strongly believed that Christ's dying to redeem humanity was the supreme act of love. In fact, the very basis of Scholasticism, of answering questions through reason rather than faith, was antithetical to Bernard's affective, mystical theology. Bernard began a campaign of letters against Abelard written to everyone from Abelard's former students to cardinals and Pope Innocent himself. At the Council of Sens in 1140, Bernard presented the case against Abelard. The council decided to condemn Abelard's errors, but not the man himself.

Sometime between 1141 and 1144 Bernard produced the *Liber de praecepto et dispensatione* (On Precept and Profession). The book began as a letter in response to the questions of two Benedictine monks at St.-Père-en-Vallée, near Chartres: Are the prescriptions of the Benedictine Rule precepts (the disobeying of which is cause for damnation) or are they simply advisory? To what extent is submission due to the superior? Are there degrees of obedience? What if an abbot makes demands that are not in the best interests of the monks' welfare? Can a monk leave a monastery after an abbot dies but before a new abbot is appointed?

Although the precise nature of the situation at St. Père is unknown, it is clear from the monks' concerns that there was some sort of crisis in obedience. As is often the case, Bernard's response was in itself a lesson in obedience. The monks had not obtained their superior's permission to write to Bernard. Conse-

Page from a thirteenth-century manuscript for a collection of Bernard's sermons (from Maggs Bros., The Art of Writing: 2800 B.C. to 1930 A.D., *1930)* quently, Bernard addressed his response not to the enquiring monks, but to their superior to be passed on to the monks at the abbot's discretion. Beyond this, however, the treatise, while rigidly maintaining the preceptual nature of the Rule, nevertheless addresses the issues in terms of a mutual obligation between monk and abbot. Bernard asserts that the phrase used in a monk's profession or vows, to obey "secundum regulam Sancti Benedicti" (according to the Rule of St. Benedict) is to be taken quite literally: that is, in the strictest accordance with that text.

After establishing the preceptual nature of the Rule and the authority of the text, he then goes on to assert that the profession is itself a contractual obligation upon both abbot and monk. The monk is not obligated to do anything beyond his promise to follow the Rule. At the same time, if he follows the Rule, the monk should have no other concerns on his mind. Hence, his is to obey. The abbot, too, is bound by the Rule to ask nothing of the monk beyond that which is stipulated by the Rule. Since the abbot, too, lives by the Rule, he has no occupation beyond the Rule and so need never to ask for anything outside the Rule. In this way, Bernard portrays obedience to the abbot and the abbot's spiritual and diurnal guidance of the monk as two inseparable parts to one act. Thus, the whole monastic community becomes the executor of God's law and will.

In 1144 or 1145 the "guardian of the Lord's house" attacked again. This time his foe was Arnold, the prior of the Augustinian foundation at Brescia. Arnold was a student of Abelard's, and he had taken a radical reform view that the Church should divest itself of all its wealth and live in strict poverty. Arnold called for armed rebellion by the people of Rome, a city with a history of driving popes away with the threat of violence. Arnold's teaching incited Bernard's ire, and not solely because Bernard sought the support of the Roman people for the papacy.

Bernard's ideals for a reformed church are to be found in his *Vitae Sancti Malachiae* (The Life of St. Malachy), written after 1148. The *Vitae Malachiae* concerns itself with the conduct of the ideal prelate, based upon the life of Bernard's friend, Malachy, bishop of Armagh, the man who was credited with bringing the sacraments back to an errant Irish Church. Bernard may have felt a special affinity for Malachy in as much as the bishop, too, desired the life of the cloister, but was he forced by circumstances into the public sphere. It is in most respects a conventional piece of hagiography, complete with the exaggerations typical of the genre. The Bernardine touch is found in the reliance upon scriptural quotation and the presence of classical quotations from Virgil, Ovid, Horace, and Apuleius.

In 1144 the northernmost crusader state, Edessa, fell to Islamic forces, alarming many in Christian Europe who saw their hold on the Holy Land threatened. At the urging of Pope Eugenius III and King Louis VIII of France, Bernard became the principal public advocate of the Second Crusade of 1147 to 1149 and traveled throughout France and Germany calling for its support. The Crusade itself was an utter failure, as the crusaders became distracted from their ostensible goal of reclaiming Edessa and instead mounted an ill-conceived and unsuccessful assault on Damascus.

Bernard's efforts in Abelard's hearing are often compared to his efforts to have Gilbert of Porrée, Bishop of Poitiers, condemned at Rheims in 1148. Gilbert appeared to hold unorthodox views regarding the divinity of Christ. In particular, Gilbert thought it incorrect to say that the Divinity became flesh; rather, only one person of that Divinity became flesh. At Rheims, Bernard first attacked Gilbert's position and then, at the request of the Pope, drew up a profession of faith regarding the Trinity to which Gilbert subscribed. Pope Eugenius III accepted Gilbert's recantation and sent him back to his bishopric without dishonor. That Eugenius's decision was not more severe was a disappointment to Bernard.

De consideratione (written between 1148 and 1153) is a companion piece to the *Vitae Malachiae* in that while the latter deals with the ideal prelate's public works, the former dwells more on how the personal and spiritual needs of the prelate can be addressed in the midst of his harried routine. The treatise is written to Pope Eugenius, himself a Cistercian and former student of Bernard. Bernard is thus addressing the pontiff, but he is also giving counsel to one of his sons. In book 1 he warns Eugenius that the daily administrative demands of his office threaten to take away the time that the Pope requires for the reflection which he needs if he is to govern wisely. Consideration must always precede action.

At the beginning of book 2 Bernard writes his apologia for the failure of the Second Crusade: the impure motives of the troops doomed the enterprise from the beginning. Bernard asserts that the cause was pleasing to God, but the men who had carried it out were not. The rashness with which the Crusade was undertaken is evidence that a pontiff needs time to reflect before acting. Bernard then asserts that consideration is different from meditation in that meditation deals directly with truth, but consideration deals with human affairs where the truth may be obscure. For a pope, consideration must always address four elements: himself as a man, his subjects, his surroundings, and the celestial hierarchy that provides the paradigm for consideration of the first three elements. Eugenius must remember that the pope is a preacher, not a sovereign, and the steward of the Church.

In book 3 Bernard casts a doleful eye on the state of Eugenius's subjects and advocates reforms. Book 4 deals with the Pope's surroundings. Rome is his diocese, the seat of the Church's government and a pilgrimage shrine, but it is also a politically troubled city from which pontiffs had been driven twice in the recent past. Nevertheless, the Pope must not allow the Church to take up arms. The Pope wields two swords: a spiritual sword, the ultimate facility of which is found in his power to excommunicate; and a temporal sword, which must be handled by secular rulers on the pontiff's behalf. If the Roman mob threatens again and no military help is forthcoming, the Pope must flee. Book 5 deals with a speculative look at the celestial model, in which God, as the principle of being, unites all. Bernard develops a metaphor of God as dimensions known to human experience. God's length is eternity; his breadth is charity; his height is majesty; and his depth is wisdom.

In 1148 Bernard set out to revise and edit his vast *operae*. Five years later, he died at the hour of terce, 20 August 1153, with the project uncompleted. Despite the fact that Bernard did not leave a systematic exposition of his theology, his influence on mysticism, religious poetry, and theology has never abated. The most complete expression of his theology may be found in Etienne Gilson's *The Mystical Theology of Saint Bernard* (1940); the extensive scholarship of Jean Leclercq is also central to the study of Bernard's works. The Cistercian Fathers Series provides reliable translations as well as excellent introductions to the individual texts.

All of Bernard's writings display distinctive traits: Bernard always scrupulously matches his form and style to his content; human experience is almost always the starting point for even his loftiest visions; and he seems to know the minds of his readers, using that knowledge to manipulate them. Bernard often chooses to break a subject down into categories and subcategories, and it was perhaps this ability that made him so effective an opponent of Scholasticism—he could employ the method himself. Bernard was canonized in 1174, declared a doctor of the Church in 1830, and was extolled in 1953 as Doctor Mellifluus, "The Honey-mouthed Doctor."

Bibliographies:

Jean de la Croix Bouton, *Bibliographie Bernardine, 1891–1957* (Paris: P. Lethielleux, 1958);

Leopold Januschek, *Bibliographia Bernardina, 1827–1898* (Hildesheim: G. Olms, 1959);

Guido Hendrix, *Conspectus Bibliographicus Sancti Bernardi Ultimi Patrum 1989–1993* (Leuven: Peeters, 1995).

Biographies:

Elphegius Vacandard, *Vie de saint Bernard, abbé de Clairvaux,* 2 volumes (Paris: Lecoffre, 1920);

Bruno Scott James, *St. Bernard of Clairvaux: An Essay in Biography* (London: Hodder & Stoughton, 1957);

William of St. Thierry, Arnold of Bonnevaux, Geoffrey and Philip of Clairvaux, and Odo of Deuil, *St. Bernard of Clairvaux: The Story of His Life as Recorded in the Vita Prima Bernardi by Certain of His Contemporaries,* translated by Geoffrey Webb and Adrian Walker (London: Mowbray, 1960);

Ailbe J. Luddy, *The Life of St. Bernard* (Dublin: Brown & Noland, 1963).

References:

Anne Astel, *The Song of Songs in the Middle Ages* (Ithaca: Cornell University Press, 1982);

Carolyn Walker Bynum, *Jesus as Mother: Studies in the Spirituality of the High Middle Ages* (Berkeley: University of California Press, 1982);

Odo J. Egres, *Bernard of Clairvaux, His Life and Teaching* (Frosinone: Casamari Abbey, 1961);

E. Rozanne Elder, ed., *The Joy of Learning and the Love of God: Studies in Honor of Jean Leclercq* (Kalamazoo, Mich.: Cistercian Publications, 1995);

G. R. Evans, *The Mind of Saint Bernard of Clairvaux* (Oxford: Clarendon Press, 1983);

Etienne Gilson, *The Mystical Theology of Saint Bernard,* translated by A. H. C. Downes (New York: Sheed & Ward, 1940);

Julia Kristeva, "Ego Affectus Est. Bernard of Clairvaux: Affect, Desire, Love," in her *Tales of Love,* translated by Leon S. Roudiez (New York: Columbia University Press, 1987), pp. 150–169;

Jean Leclercq, *Bernard of Clairvaux and the Cistercian Spirit,* translated by Claire Lavoie (Kalamazoo, Mich.: Cistercian Publications, 1976);

Leclercq, *Recueil d'études sur Saint Bernard et ses écrits* (Rome: Edizioni di Storia e Letteratura, 1962);

Leclercq, *Saint Bernard mystique* (Bruges: Desclée DeBrouwer, 1948);

L. Leloir, and others, *Bernard of Clairvaux: Studies Presented to Dom Jean Leclercq,* Cistercian Studies Series no. 23 (Washington: Cistercian Publications, 1973);

I. Vallery-Radot, *Bernard de Fontaines: Abbé de Clairvaux* (Paris: Criterion, 1990);

Watkins Williams, *Saint Bernard, the Man and His Message* (Manchester: Manchester University Press, 1944).

Bernard Silvestris

(flourished circa 1130 – 1160)

Irving A. Kelter

University of St. Thomas, Houston

WORKS: *Commentum super De nuptiis Philologiae et Mercurii* (circa 1127? – 1150?)

Manuscripts: Only one manuscript of this text is known to exist: Cambridge, University Library, Mm. 1.18., ff. 1–28. Haijo Jan Westra has attributed it to Bernard, although some scholars disagree.

First publication and standard edition: *The Commentary on Martianus Capella's De nuptiis Philologiae et Mercurii attributed to Bernardus Silvestris,* edited by Haijo Jan Westra (Toronto: Pontifical Institute of Mediaeval Studies, 1986).

Cosmographia, also known as *De mundi universitate libri duo* (circa 1150)

Manuscripts: There are approximately fifty extant manuscripts of this work. The manuscript for the modern critical edition is Oxford, Bodleian Library, Laud misc. 515, ff. 182r–219r.

First publication: *Bernardi Silvestris De mundi universitate libri duo; sive, megacosmus et microcosmus,* edited by Carl Sigmund Barach and Johann Wrobel (Innsbruck: Verlag der Wagner'sche Universitätsbuchhandlung, 1876). The editors mistakenly identified Bernard Silvestris as Bernard of Chartres.

Standard edition: *Bernardus Silvestris: Cosmographia,* edited by Peter Dronke (Leiden: E. J. Brill, 1978).

Edition in English: *The Cosmographia of Bernardus Silvestris,* edited and translated by Winthrop Wetherbee (New York: Columbia University Press, 1973).

Experimentarius (circa 1170s)

Manuscripts: Generally, only the prologue of this work is attributed to Bernard. Of the approximately twenty extant manuscripts, the major early manuscripts are Oxford, British Library: Auct. F. 3, f. 104v; Digby ff. 7v–39v; Ashmole 304 ff. 2r–30v; and Ashmole 345 f. 64v.

First publication and standard edition: "Un manuale di geomanzia presentato da Bernard Sil-

Bernard Silvestris (fourteenth-century manuscript illumination; Oxford, Bodleian Library, ms. Digby 46, f. IV.)

vestre da Tours (XII secolo): *L'Experimentarius,*" edited by Mirella Brini Savorelli, *Rivista critica di storia della filosofia,* 14 (1959): 283–342.

Commentum super sex libros Eneidos in Virgilii (date unknown)

Manuscripts: Three basic manuscripts of this text were used in the standard edition of this work. They are Paris, Bibliothèque Nationale de France, f. lat. 3804 A, ff. 233r–240b; Bibliothèque Nationale de France, f. lat. 16246, ff. 44r–68r; and Cracow, Bibliotheca Jagiellonska, 1198, ff. 91r–115v.; Paris, Bibliothèque Nationale de France. f. lat. 3804, dating from the early thirteenth century, is the oldest and primary manuscript. The editors of the standard edition question the attribution of the work to Bernard, although Peter Dronke argues for Bernard's authorship.

First publication and standard edition: *Commentum quod dicitur Bernardi Silvestris super sex libros Eneidos Virgilii*, edited by Julian Jones and Elizabeth Jones (Lincoln: University of Nebraska Press, 1977).

Edition in English: *Commentary on the First Six Books of Vergil's Aeneid*, edited and translated by Earl G. Schreiber and Thomas E. Maresca (Lincoln: University of Nebraska Press, 1979).

De cura rei familiaris, also known as *Epistola ad Raimundum de modo rei familiaris gubernandae* and as *Ultissima et maralissima de bona gubernatione familie omnibus* (date unknown)

Manuscripts: There are several extant manuscripts including Paris, Bibliothèque Nationale de France, 3195, 5698, and 6395. The work is often ascribed to St. Bernard of Clairvaux.

First publication: *De cura rei familiaris* (London?: R. Pynson?, 1505).

Edition in English: *Here begynneth a shorte monycyon, or counsayle of the cure and gouvernance of a housholde*, translated by R. Whitford? (London: Robert Wyer, 1530?).

De gemellis (date unknown)

Manuscripts: The major manuscripts for this short poem based on juridical enigmata are: Paris, Bibliothèque Nationale de France, f. lat. 6415 and Vatican, Biblioteca Apostolica Vaticana, Reg. Lat. 370. These manuscripts also include the *Cosmographia* and the *Mathematicus*. Although Mirella Brini Savorelli argues for Bernard's authorship of this work, Peter Dronke contends that there is no evidence to ascribe it to Bernard himself and argues that it emerged from a School of Bernard or a School of Tours.

Standard edition: *De gemellis*, in *Beiträge zur Kunde der Lateinischen Literatur des Mittelalters*, by Jacob Werner (Aarau, Switzerland: H. H. Saverländer, 1905); republished (Hildesheim, Germany: G. Olms, 1979).

Mathematicus (date unknown)

Manuscripts: Seventeen manuscripts are extant; those most important for the modern critical edition are Erfurt, Wissenschaftliche Allgemeinbibliothek, Ampl. 8 15, ff. 141r–148v (excerpts); Bern, Bürgerbibliothek, 710 ff. 82r–92v (excerpts); Cambrai, Bibliothèque Municipale, 977 ff. 156rb–162va; and Vatican, Biblioteca Apostolica Vaticana, Reg. Lat. 370, ff. 226va–231rb.

First publication: In *Patrologia latina*, 221 volumes, edited by Jacques-Paul Migne (Paris: Migne, 1841–1879), CLVXXI: 1365–1380.

Standard editions: *Le Mathematicus de Bernardus Silvestris et la Passio Sanctae Agnetis de Pierre Riga*, edited by B. Haureau (Paris: Klincksieck, 1895); *Mathematicus*, Latin edition and translation into German by Jan Prelog, Manfred Heim, and Michael Kiesslich (St. Ottilien: EOS Verlag, 1993).

De paupere ingrato (date unknown)

Manuscripts: A short poem based on juridical enigmata, for which the major manuscripts are: Auxerre, 243; Paris, Bibliothèque Municipale, Bibliothèque Nationale de France, f. lat. 6415; and Vatican, Biblioteca Apostolica Vaticana, Reg. Lat. 370. As with *De gemellis*, Mirella Brini Savorelli argues for Bernard's authorship of this work, but Peter Dronke ascribes it to a School of Bernard or a School of Tours.

Standard edition: *De paupere ingrato* in "Poésies latines des XIIe et XIIIe siècles (Auxerre 243)," *Études médiévales*, by André Vernet (Paris: Études Augustiniennes, 1981).

Bernard Silvestris was one of the most important writers of the twelfth-century renaissance. Best known for his magisterial *Cosmographia* (Description of the Universe, circa 1150), Bernard's works reflect the scientific and philosophical concerns of his day. In poetic form he examines the processes of creation in the macrocosm of the cosmos and in the microcosm of humanity. In his *Mathematicus* (Astrologer) and *Experimentarius* (Practitioner, circa 1170s), Bernard focuses on questions critical to late medieval and Renaissance literature and philosophy: How much of the world and of human life is controlled by the stars? Do human beings possess free will or are their lives predestined?

Details of Bernard's life are sketchy. He was probably a teacher of the *ars dictaminis* (craft of composition) and of poetry at St. Martin in Tours, France. One of his students, Matthew of Vendôme, the author of *Ars versificatoria* (Art of Versification, circa 1175), mentions learning the poetic arts from Bernard, with whom he studied from 1130 until 1140. In the *Cosmographia* Bernard refers to a visit by Pope Eugenius III to France in 1147–1148, which suggests that the work was composed around 1150. Between 1178 and 1184 Gilbert Bonceau, the son of Bernard's sister Almodis, disposed of a house in Tours that Bernard had willed to him.

Nothing else is known of Bernard's life, and the lack of information has contributed to his frequent confusion with Bernard of Chartres. This misidentification grew out of Bernard Silvestris's dedication of the *Cosmographia* to Thierry of Chartres, who had been the chancellor of Chartres in 1141. The dedication to Thierry of Chartres and the content of the work have led many scholars to associate Bernard with a "School of Chartres," which they believe had a similar philosophical approach to the cosmos. This contention is contested by the eminent scholar Richard W. Southern, who denies the very existence of a "School of Chartres."

In addition to the *Cosmographia*, the *Mathematicus*, and the *Experimentarius*, other writings have been ascribed to Bernard, although the ascriptions are controversial. The two major works in this category are *Commentum super sex libros Eneidos Virgilii* (Commentary on the Six Books of Virgil's *Aeneid,* date unknown) and *Commentum super De nuptiis Philologiae et Mercurii* (Commentary Concerning *On the Marriage of Philology and Mercury,* circa 1127?–1150?). The former work is the most extensive and important commentary on Virgil's *Aeneid* written in the High Middle Ages. Julian Jones and Elizabeth Jones, the editors of the critical edition of this work, cast doubt on the ascription to Bernard because the resemblances between this work and the *Cosmographia* are of a general nature and do not provide definitive proof that Bernard was the author of both works. The editors also note that the commentary on Martianus Capella's *De nuptiis Philologiae et Mercurii* (circa A.D. 400–439) is definitely by the same author as the Virgil commentary, but since the commentary on *De nuptiis Philologiae et Mercurii* refers to the author's connection with Orléans, a city with no association to Bernard, this is evidence against Bernard's authorship. The editors agree with Brian Stock that the doctrine of the waters above the firmament, adhered to in the Martianus commentary, is a further argument against Bernard as author of the work. This doctrine of the waters above the firmament, taken from the Bible, was a matter of debate in the twelfth century, and Bernard does not mention it in his *Cosmographia*.

Peter Dronke, however, argues in favor of Bernard's authorship of the Martianus commentary based in part on what he claims is the authenticity of the *Aeneid* commentary. Dronke also argues that the position concerning the doctrine of the waters in the Martianus commentary is close to that of Thierry of Chartres, who attempted to reconcile this doctrine with natural philosophical truth. This ideological link may support the argument for Bernard's authorship because he dedicated his *Cosmographia* to Thierry; however, two other scholars, André Vernet and E. R. Smits, have suggested that the Martianus commentary is actually the work of Bernard of Chartres. Given the variety of scholarly opinions, the attribution of either of these works to Bernard Silvestris remains controversial.

The *Commentum super sex libros Eneidos Virgilii* was certainly influenced by the late ancient Latin works of Macrobius and Fulgentius. From them, the author learned to approach the *Aeneid* as a work of poetry and philosophy in which Virgil not only tells the tale of the founding of Rome by Aeneas and his Trojans, but also reveals truths concerning mankind and the laws of human society. As the author points out in his preface, this Virgil does under the cover of poetry–specifically, an *integumentum* or spiritual allegory–wherein he describes what men do and what their spirits suffer while in the human body, and each book of the *Aeneid* is related to a stage of human existence.

The commentary on each of the first five books offers the reader a brief allegorical summary: Book 1 concerns infancy; book 2, boyhood; book 3, adolescence; book 4, early manhood; and book 5 begins the tale of Aeneas, and of all men, at the stage of maturity. Following the summary is a discussion of the allegorical significance of selected passages from Virgil's text. With book 6, however, the commentator declares that the interpretation must now deal with each and every word as in this book Virgil becomes far more philosophical.

In book 6 the crucial tale of Aeneas's descent to the underworld is told and interpreted. Influenced by Neoplatonic writings, the author sees this as dealing with the people of this world, the world of the mundane and the physical. There are several different descents to the underworld, and allegorically book 6 of the *Aeneid* can be seen as the descent of virtue. What is being described is the descent of the wise man when he considers mundane things. By doing so, he can understand their true natures and turn from them to the contemplation of invisible and higher things, and in this way, he can come to understand the creator by studying his creations, especially humanity. The commentary ends abruptly just as Aeneas is about to enter Elysium.

According to Haijo Jan Westra, an analysis of the sources for *Commentum super De nuptiis Philologiae et Mercurii* indicates a terminus ad quem, or latest possible date of composition, of approximately 1150, as the work does not reveal any acquaintance with the new works of Greek and Arabic origin available after this date. In terms of its analysis of the cosmos, a major focus of the work, the most important ancient sources

Illumination depicting man as a microcosm, a concept advanced by Bernard in his Cosmographia *(from a manuscript for* Liber Divinorum Operum *of Hildegard von Bingen; Lucca, Biblioteca Statale, ms. 1942, f. 9r.)*

influenced by the writings of Peter Abelard and Hugh of St. Victor and their respective schools. Indeed, the influence of Hugh of St. Victor's *Didascalicon de studio legendi* (Didascalicon on the Study of Reading) was so great that Westra argues that circa 1127, the putative date of the writing of the *Didascalicon*, should be seen as the terminus ad quem for the Martianus commentary.

In the *Commentum super De nuptiis Philologiae et Mercurii*, the author discusses what can be learned about the nature of the cosmos and mankind through study of the mythical tales of ancient authors. The work first gives a literal reading of a word or phrase (*sensus*) and then its significance (*sententia*). The author emphasizes the importance of the *sententia* and generally gives an excursus following each *sententia* on the subjects that flow out of the interpretations of the words and phrases of the text. As was true of the *Aeneid* commentary, this work rests on the idea of the *integumentum* or secular allegory, to be found in this case in the words of Martianus Capella.

The text is incomplete and only surveys Mercury's search for a suitable bride, the assistance of Virtue, Apollo's advice, and the approval of Philology by the gods. In an allegorical fashion similar to that followed in the *Aeneid* commentary, Mercury's quest is seen as truly about the education of the self.

Mercury with Virtue first seeks Phoebus Apollo on earth, in a search that is interpreted as the attempt to attain knowledge of the physical and mundane world, the first step to the attainment of higher forms of knowledge. The next step is the search for Apollo in the heavens, a search interpreted as the contemplation of immaterial substances. What is described here is the creation of a true philosopher, and the commentary holds up the philosopher–the *vir sapiens*–as the most praiseworthy of men.

Only when Apollo, representing human wisdom, has joined with Mercury, human eloquence, and Virtue, prudence, can one climb to the abode of the highest gods–Jupiter, Juno, and Pallas. The gods officially approve Philology, the ability and love of knowledge, as Mercury's bride. The human triad of Apollo, Mercury, and Virtue have now reached the stage of the contemplation of the highest things.

Classical allusions are linked to Christian themes, as the pagan trinity of Jupiter, Juno, and Pallas is obviously paralleled to the Christian trinity. Man's love of knowledge as represented by Philology leads him to true wisdom or *sapientia*, which is an attribute of Jesus Christ. Finally, marriage is interpreted as representing the harmony of the cosmos, and Hymen, the god of marriage, is identified with the Holy Spirit.

Bernard's most influential work, *Cosmographia*, is a mythical-scientific Creation story. Divided into two

were Calcidius's Latin translation of Plato's *Timaeus*, with commentary (fourth century A.D.), and works by Martianus Capella and Macrobius. In his analysis of music, the author of the Martianus Capella commentary draws specifically on the sixth-century writings of the philosopher Boethius, as well as classical authors, such as Cicero, Virgil, Horace, Ovid, Lucan, Juvenal, and Statius.

Earlier medieval works, such as those of Remigius of Auxerre and John Scottus Eriugena's *Glosae Martiani* (Glosses on Martianus, circa 840s), were used, as well as works by other medieval Latin authors such as Ulpricus (Helperic) and Constantinus Africanus. Works of Arabic origin, such as those of Iohannitius and Abu Ma'shar, were used, although the author appears not to have known Abu Ma'shar in the translations of either John of Seville or Herman of Carinthia.

In terms of twelfth-century works, Westra argues that the Martianus Capella commentary was highly parts, *Megacosmos* and *Microcosmos,* it has as its central themes the dualistic view of the world (spiritual and physical) and a final confirmation of the value of the physical. Greatly influenced by the philosophy of Boethius, Bernard constructed the *Cosmographia* in the Boethian form of the *prosimetrum,* a long composition in which prose and verse alternate.

The most important classical sources for the *Cosmographia* were Calcidius's fourth-century version of Plato's *Timaeus*; the Hermetic *Asclepius* (first to third century); and Martianus Capella's fifth-century *De nuptiis Philologiae et Mercurii* as well as the works of Cicero, Apuleius, Firmicus Maternus, and Seneca. In terms of medieval sources, the *Cosmographia* shows the strong influence of the *De divisione naturae* (On the Division of Nature, circa 864–866) of John Scottus Eriugena, although it is unclear whether Bernard knew this work in its original form or in the early twelfth-century abridgment of Honorius of Autun. Other twelfth-century authors, such as Adelard of Bath, William of Conches, and Thierry of Chartres, were influential in the development of Bernard's ideas about nature and the cosmos. He may also have been influenced by the astronomical and astrological works of the Islamic scholar Abu Ma'shar.

In the *Cosmographia* Bernard uses a series of "divine projections" of which the first is Noys or Providentia. Noys is the image of life and carries images of all that is to be generated. The remaining "divine projections," Silva, Urania, Natura, Physis, Endelichia, Imarmene, and others, actualize the images Noys carries.

In the opening of the *Cosmographia* everything is in chaos and Silva or Yle, the foster mother of all that is generated, cannot shape the universe. Natura appeals for aid to her mother Noys–who is the mind of God or providence–and the first-born of God. Noys is asked to restore harmony, order, and beauty for the sake of Silva and her child Mundus. Noys answers that even she is subject to the divine will, but the time has come for the fulfillment of Natura's wish.

Silva inclines more to evil (chaos, instability) than to good (order, stability), but Noys with Natura's assistance can remedy the situation. As far as is possible, Noys brings about order and balance. The four elements emerge and take their places and combine their qualities: hot, cold, moist, dry. This act of ordering is pleasing to God, for Noys brings about beauty. Then she begets Anima or Endelechia, the world soul, as a bride for Mundus, who is improved by Noys to be more fitting for his bride. Endelechia is to help Mundus and soothe him when he is ill with floods and fires. Her powers are stronger, however, in the higher realms of the stars; in the lower realms, Endelechia is obstructed by the *corporum tarditatem,* the resistance of physical bodies to order. This term was borrowed from book 6 of Virgil's *Aeneid* and was the subject of commentary by many medieval Platonists, such as William of Conches.

At this point in the narrative, the cosmos comes forth from Silva's womb, and the ether, stars, air, earth, and sea become distinct. Bernard supplies a detailed discussion of the unfolding of the universe and the forms generated in each region. Only God remains outside of the created universe, an idea which is in conformity with traditional Judeo-Christian teachings.

The highest of the heavenly regions is the region of ethereal fire and of the lesser gods or nine hierarchies of angels. In dealing with this region, Bernard characteristically emphasizes the importance of the stars, which inscribe the patterns of human behavior and foretell great events, such as the birth of Christ. The characteristics of individuals and peoples can also be brought down from the realm of the stars by souls. Thus, the majesty of Priam, the cunning of Ulysses, the skill of the Persians at astronomy, and of the Romans at war may be linked to the stars. Even the Virgin Mary and Pope Eugenius III are referred to in this section of the work.

Bernard continues with a description of the creation of the earth itself, its physical features, and animals. Animals, in particular, reveal the mind of God. The lynx is said to have a fountain of light inside it (according to legend, urine crystallizes as lynx-stone) and performs miracles associated with sight; the monkey, a deformed man, was created to make man laugh; and the beaver, squirrel, sable, and marten were created for fur. Bernard incorporates the legends of the swan that sings before death, of the phoenix who rises from the dead, of the imprudent duck, and other such tales that associate birds with virtues and vices. The life of all forms of animal life comes from the firmament, and the fire of the ether is seen as a lover and husband who pours himself into the womb of the earth. All are part of an eternal cycle of generation, corruption, and regeneration.

For this cosmos to be complete, a human being is necessary. To find a human being, Natura needs to find her sisters: Urania, the principle of celestial existence, and Physis, the principle of material existence. In the realm of the heavens known as the Aplanos, the home of the quintessence and the source for all motion below, Natura meets its governor (*Oyarses*) or guiding spirit (*Genius*) who is the All-Former (*Pantamorphos*). He writes and paints the individual forms (not the universal forms) that will be actualized below. Pantomorphos shows Natura that Urania is nearby, and Urania agrees to join with Natura and descend to the lower world, bringing with her a human mind that can distinguish between what is free, what is necessary, and what is

Pages from a thirteenth-century manuscript for Bernard's Experimentarius, *with philosophers and fortune-telling tables drawn by the English artist Matthew of Paris (Oxford, Bodleian Library, Ashmole 304, fol. 31v)*

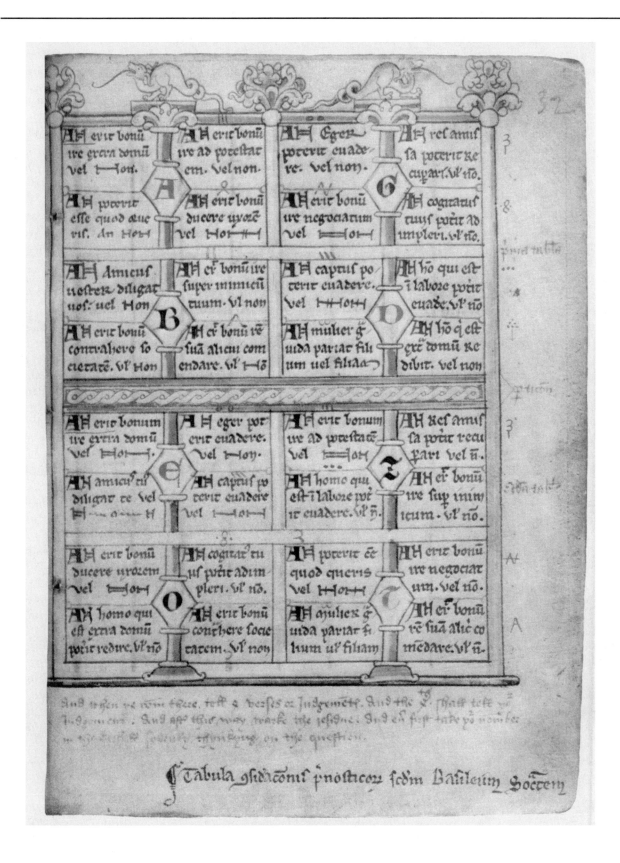

uncertain in outcome. The human mind, when the body is cast off, will ascend into heaven as a new god. Natura and Urania ascend into the highest realm of God, who is the good (*Tugaton*), to receive divine approval and then descend.

Urania and Natura go through each region of the heavens, with Urania disclosing the nature of these regions. When they reach the lunar boundary and the separation between the two major regions—the heavenly and the earthly realms—they meet a myriad of spirits, and Urania discourses to Natura on the *daemons* (supernatural beings) who exist in this realm. Urania tells Natura that the firmament has fiery stars as its angels, whereas the regions between the firmament and the earth have their own spirits—eternal like the angels and passionate like man. From the sun to the moon, there are beneficent spirits, messengers, and guiding spirits; beneath the moon there are beneficent spirits and true demons; and on earth there are also innocent spirits of forests, hills, and rivers, governed by Summanus, the lord of the shades. All of the good spirits are united by harmony and divine love.

Finally, Urania and Natura reach a spot of calm and fertility, Granusion. There they find Physis with her daughters Theorica and Practica. Reflecting once again Bernard's interest in science, Physis is represented as a scientific thinker who studies nature. She has been speculating about creating a human; however, she cannot make one by herself—this inability seems to indicate Bernard's view of the limitations of a materialistic view of the universe.

Noys gives all three a picture to work from in creating man. Urania receives the mirror of providence, which details the eternal realm. Natura receives the book of destiny, which is the record of temporal events and possible, but not totally predetermined, destinies for men. Finally, Physis receives a book which describes the nature of the physical world and its principles, though in a blurred manner. All three, Urania, Natura, and Physis, combine to form man.

In the conclusion Bernard again reveals his fascination for natural science and medicine in a discussion (drawing on material taken from Calcidius) of the functions of the parts of the body and the organs. In discussing bodily functions, Bernard is led to a disquisition on sexuality and reproduction. These passages are among the most controversial in the poem. Bernard's praise of sexuality has alternately been taken as representative of a reborn paganism—Ernst Robert Curtius's interpretation of the entire work—or as an orthodox Judeo-Christian theme based on the biblical injunction to be fruitful and multiply. Relying on a literal reading of the words, Peter Dronke has persuasively argued that this section is not indicative of a twelfth-century

revival of ancient paganism but represents Bernard's answer to the problem of human mortality: the power of generation tries to protect humans by making love pleasurable, and lovemaking is a struggle against death.

The influence of this work in the Middle Ages and early Renaissance was enormous. Testimonies to its influence can be found in the works of Matthew of Vendôme and Gervase of Melkley, a theoretician of poetry. Peter of Blois's love lyric, *A globi veteri* (On the Old World, late 1150s) used the language of the opening of the *Cosmographia*. Alain de Lille's works, the *Anticlaudianus de Antirufino* (Against Claudian's *Against Rufinus,* circa 1181–1184) and the *De planctu naturae* (On the Plaint of Nature, circa 1160–1165) also used Bernard's language and concepts.

Bernard's influence continued throughout the later Middle Ages. In the late twelfth century Giraldus Cambrensis in Wales created a work of approximately 260 lines in couplets, *De mundi creatione* (On the Creation of the World), which appears to be a plagiarism of the *Cosmographia*. In his *De naturis rerum* (On the Nature of Things, early thirteenth century), the English philosopher Alexander Neckham cites verses from Bernard. Thirteenth-and fourteenth-century authors such as Jean de Meun and Peter of Compostela were also influenced by Bernard's work.

Finally, the *Cosmographia* influenced two literary giants of the fourteenth century: Giovanni Boccaccio and Geoffrey Chaucer. Boccaccio copied the work in the manuscript Laurenziana XXXIII: 31. The influence of the work can be seen in Boccaccio's *Esposizioni sopra la Comedia di Dante* (Discourses on Dante's *Divine Comedy,* 1374), as well as in his *Il Filostrato* (circa 1350). Bernard's influence can also be seen in the "Man of Law's Tale" in Chaucer's poetic tour-de-force, *The Canterbury Tales* (circa 1387–1400). Chaucer was preoccupied with some of the same questions of determinism and freedom that so concerned Bernard.

Bernard's *Mathematicus* includes many of the same themes that run throughout the *Cosmographia*: the influence of the stars and the ability of an individual to fight against his destiny. The work is a narrative poem of almost nine hundred lines in elegiac couplets. Its plot revolves around an astrological prediction and the attempt to escape it.

In the *Mathematicus* a childless noble Roman couple consult an astrologer (a *mathematicus*), seeking a cure for their infertility. The astrologer is an expert at discovering by way of the stars the intentions of the gods and the secrets of nature. He foretells that they will have a son who will be a great Roman ruler and will kill his father. Although the husband makes his wife swear to kill the child as an infant, she sends him away and lies to her husband concerning the child's death. Indeed, she even names their son Patricida as a warning to avoid the crime of killing his father.

The child has great intellectual abilities and is able at a young age to master both astronomy and astrology—the knowledge of the movement of the stars and the understanding of the influence of the stars on human destiny. Eventually, as an adult, Patricida leads the Romans to victory against the Carthaginians. Following this victory, the Roman king abdicates in favor of Patricida.

At this point in the poem Patricida's mother reveals the truth to his father, who begs for the opportunity to see and embrace his triumphant son. He does so and informs Patricida that it has been foretold and predestined that Patricida will kill his own father. To defeat his destiny, Patricida plans his own suicide and convinces the Roman people to grant him anything he desires. When they so promise, Patricida asks to die.

The poem ends with Patricida's request. Scholars have debated whether the poem is finished or not and what its final message is. Is this Bernard's poetic expression of the doctrine of astral determinism, or is Bernard's true belief to be found in Patricida's declaration concerning his own suicide? Patricida has declared that man is not subject to the stars and sees his suicide as the only way to assert this freedom and defeat the destiny foretold for him. The existence of this work in approximately seventeen extant manuscript copies attests to its readership throughout the Middle Ages.

The *Experimentarius* is another work that deals with the role of the stars in human life. The consensus of scholarly opinion is that Bernard was the author only of the prologue to this work. The work itself consists of geomantic tables used for divination that were translated from the Arabic. Bernard appears to have been the translator, although he would have required assistance in this task. In his introduction to the critical edition of Bernard's *Cosmographia,* Dronke suggests that the renowned twelfth-century translator of Arabic scientific texts, Herman of Carinthia, could have been Bernard's partner in this endeavor, as Herman also had associations with Chartres and also dedicated a work to Thierry of Chartres. Dronke's speculation is plausible but has not been confirmed.

Two persistent themes can be identified in Bernard Silvestris's work. His work focused on the complex interrelationship of the spiritual and the physical in both man and the universe. A second, related theme was his preoccupation with the interplay of fortune and determinism in the unfolding of cosmic events. As the most important cosmographical poet of the Middle Ages, his affirmation of the physical world played a major role in encouraging the investigation of nature in the High and late Middle Ages.

References:

Charles S. F. Burnett, "What is the *Experimentarius* of Bernardus Silvestris? A Preliminary Survey of the Material," *Archives de l'histoire doctrinale et littéraire du moyen âge,* 44(1977): 79–125;

Marie-Dominique Chenu, *Nature, Man and Society in the Twelfth Century: Essays on New Theological Perspectives in the Latin West,* edited and translated by Jerome Taylor and Lester K. Little (Chicago: University of Chicago Press, 1968);

A. Clerval, *Les écoles de Chartres au moyen âge du Ve au XVIe siécle* (Chartres: Memoires de la Société archéologique d'Eure-et-Loir, 1895);

Ernst Robert Curtius, *European Literature and the Latin Middle Ages,* translated by Willard R. Trask, Bollingen Series no. 36 (New York: Pantheon, 1953);

M. Desmond, "Bernard Silvestris and the Corpus of the *Aeneid,*" in *The Classics in the Middle Ages,* edited by Aldo S. Bernardo and Saul Levin (Binghamton, N.Y.: SUNY Press, 1990), pp. 129–139;

M. T. Donati, "E ancora verosimile l'attribuzione dell'*Experimentarius* a Bernard Silvestre?" *Medioevo,* 12 (1986): 281–344;

Donati, "Metafisica, fisica e astrologia nel XII secolo: Bernardo Silvestre e l'introduzione 'Qui celum' dell'*Experimentarius,*" *Studi medievali,* third series, 31 (1990): 649–703;

Peter Dronke, *Fabula: Explorations in the Use of Myth in Medieval Platonism* (Leiden: E. J. Brill, 1974);

P. Dutton, "The Uncovering of the *Glossae super Platonem* of Bernard of Chartres," *Medieval Studies,* 46 (1984): 192–221;

R. R. Edwards, "Poetic Invention and the Medieval Causae," *Medieval Studies,* 55 (1993): 183–217;

P. Godmin, "Ambiguity in the *Mathematicus* of Bernardus Silvestris," *Studi medievali,* third series, 31 (1990): 583–648;

Godmin, "The Search for Urania. Cosmological Myth in Bernardus Silvestris and Pontano," in *Innovation und Originalität,* edited by W. Haug and B. Wachinger (Tübingen: Niemeyer, 1993), pp. 70–97;

Edouard Jeauneau, "Berkeley, University of California, Bancroft Library Ms. 2 (Notes de lecture)," *Medieval Studies,* 50 (1988): 438–456;

Jeauneau, "Note sur l'École de Chartres," *Studi medievali,* third series, 5 (1964): 821–865;

Julian Ward Jones Jr., "The So-Called Silvestris Commentary on the *Aeneid* and Two Other Interpretations," *Speculum,* 64 (October 1989): 835–848;

D. Krieger and B. Lofstedt, "Textkritische Notizen zu ps. Bernardus Silvestris' Kommentar zu Martianus Capella," *Aevum,* 65 (1991): 309–311;

Daniel Carl Meerson, "The Ground and Nature of Literary Theory in Bernard Silvester's Twelfth-Century Commentary on the Aeneid," dissertation, University of Chicago, 1967;

F. Mora, "De Bernard Silvestre à Chrétien de Troyes: Resurgences des Enfers virgiliens au XIIe siecle," in *Diesseits- und Jenseitsreisen im Mittelalter=Voyages dans l'ici-bas et dans l'au-delà au Moyen Âge,* edited by Wolf-Dieter Lange, Studium universale no. 14 (Bonn: Bouvier, 1992), pp. 129–146;

Christine Ratkowitsch, *Die Cosmographia des Bernardus Silvestris: Eine Theodizee* (Koln: Bohlau, 1995);

E. R. Smits, "New Evidence for the Authorship of the Commentary on the First Six Books of Virgil's *Aeneid* Commonly Attributed to Bernardus Silvestris?" in *Non Nova, sed Nove: Mélanges de civilisation médiévale, dédiés a Willem Noomen,* edited by Martin Gosman and Jaap van Os, Mediaevalia Groningana no. 5 (Groningen: Bouma, 1984);

G. E. Solbach, *Die Mittelalterliche Lehre von Mikrokosmos und Makrokosmos* (Hamburg: Verlag Dr. Kovac, 1995);

Richard W. Southern, *Medieval Humanism* (New York: Harper & Row, 1970);

Southern, *Scholastic Humanism and the Unification of Europe* (Oxford: Blackwell, 1995);

Brian Stock, *Myth and Science in the Twelfth Century: A Study of Bernard Silvester* (Princeton: Princeton University Press, 1972);

Lynn Thorndike, *A History of Magic and Experimental Science,* volume 2 (New York: Columbia University Press, 1923);

André Vernet, "Bernardus Silvestris. Recherches sur l'auteur suivies d'une édition critique de la Cosmographia," dissertation, École Nationale de Chartres, 1938;

Haijo Jan Westra, "Animals and Integumental Interpretation in the Commentary on Martianus Capella attributed to Bernardus Silvestris," *Reinardus,* 6 (1993): 229–241;

O. Zwierlein, "Spüren der Tragödien Senecas bei Bernardus Silvestris, Petrus Pictor und Marbod von Reims," *Mittellalteinisches Jahrbuch,* 22 (1989 for 1987): 171–196.

Charles d'Orléans

(24 November 1394 – 4/5 January 1465)

Diane R. Marks
Brooklyn College of the City University of New York

WORKS: *Poésies*

Manuscripts: Ms. O (Paris, Bibliothèque Nationale de France, f. fr. 25458), the most complete of the dozen manuscripts of Charles's poems, was the poet's personal copy and underwent various stages of development. The original manuscript, copied by a scribe in England, is a collection of poems grouped according to their lyric form: ballade, chanson, complainte, and carole. As new poems in each genre were composed, gatherings of pages were added to each section of the original manuscript. Mss. A (Paris, Bibliothèque de l'Arsenal, ms. 2070), B (Paris, Bibliothèque Nationale de France, f. fr. 19139), and C (London, British Library, Reg. 16 F. II) are selections from the first version of O without any additions. Ms. M (Carpentras, Bibliothèque de Carpentras, ms. 375, which belonged to Charles's third wife, Marie of Cleves) was copied from O between 1455 and 1458; O2 (Paris, Bibliothèque Nationale de France, f. fr. 1104, which has the Arms of Catherine de Medici) was copied from O between 1458 and 1465; and H (London, British Library, ms. Harley 6916) is another copy of O, with its later additions, made in the second half of the fifteenth century. Ms. G (Grenoble, ms. 873) was made by Charles's personal secretary between circa 1461 and circa 1464/1465; it includes all of the pre-1453 poems from O and Latin translations of them. Mss. P (Paris, Bibliothèque de l'Arsenal, ms. 3457), L (London, British Library, Lansdowne ms. 380), R (Paris, Bibliothèque Nationale de France, f. fr. 9223), S (Paris, Bibliothèque Nationale de France, f. fr. 1719), and S2 (Paris, Bibliothèque Nationale de France, nouv. acq. fr. 15771) are miscellanies comprising selections of poems by Charles and visitors to his castle at Blois.

First publication: Selections in *Le Jardin de Plaisance et Fleur de Rhétorique* (Paris: Antoine Vérard, circa 1501); *La Chasse et le départ d'amours faict et composé par reverend père en Dieu messire Octavien de Sainct Gelais evesque d'Angoulesme et par noble homme Blaise d'Auriol bachelier en chascun droit demourant a Thoulouze* (Paris: Antoine Vérard, 1509); and in *Le Triomphe de l'amant vert par Jehan Le Maire de Belges avecques plusieurs ballades et rondeaux . . .*, by Jean Le Maire de Belges, (Paris: Denys et Simon Janot, 1535).

Standard edition: *Charles d'Orléans: Poésies*, 2 volumes, edited by Pierre Champion (Paris: H. Champion, 1923, 1927; republished, Paris, 1971).

Edition in modern French: *Charles d'Orléans: Ballades et Rondeaux*, edited and translated by Jean-Claude Mühlethaler (Paris: Livre de Poche, 1992).

Editions in English: *The English Poems of Charles of Orléans, Edited from the ms. Brit. Mus. Harley. 682*, 2 volumes, edited by Robert Steele and Mabel Day, Early English Text Society nos. 215 and 220 (Oxford: Oxford University Press, 1941, 1946); republished, 1 volume (London: Oxford University Press, 1970); *The Poems of Charles of Orléans*, edited and translated by Sally Purcell (Chatham, U.K.: Carcanet, 1973); *The French Chansons of Charles d'Orléans with the Corresponding Middle English Chansons*, edited and translated by Sarah Spence (New York: Garland, 1986); *Fortunes Stabilnes: Charles of Orléans's English Book of Love*, edited by Mary-Jo Arn (Binghamton, N.Y.: Medieval and Renaissance Texts and Studies, 1994).

Canticum Amoris (date unknown)

Manuscript: A Latin religious poem attributed to Charles by Gilbert Ouy, this work is present in one manuscript, Paris, Bibliothèque Nationale de France, f. lat. 1203, ff. 48–56v.

First publication and standard edition: "Un Poème mystique de Charles d'Orléans: Le *Canticum amoris*," edited by Gilbert Ouy, *Studi Francesi*, 7 (1959): 64–84.

Charles d'Orléans (Charles of Orléans) is one of the rare poets of the Middle Ages who not only had his birth date recorded but also had his horoscope cast: he was born under a lucky star. As grandson of Gian-Galeazzo

Ducal seal and signature of Charles d'Orléans (Paris, Archives Nationales, Douët-d'Arcq, 944; and Bibliothèque Nationale de France)

Visconti, Duke of Milan, and godson as well as nephew and future son-in-law of Charles VI, King of France, good fortune might have been expected for him. In fact, however, he was unlucky and often, during his seventy years, frustrated and disappointed. The poetry that he composed when, perhaps, more-worldly pleasures and triumphs eluded him, reflects his experience. Although many of his most anthologized poems illustrate the refinement and extravagance of courtly life, his long imprisonment in England fostered an introspection that produced his characteristic psychological allegories and motivated his cultivation of *nonchaloir* (indifference).

Charles's father, Louis of Orléans, the much-indulged younger brother of King Charles VI, embraced the lifestyle of the extravagant court: he participated in the Cour d'Amours in 1401 and attended the disastrous Bal des Ardents in 1393, at which six nobles costumed as wild men, among them the king, caught fire. Louis collected books and objets d'art like his uncle, Jean, Duke of Berry, and contributed a poetic response to Jean le Sénéchal's *Le Livre de Cent Ballades* (The Book of One

Hundred Ballades, 1389). The prolific poet Eustache Deschamps was a sometime member of Louis's household, and the writer Christine de Pizan dedicated manuscripts to both him and his wife, Valentina Visconti, whom Louis married in 1389.

Louis received several apanages from the king and bought other territories to consolidate his holdings until he began to rival the wealthiest dukes of the kingdom, particularly his uncle, Philip the Bold, Duke of Burgundy. The king, after his first access of dementia in 1392, became more dependent on Louis as a result of his "absences," as his irrational periods were called, and when he could not tolerate his own wife and children, he was soothed by his sister-in-law Valentina's presence—so much so that those jealous or fearful of Louis's influence murmured charges of witchcraft against Valentina and accusations of adultery against Louis and the king's often estranged wife, Isabeau. From 1396 on, Valentina prudently resided outside of Paris and raised her children—Charles, Philippe, Jean, and Marguerite—away from the royal court. (After 1403 Valentina also raised Louis's illegitimate son, Jean, Count of Dunois, commonly but not disrespectfully known as the Bastard of Orléans, with his half brothers.) Charles's first poetic work may have been *Le Livre contre Tout Péché* (The Book against All Sin), a moralizing catalogue of the seven deadly sins written when he was ten in rhyming octosyllabic couplets on a blank leaf in the family copy of Sallust's *Catalina*.

The king's increasing reliance on his brother exacerbated the rivalry between Orléans and Burgundy. Each tried to influence the king and control the government: when Louis cemented his close relationship with his brother in 1404 by marrying his son Charles to the king's daughter Isabelle of France, fifteen-year-old widow of King Richard II of England, Philip likewise married his daughter Margaret to the dauphin, the king's eldest son.

The brutal assassination of Louis of Orléans in the Vieille Rue du Temple on the night of 23 November 1407 at the order of John the Fearless, Philip's son and current duke of Burgundy, abruptly ended Charles's childhood. Although Burgundy first privately confessed, then publicly justified, his deed, his position, wealth, power, and popularity protected him. And his eponymous audacity set against the indecisiveness of the council functioning in the king's "absence" precluded prosecution for the crime. All of Charles's teenage years were spent seeking justice for his father's death from a king who, when he was "present," was easily distracted from his purposes and usually swayed by his most recent interlocutor. In 1408 Valentina died, still attempting to have her husband's murder avenged; the following year, Charles's wife Isabelle died after the

Illumination depicting the Battle of Agincourt, where Charles was captured by the English (from a manuscript in the Bibliothèque Nationale de France)

birth of their daughter, Jeanne. No longer nominally head of the household, at fifteen Charles became truly responsible for his family, the affairs of his duchy, and bringing his father's assassin to justice. He turned to others who were alarmed or annoyed by Burgundy's growing power, lawlessness, and arrogance. Through marriage to Bonne of Armagnac in 1410, Charles allied himself with her father, the veteran fighter Bernard of Armagnac, who from 1411 led the armies of Charles's supporters against the Burgundians. In 1412 Charles contracted with Henry IV, king of England, for troops, but royal intervention forced peace on the Burgundians and Armagnacs. Annulling this contract incurred a crippling debt, and Charles was obliged to send hostages to England until the entire sum was paid.

Peace reconciled Charles with the royal family in the winter of 1414–1415, and he participated for the first time in the lavish life of the court. He exchanged poems with the marquis de Garencieres and had a garment with the words and music of the song *Madame je suis plus joyeulx* (Madame I Am More Joyful) embroidered on it with 960 pearls. This graceful existence was short-lived, however, for the following fall, on 25 Octo-

ber 1415, Charles was one of the many French knights who were casualties of the battle of Agincourt. Chroniclers recount that Charles was discovered alive under a pile of the dead whom the English soldiers were stripping of armor and valuables. He was brought to Henry V, who welcomed his "cousin" warmly and kept him in England for twenty-five years. Just twenty-one years old, Charles was the highest ranking prisoner taken that day and too valuable to be soon relinquished.

Before this time Charles had not had the leisure to compose much poetry. Charles's first collection of poems was called by Charles d'Héricault "le livre de prison" (the prison book), and perhaps aptly, for when he returned to France from England, he brought with him "plusieurs kaiers de parchemin, nouvellement escripts et enluminez apportez d'Angleterre" (several quires of parchment, newly written and illuminated, brought from England).

The volume begins with a dit, a pseudo-autobiographical love story in narrative and lyric verse. *La Retenue d'Amours* (The Homage to Love) recounts the narrator's introduction and submission to the god of Love. A letter of homage written by Cupid and Venus and dated

St. Valentine's Day identifies the narrator as the duke of Orléans, named Charles.

On a new page a series of seventy-one ballades begins. Through selection and arrangement of very conventional lyric genres—complaints, debates, epistles, and laments, all in ballade form—a narrative is suggested. Although initially reluctant to love, once conquered by Beauty, the lover begs to be admitted to her service. The lover and his heart, however, disagree on how to behave. The hasty heart has no equilibrium, swinging between elation and anguish, while the lover warns him of disappointment and failure, urges caution, and consoles him in his despair. The lover is beset not only by the traditional enemies of love such as *Dangier* or Fortune but, characteristic of Charles, even more by internal adversaries such as *Dueil* (Grief) and *Merencolie* (Melancholy). It pleases the lady and soothes the lover for him to put his distress in verse. The reader can infer from this circumstance that this writing is the only link between the two. A lack of news makes the lover anxious, so he reproaches the lady for her silence, but eventually he receives word of her death. The lover grieves, and although his heart is solicited by another lady, he continues to mourn his first love and admonishes lovers who expect love's joys without its pain.

Here the lyrics are interrupted by another narrative, *Le Songe en complainte* (The Dream in Complainte). In a dream an old man warns the lover of the approach of Old Age and recommends that he leave the service of Love if he does not wish to be mocked. The lover awakens and writes *La requeste* (The Request), a petition to Love and Venus for permission to withdraw from their service. He signs it "Charles of Orléans."

La Departie d'Amours en balades (The Departure from Love in Ballades) carries forward the narrative content of the dream vision in ten ballades. At Love's next parliament, the lover presents him with the petition. Love suggests the lover make a new conquest, but the lover declines: he will never love another. Love then agrees to release him and gives Charles of Orléans an honorable discharge dated 1 November 1437. Charles, shedding copious tears, is led by Comfort to his childhood home, *Nonchaloir,* where he will remain until Old Age comes to get him. The work concludes with two ballades summarizing the former lover's situation: no longer inspired by Love and Pleasure, he has forgotten about poetry; nonetheless, he will try again to compose poems even though he fears he is too rusty with indifference to succeed. Finally, the lover is completely cured of love's malady and laughs at those fools who suffer from it.

This sentimental autobiography is skillfully related through narratives, ballades, and fictive documents in different verse forms. It sets forth the twin themes of courtly literature: love is the central experience of life, and it is obtained through the exercise of the chivalric virtues of loyalty, courage, and endurance. Although the circumscribed story of two separated lovers, the poems are full of characters—personifications of abstractions, emotions, states of mind—who participate in the struggle of the lover toward union with his lady. The lyrics, the major part of the work, are all polished and graceful but varied in tone: from joyful to grieving, comic to ironic, impassioned to reflective.

If it were not for the persistent identification of the narrator as Charles of Orléans, there would be no obvious connection between the poet and the duke. The tumultuous and traumatic events of his adolescence, the momentous battle he so romantically survived, his long exile from home—none of these crucial episodes of his life are mentioned. In fact, he is often careful to render any references to personal experience ambiguous. In ballade 40 when he announces "prisonnier sui" (a prisoner I am), he adds "d'amour martir" (a martyr for love), forcing the reader to consider the first statement figuratively, like the second. When he speaks of his exile in ballade 63, it is in the forest of painful sadness rather than in England.

Despite this resolute ambiguity, Charles's poetry has often suffered from excessive and simplistic biographical interpretation, and since as a courtly poet his only topic is his love for his lady, her identity has been much debated. Some favor Charles's first wife, Isabelle; others, his second wife, Bonne, who died during Charles's captivity. Still others, including some of Charles's contemporaries, suggest an anonymous English lady. Evidence for each of the candidates is inconclusive. In all likelihood these poems were written for different ladies, if for any at all, during the two decades between Charles's arrival in England and the date given in the letter of discharge and only later assembled in this unified form as if written for one lady.

Also included in this manuscript are some miscellaneous topical ballades: some are part of verse correspondences that Charles exchanged with the dukes of Bourbon and Burgundy; others deal obliquely with Charles's situation in England and his desire for peace and to return home. These are followed by a series of approximately fifty chansons, a variation on the rondel, treating the same courtly subjects as the ballades in the dit: the joys and pains of love and the virtues of his lady.

So Charles passed his time as an involuntary guest of the king of England, when as he himself confesses in ballade 40: "De balader j'ay beau loisir, / Autres deduis me sont cassez" (For ballade writing I've plenty of time, / Other pleasures are denied me now). Yet, during these twenty-five years Charles was insulated not only from pleasures but also from turmoil. For

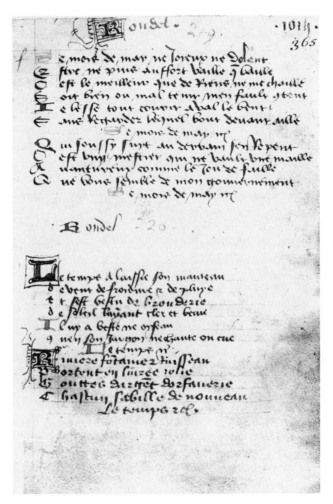

Page from a scribal copy of Charles's poems with the third stanza of the second rondeau in Charles's own handwriting
(Bibliothèque Nationale de France, f. fr. 25458)

the first year and a half of his captivity in England, he was in London and its environs. Charles lived at the king's expense and was accorded the dignities due his rank. In 1417 when Sigismond, King of the Romans, came to England in an attempt to make peace, Henry gave several celebrations, among them a great banquet in Westminster Hall. Chroniclers describe Charles and the other French prisoners of war as seated in descending order of rank in the position of honor on Sigismond's right.

During Henry's second invasion of France in 1417, Charles was sent to Pontefract, one of the largest and most prepossessing of Yorkshire castles, where Richard II had been killed. Robert Waterton, constable of the castle, was a pleasant captor and occasionally took Charles on visits to his country house.

Meanwhile, in France, Henry campaigned throughout Normandy, but no forces came from Paris to oppose him. John the Fearless, Duke of Burgundy,

out of power since the Armagnacs crushed the Cabochien uprising of 1413, had returned to the capital from a tactful five-year retreat to his own territories. Rather than leave the city to fight the invading English, Bernard of Armagnac, now constable of France, remained to defend Paris and the king from domination by Burgundy. In May 1418, however, a small force of Burgundians entered the city and massacred the Armagnacs. The dauphin escaped to territories south of the Loire, where Armagnac supporters such as Charles's brother Philippe of Vertus joined him. Burgundy declared Queen Isabeau regent, and the queen pronounced her son, the dauphin Charles, illegitimate and without authority during the king's "absences."

As a result of these Burgundian maneuvers, Henry's campaign met only local resistance. In January 1419, after a six-month siege, Rouen surrendered, and Henry ruled all Normandy. This unexpected success so alarmed both French and Burgundians that, despite their implacable enmity, John the Fearless and the dauphin agreed to meet that September; but in an attack reminiscent of the one he had ordered on Louis of Orléans a dozen years before, John the Fearless was assassinated, viciously set upon with knives and axes on the bridge at Montereau by members of the dauphin's party. This treachery eliminated the possibility of a united front against the invaders since it drove John's son, Philip, into an alliance with the English.

The English soon controlled northern France, and in 1420 Henry V and a less-than-lucid Charles VI signed the Treaty of Troyes, which made Henry V of England heir to Charles VI of France. Henry married the French king's daughter Catherine and triumphantly entered Paris that December. Then Henry returned home. Charles's brother Philippe, who had joined the disinherited dauphin and taken Charles's place opposing the Burgundians, died that year; his half brother, the Bastard Dunois, replaced Philippe in the struggle against Burgundy and the English.

In 1421 Charles was removed from Pontefract, perhaps for too great familiarity with his guard, Waterton, to Fotheringhay in Northhamptonshire. In France that year at Baugé, a combined Armagnac and Scots force defeated the English. The death of his brother the duke of Clarence in this battle brought Henry back to the battlefield in France, but he died of dysentery at Vincennes the following year. If Henry's death gave Charles any hope for release, it was ill-founded. According to the Burgundian chronicler Monstrelet, Henry gave these instructions on his deathbed: "Et si gardez que vous ne délivrez de prison beau cousin le duc d'Orléans . . . jusques à ce que beau filz Henry aura son age compétant." (Take care that you do not liberate from prison our good cousin the duke of Orléans . . . until dear son Henry comes of age.) At the time, "dear son Henry" was not yet a year old.

Charles was relocated again in 1422 to Bolingbroke in Lincolnshire, where he spent six and a half uneventful years. He was kept uninformed about events and permitted only one French-speaking servant. One of his miscellaneous ballades expresses a sense of isolation and fear of being forgotten. In the refrain he announces to both friends and enemies at home, despite rumors to the contrary, "Qu'encore est vive la souri" (That the mouse is still alive). At home, meanwhile, sporadic warfare was being waged for the dauphin against the English by Charles's half brother, Dunois, and, until his capture in 1424 at the battle of Verneuil, by his son-in-law, the duke of Alençon.

Until 1424 the expenses of Charles and the other prisoners of the king had been paid by the state, but the Council rethought this profligate policy and decided that prisoners should pay their own way. This was a

hardship for Charles, whose territories were a battleground, but a boon to scholars, whose exceptional knowledge of Charles's reading derives from inventories made for the sale of his library that these additional expenses occasioned. As of 1428, first the earl of Salisbury and then the earl of Suffolk besieged Charles's principal city of Orléans, contrary to the laws of war, as a prisoner's territory was supposed to be neutral to enable him to raise money for ransom, the most lucrative attraction of medieval warfare. Joan of Arc, generally disgusted by the depredations of war in France, was particularly aggrieved by the siege of Orléans. Accompanied by the Bastard Dunois and the duke of Alençon, she liberated the city in May 1429.

The Bastard's capture of the duke of Suffolk shortly thereafter at the battle of Jargeau unexpectedly benefited Charles. Dunois was kind to his captive, and after Suffolk's ransom and return to England in 1432, Charles was put in his custody, residing at Wingfield and Ewelme with Suffolk and his wife, Alice Chaucer, granddaughter of the English poet Geoffrey Chaucer, whose poetry may have already been familiar to Charles. He may have borrowed from his brother Jean of Angouleme, whom he had sent to England as a hostage in 1412, a copy of Chaucer's *Canterbury Tales* (known as the Paris Manuscript) that Jean had commissioned and annotated himself. Charles found a compatible custodian in Suffolk. He was not only a poetaster who had poems in both French and English attributed to him, but a leading advocate for peace, so he and Charles had similar pastimes and pursuits.

A peace conference was planned in 1433. Charles traveled to Dover waiting for his French supporters to arrive on the other side of the Channel before crossing. One of his most famous ballades must have been written at this time: *En regardant vers le païs de France* (Looking toward the Country France). The hopes for peace and repatriation that he expresses in this poem were dashed when not all the French participants appeared, canceling the conference. Charles never crossed the Channel.

Twenty years of almost constant warfare had devastated France and impoverished England. Although Philip the Good of Burgundy was less interested than his forebears had been in meddling in the affairs of the kingdom, the war threatened his lands in France and disrupted the real source of his wealth, the profitable cloth trade between his Flemish territories and England. In 1434, Philip took it upon himself to send an embassy to England to sound out Henry VI and Charles of Orléans on the prospects for peace. The failure of the previous year failure left Henry cautious, but willing. Charles, however, warmly welcomed Philip's ambassador, and despite the decades of family enmity, profusely

Charles as a prisoner in the Tower of London (detail from a manuscript; British Library, Royal 16 F II)

expressed his regard and affection for Burgundy, and vowed to do his utmost to bring about peace.

Thanks largely to the efforts of Philip's wife, Isabelle of Burgundy, a peace congress was held in Arras in 1435, and this time Charles did cross the Channel. Although this meeting did not result in peace between England and France, Charles VII's promise to punish the assassins of John the Fearless and have masses said for him reconciled the duke of Burgundy to him and ended the Anglo-Burgundian alliance.

During this decade, Charles's exile must have seemed interminable and his prospects uncertain. In the 1430s his wife, Bonne, died, as did his daughter Jeanne. From 1436 until 1439, Charles was in the care of Sir Reynold Cobham and spent much of his time in London, where he frequented the Greyfriars and read, copied, and borrowed Franciscan texts from their convent. Charles may even have been the author of a Latin religious poem that exists in his hand. The *Canticum Amoris* (Songs of Love), written in monorhyme quatrains of

thirteen-syllable lines, enumerates the signs of God's love for mankind: the beauties of creation, man's godlike faculties, and the incarnation. The poem serves both as a consolation to one who has lost much and as a reminder of what remains to him to be thankful for.

Meanwhile, a new constable in France, Arthur of Richemont, was regaining the kingdom for Charles VII. After the failure of Arras, pressure for peace came from all sides, so in the summer of 1439 Charles was once more in Calais at another peace conference orchestrated by Isabelle of Burgundy, which established commercial relations between Flanders and England and promised another conference the following year. Overwhelmed by the cost of the war, the English were ready for peace, and on 25 October 1439, they agreed that, upon payment of one third of his ransom, Charles could go to France to raise the rest of the money. He would obtain a peace agreement within a year or return, a prisoner once again. The call went out for contributions to his ransom and largely through the efforts of his hereditary enemy, the duke of Burgundy, and his persistent duchess, Charles returned to France twenty-five years after he left it. According to the English chronicler Edward Hall, Charles "was deliuered out of Englande into Fraunce at that tyme . . . speakyng better Englishe then Frenche."

Left behind in England was a manuscript similar in size, shape, and contents to the French manuscript that accompanied Charles home, but in English. Harley ms. 682 is missing its first gathering of pages, beginning with Love's letter admitting Charles to his service. A story similar to the French *Retenue d'Amours* is told in the popular late medieval English stanza form, rhyme royal.

English versions of the seventy-one ballades, the *Songe,* and the *Departie* follow. But unlike the French collection, after the ballade on the lover's cure, the book continues with a unifying narrative. A ballade invites lovers to a banquet of poetry, ninety-seven chansons, which suggest the story already familiar from the ballades: a reluctant lover falls in love with a beautiful lady who dies. A poem of thanksgiving and several short caroles for dancing conclude the banquet.

Then a delightful dream vision reminds us of the poet-lover's melancholy state after his lady's death. He has been writing a complaint to Fortune when he falls asleep in a landscape reminiscent of Dover, on a cliff overlooking the sea, and dreams he sees Venus, naked but for a kerchief, floating toward him. She addresses him as Charles and tries to dissuade him from his obstinate celibacy. Although he will not be persuaded, his shifting arguments reveal his dissatisfaction with his solitude. Charles sees Fortune descend from the sky bearing a lady on her wheel whom he at first believes is his lost lady, but this is actually another who resembles her. He wishes to approach her, so Venus lifts him up, but he awakens, grasping Venus's kerchief as a token. On his way home, he meets a company of lords and ladies playing a game. In the group is the lady Charles saw on Fortune's wheel. He joins the game and speaks to her, requesting permission to write. She agrees, they all depart, and a second series of thirty-six ballades begins.

Although half of these poems are undoubtedly translations of Charles of Orléans's French poems, the remainder (half the chansons, the dream-vision, and the second series of ballades) have only three French originals not included in Charles's French manuscript: a ballade by Christine de Pizan and two ballades by the duke of Burgundy written as part of a verse correspondence with Charles. Linguistic evidence suggests a translator would probably be French. He (or she) would need access not only to Charles's poems but to his correspondence, and would have to translate and compose narrative and lyric verse in English in Charles's favorite forms. Although Suffolk has been proposed as the translator, Anglophone critics generally believe that Charles himself, after a decade or two in England, translated and composed poems in English; most French critics, however, disagree. The history of this manuscript contributes to the uncertainty about its authorship. It was first discovered by Humphrey Wanley in 1707 when the theological manuscripts of Bishop Stillingfleet became part of the Harley collection. The largest collection of courtly lyrics in Middle English, it makes a qualitative as well as a quantitative contribution to Middle English literature.

At long last, on 11 November 1440, Charles, having disembarked in English Calais, went home to France, where he was received by representatives of King Charles VII, by the duke and duchess of Burgundy, and by his brother Dunois. Welcoming ceremonies included Charles's betrothal to Marie of Cleves, Philip the Good's fourteen-year-old niece. Following fast on the heels of the wedding, which took place on 26 November, Charles was inducted into the *Toison d'Or,* the chivalric order Philip had founded in 1430. The former adversaries, Orléans and Burgundy, were now bound together by treaties, oaths, and family ties. Charles and his bride were ceremoniously escorted south through Burgundian territories by the duke and duchess, and two months later Charles arrived in Paris. He was greeted by the constable of the city and representatives of the church, but not by the king, who demonstrated neither affection nor gratitude to the cousin who had so long endured exile in his service. Early in February Charles arrived home in Blois. He stayed there only briefly before he began a year-long circuit of France.

On his journeys throughout France, Charles had two objectives: to collect contributions for his ransom and to muster support for a peace treaty within the year. Despite Charles's best efforts, plans for a peace conference fell through. The French were reluctant to interrupt the series of victories that reclaimed the kingdom, and the English invariably refused to pay homage to the French king for the lands in Calais and Aquitaine that the French were willing to concede to them. The English were content, however, with the steady flow of payments for the liberation of Charles and his brother Jean, so even though a treaty was not forthcoming, Charles was not obliged to return to England. In 1444 an agreement was signed at Tours for a one-year truce sealed by the marriage of Margaret of Anjou to Henry VI, but this truce lasted for five years. Thanks to the combined efforts of Charles, Dunois, Suffolk, and the monetary contributions of René of Anjou, the debt Charles had incurred in 1412 during the war between

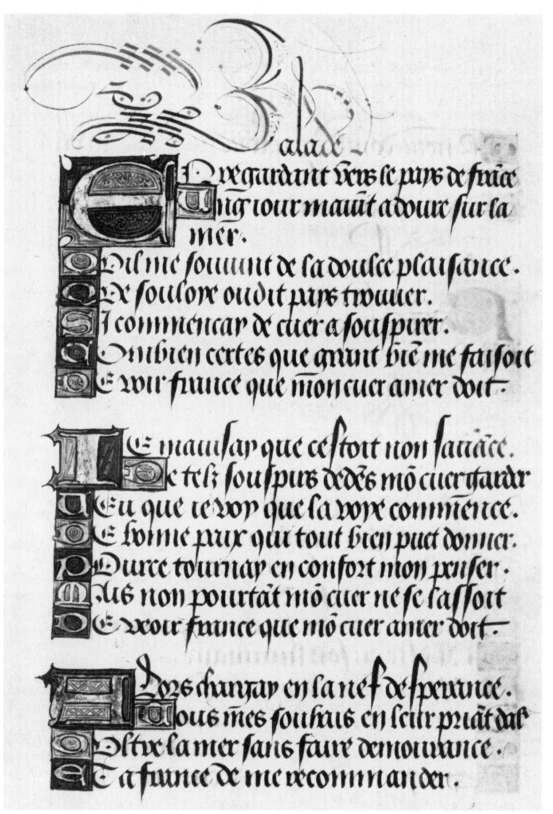

Opening page from a manuscript for Charles's En regardant vers le païs de France, *a poem expressing his desire to be repatriated to France*
(British Library, Royal 16 f. II)

the Burgundians and the Armagnacs was repaid, and Jean of Angouleme too came home in 1445.

But by 1447 Charles had a new problem. The county of Asti, part of the dowry of his mother, Valentina Visconti, had been nominally ruled by a French governor with a local Italian administration. During Charles's imprisonment in England, the Astesans sought the protection of Charles's uncle, Filippo-Maria Visconti, Duke of Milan, who promised to return the county to Charles upon his release. Visconti later claimed that at the death of Valentina, Asti had reverted to the dukes of Milan, and he named the condottiere Francesco Sforza, captain of Milan and procurer of Asti as well. To further complicate matters, when Filippo died in August 1447, he named King Alphonse of Aragon as his heir. Charles, Alphonse, and Sforza, who had by this time married Filippo's only child, an illegitimate daughter, all claimed the duchy of Milan, and neighboring rulers were eager to dismantle the extensive territories acquired by the Viscontis.

Charles set about raising an army. Once again he traversed the kingdom, this time seeking men in addition to funds. He was supported in his claim not only to Asti but to the duchy of Milan by the French king who had sent two thousand men under Regnault de Dresnay to remonstrate with Visconti. On 16 October 1447, Charles of Orléans entered Asti and was welcomed by the populace. Just two days later, however, Francesco Sforza defeated Regnault de Dresnay at Bosco, and the troops retreated to France. Not having the forces to contend with the redoubtable condottieri, Charles abandoned his military ventures but persisted in diplomatic efforts to obtain Asti and Milan. He returned to Blois in August of 1448, without an Italian county or duchy, but with a secretary from Asti, Antonio, who would translate Charles's poems into Latin. Charles continued to style himself duke of Orléans and Milan and sent letters to his subjects in Asti and copies of documents defending his right to the Italian title to his allies Burgundy, Charles VII, and the Holy Roman Emperor. He even prepared another expedition in 1448–1449, but lacking the will as well as the resources to engage in another war, Charles's Italian claim remained only a claim until 1499 when his son Louis XII captured Ludovico Sforza, and from 1500 until 1512 Milan was a French possession. François I, Louis's successor, fought with Emperor Charles V over Milan between 1515 and 1525, but in 1526 the defeat at Pavia lost the French the Visconti heritage.

After his hopes in Italy were thwarted, Charles returned to Blois and rarely left it. Since his return to France in 1440, Charles had continued to write poems despite the political events that distracted him; however, he composed only about 50 ballades as opposed to nearly 350 rondeaux, short lyrics with a refrain at the beginning, middle, and end, and usually four lines between the refrains. Many of these poems continue the courtly themes of the original manuscript although imagery in the rondeaux draws less on chivalry and warfare. Some poems chronicle the joys and pains of love or depict the world through aristocratic eyes. One of Charles's most famous poems, *Le Temps a laissié son manteau* (Time Has Left off His Cloak), depicts the change of season as a change of clothing: the winter coat of wind, cold, and rain is exchanged for one embroidered in beautiful bright sunshine. In another poem, *Petit mercier, petit pannier* (Little Merchant, Little Basketweaver), the poet identifies with these humble artisans but chides himself for wasting time talking to them when he too has his work to do.

There is a great variety of tone in the rondeaux: some poems are courtly and proclaim the virtues of loyal loving while others are cynical and mock the idea of long service to fickle ladies for an uncertain reward. The poet may praise the pleasures of life, such as *Souper ou baing et disner ou bateau* (Supper in the Bath and Dinner in a Boat), or complain about the infiltration of melancholy, care, and grief into everyday activities. Several of these later poems express regret or impatience with the process of aging: Charles complains of the ailments that assail him and of his need for glasses but concedes a desire to be done with the turbulence of youthful love and to enjoy emotional tranquility.

Although Charles never abandoned the polished, graceful musicality of his early poems, sometimes he used a laconic and elliptic style as in the four-syllable lines: "Ci pris, ci mis / Trop fort me lie / Merencolie / De pis en pis." (Taken here, put there / too tightly / Melancholy binds me / worse and worse.) Often the rondeaux replace courtly rhetoric with the jargon of different professions: of the clerk in macaronic Latin-French, of the grammarian, the lawyer, the merchant, the cook, the pilgrim, the beggar. Their language and their metaphors are turned to Charles's perennial concern: the relationship between the inconstant and uncontrollable world outside and the equally variable one within. In a few lines, these brief poems sketch the panorama of medieval life from Charles's singular viewpoint at Blois.

Charles's personal manuscript also includes several poems by others: members of Charles's household and visitors to Blois. It was not uncommon for Charles to write a poem—or perhaps just begin one—and for others to take his first line or refrain and compose their own version. The famous *concours de Blois* (Contest at Blois) is an example. A dozen ballades exist in the manuscript with the first line "Je meurs de seuf auprès de la fontaine" (I die of thirst beside the fountain), including one by François Villon, who stopped at Blois at that period. Charles's biographer Pierre Champion noted that Charles's poem was composed about the same time that repairs were made to the well at Blois. The transformation of a quotidian event like a plumbing problem into an elegant meditation on the inevitable contradictions of the human condition exemplifies the alchemy of Charles's poetry.

Charles's tranquil retirement was unexpectedly brightened in 1457 when, after sixteen years of marriage, Marie of Cleves gave birth to a daughter, Marie of Orléans. To celebrate either her birth or her ceremonious entry into the city of Orléans as a toddler on 17 July 1460, Villon composed a *dit* which suggests he was among the prisoners liberated from jail, perhaps even awaiting execution, that day of amnesty. In 1462 Marie and Charles had a son, named Louis, who later succeeded his cousins Louis XI and Charles VIII to the throne of France as Louis XII. Another daughter, Anne, was born in 1464.

Not all the events of Charles's later life were so joyful. The treason trial of his former son-in-law forced Charles from reclusion into the public eye in 1458. Jean II, Duke of Alençon, had married Charles's daughter from his first marriage, Jeanne, who died in 1432. Alençon's father had supported the Armagnacs, and Alençon himself had been fighting since his earliest teens, first for the Orléanist party and then with the Bastard for the dauphin. When he was captured at the battle of Verneuil in 1424, he sold all he had for ransom, including his castle at Fougères, and in 1427 returned to the field "the poorest man in France," according to the chronicler Chastellain. A few years later, he attempted to buy back Fougères, but the dukes of Brittany refused to sell at any price. So Alençon formed an alliance with Henry VI to invade Brittany, but he was arrested and tried for treason at the *lit de justice* (royal law proceeding) of Vendôme on 15 September 1458.

There Charles spoke eloquently on behalf of one he still regarded as a son-in-law, and for the first time expressed himself unequivocally about the events of his own life. This trial was the most displeasing event to him, he said, more painful than the loss of his father, more painful even than his imprisonment, in which he was comforted by the fact that he was taken while performing his duty, and that his countrymen were obligated not to fail him. Charles recommended mercy: put in the balance Alençon's misdeeds to be corrected and his good deeds to be rewarded.

Charles pleaded for Alençon's life. His own experience in prison proved that long imprisonment is more painful than a quick death. He suggested keeping the duke secure so he could do no ill, and confiscating his property, while providing adequately for his wife, children, and loyal servants. Although Alençon was condemned to death, his execution was indefinitely deferred, and after a few years he was released from prison.

Age and illness had stopped Charles from writing around 1461 when yet another public role fell to him: Charles VII died. Since the king had long been estranged from his son, Charles was by default the chief mourner and led the funeral procession and extensive rites. His part in the festive coronation of Louis XI that followed was subordinate to that of the duke of Burgundy, who had supported the dauphin against his father. Then in 1464, frail at the age of seventy, Charles attended an assembly called by Louis XI at Tours. He fell ill on the journey home and died at Amboise during the night of 4–5 January 1465. His body was brought home to Blois, and he was buried in the Church of Saint-Sauveur.

Charles's reputation, as lover as well as poet, is attested by his contemporaries: shortly after Charles's arrival home from England in 1440, Martin Le Franc mentions him in his *Champion des dames* (Champion of the Ladies). Several manuscript copies were made of the French poems composed in England (including the magnificently illuminated British Library Royal ms. 16 F. II, most probably made around the year 1500 for Arthur, Prince of Wales, in which Charles's poems were selected and arranged to serve as models for epistolary communication between the prince and his intended, Catherine of Aragon). Around 1453 a copy of Charles's poems was made and translated into Latin by his secretary, Antonio Astesan. Charles's wife, Marie of Cleves, had a fairly complete copy of his poems, and a similar exemplar later belonged to Marie de Medici. Early printed poetry anthologies pillaged the poems of Charles and the Blois circle and reproduced them without attribution, so when Renaissance writers purified the French language of its archaisms and abandoned fixed forms with refrains, the poet was forgotten, although some of his poems survived unattached to his name. In the early eighteenth century the antiquarian Abée Sallier praised and published samples of Charles's poems. The romantic nineteenth century took a fancy to both the figure of the melancholy, imprisoned, medieval prince and his lyrical poetry, and published four editions of his poems in the course of the century. Charles's poetry offered both the exotic in its detail and allusion to medieval life, and the familiar and intimate in the analysis of emotions the romantics believed themselves to have invented.

Although few of Charles's hundreds of poems can be dated, it is evident that over the decades Charles's poetry evolved. His first poems reflected the

Charles d'Orléans and Marie de Cleves depicted in a French tapestry of about 1450 (Paris, Musée des Arts Decoratifs)

concerns of youth and were written in a polished and precious style. In *La Retenue d'Amours* and the early ballades and chansons, Charles celebrated love, the aristocratic lifestyle, and chivalric virtues and argued against the uncourtliness signified by the allegorical personification *Dangier*. Despite his privileged social position, Charles suffered many losses and disappointments from his earliest years, and the delicacy and idealism of the courtly community is tempered by a sense of solitude and introspection. As a defense against disillusionment and frustration, even in his early poems Charles cultivated a very nonlyrical attitude—*nonchaloir*. The more expansive and polemical ballades eventually ceded to the condensed and allusive rondeaux, an expression suitable to the gallic shrug of *nonchaloir*.

Paradoxically, the voluntary restrictions Charles embraced after his return to France—his virtual confinement at Blois and his concentration on the rondel—led to greater variety in his poetry. Despite their brevity, the rondeaux are less limited than the ballades; they are not confined to themes of courtly life but adopt the language and metaphors of a wider world. Charles's acute observation and accurate representation of the world that surrounded him is joined to the expression and analysis of the most common human emotions, the quotidian and the perennial with the profound and intimate.

If Charles's aristocratic origins afforded him any pleasure in life, it was the privilege he finally had of making poetry a condition of his court at Blois. It became not only his personal solitary regimen, as it had been in England, but a social communion for the prince, his household members, and his guests. Charles's personal manuscript is a treasure: a manual of poetic forms and courtly themes, an encyclopedia of medieval life and language, and a chronicle of personal growth to maturity, from his introduction to Love and Beauty in adolescence to his surrender to Old Age. These poems offer us a window out onto the world of the Middle Ages and in on the eternal negotiations of the self with circumstance.

Bibliographies:

Edith Yenal, *Charles d'Orléans: A Bibliography of Primary and Secondary Sources* (New York: AMS Press, 1984);

Deborah Hubbard Nelson, *Charles d'Orléans: An Analytical Bibliography,* Research Bibliographies and Checklists no. 49 (London: Grant & Cutler, 1990).

Biographies:

Pierre Champion, *Vie de Charles d'Orléans* (Paris: H. Champion, 1911);

Enid McLeod, *Charles of Orléans, Prince and Poet* (London: Chatto & Windus, 1969).

References:

Jacques Drillon, *Charles d'Orléans, ou, Le génie mélancolique: théâtre à lire* (Paris: J.-C. Lattes, 1993);

David A. Fein, *Charles d'Orléans* (Boston: Twayne, 1983);

Lucien Foulet, "Villon et Charles d'Orléans," *Medieval Studies in Memory of Gertrude Schoepperle Loomis* (New York: Columbia University Press, 1927), pp. 355–380;

John Fox, *Charles d'Orléans: Choix de poésies* (Exeter, U.K.: University of Exeter, 1973);

Ann Tukey Harrison, *Charles d'Orléans and the Allegorical Mode,* North Carolina Studies in the Romance Languages and Literatures no. 150 (Chapel Hill: University of North Carolina, Dept. of Romance Languages, 1975);

Maurice Keen, *The Laws of War in the Late Middle Ages* (London: Routledge & Kegan Paul, 1965);

Henry Noble McCracken, "An English Friend of Charles d'Orléans," *PMLA,* 26 (1911): 142–180;

Jean Claude Mühlethaler, *Charles d'Orléans: Ballades et Rondeaux* (Paris: Livre de Poche, 1992);

Gilbert Ouy, "Un poème mystique de Charles d'Orléans: le 'Canticum Amoris,'" *Studi Francesi,* 7 (1959): 64–84;

Regine Pernoud, *Jeanne d'Arc* (Paris: Editions du Seuil, 1959);

Alice Planche, *Charles d'Orléans: ou, La recherche d'un langage,* Bibliothèque du XVe siècle no. 38 (Paris: H. Champion, 1975);

Daniel Poirion, *Le poète et le prince: l'évolution du lyrisme courtois de Guillaume de Machaut à Charles d'Orléans,* Publications Université de Grenoble, Faculté des lettres et sciences humaines no. 35 (Paris: Presses universitaires de France, 1965);

Desmond Seward, *The Hundred Years War: The English in France 1337–1453* (New York: Atheneum, 1982);

Italo Siciliano, *François Villon et les thèmes poétiques du Moyen Age* (Paris: Armand Colin, 1934);

Paul Strohm, "Jean of Angouleme: A Fifteenth Century Reader of Chaucer," *Neuphilologische Mitteilungen,* 72 (1971): 69–76;

Richard Vaughan, *Valois Burgundy* (London: Allen Lane, 1975).

Alain Chartier

(circa 1385 – 20 March 1430)

James Laidlaw
University of Edinburgh

WORKS: *Le Lay de Plaisance* (circa 1410)

Manuscripts: The poem is included in fourteen extant manuscripts, which include Aix-en-Provence, Bibliothèque Méjanes, 168, and Paris, Bibliothèque Nationale de France. The text in the standard edition is based on Grenoble, Bibliothèque Municipale, 874, and Bibliothèque Nationale de France, f. fr. 1127.

Standard edition: In *The Poetical Works of Alain Chartier,* edited by J. C. Laidlaw (London & New York: Cambridge University Press, 1974), pp. 147–154.

Ad fratrem suum juvenem epistola (circa 1410)

Manuscripts: This letter is preserved in only three manuscripts: Berlin, Staztsbibliothek, lat. fol. 366; Chantilly, Musée Condé, 438; and Paris, Bibliothèque Nationale, f. lat. 8757.

First publication: In *Alain Chartier: études biographiques, suivies de pièces justificatives, d'une description des éditions et d'une édition des ouvrages inédits,* edited by C. J. H. Walravens (Amsterdam: Meulenhoff-Didier, 1971), pp. 264–266.

Rondeaulx et balades (circa 1410–1425)

Manuscripts: The rondeaux and ballades are included in thirty-three manuscripts, most of which include only one or two poems. Grenoble, Bibliothèque Municipale, 874 and Toulouse Bibliothèque Municipale, 826, together with Lyon, Bibliothèque Municipale, 1235, and Berlin, Kupferstichkabinett, 78 B 17 (generally known as the *Chansonnier du cardinal de Rohan* after its eighteenth-century owner) are among the few manuscripts which have large collections of Chartier's rondeaux and ballades.

Standard edition: In *The Poetical Works of Alain Chartier,* edited by J. C. Laidlaw (London & New York: Cambridge University Press, 1974), pp. 371–392.

De libertate ecclesie oratio (1411–1412)

Manuscripts: This oration is preserved in only three manuscripts. Chantilly, Musée Condé, 438, Paris, Bibliothèque Nationale de France, f. lat. 8757 and Florence, Biblioteca Riccardiana.

Standard editions: In *Étude sur Alain Chartier,* edited by D. Delaunay (Rennes: Oberthur, 1876); in *Les Œuvres latines d'Alain Chartier,* edited by Pascale Bourgain-Hemeryck (Paris: Editions du centre national de la recherche scientifique, 1977), pp. 165–170.

Le Debat des deux fortunés d'amours (1412–1413)

Manuscripts: Twenty-seven manuscripts contain the *Debat* (also called *Le Gras et le Maigre,* The Fat and the Thin), including Aix-en-Provence, Bibliothèque Méjanes, 168; Grenoble, Bibliothèque Municipale, 874, and Paris, Bibliothèque Nationale de France, f. fr. 1127.

First publication: In *Le Jardin de Plaisance et Fleur de Rhétorique* (Paris: Antoine Vérard, circa 1501).

Standard edition: In *The Poetical Works of Alain Chartier,* edited by J. C. Laidlaw (London & New York: Cambridge University Press, 1974), pp. 155–195.

Le Debat de reveille matin (circa 1413–1424)

Manuscripts: This poem is preserved in thirty-seven extant manuscripts; the one with the most complete and regular text is the early fifteenth century manuscript: Toulouse, Bibliothèque Municipale, 826.

First publication: In *Les Fais maistre alain chartier* (Paris: Pierre Le Caron, 1489).

Standard edition: In *The Poetical Works of Alain Chartier,* edited by J. C. Laidlaw (London & New York: Cambridge University Press, 1974), pp. 305–319.

Le Breviaire des nobles (after 1415)

Manuscripts: The *Breviaire* has a complicated textual tradition; it is preserved in fifty-four manuscripts but attributed to Alain Chartier in only twelve of these.

Standard edition: In *The Poetical Works of Alain Chartier,* edited by J. C. Laidlaw (London & New

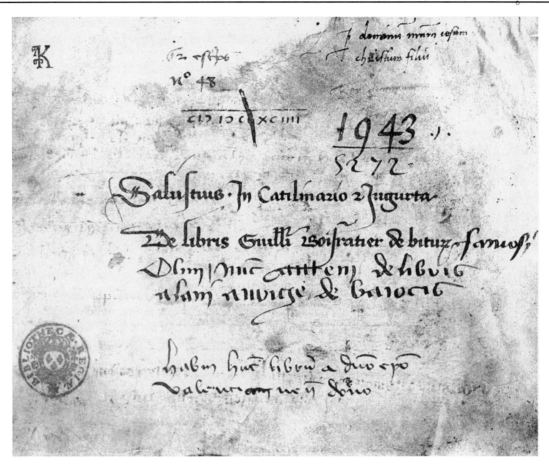

Legal document with annotations and signature by Alain Chartier (Bibliothèque Nationale de France, Salluste, lat. 5748, f. 1r.)

York: Cambridge University Press, 1974), pp. 393–409.

Le Lay de Paix (after 1415)

Manuscripts: The poem is extant in forty-eight manuscripts, including Aix-en-Provence, Bibliothèque Méjanes, 168, and Grenoble, Bibliothèque Municipale, 874, which both date from circa 1440–1470.

First publication: In *Les Fais maistre alain chartier* (Paris: Pierre Le Caron, 1489).

Standard edition: In *The Poetical Works of Alain Chartier,* edited by J. C. Laidlaw (London & New York: Cambridge University Press, 1974), pp. 410–420.

Le Livre des quatre dames (1416)

Manuscripts: Of the thirty-two surviving manuscripts, the most notable are two fifteenth-century works, London, British Library, Add. 21247, and Paris, Bibliothèque de l'Arsenal, 2940, which are probably presentation copies prepared under Alain Chartier's supervision.

Standard edition: In *The Poetical Works of Alain*

Chartier, edited by J. C. Laidlaw (London & New York: Cambridge University Press, 1974), pp. 196–304.

Ad universitatem parisiensem epistola (circa 1418–1419)

Manuscripts: This letter is preserved in nine manuscripts.

First publication: In *Epostolae Francisci Philelphi* (Paris: Felix Baligault for Jehan Petit, 1498).

Standard edition: In *Les Œuvres Latines d'Alain Chartier,* edited by Pascale Bourgain-Hemeryck (Paris: Editions du centre de la recherche scientifique, 1977), pp. 221–224.

Le Debat du Herault, du Vassault et du Villain (before 1422)

Manuscripts: Only one manuscript containing this work, Berlin, Kupferstichkabinett, 78 C 7, is known to be extant.

First publication: "Aus einer Chartier-Handschrift des Kgl. Kupferstichkabinetts zu Berlin," edited by Siegfried Lemm, *Archiv für das Studium der neueren Sprachen und Literaturen,* 132 (1914): 131–138.

Standard edition: In *The Poetical Works of Alain*

Chartier, edited by J. C. Laidlaw (London & New York: Cambridge University Press, 1974), pp. 421–435.

Le Quadrilogue invectif (1422)

> **Manuscripts:** This prose work is present in fifty extant manuscripts and was frequently copied separately (eleven manuscripts). The standard edition is based on Paris, Bibliothèque Nationale de France, f. fr. 126 with variants from Paris, Bibliothèque Nationale de France, f. fr. 1124.
>
> **First publication:** . . . *un notable et excellent traittié sur le fait de la guerre . . . lequel traittié est nommé quadrilogue* (Bruges: Colard Mansion, 1477).
>
> **Standard edition:** *Alain Chartier: le Quadrilogue Invectif,* edited by E. Droz, Classiques français du moyen âge no. 32 (Paris: Champion, 1923; revised, 1950).
>
> **Edition in English:** In *Fifteenth-Century English Translations of Alain Chartier's Le traite de l'espérance and Le quadrilogue invectif,* 2 volumes, edited by Margaret S. Blayney, Early English Text Society Original Series nos. 270 & 281 (Oxford: Published for the Early English Text Society by the Oxford University Press, 1974, 1980).

Ad detestacionem belli gallici et suasionem pacis epistola (1422–1423)

> **Manuscripts:** This text is preserved in twelve manuscripts.
>
> **First publication:** In *Epistolae francisci Philelphi* (Paris: Felix Baligault for Jehan Petit, 1498).
>
> **Standard edition:** In *Les Œuvres latines d'Alain Chartier,* edited by Pascale Bourgain-Hemeryck (Paris: Editions du centre national de la recherche scientifique, 1977).

Metra super eodem (1422–1423)

> **Manuscripts:** This text is preserved in eleven manuscripts.
>
> **Standard editions:** In *Alain Chartier: études biographiques, suivies de pièces justificatives, d'une description des éditions et d'une édition des ouvrages inédits,* edited by C. J. H. Walravens (Amsterdam: Meulenhoff-Didier, 1971), pp. 266–268; in *Les Œuvres latines d'Alain Chartier,* edited by Pascale Bourgain-Hemeryck (Paris: Editions du centre national de la recherche scientifique, 1977), pp. 242–244.

La Complainte (circa 1424)

> **Manuscripts:** Thirty-seven manuscripts include this poem; the version in Toulouse, Bibliothèque Municipale, 826, was used as the base text for the standard edition.
>
> **First publication:** In *Les fais maistre alain chartier* (Paris: Pierre le Caron, 1489).
>
> **Standard edition:** In *The Poetical Works of Alain*

Chartier, edited by J. C. Laidlaw (London & New York: Cambridge University Press, 1974), pp. 320–327.

La Belle Dame sans mercy (1424)

> **Manuscripts:** This poem is preserved in forty-four manuscripts. New York, Pierpont Morgan Library, 396, an early manuscript (late fifteenth or early sixteenth century), contains a good but incomplete text of the *Belle Dame* copied with works of Guillaume de Machaut.
>
> **Standard edition:** In *The Poetical Works of Alain Chartier,* edited by J. C. Laidlaw (London & New York: Cambridge University Press, 1974), pp. 328–360.
>
> **Edition in English:** In *Political, Religious and Love Poems: From the Archbishop of Canterbury's Lambeth ms. no. 306, and Other Sources,* edited by Frederick J. Furnivall, Early English Text Society Original Series no. 15 (London: Published for the Early English Text Society by Trübner, 1866), pp. 80–111.

L'Excusacion aux dames (1425)

> **Manuscripts:** Sometimes called *Responce* (Response), this work is preserved in thirty-one manuscripts.
>
> **Standard edition:** In *The Poetical Works of Alain Chartier,* edited by J. C. Laidlaw (London & New York: Cambridge University Press, 1974), pp. 362–370.

Ad Cesarem Sigismundum prima oratio (1425)

> **Manuscripts:** This text is preserved in eight manuscripts.
>
> **Standard editions:** In *Etude sur Alain Chartier,* edited by D. Delaunay (Rennes: Oberthur, 1876); in *Les Œuvres latines d'Alain Chartier,* edited by Pascale Bourgain-Hemeryck (Paris: Editions du centre national de la recherche scientifique, 1977), pp. 171–190.

Ad Cesarem Sigismundum altera oratio (1425)

> **Manuscripts:** This text is preserved in seven manuscripts.
>
> **Standard editions:** In *Etude sur Alain Chartier,* edited by D. Delaunay (Rennes: Oberthur, 1876); in *Les Œuvres latines d'Alain Chartier,* edited by Pascale Bourgain-Hemeryck (Paris: Editions du centre national de la recherche scientifique, 1977), pp. 191–195.

Persuasio ad Pragenses in fide deviantes (1425)

> **Manuscripts:** Preserved in eight manuscripts, including Chantilly, Musée Condé, 438, and Paris, Bibliothèque Nationale de France, f. lat. 8757.
>
> **Standard edition:** In Les *Œuvres latines d'Alain Chartier,* edited by Pascal Bourgain-Hemeryck

(Paris: Editions du centre national de la recherche scientifique, 1977), pp. 196–205.

Invectiva ad ingratum amicum (1425–1428)

Manuscripts: This prose letter is included in at least nineteen manuscripts.

First publication: (Paris: Jehan Petit, 1498).

Standard edition: In *Les Œuvres latines d'Alain Chartier,* edited by Pascale Bourgain-Hemeryck (Paris: Editions du centre national de la recherche scientifique, 1977), pp. 337–340.

Invectiva ad invidum et detractorem (1425–1428)

Manuscripts: At least seventeen manuscripts include this text; it is often copied with *Invectiva ad ingratum amicum,* and at least ten manuscripts contain only these two works by Chartier.

Standard editions: In C. J. H. Walravens, *Alain Chartier: études biographiques, suivies de pièces justificatives, d'une description des éditions et d'une édition des ouvrages inédits* (Amsterdam: Meulenhoff-Didier, 1971), pp. 268–273; in *Les Œuvres latines d'Alain Chartier,* edited by Pascale Bourgain-Hemeryck (Paris: Editions du centre national de la recherche scientifique, 1977), pp. 341–344.

De vita curiali (1425–1428)

Manuscripts: This text is preserved in ten manuscripts.

Standard edition: In *Les Œuvres latines d'Alain Chartier,* edited by Pascale Bourgain-Hemeryck (Paris: Editions du centre national de la recherche scientifique, 1977), pp. 346–375.

Edition in English: *The Curial Made by Alain Chartier; Translated Thus in Englyssh by William Caxton, 1484,* collated with the French original by Paul Meyer, edited by Frederick J. Furnivall, Early English Text Society, Extra Series no. 54 (London: Trübner, 1888; republished, London: Published for the Early English Text Society by the Oxford University Press, 1965).

Dialogus familiaris amici et sodalis super deploracione gallice calamitatis (1426–1427)

Manuscripts: The *Dialogis* is preserved in twenty-four manuscripts; in nine manuscripts it is copied between the *Quadrilogue* and the *Espérance;* the *Dialogus familiaris* is the only Latin work to be included in any of the French manuscripts.

Standard edition: In *Les Œuvres latines d'Alain Chartier,* edited by Pascale Bourgain-Hemeryck (Paris: Editions du centre national de la recherche scientifique, 1977), pp. 246–325.

Edition in English: *A Familiar Dialogue of the Friend and the Fellow: A Translation of Alain Chartier's Dialogus familiaris amici et sodalis,* edited by Margaret S. Blayney, Early English Text Society no. 295 (Oxford: Published for the Early English Text Society by the Oxford University Press, 1989).

Le Livre de l'Espérance (1427–1428)

Manuscripts: Preserved in forty-two manuscripts, the textual tradition of the *Livre de l'Espérance* is complex, partly because the work was revised, perhaps by Chartier himself. The critical edition by François Rouy is based on Paris, Bibliothèque Nationale de France, f. fr. 832, an early separate copy, which the editor describes as presenting a reliable version of the work.

Standard edition: *Alain Chartier: Le Livre de l'Espérance,* text established by François Rouy, Bibliothèque du XVe Siècle no. 51 (Paris: H. Champion, 1989).

Edition in English: In *Fifteenth-Century English Translations of Alain Chartier's Le traite de l'espérance and Le quadrilogue invectif,* 2 volumes, edited by Margaret S. Blayney, Early English Text Society Original series nos. 270 & 281 (Oxford: Published for the Early English Text Society by the Oxford University Press, 1974, 1980).

Ad Jacobum regem Scotorum oratio (1428)

Manuscripts: This work is preserved in only two manuscripts, Chantilly, Musée Condé, 438, and Paris, Bibliothèque Nationale de France, f. lat. 8757.

Standard editions: In *Etude sur Alain Chartier,* edited by D. Delaunay (Rennes: Oberthur, 1876); in *Les Œuvres latines d'Alain Chartier,* edited by Pascale Bourgain-Hemeryck (Paris: Editions du centre national de la recherche scientifique, 1977).

De Puella epistola (1429)

Manuscripts: This letter is preserved in four manuscripts in the Berlin, Chantilly, and Florence MSS and in Paris, Bibliothèque Nationale de France, f. lat. 8797.

Standard edition: In *Les Œuvres latines d'Alain Chartier,* edited by Pascale Bourgain-Hemeryck (Paris: Editions du centre national de la recherche scientifique, 1977), pp. 326–329.

Little is known about Alain Chartier's early life save that he was born in Bayeux into a bourgeois family prominent in the town's affairs, and that he studied at the University of Paris; the date of his birth is not known, nor the year in which he matriculated as a student. When Chartier addressed a letter in Latin to his alma mater toward the end of 1418 or early in 1419, he held the important post of notary and secretary to the king and was well established in the royal service. The earliest known letters which he signed in that capacity date from September 1417 and were sent on behalf of the Dauphin Charles. Chartier had almost certainly joined the dauphin's household some years earlier: Charles of France, then aged ten, was betrothed to Marie of Anjou on 18 December 1413 and, in accordance with the custom of the time, went to live with the family of his future bride. The household accounts of Yolande of Anjou, Queen of Jerusalem and Sicily, which run from February 1409 to September 1414, include the first known references to "Alain le charetier." What position Chartier occupied in the household is not known.

As the third surviving son of Charles VI and Isabel of Bavaria, Charles of France seemed destined to play only a subsidiary role in the affairs of state; however, the death of his two older brothers, on 18 December 1415 and on 4 April 1417, altered his situation dramatically. Although the members of the new dauphin's entourage no doubt benefited from the change in his circumstances, Chartier did not necessarily owe his appointment as a royal notary and secretary to the dauphin. In the prologue to *Le Quadrilogue invectif* (Four Characters in Invective Mode, 1422) Chartier describes himself as secretary both of the king (Charles VI) and of the dauphin.

The royal notaries were a select body whose number was restricted, theoretically at least, to fifty-nine, the king himself occupying a nominal sixtieth post. The important part that the notaries played in government is indicated by the king's status as the ceremonial sixtieth notary. Notaries were charged with the general correspondence of the chancellery; a select few of them were secretaries who were alone empowered to sign secret letters, as their name indicates.

Circumstances at the court of France were favorable for scholarship and literary pursuits and must have given Chartier encouragement and stimulus, particularly during his years in Paris. He probably had access to the impressive royal library, founded by Charles V and enlarged by Charles VI. Patrons, too, were at hand: the surviving manuscripts of the period include many dedicated to members of the royal family and to prominent courtiers. The influence of the chancellery itself should not be underestimated: many of the royal secretaries of this period were men of letters, interested in humanistic scholarship, and accomplished stylists in Latin and in French.

Chartier continued in office as a royal secretary for at least the next eleven years. His service brought him preferment to ecclesiastical benefices; early in 1420 he was appointed a canon of Notre Dame in Paris and was later made archdeacon. In 1424 he became rector of Saint-Lambert-des-Levées in the diocese of Angers and was allowed to defer his admission to full orders until his return from the embassy to the Emperor Sigismund. In 1425 he is described as a prebendary canon of Tours, and in 1428 as chancellor of Bayeux, his native town. The benefices in Bayeux and in Paris were more prospective than real, however, for neither city was then in territory under the control of Charles VII. The last royal letter on which Chartier's signature appears is dated 30 November 1428. He was probably promoted to the rank of royal counselor shortly thereafter, being so described in an epitaph and in one manuscript of his poetry. Chartier died in Avignon on 20 March 1430 and was buried there in the Church of Saint-Antoine. Nothing remains of his tomb or of the stone set up in his memory in 1458 by his younger brother Guillaume, bishop of Paris. What Chartier's business was in Avignon and how long he spent there are not known.

Throughout his official career Chartier was unwavering in his support of the Dauphin Charles, later Charles VII. For the royal house of Valois, these were unusually troubled times. In 1392 the dauphin's father, Charles VI, suffered the first of increasingly frequent attacks of insanity that left him unfit to rule. The government of the kingdom passed into the hands of the royal dukes, who vied for power, their struggles becoming increasingly partisan. In 1405 civil war threatened between Louis, Duke of Orleans, and Jean, Duke of Burgundy. The murder of Louis by supporters of the duke of Burgundy in November 1407 caused lasting enmity between the Orleanists (or Armagnacs, as they later became) and the Burgundians. Henry V, who succeeded to the English throne in 1413, saw the opportunity to turn the situation to his advantage. His invasion of northern France in the summer of 1415 culminated in his victory at Agincourt on 25 October when he inflicted a crushing defeat on a much larger French army.

France became a battleground, the scene of an increasingly bitter tripartite conflict between the Armagnacs, the Burgundians, and the English. In 1418 the Burgundians laid siege to Paris. When the dauphin fled the capital on 29 May, Chartier chose to follow him. He could not know that Charles's court was destined to spend the next decade and more south of the Loire in exile, as Chartier himself describes it in the opening line of *Le Livre de l'Espérance* (The Book of Hope, 1427–1428). During that time the northern provinces, including the capital, remained firmly in the hands of the English and the Burgundians.

An attempt to reconcile the duke of Burgundy with the dauphin ended disastrously in the duke's murder at Montereau on 10 September 1419. A letter and other documents associated with overtures to the new duke were signed by Chartier, who thereby committed himself irrevocably to the dauphin's cause. In the years immediately following, Chartier continued in the day-to-day work of the chancellery, signing documents that deal with finance, grants, or appointments; many of the letters that bear his name are directed to towns and institutions in France and solicit their support for the dauphin. There were further setbacks, both military and diplomatic, most often at the hands of the English. By the Treaty of Troyes, signed on 21 May 1420, Charles VI declared the dauphin to be illegitimate and, in agreeing to the marriage of Catherine of France to Henry V of England, transferred to his future son-in-law the succession to the throne of France. The dauphin suffered reverses in the military campaigns that followed. In the *Quadrilogue,* composed in the summer of 1422 when the dauphin's fortunes were at their nadir, Chartier described France as being on the verge of destruction.

After his father's death on 21 October 1422, the dauphin, now Charles VII, faced the daunting tasks of securing recognition of his right to the throne, both in France and in Europe, and of reconquering the larger part of his kingdom. From 1424 to 1428 Chartier served on several occasions as a royal envoy. An embassy to Holy Roman Emperor Sigismund early in 1425 attempted to secure imperial support for Charles VII's cause and was associated with missions to Venice and probably to Rome later that year; these diplomatic maneuvers had small effect on the progress of the war. In April 1426 Chartier was one of Charles VII's envoys in an equally unproductive mission to the duke of Burgundy. By contrast, an embassy to Scotland two years later yielded positive results: in July 1428 James I agreed to the renewal of the long-standing alliance between Scotland and France and to the marriage of his eldest daughter, Margaret, to the Dauphin Louis. He also promised to send further men-at-arms to reinforce Charles VII's army.

On each of these embassies Chartier played the subsidiary but far from insignificant role of secretary and orator: it was traditional for an oration in Latin to be given in the course of a diplomatic mission. The texts have survived of three Latin orations delivered by him: *Ad Cesarem Sigismundum prima oratio* (First oration before the Emperor Sigismund, 1425), *Ad Cesarem Sigismundum altera oratio* (Second oration before the Emperor Sigismund 1425), both pronounced during the embassy to Sigismund, and a third, *Ad Jacobum regem Scotorum oratio* (Oration before James, King of Scots, 1428), before James I. If the rubrics in four manuscripts are to be believed, *Le Lay de Paix* (The Lay of Peace) was composed in 1426, to mark the embassy to Burgundy.

Le Lay de Plaisance (The Lay of Pleasure, circa 1410), *De libertate ecclesie epistola* (Letter Concerning the Liberty of the Church, circa 1411–1412), and *Ad fratrem*

Detail from a miniature in a manuscript for Chartier's Le Quadrilogue invectif *(Bibliothèque Nationale de France)*

suum juvenem epistola (Letter to his Young Brother, circa 1410) are Chartier's earliest works, dating from the years when he was in service at the court of Anjou. The choice of form and language reflects the public to which the works were addressed. The lay is a love poem written in French for a courtly audience well versed in the *formes fixes* (fixed forms), while Chartier chose Latin for the private letter he sends to a younger brother whom he enjoins to respect his elders and avoid bad company; the advice is well-meaning, self-consciously so. Latin was the requisite medium for an open letter addressed to court officials and to the clergy, in which Chartier argues the case for the Church's traditional immunity from royal taxation. The letter may well date from March 1412, as Pascale Bourgain-Hemeryck has argued. Although the letter is presented with some spirit, the text lacks the stylistic polish of Chartier's later works.

The *Lay de Plaisance* (196 lines) is a variation on the classic New Year poem. On the day when lovers traditionally give gifts to their ladies, the poet cannot do so: he has no lady and is thus prey to solitude and sadness. He addresses his poem to an unnamed male friend whom he enjoins to avoid melancholy and to cultivate *plaisance* (pleasure or a pleasing, cheerful disposition). The stanzas that define and celebrate *plaisance* are repetitive and at times contrived, no doubt because of the need to force the poet's thoughts into the difficult and constraining mold of the heterometric lay. The poem shows a Chartier who is more rhetorician than man of feeling, more versifier than poet. It probably dates from about 1410, two or three years before the first of Chartier's debates on love, which show greater confidence and maturity.

Le Debat des deux fortunés d'amours (The Debate of the Two with Varied Fortunes in Love) was composed in 1412–1413 and comprises 1,246 lines. The stanzas are structured with three long rhyming lines followed by a short line that rhymes with the next set of three long lines. To a contemporary audience, the choice of stanza form and the structure of the debate would have recalled Guillaume de Machaut's *Le Jugement dou Roy de Behaingne* (The Judgment of the King of Bohemia, circa 1330s–1346) and, more immediately, three poems by Christine de Pizan, *Le Debat de deux amans* (The Debate of Two Lovers, circa 1400), *Le Livre des trois jugemens* (The Book of the Three Judgments, circa 1400) and *Le Livre du dit de Poissy* (The Book of the Poem of Poissy, 1400). The scene is a castle where ladies and knights have gathered, and two of the knights are persuaded to relate their fortunes in love. The first, said to be cheerful and well fed, maintains that more benefits than ills are to be derived from love; those who follow that path grow in valor, reputation, and inner worth. Love involves tests, setbacks, and disappointments, but they are greatly outweighed by the benefits that accrue from love. The contrary view is presented by the second knight, who is pensive and pale and dressed in unrelieved black. Love may indeed promise all the joys outlined by his opponent, he concedes, but these joys are transitory. There are more disadvantages than benefits: all too often the lover finds himself ensnared and falls victim to fear, suspicion, and jealousy. Listening to the fat knight, the reader gradually realizes that his views are conventional, so predictable that they provoke wry amusement. Though the thin knight's speeches also have an element of predictability, they are more lively, more pointed, and more varied. His first speech includes a memorable characterization of Jealousy and comes to a triumphant conclusion with a consciously exaggerated set of paradoxes about love.

Like Machaut and Christine before him, Chartier takes the part of spectator and reporter: he sets the scene as the poem begins and ends; he is asked to record the debate so that it can be sent for judgment. He says that he took no direct part in the discussions, partly because the joyous mood of the company contrasted with his own sadness, partly because he presents himself as one who knows love only from hearsay. The

debate is sent for judgment to Jean, Count of Foix; an allusion to his recent marriage shows that the poem was composed in 1412–1413. The dedication apart, there is no evidence of any other contact between Chartier and Jean de Foix. It may be that Chartier was following the example of Machaut and Christine in sending his poem to a patron. The dedication almost certainly had political motives also: in 1412–1413 the anti-Burgundian party, which included the house of Anjou, was anxious to secure the support of the Count of Foix.

Following the success of the *Deux fortunés,* it is not surprising that so many of the later works, in verse and also in prose, take the form of debates in which the *acteur* (author) takes a significant part. In choosing that stance, Chartier creates for himself a range of opportunities by involving the author so explicitly. He can be by turns detached, by turns involved. The mode can change; it can be narrative—giving opportunity for description and for authorial comment—or dramatic, allowing the speakers to speak for themselves and leaving the reader to interpret and to supply tone and emphasis.

Le Livre des quatre dames (The Book of the Four Ladies, 1416) is the longest (3,531 lines) and the most ambitious of Chartier's poetical works. For it, he chose a composite form: a prologue in octosyllabic stanzas of twelve or sixteen lines is followed by quatrains of the type used in the *Deux fortunés,* but here in octosyllables. Like its predecessor, the *Quatre dames* blends sentimental, political, and personal themes, but in very different proportions.

On the first morning of May, a time traditionally associated with love, the poet walks alone in the country outside Paris. Despite all the natural beauty that surrounds him, he cannot shake off his mood of melancholy. His lady is unaware of his love, for he is too timid to declare himself to her; his diffidence is the greater because of her noble qualities. A series of precise temporal references woven into the narrative suggest that it is not entirely imaginary. The reader learns that only two months have elapsed since the poet lost his heart, and so he must not lose hope. He cannot but recall, however, his previous lady who had refused him; he had waited two years for some token of her love, but to no avail. Toward the end of the poem the poet asks his lady to accept his book and to judge the debate among the four ladies. When he tells her that almost a year has gone by since he fell in love with her, he is not contradicting his earlier statement: allowance must be made for the intervening months during which the poem was composed.

As the poet walks in the countryside, his reverie is interrupted by an encounter with four ladies overwhelmed with grief. The cause of their distress is the recent disastrous defeat that the French have suffered at the hands of the English. The four have suffered contrasting fates: the First Lady mourns her dead lover, who was killed in the battle; the Second Lady lacks recent news of her beloved, knowing only that he lies captive in England. At least she has that knowledge to comfort her, whereas the Third Lady's lover is still missing after the battle. The Fourth Lady cannot rejoice at her lover's safe return, for he is one of those who fled the field, bringing disgrace on themselves and on France. Although the battle is not named in the text, it can only be Agincourt.

The poem gives no information to make it possible to identify the Third and Fourth Ladies and their lovers. More details are given of the First Lady's love; he is said to have been of high blood and royal lineage. That description, however, fits more than one of the nobles who lost their lives. By contrast the details given of the Second Lady and her beloved are circumstantial: her lover is said to be of higher rank than herself; between the ages of ten and twenty he was harried by ill fortune; and he left his sickbed, where he whiled away time composing ballades, to join the royal forces. The description points to Charles, Duke of Orleans, who was captured at Agincourt. Civil war between the Orleanists and the Burgundians had threatened in 1405 when Charles d'Orléans was ten years old. His father's murder at the hands of the Burgundians in 1407 was followed by further misfortunes–the death of his mother a year later and of his first wife a year after that. The other details also fit: in 1415 Charles was already a poet of some repute: he was still only twenty on the day of the battle, turning twenty-one a month later. The Second Lady can thus be identified with Bonne d'Armagnac, Charles's second wife.

All four ladies are fierce in their criticism of those knights who had not joined the French army or who had fled the field, the First and the Fourth Ladies being the most outspoken; their strictures echo those found in contemporary accounts of the battle. The way in which their two speeches combine expressions of private grief with scathing attacks on the behavior of the noble and knightly classes is both novel and highly effective. Less successful, however, is Chartier's decision to present the contrasting fates of the four ladies within the context of his own love affair: the final section in praise of his lady is strangely incongruous.

The role of the nobility is further addressed in the 454-line *Le Breviaire des nobles* (The Nobles' Breviary, after 1415), but here the aim is to instruct, not to criticize. The work consists of a sequence of thirteen ballades and a final rondeau. Having defined nobility in the opening poem, Chartier devotes a separate ballade to each of its twelve constituent virtues. Poems of different meters and stanza forms are carefully combined. The majority are isometric, and the only two heterometric ballades, *Droitture* (Justice) and *Courtoisie* (Courtesy), are highlighted as a result. In composing a sequence of ballades Chartier followed the example of earlier poets, including Christine de Pizan, who had recently completed two collections of *Cent balades* (One Hundred Ballads, circa 1395–1400 and 1410). The *Breviaire* is, however, shorter and more sharply focused.

The other lyrics known to be by Chartier are both fewer in number and more limited in their formal range than the works of his predecessors. The surviving poems consist of twenty-three rondeaux and five ballades; there are no virelays and no chansons royales (literally, "royal songs"–a verse form with five stanzas having identical rhyme patterns and an envoi using rhymes from the stanzas). It is not clear whether the small number is the result of accidents of transmission or lack of interest on Chartier's part. The poems themselves are traditional both in form and in subject, treating the different stages of a love affair. There is little to distinguish the majority of them from the work of contemporary medieval poets, save a particular delight and skill in shaping paradoxes of the type already highlighted in the *Deux fortunés*. The lyrics include, however, some memorable poems: a rondeau in dialogue, another rondeau in feminine voice, and a ballade on the death of the poet's lady. None of the ballades and rondeaux can be dated precisely.

The 368-line *Le Debat de reveille matin* (The Debate in the Small Hours), in which a luckless Sleeper is forced to comment on the complaints of a sleepless Lover, develops a passage in the *Deux fortunés* and was probably written between 1413 and 1424. The poem consists of octaves rhyming *ababbcbc,* a stanza form first used in French by Oton de Grandson. Chartier also uses this type of stanza in *La Belle Dame sans mercy* (The Fair Lady without Mercy, 1424) and *L'Excusacion aux dames* (Excuse to the Ladies, 1425); a variant form, rhyming *ababcdcd,* is found in *Le Debat du Herault, du Vassault et du Villain* (The Debate of the Herald, the Young Knight and the Villein, before 1422). With the exception of the *Excusacion aux dames,* the octave is used for the purpose of debate.

The author sets the scene before the debate proper begins. The protagonists then speak alternate stanzas or, much less often, two or three stanzas in succession. The rhythm of these debates is thus very different from that of the narrative poems, which are dominated by long, set speeches. Before Machaut, the *debat* had traditionally been a short poem in which the speakers alternated, stanza by stanza. Chartier is at his most original and most effective in the re-creation of that earlier form; the dialogue is well paced and shrewdly observed.

The *Debat de reveille matin* and the *Belle Dame sans mercy* (eight hundred lines) differ markedly in tone and in mood. *Reveille matin* is intended to amuse: the extreme protestations of the sleepless Lover are humorously contrasted with the prosaic statements and wise saws of his somnolent Companion. The poem has hints of irony and self-mockery, but they are less developed than in the *Belle Dame*. The author plays a more important role in the latter work, with much space being devoted to a description of his mood. He is in mourning following the death of his lady and so is reluctant to join the social gathering to which destiny brings him. As he watches the Lover and Lady whose conversation forms the centerpiece of the poem, he recalls his own love. The comparison which he draws is deliberately ambiguous. In likening himself to the Lover, does he also see a resemblance between the Lady and his dead mistress? The reader may also be left wondering about the tone in which the debate is conducted, as its different sections can be interpreted in various ways. The Lover is more finely drawn than his counterpart in *Reveille matin*: his protestations are more extravagant, his eloquence more studied. The Lady shuns rhetoric; like the Companion, she prefers to use simpler, more direct language, but her attitude to the Lover is much less sympathetic. Her intelligence and wit are more than a match for all the rhetorical fervor he can marshal. The good-natured banter of *Reveille matin* has become disillusion and self-mockery, and thus, although it is not clear when it was composed, *Reveille matin* is probably the earlier of the two poems.

On its appearance in 1424, the *Belle Dame* caused a furor, being interpreted as a criticism of courtly love and as an attack on ladies in general. In the *Excusacion aux dames* (244 lines), written in the spring of 1425 when he was engaged in the mission to the Emperor Sigismund, Chartier excused himself and his poem. The matter did not end there, however: the controversy continued for many years thereafter, inspiring a long series of imitations of the *Belle Dame sans mercy*.

The allusion to the death of Chartier's lady makes it possible to assign *La Complainte* (The Complaint) to about 1424. Its form is elaborate and demanding: stanzas of twelve or sixteen decasyllabic lines, each built on two rhymes only. Chartier addresses his complaint to untimely Death, who, in taking his mistress, has deprived the world and the poet of one who was the sum of all beauties and all virtues. This moving poem was well-known, and widely quoted and imitated.

The *Belle Dame,* the *Excusacion,* and the *Complainte* are the only love poems which can be dated after 1418, when Chartier fled from Paris. From that time onward, his works are increasingly in prose and on political and moralizing themes. *Ad universitatem parisiensem epistola* (Letter to the University of Paris), written before the murder of the duke of Burgundy in September 1419, is the first of a series of works in which Chartier sought to rally support for his master. Having described the miseries of life in war-torn France, he entreats the university to embrace the cause of peace and to urge the parties to the civil war to repent and to seek divine forgiveness. Unless they do so, the kingdom risks even harsher punishment at God's hands and faces annihilation.

Chartier returns to these themes in *Le Quadrilogue invectif* (Four Characters in Invective Mode), composed in the summer of 1422. As he surveys the calamitous state of France and asks himself whether the kingdom's destruction may not be part of the divine plan, the author falls asleep. In his dream he witnesses a dialogue between France and her three children, the estates of the realm. The three estates are depicted in different poses of inactivity in front of the house of France, which is tottering on the point of collapse. France speaks first, followed by the Knight and the People, who speak twice each, exercising their right of reply. The tone is harsh, critical, and largely negative: the Knight and the People blame each other roundly for the decline in the nation's fortunes and are reluctant to accept their full share of responsibility for the disaster that threatens. It is left to the Clergy, the estate to which Chartier himself belonged, to put forward a plan to ensure France's survival and recovery. The plan has three elements: *savance,* a sober appreciation of the current state of affairs; *chevance,* the recognition that resources are required and a readiness to provide them; and *obeissance,* willingness to subordinate self-interest and class interest to *la chose publique,* the common good, and to give unquestioning obedience. France instructs Chartier to record the debate and thus publicize it; he will fight with pen rather than sword.

The *Debat du Herault, du Vassault et du Villain* (440 lines) bears a distant resemblance to the *Quadrilogue,* for it presents a discussion on similar topics between a Herald, seasoned in war; a young Knight, prone to discouragement; and a Villein, who is reluctant to bestir himself. The poem is a much slighter work than the *Quadrilogue* and was almost certainly composed some years before. It is not clear whether the *Debat du Herault* was intended for publication, as it survives in only one copy.

Ad detestacionem belli gallici et suasionem pacis epistola (Letter Deploring the War in France and Encouraging Peace) concludes in most of the manuscripts with the poem *Metra super eodem* (Lines on the same subject); according to one manuscript the letter was written in

January 1423. The content recalls the *Quadrilogue,* but the tone is more positive. The intervening months had seen the deaths first of Henry V of England and then of Charles VI. Now that the dauphin has become king as Charles VII, has the time not come to set aside reproach and criticism, however well merited, and to look forward, to see in the new reign the prospect of a new beginning? That mood of optimism was to prove short-lived: three years later, when Chartier wrote the *Dialogus familiaris amici et sodalis super deploracione gallice calamitatis* (Familar Dialogue of the Friend and the Companion Lamenting the Calamity in France, 1426–1427), little had changed. He abandons the long speeches of the *Quadrilogue* in favor of a lively exchange, more akin to a conversation, between the Friend and his Companion. The Friend is a man of experience, pragmatic, inclined to take things as they come, to see the present crisis as only the most recent in the long series of crises that France has weathered successfully. His Companion is more reflective and more pessimistic, concerned lest the nation's sickness be terminal. France is riven by factions; each section of society looks only to protect its own interests. Everywhere vice seems to triumph over virtue. Moral decay and national decline go hand in hand, he argues, citing as examples the fall of Greece and Rome. Unless unity and lasting peace can be achieved, unless the nation as a whole repents and seeks divine forgiveness, France is in danger of suffering the same fate.

In the political works peace is a recurring theme, as Chartier contrasts the miseries of war with the order and prosperity which France had previously enjoyed. Peace is also the subject of *Le Lay de Paix* (284 lines), which has been associated with the embassy to Burgundy in 1426. The poem is addressed to all the princes of the royal house, however, and enjoins them to abandon civil war and cleanse themselves of all the associated shame and dishonor. References to the enemies who benefit from the internal strife indicate that the poem was composed after the English invasion of 1415, but they do not allow it to be dated more precisely than that.

Chartier turns from public to private morality in three Latin letters that may have been inspired by real events but can also be read as literary exercises on standard subjects. Whatever the circumstances of their composition, they are among the author's best works: the language is precise and elegant; the observations and shafts are shrewd and sharp. *Invectiva ad ingratum amicum* (Invective against an Ungrateful Friend, 1425–1428) treats the topic of ingratitude: now that he has achieved wealth, a former friend forgets the help and support he had been given. In a companion piece, *Invectiva ad invidum et detractorem* (Invective against an Envi-

Illumination from a fifteenth-century manuscript for a collection of Chartier's poetry produced by Jean Herlin, scribe of the queen of Anjou (Oxford, Bodleian Library, E. D. Clarke 34, 18395)

ous Slanderer, 1425–1428), Chartier berates one who had mocked his poverty and his learning. *De vita curiali* (On Life at Court, 1425–1428), addressed to a close friend, perhaps a brother, attempts to dissuade him from pursuing a career at court. Many earlier authors had written of the perils of life at court, highlighting the courtier's uncertain, unpredictable, uncomfortable existence. It was equally traditional to advocate the benefits of a tranquil life, characterized not by the pursuit of wealth and power but by liberty and an honest sufficiency. Chartier combines those themes with skill, laying especial stress on the moral dangers of life at court.

The only feature of these letters that helps to date them is their maturity of style. They were probably written at about the same time as the *Dialogus familiaris* and before the *Livre de l'Espérance.* Begun in the tenth year of his sorrowful exile, some time after the spring of 1427, the *Espérance* is unfinished. The work is an elaborate prosimetrum, in which passages of verse and prose alternate, on the model of Boethius's *De consolatione philosophiae* (On the Consolation of Philosophy, circa 524). In the opening poem the author contrasts the past glories of France with its current plight. He is then visited by *Melencolie* (Melancholy), and soon afterwards by three monstrous apparitions who harangue him in turn: *Indignation* makes a violent attack on the court; *Defiance* (Distrust) argues that the situations of France and of the author himself are beyond help and hope; and *Desesper-*

ance (Despair) is more brutal still and recommends suicide. Horrified by that suggestion, *Nature* awakes *Entendement* (Understanding), who opens the door of memory and admits four more allegorical figures, who bring welcome enlightenment and consolation. There follows a discussion between the author, *Entendement,* and *Foy* (Faith), who takes the largest part and succeeds in putting *Defiance* and *Desesperance* to flight. *Esperance* (Hope) then comes forward and, in a parallel conversation, brings further comfort to the author and his troubled mind; like *Foy* before her, she emphasizes the need for individuals and for the nation at large to have faith and trust in God and to seek divine intercession through constant prayer. When *Foy* and *Esperance* first appear, they are accompanied by two other figures, a third lady and a damsel described as well-born and of good bearing. While the third lady can be identified as Charity and it can be assumed that Chartier planned to include a third conversation, the identity of the noble damsel is not revealed.

In the prologue to the *Quadrilogue* Chartier describes himself as a "lointaing immitateur des orateurs" (distant imitator of the orators, that is, of the authors of antiquity). At the end of that work, when France asks the author to record the debate, she asks him to do this public service "car autant exaulça la gloire des Rommains et renforça leurs couraiges a vertu la plume et la langue des orateurs comme les glaives des combatans" (because the pen and the tongue of the orators exalted the pride of the Romans and made their hearts strive for virtue, quite as much as did the swords of the combatants).

Chartier's pride in his achievement is entirely justified. His works are eloquent and persuasive, all the more so when they are read aloud. His control of language, whether in French or in Latin, is especially impressive: the wide range of rhetorical figures at his disposal is appropriately deployed; syntax and construction are carefully varied; and the sentences are shaped and balanced for maximum effect. His control over his material and the breadth of his learning are equally striking: references to the Bible and to the Fathers are combined with quotations from classical authors, from Livy, Valerius Maximus, and Sallust in particular; they are used not for show, but judiciously, to illustrate the argument.

Chartier's later works are dominated by his passionate commitment to the survival of France and his belief that God will in the end show compassion. His courtly verse, the "joyeuses escriptures" (joyous writings) to which he devoted his youth, as he tells us at the beginning of the *Espérance,* seem to him increasingly irrelevant. Chartier lived long enough to see his prayers answered. *De Puella epistola* (Letter about the Maid), his last known work, was addressed to a foreign prince, probably the duke of Milan, in the summer of 1429. It gives an enthusiastic account of the achievements of Joan of Arc, who had raised the Siege of Orleans the previous May and escorted Charles VII to Rheims for his coronation on 17 July. Chartier's letter conveys his wonder at the divine intervention that had effected such an abrupt change in French fortunes.

A celebrated anecdote, related by Jehan Bouchet in his *Annalles d'Acquitaine* (Annals of Aquitaine, 1537), tells how the Dauphiness Margaret of Scotland, finding Alain Chartier asleep on a bench one day, kissed him on the mouth. Her action provoked comment, not least because of Chartier's reported ugliness. The dauphiness defended herself, saying that she had kissed not the man but "la precieuse bouche de laquelle sont yssuz et sortis tant de bons motz et vertueuses parolles" (the precious mouth from which so many good phrases and virtuous words have issued). That the story is apocryphal is easily demonstrated: Margaret arrived at the French court in 1436, six years after Chartier's death.

The anecdote is nonetheless important, for it shows that Chartier's reputation endured for at least a century after his death. Further evidence is provided by the large number of manuscripts in which his works have been preserved—the works of Alain Chartier survive in almost two hundred manuscripts dating from the fifteenth and early sixteenth centuries; the total is one of the largest known for any French writer of the later Middle Ages. The invention of printing made his works accessible to an even wider readership. They were scarcely out of print from 1477, when the *Quadrilogue* was first published, until 1529. *Les Fais maistre Alain Chartier,* the first collected edition, was published in Paris by Pierre le Caron on 5 September 1489; it includes all Chartier's French works in prose and verse with the exception of the *Deux fortunés,* the *Debat du Herault,* and the ballades and rondeaux. The edition was clearly popular, for it was reprinted twice by Le Caron and was also republished by other printers on at least five occasions. Galiot du Pré's two editions of 1526 and 1529 follow in the same tradition but add the *Deux fortunés,* which had first appeared in print in the *Jardin de Plaisance* about 1501.

Chartier was celebrated as a passionate defender of France, whose very existence had been threatened during his lifetime. More controversially, he was remembered as a poet whose works were marked by increasing impatience and disillusion with the artifice of courtly love. By the end of the sixteenth century, however, his works fell out of favor, and the renewed interest that followed the first critical edition of his works, published by André Du Chesne in 1617, proved to be short-lived. The title of one poem did survive to become a commonplace. John Keats's well known poem *La Belle Dame sans merci,* composed in 1819, was inspired not by the contents of Chartier's poem but by its evocative title.

Bibliographies:

E. J. Hoffman, *Alain Chartier, His Work and Reputation* (New York: Wittes Press, 1942), pp. 355–373;

C. J. H. Walravens, *Alain Chartier: études biographiques, suivies de pièces justificatives, d'une description des éditions et d'une édition des ouvrages inédits* (Amsterdam: Meulenhoff-Didier, 1971), pp. 222–261, 274–282;

J. C. Laidlaw, ed., *The Poetical Works of Alain Chartier* (Cambridge: Cambridge University Press, 1974), pp. 503–511;

Pascale Bourgain-Hemeryck, ed., *Les Oeuvres latines d'Alain Chartier* (Paris: Editions du centre national de la recherche scientifique, 1977), pp. 378–387.

References:

Pierre Champion, *Histoire poétique du quinzieme siècle,* 2 volumes, Bibliothèque du XVe Siècle nos. 27 & 28 (Paris: H. Champion, 1923), I: 1–165;

Patricia M. Gathercole, "Illuminations in the Manuscripts of Alain Chartier," *Studi Francesi,* 60 (1976): 504–510;

G. A. Jonen, *Allegorie und späthöfische Dichtung in Frankreich,* Beiträge zur romanischen Philologie des Mittelalters no. 9 (Munich: Fink, 1974);

J. C. Laidlaw, "André du Chesne's Edition of Alain Chartier," *Modern Language Review,* 73 (1968): 569–574;

Laidlaw, ed., *Alain Chartier: Poèmes,* Bibliothèque médiévale no. 10/18 (Paris: Union Gènèrale d'Editions, 1988);

Regula Meyenberg, *Alain Chartier prosateur et l'art de la parole au XVe siècle: études littéraires et rhétoriques,* volume 107, Romanica Helvetica (Berne: Francke, 1992);

Amédée Pagès, "*La Belle Dame sans merci* d'Alain Chartier: texte français et traduction catalane," *Romania,* 62 (1936): 481–531;

Arthur Piaget, *Alain Chartier: La Belle Dame sans mercy et les poèsies lyriques,* Textes littéraires Francçais (Paris: Droz, 1945; revised, Lille: Giard / Geneva: Droz, 1949);

Piaget, "*La Belle Dame sans merci* et ses imitations," *Romania,* 30 (1901): 22–48, 317–351; 31 (1902): 315–349; 33 (1904): 179–208; 34 (1905): 375–428, 559–597;

Daniel Poirion, *Le Poète et le prince: l'évolution du lyrisme courtois de Guillaume de Machaut à Charles d'Orléans,* Université de Grenoble: Publications de la faculté des lettres et sciences humaines no. 35 (Paris: Presses Universitaires de France, 1965);

Poirion, "Lectures de *la Belle Dame sans mercy,*" in *Mélanges de langue et de litterature medievales offerts à Pierre le Gentil* (Paris: SEDES, 1973), pp. 691–705;

François Rouy, *L'esthétique du traité moral d'après les oeuvres d'Alain Chartier,* volume 152, Publications romanes et françaises (Geneva: Droz, 1980);

Werner Söderhjelm, "*La Dama sanza mercede,* version italienne du poème d'Alain Chartier *La Belle Dame sans mercy,*" *Revue des langues romanes,* 35 (1891): 95–127.

Chrétien de Troyes

(circa 1140 – circa 1190)

Gerald Seaman
University of Evansville

WORKS: *Erec et Enide* (circa 1165–1170)

Manuscripts: This work is preserved in seven medieval manuscripts; six are Paris, Bibliothèque Nationale de France, f. fr. 375; Bibliothèque Nationale de France, f. fr. 794; Bibliothèque Nationale de France, f. fr. 1376; Bibliothèque Nationale de France, f. fr. 1420; Bibliothèque Nationale de France, f. fr. 1450; and Bibliothèque Nationale de France, f. fr. 24403. Chantilly, Musée Condé, 472 also includes the text in its entirety. Fragments are in Amsterdam, Universiteitsbibliotheek, 466; Brussels, Bibliothèque Royale, IV 837; Paris, Bibliothèque Ste-Geneviève, 1269; the Annonay and L'Aigle fragments are in private collections. In the eighteenth century (after 1765) Paris, Bibliothèque Nationale de France, f. fr. 375 was copied for La Curne de Sainte-Palaye and is now preserved as Paris, Bibliothèque de l'Arsenal, 3313–3318 (3317 includes *Erec et Enide*). A copy of Bibliothèque Nationale de France, f. fr. 1420 was also made for Sainte-Palaye and is classified as Bibliothèque de l'Arsenal, 3319. The *Erec et Enide* text from Bibliothèque Nationale de France, f. fr. 375 (with variants from Bibliothèque Nationale de France, f. fr. 794 and 1450) was copied (circa 1800) in a notebook belonging to Henri de Pascal de Rochegude, of Albi. This copy is now known as Albi, Bibliothèque Rochegude, Rochegude, 2.

Standard editions: *Erec und Enide,* edited by Wendelin Foerster, volume 3 of *Christian von Troyes. Sämtliche Werke nach allen bekannten Handschriften* (Halle: Niemeyer, 1890; republished, Amsterdam: Rodopi, 1965); *Erec et Enide,* edited by Mario Roques, Classiques français du moyen age no. 80 (Paris: H. Champion, 1952).

Standard edition and edition in modern French: In *Œuvres complètes de Chrétien de Troyes,* edited by Daniel Poirion, Bibliothèque de la Pléiade no. 408 (Paris: Gallimard, 1994), pp. 1–169.

Editions in modern French: *Erec et Enide,* translated by Jean-Marie Fritz (Paris: Lettres Gothiques, 1992); *Erec et Enide,* translated by René Louis (Paris: H. Champion, 1954).

Editions in English: In *Arthurian Romances by Chrétien de Troyes,* translated by W. Wistar Comfort (London & Toronto: Dent / New York: Dutton, 1914), pp. 1–90; in *Chrétien de Troyes: Arthurian Romances,* translated by D. D. R. Owen (London: Dent, 1987), pp. 1–92; *Erec and Enide,* translated by Carleton W. Carroll (New York & London: Garland, 1987); *Erec and Enide,* translated by Dorothy Gilbert (Berkeley & Los Angeles: University of California Press, 1992).

Philomena (circa 1170)

Manuscripts: Nineteen manuscripts of the *Ovide Moralisé* (a fourteenth-century text including Chrétien's *Philomena*) are cited by the editor of the standard edition.

Standard edition: In *Philomena: conte raconté d'après Ovide,* edited by Cornelis de Boer (Paris: Geuthner, 1909).

Standard edition and edition in modern French: In *Œuvres complètes de Chrétien de Troyes,* edited by Daniel Poirion, Bibliothèque de la Pléiade no. 408, pp. 915–952.

Edition in English: In *Three Ovidian Tales of Love: Piramus et Tisbé, Narcisus et Danaé, and Philomena et Procné,* translated by Raymond Cormier (New York: Garland, 1986), pp. 183–265.

Cligés (circa 1176–1178)

Manuscripts: Eight medieval manuscripts include this work: Paris, Bibliothèque Nationale de France, f. fr. 375; Bibliothèque Nationale de France, f. fr. 794; Bibliothèque Nationale de France, f. fr. 1374; Bibliothèque Nationale de France, f. fr. 1420; Bibliothèque Nationale de France, f. fr. 1450; and Bibliothèque Nationale de France, f. fr. 12560; Tours, Bibliothèque Municipale, 942; and Turin, Biblioteca Nazionale Universitaria L. I. 13 (1626). Excerpts and fragments are in Florence, Biblioteca Riccardiana, 2756; Oxford, Bodleian Library, Michael 569 (SC 24064); Paris, Bibliothèque de

Illuminated page from a fourteenth-century manuscript for Chrétien de Troyes's Le Conte du Graal, ou, Perceval, *with a depiction of a procession bearing the Holy Grail and other religious objects (Bibliothèque Nationale de France, f. fr. 12577, detail of f.74v)*

l'Institut de France 6138. *Cligés* is also transcribed in the eighteenth century (after 1765) copy of Bibliothèque Nationale de France, f. fr. 375 made for La Curne de Sainte-Palaye and now preserved as Paris, Bibliothèque de l'Arsenal, 3313–3318 (3317 contains *Cligés*). It is also preserved in the copy of Bibliothèque Nationale de France, f. fr. 1420 made for Sainte-Palaye and classified as Bibliothèque de l'Arsenal, 3319.

Standard editions: *Cligés,* edited by Wendelin Foerster, volume 1 of *Christian von Troyes. Sämtliche Werke nach allen bekannten Handschriften* (Halle: Niemeyer, 1884; Amsterdam: Rodopi, 1965); *Cligés,* edited by Alexandre Micha, Classiques français du moyen age no. 84 (Paris: H. Champion, 1957); *Cligés,* edited by Stewart Gregory and Claude Luttrell, Arthurian Studies no. 28 (Cambridge & Rochester: Brewer, 1993).

Standard edition and edition in modern French: *Cligés: Chrétien de Troyes; édition critique du manuscrit B. N. fr. 12560,* edited by Marie-Claire Gérard-Zai, translated by Charles Méla and Olivier Collet (Paris: Livre de Poche, 1994).

Editions in modern French: In *Œuvres complètes de Chrétien de Troyes* (with facing modern French translations), edited by Daniel Poirion, Bibliothèque de la Pléiade no. 408 (Paris: Gallimard, 1994), pp. 171–336; *Cligés,* translated by Alexandre Micha (Paris: H. Champion, 1957 revised, 1982).

Editions in English: In *Arthurian Romances by Chrétien de Troyes,* translated by W. Wistar Comfort (London & Toronto: Dent / New York: Dutton, 1914), pp. 91–179; in *Chrétien de Troyes: Arthurian Romances,* translated by D. D. R. Owen (London: Dent, 1987), pp. 93–184; *Cligés: Chrétien de Troyes,* translated by Burton Raffel (New Haven: Yale University Press, 1997).

Le Chevalier de la Charrette, ou, Lancelot (circa 1179–1180)

Manuscripts: This text is preserved in eight manuscripts: Paris, Bibliothèque Nationale de France, f. fr. 794; Bibliothèque Nationale de France, f. fr. 1450, Bibliothèque Nationale de France, f. fr. 12560; Chantilly, Musée Condé, 472; Madrid, Escorial, RBM M. III 21; Princeton, University Library, Garrett 125; and Vatican, Biblioteca Apostolica Vaticana, Reg. Lat. 1725. There is also a fragment: Paris, Bibliothèque de l'Institut de France, 6138.

First publication: *Roman van Lancelot (XIIIe eeuw),* 2 volumes, edited by W. J. A. Jonckbloet (The Hague: Stockum, 1846, 1849); and *Le roman du chevalier de la charrette,* edited by Prosper Tarbé (Reims, 1849).

Standard editions: In *Der Karrenritter (Lancelot) und das Wilhelmsleben (Guillaume d'Angleterre),* edited by Wendelin Foerster, volume 4 of *Christian von Troyes. Sämtliche Werke nach allen bekannten Handschriften* (Halle: Niemeyer, 1899; republished, Amsterdam: Rodopi, 1965); *Le chevalier de la charrette,* edited by Mario Roques. Classiques français du moyen Age no. 86 (Paris: H. Champion, 1958).

Standard edition and edition in modern French: In *Œuvres complètes de Chrétien de Troyes,* edited and translated by Daniel Poirion, Bibliothèque de la Pléiade no. 408 (Paris: Gallimard, 1994), pp. 505–682.

Editions in modern French: *Le Chevalier de la Charrette (Lancelot),* translated by Jean Frappier (Paris: H. Champion, 1971); *Le chevalier de la charrette,* edited and translated by Alfred Foulet and Karl D. Uitti (Paris: Bordas, 1989); *Lancelot ou le Chevalier de la Charrette,* translated by Jean-Claude Aubailly (Paris: Flammarion, 1991); *Le chevalier de la charrette, ou, le roman de Lancelot,* edited and translated by Charles Méla (Paris: Livre de Poche, 1992).

Editions in English: In *Arthurian Romances by Chrétien de Troyes,* translated by W. Wistar Comfort (London & Toronto: Dent / New York: Dutton, 1914), pp. 270–359; *Lancelot, or The Knight of the Cart,* translated by William W. Kibler (New York & London: Garland, 1981); in *Chrétien de Troyes: Arthurian Romances,* translated by D. D. R. Owen (London: Dent, 1987), pp. 185–280; *"Lancelot," or "The Knight of the Cart,"* translated by Ruth Harwood Cline (Athens: University of Georgia Press, 1990).

Le Chevalier au Lion, ou, Yvain (circa 1179–1180)

Manuscripts: This text is preserved in eight medieval manuscripts: Paris, Bibliothèque Nationale de France, f. fr. 794; Bibliothèque Nationale de France, f. fr. 1433; Bibliothèque Nationale de France, f. fr. 1450; Bibliothèque Nationale de France, f. fr. 12560; Bibliothèque Nationale de France, f. fr. 12603; Chantilly, Musée Condé, 472; Montpellier, BI, Sect. Méd. H 252; Princeton, University Library, Garrett 125; and Vatican, Biblioteca Apostolica Vaticana, Reg. Lat. 1725. A Renaissance adaptation by Pierre Sala (ca. 1455–1529) is included in Paris, Bibliothèque Nationale de France, f. fr. 1638. Fragments and excerpts are in Bruges, SA, AAJS 244, carnet scolaire; Lyon, Bibliothèque Municipale 743; Modena, AS, Archivio d'Este, Ministero Affari Esteri, Atti segreti F. 6 Miscellenea; and in a private collection for the Annonay fragments.

First publication: *Li romans dou chevalier au leon,* edited by Adelbert von Keller (Tübingen: Fues, 1841).

Standard editions: *Der Löwenritter (Yvain),* edited by Wendelin Foerster, volume 2 of *Christian von Troyes. Sämtliche Werke nach allen bekannten Handschriften* (Halle: Niemeyer, 1887; republished, Amsterdam: Rodopi, 1965). *Le chevalier au lion (Yvain),* edited by Mario Roques, Classiques français du moyen age no. 89 (Paris: H. Champion, 1960).

Standard editions and editions in modern French: In *Œuvres complètes de Chrétien de Troyes,* edited and translated by Daniel Poirion, Bibliothèque de la Pléiade no. 408 (Paris: Gallimard, 1994), pp. 337–503; *Le Chevalier au Lion, ou, Le Roman d'Yvain: édition critique d'après le manuscrit B.N. fr. 1433,* edited and translated by David F. Hult (Paris: Livre de Poche, 1994).

Editions in modern French: *Le Chevalier au Lion (Yvain),* translated by Claude Buridant and Jean Trotin, Traductions des classiques français du Moyen Age no. 5 (Paris: H. Champion, 1972); *Yvain ou le chevalier au lion,* edited and translated by Michel Rousse (Paris: Garnier-Flammarion, 1990).

Editions in English: In *Arthurian Romances by Chrétien de Troyes,* translated by W. Wistar Comfort (London & Toronto: Dent / New York: Dutton, 1914), pp. 180–269; *The Knight with the Lion or Yvain (Le chevalier au lion),* edited and translated by William W. Kibler (New York: Garland, 1985); in *Chrétien de Troyes: Arthurian Romances,* translated by D. D. R. Owen (London: Dent, 1987), pp. 281–373; *Yvain, the Knight of the Lion,* translated by Burton Raffel (New Haven: Yale University Press, 1987).

Guillaume d'Angleterre (circa 1180)

Manuscripts: This work is preserved in at least three manuscripts: Paris, Bibliothèque Nationale de France, f. fr. 375; Madrid, Escorial, H-13 (a sixteenth-century Spanish prose rendition); and a fourteenth-century manuscript, Cambridge, Saint John's College.

First publication: In *Der Karrenritter (Lancelot) und das Wilhelmsleben (Guillaume d'Angleterre),* edited by Wendelin Foerster, volume 4, *Christian von Troyes. Sämtliche Werke nach allen bekannten Handschriften* (Halle: Niemeyer, 1899; republished, Amsterdam: Rodopi, 1965).

Standard editions: *Guillaume d'Angleterre,* edited by Maurice Wilmotte, Classiques Français du Moyen Age no. 55 (Paris: H. Champion, 1927); *Guillaume d'Angleterre,* edited by Anthony J. Holden (Geneva: Droz, 1988).

Standard edition and edition in modern French: In *Œuvres complètes de Chrétien de Troyes,* edited by Daniel Poirion, Bibliothèque de la Pléiade no. 408, pp. 953–1036.

Vvlais
dist
en so
respit
Qᵉ tel
chose
a en
lan
en
despit

Qᵘi mⁱlt naue mⁱeⁱ q̄ on ne quide
pᵘ ce fait bū q̄ son estuide
a torne abien q̄l q̄ il ait
c ar qui son estuide entrelait
t ost ipuet tel chose ataisir
Qᵘi mⁱlt bendroit puis a plaisir
pᵘ ce dist crestiens de troies
Q̄ ne raisons est q̄ toctes boies
d oit chascuns penser ꞇ entendre
a bū dire ꞇ abien apᵣendre
ꞇ trait dun conte dauenture
y ne mⁱlt bele conioincture
pᵘ cõ puet prouer ꞇ sauoir
Q̄ cil ne fait mⁱe sauoir
Qᵘi sa science nabandone
t ant com dⁱeʳ grace len done
Derec le fil lac est li contes
Qᵘi deuant rois ꞇ deuant gᵘˢ
d epeⁱ꞊ ꞇ derompᵣe suolent
c il q̄ de ꞅcor buⁱre boelent

Des or q̄ menceⁱrai lestoire
Qᵘi toz iors mair ert en memoire
Tant q̄ durra crestientes
De ce sest crestiens uantes
Vn ior de pasqᵉˢ au tans nouel
a karadigan son castel
O t li rois artus cort tenue
a mes si rice ne fu beue
C ar mⁱlt ioc beax cheualiers
h ardis ꞇ corragoꞵ ꞇ fiers
E t rices dames ꞇ puceles
F illes de roi gentiⁱꞵ ꞇ beles
M ais ancois que la cort fausist
L i rois a ses chⁱꞵ dist
Qᵘil boloit le blanc cherf cachier
pᵘ le costume restauchier
M on segnor tⁱā̄ iⁱn ne plot mⁱe
Q̄ iℓ ot la pᵃrole oie
S ire fait il de ceste cache
H auerez ia ne gre ne grace
N os sauomes bien q̄ gᵘ pᵘecha
Q uel coustume li blaus cherf a
Q ui le blanc cerf ocirre puet
p ar raison baisier li estuet
D es puceles de nostre court
L a plᵘ bele a cuel quil entourt
M aus empozroit auenir grans
E ncore a il ceans ꞅ chans
D amoiseles de haus parages
F illes de roi gentiⁱꞵ ꞇ sages

Illuminated page from a manuscript for Chrétien's Erec et Enide *(Bibliothèque Nationale de France, f. fr. 24403, fol. 119)*

Edition in modern French: *Guillaume d'Angleterre,* translated by Jean Trotin (Paris: H. Champion, 1974).

Le Conte du Graal, ou, Perceval (circa 1181–1190)

Manuscripts: Fifteen extant manuscripts preserve the text of *Perceval.* Seven medieval manuscripts are: Paris, Bibliothèque Nationale de France, f. fr. 794; Bibliothèque Nationale de France, f. fr. 1429; Bibliothèque Nationale de France, f. fr. 1450; Bibliothèque Nationale de France, f. fr. 1453; Bibliothèque Nationale de France, f. fr. 12576; Bibliothèque Nationale de France, f. fr. 12577; and Bibliothèque Nationale de France, n. a. f. fr. 6614. Eight further complete manuscripts are: Bern, Bürgerbibliothek, 354; Clermont-Ferrand, Bibliothèque Municipale, I 248; Edinburgh, National Library of Scotland, Adv. 10.1.5; Florence, Biblioteca Riccardiana, 2943; London, British Library, Add. 36614; London, College of Arms, Arundel XIV; Mons, Bibliothèque Universitaire, 331/206; and Montpellier, BI, Sect. Méd. H 249. A fragment is transcribed in Prague, Národni Knihovna Ceské Republiky K I. E. 35; the Annonay and the Brussels (formerly de Lannoy) fragments are in private collections.

First publication: *Perceval le Gallois ou le conte du Graal,* 6 volumes, edited by Charles Potvin, Société des Bibliophiles Belges no. 21 (Mons: Dequesne-Masquillier, 1866–1871).

Standard editions: *Le Roman de Perceval ou le Conte du Graal,* edited by William Roach (Geneva: Droz; Paris: Minard, 1956; revised and enlarged, 1959); *Le conte du Graal (Perceval),* edited by Félix Lecoy. Classiques français du moyen age nos. 100 & 103 (Paris: H. Champion, 1973–1975).

Standard edition and edition in modern French: In *Œuvres complètes de Chrétien de Troyes,* edited and translated by Daniel Poirion, Bibliothèque de la Pléiade no. 408 (Paris: Gallimard, 1994), pp. 683–911.

Editions in modern French: *Perceval le Gallois ou le Conte du Graal,* translated by Lucien Foulet (Paris: Editions Stock, Delamain et Boutelleau, 1947; Paris: Nizet, 1970); *Le Conte du Graal (Perceval),* translated by Jacques Ribard (Paris: H. Champion, 1979); *Le conte du Graal, ou le Roman de Perceval,* edited and translated by Charles Méla (Paris: Livre de Poche, 1990).

Editions in English: *The Story of the Grail (Perceval),* translated by Robert White Linker (Chapel Hill: University of North Carolina Press, 1952); in *Chrétien de Troyes: Arthurian Romances,* translated by D. D. R. Owen (London: Dent, 1987), pp. 374–495; *The Story of the Grail (Li Contes del Graal), or Per-*

ceval, edited by Rupert T. Pickens, translated by William W. Kibler (New York & London: Garland, 1990).

Chansons

Manuscripts: The standard edition is based on fourteen manuscripts: Paris, Bibliothèque Nationale de France, f. fr. 765; Bibliothèque Nationale de France, f. fr. 844; Bibliothèque Nationale de France, f. fr. 845; Bibliothèque Nationale de France, f. fr. 847; Bibliothèque Nationale de France, f. fr. 1591; Bibliothèque Nationale de France, f. fr. 12615; Bibliothèque Nationale de France, f. fr. 20050; Bibliothèque Nationale de France, f. fr. 24406; Bibliothèque Nationale de France, n. a. f. fr. 1050; Paris, Bibliothèque de l'Arsenal, 5198; Bern, Bürgerbibliothek, 389; Modena, Biblioteca Nazionale Este., R 44; Oxford, Bodleian Library, Douce 308; and Vatican, Biblioteca Apostolica Vaticana, Reg. Lat. 1490.

First publication: In *Altfranzösische Lieder und Leiche aus Handschriften zu Bern und Neuenburg,* edited by Wilhelm Wachernagel (Basel, 1846); in *Crestien von Troies. Eine literaturgeschichtliche Untersuchung,* edited by W. L. Holland (Tübingen, 1854); in *Les plus anciens Chansonniers français publiés d'après tous les manuscrits,* edited by Jules Brakelmann (Paris, 1870–1891); in *Kristian von Troyes, Wörterbuch zu seinen sämtlichen Werken,* edited by Wendelin Foerster (Halle: Niemeyer, 1914).

Standard edition: *Les Chansons courtoises de Chrétien de Troyes,* edited by Marie-Claire Zai (Bern: Herbert Lang, 1974; Frankfurt: Peter Lang, 1974).

Standard edition and edition in modern French: In *Œuvres complètes de Chrétien de Troyes,* edited by Daniel Poirion, Bibliothèque de la Pléiade no. 408, pp. 1037–1049.

If there is a founding author not only of French literature but of medieval vernacular literature in general, it is Chrétien de Troyes, who largely inaugurated the genre of Arthurian romance and in so doing launched an entire literary tradition that has spanned more than eight centuries. Among the finest works of medieval French poetry, Chrétien's romances, composed in octosyllabic rhyming couplets, and ranging in length from approximately 6,500 to 9,300 verses, gave rise to copious and divergent Old French continuations in verse and prose.

As with most vernacular authors of the twelfth century, Chrétien's life is generally undocumented, although scholars have developed a variety of intriguing speculations on his identity based on internal and external evidence. Given his uncommon name, it has been suggested that Chrétien was a converted Jew from Troyes, the capital of the counts of Champagne and a commercial center

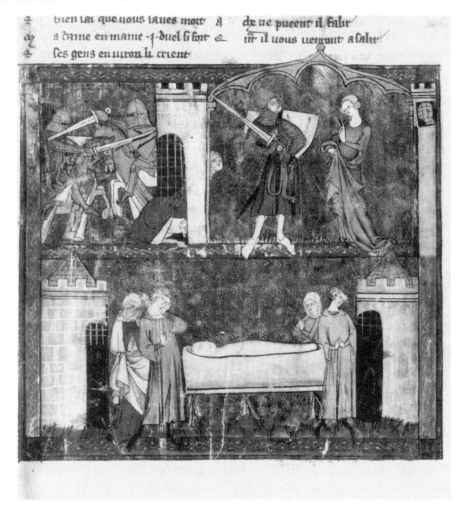

bien lai que uous laues mort · a   de ue pueent il falir
a dame en matne ·j· duel fi fort   iñ il uous uerront a falir
fes gens en utron li crient

Illuminated manuscript page for Chrétien's Le Chevalier au Lion, ou, Yvain
depicting Yvain killing Esclados, Yvain meeting Lunette, and the
funeral of Esclados (Bibliothèque Nationale de France, f. fr. 1433, fol. 69v)

with a significant Jewish presence in the twelfth century. As he indicates in the prologue to *Le Chevalier de la Charrette, ou, Lancelot* (The Knight of the Cart, or Lancelot, written 1179–1180), Chrétien at one time wrote under the patronage of Countess Marie of Champagne (daughter of Eleanor of Aquitaine and King Louis VII of France), and from this scholars have deduced that his writing began after 1159 (when Marie married Henry I of Champagne) and have estimated that he was born around 1140. He may also have been known as Chrétien de Saint-Maclou (located in Bar-sur-Aube, twenty-five miles from Troyes), a man who received a benefice in 1172 from Marie and Count Henry. Other evidence, from 1173, suggests that he may have been canon of the Abbey of Saint Loup at Troyes. A second of Chrétien's patrons is named in the prologue to his unfinished *Le Conte du Graal, ou, Perceval* (The Story of the Grail, or, Perceval, circa 1181–1190): Philip of Alsace, Count of Flanders, who died on crusade at Acre in 1191; his death may serve as a terminus for

Chrétien's literary life. It has been inferred from Chrétien's work that he had traveled extensively and was perhaps a herald-at-arms.

While Chrétien's biography remains uncertain and largely undocumented, his literary career is neatly indexed in the prologue to his second romance, *Cligés* (circa 1176–1178), where he catalogued his literary production to date. These works included: *Erec et Enide* (circa 1165–1170), a translation of Ovid's *Ars Amatoria* (Art of Love), the *Shoulder Bite* (a story of Pelops, Tantalus's son, taken from Ovid), another story from Ovid, *Philomena,* and a tale of King Mark and Iseut. Although only *Erec et Enide* has been positively identified, the list of other works indicates that Chrétien was educated in Latin and was perhaps a clerk in minor orders and that his work stood astride vernacular culture and the culture of the ancients. The reference to King Mark and Iseut indicates that Chrétien was familiar with the legend of the tragic love of Tristan and Iseut, who accidentally ingest a love potion and are forced, through their mutual passion, into betraying King Mark, who is Tristan's uncle and liege and Iseut's husband. From his position at the court of Champagne, it may also be presumed that Chrétien, though perhaps not noble himself, represents in his works the cosmopolitan nature of the city of Troyes and the habits and ideals of the cultured aristocracy of Champagne, especially in chivalry and courtliness.

Probably educated in the seven liberal arts of the trivium and quadrivium, and certainly familiar with rhetorical tradition dating to Cicero and Quintillian, Chrétien employs a poetic technique that borrows from and elaborates on classical models. The opening verses of *Erec et Enide* situate Chrétien's craft within the context of the feudal court, where oral and written cultures coexisted and where minstrels and authors competed at recounting similar tales. In verse 9, Chrétien provides the only extant "signature" of his full name, and in verses 13–14 he rhymes his signal poetic term *conjointure* (composition) with the defining impulse of Arthurian chivalry, *avanture* (adventure):

> Por ce dist Crestïens de Troies
> que reisons est que totevoies
> doit chascuns panser et antandre
> a bien dire et a bien aprandre
> et tret d'un conte d'avanture
> une molt bele conjointure
>
> (For this reason, Chrétien de Troyes claims
> That it is always right
> For individuals to devote their thoughts and efforts
> To telling and teaching what is good
> And from a tale of adventure
> He fashions a very elegant composition)

The distinguishing characteristic of conjointure lends to *Erec et Enide* a structural unity that is lacking in the tales of Chrétien's peers and rivals who, the poet claims, work negligently and purely for material gain. By contrast, Chrétien is highly aware of his art and concerned with its quality and craftsmanship. This concern is perhaps a reflection of his dedication and character, but it may also result from his formal training. Geoffrey of Vinsauf's *Poetria nova* (New Poetry, circa 1200), for example, compared the writer in the twelfth and thirteenth centuries to an architect and insisted that narrative structure, like building structure, be conceived and developed in advance of composition with the aim of producing a coherent and harmonious whole—which is similar to Chrétien's "bele conjointure," or "very elegant composition." Beyond reference to narrative order and arrangement, conjointure, which has no perfect equivalent in English or clear antecedent in Latin, may also have thematic resonances in Chrétien, for whom marriage and the couple are central themes; the notion of a well-ordered

tale has been thematically linked by scholars to the blissful union of husband and wife, or to the consonance of two lovers. While Chrétien may treat this union in a comic, ironic, or serious mode, it remains a consistent motif in his romances.

The desire to place his romances in a textually based tradition descended from ancient Greece and Rome is clearly expressed in the "translatio" topoi of the prologue to *Cligés*. Here Chrétien distances himself from itinerant storytellers by establishing a genealogy for chivalry and knowledge (*clergie*) that makes the knights and clerks of his France the descendants of the great soldiers and poets of the past. Though Chrétien's "France" likely referred to a broad cultural and linguistic setting (including Champagne, Flanders, England, Normandy, and Paris) rather than an exact geopolitical entity (that is, the kingdom of France, which was small and weak in comparison to either the realm of the British king Henry II or other continental kingdoms), it is significant that in his prologue Chrétien downplays chivalry and chooses instead to end on a note of literary triumphalism. If *translatio studii*, the transferal of knowledge from the ancients in the East to the moderns in the West, was a mechanism for poetic self-authentication through an authoritative origin, it allowed Chrétien at the same time to celebrate the present and to relegate the past to a place of honorable, but permanent, repose. The fact that *clergie* had arrived in France, and that Greek and Roman culture was supplanted, was equated by Chrétien to an ennobling eclipse of his predecessors and was necessary for the establishment of a new vernacular literary paradigm.

Further key elements of Chrétien's craft can be found in the prologue to his *Le Chevalier de la Charrette, ou, Lancelot*, where they figure prominently in his dedication to Marie de Champagne:

> Del Chevalier de la Charrette
> comance Crestïens son livre;
> matiere et san li done et livre
> la contesse, et il s'antremet
> de panser, que gueres n'i met
> fors sa painne et s'antancïon
>
> (Chrétien begins his book
> About the Knight of the Cart
> The subject matter and treatment
> Were given to him by the Countess
> And he undertakes to do no more in the telling
> Than to apply his effort and application)

Though there has been some debate on the meanings of *matiere, san,* and *antancïon,* their paradigmatic significance for Chrétien has never been in doubt. "Matiere"–translated by D. D. R. Owen as "matter"–is the least cryptic of the three, and it points plainly to Chrétien's

Yvain and Laudine reconciled (illustration from a manuscript for Le Chevalier au Lion, ou, Yvain; *Bibliothèque Nationale de France, f. fr. 1433, fol. 118)*

story materials: legendary Arthurian narratives of Celtic origin that Chrétien may have discovered in a variety of sources and forms. In *Erec et Enide,* for example, he draws on the "conte d'avanture" (tale of adventure), and the text may constitute an assembly of materials from an oral tradition, while the prologues to *Cligés* and the *Conte du Graal* list *livres* (books) as their points of origin. None of these source books is extant, and, for that reason, some scholars have suggested that references to written sources may carry more rhetorical than historical significance. Unlike "matiere," the term "san" is more difficult to define and perhaps cannot be completely or justly rendered in English. Owen suggests that it is the poem's meaning, or signification, that the poet applies to his material. This is a generally accepted view of *san,* but it remains at least partially incomplete until the role of Marie of Champagne is taken into account. Because Chrétien contends that Marie in fact conferred *san* on his story, it may be deduced that *san* denotes the guiding principle or "controlling purpose"

of the *Charrette,* which cannot in the end be separated from its moral or signification. Notwithstanding this caveat, scholars have been unable to reduce *san* to a fixed meaning or set of meanings in the *Charrette.* What is certain, however, is that it is an essential component of the deep structure of Chrétien's art and of medieval narrative in general.

In his first romance, *Erec et Enide,* Chrétien defines the Arthurian setting for his romances and, in detail or in brief, indicates some essential themes, issues, and tensions that will be shared by all or most of his texts. From the outset this first work juxtaposes the duty and measure of knights in battle over and against the terms that define their relationships to ladies, a dominant motif that will recur in all romances of chivalry. The uneasy blending of battlefield prowess (military chivalry) with courtliness (proper service to the lady) comes to the fore in two opening instances connected to Arthur's hunt for the white stag. According to custom, the victor in the hunt is rewarded with a kiss from the most beautiful damsel at court. Erec, a most noble, valorous, and handsome knight of the Round Table, chooses to forego the hunt and instead (armed only with his sword) accompanies Guenevere and her damsel on a courtly trot through the forest. When they lose contact with the hunting party, they retreat to a clearing, where they encounter a heavily armed knight (Yder), his dwarf, and a damsel. Upon approach, first the queen's damsel, and then Erec, suffer the lash of the dwarf's whip. With only his sword, Erec is no match for Yder, and so must refrain from attacking the insulting dwarf, for fear of deadly reprisal from his knight companion. When Yder and his party depart, Erec pledges to pursue them and so avenge his shame. Meanwhile, having slain the white stag and thereby winning the customary kiss, Arthur is faced with a dilemma of his own, as none of the more than five hundred knights at court are willing to admit, without trial at arms, that his damsel or lady is not the most beautiful. Chrétien neatly resolves this problem through Guenevere, who intercedes with the suggestion that the kiss be put off until Erec returns. Eventually, Erec defeats Yder in the contest of the sparrowhawk, which contest also serves the dual purpose of distinguishing the best knight through arms and, consequently, indicating the most beautiful damsel, in this case Enide. While underlining Enide's beauty, Chrétien takes this opportunity to criticize social and political institutions based on violence. Although of noble stock, Enide is poorly dressed and lives in a shabby house because her father has spent all of his wealth on arms and fighting, and has lost his land in continual warfare. In the end Erec decides to take Enide as his bride, a commitment that implies a rarefied form of love, as she will bring him no material or political advantage. Upon their return to Arthur's court, Enide is recognized as the most beautiful damsel, and so she receives Arthur's kiss, which brings the custom of the stag and the first portion of the tale (the *premier vers*) to a peaceful resolution.

This apparent happy ending is merely a prelude to more tribulations, however. In the text that follows, Erec abandons his chivalric duties in favor of his relationship to his wife, with whom he frequently dallies in bed, thus earning the title of "recreant" (one who fails at, or abdicates from, knighthood) from his peers and vassals, who mock him behind his back. One morning, Enide, thinking Erec is asleep, loudly grieves at her husband's lost honor and reputation. Erec hears her words and chides her severely for them. To redeem himself, and to punish his wife's impertinence, Erec decides that they will ride off together to seek adventure, with the condition that she not speak to him for the duration. The balance of the text concerns these adventures, which culminate in Enide's abduction and forced marriage to the count of Limors, when Erec, believed to be dead, has gone comatose from his accumulated wounds. Resurrected, Erec strikes fear into the count's company, slays the count at table, and rides off with Enide. With the help of his friend Guivret, Erec is healed and prepared for his last adventure, the "Joy of the Court." Here Chrétien pulls out all the stops in an effort to reconcile knightly prowess and courtly loyalty to a lady by matching the redeemed Erec against the tall Mabonagrain, a nephew of King Evrain, whose valor at arms has been vitiated by his commitment to carry out the will of his damsel. When Erec vanquishes Mabonagrain and returns joy to the court, however, Chrétien reveals the essential conundrum in the text: to win the lady, one must display military chivalry and faithfulness, but if loyalty to the lady results in an abandonment of knightly activities (tournaments, adventure, battle), then knightly prowess quickly turns to *recreantise*, or knightly failing.

In Chrétien's second romance, *Cligés*, questions of knighthood, love, feudal loyalties, and marriage are intertwined in a narrative that mixes Byzantine and Arthurian elements. Scholars such as Michelle A. Freeman and Peter Haidu have labeled *Cligés* a comedy and have also called it an anti-Tristan, as W. W. Comfort noted, because of its belittling comments on the love story of Tristan and Iseut. Alexander, son of the emperor and empress of Greece and Constantinople, chooses to leave his homeland for Arthur's court, where he will be initiated into the highest order of chivalry. Upon his arrival, Alexander and his companions are made members of the British court and immediately afterward they embark with King Arthur across the sea to Brittany, leaving England in the care of Count Angrés of Windsor. During the ocean voyage, Guenevere notices that Alexander and Soredamors, one of her maidens, have become visibly ill. Pale, trembling and sighing, Alexander and Soredamors have the symptoms of sea-sickness, but are actually afflicted by love. Chrétien cleverly translates Ovidian lovesickness, with its plaints and antitheses, to a medieval context and finishes by punning on the maiden's name, explaining that Soredamors means "gilded over with love." When Arthur is forced to return to England in order to avert the rebellion of Count Angrés, Alexander gains the chance to prove his knightly ability to both his lord and to his lover. Wearing armor over a white silk shirt (sewn with gold thread and strands of Soredamors's golden hair), Alexander acquits himself well in battle, but neither he nor his beloved can bring themselves to confess their love. When he overhears the maiden admit she sewed the shirt, Alexander knows that his love is requited and is overjoyed. More battle, however, awaits before they can be united, and Alexander heroically contributes to the victory by disguising himself and thirty of his men in the shields, lances, and garb of their enemy and thus gaining entrance to their stronghold. Here Chrétien provides telling commen-

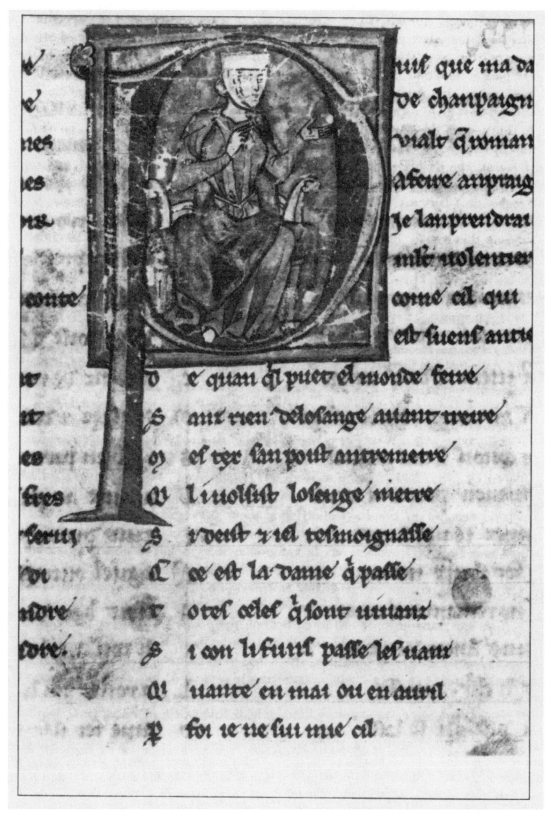

Countess Marie of Champagne depicted in an illuminated initial in an early thirteenth-century manuscript for Chrétien's Le Chevalier de la Charette, ou, Lancelot, *which was dedicated to her (Bibliothèque Nationale de France, f. fr. 794, fol. 27r)*

tary on feudal customs linking lords and vassals through fiefs, and he also underscores generosity as one of Arthur's defining characteristics. In return for Alexander's role in quelling the rebellion, Arthur rewards him with the castle, the best kingdom in Wales, and the hand of Soredamors in marriage. Within five months, Soredamors is expecting their child, the eponymous hero of the romance, Cligés.

The remainder of the tale plays out the political and emotional drama of succession and marriage in the empire of Greece and Constantinople, first pitting Alexander against his brother Alis for the title of emperor and later (after Alexander dies) pitting his son Cligés against Alis not only for the empire but also for the love and hand of the same woman, Fenice. The initial rivalry of Alexander and Alis is induced by a scheming messenger from Greece, the sole survivor of a crew who had embarked for England to bring Alexander news of his father's death but whose ship was sunk in a storm prior to arrival. Because the messenger (who favored Alis) returns to Greece and claims that the ship, with Alexander on board, has sunk while returning from England, Alis innocently takes the crown his brother was to inherit. When Alexander gets this news, however, he sets out immediately to settle affairs with his brother. After some disagreement, the brothers decide that Alexander will rule over the land in all matters, while Alis will retain the title of emperor on the condition that he never take a bride, thereby assuring that Cligés will become the next emperor. On his deathbed, Alexander advises Cligés to go to Arthur's court to test his knightly mettle, but before he can do so, Alis decides to follow the wicked advice of his vassals and to take Fenice ("Phoenix"), the daughter of the emperor of Germany, as a bride. In a coup de théâtre, Cligés and Fenice instantly fall in love, and to complicate matters further, the duke of Saxony warns the German emperor to expect war unless he delivers his daughter over to him in marriage.

While Chrétien admits that he is rewriting the Tristan story by obliging Alis and Fenice to marry but refusing to allow her to consummate her love for Alis's nephew, scholars have also suggested that a contemporary example (circa 1170–1174) may be the inspiration for this tense wedding scenario. To ally the Holy Roman Empire with the Byzantine empire, the Emperor Frederick Barbarossa had attempted to wed his son to the Greek princess. As in *Cligés,* a third party was involved, Henry the Lion, duke of Saxony and Bavaria, who later became antagonistic toward Frederick, though not for spurned love. In Chrétien's text, Cligés's battlefield ability helps to repel the threat of the Saxons, and love sickness returns as a dominant motif. In Fenice this sickness is finally diagnosed by her nurse, Thessala, who later concocts a potion that will preserve Fenice's maidenhood by inducing vivid

dreams in her husband that convince him that their marriage has been consummated. Cligés and Fenice love each other with mutual passion, but he eventually departs for Arthur's court, where, in a tournament, he competes in a sequence of contests and proves himself to be the equal of Gawain. When Cligés returns to Constantinople, he confesses to Fenice that he had left his heart with her, and they devise a plan to feign her death and afterward to flee to an isolated tower built by his vassal John and live out their days together in hiding. After an ordeal at the hands of torturous physicians who realize she is not truly dead, Fenice is "buried," then retrieved by Cligés, repeating the motif of resurrection from *Erec et Enide,* and playing out the full significance of her name, Phoenix. For a short time, they enjoy their life together, until they are discovered in a garden, and John eventually is made to confess the entire scheme to Alis. Cligés flees with Fenice to Arthur's court, where he raises an invasion army against his uncle; however, just prior to its departure, a messenger arrives to announce that Alis has died of grief, a madman. Fenice and Cligés return triumphant to Greece, where they are married in one of Chrétien's typical, but somewhat incongruous, happy endings. Chrétien's curiously negative gloss on his own ending, however, underscores that his rewriting of the Tristan legend is an artful and optimistic fiction, as he points out in his final verses that no husband will ever be able to trust his wife, so long as he believes that there are deceptive potions like Thessala's, and that the passion of lovers such as Cligés and Fenice can undermine the political institution of marriage. Notwithstanding this final comment, it is clear that Chrétien does not endorse such suspicions. For him, Cligés and Fenice, like Erec and Enide, express a rarefied form of love, one whose union transcends immediate worldly concerns to embrace far more enduring spiritual, and courtly, ideals.

Chrétien's virtuosity as a storyteller reaches a high point of maturity and complexity in *Le Chevalier de la Charrette, ou, Lancelot* and *Yvain, ou, Le Chevalier au Lion* (Yvain, or, The Knight with the Lion), two romances apparently composed simultaneously, circa 1179–1180 (a coda to the former announces that the ending was written, per Chrétien's instructions, by Godefroi de Leigni). Weaving together events and themes, in these two works Chrétien points out the pitfalls and dilemmas of the knight's divided loyalties in the systems of military chivalry and courtliness. Lancelot and Yvain are both prototypical characters of supreme military prowess whose promise to serve their ladies results in a profound personal failure that leaves them initially disgraced and nearly suicidal as knights and as lovers. In this sense, they are unlike Erec, in that their ladies have put their loyalties on trial, and yet like him in that it is through battlefield exploits that they seek redemption. From the tale of Lancelot and Guenevere, Gaston Paris and other scholars have developed the term *amour cortois* (courtly love), which presumes a sort of rigid service to the lady, a love that is recognized but unrequited, and an inaccessible, capricious, and even disdainful lady lover. The historical validity of this doctrine has been questioned, and its inflexible application may be of limited utility. Nonetheless, Chrétien apparently explores in each text a kind of love that substituted the lady for the lord and required the knight to serve as vassal to her sovereign. In the end, Lancelot and Yvain are successful lovers at least in part because they are successful vassals, but no amount of chivalry can atone for their courtly failures, and redemption is considered the ladies' prerogative.

In *Le Chevalier de la Charrette* a strange knight named Meleagant challenges the court of King Arthur, saying that he has many of Arthur's people in captivity, and will release them only if Arthur gives him Queen Guenevere and sends a champion to rescue her. Lancelot, who is not named until well into the story, is among those seeking to rescue Guenevere. Meeting a dwarf pulling a cart of the sort used to transport criminals, he asks the dwarf about the queen and is told to get in the cart. Although Lancelot does get in the cart, he hesitates, fearing the dishonor of riding in the cart, and this hesitation leads him down a path of trials and temptations. When he single-handedly lifts the slab off a tomb, a feat that legend says can be only done by the one who will free the people held captive in the kingdom from which none escape, and later crosses the Sword Bridge with bare hands and feet, Lancelot is obviously being made to perform in a ritual of redemption for his lady that has clear resonances of a Christian model. The reader may sense, however, a playful irony here in Chrétien, and when, after the two consummate their love, Guenevere obliges Lancelot to perform at his worst in a tournament, one may also suspect that the ritual entails humiliation more than it does Christian humility, or feudal loyalty. Deceived and captured by Meleagant, who has imprisoned Arthur's people, Lancelot is locked in a tower from which he is eventually released by Meleagant's sister. This somewhat forced incarceration device allows the story to effectively skirt the difficult issue of Lancelot and Guenevere's adultery and thereby diminishes any threat that their love may represent to Arthurian order. Instead, in typical Chrétien fashion, the text closes with a happy ending, satisfying the reader with Lancelot's liberty and the story of his beheading of Meleagant, an act that once and for all avenges the queen's abduction and that can be read on two levels: as service either to Arthur or to Guenevere. Unlike the protagonists of Chrétien's first two romances, Lancelot and Guenevere cannot marry; however, unlike Tristan and Iseut, they have not completely shirked their loyalties to the king, indicating perhaps that, for Chrétien, even the most passionate and overwhelming sort of love must in the end bend to accommodate prevailing power structures.

In the *Chevalier au Lion* the themes of knightly prowess, *recreantise,* and feudal service to the lady recur. Chrétien fills his text with marvels that will become the stock of later romances and fantasy literature: a mysterious fountain that causes tremendous tempests, a ring of invisibility, serpents, lions, giants, and goblins. Chrétien's basic story line, however, shares much with his prior works. Yvain seeks the fountain adventure to avenge his kinsman Calogrenant, who was shamed by Esclados, the knight who keeps the fountain. Yvain defeats Esclados; then, hidden by the power of the magic ring, he manages to dwell in his opponent's castle long enough to fall deeply in love with his mourning widow, Laudine. Although Chrétien employs the standard motifs of the lovestricken, there is something more earthy about the eventual joining of Yvain and Laudine. As the servant Lunete persuades her lady, Yvain's victory does not indict him but rather invests him with the power to replace her husband, precisely because he proved himself better at arms (and, therefore, a superior defender of the fountain and her realm). In this sense the couple appears more a product of expedience and logic than of desire and courtly ideals. Like Erec, Yvain after his marriage is accused of potential *recreantise* and is given leave of his lady for one year, during which he will seek adventure and acquit himself of his knightly duties. When, however, Yvain fails to return to his lady on time, an entire sequence of negative events ensues that suggests that Chrétien is reviving the conundrum first discovered in *Erec et Enide,* with an additional emphasis placed on a knight's imprisoning commitment not to the lady but to military chivalry. When Laudine rejects her disloyal husband, he goes mad and lives naked like a beast in the forest. Meanwhile, Lunete, for her recommendation of Yvain as a mate, is sentenced to be burned at the stake. Yvain is eventually revived, however, and reborn into chivalry by means of a magic ointment. Accompanied now by a lion, whom he saved from a serpent, he defeats a giant, frees Lunete at the last minute, and liberates the toiling damsels from Pesme Avanture. After nearly killing off Yvain and Gawain in a judicial duel over the inheritance dispute of the two daughters of Lord Noire Espine, Chrétien appears to retreat from the rule of the strongest to the rule of Arthur's reason. This retreat is only partial, however, since Lunete uses the same reasoning in the end to persuade (really to trick) Laudine into reconciling with the Knight with the Lion. Since only he can guarantee the security of her realm and of her fountain, Laudine must choose this strongest knight for her new mate. When she discovers the ruse, Laudine is briefly angered but accepts Yvain as a redeemed vassal who will not in future fail to love and defend her with honor. The resolution is clearly artificial, but it convincingly indicates nonetheless that the seamless fusion of military prowess and courtly love was a vital theme for Chrétien and perhaps even a cultural ideal of his times.

There is no happy ending to Chrétien's *Le Conte du Graal*. Unfinished, this longest of Chrétien's romances spawned the Grail legend and, for that reason alone, can be considered his best-known and most influential work. It is preserved in more manuscripts than any of his other romances, and many of these are richly illustrated, indicating its treasured importance in aristocratic circles. The *Conte du Graal* was clearly a literary phenomenon in its day and can be justifiably invoked as one of the most enduring and alluring cultural representations of the Middle Ages. In some ways, though, it is an atypical romance for Chrétien. The displacement from an eponymous hero or central character to the Grail, with the subsequent bifurcation of the text into the tale of Perceval and the tale of Gawain, is clearly a new departure for him, one that may or may not have been intended or successful. Some scholars, such as Owen, have suggested that Chrétien was composing two romances that were later combined into one, and it is commonly believed that the *Conte du Graal* remains unfinished because Chrétien died while composing it. It has also been suggested, however, that the story demonstrates no clear narrative resolution and so was abandoned by the author and left to continuators. What does seem obvious, however, is that the extant text contrasts worldly chivalry, represented by Gawain, to spiritual chivalry, represented by Perceval. Feudal allegiance is an issue as well. Perceval's mother strongly desires that her son have no part in chivalry or royal courts (which were the bane of her husband and two other sons), and she in fact dies of grief when he leaves her to be knighted by King Arthur. Chrétien suggests that this lack of fealty on Perceval's part represents a profound transgression of cultural norms. Beyond this, many of Perceval's accumulated errors (kissing a maiden, taking her ring, eating and drinking from her provisions, for example) may be considered necessary elements in his initiation to knightly and courtly culture. For that reason, the *Conte du Graal* can be considered at least partially a bildungsroman, and the instruction Perceval receives from his mother, and later from Gornemant of Gohort (whom Chrétien employs to articulate the doctrine of chivalry and who dubs Perceval a knight by fastening on his spurs), certainly bears out this consideration.

The Arthurian adventure materials for the Gawain story cohere well with the story elements of Chrétien's prior romances, as do those portions of Perceval's story that do not concern the Grail castle or its Christian allegorical context. After he is dubbed a knight, then single combat, defense of the lady, and defense of his honor define Perceval's relationship to the world, as he defeats opponents for his lady, Blancheflor. When Guigambresil accuses Gawain of treason (that is, of killing a knight without proper challenge), Gawain embarks on a series of tournaments, jousts, and adventures that culminates in his discovery of a cliff castle, the Rock of Champguin. Here, after the adventure of the Wondrous Bed (where Gawain survives attack by hundreds of arrows and a hungry lion), Gawain finds two queens and a maiden: Arthur's mother (Ygerne), his own mother, and his sister. After Gawain dubs five hundred new knights with his own hands, Chrétien's story briefly returns to Arthur's court by way of a messenger Gawain has sent there. In the final lines of the romance, a powerful narrative resolution is portended in the joining of Arthur's court with Gawain's new domain, but Chrétien's text breaks off, leaving the reader with no closure. Perceval's story is also incomplete; however, unlike Gawain's story, indications of its potential conclusion are far less clear, and the Christian allegorical nature of the Grail lends it a level of complexity that sets Perceval's story apart from Chrétien's prior narratives. Beginning with the scriptural paraphrasings of the prologue, the hints at religious allegory are frequent throughout the text. The Fisher King, the bleeding lance, the Grail itself, the communion wafer, and discourses on confession and proper knightly conduct on Good Friday—all announce a Christian grounding to Chrétien's narrative. Like the Celtic legends, these are Chrétien's *matiere,* furnished to him perhaps by his patron Philip of Alsace, the crusader. By contrast, the *san* of the story may be more elusive. It has been argued that Chrétien's quotation from Scripture is erroneous enough to make use of the Bible as an interpretive overlay somewhat unreliable, and there seems to be some confusion about Christian doctrine as well, as Brigitte Cazelles has pointed out. For example, if the Grail was a holy relic, why was it carried by a maiden? The handling of relics by a woman in a religious procession could have been considered a heretical gesture in the twelfth century. Further, could Perceval be guilty for failing to make confession in Chrétien's romance (written circa 1180–1190), when confession was not officially joined to religious obligation until the Fourth Lateran Council of 1215? Notwithstanding these con-siderations, it would be an overstatement, and an historical fallacy, to deny the religious character of the *Conte du Graal*. If it took Robert de Boron and the other thirteenth-century continuators to invent the Grail's heritage as the cup of Christ, passed at the Last Supper and used by Joseph of Arimathea to collect his blood as he died on the cross, it was nevertheless Chrétien's text that provided the impulse to that invention. Without an ending, it is impossible to know what Chrétien would have made of his Grail; however, those who came after him made it into an undeniable literary and religious icon.

The minor romance *Guillaume d'Angleterre* (William of England, circa 1180) is thought by some scholars to have been written by Chrétien, as are at least two minor songs, but it is through his reshaping of the Celtic Arthurian legends that Chrétien is remembered. Throughout the Middle Ages, Chrétien's influence crossed linguistic and geographic boundaries. In the twelfth and thirteenth centuries, adaptations of his Arthurian romances were made in German by Hartmann von Aue and Wolfram von Eschenbach. In English, Sir Thomas Malory's fifteenth-century *Le Morte d'Arthur* (circa 1470) owes much to Chrétien and his literary disciples; Arthurian material was prominent in sixteenth-century Italy as Ludovico Ariosto composed his *Orlando furioso* (1516). The myths Chrétien related of the Knights of the Round Table, of the love of Lancelot and Guenevere, and of the Holy Grail, are the stuff of enduring legend, and they remain a part of contemporary popular culture, reappearing in children's books, fantasy literature, and motion pictures.

Bibliography:

Douglas Kelly, *Chrétien de Troyes: An Analytic Bibliography*, Research Bibliographies and Checklists no. 17 (London: Grant & Culter, 1976).

References:

L. D. Benson, "The Tournament in the Romances of Chrétien de Troyes," in *Chivalric Literature,* edited by Benson and J. Leyerle (Kalamazoo, Mich.: Medieval Institute Publications, 1980), pp. 1–24;

Keith Busby and others, ed., *Les Manuscrits de Chrétien de Troyes = The Manuscripts of Chrétien de Troyes,* 2 volumes (Amsterdam & Atlanta: Editions Rodopi, 1993);

Brigitte Cazelles, *The Unholy Grail: A Social Reading of Chrétien de Troyes's "Conte du Graal"* (Stanford, Cal.: Stanford University Press, 1996);

Edmond Faral, *Les Arts Poétiques du XIIe et du XIIIe siècle: Recherches et documents sur la technique littéraire du Moyen Age* (Paris: H. Champion, 1971);

Jean Frappier, *Chrétien de Troyes: l'homme et l'œuvre* (Paris: Hatier, 1968); translated by Raymond J. Cormier as *Chrétien de Troyes: The Man and His Work* (Athens: Ohio University Press, 1982);

Frappier, "Le prologue du *Chevalier de la Charrette* et son interprétation," *Romania,* 93 (1972): 337–377;

Michelle A. Freeman, "Cligés," in *The Romances of Chrétien de Troyes: A Symposium,* edited by Douglas Kelly (Lexington, Ky.: French Forum, 1985), pp. 89–131;

Freeman, *The Poetics of "Translatio Studii" and "Conjointure": Chrétien de Troyes' "Cligés"* (Lexington, Ky.: French Forum, 1979);

Peter Haidu, *Aesthetic Distance in Chrétien de Troyes: Irony and Comedy in "Cligés" and "Perceval"* (Geneva: Droz, 1968);

Sandra Hindman, *Sealed in Parchment: Readings of Knighthood in the Illuminated Manuscripts of Chrétien de Troyes* (Chicago: University of Chicago Press, 1994);

Urban Tigner Holmes and M. Amelia Klenke, *Chrétien, Troyes, and the Grail* (Chapel Hill: University of North Carolina Press, 1959);

Holmes, *Chrétien de Troyes* (New York: Twayne, 1970);

Tony Hunt, "The Emergence of the Knight in France and England 1000–1200," in *Knighthood in Medieval Literature,* edited by W. T. H. Jackson (Woodbridge, U.K.: Brewer, 1981), pp. 1–22;

Hunt, "The Rhetorical Background to the Arthurian Prologue: Tradition and the Old French Vernacular Prologues," *Forum for Modern Language Studies,* 6 (January 1970): 1–23;

Douglas Kelly, *The Art of Medieval French Romance* (Madison: University of Wisconsin Press, 1992);

Kelly, "Chrétien de Troyes: The Narrator and His Art," in *The Romances of Chrétien de Troyes: A Symposium,* edited by Kelly (Lexington, Ky.: French Forum, 1985), pp. 13–47;

Kelly, "The Scope and Treatment of Composition in the Twelfth- and Thirteenth-Century Arts of Poetry," *Speculum,* 41, no. 2 (1966): 261–278;

Kelly, *Sens and Conjointure in the "Chevalier de la Charrette"* (The Hague & Paris: Mouton, 1966);

Roger Sherman Loomis, *Arthurian Tradition and Chrétien de Troyes* (New York: Columbia University Press, 1949);

Donald Maddox, *The Arthurian Romances of Chrétien de Troyes: Once and Future Fictions* (Cambridge: Cambridge University Press, 1991);

Alexandre Micha, *La Tradition manuscrite des romans de Chrétien de Troyes,* second edition (Geneva: Droz, 1966);

William A. Nitze, "*Sans* et *Matiere* dans les œuvres de Chrétien de Troyes," *Romania,* 44 (1915): 14–36;

Gaston Paris, "Etudes sur les romans de la Table Ronde: Lancelot du Lac. II. *Le Conte de la Charrette,*" *Romania,* 12 (1883): 459–534;

Jean Rychner, "Le prologue du *Chevalier de la Charrette,*" *Vox Romanica,* 26 (1967): 1–23;

L. T. Topsfield, *Chrétien de Troyes: A Study of the Arthurian Romances* (Cambridge: Cambridge University Press, 1981);

Karl D. Uitti, "Autant en emporte *Li funs:* Remarques sur le prologue du *Chevalier de la Charrette* de Chrétien de Troyes," *Romania,* 105, no. 2 (1984): 270–291;

Uitti and Freeman, *Chrétien de Troyes Revisited* (New York: Twayne, 1995);

Paul Zumthor, *Speaking of the Middle Ages,* translated by Sarah White (Lincoln & London: University of Nebraska Press, 1986).

Christine de Pizan

(circa 1365 – circa 1431)

Earl Jeffrey Richards
University of Wuppertal

WORKS: *Les Cent Balades* (1395–1400)

Manuscripts: The text of this work survives in seven manuscripts. The five most important manuscripts are those that include all the major lyrical works by Christine de Pizan, representing three major redactions made by Christine to her works. The first version of what is known as *Le Livre de Christine* (The Book of Christine), begun in 1399 and completed in June 1402, survives in three manuscript copies: Chantilly, Musée Condé, 492–493 (the rubrics of 492 are dated "1399 to June 23, 1402"; 493 includes works from 1402–1405); Paris, Bibliothèque Nationale de France, f. fr. 12779, and Bibliothèque Nationale de France, f. fr. 604 (a later copy). *Cent Balades* is copied in Chantilly 492, ff. 2r–22v; Paris, Bibliothèque Nationale de France, f. fr.12779, ff. 1t–21v; and Paris, Bibliothèque Nationale de France, f.f. 604, ff. 2r–18r. Christine revised her lyrics before transcribing them in the Duke's Manuscript (Paris, Bibliothèque Nationale de France, f. fr. 835, 606, 836, 605 and 607), acquired by the duke of Berry in 1408 or 1409; *Cent Balades* comprises Paris, Bibliothèque Nationale de France, 835, ff. 1r–16v, 18r–v. Additions were made for the final redaction, the Queen's Manuscript (London, British Library, Harley 4431), presented to Isabeau de Bavière and completed in 1410 or 1411; *Cent Balades* comprises Harley 4431, ff. 4r–21r.

Standard edition: In *Œuvres poétiques de Christine de Pisan,* 3 volumes, edited by Maurice Roy (Paris: Firmin-Didot, 1886–1896), I: 1–100.

Editions in English: Selections in *The Writings of Christine de Pizan,* edited by Charity Cannon Willard (New York: Persea, 1994), pp. 41–48; and in *The Selected Writings of Christine de Pizan,* edited by Renate Blumenfeld-Kosinski (New York: Norton, 1997).

Virelais (1395–1400)

Manuscripts: The text of the *Virelais* is extant in the same seven manuscripts as the *Cent Balades* and is always copied immediately following that text.

Standard edition: In *Œuvres poétiques de Christine de Pisan,* 3 volumes, edited by Maurice Roy (Paris: Firmin-Didot, 1886–1896), I: 101–118.

Edition in English: Selections in *The Writings of Christine de Pizan,* edited by Charity Cannon Willard (New York: Persea, 1994), pp. 55–56.

Epistre au Dieu d'Amours (May 1399)

Manuscripts: This text is present in eight extant manuscripts. It is included in the five manuscripts representing *Le Livre de Christine;* in addition, it is in London, Westminster Abbey Library, MS. 21, ff. 52a–64b; Paris, Bibliothèque de l'Arsenal 3295, ff. 128r–140v; and Paris, Bibliothèque Nationale de France, Moreau 1686, ff. 126r–138v.

Standard edition: In *Œuvres poétiques de Christine de Pisan,* 3 volumes, edited by Maurice Roy (Paris: Firmin-Didot, 1886–1896), II: 1–27.

Standard edition and edition in English: In *Poems of Cupid, God of Love: Christine de Pizan's "Epistre au dieu d'Amours" and "Dit de la Rose"; Thomas Hoccleve's "The Letter of Cupid,"* edited by Thelma S. Fenster and Mary Carpenter Erler (Leiden: Brill, 1990).

Editions in English: Selections in *The Writings of Christine de Pizan,* edited by Charity Cannon Willard (New York: Persea, 1994), pp. 145–150; and in *The Selected Writings of Christine de Pizan,* edited by Renate Blumenfeld-Kosinski (New York: Norton, 1997), pp. 15–28.

Enseignemens et Proverbes moraulx (circa 1400)

Manuscripts: This work is represented in at least twenty-three extant manuscripts, including all major manuscript families of Christine's works.

Standard edition: In *Œuvres poétiques de Christine de Pisan,* 3 volumes, edited by Maurice Roy (Paris: Firmin-Didot, 1886–1896), III: 27–57.

Edition in English: *The Morale Proverbes of Cristyne,* translated by Richard Wydeville, Earl Rivers

(Westminster: William Caxton, 1477); republished (Amsterdam: Theatrum Orbis Terrarum / New York, Da Capo Press, 1970).

Le Debat de deux asmans (circa 1400)

Manuscripts: Paris, Bibliothèque Nationale de France, f. fr. 835: Paris, Bibliothèque Nationale de France, f. fr. 1740, British Library, Harley 4431; Brussels, Bibliothèque Royale/Koninklijke Bibliotheek, 11034.

Standard edition: *Œuvres poétiques de Christine de Pisan,* 3 volumes, edited by Maurice Roy (Paris: Firmin-Didot, 1886–1896), II: 49–109.

L'Epistre d'Othea (circa 1400)

Manuscripts: The work survives in forty-three manuscripts: the six most important include the earliest redaction found in *Le Livre de Christine*; the next version is Paris, Bibliothèque Nationale de France, f. fr. 848; the third redaction is Paris, Bibliothèque Nationale de France, f. fr. 606, the Duke's Manuscript, virtually identical to that of the Queen's Manuscript.

Standard edition: *Les Cent histoires de Troye* (Paris: Phillippe Pigouchet, 1490; Philippe Le Noire, 1522); republished as *Lepistre de Othea deesse de Prudence, moralisee . . .* (Paris: Trepperel, 1518, 1522; Rouen: Raulin Gaultier, before 1534); in "Classical Mythology in the Works of Christine de Pisan, with an edition of *L'Epistre Othea* from the manuscript Harley 4431," by Halina Didycky Loukopoulos, dissertation, Wayne State University, 1977.

Editions in English: *Here foloweth the C. hystoryes of Troye, Lepistre de Othea deesse de Prudence envoyee a l'esprit chevalereux Hector de Troye,* translated by Robert Wyer (London: Robert Wyer, circa 1540); *The Epistle of Othea to Hector: A 'Lytil Bibell of Knyghthod' : Edited from the Harleian Manuscript 838,* translated by Anthony Babyngton, edited by James D. Gordon (Philadelphia: Privately printed, 1942); *The Epistle of Othea, Translated from the French Text of Christine de Pisan by Stephen Scrope,* edited by Curt F. Bühler, Early English Text Society no. 264 (London: Oxford University Press for the Early English Text Society, 1970); *Christine de Pizan's Letter of Othea to Hector,* translated, with an introduction and notes, by Jane Chance, Focus Library of Medieval Women (Newburyport, Mass.: Focus, 1990; Cambridge: Brewer, 1997).

Le Livre du Dit de Poissy (April 1400)

Standard editions: In *Œuvres poétiques de Christine de Pisan,* 3 volumes, edited by Maurice Roy (Paris: Firmin-Didot, 1886–1896), II: 159–222; in *The Love Debate Poems of Christine de Pizan,* edited by Barbara K. Altmann (Gainesville: University

Christine presenting her book to her patron, Louis, Duke of Orléans, (illumination in a manuscript for her L'Epistre d'Othea; *British Library, Harley ms. 4431, fol. 95r)*

Press of Florida, 1998).

Edition in English: In *The Writings of Christine de Pizan,* edited by Charity Cannon Willard (New York: Persea, 1994), pp. 61–69.

Epistres sur "Le Roman de la Rose" (1401–1402)

Manuscripts: Eight manuscripts exist, including two versions of Christine's lost autograph: Paris, Bibliothèque Nationale de France, f. fr. 1563, ff. 178r–199r comprises the most extensive text, whereas *Le Livre de Christine* and Brussels, Bibliothèque Royale/Koninklijke Bibliotheek, ms. 9559–9564 (9561), ff. 97r–109v present Christine's first redaction; the Duke's and Queen's Manuscripts and Berkeley, University of California, 109 present the second redaction.

Standard edition: Christine de Pizan, Jean Gerson, Jean de Montreuil, Gontier and Pierre Col, *Le Débat sur le "Roman de la Rose,"* edited by Eric Hicks (Paris: H. Champion, 1977).

Edition in English: *La Querelle de la Rose, Letters and Documents,* translated by Joseph L. Baird and

John R. Kane (Chapel Hill: University of North Carolina Press, 1978).

Le Livre des trois jugemens (1402)

Manuscripts: Paris, Bibliothèque Nationale de France, f. fr. 835; London, British Library, Harley 4431.

Standard edition: *Œuvres poétiques de Christine de Pisan,* 3 volumes, edited by Maurice Roy (Paris: Firmin-Didot, 1886–1896, II: 111–57.

Le Dit de la Rose (14 February 1402)

Standard edition: In *Œuvres poétiques de Christine de Pisan,* 3 volumes, edited by Maurice Roy (Paris: Firmin-Didot, 1886–1896), II: 29–48; edited and translated in *Poems of Cupid, God of Love: Christine de Pizan's "Epistre au dieu d'Amours" and "Dit de la Rose"; Thomas Hoccleve's "The Letter of Cupid,"* edited and translated by Thelma S. Fenster and Mary Carpenter Erler (Leiden: Brill, 1990);

L'Orayson Nostre Dame, Les Quinze Joyes Nostre Dame, L'Oroyson Nostre Seigneur (1402–1403)

Manuscripts: These three short prayers are generally copied together. All three are extant in four manuscripts: Chantilly, Musée Condé 492; London, British Library, Harley 4431; Paris, Bibliothèque de l'Arsenal, 3295; and Paris, Bibliothèque Nationale de France, f. fr. 836. The *Orayson Nostre Dame* and *Les Quinze Joyes* are further represented in Paris, Bibliothèque Nationale de France, f. fr. 12779.

Standard edition: In *Œuvres poétiques de Christine de Pisan,* 3 volumes, edited by Maurice Roy (Paris: Firmin-Didot, 1886–1896), III: 1–26.

Edition in English: Selections in *The Writings of Christine de Pizan,* edited by Charity Cannon Willard (New York: Persea, 1994), pp. 323–324.

Le dit de la pastoure (May, 1403)

Manuscripts: The text surives in six manuscripts: Paris, Bibliothèque Nationale de France, f. fr. 12779; Paris, Bibliothèque Nationale de France, f. fr. 836; Paris, Bibliothèque Nationale de France, f. fr. 2184; Paris, Bibliothèque Nationale de France, f. fr. Ashburnham MS. 72 (Barrois); London, British Library, Harley 4431; Westminster Abbey, MS. 21.

Standard edition: *Œuvres poétiques de Christine de Pisan,* 3 volumes, edited by Maurice Roy (Paris: Firmin-Didot, 1886–1896), II: 223–94.

Le Livre de la Mutacion de Fortune (August 1400 – November 1403)

Manuscripts: The most important of the surviving ten manuscripts (complete versions or fragments) are: Brussels, Bibliothèque Royale/Koninklijke Bibliotheek 9508, 190 ff., copied during 1403 and presented to Philip the Bold, Duke of Burgundy,

on 1 January 1404; in *Le Livre de Christine* (Paris, Bibliothèque Nationale de France, f. fr. 604, 160v–314; Chantilly, Musée Condé 493, ff. 232r–427r); Paris, Bibliothèque Nationale de France, f. fr. 603, ff. 81–242; and The Hague, Koninklijke Bibliotheek, 78. D 42, 170 ff. (with the signature of Jean, Duke of Berry, dating its presentation, March 1403).

Standard edition: *Le Livre de la Mutacion de Fortune,* 4 volumes, edited by Suzanne Solente, Société des anciens textes français (Paris: A. & J. Picard, 1959–1966).

Edition in English: Selections in *The Writings of Christine de Pizan,* edited by Charity Cannon Willard (New York: Persea, 1994), pp. 109–136.

Le Livre du Chemin de long estude (5 October 1402 – 20 March 1403)

Manuscripts: Seven manuscripts survive: Paris, Bibliothèque Nationale de France, f. fr. 604, ff. 122r–160v (from the family of manuscripts called *Le Livre de Christine*); Brussels, Bibliothèque Royale/Koninklijke Bibliotheek 10982, 100 ff. and Brussels, Bibliothèque Royale/Koninklijke Bibliotheek 10983, 96 ff. (both from the library of the dukes of Burgundy); Paris, Bibliothèque Nationale de France, f. fr. 1643, 93ff (a fifteenth century manuscript that belonged to Charles d'Orléans); Paris, Bibliothèque Nationale de France, f. fr., 836, ff. 1–41v; Paris, Bibliothèque Nationale de France, f. fr. 1188; Cracow, Bibliotheca Jagiellonska, Gall. fol. 133 (earlier Berlin, Preußische Staatsbiblik, fr. 133).

Standard editions: *Le chemin de long estude de dame Christine de Pise ou est descrit le debat esmeu au parlement de Raison, pour l'élection du Prince digne de gouverner le monde,* prose version by Jean Chaperon (Paris: Estienne Groulleau, 1549); *Le Livre du Chemin de long estude, publié pour la premiere fois d'après sept manuscrits de Paris, de Bruxelles et de Berlin,* edited by Robert Püschel (Berlin: Damköhler / Paris: Le Soudier, 1881; republished, Geneva: Slatkine, 1974); "An Edition of Christine de Pisan's *Livre du chemin de long estude,*" edited by Patricia Bonin Eargle, dissertation, University of Georgia, 1973.

Editions in English: Selections in *The Writings of Christine de Pizan,* edited by Charity Cannon Willard (New York: Persea, 1994), pp. 104–108; and in *The Selected Writings of Christine de Pizan,* edited by Renate Blumenfeld-Kosinski (New York: Norton, 1997), pp. 59–87.

Le Livre du Duc des Vrais Amans (between 1403 and November 1405)

Standard editions: In *Œuvres poétiques de Christine*

de Pisan, 3 volumes, edited by Maurice Roy (Paris: Firmin-Didot, 1886–1896), III: 59–208; *Le livre du duc des vrais amans,* edited by Thelma S. Fenster, Medieval & Renaissance Texts & Studies no. 124 (Binghamton, N.Y.: Medieval and Renaissance Texts and Studies, 1995).

Edition in English: *The Book of the Duke of True Lovers: Now First Translated from the Middle French of Christine De Pisan,* translated by Laurence Binyon and Eric R. D. Maclagan, introduction by Alice Kemp-Welch, The New Medieval Library (London: Chatto & Windus, 1908; republished, New York: Cooper Square Publishers, 1966); *The Book of the Duke of True Lovers,* translated, with an introduction, by Thelma S. Fenster, lyric poetry translated by Nadia Margolis (New York: Persea, 1991).

Epistre a Eustache Morel (10 February 1404)

Manuscripts: This text survives in two manuscripts: London, British Library, Harley 4431, ff. 255–257r; and Paris, Bibliothèque Nationale de France, f. fr. 605, ff. 2v–3v.

Standard edition: In *Œuvres poétiques de Christine de Pisan,* 3 volumes, edited by Maurice Roy (Paris: Firmin-Didot, 1886–1896), II: 295–301.

Edition in English: In *The Selected Writings of Christine de Pizan,* edited by Renate Blumenfeld-Kosinski (New York: Norton, 1997), pp. 109–112.

Le Livre des Fais et bonnes meurs du sage roy Charles V (January–November 1404)

Manuscripts: Four fifteenth-century manuscripts survive: Paris, Bibliothèque Nationale de France, f. fr. 10153, 107 ff.; Bibliothèque Nationale de France, f. fr. 5025, 99 ff.; Modena, Biblioteca Estense, 8.7, 106 ff.; Vatican, Biblioteca Apostolica, Reg. lat. 920, 111 ff. Two seventeenth-century copies also survive.

Standard edition: *Le Livre des Fais et bonnes meurs du sage roy Charles V,* 2 volumes, edited by Suzanne Solente, Société de l'histoire de France: Série anterieure à 1789 nos. 437 & 444 (Paris: H. Champion, 1936, 1940; republished, 1977).

Edition in modern French: *Le Livre des faits et bonnes moeurs du roi Charles V le Sage,* translated by Eric Hicks and Thérèse Moreau, Série "Moyen Âge" (Paris: Stock, 1997).

Le Livre de la Cité des Dames (13 December 1404 – April 1405)

Manuscripts: The most important of the surviving twenty-seven manuscripts and/or fragments are: London, British Library, Royal 19 A. XIX, ff. 2a–172d (first redaction); Paris, Bibliothèque de l'Arsenal 2686, ff. 1–140d (second redaction); Paris, Bibliothèque Nationale de France, f. fr. 607,

ff.1a–79b and London, British Library, Harley 4431, ff. 288c–374a (final redaction); Paris, Bibliothèque Nationale de France, f. fr. 1178, ff. 2a–159c (with corrections probably in Christine's own hand); and Brussels, Bibliothèque Royale/ Koninklijke Bibliotheek 9393, ff. 2a–87d.

Standard editions: "Le Livre de la Cité des Dames, Eine kritische Textedition auf Grund der sieben überlieferten 'manuscrits originaux' des Textes," edited by Monika Lange, dissertation, University of Hamburg, 1974; "The 'Livre de la Cité des Dames' of Christine de Pisan, A Critical Edition," edited by Maureen C. Curnow, dissertation, Vanderbilt University, 1975; in *La Città delle dame,* edited by Earl Jeffrey Richards, translated into Italian, with an introduction, by Patricia Caraffi (Milan: Luni Editrice, 1997).

Edition in modern French: *Le Livre de la Cité des Dames,* translated by Thérèse Moreau and Eric Hicks (Paris: Stock, 1986).

Editions in English: *The Boke of the Cyte of Ladyes,* translated by Bryan Anslay (London: H. Pepwell, 1521); *The Book of the City of Ladies,* translated by Earl Jeffrey Richards (New York: Persea, 1982; revised, 1997).

L'Avision-Christine (1405)

Manuscripts: This text is preserved in three manuscripts: Brussels, Bibliothèque Royale/Koninklijke Bibliotheek, 10309, 79 ff.; Paris, Bibliothèque Nationale de France, f. fr. 1176, 81 ff.; and ex-Philipps 128 (now in a private collection).

Standard Editions: *L'Avision-Christine,* edited by Mary Louis Towner (Washington, D.C.: Catholic University of America, 1932); *L'Avision-Christine, Manuscrit ex. Philipps 128,* edited by Christine Reno and Liliane Dulac (Paris: Champion, 1999).

Editions in English: Preface translated in *Reinterpreting Christine de Pizan,* edited by Earl Jeffrey Richards (Athens: University of Georgia Press, 1992); *Christine's Vision,* translated by Glenda K. McLeod, Garland Library of Medieval Literature no. 68 (New York: Garland, 1993); selections in *The Writings of Christine de Pizan,* edited by Charity Cannon Willard (New York: Persea, 1994), pp. 6–26; and in *The Selected Writings of Christine de Pizan,* edited by Renate Blumenfeld-Kosinski (New York: Norton, 1997), pp. 173–200.

Epistre a Isabelle de Baviere, Reine de France (5 October 1405)

Manuscripts: This work is represented in at least six manuscripts; the two most important are: Paris, Bibliothèque Nationale de France, f. fr. 580, ff. 53r–54v; and Oxford, All Souls College, ms. 182 ff. 230–232.

Standard editions: In *Essai sur les écrits politiques de Christine de Pisan,* edited by Raymond Thomassy (Paris: Debécourt, 1838), pp. 132–140; in *Anglo-Norman Letters and Petitions from All Souls ms. 182,* edited by M. D. Legge (Oxford: Blackwell, 1941), pp. 144–150; *Epistre a la Reine,* edited by Angus J. Kennedy, in *Revue des Langues Romanes,* 92, no. 2 (1988): 258–264.

Standard edition and edition in English: *The Epistle of the Prison of Human Life; with, An Epistle to the Queen of France; And; Lament on the Evils of Civil War,* edited and translated by Josette A. Wisman, Garland Library of Medieval Literature no. 21 (New York: Garland, 1984).

Le Livre des Trois Vertus (April–November 1405)

Manuscripts: Boston, Public Library, 1528, 98 ff. (probably belonged to Diane de Poitiers) gives the only complete text. Other important manuscripts of the surviving twenty-one include: Brussels, Bibliothèque Royale/Koninklijke Bibliotheek, ms. 10973, 90 ff.; New Haven, Yale University, Beinecke Library, ms. 427, 95 ff.; Oxford, Bodleian Library, ms. Fr. D 5, 208 ff.; and Paris, Bibliothèque Nationale de France, f. fr. 452, 93 ff.

Standard editions: Three printed versions, based on fragments and entitled *Le Tresor de la Cité des Dames* (Paris: Antoine Vérard, 1497; Paris: Michel le Noir, 1503; Paris: Jehan André & Denis Janot, 1536); *Le Livre des Trois Vertus,* edited by Charity Cannon Willard and Eric Hicks, Bibliothèque du XVe siecle no. 50 (Paris: H. Champion, 1989).

Translations in English: *The Treasure of the City of Ladies: or, The Book of the Three Virtues,* translated by Sarah Lawson (Harmondsworth: Penguin, 1985); *A Medieval Woman's Mirror of Honor: The Treasury of the City of Ladies,* translated by Charity Cannon Willard, edited by Madeleine Pelner Cosman (Tenafly, N.J.: Bard Hall Press / New York: Persea, 1989).

Livre de Prudence, also known as *Livre de la Prod'hommie de l'homme* (1405 – 1406)

Manuscripts: The work, surviving in two versions, is unedited. Four manuscripts of the first version survive: Brussels, Bibliothèque Royale/Koninklijke Bibliotheek, ms. 11065–73, ff. 236r–272r. and Bibliothèque Royale/Koninklijke Bibliotheek, ms. 11074–78, ff. 72r–115r.; London, British Library, Harley 4431, ff. 268a–287c; Paris, Bibliothèque Nationale de France, f. fr. 605, ff. 5v–22r; the second, expanded version in two manuscripts, Paris, Bibliothèque Nationale de France, f. fr. 5037, ff. 182–221; and Vatican, Biblioteca Apostolica Vaticana, Reg. lat 1238, ff.1r–46r.

Edition in English: Selections in *The Writings of Christine de Pizan,* edited by Charity Cannon Willard (New York: Persea, 1994).

Le Livre du Corps de policie (1406–1407)

Manuscripts: Nine manuscripts survive: Besançon, Bibliothèque Municipale, ms. 423, 81 ff.; Brussels, Bibliothèque Royale/Koninklijke Bibliotheek, 10440, 59 ff.; Chantilly, Musée Condé 294, 100 ff.; London, British Library, Harley 4410, 72 ff.; New York Public Library, Spencer Collection 17, ff. 127–186; Paris, Arsenal 2681, 94ff; Paris, Bibliothèque Nationale de France, f. fr. 1197, 106ff; Bibliothèque Nationale de France 1198, 62 ff.; Bibliothèque Nationale de France 1199, 58 ff.; and Bibliothèque Nationale de France 12439, ff. 46v–225.

Standard edition: *"Le Livre du Corps de policie" of Christine de Pisan: A Critical Edition,* edited by Robert Harold Lucas, Textes littéraires français no. 145 (Geneva: Droz, 1967); *Le Livre da corps de policie,* edited, with an introduction by Angus J. Kennedy (Paris: H. Champion, 1998).

Editions in English: *The Body of Polycye* (London: John Skot, 1521; republished, Amsterdam, Theatrum Orbis Terrarum / New York: Da Capo Press, 1971); *The Book Of The Body Politic,* edited and translated by Kate Langdon Forhan (Cambridge & New York: Cambridge University Press, 1994); selections translated in *The Writings of Christine de Pizan,* edited by Charity Cannon Willard (New York: Persea, 1994), pp. 275–291.

Sept Psaumes allegorisés (26 June 1409 – 1 January 1410)

Manuscripts: The *Sept Psaumes* survives in at least three manuscripts: Paris, Bibliothèque Nationale de France, nouv. acq. fr. 4792, 1r–88r; Brussels, Bibliothèque Royale/Koninklijke Bibliotheek, 10987, 87 ff. and BR, IV 1093, 97 ff.

Standard edition: *Les Sept Psaumes Allegorisés of Christine de Pisan, A Critical Edition from the Brussels and Paris Manuscripts,* edited by Ruth Ringland Rains (Washington, D.C.: Catholic University of America Press, 1965).

Edition in English: Selections in *The Writings of Christine de Pizan,* edited by Charity Cannon Willard (New York: Persea, 1994), pp. 325–337.

Cent Balades d'Amant et de Dame (1410)

Manuscript: This text is represented in only one manuscript, London, British Library, Harley 4431, 376r–398r; however, based on the existence of two fragments (Leiden, ms Ltk. 1819 and ex-Philipps 128), there is good reason to believe that a now lost collectanea of Christine's works (called the "Burgundy Manuscript" because Christine enjoyed the patronage of the dukes of Burgundy) was transcribed that included the *Cent balades d'amant et de dame.*

Standard Editions: In *Œuvres poétiques de Christine de Pisan,* 3 volumes, edited by Maurice Roy (Paris: Firmin-Didot, 1886–1896), III: 209–317; *Cent Balades d'Amant et de Dame,* edited by Jacqueline Cerquiglini, Collection 10/18: Bibliothèque Médiévale, no. 1529 (Paris: Union Générale d'Éditions, 1982).

Edition in English: Selections in *The Writings of Christine de Pizan,* edited by Charity Cannon Willard (New York: Persea, 1994), pp. 261–268.

Livre des Fais d'Armes et de Chevalerie (1410)

Manuscripts: The most important of the surviving twenty-two manuscripts are: Paris, Bibliothèque Nationale de France, f. fr. 585, 132 ff.; Bibliothèque Nationale de France, f. fr. 603, ff. 1–80; Brussels, Bibliothèque Royale/Koninklijke Bibliotheek, 10205, 162 ff.; and Bibliothèque Royale/Koninklijke Bibliotheek, 10476, 132 ff.

Standard edition: *L'Art de chevalerie selon Végèce* (Paris: Antoine Vérard, 1488); *L'Arbre des batailles et Fleur de chevalerie selon Végèce, avecques plusieurs hystoires et utilles remonstrances du fait du guerre* (Paris: Philippe Le Noir, 1527).

Edition in English: *The Boke of the Fayttes of Armes and Chyualrye,* translated by William Caxton (Westminster: Caxton, 1489); republished as *The Book of Fayttes of Armes and of Chyualrye, Translated and Printed by William Caxton from the French Original by Christine de Pisan,* edited by A. T. P. Byles (London: Published for the Early English Text Society by H. Milford, Oxford University Press, 1932, revised 1937).

Lamentacion sur les maux de la France (23 August 1410)

Manuscript: The text survives in a single manuscript: Paris, Bibliothèque Nationale de France, f. fr. 24864, ff. 14r–18r.

Standard editions: In *Essai sur les écrits politiques de Christine de Pisan,* edited by Raymond Thomassy (Paris: Debécourt, 1838), pp. 141–149; *Lamentacion sur les maux de la France,* edited by Angus J. Kennedy, in *Mélanges de langue et littérature françaises du Moyen Âge et de la Renaissance offerts à Charles Foulon* (Rennes: Institut français, Université de Haute-Bretagne, 1980), I: 177–185.

Standard edition and edition in English: In *The Epistle of the Prison of Human Life; with, An Epistle to the Queen of France; and, Lament on the Evils of Civil War,* edited and translated by Josette A. Wisman, Garland Library of Medieval Literature no. 21 (New York: Garland, 1984); and in *The Selected Writings of Christine de Pizan,* edited by Renate Blu-

menfeld-Kosinski (New York: Norton, 1997), pp. 224–228.

Le Livre de la Paix (September 1412–late 1413)

Manuscripts: The text survives in at least two extant manuscripts: Paris, Bibliothèque Nationale de France, f. fr. 1182, ff. 1–108; and Brussels, Bibliothèque Royale/Koninklijke Bibliotheek, 10366, ff. 1–108. The latter manuscript was produced in the atelier of the "Master of Christine de Pizan" and is most likely the 1414 presentation copy for the duke of Berry.

Standard edition: *The "Le Livre de la Paix" of Christine de Pisan,* edited by Charity Cannon Willard (The Hague: Mouton, 1958).

Edition in English: Selections in *The Writings of Christine de Pizan,* edited by Charity Cannon Willard (New York: Persea, 1994), pp. 310–317; and in *The Selected Writings of Christine de Pizan,* edited by Renate Blumenfeld-Kosinski (New York: Norton, 1997), pp. 310–317.

La Ditié de Jehanne d'Arc (31 July 1429)

Manuscripts: Three manuscripts survive: Bern, Stadtbibliothek, Sammlung-Jacques Bongars, ms. 205, ff. 62r–68r (most complete version); Carpentras, Bibliothèque Municipale, ms. 390, ff. 81r–90v; Grenoble, Bibliothèque Municipale, u. 909. Rés., ff. 98r–102r (fragment).

Standard editions: Charles de Roche and Gustave Wissler, "Documents relatifs à Jeanne d'Arc et à son époque d'un manuscrit du XVe siècle de la Bibliothèque de la ville de Berne" in *Festschrift Louis Gauchat* (Aarau: Sauerländer, 1926), pp. 329–376; and *La Ditié de Jehanne d'Arc,* edited by Angus J. Kennedy and Kenneth Varty, "Medium Aevum" Monographs, new series (Oxford: Oxford Society for the Study of Medieval Languages and Literatures, 1977).

Editions in English: Selection in *The Writings of Christine de Pizan,* edited by Charity Cannon Willard (New York: Persea, 1994), pp. 352–363; complete prose translation in *The Selected Writings of Christine de Pizan,* edited by Renate Blumenfeld-Kosinski (New York: Norton, 1997), pp. 252–262.

Epistre de la prison de vie humaine (25 October 1415 – 20 January 1418)

Manuscript: One manuscript is extant: Paris, Bibliothèque Nationale de France, f. fr. 24786, ff. 36r–97r.

Standard edition: *Epistre de la prison de vie humaine,* edited by Angus J. Kennedy (Glasgow: University of Glasgow, French Department, 1984).

Standard edition and edition in English: In *The Epistle of the Prison of Human Life; with, An Epistle to the Queen of France; and, Lament on the Evils of Civil*

Page from a manuscript for Christine's L'Epistre d'Othea *(New York, Pierpont Morgan Library, M 775, f. 209)*

War, edited and translated by Josette A. Wisman, Garland Library of Medieval Literature no. 21 (New York: Garland, 1984), pp. 338–346.

Les Heures de Contemplation sur la Passion de Nostre Seigneur (1425)

Manuscript: The text is represented only in Paris, Bibliothèque Nationale de France, nouv. acq. 10059, f. 114–144, and The Hague, Koninklijke Bibliotheek, 73. J. 55, flo. 51–92v.

Edition in English: Selections in *The Writings of Christine de Pizan,* edited by Charity Cannon Willard (New York: Persea, 1994), p. 347.

Almost everything known of Christine de Pizan's life is derived from references she makes in her works. The year of her birth—either 1364 or 1365—has only been determined from her statement that she was widowed at the age of twenty-five when her husband died while accompanying the French king Charles VI to Beauvais. Since a royal visit there occurred between 29 October and 7 November 1390, this produces an approximate date, which is confirmed by Christine's remark from 1403 that she had then mourned her husband for thirteen years.

She was born in Venice, where her father, Tommaso da Pizzano, was a salaried counselor. Christine benefited all her life from her father's connection to northern Italian intellectuals, especially at the University of Bologna. Her Parisian contemporaries regarded her as a link to the new ideas coming from Italy that were later referred to as "humanism": the return to pagan Latin and Greek authors; a reconsideration of the work of St. Augustine in light of the writings of St. Thomas Aquinas; a new respect for the individual; and the search for an ideal state. Unlike her courtly predecessors, Christine assigns an unprecedented importance to questions of authority, legitimacy, power, and the positions and roles occupied by women and men in society, expressed in her shift from a lyric poet who had mastered courtly forms to a political writer who addressed issues of peace and justice in human society at large.

The French king Charles V invited Tommaso to come to Paris as court astrologer shortly after Christine's birth. His family—wife, daughter, and two sons—followed him to Paris three years later and was formally presented to the king at the Louvre in December 1368. Thus Christine grew up in one of the most intellectually flourishing environments in contemporary Europe and enjoyed access to the excellent royal library. Christine knew many intellectuals at the court, including Jean Gerson, provost of Notre Dame and chancellor of the Sorbonne, and Gilles Mallet, the royal librarian.

Married at the age of fifteen to Estienne de Castel, a court notary, Christine had ten happy years of marriage and bore a daughter (Marie, born in 1381, who in 1397 entered the Dominican convent of Poissy), and two sons (Jean, born in 1383, survived to adulthood; the other son's name is unknown). The death of Charles V in 1380 dramatically changed Christine's fortunes. Her father lost royal favor and died shortly after 1385. Christine's brothers, Paolo and Aghinolfo, returned to Bologna, leaving her to care for their mother in Paris. In 1390 the death of Christine's husband left her and their children with large debts and no inheritance. Christine frequently discussed her subsequent decision not to remarry, citing her affection for her husband, her need to settle the financial difficulties following his death, and the necessity of solitude to gain the erudition required as a writer.

Christine's literary career roughly falls into three overlapping periods, which might be termed lyrical, allegorical, and political. These divisions designate her experiments with literary form and content. Writing dominated the twenty-three years in Christine's life after the first publication of her lyrics around 1395, when she was thirty, until she was fifty-three in 1418. In her most autobiographical work, *L'Avision-Christine* (The Vision of Christine, 1405), she explains that she chose to retire to her study to write. Even allowing for self-fictionalization, this portrayal of her choice of the contemplative over the active life speaks volumes about the kind of life she could actually lead.

Apart from her legal and financial difficulties, and those experienced in placing her surviving son in a noble household (she succeeded in 1396 with the earl of Salisbury), Christine's life was largely spent thinking and writing in her study. She enjoyed the support of the French king's brothers, Louis, Duke of Orléans (and of his Italian wife, Valentina Visconti); Jean, Duke of Berry; and Philip, Duke of Burgundy; and of the French queen herself, Isabeau de Bavière (Isabella of Bavaria). Handwriting evidence suggests that Christine may have either worked for a short time in the royal chancery copying documents or have begun her "chemin de long estude" (road of long study) by copying the works of other authors on commission: one surviving hand that seems to be hers resembles the notarial hand of contemporary scriptoria. This kind of work would explain both her familiarity with a vast range of sources and the possibility that several surviving manuscripts of her works are autographs.

Christine was one of the most linguistically innovative authors in the history of French literature, coining words still in use. Computer-generated concordances of her works reveal that Christine deployed an enormous vocabulary, ranging from rare diminutives and femi-

Illumination from a manuscript for Christine's L'Epistre d'Othea, *depicting the Wheel of Fortune (Bibliothèque Nationale de France, f. fr. 606, fol. 35r)*

nized substantives to specialized military, architectural, and legal terms. She came to know many scribes and manuscript illustrators. When she began writing lyrics around 1395, she was very much on her own, but when Philip of Burgundy commissioned her in 1403 to write a biography of his father, King Charles V, she arrived at the Louvre "avec mes gens" (with my staff). This staff may account for both her productivity and the care that she was able to take in the copying, revising, expanding, and illustrating of her works.

Christine's early works exhibit a subtlety in her cultivation of a narrator's voice distinguishable from the voices of the various lyrical protagonists that is hardly an apprentice's work. In a characteristically modest way, Christine later called these pieces "lighter matters." Remarkably, between 1399 and 1402, some five to eight years after beginning to write lyric poetry, she supervised the production of two copies of her collected verse works known as *Le Livre de Christine* (The Book of Christine). Both copies begin with *Les Cent Balades* (The One Hundred Ballads, 1395–1400), and both are introduced by Christine's trademark minia-

ture, showing her writing in her book-lined *estude* (study) or *cele* (cell).

In *Les Cent Balades* Christine tells a complex story using individual poems to form a narrative. After an evocative, autobiographical introductory section, Christine presents a series of love affairs from a woman's perspective, emphasizing how short-lived the joy of love is. The second half of the collection is a parallel series of love affairs, told from a man's perspective, all also ending in disappointment. Ballades 91 through 99 show the plight of contemporary society, paralleling the autobiographical introduction. Christine skillfully sets up a series of parallel situations depicting the moral folly of individuals, framed by a self-portrait and a portrait of society. This rigorous combination of courtly forms with a noncourtly content announces Christine's departure from the pattern of earlier poets.

In her first virelay, composed immediately after *Les Cent Balades,* Christine speaks of the "cover" she must wear in writing according to prescribed compositional rules of courtly poetry. Her highly charged remark "je chante par couverture" (I sing through a cover, or mask) uses *couverture* to refer not only to a courtly lover's prescribed dissimulation but also to the covering or simulacrum of allegorical poetry, and it typifies Christine's dissatisfaction with both contemporary French lyric and the potential confusion between poetic persona and historical personality in courtly poetry. Christine resolves this problem by unmasking artificial courtly conventions in the name of literal or historical truth within the context of fourfold allegory. She stresses the historical veracity of her works as an allegory of moral teaching and of the history of salvation and sees her historical situation as a woman and as a widow as part of the divine plan in history. Medieval French lyric is delicate, skillful, witty, and beautiful (at its best) but almost never actually autobiographical: medieval French poets usually relied instead on biographical commonplaces such as being either lovelorn or penniless. During the first ten years of her career, Christine undisputedly wrote lyric as sophisticated as that of her predecessors and contemporaries; yet, her keen sense of the formal and spiritual limits of this aristocratic, frozen, and self-absorbed lyrical tradition separates her from her medieval French counterparts. When Christine speaks of her real loneliness as a widow and turns her widowhood into an integral part of her identity as a woman writer, she has given a biographical fact a new twist within the context of the stereotypical desolation of the courtly lover. She speaks not of adulterous love mourning for a consummation not yet achieved but of married love mourning for the irreparable loss of the beloved. The contrast between her life and poetic convention could not be more striking. While she knew that her initial success among courtly readers stemmed from the curiosity of her being a woman writer, she was hardly taken in by this superficial reception of her work and thought.

From this biographical context arises a recurrent critique of courtly love in Christine's works. For example, in *Le Livre du Dit de Poissy* (The Book of the Tale of Poissy, April 1400), the biographical point of departure is Christine's visit to her daughter in the convent of Poissy in the spring of 1400. In the first part of the book, several women, including a nun (Christine's daughter), are met in a seemingly courtly assembly to discuss the desirable physical traits of male beauty, and in their discussion invert and unmask courtly conventions of female beauty. The second part is a dispute over finer points in courtly love.

The context here was the recurrent theme in courtly literature of avoiding *fole amour,* "foolish love." Love's folly was a source of amusement in courtly literature, but for a stern cleric such as Jean Gerson, who called *fole amour* unambiguously *amor insanus* (insane love), it was a source of insanity. For Guillaume de Lor-

ris and Jean de Meun, in *Le Roman de la Rose* (The Romance of the Rose), a work begun by Guillaume between 1225 and 1230 and continued by Jean (circa 1269–1278), *fole amour* was an inexhaustible source of irony and creativity. For all its playful qualities, their work rests firmly on male clerical misogyny, male self-absorption, and French cultural superiority as the projection of the individual male ego. Christine's remaining career was a reaction to these issues. For Christine, the popularity of the *Rose* was symptomatic of lyric's formal perfection and empty content. She notes in *Le Livre de la Cité des Dames* (The Book of the City of Ladies, written between 13 December 1404 and April 1405) that many contemporaries wrote about women in "dictiez de eaue sans sel" (poems of water without salt) and "balades sans sentement" (ballades empty of feeling). Formal perfection, devoid of content and feeling, led to a false representation of women in poetry.

The literary controversy known as the *Querelle de la Rose* (Quarrel of the Rose) marks the major turning point in Christine's career. The first part of the *Rose,* the four thousand lines composed by Guillaume de Lorris, introduces a superficially allegorical dream in which the protagonist Amant (Lover) pursues but does not obtain his beloved Rose. In the approximately seventeen thousand lines in the second part, written as a continuation by Jean de Meun, the format switches from lyrical reflections on love to long speeches, by various allegorical figures purporting to advise Amant, that allow Jean to incorporate scholastic, generally misogynist material on women, love, and marriage into the work. What the *Rose* "means" is secondary to Jean's teasing play with the concept of meaning. When Jean has one character call all women whores, it is unclear whether Jean believes what his speaker says. The Italian poet Dante, who borrows from the *Rose* in his *Commedia* (Comedy, circa 1308–1321), never mentions the French work, partially because he probably recognized that Jean's playing with the paradoxes of literary self-referentiality ultimately subverted the possibility of meaning. For Christine, the *Rose* represented the combination of lyrical narcissism—the tendency of lyric to call attention to its own formal devices—and misogyny. As such the *Rose* epitomizes the self-absorbed, self-aggrandizing, and misogynist currents of the male clerical tradition.

Christine wrote her first letter against the *Rose* in 1401. Prominent Parisian intellectuals rushed to Jean's defense. She explained that while Dante spoke of all things in heaven, earth, and hell, using an allegory consistent with his serious moral purposes, Jean's allegory was superficial, and his wit hid his hatred of women. She criticized Jean's use of the words *coilles* (balls) and *pute* (whore) as linguistic sophistry: since language

Page from a manuscript for Christine's Le Livre du Chemin de long estude,
*depicting Christine and the Sybil of Cumae in the Court of Reason
(Bibliothèque Natioinale de France, f. fr. 836, fol. 19)*

reflected social hierarchies, a cleric's derogation of women mirrored the general oppression of women.

Christine's ally in the Quarrel, Gerson, was even less tolerant: he proposed burning every copy of the work. Before one condemns Gerson's position, one might recall that medieval France was not a democratic society with a tradition of free speech but a hierarchical feudal state in which literacy was limited and a basic prerogative of power. Christine's reaction is more subtle: the patristic writers and scholastic philosophers represented the single literary tradition linked to power and authority, offering a vaster intellectual system with possibilities for conceptualizing freedom not found in courtly literature.

Christine's critique of the *Rose* was hatched, significantly, at about the same time she wrote *L'Epistre d'Othea* (The Letter of Othea, circa 1400). The *Othea* consists of one hundred illuminations of scenes borrowed from classical mythology. Christine systematically treats these myths as history, scriptural allegory, and morality. To each miniature Christine appends a verse text, a gloss, and an allegory to set the pattern for allegorical exposition contrasting with the lightweight allegory of the *Rose*. This historicizing and allegorizing approach means Christine rejects any form of archetypal (that is, ahistorical) mythology and situates the events of history squarely within the intersection of human history with the divine as embodied in the notion of the Incarnation. Christine follows Dante's pattern of portraying individual sinners as embodying an internal spiritual state of being, consistent—as Erich Auerbach demonstrated in his 1929 work on the Italian poet—with the concept of the Incarnation as Thomas of Aquinas explained it in his theory of the *habitus* (state of mind).

Just as the *Othea* establishes Christine as a skillful allegorical writer, much of her subsequent prose reveals her to be a careful historian. Allegory and history were necessarily complementary aspects of the Incarnation for Christine, as they had been for Dante. In order to reveal the omnipresence of the Incarnation—human history intersecting with the timeless divine—*allegoresis* (allegorization) couples history with the anagogical. Therefore, Christine as an allegorical authority is inseparable from Christine as a historian.

The *Othea* was originally dedicated to Louis, Duke of Orleans. Another early work, composed like the *Othea* around 1400, *Le Debat de deux amants* (The Debate of Two Lovers) is also addressed to this duke. Here Christine has two lovers, a knight and a squire, each express their conventional, though opposing (and male-centered) views on love. The older knight argues that love destroys reason and honor, whereas the younger, and presumably less experienced, squire claims love is ennobling. In an interesting twist, Christine introduces a young woman who pointedly observes that in fact men suffer less than they claim. This technique of a somewhat modifed love casuistry allows Christine to deflate the stereotypes surrounding courtly love.

Christine follows a similar tack of contrasting oppsing views of love in *Le Livre des trois jugemens* (The Book of Three Judgments), written around 1402. In this poem three aggrieved lovers plead their cases. The first case touches on a woman abandoned by her lover who in turn takes a new lover: has she perjured her original vows? The second case concerns a knight who is prevented from seeing his lady by her jealous husband: would he be disloyal if he then loved anoither woman? The third case recounts the plight of a young woman who is first jilted by her knight-lover for a noble lady and then a year later is confronted by her former lover asking for pardon: should the lady pardon him? Christine blithely recounts all of these situations with tongue firmly in cheek and refrains from passing judgment, for which she defers tot the Sénéchal de Hainault to whom the poem is dedicated. These two works demonstrate that Christine manipulated courtly concentions with ease and skill, clearly aware of their lack of seriousness.

Christine's *Le Dit de la Rose* (The Tale of the Rose), written 14 February 1402, transposed and translated the polemics of the Quarrel into a courtly context. The work, also dedicated to the duke of Orléans, recounts a celebration at the duke's Paris residence where the goddess Loyalty, representing fidelity, appears. Loyalty explains that she has commissioned Amor to support his true supporters in their fight against deceptive lovers. Each male guest must promise to swear fidelity to women. Christine then retires to her chamber, falls asleep, and in a dream sees Loyalty who announces the founding of a new "Order of the Rose"—one based on nearly every possible chivalric convention—for the defense of women. For all its charm, the appeal made in the poem, that true chivalry take up the cause of women, remained unheeded. Feudal society and its supporting ideologies fell apart during the early fifteenth century. Traditional chivalry was as unsuited to defend women in the late Middle Ages as it was to repulse the new form of warfare unleashed at Agincourt in 1415. Christine's later reflections on virtue as the origin of true nobility rather than bloodlines show she was sensitive to the collapse of earlier feudal ideals.

Just as in the *Othea* Christine attempts to show what allegoresis required in serious literature in order to underscore the shortcomings of the *Rose,* in the 23,636-verse *Le Livre de la Mutacion de Fortune* (The Book of the Mutation of Fortune, circa August 1400 – November 1403) she strives to show how a proper universal history must be written. Jean had claimed that the entire art of love was enclosed in his poem; Christine endeavored instead to summarize all of human history, a more serious subject than the art of love, believing as Dante had that the meaning of human history was allegorically subsumed in the history of salvation. The *Mutacion de Fortune* also includes a celebrated description of her transformation from a woman to a man clearly indicating that Christine saw women's identity as socially and not biologically determined.

Christine makes her final argument against equating Jean with Dante in the *Le Livre du Chemin de long estude* (The Book of the Road of Long Study), written between 5 October 1402 and 20 March 1403. The last line of the *Chemin de long estude,* "car tart estoit, et je m'esveille" (for it was late, and I awoke), alludes to the last line of the *Rose.* In this allegorical dream vision, Christine is led by the Sybil of Cumae to the court of Reason (an altogether different allegorical personification than in the *Rose*), where the question of the ideal ruler for a world empire is under discussion.

Christine shows her mastery of the conventions of pastoral lyric in *Le dit de la pastoure* (The Tale of the Shepherdess), dated to May 1403. In this work, a shepherdess named Marotele meets and falls in love with a knight who, of course, ends up by abandoning her. Marotele is disconsolate at the end of the work, appealing for the prayers of all courtly lovers (fins amans) on behalf of her lover, who she stupidly remains convinced, is good and valiant and loved by the brave. The gap between this work's formal perfection and its content could not be more blatant.

Written between 1403 and November 1405, *Le Livre du Duc des Vrais Amans* (The Book of the Duke of True Lovers) is a work of 3,500 verse lines with intercalated prose epistles, composed at the request of an unnamed duke, who instructed Christine to tell the story of his love for his married cousin. The affair had

Illumination in a manuscript for Christine's Le Livre de las Cité des Dames, *with the three goddesses greeting Christine on the left and Christine and Rectitude building the City of Ladies on the right (British Library, ms. Harley, 4431)*

lasted some twelve years, with a stereotypical happy beginning, hackneyed dilemmas, and an inevitable and programmatic unhappy end. In her story Christine added a new twist by condemning the lures of foolish love in a letter written to the younger woman by an older woman. Christine also includes the letter in *Le Livre des Trois Vertus* (The Book of the Three Virtues, circa April–November 1405). In practical terms Christine sees courtly love as a threat to the honor of women (and by extension to what little power they had). She allows women to speak more than in most courtly lyrics, where their role as dupes and victims of courtly love had been to lament their lovers' infidelity.

Christine's fame prompted Philip, Duke of Burgundy, to commission her to write a biography of his father, Charles V. In the resulting work, written circa January–November 1404, *Le Livre des Fais et bonnes meurs du sage roy Charles V* (The Book of the Deeds and Good Conduct of the Wise King Charles V), Christine writes in a spirit consistent with her search for an ideal ruler in the *Chemin de long estude*. This topically arranged mirror for princes posits Charles V as the model for the ideal ruler for France. Christine's political rhetoric entailed the representation of ideal models, and her vision of a female utopia in her next work is no exception to this rule.

No sooner had she finished this royal biography than she began a universal history of women, *Le Livre de la Cité des Dames* (The Book of the City of Ladies, 1404–1405), the crowning achievement of Christine's career. Christine recounts how three celestial beings came to comfort her in her despair over the long history of misogyny. Christine interweaves stories from ancient and contemporary sources to demonstrate the affinity of women for letters. Sitting in her book-lined study, Christine associates herself with the traditional iconography of the Annunciation in which the Virgin sits at a desk with a book. The term *cele* also alludes to the cloistered lives of learned women: her vision of the "City of Ladies," where a new positive concept of freedom or *libertas,* associated in fourteenth and fifteenth centuries with the rise of independent cities, replaces the negative freedom associated with the autonomy of ecclesiastical institutions, defined as *immunitas* (a freedom from outside jurisdiction). Christine's "city" not only represents an allegory of the City of God but also looks to the newly won autonomy of late medieval cities as a metaphor for the ideal freedom women achieve through virtue. The noble ladies who inhabit this city are not members of a hereditary nobility but are women whose nobility is founded on virtue, a claim consistent with late medieval disputes on the nature of nobility itself.

Illuminated page from a manuscript for Christine's collected works; Christine is depicted presenting her book to her patron, Isabeau de Bavière, Queen of France (British Library, ms. Harley 4431, fol. 1r)

Christine composed *Le Livre des Trois Vertus* (The Book of the Three Virtues) in 1405 as a sequel to the *Cité des Dames*. The practical hints for following virtue given in the *Trois Vertus* supply the criteria for true nobility. Although conceived as a companion to the *Cité des Dames*, Christine did not include it in her collected manuscripts. Often entitled *Le Tresor de la Cité des Dames* (The Treasure of the City of Ladies), its success was roughly comparable to that of the *Cité des Dames*, and it is one of the few vernacular books printed in France before 1500, probably because it was seen as a practical and didactical treatise guiding women's conduct. It is as active and practical in its content as the *Cité des Dames* is contemplative and theoretical.

Christine marked the turning point in her career at the end of 1405 by composing her most autobiographically introspective work, the prose *L'Avision-Christine*. Following a dream-vision format common in medieval Latin literature, Christine meets several allegorical figures, including "Libera" (literally, "the free woman," perhaps an allusion to the dream of freedom in the *Cité des Dames*), who represents France mourning over the unrest arising from Charles VI's bouts of madness, "Opinion" and "Philosophie," to whom Christine narrates her life.

Charles VI's madness left a political vacuum in the midst of intrigues and wars. On 5 October 1405 Christine composed a letter to the queen of France in which she called on Isabeau to mediate among rival court factions. One month later, Christine's ally, Gerson, made a similar appeal directly to the princes in a sermon entitled *Vivat rex* (Long Live the King).

Christine's turning from courtly lyric to political prose was virtually complete, with the exception of the *Cent Balades d'Amant et de Dame* (One Hundred Ballads of the Lover and the Lady, 1410), although she continued to revise the collections of her works. The *Cent Balades d'Amant et de Dame* uses the same techniques of symmetry as the *Cent Balades*, except that it focuses on the single story of the love between a knight and a lady, with the voices of the knight and lady alternating throughout. After granting the knight her favors, the lady despairs when the affair fails. While formally excellent, the work seems like an afterthought to Christine's political writings between 1405 and 1410.

The major works of this period echo with the recurrent theme of peace. The clear message was that the rival factions must make peace; the different estates of society must strive to fulfill their duties to one another; and corrupted knights must return to the original ideals of chivalry. Christine's call for peace was drowned out in the political chaos of the second decade of the fifteenth century. The English defeat of the French at Agincourt on 25 October 1415 and the death

of the duke of Berry in 1417 resulted in increasing turmoil within France. Christine's reaction was to console the survivors and widows of Agincourt in her *Epistre de la prison de vie humaine* (Letter on the Prison of Human life) written sometime between the battle and 20 January 1418. In Paris her life was in danger as the city became a battleground for rival factions, and she sought refuge with her daughter at the convent of Poissy at some point in 1418.

Except for her *Les Heures de Contemplation sur la Passion de Nostre Seigneur* (The Hours of Contemplation on the Passion of Our Lord, 1425) portraying Mary at the foot of the Cross—far different from the triumphant Virgin ruling the City of Ladies—which was probably written as a response to her own son's death in 1425, Christine wrote nothing until 31 July 1429, when she celebrated the first military victories of Joan of Arc over the English. *La Ditié de Jeanne d'Arc* (The Tale of Joan of Arc) portrays Joan as the successor of Old Testament women who saved the people of Israel. Joan, writes Christine, will drive the English out of France and unite Christendom in a crusade to free Jerusalem. Whether Christine survived until Joan's capture and execution in 1431 is unclear. In 1434 Guillebert de Mets, a member of the court of Burgundy, wrote about Christine in the past tense, and therefore she must have died sometime before this date.

Until the twentieth century Christine's works enjoyed a limited reception throughout Western Europe, although many of them were translated into English, Dutch, and Portuguese and were among the first printed books in both France and England. Scenes from the *Cité des Dames* woven into fifteenth-century tapestries for noblewomen in Burgundy attest to the chord Christine's work had struck in its treatment of the question of women and power. In the seventeenth and eighteenth centuries French royal historians were drawn to Christine's account of Charles V, and late-eighteenth-century interest in women writers in France, Germany, and England led to a rediscovery of some of her works. The rise of women's rights movements in the late nineteenth century sparked interest in Christine as a feminist writer, an interest that was rekindled in the 1970s. The publication of the first modern English translation of the *Cité des Dames* in 1982 initiated a veritable renaissance of Christine de Pizan scholarship, which continues to grow, as does the understanding that Christine's work has lost none of its provocative challenge since it was first written.

Bibliographies:

Angus J. Kennedy, *Christine de Pizan: A Bibliographical Guide*, Research Bibliographies & Checklists no. 42 (London: Grant & Cutler, 1984);

Edith Yenal, *Christine de Pizan: A Bibliography,* 2nd edition (Metuchen: Scarecrow Press, 1989);

Kennedy, "A Selective Bibliography of Christine de Pizan Scholarship, circa 1980–1987," in *Reinterpreting Christine de Pizan,* edited by Earl Jeffrey Richards (Athens: University of Georgia Press, 1992), pp. 285–298;

Kennedy, *Christine de Pizan: A Bibliographical Guide, Supplement I,* Research Bibliographies & Checklists no. 42, I (London: Grant & Cutler, 1994).

Biographies:

Suzanne Solente, "Christine de Pisan," in *Histoire littéraire de la France,* 40 (1974): 335–422;

Charity Cannon Willard, *Christine de Pizan, Her Life and Works* (New York: Persea, 1984).

References:

Erich Auerbach, *Dante, Dichter der irdischen Welt* (Berlin: de Gruyter, 1929);

Margaret Brabant, ed., *Politics, Gender and Genre: The Political Thought of Christine de Pizan* (Boulder, Colo.: Westview Press, 1992);

Liliane Dulac and Bernard Ribémont, eds., *Une femme de Lettres au Moyen Age, Études autour de Christine de Pizan* (Orléans: Paradigme, 1995);

James C. Laidlaw, "Christine de Pizan: An Author's Progress," *Modern Language Review,* 78 (1983): 532–550;

Laidlaw, "Christine de Pizan: A Publisher's Progress," *Modern Language Review,* 82 (1987): 37–75;

Nadia Margolis, "Christine de Pizan: The Poetess as Historian," *Journal of the History of Ideas,* 47 (1986): 361–375;

Glenda K. McLeod, ed., *The Reception of Christine de Pizan from the Fifteenth through the Nineteenth Centuries, Visitors to the City* (Lewiston, N.Y.: Edwin Mellen, 1991);

Gianni Mombello, *La tradizione manoscritta dell' "Epistre Othea" di Christine de Pizan, Prolegomeni all'edizione del testo* (Turin: Accademia delle Scienze, 1967);

Patricia A. Philippy, "Establishing Authority: Boccaccio's *De Claris Mulieribus* and Christine de Pizan's *Le Livre de la Cité des Dames,*" *Romanic Review,* 77 (1986): 167–193;

Christine Reno, "Christine de Pizan: Feminism and Irony," in *Seconda miscellanaea di studi et ricerche sul Quattrocento francese,* collected by Franco Simone and edited by Jonathan Beck and Gianni Mombello (Chambéry & Turin: Centre d'Etudes Franco-Italien, 1981), pp. 125–133;

Earl Jeffrey Richards, Joan Williamson, Nadia Margolis, and Christine Reno, eds., *Reinterpreting Christine de Pizan* (Athens: University of Georgia Press, 1992);

Richards, "Rejecting Essentialism and Gendered Writing: The Case of Christine de Pizan," in *Gender and Text in the Later Middle Ages,* edited by Jane Chance (Gainesville: University Press of Florida, 1996), pp. 96–131;

Margarete Zimmermann and Dina de Rentiis, eds., *The City of Scholars, New Approaches to Christine de Pizan* (Berlin: de Gruyter, 1994);

Bärbel Zühlke, *Christine de Pizan in Text und Bild, Zur Selbstdarstellung einer frühhumanistischen Intellektuellen* (Stuttgart: Metzler, 1994).

Philippe de Commynes

(circa 1447 – 18 October 1511)

Yvonne LeBlanc
Culinary Institute of America

WORKS: *Les Mémoires* (Books 1–6, circa 1489–1493; Books 7–8, circa 1496–1498).

Manuscripts: No original or authorized manuscript exists of the *Mémoires*. Of the five extant manuscripts from the first half of the sixteenth century, all include a significant number of errors and lacunae. Two of these manuscripts have been, however, of particular interest editing the *Mémoires*. The first is Nantes, Musée Dobrée, ms. 18. Manuscript Dobrée (circa 1524) is the only manuscript version divided into books and chapters although these divisions were not always respected in subsequent printed editions; this elaborate manuscript, with its fourteen miniatures, has only the first six books of the *Mémoires*. The second important manuscript is Paris, Bibliothèque Nationale de France, nouv. acq. fr. 20960 (ms. Polignac), the only manuscript to comprise all eight books of this text and originally belonged to the niece of Philippe de Commynes, Anne de Polignac. Of the three other extant manuscripts, the ms. Montmorency-Luxembourg belonged first to Diane de Poitiers before entering into the private collection of the Montmorency-Luxembourg family; the other two are Paris, Bibliothèque Nationale de France, f. fr. 3979 and Bibliothèque Nationale de France, f. fr. 10156.

First publications: *Chronique et hystoire faicte et composée par feu messire Philippe de Commines* (Paris: Gaillot de Pré, April 1524); *Mémoires de Philippe de Commines,* edited by Denys Sauvage (Paris: Jean de Roigny, 1552).

Standard editions: *Philippe de Commynes: Mémoires,* edited by Joseph Calmette and G. Durville, 3 volumes (Paris: H. Champion, 1924–1925).

Edition in modern French: *Mémoires sur Louis XI: 1464–1483,* edited by Jean Dufournet (Paris: Gallimard, 1979).

Editions in English: Books 1–6 in *The Reign of Louis XI, 1461–83,* translated by Michael Jones (Harmondsworth, U.K.: Penguin Books, 1972);

The Memoirs of Philippe de Commynes, edited by Samuel Kinser and translated by Isabelle Cazeaux, 2 volumes (Columbia: University of South Carolina Press, 1969, 1973).

Celebrated as the first modern French historian, Philippe de Commynes not only recorded the political events surrounding the French court at the close of the fifteenth century; he also played an active role in them. The professional life of Commynes as political adviser and diplomat to the French king became the raw material of his writings; yet, he did not begin his career intending to become a writer but rather a man of action, a soldier, and a political agent. His *Les Mémoires* (The Memoires, circa 1489–1498), is the work of his later years when he was removed from the center of power, are a retrospective evaluation of battles, political intrigues, and most importantly, of the princes who shaped history. What Commynes began to write as a simple eyewitness account of the monarchy of Louis XI developed into a political and psychological analysis of the role of the prince and a guide for future leaders, a *miroir des princes* (mirror for princes). Commynes's work differs from that of his contemporaries in that it is in general devoid of mythological and historical allusions, chivalric portrayals of heroism, or the fulsome flattery of the court poet. His unembellished and, at first glance, simple style masks a complex and subtle work. The *Mémoires* are no mere descriptive chronology of events that the author was privileged to observe: they represent a study of political power and its effects on the men who possess it. Through an analysis of the different events and personalities of his day, Commynes searched for eternal truths that transcend a world ruled by political ambition and deception, a rational explanation for the triumphs and catastrophes he had witnessed.

Philippe de Commynes was born in Commines, Flanders, in about 1447 to an impoverished Flemish family of the lesser nobility. He was the only legitimate son of Colard van den Clyte and Marguerite d'Armuy-

Philippe de Commynes, after 1473 (anonymous chalk drawing, Musée d'Arras, France)

den. His mother died when he was an infant, and his father died six years later. Little is known of his childhood years, but they must have been a period of intense loneliness and financial instability. His father had been a knight of the Order of the Golden Fleece, and the bailiff of Cassel under Duke Philip the Good of Burgundy. Despite Colard's social standing, he died impoverished, and the family castle of Renescure was sold to pay debts. The orphaned Commynes went to live with his paternal uncle, Jean de Commynes, and received the traditionally limited education reserved for members of his class. At about the age of fifteen he began his career by entering the service of Charles, the count of Charolais, who was the son of Duke Philip (and would later become known as Charles the Bold). Commynes quickly rose in power and influence at the count's court, becoming a close adviser to Charles on many diplomatic and military missions for the house of Bur-

gundy. The prominence of Commynes at the ducal court was undoubtedly due to his ability and charm, for he had neither fortune nor powerful relatives to recommend him. In the duke's service he regained his father's family home and was known thereafter as the lord of Renescure. He also received the titles of knight, chamberlain, lord, and captain.

As an adviser to the duke, Commynes witnessed many important events, such as the battle of Montlhéry in 1468 and the brutal suppression of the revolt of Liège that same year, after Louis had incited the citizens to chase the duke's representatives from the city. The closeness between Charles and his adviser is demonstrated in the famous episode that transpired at Péronne, also in 1468. There Commynes reports sharing a bed chamber with the restive count and trying to soothe his rage against Louis XI, who had foolishly come to negotiate a peace treaty at Péronne, a town under the duke's control, without adequate protection. This potentially dangerous situation grew critical when Charles learned of Louis's alleged treachery in inciting the citizens of Liège to revolt, and in effect he took the king prisoner. Commynes saved the king's life by advising Louis to accept Charles's demand to accompany him with an army to Liège and put down the rebellion.

During the next four years Commynes continued in the duke's service and was entrusted with important diplomatic missions. For part, if not all of this time, he was playing a double game: pretending to serve Charles while secretly supporting the political machinations of the king. In 1471 Charles dispatched Commynes to Brittany to secure the loyalty of Duke François I in an alliance against Louis. From there Commynes traveled to Spain, purportedly on a pilgrimage to Santiago de Compostela. On the way he visited the king at Tours, probably to discuss his future defection from Burgundy. There he secretly accepted a pension of 6,000 livres, considerably more money than he was receiving from the duke. Deeply materialistic, Commynes strove his whole life to increase both his influence at court and his financial worth. In offering Commynes a sizable pension Louis correctly read the character of his future principal adviser.

The next year Commynes was horrified by Charles the Bold's barbaric behavior at Nesle, where the duke had the king's *francs archers* (regular soldiers) slaughtered after they had surrendered. His severe condemnation of Charles may have been partially motivated, however, by a desire to belittle the man he would soon betray, for during the night of 7 August 1472 Commynes secretly left the duke's service while stationed in Normandy. Whether he deserted his post in disgust at Charles's cruelty at Nesle or whether Louis's confiscation of the author's pension earlier that year ultimately provoked this decision is unclear. Charles must have taken his defection personally, for he never pardoned the former lord of Renescure as he did several other courtiers who abandoned him. Despite his betrayal of the Burgundian cause, Commynes always remained attached to his native Flanders and tried over the years to regain his father's lands.

Was Commynes's defection a betrayal or a career move, and to what degree did this act color his historical writings? The memoirs do not directly address these questions. Indeed, Commynes's relative silence on the issue—all he ever says about this watershed event is: "Environ ce temps, je vins au service du roy . . ." (About this time, I entered the king's service . . .)—only adds to an already ambiguous situation. In his many works on Commynes, Jean Dufournet treats this personal drama as the key to understanding the *Mémoires*. He points out the numerous cases of betrayal exposed in his work,

which he calls an "anthology of treason," and accounts for their frequency as a device for justifying Commynes's own defection by depicting his era as one in which courtiers were constantly being bought and sold. Other critics, such as Joël Blanchard, believe that desertion was much less an issue in a still-feudal France where intersecting and conflicting allegiances among vassals and lords were common. From this perspective, Louis as king of France was as much—if not more—Commynes's suzerain as was the duke of Burgundy.

Commynes was only twenty-five when he entered the service of the king. During the next four years his professional and financial fortunes both rose rapidly, and he became Louis's closest and most influential adviser, occupying a position roughly equivalent to that of prime minister today. Commynes also made an advantageous marriage on 27 January 1473 to a rich heiress, Hélène de Chambes. For the writer's service to the crown, Louis rewarded him with a sizable pension, several titles, and important properties. He was made lord of Argenton and prince of Talmont, a large income-producing territory in southwestern France. Louis XI had earlier seized Talmont on dubious grounds from the duke of Nemours, an action that would leave its legitimate ownership in question for many years after the monarch's death. After many legal battles and delays, this rich principality would be stripped from Commynes and given to the La Trémoïlle family.

The death of Charles the Bold on the battlefield of Nancy in 1476 signaled not only the end of Burgundy's hope for a unified and independent state but also the decline of Commynes's influence at the French court. Exactly why Louis decided at this time to replace him with other advisers is open to question; however, it appears that Louis wanted to distance the lord of Argenton from the Burgundian theater either because the king felt uncertain as to his loyalty or because he feared that Commynes the Fleming might act more out of regional interest than in the interest of France. In August 1478 Commynes was ordered to Poitou, far from Flanders, the primary sphere of political activity. Though Louis continued to appease his adviser's pride—for example, Commynes was inducted into the prestigious Order of Saint Michael—Commynes had no real power at court and was essentially living in exile.

During this time Commynes was sent to Florence on a diplomatic mission for the king. While in Italy, Commynes began a long and cordial relationship with the Medici family, in particular, with Lorenzo de' Medici, whom he held in high esteem. He was also exposed to the culture of Renaissance Italy. Blanchard argues that although humanist ideals in literature and art may not have had a direct influence on Commynes, the political and mercantile cultures of the Italian peninsula dramati-

Commynes's patrons, Louis XI and Charles the Bold (portrait of Louis attributed to Jean Fouquet, Brooklyn Museum, New York; anonymous portrait of Charles, Avignon Museum, France)

cally shaped his pragmatic and relativist view of power. During his missions to Florence and Milan, Commynes learned not only to speak Italian but also to appreciate the subtleties of Italian diplomacy and intricate banking practices.

On 30 August 1483 Louis died of apoplexy. Prior to his death the king recommended five of his most valued aides to his son's regents, his daughter Anne and son-in-law Pierre de Bourbon, seigneur de Beaujeu; Commynes's name was conspicuously absent. This omission doomed him to second-class status during the new regime. The usually prudent Commynes conspired against the monarchy with other dissatisfied and ambitious nobles, most notably Louis, Duke of Orleans (the future King Louis XII), as well as several foreign princes, including Richard III of England and Maximilian of Austria. Commynes, who had earlier decried Charles the Bold's disloyalty to the monarchy, now plotted in a similarly perfidious manner against the Beaujeu regency. He even conspired to kidnap the young king. The plot was thwarted, and Commynes, accused of lèse-majesté, was condemned to prison. He spent the first six months (January–July 1487) shackled

in one of Louis XI's infamous iron cages in the castle of Loches. He was then transferred to a dark, vermin-infested cell in the Conciergerie prison in Paris, where he was incarcerated until 24 March 1489. Upon his release he was exiled to his remaining property at Dreux.

Although this period of imprisonment and disgrace marks the nadir of Commynes's professional life, some critics, Jean Liniger in particular, suggest that it led to a deepening of his religious faith. According to Liniger, Commynes did not reflect on his own actions while imprisoned but pondered on the role of God in the political machinations of princes. Whether or not Commynes's confinement nurtured a mind already receptive to see God's hand in the rise and fall of monarchs is uncertain. It did, however, give him time to contemplate the events he had witnessed and to seek explanations for them. Shortly after his release he began writing the *Mémoires,* an examination of political ambition and maneuvering that would intermittently occupy him over the next ten years.

Commynes continued to try to regain his former position at court. In pursuit of this aim he arranged a marriage in 1491 between his only daughter and a Breton noble, a family relationship that brought him closer to Anne of Brittany, the next queen of France; however, it was not until 1494, when the young king Charles VIII decided to invade Italy to claim the kingdom of Naples, that Commynes was once again able to play a significant role on the political stage.

Commynes began the Italian campaign skeptical of the benefits that France could derive from such a military venture. He thought the king too inexperienced and under the influence of untrustworthy and unproven advisers. Commynes's mission was to prevent neutral Venice from aligning itself with France's enemies, but he failed, for Venice joined the Holy League, an anti-French alliance comprised of formidable foes: Aragon (Spain), the Holy Roman Empire, Milan, and the Papal States. The consolidation of France's opponents into one powerful force impelled Charles to abandon his enterprise in haste. Although the king avoided a military disaster, he had no tangible gains to show for his efforts, and Commynes could claim no reward for his services. At the peace treaty of Vercelli in July 1495, Commynes's efforts as the main French negotiator floundered again, for the agreement included only Milan and not the other members of the League. To aggravate the situation, the duke of Milan, Ludovico Sforza, entered into this treaty in bad faith and never had any intention of fulfilling its terms. The fiasco of the Treaty of Vercelli sealed Commynes's descent into obscurity.

After Charles VIII's premature death in 1498, Commynes's former conspirator, Louis of Orleans, became king. Although Commynes could not expect any special favor from the new monarch, whose cause he had deserted after his release from prison, through his daughter's marriage Commynes was able to gain the support of Charles VIII's widow, Anne, who had married the new king, thus becoming queen to two consecutive monarchs. The access Commynes had to the court was limited, however, and he died, relatively forgotten, at Argenton-Château on 18 October 1511.

Although probably completed by 1498, the *Mémoires* were not published until 1524, some thirteen years after Commynes's death. The prologue is addressed to Angelo Cato, the Neapolitan archbishop of Vienne who had served Louis XI as doctor and astrologer, and states that the work was written to provide information for a future life of the king in Latin. Commynes directly addresses Cato at various intervals in the *Mémoires,* and this use of apostrophe, coupled with a simple style, imbues the text with a conversational and personal tone. The absence of any literary pretensions separates the *Mémoires* from most other histories written at the time, but if an elegant style rife with poetic images is not

Commynes's prime objective, veracity and accuracy are. He explains that his work will contain nothing that he does not know personally to be true, and in pursuit of an objective picture of the past, he establishes from the outset his evenhandedness as a reporter and judge. Although he celebrates Louis as the most praiseworthy of all leaders he has known, he declares his intention to tell the unvarnished truth. He deflates the image of the ideal prince by emphasizing how difficult it is for any ruler surrounded by obsequious advisers to be consistently virtuous.

Commynes's insistence on truth even if it is unflattering separates his work from that of his Burgundian counterpart, Georges Chastellain, whose historical writings are encomiastic in nature, composed to raise the deeds of the dukes of Burgundy to the lofty realm of legend. Though some scholars have taken issue with Commynes's claim of neutrality, his history does have a modern tone, for the world presented in the *Mémoires* is not one of heroic deeds but a dark landscape of betrayal, doubt, and self-interest, where rulers are judged by their political successes, not by their bravery in battle or moral principles. The cynical realism that pervades the *Mémoires,* coupled with its unpretentious style, has attracted readers over the centuries, long after the chronicles of Chastellain became the domain of scholars.

The *Mémoires* function in large measure as a *miroir des princes,* a work from which future monarchs can observe the actions of past rulers and profit from a study of their errors and successes. In real life it did serve as an instructional book for Charles V, the great-grandson of Charles the Bold, an irony that would have probably intrigued Commynes. More than any other early French chronicler, Commynes tried to make his *miroir* an undistorted reflection of the real world in which facades are deceptive, truth elusive, and change inevitable. Unlike Chastellain's portrait of Philip of Burgundy, who remains constant and pure in substance and intention, the main actors in the Commynian universe are transformed by the vicissitudes of time.

Through an examination of the rulers and advisers he knew, Commynes searched for an understanding of the political world that resisted the assaults of change. In his *Seven French Chroniclers: Witnesses to History* (1974) Paul Archambault describes Commynes's world as one of "time, motion and sense [that] once stripped of its outer shell, reveals a structured, irreducible core of timeless truth." Though not trained as a clerk, Commynes saw books as preserving in concentrated form the experiences of many lifetimes. He constructs his history by isolating the causes and effects of political events and the psychological motivations of the players involved. He tries to identify ways of dealing success-fully and of getting the upper hand in personal relation-ships, especially diplomatic negotiations. The *Mémoires* are replete with long digressions in which Commynes dissects and judges the actions and actors he observed during his service. In her book *Commynes mémorialiste* (1975), Jeanne Demers argues that his use of the digres-sion is a kind of "verbal tic" that reveals the moralistic intent of the author. Through his asides of varying length Commynes is able to shade, interpret, and cate-gorize the events and people he knew.

The focus of the first six books of the *Mémoires* is the reign of Louis XI, the ruler who comes closest to embodying Commynes's ideal of the successful prince. In book 6 he sums up Louis's life by stating that: "Quelque grace luy feït Dieu, car comme il l'avoit créé plus saige, plus liberal et plus vertueux en toutes choses que les autres princes qui regnoyent avec luy et de son temps . . ." (God had endowed him with more sagacity, liberality, and virtue in all matters than any other prince who ruled at the same time as he.) It is through his memories and critique of this king that he constructs the image of the almost perfect ruler. The attributes of the wise prince derived from Commynes's portrayal of Louis in the *Memoires*, a flesh-and-blood human being, closely parallel Niccolò Machiavelli's hypothetical prince in his *Il principe* (The Prince, 1513). According to Kenneth Dryer, what distinguishes Machiavelli from Commynes is not the type of leader each admires but how each author approaches his subject. Whereas Machiavelli, the learned clerk, applies a theoretical per-spective to the political sphere, Commynes, the man of action, draws his knowledge from personal experience.

What traits did Commynes perceive as indispens-able for a successful ruler? First and foremost is *saigesse* (wisdom), a quality Louis possessed in abundance. The word *saige* (wise) and its adverbial form *saigement* (wisely) figure more frequently than any other significant word in the *Mémoires*. In his 1967 article on *saigesse*, Archam-bault explains that during the late fifteenth century the notion of *saige* acquired, in addition to its classical and moral sense, a secularized and even "neutrally moral" range. In the *Mémoires*, *saige* can signify not only wise and virtuous but also shrewd, cunning, and calculating, especially when employed in a political context. In praising Louis's *saigesse*, Commynes illustrates the prag-matic aspect of this trait:

> entre tout ceux que j'ay jamais congneu, le plus saige pour soy tyrer d'un mauvais pas en temps d'adversité, c'estoit le roy Loys unziesme, nostre maistre, et le plus humble en parolles et en habitz, qui plus travailloit à gaigner ung homme qui le povoit servir ou qui luy pov-oit nuyre. Et ne se ennoyoit point à estre reffusé une fois d'un homme qu'il pratiquoit à gaigner, mais y con-

tinuoit en luy promectant largement et donnant par effect argent et etatz . . . , il les rachatoit bien chere quand il en avoit besoing, et s'en servoit et ne les avoit en nulle hayne pour les choses passées.

> (Among all those that I have ever known, the one who knew best how to extricate himself from a bad situation was King Louis XI, our master, the most humble in speech and dress, who worked harder to win over a man who could serve him or cause him harm. He was not deterred by a refusal from a man he was trying to gain as an ally, but would continue to make him gener-ous promises and offer him money and lands . . . , he paid dearly to buy their loyalty when he needed them, and made use of them without any bitterness over past differences.)

Louis's *saigesse* is demonstrated in his dislike of war, not for its cruelty or immorality, but for its wasteful and capricious nature. In discussing the battle of Montlhéry in 1468, Commynes remarks on how, despite man's best efforts, battles are often won by chance. In a passage far removed from the chivalric ideal that had earlier cap-tured the medieval imagination, the glory of war is depicted at Montlhéry as not only illusory but deleteri-ous, for it was during this battle that Charles the Bold discovered his predilection for soldiering, a fascination that led to his ignominious end before the walls of Nancy and the near destruction of the House of Bur-gundy.

For Commynes, battlefields offer deceptive victo-ries as opposed to those achieved through diplomacy and the ability to read one's adversaries. Louis XI was an expert at the latter and made an art of identifying and exploiting the foibles of his enemies, taxing his sub-jects heavily in order to buy information from spies and to pay for the loyalty of advisers and informants at other courts. Even the king of England, Edward IV, received gifts from the French crown with the under-standing that he would abandon the cause of the Bur-gundians.

In the first five books of the *Mémoires*, Commynes contrasts the shrewd, perspicacious Louis with the stub-born, irrational Charles the Bold. Demers perceives the portraits of these two rulers as creating a diptych in which one panel represents Louis, the successful and *saige* ruler, and the other Charles, the failed and *fol* (fool-ish) prince. To a large extent it seems that Commynes has exaggerated these portrayals in order to create two diametrically opposed examples. Whether he did this to foster the political message of his work or, as Dufournet has suggested, to justify his own betrayal of Charles is a question that continues to intrigue critics and histori-ans.

Although Louis may have been the most laudable of the princes Commynes had known, he is far from a

Frontispiece from a manuscript for Commynes's Memoires, *depicting the author seated at the feet of the king of France and dictating the work to his secretary (Nantes, Musée Dobrée, ms. 18, fol. 1r)*

paragon in Commynes's work. Louis's ego foolishly placed him in the power of his enemy at Péronne, where only Commynes's wise counsel and the king's willingness to listen saved the monarch's life. In fact, Louis's weaknesses made his final moments on earth a purgatory, and book 6 describes in detail the last pitiful days of a once mighty monarch in a sort of case study in paranoia, as the king who spent his life expanding his territorial boundaries is now reduced to a small chamber in the barricaded castle of Plessis-les-Tours, surrounded by uncaring and self-promoting advisers. He is the willing victim of a greedy and callous doctor and cannot even trust his own son and heir. In order to keep his grip on the kingdom he maintains a reign of fear so that his subjects will know that he is still in command. Despite his illness, Louis clings to life with a pathetic ferocity. He tries to influence God through large gifts to the Church and even summons a holy man, St. Francis

of Paola, to come and pray at his bedside in the futile hope of extending his life a few hours. Louis's faith is rooted in suspicion and fear. In his portrait of a dying prince Commynes underlines the precariousness of a world where even the great can be reduced to a lowly and pusillanimous end.

The last two books of the *Mémoires* differ somewhat in style and function from the first six. With fewer digressions and in more elegant prose Commynes emphasizes the historical narrative of Charles VIII's Italian campaign rather than the psychological drama of the participants. In place of the mortal struggle between King Louis XI and Duke Charles, here a young, amiable, and ineffective King Charles takes center stage to head an armed expedition supported by largely inexperienced aides. Ill-prepared and poorly advised, the king is spared a monumental defeat only by the intercession of God. In Commynes's narrative, Charles is the Lord's instrument for dealing with the feuding Italian princes. This divine justification for the French descent into Italy is seconded by Girolamo Savonarola, whom Commynes met and admired while in Florence. The religious zealot explains that though God will save Charles from a terrible defeat, he will not give him victory, as the French king has failed to pursue the reform of the Catholic Church.

The role of God in the affairs of men continues to preoccupy the author's thoughts in the last two books. The God of Commynes is not an accessible and merciful father, but rather the great equalizer who keeps rulers in their place and establishes a balance of power in international affairs; he functions like a supreme feudal lord who keeps his vassals in line while he maintains order in his realm, and he has little to do with ordinary people, whose existence remains largely outside the scope of the *Mémoires*. In the earlier books Commynes asserts that Charles the Bold was punished by God for his vanity and egoism; it was God who upset his reason, bringing about his fall and with it that of the proud but decadent House of Burgundy. Although Commynes's analysis of political events is sophisticated, his theological interpretation is somewhat simplistic.

Unlike many late-medieval writers whose works were admired during their lifetimes but did not find a wide readership past 1550, Commynes has continually attracted an audience despite evolving historical and literary expectations. During the sixteenth century many editions and translations of the *Mémoires* were printed, and such prominent Renaissance writers as the essayist Michel de Montaigne and the poet Pierre de Ronsard praised Commynes the historian. Montaigne admired the impartiality and conversational style of the Lord of Argenton and cited him in his *Essais* (Essays, 1580). Ronsard, the leader of the elite French literary circle known as the Pléiade, shared Montaigne's respect for Commynes as a writer and historian. In an epitaph dedicated to Commynes he paints an idealized image of the soldier-writer who excels equally in the worlds of the sword and the pen: ". . . [le] premier gentilhomme/Qui d'un coeur vertueus, fit à la France voir/Que c'est honneur de joindre aus armes le savoir." (The first gentleman / who with a virtuous heart made France see / the honor of joining knowledge to soldiering.)

Commynes was generally esteemed throughout both the seventeenth and eighteenth centuries, though he had his detractors, notably Voltaire, who perceived him as a traitor and his writings as superficial. It was not until the nineteenth century, however, that Commynes the historian made his first appearance as a fictional character. In Sir Walter Scott's *Quentin Durward* (1823) the medieval writer is a protagonist in an historical novel that portrays the rivalry between Louis XI and Charles the Bold. Commynes the character is described as a clever and shrewd diplomat, yet a man vulnerable to the king's flattery. Commynes also appears as a character in the historically inaccurate play *Louis XI* (1832) by Casimir Delavigne. Of all the nineteenth-century readers of the *Mémoires*, perhaps the most influential and the most frequently quoted was the literary critic Charles Augustin Sainte-Beuve. It was he who dubbed Commynes a "Machiavelli en douceur" (a gentle Machiavelli) in one of his *Causeries du lundi* (Monday Chats, 1851). Sainte-Beuve brought the *Mémoires* of Commynes back to the forefront of literary debate and evoked the similarities between the Florentine theorist and the French historian.

One of the first purely political thinkers of the Western world, Commynes announced through his writings the advent of the modern secular age. His evaluation of the princes who shaped his era was remarkably free of the moral dogma and literary aspirations that characterized earlier works by French historians. He was the quintessential pragmatist who based his portrait of the wise king on policies he personally observed to be productive in purpose and efficient in outcome. His ideal prince is neither a protective father nor a heroic knight but a clever politician who surrounds himself with equally shrewd advisers and then listens to their counsel. Through his analysis of actual leaders Commynes isolated those traits and patterns of conduct that proved successful in the political arena and those that resulted in lost opportunities and failure, for in his world a handful of princes controlled the destiny of nations and their actions and attitudes fixed the fate of their subjects.

Letters:

Kervyn de Lettenhove, ed., *Lettres et négociations de Philippe de Commynes*, 3 volumes (Brussels: Matthieu Closson, 1867–1874);

Joel Blanchard, ed., *Commynes et les Italiens. Lettres inédites du mémorialiste* (Paris: Klincksieck, 1993).

Bibliography:

Albert Pauphilet, ed., *Historiens et Chroniqueurs du Moyen Age*, volume 2, Bibliothèque de la Pléiade no. 48

(Paris: Editions de la Nouvelle Revue Française, 1938), pp. 948–1448.

Biographies:

Jean Dufournet, *Vie de Philippe de Commynes* (Paris: Société d'Edition de l'Enseignement Supérieur, 1969);

Jean Liniger, *Philippe de Commynes* (Paris: Perrin, 1978).

References:

Paul Archambault, "Commynes' *Saigesse* and the Renaissance: Idea of Wisdom," *Bibliothèque d'Humanisme et Renaissance,* 29 (1967): 613–632;

Archambault, *Seven French Chroniclers: Witnesses to History* (Syracuse: Syracuse University Press, 1974);

Joël Blanchard, *Commynes l'européen, l'invention du politique* (Geneva: Droz, 1996);

Blanchard, "Commynes et la nouvelle histoire," *Poétique,* 79 (1989): 286–298;

Blanchard, "La moralité juge du pouvoir: théâtre et politique aux lendemains du règne de Louis XI," *Romania,* 109 (1988): 354–377;

William J. Bouwsma, "Commynes et la nouvelle histoire," *Poétique,* 23 (1951): 315–328;

Joseph Calmette and G. Périnelle, *Louis XI et l'Angleterre (1461–1483)* (Paris: Auguste Picard, 1930);

Gustave Charlier, *Commynes* (Brussels: Renaissance du Livre, 1945);

Jeanne Demers, *Commynes mémorialiste* (Montreal: Presses de l'Université de Montréal, 1975);

Kenneth Dryer, "Commynes and Machiavelli: A Study in Parallelism," *Symposium,* 5 (1951): 38–61;

Jean Dufournet, "Apropos des lettres inédites de Commynes à Gaddi," *Bibliothèque d'Humanisme et Renaissance,* 26 (1966): 583–604;

Dufournet, "Art et déformation historique dans les *Mémoires* de Philippe de Commynes," *Romania,* 90 (1969): 145–273;

Dufournet, *La Déstruction des mythes dans les "Mémoires" de Philippe de Commynes* (Geneva: Droz, 1966);

Dufournet, *Etudes sur Philippe de Commynes* (Paris: H. Champion, 1975);

Dufournet, *Philippe de Commynes, un historien à l'aube des temps modernes* (Brussels: DeBœck Université, 1994);

Dufournet, "Sur le texte des *Mémoires* de Commynes," *Revue des langues romanes,* 78 (1969): 97–108;

Dufournet, *Sur Philippe de Commynes: quatre études* (Paris: Société d'Edition d'Enseignement Supérieur, 1982);

Johan Huizinga, *The Autumn of the Middles Ages,* translated by Rodney J. Payton and Ulrich Mammitzsch (Chicago: University of Chicago Press, 1996);

Paul Murray Kendall, *Louis XI: "The Universal Spider"* (New York: Norton, 1971);

Michel de Montaigne, *Essais,* 4 volumes (Paris: Garnier, 1925);

Pierre de Ronsard, *Œuvres complètes de Pierre de Ronsard,* edited by Paul Laumonier, volume 6 (Paris: Garnier frères, 1930);

Charles Augustin Sainte-Beuve, *Causeries du lundi,* volume 1 (Paris: Garnier Frères, 1851);

Richard Vaughan, *Charles the Bold, the Last Valois Duke of Burgundy* (London: Longman, 1973).

Eustache Deschamps
(1340? – 1404)

Ian S. Laurie
Flinders University

and

Deborah M. Sinnreich-Levi
Stevens Institute of Technology

WORKS: Poems, including ballades, chansons royales, lays, pastourelles, rondeaux, sirventes, and virelays; and a work on prosody, *L'art de dictier,* and a work on marriage, *Le Miroir de mariage.*

Manuscripts: A unique complete manuscript containing 1,501 works has been preserved, as well as several partial manuscripts. Paris, Bibliothèque Nationale de France, f. fr. 840 was possibly commissioned within a few years of Deschamps's death and is the base text for all modern editions and translations. Paris, Bibliothèque Nationale de France, nouv. acq. fr. 6221, of the same family as Bibliothèque Nationale de France f. fr. 840, includes *L' Art de dictier* and 155 other pieces, the majority by or attributable to Deschamps; the balance to Guillaume de Machaut, Alain Chartier, and Oton de Grandson. There are also several lesser manuscripts, of which the most important are Bibliothèque Nationale de France, nouv. acq. fr. 6221; Bibliothèque Nationale de France, nouv. acq. fr. 6235; Bibliothèque Nationale de France, f. fr. 850; and Bibliothèque Nationale de France nouv. acq. fr. 20029, which includes two miniatures of Deschamps.

First publications: *Poésies morales et historiques d'Eustache Deschamps publiées pour la première fois,* edited by Eduard Crapelet (Paris: Crapelet, 1832); *Œuvres inédites d'Eustache Deschamps,* 2 volumes, edited by Prosper Tarbé (Paris: Techener, 1849); *Le Miroir de mariage,* edited by Tarbé (Reims: P. DuBois, 1865; Reims: Brissart-Binet, 1865; and in *Travaux de l'Académie de Reims,* 40 [1863–1864]: pp. 1–214); "Le Lay des douze estats du monde" and "Le Lay de vaillance," edited by Tarbé, *Travaux de l'Académie de Reims,* 47 (1867–1868): pp. 205–249; *Le Lay des douze estats du monde,* edited by Tarbé (Reims: P. DuBois, 1870); *Le Traicté de Getta et d'Amphitrion poème dialogué du XVe siècle,* edited by Auguste Henri Edouard (Paris: Librairie des Bibliophiles, 1872); "Quant reviendra nostre roy à Paris?" edited by Tarbé (Reims: L. Jacquet, 1849); *Specimens of Old French,* edited by Paget Toynbee (Oxford: Clarendon Press, 1892); "Variantes inédites de sept poésies d'Eustache Deschamps," edited by Jean-Claude Faucon, *Littératures,* 16 (Spring 1987): 139–151.

Standard editions: *Œuvres complètes de Eustache Deschamps,* 11 volumes, edited by Gaston Raynaud and Auguste Henri Edouard Sainte-Hilaire, Société des Anciens Textes Français (Paris: Firmin-Didot, 1878–1903; republished, New York: Johnson, 1966); "Le Miroir de mariage," edited by Monique Dufournaud-Engel, dissertation, McGill University, 1975; *L' Art de dictier,* edited and translated by Deborah M. Sinnreich-Levi (East Lansing, Mich.: Colleagues Press, 1994).

Eustache Deschamps is arguably the best and certainly one of the most prolific French poets of the fourteenth century. A disciple of the last great poet-musician, Guillaume de Machaut, Deschamps is the first major French lyric poet known to have dismissed the need for musical settings for his poems. He explains divorcing the lyric from music in *L' Art de dictier* (The Art of Poetry), the first book on prosody in French. His *Le Miroir de mariage* (The Mirror for Marriage), a discussion of the advisability of marriage, includes scenes worthy of Geoffrey Chaucer. Respected by his contemporaries for the range and wit of his many short works, yet demeaned by nineteenth-century critics, in recent years Deschamps has received critical attention both for his vivid glimpses of fourteenth-century life and for the vivacity and humor of his 1,500 poems.

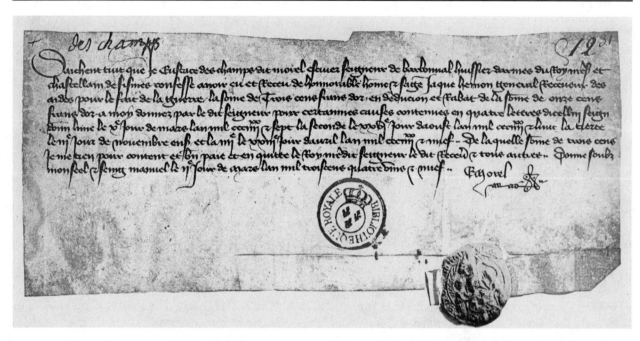

Legal document signed by Deschamps (Bibliothèque Nationale de France)

Born in Vertus in Champagne circa 1340, he was always referred to simply as Eustache Morel until 1389, by which time he had adopted the name Eustache Deschamps and claimed to be a nobleman. Less formally, he was probably called Eustache Morel for the whole of his life. His friend the poet Christine de Pizan calls him that in her verse epistle to him in 1404. The name "Deschamps" is connected with a property he owned near Vertus, but neither it nor the name Morel prove that he was born into the nobility. He may have had fairly humble origins and records in his Ballades 803 and 1199 that his enemies at court dismissed him as a mere cobbler. His family did, however, have the money to send him to Rheims and Orléans to study the trivium and law. In later life, he claimed to have wasted his time there in debauchery (in his Ballade 1105) and was never credited with a degree, even in the most formal documents. In Lay 310 he gives himself the title of "Magister," but in Ballade 878 he excuses himself for having little academic learning to recommend him. Given the fact that during his later career in the royal service he was a *bailli* (bailiff), an office that lies somewhere between that of a modern judge or magistrate and even has certain analogies to the post of a colonial governor of a small province, it is likely that he owed his successful career in the royal service to the authority given him by his poetry rather than to any academic qualifications or outstanding administrative skills. Still, many of his poems as well as *L' Art de dictier* reflect his study of the liberal arts, astrology, and law, or at least his observation of their practical applications.

Unfortunately, most of Deschamps's poems cannot be reliably dated. His *Geta et Amphitrion, Dit* (Geta and Amphitrion, Tale, 1494) may be an early work. It is based on Vitalis of Blois's twelfth-century work *Geta and Birria* or *Amphitryoneïde*. In this anti-Scholastic tract, ultimately derived from the work of Plautus, good sense is overruled in a simple mind when Scholastic reasoning takes over.

By 1365, if he is to be believed, Deschamps had already been appointed to his first official office, that of Emperor of the Society of Dreamers (*Fumeux*) at Vertus. This droll claim, sustained with all his legal learning in drafting constitutions (in Chartre 1398, written from Vertus in 1368), was to be typical of his poetry throughout his career: he was not inclined to take himself, his professional duties, his patrons, and even his own poetry with the humorless pomposity and arrogance of the career administrator. He was a juror of the count of Vertus (John Galeas Visconti, Duke of Milan) from 1367 until about 1370. When the count and his French wife, Isabelle of France, his first patrons, took Deschamps with them to Italy, it is probably because they liked his verse and his company rather than because anything on the trip involved his official duties.

More important posts followed: in 1368 he was appointed as an *escuyer* (squire) of Charles V, and later, under Charles VI, Deschamps was to remain in royal service for the rest of his life. It is not likely that he owed this post to his comic verse, and later (in 1396) he presented himself as having been something of an official court poet to Charles, with privileged entrée to state occasions that enabled him to write a chronicle in verse of the royal house. There is no way of testing this assertion, particularly since the chronicle, the *Livre de mémoire* (Book of Memory) as he calls it in his Ballade 1148, is now lost, although Deschamps may have recycled some parts of it into other works. He did, however, produce patriotic poetry in the 1370s, celebrating the victories of Bertrand du Guesclin in his Chanson Royale 362; condemning the lawless activities of Breton mercenaries in his Virelai (virelay) 735; claiming to have been one of the traveling companions of the chancellor, Jean de Dormans, in his Rondeau 662; and also presenting himself as having been in the service of the royal children, Charles and Louis, in their infancy (in his Ballades 1146, 1190, 1379, and 1459). He had become bailiff of Valois, in the service of Philippe d'Orléans by 1375, and, probably by 1378, *huissier d'armes* (royal sergeant-at-arms) of Charles V. This post gave him privileged personal access to the king, and Deschamps viewed it as being of critical importance in his career as a court poet. He was to retain this position under Charles VI, even after the king's first fit of madness in August 1392, and kept it until he retired two or three years before his death.

Deschamps had married by 1373 but lost his wife in childbirth in 1375 or 1376. The marriage produced at least three children, and Deschamps did not hesitate to use his verse, his administrative offices, and his personal wealth to advance their fortunes, making a request to the Pope for a benefice for his son Gilles in Ballade 1038, getting his other son Laurent appointed as his lieutenant when he later became bailiff of Senlis, and even lending his son-in-law money to get him out of debt on his wedding day in 1393, on which occasion he went to great lengths to praise his daughter and also his wife, who had died nearly twenty years earlier (in his Ballade 1151). He may have been the first author in French literature to have had positive things to say about his family in his verse. Also of interest are his sixty-some poems written in women's voices, remarkable for their sympathetic presentation of a sex whose voice was seldom heard favorably: unhappily married women, disgruntled nuns, a servant, ladies, bourgeois women, and peasants. Among the best poems are Ballades 1252, 1144, Virelays 751 and 752, and Virelay 554, "Sui je belle?" (Am I beautiful?).

The question of Deschamps's family is also critical in his relationship to Guillaume de Machaut, the greatest French poet and composer of his generation. Modern biographers, following a fifteenth-century tradition, sometimes state that Deschamps was Machaut's nephew. Deschamps made no such claim himself despite his stated ambition to inherit not only Machaut's position as the leading French poet of his day (as expressed in Ballades 123 and 124) but also Machaut's mistress, the

Péronne featured in Machaut's poem the *Voir Dit* (True Tale), 1365, after the great man died in 1377, the latter ambition expressed in Ballades 447 and 493. Deschamps did, however, point out in his Ballade 447 that Machaut befriended him, perhaps confusing later scholars. This close friendship has some independent confirmation in that Machaut entrusted Deschamps with a commission to present the *Voir Dit* in Bruges to Louis III of Flanders at some time between 1365 and 1377; Deschamps reported back, in his Ballade 127, that the work had a favorable reception there. How close this association was, whether Machaut actually tutored the young Deschamps as a poet, whether Deschamps sent him his works for comment, cannot now be known. Thematically, Machaut's verse was different from Deschamps's since it was largely confined to the courtly tradition. Metrically, however, Deschamps appears to have followed Machaut's example fairly closely, using in most of his verse the fixed forms of fourteenth century verse that, although largely created before Machaut, were nevertheless perfected and popularized by him. These forms, the most common of which are the ballade, chanson royale, virelay, rondeau, and lay, were admittedly much developed by Deschamps, notably with longer lines and strophes, the standardization of an envoy in the ballade and a refrain in the chanson royale. There is little here, however, that marks a significant break with Machaut. It is therefore possible that, at least at the early stages of his career, Deschamps viewed himself as Machaut's disciple.

Deschamps's career in the royal service from 1380 until his death in 1404 took him to many countries in Europe, notably to Italy and also to Eastern Europe, sometimes as an ambassador. He also accompanied his patrons on military campaigns against the English. His great contribution was that, unlike Machaut, he regularly included these experiences in his verse, thus greatly increasing the traditional thematic range of the French lyric. Much of this poetry is among the best comic verse in the French language. Deschamps could be generous in his praise of foreign cities, speaking favorably of Prague in his Rondeau 1330, but did not allow foreign travel to alter his view that all sensible people live in Paris (or at least in Senlis, according to Ballade 924). In his works he produces a colorful gallery of the people he met in Paris and in the course of his duties as bailiff at Senlis in Champagne. He also wrote much poetry of a moralizing kind, presenting himself as something like a prophet of doom, which has given him an unduly somber reputation.

In the course of Deschamps's travels in the royal service, he met and mentioned notables great and small, abroad and at home, including Enguerrand de Coucy, whose castle is of note for its decoration, described in Ballade 144 and Chanson Royale 383: a Salle des Preux

(Hall of the Nine Worthies) as well as a Salle des Preuses (Hall of the Nine Women Worthies), which were decorated with tapestries depicting these eighteen heroes. The vogue of the Nine Worthies had begun early in the fourteenth century; Deschamps may well have invented the female list which came to be popularized in poetry, tapestry, and courtly spectacle.

Deschamps also is significant in the separation of the French lyric from music. At least in theory, earlier lyric poets in the north and south of France had subscribed to the view that the lyric and music were indivisible; Machaut shared this view. Deschamps, however, in his *L' Art de dictier,* written in 1392, claims that music was an unnecessary complication to the private enjoyment of verse since, according to him, poetry has its own "natural music," superior to the "artificial," that is, instrumental variety, an inversion of the usual medieval definitions, and a view shared by most French poets ever since.

L' Art de dictier consists of two main parts: a treatise on the seven liberal arts and a prescriptive poetics. The liberal-arts section treats all of the arts except music very briefly. Grammar is noted for its antiquity and for being the tool by means of which all the other arts are studied. All the arts are presented with an eye toward their practical applications: logic helps produce subtle arguments, the ability to distinguish the truth, and men more skilled than their fellows; rhetoric, correct speech. Geometry is credited with multitudinous practical applications, from architecture to shipbuilding; arithmetic is useful to these as well as other professions, most notably coinage and moneychanging, and is also useful to those who are concerned with questions related to the passage of time; astronomy's applications are medical and agricultural.

The section on music is more than twice as long as the first six sections combined. Music is the "medicine" of the liberal arts, restoring those exhausted by the pursuit of the other sciences as well as those exhausted by hard work. Music is either natural or artificial. Artificial music consists of melodies produced either by instruments or the human voice, but natural music is lyric poetry. Although the two species of music are well suited to each other, Deschamps finds natural music superior since it cannot be learned unless the student is talented, and since it can be performed under more conditions than artificial music, for example, in the private chambers of lords and ladies, or before the ill for whom it is presumably therapeutic. The section on music concludes with a discussion of linguistics and euphonics.

The balance of the text is comprised of brief prescriptions for and examples of the composition of various genres of poetry. The genres discussed are the various forms of the ballade, the sirventes, the virelay, the rondeau, and the lay. Other genres mentioned include the chanson royale and the pastourelle. The description of the ballade provides an indication that Deschamps may have been the first to add envoys to ballades as had previously only been done with chansons royales. Deschamps also advocated the mixture of lines of odd and even numbers of syllables, that is, masculine and feminine lines, an innovation that became standard in French prosody and for which sixteenth-century writers are unjustly credited.

L' Art de dictier, written under duress at the request of a powerful patron whom Deschamps does not even name, can only have been intended for an educated audience—for people who, if not themselves poets, were conversant with poetic theory. It is a remarkable window into the mind of a practicing and respected fourteenth-century poet. Deschamps did not always follow his own prescriptions and left confused descriptions of some musical and poetic forms, even expressing impatience with the whole exercise, but *L' Art de dictier* is a valuable document nevertheless. Its most important feature is that it underlines the growing importance of poetry as written word, separate from musical or oral performance.

It may well be that the most significant aspect of Deschamps's literary career is the extent to which he turned what he claimed to have been the events of his own life into verse. If his major objection to instrumental music was that it made the purely private reading of poetry impossible, his expansion of the place of the author's private life in French poetry assumes its full significance. The question of how far his poetic persona corresponded with his real-life personality and experiences cannot be avoided, given the nature of much of his verse. Names of real people and places abound, and the details of journeys, complete with itineraries, dates, and traveling companions, are supplied. He was not above reminding his patrons of sums of money they had promised him, calculating the exact financial damages he had incurred when his house at Vertus was burned by an English raiding party, and even versifying his salary and privileges in his posts in the royal service. There is no reason to doubt that much of this detail corresponds fairly closely to the facts. It even offers some interest to social historians, who, earlier in this century, gave Deschamps more attention than literary scholars. What is more doubtful is the value it has as poetry and whether it is anything more than versified prose. Deschamps had the misfortune to be a compulsive writer, seizing even the most inappropriate moments to express himself, for example to rescue himself from the tedium of his own law courts, where he depicted himself as a clay idol. He must also have been a compulsive collector of his own verse, complaining about friends who borrowed manuscripts from him rather than making their own copies and, according to the copyists of Bibliothèque Nationale

Eustache Deschamps presenting his Double lai de la fragilité humaine *to King Charles VI of France, from a manuscript for the work (Bibliothèque Nationale de France, f. fr. 20029)*

de France f. fr. 840, the very large manuscript in which most of them now survive, he left many works among his papers after his death for his friends to find.

The resulting profusion of poems has not always been positive for his reputation in modern times. It is perhaps the sheer bulk of his output, coupled with its unevenness, which has discouraged some readers. Deschamps's collected works occupy nine volumes in the Société des Anciens Textes Français edition, 1,501 works of poetry and prose in all, some of which appear two or even three times, and some are difficult to categorize. The works include: 1,014 ballades, 138 chansons royales, 173 rondeaux, 84 virelays, 14 lays, 34 nonstrophic dits, 10 nonfixed form lyrics, and 11 pieces in Latin. There are also four prose works, one in Latin, of which the most important is *L'Art de dictier*. Deschamps also tried his hand at translations from Latin, versifying Pope Innocent III's *De contemptu mundi* (On Despising the World), which he presented to Charles VI in 1383 in the *Double Lai de la fragilité humaine* (Double Lay on Human Frailty, Lays 309 and 310), and *Geta and Amphitrion*. When one adds to this enormous output his enthusiasm for moralizing poetry of the kind that praises time past at the expense of time present, it becomes clear that no

medieval French poet ever stood in greater need of the services of a modern editor.

That said, no medieval French poet has left a better gallery of characters. Most of his best work is to be found in the short verse forms, notably in certain ballades and chansons royales as well as in some of the shorter *dits,* composed as comic letters in verse to his friends and patrons. His vision was, at its best, comic rather than condemnatory or moralizing. Some of it has a claim to offer, along with Villon, the most hallucinatory pictures in all of medieval French literature: peasants in Brie hopping like grasshoppers over their ditches into the fog to avoid answering his questions, hypochondriacs at court breathing hot spices on all who approach, Parisian women of fashion cataloguing their own charms, the grimaces made by diners at court, an analysis of the different styles of laughing, the exaggerations of urban politeness, the horrors of dining rooms and bedrooms in central European inns, and the endless miseries of senescence and disease. He found himself to be the most comic character of all, rejoicing in his own capacity for self-contradiction, aberrant conduct, and eccentricity; mocking his own poetry with as much good humor as his own posts in the administration. Some of his work, for example, his dialogue lyrics, which present arguments among many sections of society, from thieves and judges to peasants in the fields making satirical comments about French indecision in waging war against the English invaders, almost invite dramatic performance despite the fact that they operate within the chanson royale's tight grid of five strophes and an envoy.

Deschamps moved closer to the theater in a dit that the fifteenth-century copyists of Bibliothèque Nationale de France, f. fr. 840, called a farce in their table of contents: *Trubert et Antroignart* (Trubert and Antroignart, poem 1359). Its subject is the alleged theft of an almond from the property of a falsely gullible, rural confidence man who is outwitted by greater pretense at gullibility made by the vain, thieving lawyer hired to prosecute the case.

In his longest work, *Le Miroir de mariage* (poem 1498), incomplete in spite of its 12,103 lines and on which he was still working in 1404, the theme is whether the protagonist ought to consider getting married; the best passages, at least for most modern readers, are those in which the trials and tribulations of domestic life are presented as being at least as difficult for women as for men, couched as colorfully as any medieval French farce. The *Miroir* is one of the three works Deschamps left incomplete at the time of his death. (*La Fiction du lion* [The Lion's Story] and *L'Art de dictier* are the others.) It is an erudite, antifeminist tract in which allegorical figures debate the advisability of marriage. *Franc Vouloir*'s (True Heart) false friends, *Désir* (Desire), *Folie* (Madness), *Servitude* (Slavery), and *Faintise* (False Heart), urge marriage citing biblical reasons. *Franc Vouloir* is afraid of making a quick decision, but eventually expresses fervent hopes of finding a youthful, rich, obedient wife who will care for him in his old age and pray for his soul after his death; however, *Franc Vouloir*'s only true friend, *Répetoire de Science* (Fund of Knowledge), answers *Franc Vouloir*'s lingering doubts in a misogamist, misogynist disquisition rooted in classical arguments. Significant sections of this part are based on the continuation of the *Roman de la Rose* (Romance of the Rose) written by Jean de Meun, circa 1268–1285. The false friends then rejoin the discussion, which breaks off abruptly.

The most likable element in Deschamps's comic verse is that he found no character to be stranger, more self-contradictory, more eccentric than his own. He warned his readers that his political or moralizing verse had no practical effect on the course of events. Atypical for a public servant who survived in his offices until his death, he had no inclination to take himself or his duties too seriously. The liberty with which he expressed his discontent to his patrons, who included the king of France and his brothers, and the fact that he saw no reason not to rebuke them for what he saw as their errors of judgment or moral flaws are indications of the power conferred on him by his writing as well as a tribute to his character.

The question of Deschamps's influence is difficult to resolve. He certainly made it his business to make contact with other French writers, for example Oton de Grandson, Christine de Pizan, and possibly also Jean Froissart. It could be argued that his free importation of the details of his private life into the lyric and also his epistles in verse influenced Christine, but her tribute to him has nothing to do with such matters: in the verse epistle that she sent to the man she called her "cher maitre et ami" (dear master and friend) in 1404, to which he made courteous reply in Ballade 1242, her praise is for the weighty and moral elements of his work. One implication of Christine's judgment may be that the liberation of the French lyric from a musical accompaniment, defended in *L'Art de dictier,* had assisted this process of giving it more weight and substance since it was no longer confined to the status of a trite, conventional love song. After Christine, it is also possible that the great fifteenth-century poet Charles d'Orléans knew Deschamps's work if only because Deschamps had been closely affiliated with both Philippe d'Orléans and Louis d'Orléans from 1375 to 1404 and had also been a close friend of Louis's wife Valentina. If Charles indeed knew the work of his family's favored poet, any lessons he drew from it may have been negative as well as positive. The aesthetic distance between the presentation of Deschamps's private life in his poetry and its realities is often very small whereas in the works of Charles d'Orléans, it tends to be much greater and more elusive. Thematically, the two authors have little in common, although Charles's extraordinary miniatures in verse of peddlers and of young men rashly displaying their horsemanship are strongly reminiscent of Deschamps's poetry. There is, however, no sure evidence that Deschamps exercised such an influence any more than that François Villon, some of whose urban poetry is also reminiscent of Deschamps, knew his work. It may be that he had an influence on the fifteenth-century farce, in particular on the anonymous *Pathelin* (between 1456 and 1469), which presents some distant analogies with *Trubert et Antroignart.*

One of the more interesting questions concerns Deschamps's possible influence on foreign writers, notably Chaucer. Much has been written on this question, the consensus appearing to be that some of Chaucer's shorter poems may have been influenced by Deschamps's lyrics and that *Prologue to the Legend of Good Women* (circa 1385) may have been influenced by Deschamps's *Lay de franchise,* a work presented to Charles VI in May 1385. None of this is impossible, although one must have doubts that Deschamps's *Miroir de mariage* influenced Chaucer's *Merchant's Tale* and his *Wife of Bath's*

Prologue (circa 1387–1400) if for no other reason than that Deschamps, according to the copyists of the manuscript Bibliothèque Nationale de France f. fr. 840, was still writing the *Miroir* in 1404, four years after Chaucer's death. Chaucer may have seen early sections of the work, but there is no evidence that Deschamps was in the habit of circulating incomplete works. He did indeed send Chaucer copies of some of his works, probably in the 1380s, writing Ballade 285 to accompany them. There is no indication in this poem what these works were, but the idea that sections of an incomplete work such as the *Miroir* might have been included in this or other packages seems strained.

There is also the difficulty that Deschamps, in his "Ballade to Chaucer," does not assume the role of the greatest living poet: rather, with disarming authorial modesty and an irrepressible comic sense, Deschamps actually tells Chaucer that he feels he is worthy to be no more than a weed in Chaucer's own garden. Nowhere else, except in the case of his own master Machaut, does Deschamps adopt the role of awed disciple (as he did in Ballades 127 and 447, and in Lay 306). This is remarkable given that Deschamps was no older than Chaucer and that England and France were at war at the time. It is very possible that Chaucer may have been influenced by Deschamps, but it is equally likely that Deschamps learned from Chaucer and may even have had Chaucer's work before him while composing the *Miroir*. The astonishing thematic variety of Deschamps as compared with every other earlier French lyric poet and his extraordinary capacity to construct character lyrics, both of which altered French poetry permanently, may well have had at least some English roots. It is also possible that it may have had some Italian ones, but the question of whether Deschamps, who visited Italy several times, learned anything from Italian poets or even influenced them in his turn has never yet been the subject of systematic enquiry.

Deschamps was forgotten by the sixteenth century. Even his seventeenth-century descendants who used his title to nobility as a means to avoid taxation gave no indication that they knew his poetry. The lexicographer La Curne de Sainte-Palaye made a fair copy of the manuscript Bibliothèque Nationale de France, f. ff. 840 in the eighteenth century, largely for the linguistic and historical interest it provided. Nineteenth-century scholars who first edited Deschamps's work tended to use it as a means of defending traditional values, which they believed had been damaged by eighteenth-century Enlightenment and two or three French revolutions. In the twentieth century Deschamps's moral values won more blame than praise from his principal editor, Gaston Raynaud, as well as Johannes Huizinga in *The Autumn of the Middle Ages* (1919). However, Deschamps's work has been much admired in recent years for its historical and sociological interest. Deschamps's greatest claim to fame as a poet may well be that he constructs characters and situations with an immediacy and verve that restore life to a vanished society. He reinvented every genre he touched and was one of the most original as well as one of the most colorful French poets of the later Middle Ages.

Bibliography:

Deborah M. Sinnreich-Levi, ed., *Eustache Deschamps Fourteenth-Century Courtier-Poet, His Work and His World* (New York: AMS Press, 1998), pp. 253–267.

References:

Karin Becker, *Eustache Deschamps: L'etat actuel de la recherche,* Medievalia no. 21 (Orléans: Paradigme, 1996);

Jean-Patrice Boudet and Hélène Millet, eds., *Eustache Deschamps en son temps* (Paris: Publications de la Sorbonne, 1997);

Ernest Hoepffner, *Eustache Deschamps: Leben und Werke* (Strassburg: Trübner, 1904; republished, Geneva: Slatkine, 1974);

I. S. Laurie, "Deschamps and the Lyric as Natural Music," *Modern Language Review,* 59 (1964): 561–570;

Laurie, "Eustache Deschamps: His Life and His Contribution to the Development of the Rondeau, the Virelay, and the Ballade," dissertation, Cambridge University, Clare College, 1962–1963;

Ann McMillan, "Men's Weapons, Women's War: The Nine Female Worthies, 1400–1600," *Medievalia,* 5 (1979): 113–139;

Glending Olson, "Deschamps' *Art de dictier* and Chaucer's Literary Environment," *Speculum,* 48 (1973): 714–723;

Daniel Poirion, "Eustache Deschamps et la société de cour," in *Littérature et société au Moyen Age: Actes du colloque des 5 et 6 mai 1978,* edited by Danielle Buschinger (Paris: Champion, 1978), pp. 89–119;

Poirion, *Le poète et le prince: l'évolution du lyrisme courtois de Guillaume de Machaut à Charles d'Orléans* (Paris: Presses Universitaires de France, 1965; republished, Geneva: Slatkine, 1978);

Deborah M. Sinnreich-Levi, ed., *Eustache Deschamps Fourteenth-Century Courtier-Poet, His Work and World* (New York: AMS Press, 1998).

Jean Froissart

(circa 1337 – circa 1404)

R. Barton Palmer
Clemson University

WORKS: *Le Paradis d'Amour* (circa 1361–1362)

Manuscripts: Most of Froissart's poetical works, lyric as well as narrative, are preserved in two manuscripts devoted entirely to them and likely prepared under the poet's supervision for presentation to noble patrons. These are: Paris, Bibliothèque Nationale de France, f. fr. 831 (ancien 7215), generally assigned the siglum *A;* and Paris, Bibliothèque Nationale de France, f. fr. 830 (ancien 7214), generally assigned the siglum *B,* which is more complete than *A.*

First publication: In *Poésies de J. Froissart, extraites de deux manuscrits de la Bibliothèque du Roi et publiées pour la première fois,* edited by J. A. Buchon (Paris: Verdière, 1829).

Standard edition: In *Le Paradis d'Amour; L'Orloge amoureus* [de] *Jean Froissart,* edited by Peter Dembowski, Textes Litteraires Français no. 339 (Geneva: Droz, 1986).

Les chroniques de France, d'Engleterre, et des païs voisins (circa 1361–1400)

Manuscripts: A complex textual tradition, with several extant variants including probable authorial redactions. A useful description of the manuscript survivals is in Kervyn de Lettenhove's edition, I: 188–438.

Standard editions: *Œuvres de Froissart: Publiées avec les variantes des divers manuscrits—Chroniques,* 25 volumes in 26, edited by Kervyn de Lettenhove (Brussels: Devaux, 1867–1877); *Chroniques,* edited by George T. Diller (Geneva: Droz, 1971–).

Edition in modern French: *Chroniques: Jean Froissart,* translated and edited by Andrée Duby (Paris: Stock, 1997).

Editions in English: *The Chronicle of Froissart: Translated out of French by Sir John Bourchier, Lord Berners, annis 1523–25,* 6 volumes, edited, with an introduction, by William Paton Ker, The Tudor Translations nos. 27–32 (London: David Nutt, 1901–1903; republished, New York: AMS Press, 1967); selections in *Contemporary Chronicles of the Hundred Years' War: From the Works of Jean le Bel, Jean Froissart & Enguerrand de Monstrelet,* translated and edited by Peter E. Thompson (London: Folio Society, 1966); selections in *Chronicles: [by] Froissart,* translated and edited by Geoffrey Brereton (Harmondsworth, U. K.: Penguin, 1968).

Lyric Poetry:

Manuscripts: In *A* and *B.*

First publication: In *Œuvres de Froissart (Poésies),* edited by August Scheler (Bruxelles: Devaux, 1870).

Standard edition: *The Lyric Poems of Jehan Froissart: A Critical Edition,* edited by Rob Roy McGregor Jr., North Carolina Studies in the Romance Languages and Literatures no. 143 (Chapel Hill: University of North Carolina Department of Romance Languages, 1975).

Le Temple d'Honneur (circa 1363)

Manuscripts: In *A* and *B.*

First publication: In *Poésies de J. Froissart, extraites de deux manuscrits de la Bibliothèque du Roi et publiées pour la première fois,* edited by J. A. Buchon (Paris: Verdière, 1829).

Le Joli mois de Mai (circa 1363)

Manuscripts: In *A* and *B.*

First publication: In *Poésies de J. Froissart, extraites de deux manuscrits de la Bibliothèque du Roi et publiées pour la première fois,* edited by J. A. Buchon (Paris: Verdière, 1829).

Le Dit de la margheritte (circa 1364)

Manuscripts: In *A* and *B.*

First publication: In *Poésies de J. Froissart, extraites de deux manuscrits de la Bibliothèque du Roi et publiées pour la première fois,* edited by J. A. Buchon (Paris: Verdière, 1829).

Le Dit dou bleu chevalier (circa 1364)

Manuscript: Only in *B.*

First publication: In *Poésies de J. Froissart, extraites de deux manuscrits de la Bibliothèque du Roi et publiées pour la première fois,* edited by J. A. Buchon (Paris: Verdière, 1829).

Jean Froissart presenting a copy of his Chroniques *to Richard III of England (British Library, ms. Harley 4380 fol. 23)*

Le Debat dou cheval et dou levrier (circa 1365)

Manuscript: Only in *B.*

First publication: In *Poésies de J. Froissart, extraites de deux manuscrits de la Bibliothèque du Roi et publiées pour la première fois,* edited by J. A. Buchon (Paris: Verdière, 1829).

Standard edition: *Jean Froissart: "Dits" et "débats,"* edited by Anthime Fourrier (Geneva: Droz, 1979).

L'Orloge amoureus (1368)

Manuscript: Only in *B.*

First publication: In *Poésies de J. Froissart, extraites de deux manuscrits de la bibliothèque du Roi et publiées pour la première fois,* edited by J. A. Buchon (Paris: Verdière, 1829).

Standard edition: *Le Paradis d'Amour; L'Orloge amoureus,* edited by Peter Dembowski, Textes litteraires français no. 339 (Geneva: Droz, 1986).

L'Espinette amoureuse (circa 1369)

Manuscripts: In *A* and *B.*

First publication: In *Poésies de J. Froissart, extraites de deux manuscrits de la Bibliothèques du Roi et publiées pour la première fois,* by J. A. Buchon (Paris: Verdière, 1829).

Standard edition: *Jean Froissart: L'Espinette Amoureuse,* edited by Anthime Fourrier, revised edition (Paris: Klincksieck, 1972).

La Prison amoureuse (circa 1372–1373)

Manuscripts: In *A* and *B.*

First publication: In *Poésies de J. Froissart, extraites de deux manuscrits de la bibliothèque du Roi et publiées pour première fois,* edited by J. A. Buchon (Paris: Verdière, 1829).

Standard edition: *Jean Froissart: La Prison Amoureuse,* edited by Anthime Fourrier (Paris: Klincksieck, 1974).

Edition in English: *La prison amoureuse = The Prison of Love,* translated and edited by Laurence de Looze, Garland Library of Medieval Literature no. 96 (New York & London: Garland, 1994).

Le Joli buisson de jonece (circa 1373–1374)

Manuscripts: In *A* and *B.*

First publication: In *Poésies de J. Froissart, extraites de deux manuscrits de la bibliothèque du Roi et publiées pour première fois,* edited by J. A. Buchon (Paris: Verdière, 1829).

Standard edition: *Jean Froissart: Le Joli Buisson de Jonece,* edited by Anthime Fourrier, Textes litteraires français no. 2 (Geneva: Droz, 1975).

Edition in modern French: *Le joli buisson de Jeunesse: Jean Froissart,* translated by Marylene Possamai-Perez, Traductions des classiques français du Moyen Age no. 57 (Paris: H. Champion, 1995).

Méliador (after 1373)

Manuscript: The text is preserved in one manuscript: Paris, Bibliothèque Nationale de France, f. fr. 12557; some fragments are in Paris, Bibliothèque Nationale de France, f. fr. 2374.

First publication: *Méliador: Roman comprenant les poésies lyriques de Wenceslas de Bohême, duc de Luxembourg et de Brabant,* 3 volumes, edited by Auguste Longnon, Société des Anciens Textes Français no. 36 (Paris: Didot, 1895–1899).

Le Dit dou florin (circa 1388)

Manuscript: Only in *B.*

La Plaidoirie de la rose et de la violette (after 1388?)

First publication: In *Poésies de J. Froissart, extraites de deux manuscrits de la Bibliothèque du Roi et publiées pour la première fois,* edited by J. A. Buchon (Paris: Verdière, 1829).

Standard edition: *Jean Froissart: "Dits" et "débats,"* edited by Anthime Fourrier (Geneva: Droz, 1979).

Jean Froissart was a noted poet and chronicler from northern France who thrived on the patronage of the wealthy and famous. Froissart came from a bourgeois family of limited means—or so one may surmise from the brief autobiographical indications in the poems and chronicles that constitute the most important surviving evidence for the course of his life. Born in Valenciennes, probably in 1338 (the poet's own testimony is inconsistent), Froissart received there the education for a clerical career; however, his literary and personal talents turned

him away from a life in church administration. Sponsored by Jean de Beaumont, the brother of the count of Hainaut, Froissart was recommended to their niece, Philippa of Hainaut, then queen of England, and Froissart went to the English court in 1361. Though still a comparatively young man, he had already achieved some literary success under the patronage of Robert de Namur, Lord of Beaumont, who had commissioned him to write about the hostilities between France and England, especially the battles of Crécy and Poitiers.

Philippa evidently found pleasing the service of her countryman (she had also been born in Valenciennes), for after a brief return to Hainaut, Froissart was engaged as the queen's secretary, a post he occupied until her death. His position as secretary afforded Froissart two opportunities of which he took full advantage: the leisure to write verse, for which the court provided an appreciative audience; and the chance to travel on official business. During this period Froissart journeyed to Scotland to meet King David II and visited other parts of what is today the United Kingdom. He also returned to the Continent on several trips; on one trip to Brussels he met his future patron and literary collaborator, Duke Wenceslas of Brabant. Froissart also met and traveled with Edward, the Black Prince (son and heir apparent of Edward III of England), later accompanying the royal party to Milan for the marriage of Lionel, Duke of Clarence.

Froissart was in Brussels when he learned of Philippa's death in 1369. Determining to remain on the Continent where he enjoyed the generosity of many noble protectors, Froissart entered holy orders and became the pastor of Lestines, a small town in Hainaut. His connection with Wenceslas, resident not far away, grew stronger, and in 1381 Froissart became the duke's secretary, beginning collaboration on *Méliador* (a work already in progress), whose completion in 1384 Wenceslas did not live to see, having died the previous year.

Froissart, however, found another noble employer in Guy de Blois, whose chaplain he soon became, abandoning the rectorate at Lestines and acquiring, with Guy's assistance, a position as canon in Chimay, a town nearby. Freed from daily church duties, Froissart resumed his travels, visiting, among other places, Avignon, Auvergne, Bruges, and Paris. He also worked constantly on the *Chroniques* and prepared a manuscript of collected poems he intended to present to Richard II of England. The meeting between poet and king took place in 1395, with Froissart richly rewarded by Richard for his literary efforts. Returning to the Continent, Froissart spent his last years in residence at Chimay. Though the exact date is unknown, he probably died not many years after the death of Richard in 1400.

Froissart is best known to modern readers as a historian rather than a literary figure. Froissart, in fact, holds the distinction of being the author of the only medieval chronicle that is today still widely read and admired: *Les chroniques de France, d'Engleterre, et des paїs voisins* (The Chronicles of France, of England, and of Neighboring Countries, circa 1361–1400), an immense work usually referred to simply as Froissart's *Chronicles*. Incorporating and continuing earlier accounts by Jean le Bel, the *Chronicles* narrates a wide sweep of northern European history, from 1325 to about 1400, and are perhaps most famous for their accounts of important events in what modern historians term the Hundred Years' War. Unlike many other medieval works of this type, Froissart's text has an unmistakably personal, often idiosyncratic style. This is because the *Chronicles* relies less on documents than on the writer's experiences as servant of the wealthy and influential as well as reports he diligently obtained from reliable informants. The result is a vivid, detailed, and lively portrait of an aristocratic world, many of whose luminaries the historian knew personally. Though not of noble birth himself, Froissart reflects the values of the aristocracy, especially the attempts of some to restore to practice and eminence the chivalric tradition, which was fast becoming a code of behavior unsuited to contemporary circumstances. His history shares with that of Jean le Bel a desire to glorify noble deeds regardless of political allegiance rather than, as do other chroniclers of the period, to shape the reporting of events for the cause and interests of a particular dynasty. With their universal, frankly ideological outlook and their detailed accounts of important events, the *Chronicles* has proved fascinating to many generations of readers since their original publication in Froissart's own time. Perhaps more than forty years in the making, the *Chronicles* is an immense work with a complicated textual history, including several installments and, for some of these, several different redactions overseen by the author himself. The somewhat unwieldy nature of the *Chronicles* reflects in part Froissart's enthusiasm for the task—which he quite freely proclaims—and his aims: to delight and entertain the same noble audience he thought would appreciate his poetry; and, perhaps more important, to leave behind a full, accurate record of those deeds he, along with his readers, thought worthy of both emulation and memorial. Thus the *Chronicles* do not attempt, as a modern history might, an overall analysis of the period itself, with discussion of "trends" and "developments." Instead Froissart imagines the unfolding passage of time as a canvas upon which the noble have the opportunity to inscribe their courage and worthiness; the vicissitudes of the intermittent war between the French and English, for example, are not worth recording as "events" but as the settings for notable feats of arms and gallantry.

To fulfill these aims required a narrative in some depth, not a simple outline of facts. Despite the title

Illumination from a manuscript for Froissart's Chroniques, *depicting civil unrest during the Hundred Years' War (British Library, ms. Harley 4379, fol. 12b)*

accorded his writing, the work is not a "chronicle" properly speaking, but a history; yet, if his account were to be as true as he could make it (a quality whose importance Froissart often emphasizes), he would have to spend no little energy in collecting reliable accounts of those important events at which he had not been personally present. Froissart appears to have done so and, in fact, often mentions the sources he used: all people with a story to tell, in an age that possessed no research libraries. His many travels on behalf of his various patrons facilitated this work, which for the curious and inquisitive Froissart was self-evidently a labor of love. Those he talked to were principally men, for despite his service to Philippa, Froissart's history is an elaborate account of aristocratic male accomplishment. Only seldom do other subjects intrude. He has something to say about the papal schism that was a major event in the century's last decades, but only insofar as it impinges upon the noble realm of virtue and accomplishment. Though himself a priest, he in fact mentions religion only in passing, generally whenever the proper characterization of a worthy knight requires an account of his piety. The common people figure only fleetingly in his account, most notably in the Peasants' Revolt of 1381, an event with important consequences for the nobility who were his readers.

Despite his unwavering loyalty to patrons personal and literary, Froissart deals fairly with John Ball, the mad priest who speaks convincingly in Froissart's pages of the oppression felt by many commoners. Although different redactions evidence a slight national bias (which varies, depending on who was Froissart's patron at the time), the *Chronicles* treats the battles, campaigns, and tournaments that are their main subject matter with remarkable evenhandedness. Throughout, Froissart is true to his own stated aim to recount in an edifying way the admirable deeds of a warrior caste that was truly international. It is this wide scope, frankly ideological, that contributed the most to the work's enduring popularity.

Froissart, however, was also much celebrated by his contemporaries for a different kind of writing, one not as well known to his modern readers. By the end of his life Froissart had become one of the most noted and prolific poets of French-speaking Europe, and to judge from the two surviving omnibus manuscripts of his poetry (one of which is either the presentation copy intended for Richard II of England or a copy of that book), he succeeded in finding readers among the nobility. Like many of his contemporaries, including Christine de Pizan and Eustache Deschamps, Froissart was heavily influenced by the example and works of the century's most famous French poet-musician, Guillaume de Machaut. Although Froissart apparently composed no music, he devoted much literary labor to continuing two other traditions Machaut had advanced and popularized. The first was lyric verse in more or less elaborate fixed forms, of which Froissart wrote a substantial corpus: 13 lays, 6 chansons royaux, 40 ballades, 13 virelays, 20 pastourelles, and 107 rondeaux. Froissart also wrote twelve *dits amoureux* (love narratives), most with a strong allegorical component, that treat *fin'amors* (refined love) and utilize and often explore conventions first developed in the thirteenth-century masterpiece *Le Roman de la Rose* (The Romance of the Rose).

Froissart also was interested in another, earlier tradition, that of verse romance with Arthurian themes, the kind of poetry made most famous by the twelfth-century writer Chrétien de Troyes. *Méliador,* Froissart's contribution to this genre, is an enormous work, more than thirty thousand verses in length, that took the poet more than two decades to complete. Though Froissart connects his story of a knight who exemplifies the highest aspirations of the chivalric life with an Arthurian milieu derived from earlier literary traditions, the poem is most unusual in consisting largely of story elements that were Froissart's own invention and, like the *Chronicles,* the poem reflects his wide experience in the world of politics. *Méliador* also offers an extraordinary form of collaboration between the poet and his patron, Wenceslas of Luxembourg, Duke of Brabant: some seventy-nine of the nobleman's lyric poems are inserted into the narrative.

Nineteenth-century scholars generally dismissed authors of the later Middle Ages as overly conventional and mannerist imitators, who, lacking originality or talent, simply recycled familiar conventions and themes. In fact, such a characterization is unfair and inaccurate; the many poems Froissart produced are often strikingly original. In particular, his works offer interesting variations on and reworkings of traditional material (largely derived from the *Roman de la Rose*), and also of contemporary works devoted to *fin'amors*. Although his lyric production by no means lacks value or interest, his narrative works are undoubtedly more significant.

At the beginning of his career, however, Froissart was interested not only in chronicling the grand and regrettable great events of his time, but in composing the light allegorical verse narrative then so popular with aristocratic audiences and readers. Nothing could be further from the grim realities of Richard's dethronement and subsequent miserable death in prison than the ideal setting and characters of *Le Paradis d'Amour* (The Paradise of Love, circa 1361–1362), probably composed for Philippa of Hainaut soon after Froissart's installation at court, though it may have been written a year or so earlier, just after the manuscript publication of Machaut's *Dit de la Fonteinne amoureuse* (Story of the Fountain of Love, 1361), to which it is extensively and obviously indebted. The poem is a well-conceived mixture, like its model, of narrative and lyric (1,252 verses in octosyllabic couplets and six lyric inserts, namely a complainte (complaint) and lengthy lai, two rondels, a virelai, and a ballade). In structure, the *Paradis* closely resembles Machaut's *Fonteinne amoureuse*. The poem's narrative design, however, derives more from Machaut's initial composition in the *dit amoureus* (tale of love) genre, *Le Dit dou vergier* (Story of the Orchard, 1330), a bildungsroman of the love experience in which a young man has a revelatory vision and therein learns from allegorical personifications about the nobler aspects of a lover's life.

Froissart provides an allegorical cadre of some complexity and finesse. The *Paradis* relates the adventures of an unhappy young lover who finds himself in the traditional *locus amoenus* (pleasant place, a literary topos) of love-vision poetry, a pleasant springtime paradise that does not soothe him because of his sorrow over his love affair. Aided by *Dame Esperance* (Lady Hope) and *Dame Plaisance* (Lady Pleasure), the young man, who has blasphemously adjured the teachings of the god of love, is reminded of the god's power. In the company of famous medieval and classical lovers and his allegorical guides, the young man rededicates himself to love's service and is welcomed by his lady under the guise of her most characteristic virtue—*Biel Aquel* (Fair Welcome). The lover

Froissart (second from left) being shown where the wall of the town of Cazeres was breached during a battle (from F. S. Shears, Froissart, Chronicler and Poet, *1930)*

convinces her readily that all he wishes is to serve her and have her speak to him. In the presence of his two mentors, he then sings a virelay expressing his gratitude for their help in this love affair. *Esperance,* no longer needed, then departs, and the lover, greatly moved, sings a ballad in honor of the *marguerite* (daisy), as the lady weaves from the same flowers a wreath they in turn kiss and place on his head. The couple leave in eagerness to enjoy themselves elsewhere, but the dreamer, startled by joy, at this moment awakes.

Though in large part derived from several *dits* of Machaut, the *Paradis* differs substantially from its immediate sources in developing and maintaining a coherent and interesting allegorical cadre, providing in the process a charmingly reduced version of the lover's progress from immaturity to satisfaction as detailed in the *Rose.* Froissart uses this traditional form to depict a lover whose ultimate success derives largely from his abilities

to give his emotions a correct and pleasing lyric form. The lyrical inserts are recited at crucial points in the narrative. As in Machaut's *dits,* the lover is the poet's intratextual alter ego; by implication, the poem itself is then not so much a story as a performance, the proof of the author's finesse and talent. Significantly, five of the six lyrics are favorably commented upon by characters within the story world, modeling the reaction the poet must have hoped to receive from his aristocratic hearers and readers.

While in Philippa's service Froissart composed several shorter narrative poems, all indebted, more or less, to either Machaut or other poets who worked within the *dit amoureus* genre. None of these is as accomplished as the *Paradis.* The longest (1,076 octosyllabic couplets) is *Le Temple d'Honneur* (The Temple of Honor), an occasional piece most likely written to help celebrate the marriage in May 1363 of young Humphrey X of Bohun, one of the great lords of England. Suiting its occasion, the poem is in effect a *regimen principum* (guide for princes), though Froissart offers the code of conduct for an ideal lover (this accords, in part, with the then-current truism that the noble person should occupy himself with two matters: arms and love). Significantly, the manuscript rubrics identify the poem as a *trettié de moralité,* literally, a moral treatise (though Froissart does elsewhere use *dit* or *ditté* more or less interchangeably with *trettié*). The poet-narrator recounts a dream in which he is invited to a feast where Honor has arranged for the marriage of his son Desire to Pleasure, whose father is Courtesy. The narrative gives way to allegorical exposition of the fourteen virtues (Humility, Bravery, Justice, Good Manners, Charity, Pity, Faith, and so on) that guide the behavior of perfect lovers. Honor proceeds to explain the male virtues to the bridegroom and, subsequently, the female virtues to the bride. After this ceremony the poet gets a good look at the happy couple, whom he thinks he recognizes; however, as it is now morning he wakes up before he can be certain. Although by no means profound or formally complex, the *Temple d'Honneur* manifests Froissart's virtuosity in adapting the matter of *fin'amors* to its occasion, producing an interesting "doctrinal" epithalamium in the process.

Le Joli mois de Mai (The Pretty Month of May) is a much shorter (464 lines) and less ambitious work, probably composed in 1363. On a May morning the narrator enters a beautiful garden filled with flowers where he listens to the pleasant song of the birds. He sings two ballades and a virelay of his love for his lady, promising her his undying service, and comparing his happiness to the new season. Here the narrative is little more than a setting for a group of lyrics, a formal structure much unlike the *Paradis,* where the lyrics are integrated into a more complex narrative. The *Joli mois de Mai,* though a poetic meditation on the conventional theme of *reverdie* or "re-greening," is dominated by lyric rather than narrative features. The most important of these is its ingenious and complex strophic form; similarly, the lyrics are of an intricate, unusual design. *Le Dit de la margheritte* (The Story of the Daisy, 1364) is also barely narrative; its 192 lines offer little more than an extended praise of the daisy and the lady named for the flower. Froissart here continues a specific poetic type created by Machaut, whose two *marguerite* poems were composed for noble patrons (the form enjoyed an even wider popularity, with, among other continuators, Geoffrey Chaucer). Froissart shows considerable originality in inventing a kind of mythology (based on classical motifs he likely found in Ovid) for the flower, and *Le Dit de la Margheritte* testifies to his developing interest in classical mythology and its usefulness for instructive poetic exempla, an enthusiasm and poetic practice he shares with Machaut and other writers of the time.

Froissart's next effort, composed perhaps a year later, was *Le Dit dou bleu chevalier* (The Story of the Blue Knight), which returns to the thematic and storytelling concerns of the *Paradis.* As in his first narrative work, Froissart is again here much indebted to Machaut, particularly the older poet's famous and popular *Fonteinne amoureuse.* Froissart's innovation (highly influential on Chaucer, who used this work in composing *The Book of the Duchess,* circa 1368–1369) is to deepen the relationship between the two interlocutors, a sorrowing nobleman and a sympathetic poet-narrator, who discuss the nature of the nobleman's feelings and loss. The narrator assumes a traditionally clerical role, advising his chance companion to resist the hardships Fortune brings. The sorrowing man asks the narrator to transform their adventure into a book that the lady will perhaps read or listen to and thus learn of his love and devotion. Froissart replaces the traditional divine figure who offers consolation with the poet-narrator, his alter ego, whose well-known and appreciated writing is granted the power to celebrate and therefore mitigate the love sorrows of his patron.

The last short (92 lines) narrative poem from the period of Froissart's service to Philippa enjoyed more favor in the nineteenth century than his other poetry, primarily because of its amusing blend of real and traditional elements. Composed toward the end of 1365, *Le Debat dou cheval et dou levrier* (The Debate between the Horse and Greyhound) uses a real event–Froissart's journey back from Scotland with the royal party–as the setting for a *conflictus,* a debate between opponents, who are sometimes people but usually animals or inanimate objects, over the relative merit of their qualities. The *conflictus* is one of the oldest of medieval forms, with its origins in Virgil's *Eclogues* (circa 42–37 B.C.) and Latin school verse of the Carolingian period. Froissart demonstrates some familiarity with this tradition, as witnessed by the pithy and sharp repartee contained in the dialogue, as the two animals of this *conflictus* debate the difficulties of their voyage with Froissart. More like the Latin than the vernacular examples of this genre, the poem is witty, sophisticated, and subtle–a masterpiece of sly humor.

Froissart's next major work, probably finished not long before Philippa de Hainaut's death in 1369, abandons the love-vision genre for a tour de force of allegorical exposition. Unlike the *Paradis,* which has strictly literary sources, *L'Orloge amoureus* (The Clock of Love, 1368) was inspired by the poet's own experience. Froissart's post as Philippa's secretary did not preclude him from traveling, and during several visits to Paris, he had the opportunity to examine what was fast becoming one of that city's most notable attractions: a huge clock with a bell mechanism Charles V was having built in his palace tower by the German craftsman Heinrich von Wieck. The project took nearly eight years to complete and was not finished until

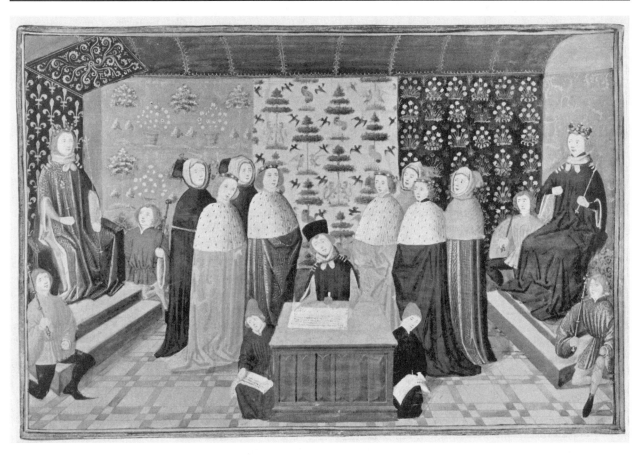

Signing of a treaty between France and England that brought about a temporary truce in the Hundred Years' War (illumination from a manuscript for Froissart's Chroniques*, British Library, ms. Harley 4380, fol. 10b)*

1370, but would have been largely operational by 1368 when Froissart visited the city during a truce in the hostilities between France and England. The poem was likely written soon afterward. In a sense, the *Orloge amoureus* is a tribute to both the clock and the poet's understanding of its intricate workings (which are so faithfully rendered that the text is important for the history of clockmaking); yet, the purpose of the *Orloge* is not so much to describe a notable object as it is to exemplify the poet's ingenuity in developing and sustaining at some length an unlikely, but ultimately revealing analogy between the Paris clock and himself as a lover. Love forces him to see the appropriateness of this comparison, he says, and desire for his lady encourages him to set it into verse.

At times somewhat forced and strained, Froissart's development of the clock analogy is nonetheless often ingenious and striking; the poem offers a startlingly original reanimation of the thematic conventions, the "doctrine" of late medieval poetry. The *Orloge* is a bravura production, a performance that demonstrates the poet's abilities to work competently within an unlikely and difficult format of his own choosing. Even formal structure and versification are adapted to the purpose at hand.

Froissart eschews lyric inserts and employs a decasyllabic line more suited because of its length to the detailed, technical description the subject requires.

Froissart's next major work, *L'Espinette amoureuse* (The Hawthorn Bush of Love, circa 1369), abandons this static, allegorical description for a novelistic account of an affair the narrator confesses was his introduction to the experience of love. The work's obvious debts to Machaut's *Fonteinne amoureuse* and *Le Livre dou Voir-Dit* (The Book of the True-Tale, circa 1363–1365) are to some degree an homage to an acknowledged master; however, these recycled motifs also effectively mark out the quite different emphases and themes Froissart pursues. The young narrator, daydreaming under a hawthorn bush, imagines himself as a judge in a classical beauty contest, selecting among the goddesses Juno, Venus, and Pallas. The narrator's selection of Venus is rewarded by the goddess, who promises him the love of a woman even more beautiful than Helen.

In the *L'Espinette amoureuse* the dream sequence sets the emotional stage for a relationship in the waking world whose complex, realistic vicissitudes take the lovers far from the idealized, conventional doctrines and practices of dream vision. The promise of Venus is fulfilled: the narrator meets a beautiful young woman. They exchange gifts, a lyric, and a rose. The lover, encouraged by his confidante, one of the lady's women friends, continues to seek out the lady even as he begins to suffer the ills of lovesickness. He journeys abroad, hoping to mend his health, carrying the lady's mirror, a gift from his confidante. He thinks he sees his lady's face in the mirror and relates in some detail the story of Papirus and Idorée, drawn from Ovid. He dreams that his lady addresses him from the mirror, with a long *reconfort* or lyric consolation, and he replies with a virelay. Emboldened, he returns home, but even multiple meetings with his lady do not advance his cause.

Although shaken by the sudden death of his confidante he continues his suit, and the next May finds the pair under the flowering hawthorn bush where they exchange vows of love. Their happiness is threatened by an older woman, *Male Bouche* (Evil Tongue), who does her best to frighten off the poet-narrator. A final and ambiguous meeting ends the narrator's tale of the relationship. Meeting the lady by chance, the narrator greets her and is rebuffed; however, shortly thereafter she passes by his side, smiling as she embraces him and grasps his head by the hair, pulling out some and, without saying a word, going back inside her dwelling. The lover is unsure of the meaning of this gesture, but concludes that the lady still cares for him.

The narrative of Froissart's poem serves, in part, as a showcase for expertly retold stories of classical mythology, drawn from the *Ovide moralisé* (Ovid Moralized), an immensely popular work by an anonymous thirteenth-century author. The *Espinette amoureuse,* like the *Paradis d'Amour,* also betrays the extensive influence of Machaut's *Voir-Dit,* in which several lyric poems are expertly integrated into a story frame. Froissart always sought to modify in interesting ways the models provided him by Machaut. In the *Espinette amoureuse* the narrative, though intriguingly novelesque, is not developed in sufficient detail to sustain the lyric moments, which are frequently overlong or digressive, and Froissart does not achieve the charm, subtlety, and complexity of his model.

In some cases, however, Froissart's *dits* equal or even surpass the sources to which he pays homage. *La Prison amoureuse* (The Prison of Love), written in 1372–1373 or about a decade after the success of Machaut's *Voir-Dit,* borrows that work's innovative fundamental structure: an exchange of letters between correspondents who frequently append poetical works to their messages, the whole framed by a first-person narrative that details the relationship between the two writers.

The *Prison amoureuse* begins with the poet's unhappy relationship with his beloved who, it seems, not only slights his work at a party by reciting someone else's

virelay rather than his own but also recites a virelay that proclaims she is never happier than when she sees her lover burdened with melancholic thought. Puzzled by her attitude, the lover resists the temptation to sink into despair and anxiety but remains upset though he goes on with his life. Froissart's poem departs from the conventional motif of the gracious lady comforting the poet. One of his closest male friends, using the pseudonym "Rose," writes to ask advice for his romantic troubles: he is reticent to tell his lady he loves her. The man proposes a correspondence and an exchange of poetry, including a ballade with his letter. The narrator accepts the offer, writes a letter advising Rose to send the lady messages if he does not have the courage to face her with his feelings, and appends a ballade of his own. Like his fellow, the narrator chooses a pseudonym more appropriate for a woman than a man, *Flos* (flower), by which he intends the *marguerite* in honor of his beloved. The correspondence, which includes several poems, comes into the possession of several ladies, whose approbation incites more poetry. The exchange of letters breaks off, but *Flos* later receives a chest from Rose containing two letters and a *dit* that, the first letter explains, puts into verse the dream that Rose experienced after reading the narrative of Pynoteüs and Neptisphelé that *Flos* had sent him. Rose's allegorical dream includes a military campaign, with a fully detailed *psychomachia* or "battle within the mind" in the manner of the Christian Latin poet Prudentius and the *Roman de la Rose.* Rose asks *Flos* to comment on this dream vision, and Flos's answer includes a lengthy interpretation of Rose's *dits* and ballades. Rose then asks *Flos* to fulfill his lady's desire and transform their correspondence and verse into a work he can present to her. *Flos* agrees, produces a work he calls the *Prison amoureuse,* explains his choice of title, and emends his interpretation to suit his friend. The poem ends with *Flos* expressing his hope that the work will please his friend and earn his gratitude.

The *Prison amoureuse* is more literary and more concerned with composition and interpretation than its primary source, the *Voir-Dit.* The separate love relationships in which *Flos* and Rose are involved serve merely as the pretext for their correspondence and exchange of poetry. In the *Prison amoureuse* Rose's delayed rejoinder to *Flos* is a miscommunication that interrupts the flow of texts rather than that of emotions. The emphasis of the work on writing, moreover, is reflected in its altered sexual politics, with the exchange between a man and woman who are eager to consummate their love becoming the mutual support and reinforcement of two men who, it is obvious, are more enthusiastic about the literary game of love than its reality. Although messages to their individual beloveds in one sense, their works are also to be enjoyed as verbal artifacts that elicit appreciative commentary.

Thus, in contrast to the *Voir-Dit,* the *Prison amoureuse* emphasizes both literary production and reception, with Rose's dream-vision poem a specific response to the experience of reading another text. Like several of Froissart's other works, this self-reflexive work thematizes the joys and discontents involved in the practice of authorship, even as it is traditional in suggesting that the writing of love poetry results in some sense from the actual experience of love. Not only does the *Prison amoureuse* play an intricate literary game, it also advertises the poet's considerable abilities in the process, especially his wit and sophistication. The poem is undoubtedly Froissart's masterpiece and compares favorably with the best work of his more celebrated contemporaries, not only Guillaume de Machaut, but also Christine de Pizan and Geoffrey Chaucer.

Froissart's last major *dit* (5,442 verses, including 28 interpolated lyrics totaling 1,135 verses), *Le Joli buisson de jonece* (The Pretty Bush of Youth, circa 1373–1374), takes up many of the themes that dominate the *Prison amoureuse,* especially the importance of revelatory dreams and instructive exempla for an understanding of the meaning of both life and love. These themes, however, are developed in a radically different fashion. The poem opens with a long (nearly 900 verses) dialogue between Philosophy and the narrator that is obviously indebted to Boethius's *De Consolatione philosophiae* (On the Consolation of Philosophy, circa A.D. 520). The narrator laments the fallen state of the world, particularly the niggardliness of potential benefactors. Philosophy counters with a defense of the importance of a writer's career and encourages him to be reinspired by his youthful works and experiences; in particular, the poet is to contemplate a painting of the lady he loved in his youth.

Thinking of the past provokes a dream of love when the poet retires that night. Guided by Venus, he moves through a lovely garden setting until he arrives at the *buisson de jeunesse* (bush of youth) a beautiful plant whose dimensions and features are constantly shifting. There the dreamer meets *Jeunesse* (Youth), who becomes his close companion and explains the seven branches of the plant, each under the influence of one of the planets. The poet moves into one of the areas inside this living plant where he meets again his lady love, who seems as young as when they first met, the result of the permanence of the emotions and attractions of love. The dreamer is received courteously by certain of the lady's companions, including *Doux Semblant* (Fair Welcome) and *Pitié* (Pity), and rebuffed by others, including *Danger* (Haughtiness) and *Escondit* (Shame). *Desir* (Desire) joins the group and overwhelms the narrator, whose intellectual equilibrium is restored by *Jeunesse.* The dreamer speaks at last to the lady; his long and rhetorically elaborate plea is met with a laconic, evasive response. A contest in the composition of lyric poetry follows in which

Followers of Froissart's patron, Richard II of England, being executed after the king was overthrown (illustration from a manuscript for Froissart's Chroniques, *British Library, ms. Harley 4380, fol. 193b)*

the various allegorical characters offer brief *souhaits* (wishes) to be judged. The dreamer refuses, and the vision ends with the company approaching the god of love for a decision. Awake and back in the present where he is old and the season is winter, the poet decides to abandon the frivolous thoughts of youth. He plans to devote himself to examining his soul, in which task he will ask for the intercession of the Blessed Virgin; the poem ends with a lay in her honor. With its melancholic meditations on the joys and discontents of authorship and love, *Le Joli buisson de jonece* offers a fitting coda to Froissart's engagement with the tradition of love-vision poetry. As in the *Prison amoureuse,* the *Espinette amoureuse,* and the *Paradis d'Amour,* Froissart here expertly combines the themes and structures of the *Roman de la Rose* and Machaut: the dream vision animated by lively personification allegory; the ornamental classical exemplum; appropriate lyric inserts; and the humorous interrogation of authorial experience defined by both textual and amorous encounters or, more precisely, by encounters that are both amorous and textual.

Two late works were completed after Froissart's period of service to Philippa (they are placed after *Joli buisson de jonece* late in both mss. *A* and *B*, which appear to follow the chronology of composition). Both probably dating sometime after 1388, they are *Plaidoirie de la rose et de la violette* (Debate Between the Rose and the Violet), a 342-line *conflictus* between the two flowers as to their relative merits, and *Le Dit dou florin* (The Story of the Florin), a charming account of a mission the poet undertook in 1388 on behalf of his patron Guy de Blois.

Far removed from the precious self-reflexivity of Froissart's *dits* is the energetic narrative of knightly adventure in his *Méliador,* the author's significant contribution to the *roman d'aventure* (romance of adventure) genre and his final major poem. It seems likely that Froissart grew tired of Machaldian verse narrative and took up again work on *Méliador,* whose thematic emphasis on knightly glory and renown was very similar to that of the *Chronicles,* whose composition much occupied him in the early 1370s. Froissart was perhaps also encouraged to finish his verse romance by Wenceslas of Brabant, who is the author of the lyric poems inserted in the text. For the overall plan and style of this work Froissart is obviously much indebted to the so-called Vulgate cycle of prose Arthurian romances (composed in the thirteenth century), which are structured by multiple lines of narrative whose separate elements are interlaced with one another. Despite the title, then, Froissart's poem does not feature a single main character (though Méliador plays a prominent role); the narrative is focalized at various points by a series of primary and secondary heroes, each of whom represents the chivalric ideal in a different way.

Although romantic elements are by no means absent, *Méliador* concentrates much more on detailed description of tournament fighting and other martial encounters, in this way catering to the sensibilities of Froissart's fourteenth-century courtly audience. Like the chronicles, the poem offers marvelous representations of a world devoted to the expression of knightly virtue, only here those sentiments can be given a more ideal shape than the chronicling of reality permits. Because of its prolixity and interlaced organization, *Méliador* has not found many appreciative modern readers, but it was certainly popular in its own time. Froissart reports that he recited the entire text, in seven hundred line installments, to Count Gaston Phoebus and his court.

Like Froissart's considerable body of lyric verse in the fixed forms popularized by Machaut, *Méliador* is more conventional than original, more a tribute to a literary tradition and the values that energized it than an influential revision of a genre through the infusion of new ideas. Much the same might be said of Froissart's poetry as a whole. Though his love narratives and verse romance never lack interest and occasionally explore in depth the possibilities of received forms (this is especially true of the *Prison amoureuse*), they did not substantially affect the course of literary history by providing compelling models for later authors to follow. A competent, talented writer with a knack for writing intricate and pleasing verse, Froissart undoubtedly entertained and fascinated the aristocratic audiences of the time with his poetry, but he influenced that culture much more through his historical works, which achieved a widespread, enduring popularity and acceptance that his poetry never did.

References:

Peter F. Ainsworth, *Jean Froissart and the Fabric of History: Truth, Myth, and Fiction in the Chroniques* (Oxford: Clarendon Press / New York: Oxford University Press, 1990);

Peter F. Dembowski, *Jean Froissart and His Méliador: Context, Craft, and Sense,* Edward C. Armstrong Monographs on Medieval Literature no. 2 (Lexington, Ky.: French Forum, 1983);

Kristen Mossler Figg, *The Short Lyric Poems of Jean Froissart: Fixed Forms and the Expression of the Courtly Ideal,* Garland Studies in Medieval Literature no. 10 (New York: Garland, 1994);

Georg Jäger, *Aspekte des Krieges und der Chevalerie im XIV. Jahrhundert in Frankreich: Untersuchungen zu Jean Froissarts* Chroniques (Bern & Las Vegas: Peter Lang, 1981);

Laurence de Looze, *Pseudo-autobiography in the Fourteenth Century: Juan Ruiz, Guillaume de Machaut, Jean Froissart, and Geoffrey Chaucer* (Gainesville: University Press of Florida, 1997);

Donald Maddox and Sara Sturm-Maddox, eds., *Froissart Across the Genres* (Gainesville: University Press of Florida, 1998);

J. J. N. Palmer, ed., *Froissart, Historian* (Woodbridge, U.K.: Boydell Press / Totowa, N.J.: Rowman & Littlefield, 1981);

Jacqueline Picoche, *Le vocabulaire psychologique dans les Chroniques de Froissart,* 2 volumes (Paris: Klincksiek, 1976, 1984);

Beate Schmolke-Hasselmann, *The Evolution of Arthurian Romance: The Verse Tradition from Chrétien to Froissart,* translated by Margaret and Roger Middleton, Cambridge Studies in Medieval Literature no. 35 (Cambridge & New York: Cambridge University Press, 1998).

Jean Gerson

(14 December 1363 – 12 July 1429)

B. Gregory Hays
University of Illinois, Urbana-Champaign

WORKS: *De modo se habendi tempore schismatis* (1398)

Manuscripts: The work is extant in at least eighteen manuscripts. The standard edition is based on Paris, Bibliothèque Nationale de France, f. lat. 3126, f. 105v–107, a fifteenth-century collection of Gerson's works.

Standard edition: In *Œuvres Complètes,* 10 volumes in 11, edited by P. Glorieux (Paris, Tournai, Rome & New York: Desclée, 1960–1973), VI: 29–34.

Montagne de contemplation (1400)

Manuscripts: Approximately twenty-five manuscripts are extant. The standard edition is based on Paris, Bibliothèque Nationale de France, f. fr. 1003.

Standard edition: In *Œuvres Complètes,* 10 volumes in 11, edited by P. Glorieux (Paris, Tournai, Rome & New York: Desclée, 1960–1973), VII, pt. 1: 16–55.

Epistola prima ad Bartholomeum (1402)

Manuscripts: Glorieux's edition is based on Brussels, Bibliothèque Royale/Koninklijke Bibliotheek, 2384, ff. 160–165v. Other manuscripts include Paris, Bibliothèque Mazarine, 921, f. 100 and Trier, Stadtbibliothek, 719, f. 39v–42.

Standard editions: In *Essai sur la critique de Ruysbroeck par Gerson,* 3 volumes in 4, edited by André Combes (Paris: J. Vrin, 1945–1972), I: 615–635; In *Œuvres Complètes,* 10 volumes in 11, edited by P. Glorieux (Paris, Tournai, Rome & New York: Desclée, 1960–1973), II: 55–62.

Traité contre le Roman de la Rose (1402)

Manuscripts: The work is preserved in nine manuscripts in whole or in part. The standard edition is based on Paris, Bibliothèque Nationale de France, f. fr. 1797, f. 1–23.

Standard edition: In *Œuvres Complètes,* 10 volumes in 11, edited by P. Glorieux (Paris, Tournai, Rome & New York: Desclée, 1960–1973), VII, part 1: 301–316.

Notulae super quaedam verba Dionysii De Coelesti Hierarchia (1402)

Manuscripts: Preserved only in Paris, Bibliothèque Nationale de France, lat. 14905, f. 264–274v. This manuscript is a fifteenth-century compilation of theological works, mostly by Gerson.

Standard edition: In *Jean Gerson. Commentateur Dionysien,* edited by André Combes (Paris: J. Vrin, 1940), pp. 28–47; in *Œuvres Complètes,* 10 volumes in 11, by P. Glorieux (Paris, Tournai, Rome & New York: Desclée, 1960–1973), III: 203–224.

Contra curiositatem studentium (1402)

Manuscripts: The standard edition is based on Paris, Arsenal 523, f. 282, 287v–296. This manuscript is a fifteenth-century collection of Gerson's writings.

Standard edition: In *Œuvres Complètes,* 10 volumes in 11, edited by P. Glorieux (Paris, Tournai, Rome & New York: Desclée, 1960–1973), III: 224–249.

Translation: Select passages in *Jean Gerson. Selections from A Deo Exivit, Contra curiositatem studentium and De mystica theologia speculativa,* edited and translated by Steven E. Ozment (Leiden: E. J. Brill, 1969).

De mystica theologia speculativa et practica (1402, probably revised 1407)

Manuscripts: More than sixty manuscripts preserve one or both parts of this work. Of these Paris, Bibliothèque Nationale de France, f. lat. 3623, fol. 68r–118v is particularly noteworthy, since it may have been written by Gerson's brother Jean the Celestine.

Standard edition: *Ioannes Carlerii de Gerson De Mystica Theologia,* edited by André Combes (Lugano, Switzerland: Thesaurus Mundi, 1958).

Translation: Select passages from the first half in *Jean Gerson. Selections from A Deo Exivit, Contra curiositatem studentium and De mystica theologia speculativa,* edited and translated by Steven E. Ozment (Leiden: E. J. Brill, 1969).

Epistola secunda ad Bartholomeum (1408)

Manuscripts: The standard edition is based on Paris, Bibliothèque Mazarine, 921, f. 114v–116v. The work is also preserved in Trier, Stadtbibliothek, 719, f. 51–53.

Standard edition: In *Œuvres Complètes,* 10 volumes

Jean Gerson (engraving by Montcornet, 1658)

in 11, edited by P. Glorieux (Paris, Tournai, Rome & New York: Desclée, 1960–1973), II: 97–103.

Propositio facta coram Anglicis (1409)

    Manuscripts: The standard edition is based on Paris, Bibliothèque Nationale de France, f. lat. 14902, f. 12–19, a fifteenth-century collection of Gerson's works. Other manuscripts in which the sermon is found include Bibliothèque Nationale de France, f. lat. 1573, A. n. 2; Bibliothèque Nationale de France, f. lat. 3126, f. 44–48; Bibliothèque Nationale de France, lat. f. 17489, f. 62v–67; Tours, Bibliothèque Municipale, 384, f. 20v–27, a fifteenth-century collection of theological works, mostly by Gerson; and Bordeaux, Bibliothèque Municipale, 117–118, f. 7–19.

    Standard edition: In *Œuvres Complètes,* 10 volumes in 11, edited by P. Glorieux (Paris, Tournai, Rome & New York: Desclée, 1960–1973), VI: 125–135.

Josephina (circa 1414–1418)

    Manuscripts: The standard edition is based on two

manuscripts: Tours, Bibliothèque Municipale, 378, f. 67–105v (a fifteenth-century collection of Gerson's works) and Paris, Bibliothèque Nationale de France, lat. 14902, f. 182–233. Other manuscripts include Paris, Bibliothèque Nationale de France, f. lat. 3126, fol. 2–15; Bibliothèque Nationale de France, f. lat. 17488, fol. 245–282v; Bibliothèque Nationale de France f. lat. 18572, fol. 1–47v.; Paris, Bibliothèque Mazarine, 3895, n. 2; Prague Univ. 2774; and Wolfenbüttel 2338, f. 97v.

    Standard edition: In *Œuvres Complètes,* 10 volumes in 11, edited by P. Glorieux (Paris, Tournai, Rome & New York: Desclée, 1960–1973), IV: 31–100.

Ambulate dum lucem habetis (1415)

    Manuscripts: The standard edition is based on Tours, Bibliothèque Municipale, 384, fol. 1–8. Other manuscripts include Paris, Bibliothèque Nationale de France, f. lat. 3126, fol. 34–37v; Paris, Bibliothèque Mazarine, 940, fol. 1–9; and Bibliothèque Nationale de France, f. lat. 17489, fol. 49–

53v.

Standard edition: In *Œuvres Complètes,* 10 volumes in 11, edited by P. Glorieux (Paris, Tournai, Rome & New York: Desclée, 1960–1973), V: 39–50.

Prosperum iter faciat nobis (1415)

Manuscripts: The sermon appears in at least forty manuscripts. The standard edition is based on Paris, Bibliothèque Nationale de France, f. lat. 14902, f. 29–35v.

Standard edition: In *Œuvres Complètes,* 10 volumes in 11, edited by P. Glorieux (Paris, Tournai, Rome & New York: Desclée, 1960–1973), V: 471–480.

De consolatione theologiae (1418)

Manuscripts: More than forty manuscripts are extant. The standard edition is based on Paris, Bibliothèque Nationale de France, f. lat. 14581, f. 253–275, a fifteenth-century collection of Gerson's works.

Standard edition: In *Œuvres Complètes,* 10 volumes in 11, edited by P. Glorieux (Paris, Tournai, Rome & New York: Desclée, 1960–1973), IX: 185–245.

De puella Aurelianensi (1429)

Manuscripts: Nine manuscripts are extant. The standard edition is based on the text in Paris, Bibliothèque Nationale de France, f. lat. 14904, f. 201–203v.

Standard edition: In *Œuvres Complètes,* 10 volumes in 11, edited by P. Glorieux (Paris, Tournai, Rome & New York: Desclée, 1960–1973), IX: 661–665.

Jean Gerson is a figure of contradictions: at once a shrewd politician and a convinced mystic, a radical reformer and a conservative theologian, a university chancellor and a poet as well as a preacher, a humanist, and an extraordinarily prolific writer in both Latin and French. He was a complex man, and one whose thought changed and developed considerably over his career; yet, the contradictions in the man also offer a mirror on the tumultuous and confusing age in which he lived.

Jean Charlier de Gerson was born 14 December 1363 at Gerson-les-Barby in Champagne, the son of Arnoul le Charlier and Elizabeth la Chardenière. He was the oldest of twelve children, several of whom died in childhood. Of the remainder, many pursued religious vocations; Gerson remained especially close to his youngest brother, who later became a Celestine monk. All but one of the Charlier sons were named Jean, a name which may have had family significance. The addition of the place name, Gerson, was significant in another way. The name means "pilgrim" in Hebrew, and the coincidence was meaningful to Gerson, who often depicted himself as a pilgrim in his writings.

Gerson's early schooling took place at Rethel and under the Benedictines at Rheims. This instruction would have been first of all religious, but it was probably at this

Jean Gerson, depicted as a pilgrim (illustration from Opera Johannis Gerson, *published in Strasbourg in 1488)*

stage also that Gerson acquired the grounding in the Latin classics–Cicero, Seneca, Virgil, and Horace–that is reflected in his works. At the age of fourteen he was enrolled in the university at Paris. He received his arts degree four years later in 1381, and proceeded on to a doctorate in theology. As *baccalarius biblicus* in 1387, he was required to lecture on two books of the Bible, one from the Old and one from the New Testament. In 1389 he became a *baccalarius sententiarius,* delivering a mandatory series of lectures on the *Sententiarum libri IV* (Four Books of Sentences, circa 1148–1151) of Peter Lombard. These lectures do not seem to have been preserved; the attribution to Gerson of an extant manuscript commentary on the *Sententiarum libri* (Paris, Bibliothèque Nationale de France, f. lat. 15156) is probably mistaken.

The influence of his university training on Gerson is clear, particularly in his tendency to present an argument as a series of disjunct propositions and in his frequent invocation of the Aristotelian model of causation with its efficient, final, formal, and material causes. Though no student at this time could have remained unaffected by the new and exciting writings of William of Ockham, Gerson's response seems to have been cautious. Like Ockham, Gerson endorses the formal separation of philosophy from theology; but while Ockham tried to empower philosophy by freeing it from theological constraints, Gerson consistently privileged theology over philosophy, whose influence on the students of the Sorbonne he later criticized in his *Contra curiositatem studentium* (Against Excessive Curiosity in Students, 1402).

As important to Gerson's future career as any formal instruction, however, was his relationship with Pierre d'Ailly, first as student and protegé, later as friend and colleague. D'Ailly became rector of the college of Navarre in 1384 and chancellor of the university five years later. As d'Ailly rose in the university hierarchy, Gerson followed in his wake. In 1383 or 1384 he had been elected proctor of the French Nation (one of the university's four student divisions). In 1388 he was selected to accompany d'Ailly and others on an embassy to Pope Benedict XIII at Avignon, where they secured papal condemnation of the Dominican John de Monzon, who had argued against the doctrine of the Immaculate Conception. In 1391 Gerson preached his first sermon at court.

Gerson came of age at a troubled time. The Hundred Years' War had taken its toll on France, both in military and political terms. Within the country, rivalry between the king's brother, the duke of Orléans, and his uncle, the duke of Burgundy, produced constant outbreaks of violence. The situation worsened after August 1392 when King Charles VI suffered the first of many attacks of insanity, creating a power vacuum that the feuding dukes hastened to take advantage of.

The political divisions within France mirrored an equally deep rift in the church. Pope Gregory XI had ended the so-called Babylonian Captivity by returning the seat of the papacy from Avignon to Rome, where he died on 27 March 1378. The conclave of cardinals there elected Urban VI to succeed him. It was alleged by the French cardinals, however, that the choice had been dictated by force. Once safely back at Avignon, they held a new conclave and elected an Antipope, Clement VI, on 20 September. With this election the Great Schism began; attempts to resolve it were to preoccupy Europe for the next forty years. These two issues—the schism and the struggle between the Burgundian and Orleanist factions—would become the leitmotifs of Gerson's career.

In 1393, Gerson became almoner to the duke of Burgundy and received a benefice at Bruges, in what is now Belgium. A still greater honor followed. On 13 April 1395, shortly after receiving his doctorate, Gerson was elected chancellor of the university in succession to d'Ailly. The appointment made Gerson a major player in attempts to resolve the schism. At this stage of his career he appears as an advocate of quiet diplomacy directed toward the voluntary abdication of both claimants and a new election. A

brief treatise written in 1398, *De modo se habendi tempore schismatis* (On How to Conduct Oneself at a Time of Schism) strikes a remarkably moderate note in this regard. At this difficult time, Gerson writes, Christians are free to align themselves as their consciences dictate, but the validity of rites performed by the other side should not be questioned, nor should the tactic of excommunication be abused. Not all were so reasonable: in the same year more radical supporters of the *via cessionis* (way of abdication) within the university tried to force the obstinate Benedict's hand by refusing to acknowledge his authority. Gerson was among those who worked for the restoration of obedience, which was finally achieved in 1403.

In 1399 Gerson journeyed to his benefice in Bruges, remaining there until September of the following year. This extended absence seems to have coincided with a spiritual crisis, perhaps brought on by the continuing impasse over the Schism. At one point Gerson even considered resigning his chancellorship. Certainly his interest in inner spirituality grew more pronounced at this point, and during the Bruges period he composed several major theological works.

The most notable of these is perhaps the *Montagne de contemplation* (Mountain of Contemplation, 1400). Addressed to Gerson's sisters, the work is written in French rather than Latin, with the deliberate goal of accessibility. Gerson draws a distinction between intellectual and affective contemplation. In the latter, which is to be preferred, the learned cleric has no advantage over the simple Christian. Gerson, indeed, claims no special authority in discussing the contemplative life; as he puts it later in the treatise: "j'en parlerais comme un aveugle de couleurs" (I will be describing it as a blind man describes colors).

The beginning and end of contemplation, Gerson tells us, is the love of God; however, the path up the mountain of contemplation is steep and marked by three stages: first, by penitence; second, by solitude and silence; and last, by perseverance. The process is a gradual one, comparable to the slow smoldering of a flame before it catches fire or to the slow growth of a seed in the earth. After digressing to refute potential objections to the contemplative life, Gerson returns to the theme of perseverance. In the ascent of this mountain, Gerson writes, "reposer est descendre ou reculer aval" (to rest is to descend or to fall back). Hence, those who reach the summit are few, and the majority (described in a vivid extended allegory) are sidetracked or give up, daunted by terrors, burdened by worldly cares, or distracted by temptation and pride.

Gerson stresses once again that there is no single method or experience of contemplation. For models the reader is directed to the accounts of various church fathers, especially St. Bernard of Clairvaux. Though Gerson does offer a sample contemplative exercise employed

Opening page of a manuscript for Gerson's Josephina *(Bibliothèque Nationale de France, f. fr. 18572, fol. 1)*

by an anonymous friend (in fact, almost certainly Gerson himself), he reiterates that prescription is no substitute for practice: "vrai est que toutes les escriptures dou monde ne feroient mie tant a venir ou le contemplatif doibt venir" (it is a fact that all the writings in the world will not suffice to bring one where the contemplative must go). The treatise closes with a final image for contemplation, adapted from the allegory presented earlier. On the shore of a stormy sea, the reader is to imagine an immense mountain giving a view of travelers tossed on the waves below. The mountain has three levels: faith, hope, and charity. Above is God, but one cannot know him in this world, nor can he be described except in negative terms. Gerson leaves open the possibility of contemplative union with God, "mais de ceste maniere ne suis je mie digne d'en ouvrir ma bouche; ie la laisse aux plus grans" (but of this I am not worthy to open my mouth; I leave it to those greater than I).

Gerson returned to Paris in September 1400, apparently reconciled to continuing as chancellor. At the same time, however, he continued to develop his interest in mysticism. In early March 1402 he composed a letter, now known as the *Epistola prima ad Bartholomeum* (First letter to Barthelemy), to a certain Barthelemy Clantier, who had written to ask about a point of theology in the writings of the contemporary Flemish mystic Jan van Ruysbroeck. Though largely sympathetic to Ruysbroeck's approach, Gerson scented heresy in a few points. Ruysbroeck's writings found defenders, and Gerson discussed the issues further six years later in the *Epistola secunda ad Bartholomeum* (Second letter to Barthelemy, 1408). As this exchange shows, Gerson's attitude to mysticism was one of thoughtful adhesion rather than uncritical acceptance (among his other writings of this period is a short treatise on distinguishing true visions from false ones).

Meanwhile, a rather different controversy at-tracted Gerson's attention. Since 1400, literary circles had witnessed a pitched battle over *Le Roman de la Rose* (The Romance of the Rose), a work whose first half was written circa 1225–1230 by Guillaume de Lorris, with a second part added by Jean de Meun circa 1269–1278. First, Christine de Pizan attacked Jean de Meun's continuation of the *Rose* for its portrayal of women; the work was then defended in turn by the humanist Jean de Montreuil and the brothers Gontier and Pierre Col. On 18 May 1402 Gerson entered the fray on Christine's side with his *Traité contre le Roman de la Rose* (Treatise against the *Romance of the Rose*). The treatise wittily mimics the allegorical form of the *Roman de la Rose* itself; Gerson portrays himself as having been transported in a vision to "la court saincte de Crestienté" (the holy court of Christianity), presided over by *Justice canonique* (Canon Law). The indictment of the *Fol Amoureux* (Fool for Love) is read by the figure of *Chasteté* (Chastity). The defendant is accused of defaming marriage and religion and leading the young astray with erotic

visions. Witnesses for the defense are heard but are confuted by a long speech from *Eloquence Theologienne* (Theological Eloquence). The author returns to reality before he can hear the sentence pronounced. Although Gerson's disapproval is clear, the treatise is no rigid, moralistic condemnation, but rather an entertaining pastiche in which Gerson critiques the *Roman de la Rose* using the same rhetorical weapons as had Jean de Meun. The *Traité* provoked a substantial response from Pierre Col, to which Gerson replied in a letter dated October 1402, laying out in more conventional form his objections to the work. Some texts, he argues, are genuinely dangerous, and young people ought to be protected from them.

This episode, however, was only an interlude in a series of more serious compositions. In late 1402, Gerson completed the first part of his single most influential work, the long treatise *De mystica theologia speculative at practica* (On Mystical Theology Speculative and Practical). The work reiterates in a more formal manner many of the themes expressed in the *Montagne de Contemplation*. The superiority of faith to reason, of the affective to the intellectual powers, is stressed: rational understanding is subordinated to the ultimate goal of mystical union with God. The second, "practical" part of the treatise (which Gerson added as a sort of sequel in 1407) again expands on Gerson's earlier works, emphasizing the inner discipline necessary to contemplation and even offering suggestions derived from St. Jerome on diet and sleep.

The combination of speculative and practical advice can be explained by Gerson's desire to see mysticism incorporated into the daily life of ordinary, secular Christians. This aim is what distinguishes Gerson's mystical theology from that of movements such as *Devotio Moderna* (Modern Devotion), a movement within the Catholic Church from the late fourteenth to sixteenth centuries that promoted mysticism in the context of a religious community set apart from the world. At the same time, the treatise seems to have been intended as the keystone of Gerson's program to reform the university, then overwhelmingly dominated by the Scholastic tradition, by providing both an introduction and an invitation to a different tradition of theological thought.

A central influence is the author known as Pseudo-Dionysius the Areopagite, a sixth-century mystic posing as one of St. Paul's converts. His treatises, originally written in Greek, had been translated into Latin by the ninth-century scholar John Scottus Eriugene and exercised an enormous influence on European mysticism, in particular through their insistence that the experience of God cannot be expressed in other than negative terms. Gerson seems to have contemplated a set of lectures on Pseudo-Dionysius's *Caelestis Hierarchia* (On the Celestial Hierarchy) at the same time that he was working on the *De mystica theologia,* and his notes, preserved in a Paris

Page from a manuscript for a theological work by Gerson; the Soul, depicted as a naked woman with a pilgrim's staff, converses with a monk and a nobleman (Gotha, Landesbibliothek, ms. I. 118, fol. 1r)

manuscript, have been published as *Notulae super quaedam verba Dionysii De coelesti Hierarchia* (Notes on Certain Passages of Dionysius's Celestial Hierarchy, 1402).

Though an important model, Pseudo-Dionysius was by no means Gerson's only source. Equally important were several lesser-known twelfth- and thirteenth- century authors working in the Dionysian tradition, notably Hugues de Balma and Thomas Gallus. Gerson invokes a wide variety of other predecessors, among them St. Augustine, St. Bernard of Clairvaux, St. Bonaventura, and Hugh and Richard of St. Victor. The frequent appeal to earlier authorities is not accidental: Gerson saw his advocacy of mysticism not as a radical innovation but as a return to a tradition with roots deep in the history of the church.

In the meantime the world continued to exert its claims on the chancellor. On 27 April 1404 Gerson's patron Philip the Bold died and was succeeded by his son, John the Fearless. Gerson's relations with John quickly deteriorated, and within three years an event took place that would eventually lead to open hostilities between the chancellor and the House of Burgundy. In March 1407 Gerson left Paris as part of a royal commission charged with negotiating an end to the Schism. During Gerson's absence, on 23 November the duke of Orleans was assassinated by Burgundian partisans. A few months later, in March 1408, a supporter of the duke of Burgundy, one Jean Petit, published a treatise justifying the murder (partly on biblical grounds) as a legitimate act of tyrannicide.

Meanwhile, the commission found itself mired in frustration. The popes, Benedict and Gregory, temporized and equivocated, at one point coming within a few hours' journey of one another but never actually meeting. In the end, Gerson and his fellow commissioners returned empty-handed. Their failure seems to have marked a major turning point in Gerson's attitude to the Schism. From this point on he becomes a firm advocate of the *via concilii* (conciliar way), which called for a church council to resolve the issue, with or without the consent of the two contending parties. Though he did not himself take part in the Council of Pisa, which opened in March of 1409, Gerson's views were put forward unequivocally in the sermon he addressed on 29 January 1409 to the English delegation to the Council, which was passing through Paris on its way to Italy.

In *Propositio facta coram Anglicis* (Discourse before the English) Gerson takes as his starting point Hosea 1:11, "Then shall the children of Judah and the children of Israel be gathered together, and appoint themselves one head. . . ." The interpretation of the passage lays the groundwork for a decisive statement on Gerson's part: "The church assembled, though it may not create or destroy the papacy as an institution, may nevertheless either in its own right or through a council acting as its representative decree another method of choosing a pope than is customary. . . . It may even depose a duly elected pope and choose another if this seems likely to be expeditious for the growth of the church." A council, Gerson further argues, may assemble in the absence of a pope, as it had before St. Peter first assumed that office. It may assemble also in other special cases, as when the pope has lost his reason, or when he embraces heresy or immorality. And surely this schism, "fera pessima, monstrum horrendum ingens" (that dreadful beast, that great and fearful monster) as Gerson had earlier described it, is such a case. The English delegation is blessed and encouraged as it departs, carrying with it the hopes of the University of Paris.

Gerson's hopes for the Pisan Council were to be only partially fulfilled. The Council duly deposed Benedict and Gregory and elected in their place Alexander V. This failed to settle matters. Indeed, it had the net effect of worsening the schism since neither of the deposed Popes accepted his deposition. To complicate matters still further, Alexander died on 6 May 1410 and was succeeded by the shrewd and ambitious Pope John XXIII, who would prove as stubborn an obstacle to reconciliation as either of his rivals. Negotiations continued, but little progress was made.

Meanwhile, relations between the Burgundians and Orleanists had worsened still further. In late spring and summer 1413, Paris was effectively in a state of civil war. Gerson's house was burned by the Burgundian faction, and he was briefly forced to take refuge in the cathedral of Notre-Dame. The experience seems to have hardened his anti-Burgundian stance, and in the years that followed he pursued as a kind of personal crusade the refutation of the Burgundian apologist Jean Petit, issuing a series of attacks on Petit's theory of justifiable tyrannicide.

By this time, the prospects for resolving the schism appeared somewhat brighter. Under pressure from the Holy Roman Emperor Sigismund, Pope John XXIII was eventually persuaded to endorse the *via concilii*, and on 16 November 1414 the Council of Constance opened; Gerson arrived in February 1415. Events were already moving toward a climax. On 21 March 1415, recognizing that his deposition was imminent, John XXIII fled the city, leaving the Council in a quandary: without the presence of the Pope who had summoned it, did it still retain any authority? On 23 March, Gerson delivered his famous sermon *Ambulate dum lucem habetis* (Walk While Ye Have the Light).

The sermon takes its starting point from John 12:35, "walk while ye have the light, lest darkness come upon you." This light, according to Gerson, is first of all Christ, but it is also the members of the Council insofar as they follow the injunction of Matthew 5:14, "You are the light of the world." Gerson then sets forth twelve propositions, which together constitute a manifesto of conciliar suprem-

Gerson preaching a sermon (illumination from a manuscript in the Bibliothèque Municipale de Valenciennes)

acy. Any church council, Gerson argues, is entitled to obedience from all Christians, including the pope himself. A council may depose even a properly elected pope and may assemble without being convoked by a pope in certain cases, as when the pope is accused of wrongdoing, when there are multiple claimants to the papal throne, or–in a remarkably broad clause–when the pope "contumaciously refuses" to summon a council despite circumstances that demand one. Finally, Gerson turns to the correction of error and heresy, the "shadows" of his opening text. Here too, the Council's duty to shed light is pressing; heresy is to be extirpated–together with those who preach it.

The sermon seems to have had its intended effect. Six days later, on 29 May, the Council voted to depose John XXIII. A few weeks later, on 4 July, Gregory XII abdicated voluntarily at Rome, leaving only the recalcitrant Benedict to be dealt with. In the meantime, the Council faced another issue. The dissident preacher Jan Hus had arrived at Constance under a guarantee of safe conduct from the emperor. It did him little good. He was officially condemned by the Council and burned at the stake on 6 July, with Gerson playing a leading role in the

condemnation. In his eyes, ecclesiastical unity was threatened by heresy no less than by schism; the Council's ruthlessness was justified by the danger Hus presented.

On 18 July, Sigismund left Constance for Aragon to negotiate with Benedict. Three days later Gerson delivered the sermon *Prosperum iter faciat nobis*. It begins with a kind of fugue on its opening words, which also serve as the title (taken from Psalm 67), "let him make a prosperous journey for us." The phrase is applied in the first instance to the absent Sigismund. Gerson then describes a more abstract journey, one made by the mind's two "feet," cognition and volition, on which progress is made by the keeping of the Lord's commandments. To this end, the stumbling blocks that impede this journey–schism, heresy, and corruption–must be removed. Here the Council can take pride in its achievements. It had asserted firmly the authority of church councils over the pope, and even its authority to depose the pope. It had acted to correct and punish heresy, notably in the case of the unfortunate Hus, whose writings had taken in so many. "The freedom to speak wrongly and erroneously is an evil freedom," asserts Gerson ominously. Finally, the Council had worked for general reform, as witnessed by its condemnation of John XXIII and its regulation of the future exercise of papal power. In this connection Gerson digresses briefly to argue for a conciliar organization as the ecclesiastical equivalent of Aristotle's "mixed constitution," with the Pope acting as its executive arm. Before closing, Gerson expresses the hope that the Council might play a unifying role between the various kingdoms of Christendom and that it might arrange for more frequent councils in future. Thus will the spiritual journey envisioned earlier in the sermon reach its goal more swiftly.

On 26 July 1417, Benedict XIII was deposed by the Council, and on 11 November of the same year, Martin V was elected the sole, legitimate Pope. Gerson's star might have seemed to be in the ascendant. In actual fact, the end of the schism marked the high watermark of his career, which was soon to take a new downturn. The Council disbanded on 22 April 1418, and Gerson left Constance a few weeks later. Almost simultaneously, on 6 May, the forces of John the Fearless entered Paris, and in the weeks that followed the Burgundians rampaged through the city, looting and killing. The dead included Jean de Montreuil and Gontier Col, Gerson's old sparring partners in the controversy over the *Roman de la Rose*. Under these circumstances it was clear that France was no safe place for Gerson. He spent the summer of 1418 in Bavaria and at the abbey of Melk in Austria, whose abbot he had met at Constance. Here Gerson's depression over the sack of Paris found expression; several poems from this period offer moving laments for the destruction visited upon the city and the university. It was here too that he put the finishing touches on the long poem *Josephina* (circa 1414–1418) on which he had been at work intermittently throughout the Council.

The poem, a narrative of the early life of Christ seen from the perspective of St. Joseph, is divided into twelve books or *distinctiones*. It begins with a prologue, which includes a stylized self-portrait–Gerson as pilgrim–as well as an invocation of St. Joseph. The work proper then opens dramatically with the flight into Egypt. By night, the figure of *Tribulatio* (Tribulation) appears to Joseph in a vision, which is explained to him the following morning by the Virgin. The two continue their theological discussion as they go. Their arrival in Egypt is greeted with excitement by the populace, and they are taken before the pharaoh, for whose help Joseph successfully appeals.

The next two books cover the events of the first seven years of Jesus' life. He learns from his mother, Mary, the story of the Fall and the fate that awaits him. Jesus weeps, and his mother weeps with and for him. In the beginning of the third book, Joseph returns to Israel, where a glad reunion with friends and family takes place. At this point Gerson digresses briefly to discuss the issue of sources: he has invented nothing, he stresses, but has

felt at liberty to extrapolate from the transmitted accounts; thus the canonical story of the young Jesus preaching in the temple is juxtaposed with a quaint imagined picture of the various household chores the boy might have performed. When Jesus asks his father about his ancestry, Joseph explains it and proceeds to instruct the boy in ethics, stressing particularly the importance of chastity, adducing his own relationship with Mary as an example.

Books 4 to 10 retell the story of the nativity, in a kind of flashback. This retrospective narrative begins with the annunciation and Mary's decision to inform Joseph of it. He is troubled, but is reassured in a nocturnal vision by the twin figures of *Virginitas* (Virginity) and *Phronesis* (Wisdom). The account of Jesus's birth in book 7 is preceded by the appearance of *Gratia* (Grace) to Joseph. The book closes with an address directed by *Gratia* to man, rebuking him for his slowness in accepting the salvation offered by Christ's incarnation.

In book 8, Mary and Joseph make arrangements for the child's circumcision and confer his name on him. Joseph and Mary reflect on the allegorical significance of circumcision, and the Magi arrive. Joseph ponders on the star that guided them and is enlightened by another nocturnal vision, this time of the figure of *Natura* (Nature), who disclaims all responsibility for the phenomenon. Book 10 deals with the presentation of Jesus in the temple and the mysterious prophecy of Simeon, which Joseph and Mary discuss on the way back to Nazareth. The flashback closes on a peaceful note (following a vivid description of the slaughter of the innocents) with an odd discussion of the process by which a preexisting pagan festival was transmuted into the Christian feast of Candlemas.

Book 11 focuses on Jesus' twelfth year and his three-day sojourn in the temple. The story is presented through the conversation between Jesus and his parents on the way back to Nazareth. Gerson passes over the remainder of Jesus' childhood, moving ahead to his departure from home at the age of thirty and his emotional leave-taking from the aged Joseph. The final book briefly describes Joseph's death; the widowed Mary is consoled by her son, who promises a reunion with Joseph in the afterlife. The poem closes with an epilogue invoking St. Joseph and requesting his favor on Gerson's behalf.

It cannot be denied that the *Josephina* as a whole is an uneven work. At some points Gerson's own preoccupations intrude awkwardly, as when the narrator exclaims of the slaughter of the innocents in book 10: "si fas saevos jugulare tyrannos / Cur sceleratus, cur truculentus vivit Herodes? / Sed non fas; tibi vindictam, Deus alme, reservas" (if it be right to slay savage tyrants / why did the evil, vicious Herod live? But it is not right; you reserve vengeance for yourself, o Lord,)–here the echo of the Petit controversy is clear. Particularly intrusive is the brief book

5, a digression that can be dated to the summer of 1417; it begins by giving thanks for the settlement of the schism, then offers a typological interpretation of the marriage of Mary and Joseph, and closes with a theological invective directed in particular at the Flagellants and Beghards. The characters are also prone to speak in suspiciously Gersonian accents, as when the Virgin learnedly distinguishes between philosophy and theology in the first book.

The work still holds much of interest, however. The picture of the holy family's domestic life is often charming; Gerson makes good use of the material provided by various apocryphal gospels. The overall structure of the poem, with its dramatic opening and central flashback, shows a sure grasp of narrative technique, probably derived from Virgil. Above all, the presentation of this familiar story from an unfamiliar perspective is a remarkable imaginative stroke. If the individual parts do not always cohere, the poem nevertheless deserves more attention than it has received.

Gerson's depression over the situation in France prompted the composition of *De consolatione theologiae* (On the Consolation of Theology, 1418), a prosimetrum, or work in alternating prose and verse, modeled on *De consolatione philosophiae* (On the Consolation of Philosophy, circa 525) of Boethius. It presents a discussion, spread over four days, between two characters. The first, *Volucer* (Traveler), has recently returned from the Council of Constance, bringing tidings of the absent chancellor. His interlocutor, *Monicus* (Monk), represents Gerson's brother. The two begin by discussing the sad state of political and ecclesiastical affairs. In these circumstances, *Volucer* reports, Gerson has turned to theology, which provides consolations more surely grounded than those philosophy had offered Boethius. The first conversation then details how man is drawn to God through fear of judgment and hope of grace (the tricky issue of predestination is dealt with in this connection); it closes with a poem in which Gerson's state is compared to that of a storm-tossed sailor.

The second conversation similarly begins with Gerson's own situation. Gerson places his hope in God and is grateful to have escaped experiencing and witnessing the civil war in France; yet, how can he not be grieved over the fates of friends? This leads into a discussion of man's will. Gerson distinguishes multiple wills. Often one's higher and lower wills conflict; the task for a Christian is to bring his will into harmony with the divine will, which is by definition good.

The third day's discussion centers on patience, which is contrasted with misdirected zeal. This leads into a discussion of the Christian's conduct in public life and in relation to other Christians, and the book closes with a long speech by *Volucer* extolling the rewards of patience, capped by a poem retelling the story of Job. The fourth day begins with a question from *Monicus:* Does Gerson feel no misgivings about his public life? Would it not be better to abjure the world altogether? No, replies *Volucer,* one must persevere, using one's judgment, trusting in God's mercy, and with the help of theology. Although *Monicus* objects that theologians generally seem no better than other men, *Volucer* explains that not all who study theology profit from it. The work then closes with a virtuoso speech delivered by *Volucer* in the character of Theology herself. Why such complaints? she demands. History is filled with catastrophes as great as those now being suffered by France, and all took place by God's will.

The dialogue as a whole is among the most accessible and attractive of Gerson's theological works. Throughout the treatise the prosimetrical element enlivens the theological discussion; it also serves to display both Gerson's metrical virtuosity and his acquaintance with the classical poets. At the same time the dialogue form prevents the prose sections from becoming monotonous. Here Gerson seems to have been influenced not only by Boethius but also by St. Augustine's dialogues with himself in his *Soliloquia* (Soliloquies, circa 386–387), which are explicitly referred to several times in the course of the work.

The *De consolatione theologiae* was to be Gerson's last major work. In the autumn of 1418 he was invited to teach at Vienna, but he remained there for only a year. On 10 September 1419 John the Fearless was assassinated by partisans of the dauphin, soon to be crowned as Charles VII. The way was now clear for a return to France; however, Gerson chose to settle at Lyons in November of the same year. He would never return to Paris or to the university whose chancellor he remained.

The years at Lyons were by and large spent quietly. No longer a player on the international stage, Gerson filled a more modest role as the preceptor of the choirboys at the church of St. Paul, but he had by no means renounced literary activity. He continued to write on spiritual questions and conducted an active correspondence with the monks of the Grande Chartreuse. Nor did Gerson hold himself entirely aloof from political controversy; among his last works is *De puella Aurelianensi* (On the Maid of Orléans, 1429), a treatise in defense of Joan of Arc, who would soon lead the way to a stronger and more independent France and in whom (as in Gerson himself) mysticism and political activity were combined. He died soon afterwards, on 12 July 1429.

To summarize Gerson's importance is no easy matter. His thought changed and developed over his career (his attitude to the schism is a notable example), while the sheer variety of his writings and his extraordinary productivity (more than four hundred works in the standard edition) make it difficult to take the measure of the man. The variety of his body of work is mirrored by an equally wide range of responses to it. In his own lifetime he was a figure of controversy, hated by the Burgundians and revered by contemporaries such as Nicholas de Clamanges, who described the chancellor as "the greatest of my teachers, burning with pious zeal for the salvation of souls, the best of leaders and guides on the spiritual road." The chancellor's continuing relevance and influence in the generations immediately following his death is clear. In 1483, only a few years after the invention of printing, Johannes Koelhoff of Cologne published a multivolume collection of Gerson's works; by the end of the century six such collections had appeared.

Gerson's attempts at ecclesiastical reform exercised at least some influence on a still greater reformer, Martin Luther. In the sixteenth and seventeenth centuries, the rise of Gallicanism—a movement in the conciliar tradition which denied papal authority over the French church—enhanced Gerson's reputation and prompted several comprehensive editions of his works, notably that of Ellies du Pin (Anvers, 1706 in five volumes). This proved, however, to be the high watermark of Gerson's influence in this area. His ecclesiastical doctrine remains suspect to Catholic theologians, and scholars have tended to view the chancellor's conciliarist writings as an isolated reaction to a specific historical circumstance, rather than works of real theoretical importance.

By contrast, Gerson's strictly theological writings have generally met with approval, even winning him the sobriquet of *Doctor Christianissimus* (Most Christian Doctor). Indeed, his reputation as a mystic was such that for many years he could plausibly be credited with the authorship of the influential mystical treatise *Imitatio Christi* (Imitation of Christ, circa 1390–1440), now generally attributed to Thomas à Kempis. He was not an original thinker, nor would he have claimed to be. His importance lies rather in his gift for synthesis, and in his insistence on making mystical thought accessible to ordinary people. Though now less well-known than the *Imitatio Christi* or the anonymous fourteenth-century work *The Cloud of Unknowing*, Gerson's works retain an important place in the history of European religious thought.

Letters:

Jean Gerson, *Œuvres Complètes,* 10 volumes in 11, edited by P. Glorieux (Paris, Tournai, Rome & New York: Desclée, 1960–1973), II.

Bibliography:

Jean Gerson, *Œuvres Complètes,* 10 volumes in 11, by P. Glorieux (Paris, Tournai, Rome & New York: Desclée, 1960–1973), I: 153–166.

Biographies:

J. B. Schwab, *Johannes Gerson* (Würzburg: Stahel'sche Buchhandlung, 1858);

J. L. Connolly, *John Gerson, reformer and mystic* (Louvain: Librairie Universitaire, 1928);

P. Glorieux, "La Vie et les Œuvres de Gerson," *Archives d'histoire doctrinale et littéraire du moyen age,* 25–26 (1950–1951): 149–192.

References:

Catherine D. Brown, *Pastor and Laity in the Theology of Jean Gerson* (Cambridge: Cambridge University Press, 1986);

Christoph Burger, *Aedificatio, Fructus, Utilitas: Johannes Gerson als Professor der Theologie und Kanzler der Universität Paris* (Tübingen: Mohr, 1986);

Mark S. Burrows, *Jean Gerson and "De Consolatione Theologiae"* (Tübingen: Mohr, 1991);

André Combes, *Essai sur la critique de Ruysbroeck par Gerson,* 3 volumes in 4 (Paris: J. Vrin, 1945–1972);

Combes, *Jean Gerson. Commentateur Dionysien* (Paris: J. Vrin, 1940);

Combes, *Jean de Montreuil et le chancelier Gerson* (Paris: J. Vrin, 1942);

Combes, *La Théologie Mystique de Gerson. Profil de son Évolution,* 2 volumes (Rome, Paris, Tournai & New York: Desclée, 1963);

M. Lieberman, "Chronologie Gersonienne, I–X," *Romania,* 70 (1948/1949): 51–67; *Romania,* 73 (1952): 480–496; *Romania,* 74 (1953): 289–337; *Romania,* 76 (1955): 289–333; *Romania,* 78 (1957): 433–462; *Romania,* 79 (1958): 339–375; *Romania,* 80 (1959): 289–336; *Romania,* 81 (1960): 44–98; *Romania,* 82 (1961): 338–379; *Romania,* 83 (1962): 52–89;

John B. Morrall, *Gerson and the Great Schism* (Manchester: Manchester University Press, 1960);

Steven E. Ozment, *Homo Spiritualis. A Comparative Study of the Anthropology of Johannes Tauler, Jean Gerson and Martin Luther (1509–16) in the Context of their Theological Thought,* Studies in Medieval and Reformation Thought, no. 6 (Leiden: E. J. Brill, 1969);

Louis B. Pascoe, S. J., *Jean Gerson: Principles of Church Reform* (Leiden: E. J. Brill, 1973);

Charles Frederick Ward, "Epistles on the Romance of the Rose and other Documents in the Debate," dissertation, University of Chicago, 1911.

Oton de Grandson
(circa 1345 – 7 August 1397)

Sally Tartline Carden
University of Missouri–Rolla

WORKS: *Cinq balades ensuivans* (circa 1372–1374)

Manuscripts: This ballade series is transmitted in at least four manuscripts, all of which date from the fifteenth century: Barcelona, Biblioteca Catalunya 8 was copied in Catalonia but written in French; Paris, f. fr. 2201, upon which Arthur Piaget based his edition, represents one of the earliest of the manuscripts containing Oton de Grandson's poems; Lausanne, Bibliothèque Cantonale et Universitaire, 350, comprises nearly sixty percent of all poems attributed to Grandson, including the "Songe Saint Valentin"; and Philadelphia, University of Pennsylvania, French 15, probably transcribed circa 1400.

Livre Messire Ode (circa 1386–1392)

Manuscripts: A complete version of this work is preserved in two manuscripts: Brussells, Bibliothèque Royale, 10691–10970, which dates from the first half of the fifteenth century, and Paris, Bibliothèque Nationale de France, f. fr. 1727, dating from the mid-fifteenth century. An early, incomplete version of the *Livre* survives in Paris, Bibliothèque Nationale de France, f. fr. 1952, the only known manuscript of Grandson's work dating from the sixteenth century; and a fragment of the text appears in Karlsruhe, Badische Landesbibliothek, MS 410.

Fixed-form lyrics and *Valentine's Day Poems*

Manuscripts: No holograph manuscript exists, since none of the surviving manuscripts predate Grandson's death in 1397. In addition to Paris, Bibliothèque Nationale de France, f. fr. 1727, Bibliothèque Nationale de France, f. fr. 1952, and Bibliothèque Nationale de France, f. fr. 2201, works by Grandson are also preserved in Paris, Bibliothèque Nationale de France, f. fr. 1131 and Bibliothèque Nationale de France, f. fr. 24440. Forty of Grandson's poems survive in these five manuscripts, including the "Complainte amoureuse de Sainct Valentin Gransson" and the "Pastourelle Gransson." A manuscript of the works of Guillaume de Machaut found in the library of Leo S. Olschki in Florence includes twenty-six poems by Grandson. Several of Grandson's poems are in London, Library of Westminster Abbey, ms. 21, a volume of poems by Christine de Pizan. The group of poems entitled *Recueil de Galanteries* (Collection of Gallantries), which includes five poems by Grandson, is preserved in Turin, Archivio di Stato, J. b. IX 10. The only manuscript known to consist exclusively of poems by Grandson is Lausanne, Bibliothèque Cantonale et Universitaire, IS 4254, which comprises only seven short poems.

First publications: "Pastourelle Gransson" and the "Complainte de Saint Valentin Gransson," in *Les Fais maistre Alain Chartier* (Paris: Pierre Le Caron, 5 September 1489); "Ballade de Saint Valentin double" and "Balade de Saint Valentin," in *Le Jardin de Plaisance et Fleur de Rhétorique* (Paris: Antoine Vérard, circa 1501).

Standard editions: *Oton de Grandson: Sa vie et ses poésies,* edited by Arthur Piaget (Lausanne & Geneva: Payot, 1941); *Recueil de Galanteries,* edited by A. Vitale Brovarone in *Le Moyen Français,* 6 (1980); "A Critical Edition of the Poetry of Oton de Grandson, MS. L," edited by Caroline A. Cunningham, dissertation, University of North Carolina, Chapel Hill, 1987.

Oton de Grandson, lord of Sainte-Croix, Cudrefin, Grandcour, Aubonne, and Coppet, was a well-known figure at courts throughout Europe during the second half of the fourteenth century. His reputation as an exemplary knight and lover is preserved in several texts written by contemporaries, such as *Epistre au Dieu d'Amours* (Letter to the God of Love, May 1399) by Christine de Pizan, who called him "Le bon Othe de Grançon le vaillant, / Qui pour armes tant s'alia traveillant" (The good and valiant Oton de Grandson, / who tirelessly devoted himself to feats of arms), and praised him highly as "Courtois, gentil, preux, bel et gracieux"

Seal of Oton de Grandson's great-great-uncle and namesake (Archives Cantonales Vaudoises)

(courteous, good, noble, brave, handsome and gracious).

Although best known to his contemporaries for his military exploits, Grandson participated actively in the literary culture of the period. He occupies a transitional role as perhaps the first prince-poet of the late Middle Ages, continuing the lyric traditions of Guillaume de Machaut while foreshadowing the arrival of Jean de Garencières, René d'Anjou, and Charles d'Orléans. While much of his lyric production echoes the conventional forms and subject matter of the period, his Valentine's Day pieces and the *Livre Messire Ode* (Sir Oton's Book, circa 1386–1392) offer profoundly influential and enduring literary innovations.

Oton de Grandson was born to Guillaume de Grandson and Jeanne de Vienne between 1340 and 1350, in what is now the canton of Vaud in Switzerland, but was then part of the independent county of Savoy. On 25 September 1365, he married Jeanne d'Allamand. Little else is known of his early life. In 1368, however, his name appears in historical documents as part of a group of Savoyard knights battling a detachment of Burgundian troops. By 1372, he must have already gained a reputation as an exceptional soldier, for he was chosen by Edward III, the king of England, to accompany John Hastings, 2nd Earl of Pembroke (the king's son-in-law) to relieve the French siege of La Rochelle.

According to Jean Froissart's account in his *Chroniques* (Chronicles, circa 1361–1400), included among these elite individuals was "Premierement, messire Othe de Grantson" (First, Sir Oton de Grandson).

Just before reaching La Rochelle, however, the earl of Pembroke and his companions encountered a strong Spanish fleet, sent by Henry II of Castille in support of the French, and after a fierce two-day naval battle were defeated on 23 June. Grandson was captured and sent to Santander in Spain, where he was imprisoned for the next two years. During his captivity the Savoyard poet composed several ballades and participated in a poetic debate with fellow prisoner Florimont de Lesparre, which appears in several manuscripts as the *Cinq balades ensuivans* (Five Consecutive Ballades, circa 1372–1374). In the Barcelona manuscript, the responses written by Lesparre appear alongside Grandson's poems. Grandson's literary reputation on the Iberian peninsula most probably dates from this period. The *Proemio e carta* (Preface and Letter, circa 1448–1449), considered to be the earliest example of literary criticism written in Spanish, testifies to Grandson's popularity in Spain. In this letter written to the constable of Portugal, the marquis of Santillana praises Grandson along with Guillaume de Lorris, Jean de Meun, Guillaume de Machaut, and Alain Chartier as masters of the art of poetry.

The *Cinq balades ensuivans* reappear in England following Grandson's release from prison in 1374 as the inspiration for Geoffrey Chaucer's *Complaint of Venus,* which was written sometime between 1374 and 1392. Chaucer most probably became acquainted with these poems around 1374, when Grandson entered the service of John of Gaunt, Duke of Lancaster. The original French ballades present a rather conventional love complaint, including the lamentations of a love martyr directed toward his disdainful mistress. Unable to speak with his beloved, Grandson contents himself with reflections on her unrivaled beauty and character. In his opinion, God, Nature, and Reason combined to create a woman possessed of every good quality, grace, and moral virtue. Even the God of Love himself would look no further when seeking a lover. However, one major flaw tempers this perfection: her stubborn refusal to submit to love. The poet goes on to explain that he has served her faithfully for seven years, receiving nothing in return. Instead of enjoying the sweet rewards of love, the devoted Grandson experiences only suffering.

Although Chaucer describes the *Complaint of Venus* as a "word by word" translation of Grandson's ballades, the Englishman's version represents a rewriting that significantly diverges from the originals, including a switch of the gender of the narrator from male to female. The most interesting aspect of Chaucer's *Complaint of Venus* appears in an attached envoy, which has no counterpart in the French ballades. In these ten verses, Chaucer offers a commentary on his literary endeavor as well as on his relationship with Grandson. Adopting the self-deprecating tone of a nonnoble clerk, Chaucer complains of the scarcity of rhyme in English to accommodate the "curiosite" of Grandson's French originals; he does this, however, while using a much more difficult rhyme scheme than that found either in the *Complaint of Venus* itself or in the *Cinq balades ensuivans*, thus subtly valorizing his skill as a poet despite his claims of inadequacy. In the closing line Chaucer identifies and praises his literary source as "Graunson, flour of hem that make in France," (Grandson, flower of those who compose poetry in France)."

Another short ballade series, *Six balades ensuivans* (Six Consecutive Ballades), follows Grandson's *Cinq balades* in several manuscripts. These ballades develop an extended complaint, building upon the dynamic established in the first five. All of the conventional lover's arguments find their way into these poems that seek to move the poet's beloved to mercy. The series ends with an envoy addressed directly to the lady, requesting her to soothe the lover's misery with a tender thought. This envoy represents a structural anomaly, as it replaces the third stanza of the sixth ballade, leaving it formally incomplete in spite of the traditional closure signaled by the envoy. These two ballade series establish Grandson as one of the earliest practitioners of this literary form and signal a key development in the evolution of lyric discourse. The lyric series found at the end of the *Livre Messire Ode* experiments with another version of the collection, with an increased emphasis on narrative coherence.

Evidently Grandson and Chaucer enjoyed a strong personal friendship and a mutually beneficial literary association. The *Complaint of Venus* testifies to Chaucer's interest in and respect for Grandson's work; similarly, many of Grandson's poems reveal the direct influence of Chaucerian ideas. Perhaps their most famous collaborative effort resulted in the development of the tradition of Valentine's Day poetry, which enjoyed considerable success among their contemporaries and subsequent generations. Among Grandson's relatively limited corpus are found seven works whose rubrics identify them explicitly as Valentine's Day poems: the "Songe Saint Valentin," (The Saint Valentine's Day Dream, circa 1386–1392), two different pieces entitled "Complainte de Saint Valentin" (The Saint Valentine's Day Complaint), "Balade de Saint Valentin" (The Saint Valentine's Day Ballade), "Balade de Saint Valentin Double" (The Double Ballade of Saint Valentine), the "Souhait Saint Valentin" (The Saint Valentine's Wish), and the "Complainte Amoureuse de Sainct Valentin Gransson" (Grandson's Love Complaint on Saint Valentine's Day). As with the majority of Grandson's poetic production, it is impossible to date these poems with any certainty, with the exception of the "Songe Saint Valentin," which was probably written circa 1386–1392.

Grandson and Chaucer popularized in literature the tradition of choosing one's beloved on the feast of St. Valentine. Grandson's first "Complainte de Saint Valentin" dramatizes this occasion, as the God of Love and St. Valentine appear before the narrator, who refuses to participate in the festivities due to the recent death of his lady. His resistance is short lived, however, as love's champions introduce him to a new lady who surpasses all others, whom he promises to serve for life. The "Balade de Saint Valentin" offers a lyric rendering of this promise, with each verse beginning "Je vous choisy" (I choose you). This ballade may represent the earliest of the occasional poems, based on its appearance in the Barcelona manuscript, which probably includes those works written by Grandson prior to 1374. The much-debated question as to which poet was the originator of the Valentine literary tradition was resolved by James I. Wimsatt, who declared it a joint effort between the two poets, with Grandson being the first to write love poems on Valentine's Day and Chaucer introducing the convention of birds choosing their mates. In support of this conclusion, Wimsatt cites the fact that the first English poets to write Valentine's Day verse after Chaucer refer to the birds choosing their mates, whereas birds do not appear at all in the next generation of French Valentine's Day poetry.

The identity of the lady to whom Grandson addresses his poems has inspired a great deal of speculation by both literary critics and historians; however, the value of these texts as autobiography remains highly questionable, especially given their adherence to conventional forms and ideas. The tenets of courtly love mandated discretion on the part of all romantic partners. Consequently, there are no overt references to any particular lady in any of Grandson's poems. Nonetheless, the presence within the texts themselves of the acrostic "ISABEL," woven into the initial verses of the "Souhait Saint Valentin," the "Songe Saint Valentin," and the opening letter of each stanza of the "Complainte de Gransson" suggests that perhaps the poet did indeed write at least some of his poems for a particular individual. Several different women have been identified as this Isabel, including Isabel de Portugal, Isabel of York, Isabel de Castille, and Isabeau de Bavière (Isabel of Bavaria), Queen of France. A fifth Isabel, Isabel de Neuchâtel, should also enter into consideration, as records indicate that Grandson spent time with her as an escort in her retinue as well as at court. Historical realities eliminate the princess of Portugal, for she was born several months after the death of Grandson, but the other cases can be neither confirmed nor denied based on existing evidence.

Perhaps the most attractive candidate for the romantic imagination is Queen Isabel of Bavaria. Her royal status corresponds to Grandson's description of "la non per de France," (the lady without equal in France) of whom he declares himself unworthy. In addition, court documents indicate that the French queen possessed a manuscript of the "livre des balades messire Othe de Grantson" (Book of the Ballades of Sir Oton de Grandson), which she had bound with two gold clasps. Wimsatt has suggested that this manuscript is now the University of Pennsylvania manuscript French 15. Unfortunately, a lack of solid historical evidence makes it impossible to reach any absolute conclusions concerning the identity of Grandson's "belle sans per" (beauty without equal).

The fixed-form lyrics—including ballades, rondeaux, complaints, lays, virelays, pastourelles, and chansons—scattered throughout the many manuscripts containing Grandson's works give voice to the unhappy victim of unrequited love. Despite the efforts of some critics, most notably Arthur Piaget, to read them as a chronologically organized, pseudo-autobiographical narrative, no solid evidence exists to encourage such a reading. Instead, these thematically related poems reflect a variety of perspectives on the courtly love relationship, be it real or imagined. Several of Grandson's ballades are conceived as a sort of *ars amatoria* (art of love), directed toward those who count themselves among the servants of the God of Love. Grandson, recognized by his contemporaries as among the worthiest of noble lovers, proclaims that loyalty, discretion, generosity, and honor are among the most essential qualities for an aspiring lover. Having followed his own good advice, devoting himself exclusively to one woman, "des belles la meillour" (the best of the most beautiful), for a period of years, Grandson laments her unresponsiveness to his amorous overtures as well as to his loyalty. As a symbolic testament to his unhappy state, he conducts himself as one in mourning, "vestu de noir" (dressed in black). However, he repeatedly and graciously accepts his beloved's indifference, as befitting a nobleman of his status and reputation and remains dedicated to her in spite of his suffering. As the lover explains, his lady so surpasses all others

Qui il me vault mieulx trestous les maulx avoir
En vous servant que d'autre recevoir
Tous les grans biens que jamais homme aura.

(That it is better for me to endure endless suffering
while serving you than to receive from another
all of the great rewards that a man could ever have.)

In his quest for mercy, Grandson enlists the aid of many of the conventional allegorical figures who populate the literature of the Middle Ages. The lover is inspired and encouraged by Espoir (Hope) and hopes that along with Pitié (Pity), Courtoisie (Courtesy) and

Franchise (Openness), he may vanquish Dangier (Resistance). The scope of the allegory remains limited in Grandson's poetry, never approaching the global narrative coherence found in the works of later authors, such as Charles d'Orléans.

In a few ballades, Grandson gives voice to a female narrator. The woman who speaks in most of these poems has, like her male counterpart, experienced loss or betrayal; however, in one intriguing departure from this norm, a lady who has taken a new lover responds to her former lover's accusations. She not only shows no sympathy toward him, claiming to not even remember who he is, but also berates him for his inflexibility and lack of gratitude for the pleasures he enjoyed while in Love's favor. A similar attitude characterizes the female protagonist of the *Pastourelle Gransson* (Grandson's Pastourelle), "la bien saichant pasteure" (the clever shepherdess) who reveals herself to be much more sophisticated than her companion, a "simple, loyal bergier" (simple, faithful shepherd). This poem scarcely resembles the traditional pastourelle, for it is the woman who controls the erotic dynamic. The shepherd complains of his beloved's indifference to him and the attention she has accorded other men—"un ou deux, / Ou cinq ou dix ou vint ou trente" (one or two, / or five or ten or twenty or thirty). She responds that in order to hide her intentions, she must flirt with more than one man and, furthermore, that he should content himself with the favors he receives without concerning himself with anyone else.

The static, imaginary universe that provides the setting for almost all of Grandson's poetry contrasts sharply with the poet's active military and political career. During the late 1370s and early 1380s, the Savoyard knight enjoyed a period of activity which included a campaign at Cherbourg in 1379 and a mission to Portugal as the envoy of the king of England in 1382.

After returning to England in 1384, he participated in peace negotiations between the French monarch, Charles VI, and King Richard II. The poet Eustache Deschamps, a member of the French entourage at these negotiations, recounts an anecdote concerning a visit to Grandson, revealing a lighter side to this noble personality. Deschamps arrived at Calais, having forgotten to bring his pass. Grandson decided to play a practical joke on his friend by refusing to identify him to the English authorities, who promptly arrested him. Dechamps writes: "De paour la face me ride, / De tel amour ma mort me cuide. / Au derrain leur dist: 'Je l'adveue.'" (My face creased with fear, / With such friendship, I thought I would die. / At last, he said to them: "I acknowledge him.")

Grandson returned to Savoy in 1386 upon the death of his father. A judicial challenge was brought against his inheritance, and he spent several years resolving this dispute. In 1389 court records identify Grandson as a prisoner, held first at the château of Morges and then the château of Chillon, although the reasons for his detention are unknown. During this time, while defending his inheritance and becoming enmeshed in even greater political troubles, Grandson likely composed his two longest works, the *Songe Saint Valentin* and the *Livre Messire Ode*.

The *Songe Saint Valentin* fits loosely into the generic category of the *dit amoureux*, as it highlights the first-person discourse of a clerkly writer who uses his exemplary tale to instruct his audience. As its title suggests, the *Songe* also belongs to the category of dream visions. The narrator opens with a prologue of approximately thirty lines that reflects on the pleasures of letting the mind wander to pass the time, but warns that one has little control over these musings, and they may lead to either "fouleur ou sçavoir" (folly or wisdom). The narrator then offers a dream he had on Valentine's Day as evidence of this phenomenon. In this dream, the narrator goes in search of a ruby and a diamond he had left in a garden the previous day and happens upon an assembly of birds of all varieties. Moved by this spectacle and the charming songs of the participants, he immediately abandons his search for the jewels, turning his attention instead to the activities of the birds. Following the Valentine's Day tradition, each of these birds "choisist a per en son degré, / Cellui qui mieulx lui vient a gré" (chooses as mate according to his rank, / the one which pleases him the most). The narrator then notices one bird, a very noble, richly appareled peregrine falcon who remains apart from the others, perched atop a pine tree. When confronted by the eagle who presides over the avian assembly, the falcon explains that he has indeed already dedicated himself to the most worthy bird. The falcon recounts a story which portrays him as a fine courtly lover who suffers as the victim of an impossible love. Like Grandson, who was suspected of amorous inclinations toward "la non pareille de France," Queen Isabel of Bavaria, the falcon loves above his social condition. The eagle offers a favorable judgment of the falcon's case, and the assembly suddenly disperses, flying away in pairs. The narrator awakens as the birds depart.

The *Songe Saint Valentin* concludes with a lengthy epilogue in which the narrator reflects upon the love experience of the birds and of men. In his opinion, no one should be blamed for loving the one he or she chooses. Grandson's narrator is moved to tears, sharing the anguish of unhappy lovers; however, he claims to possess no firsthand knowledge of such affairs, having

been "n'amé n'amis" (neither loved nor lover) and writing only from "l'ouy-dire" (hearsay). Paradoxically, this claim of inexperience enhances Grandson's status as a lover by displaying his courtly discretion. As a poet, he skillfully incorporates his own love experience into the words of the *Songe,* which seem to deny this very possibility. After reiterating his "simplece" (naïveté) in matters of love, the narrator again expresses sympathy for all those wounded by love:

> Tant est navré qui amours blesse,
> Que j'ay pitié de tous amans,
> Soyent englois ou alemans,
> De France né ou de Savoye.
>
> (He who is wounded by love is so destroyed
> that I have pity on all lovers,
> be they English or German,
> born in France or in Savoy.)

His choice of adjectives here offers yet another subtle hint concerning the poet's love relationship. The four terms identify Grandson himself and Isabel of Bavaria. Grandson, a native of Savoy, spent much time in England in the service of John of Gaunt and Richard II. Isabel, a native of Bavaria (and therefore "alemans," that is, German), became queen of France. His text thus conforms to the rule of courtly discretion that binds all lovers, proving his worthiness in the eyes of his lady, to whom he addresses his poem in the opening acrostic.

The *Livre Messire Ode,* composed during the same period as the *Songe Saint Valentin,* represents the longest and most complex work written by Grandson. This text combines the poetics of the lyric collection developing out of the *Cinq balades ensuivans* with the techniques of the *dit* and the dream vision that characterize the *Songe Saint Valentin.* While the love situation that inspires the writing of the *Livre Messire Ode* offers little in the way of originality, the hybrid and fragmentary structure of this text represents a major and influential innovation, as Grandson explores the relationship between lyric identity and poetic form in these 2,645 lines, divided almost equally between lyric and narrative verse.

As a text about writing and the role of the poet, Guillaume de Machaut's *Le Livre dou Voir-Dit* (The Book of the True Tale, circa 1363–1365) serves as the principal model for Grandson's *Livre.* The fundamental importance of the first-person voice reveals itself in the opening verses of the text, which also comment on the role of the poetry he sets out to compose:

> Je vueil ung livre encommencier
> Et a ma dame l'envoyer,
> Ainsi que je luy ay promis,
> Ou seront tous mes faiz escripz

(I want to begin a book
in which all of my deeds will be written,
and send it to my lady,
just as I have promised her.)

This text will be "escripz" (written) rather than sung or said, a defining feature of the lyric production of the fourteenth century. As opposed to general lamentations vaguely directed toward the lady, which are found throughout Grandson's ballades, this account is conceived with the specific purpose of creating a book. Writing thus forms an integral part of the poet's love service; the poet's desire is sublimated through the pages of a book, which he will then offer to his lady as testament to and material proof of this love.

The first-person voice in the *Livre Messire Ode* is characterized by a fundamental ambiguity resulting from the instability inherent in Grandson's dual identity as aristocrat and poet. Grandson was acutely aware of the social and literary roles that distinguished the noble knight from the court poet since he himself embodied aspects of both figures. The aristocratic poet Grandson who composes fixed-form love lyrics need never question the authenticity of his poetic voice, since according to poetic convention, the noble lover has the right—or indeed the obligation—to sing about his love experiences. His status becomes complicated, however, when he ventures into the genre of the *dit,* a form characterized by the fictionalized discourse of the *clerc-écrivain* (clerkly writer). Grandson reverses poetic convention by initially adopting the anonymous voice of the professional poet, whereas professional poets, such as Guillaume de Machaut, seek to appropriate the privileged voice of the noble lover. Following the conventions of the *dit,* Grandson attempts to differentiate the clerkly narrator from the protagonist engaged in love adventures; however, the two manifestations of the first-person voice—poet and lover—merge in the lyric series that closes the text.

The status of the first-person voice becomes increasingly complex as the text develops. The *Livre Messire Ode* consists of two dream sequences, each of which is introduced and followed by a waking episode. The author alternates lyric and narrative verse in an unsystematic fashion until the final section of the *Livre,* which is comprised exclusively of fixed-form poems. The events of the first dream, the product of a troubled sleep, include sixteen intercalated lyric pieces and two letters, one in verse and one in prose. The appearance of three secondary characters marks the major narrative episodes of this dream: a happy lover, a young squire who begins a lament but is immediately comforted by a young lady, and an unhappy lover. The first two characters serve essentially to highlight the unfavorable love situation of the narrator-protagonist, while the unhappy lover, on the contrary, plays a fundamental role in the development of the story, introducing an important dialogic dynamic modeled on the *jeu-parti,* and commenting on appropriate strategies for reading metaphorical discourse.

The encounter between Grandson and the bird lover disrupts the formal and generic system based on the *dit,* which defines the first dream sequence, with narrative verses framing lyrics, identifying the love situation out of which they develop and emphasizing the act of transcribing them into the book. When the bird lover recounts the tale of his amorous adventures, he begins not in the narrative octosyllabic couplets used previously, but rather with a narrative fixed-form ballade. The narrator's response follows a similar pattern, thus undoing the previous distinctions between lyric and narrative discourse. While lyric forms reject traditional lyric material, however, the narrative translates nothing other than lyric experience—the suffering of two unhappy lovers.

The second dream, which is significantly shorter than the first, comprised of a brief introduction and a complaint, results from a combination of fatigue and the narrator's desire to have the opinions of his lady revealed to him in a dream. The third and final waking scene consists of a series of thirteen lyric poems that do not advance the narrative, but comment on various elements of it. The lyric finale is an amplification of the return to lyric discourse found at the end of the dream-vision poems, and the first-person voice speaking in these fixed-form poems recalls and echoes all of the other first-person utterances throughout the entire work. Defining his *Livre* initially according to the principles of the *dit* while moving progressively toward the poetics of the lyric collection, Grandson creates a literary dialogue among individual voices, poetic forms, and modes of writing.

Perhaps the strangest events in Grandson's history relate to the death on 2 November 1392 of the Red Count, Amédée VII of Savoy. While hunting wild boar, the count fell from his horse and suffered a wound to his thigh. Initially left untreated, the wound worsened, eventually leading to his death by what has since been identified as tetanus. Before dying, however, Amédée revealed his belief that he had been poisoned. In a bizarre series of unfounded assumptions and accusations, Bonne de Bourbon, the count's mother, and Jean de Grandville, the attending physician, were accused of conspiracy and murder. Inculpated as an accomplice was Grandson.

Political rivalries and economic interests fueled the rumors of murder in the absence of any convincing evidence. Jean de Grandville's forced confession under

*Opening page from a manuscript that may have been compiled by Grandson for Isabelle of Bavaria
(University of Pennsylvania ms. French 15)*

torture provided factions hostile to the regency of Bonne de Bourbon (including the regent's daughter-in-law, Bonne de Berry) adequate material to inflame public opinion. Although Grandson had served as a trusted advisor to the Red Count (a distant relative), he was unable to quiet the accusations against him, even though he had been absent from the court at the time the alleged conspiracy was developed.

In order to escape the hostile environment in Savoy, shortly after the count's death Grandson returned to England, where he entered the service of Richard II. From 24 July 1392 through 5 July 1393, Grandson participated in the military campaign of Henry Bolingbroke, the earl of Derby, in Prussia and the Upper Palatinate. In 1393 Grandson's properties were seized although there exists no record of any judgment against him. Rodolphe de Gruyère and Jean de la Baume, who had previously challenged the legitimacy of Grandson's claims to Aubonne and Coppet, purchased these domains. Gérard d'Estavayer took over the administration of Cudrefin and Grandcour on behalf of François Corneri, the new proprietor. Grand-

son seems to refer to this dispossession and flight to England in two ballades whose subject matter distinguishes them from the poet's typical works, declaring that folly reigns as

Gens ennuyeux et commun trop puissant,
M'ont eforcé, du mien desherité,
Et vont toudiz mon honneur chalangant.

(Bothersome common people with too much power
have forced me to lose my possessions
and go about challenging my honor.)

In 1395 Grandson received a complete and unconditional pardon from the French king, Charles VI. Despite the challenges to his character in the wake of Amédée VII's death, Grandson still commanded a great deal of respect, at least outside of Savoy. In addition to the king's pardon, Philippe de Mézières named Grandson as one of the four principal "Evangelists" in *La substance abregee de la Chevalerie de la Passion de Jhesu-Crist* (The Condensed Charter of the Knightly Order of the Passion of Jesus Christ, 1396), which formally outlined the obligations and purpose of this knightly order he envisioned for a new crusade in defense of Christianity.

This noble recognition held little sway among the general public in Savoy, however. In order to restore his claims on Grandson's lands, Gérard d'Estavayer revived the accusations of murder against him, including not only that of the Red Count, but also adding the absurd claim that Grandson had murdered his uncle, Hugues de Grandson, a convicted felon who had actually died in prison. Gérard d'Estavayer challenged Grandson to a judicial duel, a "jugement de Dieu" (judgment of God) in order to determine his guilt or innocence. After many delays, the duel finally took place on 7 August 1397 at Bourg-en-Bresse, and Grandson was killed by his younger opponent. Only one account of the duel survives, written almost one hundred years later by Olivier de la Marche in his *Livre de l'advis du gaige de bataille* (Book of Battle Engagement Protocol, 1494) and of questionable accuracy.

The life of this Savoyard nobleman-poet offers a colorful history of power, glory, intrigue, and ultimately, defeat, which inspired many legends for centuries after his death. Neglected since the laudatory testimonies of his contemporaries, the works of Oton de Grandson have much to offer as textual artifacts of the changing literary climate of the late fourteenth century. Influenced by the dominant literary trends of the late Middle Ages, the poet Grandson adapts conventional elements in innovative ways, experimenting with hybrid and fragmented forms that significantly influenced the evolution of lyric poetry. Through all aspects of his life and letters, Grandson's voice proudly resonates with the family motto: "A petite cloche, grand son" (a great sound for a small bell).

References:

G. Bertoni, "Liriche di Oton de Grandson, Guillaume de Machaut e di altri poeti in un nuovo canzoniere," *Archivum romanticum,* 16 (1932): 1–20;

Haldeen Braddy, "Chaucer and Graunson: The Valentine Tradition," *PMLA,* 54 (1939): 359–368;

Braddy, *Chaucer and the French Poet Graunson* (Baton Rouge: Louisiana State University Press, 1947);

Braddy, "Chaucer's *Book of the Duchess* and Two of Graunson's Complaintes," *Modern Language Notes,* 52 (1937): 487–491;

Braddy, "Flour of hem that make in France," *Studies in Philology,* 35 (1938): 10–24;

Sally Tartline Carden, "Le *Livre Messire Ode* d'Oton de Grandson: Un interrogatoire poétique," *Le Moyen Français,* 35–36 (1996): 79–89;

Normand R. Cartier, "Oton de Grandson et sa princesse," *Romania,* 85 (1964): 1–16;

A. Henry, "Une copie inconnue du 'Lay de désir en complainte' d'Oton de Grandson," in *Mélanges de philologie romane offerts à Karl Michaëlsson* (Göteborg: University of Göteborg, 1952), pp. 250–255;

Stefan Hofer, "Zu den dichtungens Otons de Granson," *Zeitschrift für französische Sprache und Literatur,* 54 (1930): 168;

France Igly, *Oton de Grandson, chevalier-poète du XIVe siècle* (Sierre: Nouvelle Bibliothèque Travers, 1969);

James C. Laidlaw, "An Unidentified Fragment of *the Livre Messire Ode* de Granson," *Scriptorium,* 24 (1970): 53–54;

L. Mourin," Le débat des deux grands amis," *Scriptorium,* 1 (1946–1947): 151–154;

Amédée Pagès, "Le thème de la tristesse amoureuse en France et en Espagne du XIVe au Xve siècle," *Romania,* 58 (1932): 29–43;

Arthur Piaget, "La *Belle Dame sans Mercy* et ses imitations. VI. La Belle Dame qui eut merci," *Romania,* 33 (1904): 200–206;

Piaget, "Oton de Grandson amoureux de la reine," *Romania,* 61 (1935): 72–82;

Piaget, " Oton de Grandson et ses poésies," *Romania,* 19 (1890) : 237–259, 403–448;

Piaget, *Oton de Grandson: Sa vie et ses poésies* (Lausanne & Geneva: Payot, 1941);

G. Ludwig Schirer, *Oton de Graunson und seine Dichtungen* (Strassburg: M. Du Mont-Schauberg, 1904);

Jaume Massó Torrents, "Oto de Granson i les balades de Lluís de Vilarasa," in *Mélanges de linguistique et de littérature offerts à M. Alfred Jeanroy* (Paris: Droz, 1928), pp. 403–410;

James I. Wimsatt, "Chaucer and Oton de Granson" in *Chaucer and His French Contemporaries: Natural Music in the Fourteenth Century* (Toronto: University of Toronto Press, 1991), pp. 210–241;

Wimsatt, *Chaucer and the Poems of "Ch" in the University of Pennsylvania MS French 15* (Cambridge: D. S. Brewer / Totowa, N.J.: Rowman & Littlefield, 1982).

Hugh of St. Victor

(circa 1096 – 11 February 1141)

Edgar Laird

Southwest Texas State University

WORKS: *Commentaria in Hierarchiam celestem* (before 1125)

Standard edition: In *Patralogia latina,* 221 volumes, edited by Jacques-Paul Migne (Paris: Migne, 1841–1879), CLXXV: 923A–1154C.

Didascalicon de studio legendi (before 1125)

Standard editions: In *Patralogia latina,* 221 volumes, edited by Jacques-Paul Migne (Paris: Migne, 1841–1879), CLXXVI: 770C–812B; *Hugonis de Sancto Victore Didascalicon de studio legendi, a Critical Text,* edited by Charles Henry Buttimer, Studies in Medieval and Renaissance Latin no. 10 (Washington, D. C.: Catholic University of America, 1939).

Edition in English: *Didascalicon: A Medieval Guide to the Arts,* translated by Jerome Taylor, Records of Civilization, Sources and Studies no. 64 (New York: Columbia University Press, 1961).

Epitome Dindimi in philosophiam (before 1125)

Standard edition: In *Hugonis de Sancto Victore opera propaedeutica:* Practica geometriae, De grammatica, Epitome Dindimi in philosophiam, edited by Roger Baron, University of Notre Dame Publications in Mediaeval Studies no. 20 (Notre Dame, Ind.: University of Notre Dame Press, 1966).

Practica geometrie (before 1125)

Standard edition: In *Hugonis de Sancto Victore opera propaedeutica:* Practica geometriae, De grammatica, Epitome Dindimi in philosophiam, edited by Roger Baron, University of Notre Dame Publications in Mediaeval Studies no. 20 (Notre Dame, Ind.: University of Notre Dame Press, 1966).

Edition in English: *Practical Geometry = Practica geometriae, Attributed to Hugh of St. Victor,* translated by Frederick A. Homann, Mediaeval Philosophical Texts in Translation no. 29 (Milwaukee: Marquette University Press, 1991).

De arca Noe morali and *De arca Noe mystica* (circa 1126–1129).

Standard editions: In *Patralogia latina,* 221 volumes, edited by Jacques-Paul Migne (Paris: Migne, 1841–1879), CLXXVI: 618C–680D; *Hugo de Sancto Victore: De arch Noe pro arch sapientie cum arch Ecclesi et archa matris gratie. Libellus de formatione arche,* edited by Patrice Sicard, Corpus Christianorum, Continuo Mediaevalis no. 161 (Turnhout, Belgium: Brepols 1994).

De vanitate mundi (before circa 1130–1131)

Standard editions: In *Patralogia latina,* 221 volumes, edited by Jacques-Paul Migne (Paris: Migne, 1841–1879), CLXXVI: 703A–740C; in *Hugo von St. Viktor: "Soliloquium de arrha animae" und "De vanitate mundi,"* edited by Karl Müller, Kleine Texte für Vorlesungen und Ubungen (Bonn: A. Marcus and E. Weber, 1913).

Chronicon, with prologue *De tribus maximus circumstantiis gestorum* (circa 1130–1131)

Standard editions: *Chronica: quae dicitur Hugonis de Sancto Victore,* edited by G. Waitz (Hanover: Hahn, 1879): 88–97; "Hugo of St. Victor *De tribus maximis circumstantiis gestorum,*" edited by William M. Green, *Speculum,* 18 (1943): 484–493.

De sacramentis christiane fidei (circa 1131–1135)

Standard edition: In *Patralogia latina,* 221 volumes, edited by Jacques-Paul Migne (Paris: Migne, 1841–1879), CLXXVI: 173A–618B.

Edition in English: *Hugh of Saint Victor on the Sacraments of the Christian Faith: English Version,* translated by Roy. J. Deferrari (Cambridge, Mass.: Medieval Academy of America, 1951).

Soliloquium de arrha anime (circa 1139–1140)

Standard edition: In *Patralogia latina,* 221 volumes, edited by Jacques-Paul Migne (Paris: Migne, 1841–1879), CLXXVI: 951B–970D; in *Hugo von St. Viktor: "Soliloquium de arrha animae" und "De vanitate mundi,"* edited by Karl Müller, Kleine Texte für Vorlesungen und Ubungen (Bonn: A. Marcus and E. Weber, 1913).

Annotationes in Pentateuchum

Standard edition: In *Patralogia latina,* 221 volumes, edited by Jacques-Paul Migne (Paris: Migne, 1841–1879), CLXXVI: 29A–86D.

Annotationes in librum Iudicum

> **Standard edition:** In *Patralogia latina,* 221 volumes, edited by Jacques-Paul Migne (Paris: Migne, 1841–1879), CLXXVI: 87A–96C.

Annotationes in libros Regum

> **Standard edition:** In *Patralogia latina,* 221 volumes, edited by Jacques-Paul Migne (Paris: Migne, 1841–1879), CLXXVI: 95D–114B.

Annotationes in Threnos

> **Standard edition:** In *Patralogia latina,* 221 volumes, edited by Jacques-Paul Migne (Paris: Migne, 1841–1879), CLXXVI: 255D–322B.

Descriptio mappe mundi

> **Standard edition:** *La 'Descriptio mappe mundi' de Hugues de Saint-Victor: Texte inédit avec introduction et commentaire,* edited by Patrick Gautier Dalché (Paris: Etudes Augustiniennes, 1988).

Epistula ad canonicos Lucensis

> **Standard edition:** "*Epistula ad canonicos Lucensis,*" edited by J. F. Croyden, in *Journal of Theological Studies,* 40 (1939): 251.

De sapientia Christi

> **Standard editions:** In *Patralogia latina,* 221 volumes, edited by Jacques-Paul Migne (Paris: Migne, 1841–1879), CLXXVI: 845C–856D; "De sapientia Christi. Ad Gualterum de Mauritania," edited by Ludwig Ott in *Untersuchungen zur theologischen Briefliteratur der Frühscholastik,* Beiträge zur Geschichte der Philosophie und Theologie des Mittelalters no. 34 (Münster: Aschendorff, 1937), pp. 353–354.

Sententie de divinitate

> **Standard edition:** "Hugo di San Vittore, 'auctor' delle *'Sententie de divinitate,'*" edited by A. M. Piazzoni in *Studi Medievali,* 23 (1982): 861–955.

De uirtutibus et uitiis

> **Standard edition:** *De uirtutibus et uitiis,* edited by Roger Baron in his *Études sur Hugues de Saint-Victor* (Bruges: De Brouwer, 1963), pp. 248–255.

Hugh of St. Victor has been called by modern historians the leading and most influential theologian of the twelfth century. In his *Divine Comedy* (early fourteenth century), the poet Dante situates him in the fourth sphere of Paradise, among the intellectual and spiritual lights associated with the Sun. The thirteenth-century Italian theologian Bonaventura ranked Hugh among his approximate contemporaries by saying that whereas Anselm of Canterbury was great in rational argumentation, Bernard of Clairvaux was great in preaching, and Richard of St. Victor was great in mystic vision, Hugh was great in all three areas at one and the same time. In his own day, Hugh was sometimes called *alter Augustinus,* a "second

Augustine." He was a teacher, philosopher, theologian, and mystic whose extensive and varied writings do not fit readily into literary genres. They may, nevertheless, be grouped into the following categories: commentaries (chiefly scriptural), educational handbooks, theological works (treatises and brief teaching summaries), spiritual writings, letters, and sermons.

The canon and chronology of Hugh's works have been difficult to establish. Some works, such as the treatise *De astronomia* (On Astronomy) that Hugh himself claims to have written, are no longer discoverable. Moreover, there has been a tendency over the centuries to attach Hugh's name to anonymous works written by others, for example, the treatise *De bestis et aliis rebus* (On Animals and Other Creatures) that is sometimes cited to demonstrate Hugh's familiarity with anatomical texts of the Salernitan school of medicine is probably not by Hugh.

Owing to a scantiness and contradictoriness of surviving data concerning Hugh's early life, his origins remain obscure; most details of his life are derived from an account assembled by the Victorines (canons of the order of St. Victor) who published an edition of his works at Rouen in 1648. Hugh belonged to the family of the counts of Blankenburg in the German diocese of Halberstadt. He was born in the last decade of the eleventh century, possibly in 1096, and was sent at an early age to the Augustinian house of St. Pancras at Hamersleben. While still a youth, he was sent by his uncle Reinhard, Bishop of Halberstadt, to the newly established abbey of St. Victor in Paris. Traveling in the company of another uncle (himself named Hugh), who was an archdeacon of the church at Halberstadt, the young Hugh went first to the monastery of St. Victor at Marseilles, where he and his uncle obtained relics of the saint. From there, possibly as early as 1115, the two Hughs arrived at St. Victor in Paris and presented the relics along with other donations to the abbot, Gilduin. Hugh and his uncle entered the abbey, and soon, certainly by the early 1120s, Hugh was teaching, writing, and attracting a following among students and fellow scholar-teachers. He remained there until his death on 11 February 1141.

Substantial details of this sketch of Hugh's early life have been questioned, chiefly on the basis of statements in manuscripts dating from as early as 1154 that he came from Lorraine or the Low Countries rather than from Germany. The question of his national origin was once hotly debated by historians, some of whom saw in his life and work an expression of "racial genius." That question now seems less important than the fact of his early association with the canons regular, with their communal life of monastic observance, pastoral duty, and teaching. Hugh tended to minimize the importance of origins, remarking, in his *Didascalicon de studio legendi* (Didascalicon on the Study of Reading, before 1125) that he has lived in a foreign land since he was a boy, and asserting that, for a perfect philosopher, all the visible and transitory world should be a foreign land.

During Hugh's earliest years at St. Victor, the abbey and school were new. St. Victor had been founded in 1108 by William of Champeaux, former master of the cathedral school in Paris, where he had lectured for many years on dialectics and theology. His move to the old chapel and hermitage of St. Victor outside the walls of Paris expressed his intention to retire with some of his disciples in order to lead a life of prayer and contemplation; but before long, perhaps under pressure, he had resumed teaching and had reorganized the hermitage under the Rule of St. Augustine. Thus he early established for St. Victor that association of the contemplative and the academic which Hugh encountered and found entirely congenial when he arrived. In 1113 William had become bishop of Châlons-sur-Marne, and in 1114 King Louis VI made St. Victor a royal abbey with Gilduin as abbot, a position he was to hold until 1155, that is, throughout Hugh's life at St. Victor, and it was Gilduin who first assembled Hugh's collected works. By the 1120s when the two Hughs arrived, a building program was underway.

One of Hugh's most influential works was also one of his earliest. Written before 1125, the *Didascalicon* is a sort of educational outline, or encyclopedia, of which the first three books deal mainly with secular arts and the remaining three deal with the study of Scripture. Its influence can be seen not only on the work of others but also on Hugh's own later works, as it treats subjects and develops themes that are of enduring importance to him, so that many of his later works, though widely various in form and function, manifestly exploit or develop its text. Hugh's development as a scholar and writer was not a discursive movement from one study to another, but a continuing act of studying and elaborating all things whose study can lead to wisdom, which is held to be divine. It is in that spirit that he says at the opening of the *Didascalicon,* "Learn everything; you will see afterwards that nothing is superfluous."

As an educational preliminary, *Didascalicon* is a study guide for learning everything, which establishes a schema that will encompass all knowledge. Drawing upon various Greek schemata as they came to him through Latin intermediaries, Hugh organizes arts, sciences, and all disciplines into four categories: the theoretical, the practical, the mechanical, and the logical.

His most conspicuous contribution here was the very un-Greek inclusion of the mechanical arts alongside the other three. He may have been moved to include them by their usefulness in the urban setting of his school. That contribution, however, did not catch on among his contemporaries and successors; William of Conches, for example, argued for an alternative schema of his own. In any case, it was not this innovation, which Hugh himself ignored in later works, that was of lasting importance. What was important was Hugh's treatment of the theoretical sciences of mathematics, physics, and theology so as to condition Western thinking for reception of the thirteenth-century translations of Aristotle's *Physics* and *Metaphysics.*

Hugh was not the first to adopt such a division and treatment of theoretical sciences. A version of the division is succinctly presented in Boethius's short treatise *De Trinitate* (On the Trinity, circa A.D. 520), which, not coincidentally, Hugh lectured on, according to Clarembaud of Arras, in his commentary on *De Trinitate;* however, Hugh's schema, which included the seven liberal arts, influenced such important theorists as Dominicus Gundissalinus, John of Salisbury, Robert Kilwardby, and Albertus Magnus.

A second major theme in Hugh's works that first appears in the *Didascalicon* is that there is a difference between reading Holy Scripture and reading anything else. The Augustinian distinction between other texts, in which words signify things, and Scripture, in which both words and things signify, was often stated in Hugh's time, but it was not always observed. Hugh's insistence on making the distinction sounds much like one side of a debate in which he is responding to those who would explicate secular literature—even pagan poetry—as if it were the product of an all-knowing mind, capable of yielding philosophical, metaphysical, or theological truth. A statement of St. Paul's that "all that is written is written for our doctrine" (Romans 14:4) was sometimes taken in the Middle Ages as an excuse for extracting doctrine from poetry, with Geoffrey Chaucer going so far as to apply it to some of his *Canterbury Tales* (circa 1387–1400); however, while his contemporaries were writing commentaries on Virgil, Juvenal, Martianus Capella, and Plato, Hugh confined his own commentaries to Scripture and one or two religious texts.

In addition to distinguishing Scripture from other texts, Hugh also distinguished between history (what truly occurred) and fable (fictional narrative). His contemporaries made a similar distinction, but Hugh had much less use for fables than some of them did. William of Conches and others who have been grouped under the heading "Chartreans" thought it possible to extract natural philosophy from fable. In *Didascalicon,* again sounding somewhat adversarial, Hugh rejects as tangential to philosophy not only the songs of poets, but also the prose of those who are called philosophers but who in their writing lump fiction and fact together. Natural philosophy itself, moreover, has less explanatory power for Hugh than for the Chartreans. He never treats the cosmos as a closed system functioning independently of its Creator, according to wholly intelligible and fully explanatory laws. For him, the efficient cause of processes in the created world often turns out to be divine power.

An important aspect of Hugh's teaching and practice is his emphasis on the literal and historical sense of words in Scripture, a continuing theme that is first fully propounded in *Didascalicon*. Whether his "scientific" attention to the literal was something new in the history of exegesis or was an attempt to preserve an older tradition, it was certainly emphatic enough to have the appearance and effect of novelty. The experience of teaching young students, in which he was chiefly engaged at the time of writing *Didascalicon*, probably taught him that a show of theoretical sophistication can be dangerous for those who have an imperfect grasp of the verbal meaning of a text or, worse, an indifference to it. Hence, he insists in *Didascalicon* that "we follow the letter in such a way as not to prefer our own sense to the divine authors." When he says in the same discussion that others teach a different way of reading and that he will not argue with them, he shows himself to be keeping up with developments in his profession. If he is not quite arguing with those whose methods he cannot accept, he is at least responding to their teaching. Both this awareness of what others are doing elsewhere and this disinclination to engage in personal polemics are characteristic of Hugh.

Although *Didascalicon* is an early work, and many of its materials were later reworked, it should not be regarded as embryonic or inchoate. It is well informed and fully accomplished because it is built on the experience of teaching and also on the experience of having written several annotations of the early books of the Old Testament, collectively called *Adnotationes elucidatoriae* (Elucidatory Annotations) or, alternatively, *Notulae* (Brief Notes).These annotations may have begun as isolated notes on individual passages of Scripture, or they may have been extracted from larger, more systematic commentaries. It is possible, too, that Hugh's students collected them. In any case, as Beryl Smalley has shown, they represent an important stage in the development of Scriptural exegesis. They can be seen to be closely tied to Hugh's teaching function and to the study of reading as set forth in his *Didascalicon*.

The *Commentaria in Hierarchiam celestem* (Commentary on the *Celestial Hierarchy*, before 1125) is probably the next major work in time after *Didascalicon*—if, that is, *Epitome Dindimi in philosophiam* (Epitome of Dindimus on Philosophy) and *Practica geometrica* (Practical Geometry) are excepted. The former, a dialogue in which one of the interlocutors is called Dindimus, is in large part an epitome of *Didascalicon;* the latter, a simple geometry text now of some interest to historians of science and mathematics, probably looked less important in Hugh's time. *In Hierarchiam celestem* is considerably more consequential than either. It is a commentary on a Latin version of the *Celestial Hierarchy,* a treatise written in Greek in the fifth or sixth century by the Pseudo-Dionysius—someone pretending to be Dionysius (or Denis) the Areopagite, who had been converted by Paul in the first century A.D. and was identified with St. Denis. The *Celestial Hierarchy* is a work whose Neoplatonism would appeal to—and meld with—Hugh's own Augustinian sort of Neoplatonism. He attaches it to his habitual way of thinking by positing, at the beginning of his commentary, that there are three parts of theoretical science—mathematics, physics, and theology—whereby contemplation ascends to the heights as if by steps. The hierarchy provides a framework by which Hugh can show what he had earlier asserted, that there is a true progression of spirit which mounts toward knowledge of the true through visible forms of visible things (mathematics) and through invisible causes of visible things (physics) in an arising toward invisible substances (theology). The world, Hugh believes, can be a bait drawing us to false worldly goods and beauties; or it can be a sacramental guide drawing us toward divine goodness and beauty.

In Hierarchiam belongs in the main to the period before 1125, and parts of the later *De sacramentis christiane fidei* (On the Sacraments of the Christian Faith, circa 1131–1135) are borrowed from it; however, a subtitle added to *In Hierarchiam,* indicating that Hugh was writing at the desire of King Louis VII, suggests that he was revising or completing it at least as late as 1137, when Louis ascended the throne. Hugh's continuation or resumption of work on the commentary provides another instance of his reluctance to abandon an important topic in favor of something new. The work itself is an instance of the influence of reason on mysticism, and, as such, it is typical of Hugh and other Victorines.

Within a few years of his initial work on *In Hierarchiam,* Hugh wrote three impressive treatises whose mystical and symbolic character has given rise in some quarters to the view that he belongs more properly to the history of mysticism and theology than to that of philosophy or science or education. The treatises, all written before circa 1130–1131, are traditionally discussed under the titles *De arca Noe morali* (On the Moral Ark of Noah), *De arca Noe mystica* (On the Mystic Ark of

Hugh of St. Victor (illuminated page from a twelfth-century manuscript for his
Didascalicon, *Leiden, Bibliothek der Rijksuniversiteit, ms.*
Vulcanianus 46, f. 130)

Noah), and *De vanitate mundi* (On the Vanity of the World). Of these, the two ark-treatises are now usually called *De archa Noe* (On the Ark of Noah) and *Libellus de formatione arche* (Book of the Design of the Ark). Relations among the three are marked by reference in *De vanitate* to *De arca mystica* and reference in the latter to *De arca morali.*

The ark-treatises are remarkable for their employment of diagrammatic representation of the literal, material ark in a form that can be held in memory and that can also be exploited for its symbolic value because it is, in Hugh's sense of the term, mathematical: that is, it is a visible representation of visible things. A spiritual meaning of a Scriptural text requires a firm foundation in the literal, so it is with visual symbolism that an abstract or spiritual lesson requires something concrete that a student can grasp. Hugh tells us that his discus-

sion of the ark grew out of a monastic collation in the cloister where, as master, he was asked questions that led to the writing and to the drawing of diagrams for pedagogical purposes.

De vanitate mundi is, as the title suggests, a rejection of all things worldly, though with a flair and originality unusual in medieval rejections of the world. One must, in abandoning all the world, abandon at last even that precious knowledge acquired in pursuit of arts, sciences, and disciplines. This attitude separates Hugh from his Chartrean contemporaries who distinguish themselves by the quality of their attention to natural philosophy, but it does not make him a skeptic. He is simply warning against the world as bait, against the taking of natural knowledge as a good in itself. *De vanitate mundi* turns away from secular learning because, like the ark-treatises, it is an exercise in spiritual pedagogy.

During this same period, in the midst of writing the three mystical treatises, Hugh also composed his *Chronicon,* a work of historical chronology that is more secular, although not unrelated to the mystical treatises. In *De archa morali,* Hugh sets forth a quadripartite history of the world, moving from Eden through a conflated Assyrian, Babylonian, and Median empire to the Greeks and thence to the Romans, whose empire Hugh extended to include the Roman Catholic Church. In the last two of the four books of *De vanitate mundi,* Hugh reviews the chief personages of sacred history.

The *Chronicon* is not a chronicle–it makes no attempt to be a record of events–but is, rather, a compendium of historical materials designed to introduce young boys to the first stage of Scriptural study, which is the historical and literal interpretation of sacred text. It consists of a prologue and a fairly extensive set of tables (occupying about forty folios in the best manuscripts) that present, in compact form, the essentials of revelation history, together with their principal ramifications in secular history, ancient as well as Christian. The prologue has its own heading or title that constitutes a virtual thesis statement for the whole work: *De tribus maximis circumstantiis gestorum, id est personis locis temporibus* (Three Great Elements in Histories of Events: Persons, Places and Times). The prologue first gives rules for memorizing data; then it announces the three methods of Scriptual exposition already explained in *Didascalicon:* the historical, the allegorical, and the tropological, with the historical being selected here as the foundation of all doctrine and the concern of the present work. The prologue ends with a rehearsal of the six days of creation, and the historical tables follow.

Considerations of historical development have a determining influence on the structure of Hugh's longest and most celebrated work, the *De sacramentis christiane fidei.* It is innovative and important in its systematizing of theological thought according to a temporal schema. The text of *De sacramentis* is in large part a compilation and modification of materials from Hugh's earlier writings, and its general plan had been drawn as early as *Didascalicon* where, in book 6, he describes the foundational and doctrinal studies necessary for the informed reading of divine Scripture. Each study, as there described, corresponds to a section of *De sacramentis.* As the *Chronicon* was an introduction to the literal sense of Scripture, so *De sacramentis,* as Hugh explains, is an introduction to the spiritual or allegorical sense. Thus *Didascalicon* prescribes and *De sacramentis* completes a course in divinity.

In the late 1120s, between the writing of *Didascalicon* and that of *De sacramentis,* Hugh gave a course of theological lectures, perhaps the first course in systematic theology not directly based on Bible commentary.

These lectures were transcribed by a student named Lawrence (possibly Lawrence of Durham, later abbot of Westminster), and the transcriptions were checked and revised by Hugh each week as the course progressed. These lectures are an early, fairly elaborate sketch of *De sacramentis,* which itself was composed over a period of more than five years, beginning in 1130 or 1131.

At this time, Hugh was at the height of his powers, but he was also, as he indicates in prefaces and letters, feeling somewhat burdened by the demands being made of him. He was occupied as master of the school of St. Victor, which was responsible for educating members of the community and was attracting external students as well. There were pastoral obligations that the canons had assumed, including preaching and acting as confessors to students in Paris, and Hugh was also being called upon from time to time to assess difficult theological questions. Following the death of Prior Thomas in 1133, Hugh may for a time have taken on some of a prior's duties. He could have used his level of activity as an excuse for the expedient of incorporating earlier writing into *De sacramentis.* (he did use it to excuse his tardiness in replying to a letter). He did not regard any excuse as necessary, however–on the contrary, his concern was justifying the alteration of older material in the process of incorporating it.

In *De sacramentis* Hugh makes use of the works of others as well as his own. He is, however, sparing in his use of direct quotations and reticent about his sources, which probably include the church fathers, especially Augustine, and later writers, including Hugh's contemporaries. He makes use of Anselm of Canterbury, Anselm of Laon, William of Champeaux and, in oblique but important ways, Peter Abelard. It might be said, in fact, that one of the salient circumstances of Hugh's intellectual life was the existence of Abelard, although Hugh never mentions him by name. In the 1130s, Hugh and Abelard were simultaneously preeminent in the scholastic milieu in and around Paris, and Hugh had long been aware of Abelard's teaching. While the two were in agreement in many things, where Hugh did not agree with Abelard, he simply but firmly set down the views he believed to be correct. He did not, like Bernard of Clairvaux, declare Abelard a persecutor of the Catholic faith and an enemy of the cross of Christ; but he did at times (especially in *De sacramentis* but also as early as *Didascalicon*) clearly dissociate himself from Abelard, as from one of those peddlers of trifles who, he says, accuse their forefathers of simplicity and suppose that wisdom was born with themselves.

During the years from 1123 to 1127, Abelard gave a course of lectures at Quincey, and it was probably these that prompted Hugh to write to Bernard of Clairvaux concerning certain views that Abelard held, especially the view that some pre-Christians had attained a high degree of precise knowledge about the Incarnation and the virgin birth of Christ. Hugh offered a refutation of these views, and Bernard, in a reply, accepted Hugh's arguments and added others of his own, chiefly citations of Scriptural texts. Hugh incorporated Bernard's reply into *De sacramentis* as a discussion of the question whether faith changed according to changes of times. Other parts of *De sacramentis* can be seen to respond to other Abelardian teachings; in addition, other exchanges of correspondence can be seen to affect it, as when Hugh incorporates into it his own letters to Gautier de Mortagne and Ranulphe du Mauriac.

De sacramentis amounts to more than an arrangement of Hugh's old and new teachings, more than a collection of *sententiae* (sentences), although Alexander of Hales, Thomas Aquinas, and Henry of Ghent all refer to the work as Hugh's sentences. It is better described as a *summa,* in the sense of a systematic treatise covering an entire field of learning, and it is the first such *summa* of the Middle Ages. It is not organized dialectically, as later *summae* tended to be, but it is not irrational. Indeed, reason is the standard by which it orders discourse: some enunciations, Hugh says, are from reason and are necessary; some are according to reason and are probable; and some are above reason and are marvelous. The treatise's exclusive concern with divinity does not mean that it is unconcerned with this world. On the contrary, it is deeply concerned with spiritual and sacramental life in this world, often in quite practical ways, as when it specifies that one appointed to read the lessons in the order of worship must first know the alphabet or when it deals with legalistic niceties arising from problems with clandestine marriage. The rationality and practicality of its spiritual teaching lead even critics who are generally unreceptive to spiritual writing to regard *De sacramentis* as the work that best supports Hugh's fame.

More affective than *De sacramentis* and more inward in its spirituality is *Soliloquium de arrha anime* (Soliloquy on Earnest Money of the Soul, circa 1139–1140), a small treatise on love which Hugh sent, along with an affectionate letter, to the brothers at Hamersleben, where in early youth he had first known the canonial life. It is a soliloquy in the sense that it represents a private, interior meditation in which no secrets are hidden; however, in form it is a dialogue, like Augustine's *Soliloquia* (Soliloquies, circa 386–387). The interlocutors are *homo* (a man)—or, in some manuscripts, Hugo—as the voice of Reason and *anima* (soul) as the Soul, the individual subject or person. Written near the end of Hugh's life, in 1139 or 1140, *De arrha* is a final

reworking of yet another theme he had introduced earlier: the rewards of love with which God the divine Bridegroom fills the human soul. These rewards are "the earnest money" given to the world in common and to each person in particular, so that the soul may be drawn upward towards God in each life and in the history of human salvation. Critics have noted in *De arrha* more individuality of style and, especially in the confession that concludes it, a more personal note than is usual with Hugh. It remains true, nevertheless, that Hugh's meditations are generally on communicable knowledge, and his mysticism, even in *De arrha,* is of a sort best described as objective, because it is more Scriptural than psychological.

It appears that there were many constants in Hugh's life, the most fundamental being his commitment to the life of a Victorine canon. He never took high ecclesiastical office, was never in continuous secular employment, and he never joined the ranks of the wandering scholars of his time. The life of a canon in the twelfth century carried with it a consciousness of obligation to teach, as well as to study and contemplate, and that consciousness appears to have been especially strong in Hugh. Whatever innovations may have emanated from Chartres and whatever anxieties might have been raised by Abelard and others, boys still had to be taught their letters and geometry and the persons, places, and times of history. In order to see the spiritual sense in Scripture, students always needed to be solidly grounded in doctrine. It is not surprising, therefore, that even in Hugh's most advanced work there was so often room for a return to the literal, the visible, and the historical.

References:

Roger Baron, *Etudes sur Hugues de Saint-Victor* (Paris: Desclee, De Brouwer, 1963);

Baron, *Science et sagesse chez Hugues de Saint-Victor* (Paris: Lethielleux, 1957);

Caroline Walker Bynum, *Jesus as Mother: Studies in the Spirituality of the High Middle Ages* (Berkeley: University of California Press, 1982);

F. E. Croyden, "Notes on the Life of Hugh of St. Victor," *Journal of Theological Studies,* 40 (1939): 232–253;

Joachim Ehlers, *Hugo von St. Viktor: Studien zum Geschichtesdenken und zur Geschichtsschreibung des 12. Jahrhunderts,* Frankfurter Historische Abhandlungen no. 7 (Wiesbaden: Steiner, 1973);

Damien van den Eynde, *Essai sur la succession et la date des écrits de Hugues de Saint-Victor,* Spicilegium Pontificii Athenaei Antoniani no. 13 (Rome: Apud Pontificium Athenaeum Antonianum, 1960);

Tullio Gregory, "La nouvelle idée de savoir scientifique au XIIe siècle," in John E. Murdoch and Edith D. Sylla, eds., *The Cultural Context of Medieval Learning: Proceedings of the first International Colloquium on Philosophy, Science, and Theology in the Middle Ages—September 1973,* Boston Studies in the Philosophy of Science no. 26 (Dordrecht, The Netherlands & Boston: D. Reidel, 1975), pp. 195–218;

Barthelmy Hauréau, *Les œuvres de Hugue de Saint-Victor: Essai critique* (Paris: Hachette, 1866; republished, Frankfurt am Main: Minerva, 1963);

Robert Javelet, "Considérations sur les arts libéraux chez Hugues et Richard de Saint-Victor," in *Arts Libéraux et philosophie au moyen âge,* Actes du quatrième congrès international de philosophie médiévale (Montreal: Institute d'études médiévales/ Paris: J. Vrin, 1969), pp. 557–568;

Maxwell S. Luria, "Some Literary Implications of Hugh of St. Victor's Didascalicon," in *Arts Libéraux et philosophie au moyen âge,* Actes du Quatrième Congrès International de Philosophie Médiévale (Montreal: Institute D'Études Médiévales, 1969), pp. 541–549;

D. E. Luscombe, *The School of Peter Abelard: The Influence of Abelard's Thought in the Early Scholastic Period,* Cambridge Studies in Medieval Life and Thought, n.s., no. 14 (London: Cambridge University Press, 1969);

Bernard McGinn, *The Growth of Mysticism* (New York: Crossroad, 1994);

A. J. Minnis, A. B. Scott, and Daviel Wallace, editors, *Medieval Literary Theory and Criticism, c. 1100–c. 1375: The Commentary Tradition,* revised edition (Oxford: Clarendon Press, 1991);

George Ovitt Jr., "The Status of the Mechanical Arts in Medieval Classification of Learning," *Viator,* 14 (1983): 89–105;

Heinz Robert Schlette, *Die Nichtigkeit der Welt: Der philosophische Horizont des Hugo von St. Viktor* (Munich: Kösel-Verlag, 1961);

Patrice Sicard, *Diagrammes médiévaux et exégèse visuelle: Le Libellus de formatione arche de Hugue de Saint-Victor,* Bibliotheca Victorina, no. 4 (Turnhout, Belgium: Brepols, 1993);

Sicard, *Hugues de Saint-Victor et son école* (Turnhout, Belgium: Brepols, 1991);

Beryl Smalley, *The Study of the Bible in the Middle Ages* (Notre Dame, Ind.: University of Notre Dame Press, 1964);

R. W. Southern, "Aspects of the European Tradition of Historical Writing: 2. Hugh of St. Victor and the Idea of Historical Development," *Transactions of the Royal Society,* fifth series, 2 (1971): 159–179;

James A. Weisheipl, "Classification of the Sciences in Medieval Thought," *Mediaeval Studies,* 27 (1965): 54–90;

Grover Zinn, "Hugh of St. Victor and the Ark of Noah: A New Look," *Church History,* 40 (1971): 261–272;

Zinn, "Hugh of St. Victor and the Art of Memory," *Viator,* 5 (1974): 211–234.

Jacques de Vitry

(circa 1160/1170 – 1 May 1240)

Walter Simons
Dartmouth College

WORKS: *Vita Mariae Oigniacensis* (1215)

Manuscripts: This work is preserved in at least twenty-six manuscripts, eight of which date from the thirteenth century. The manuscript Brussels, Bibliothèque Royale/Koninklijke Bibliotheek, II, 700, belonged to the monastery of Oignies and may have been written there between 1215 and 1230.

First publication: In *Acta Sanctorum quotquot toto orbe coluntur vel a Catholicis scriptoribus celebrantur,* June, volume 4, edited by Daniel Papebrochius (Antwerp: Joannes Meursius, 1707), pp. 636–666, republished in *Acta Sanctorum quotquot toto orbe coluntur vel a Catholicis scriptoribus celebrantur,* June, volume 5 (Paris: Palme, 1867), pp. 542–572.

Edition in English: *The Life of Marie d'Oignies by Jacques de Vitry,* translated by Margot H. King, revised edition (Toronto: Peregrina, 1993).

Letters (1216–1221)

Manuscripts: Seven letters by Jacques are extant in fourteen manuscripts that include one or more letters each; five of the manuscripts date from the thirteenth century.

First publication: "Briefe des Jacobus de Vitriaco, 1216–1221," edited by R. Röhricht, *Zeitschrift für Kirchengeschichte,* 14 (1892–1894): 97–118; 15 (1894–1895): 568–587; 16 (1895–1896): 72–114.

Standard edition: *Lettres de Jacques de Vitry (1160/ 70–1240) évêque de Saint-Jean-d'Acre,* edited by R. B. C. Huygens (Leiden: E. J. Brill, 1960).

Historia Hierosolimitana Abbreviata (1219–1223)

Manuscripts: About 150 manuscripts containing the work in more or less complete form have been identified. The critical edition of the first book was mainly based on London, British Library, Add. ms. 40075, which dates from the first half of the thirteenth century and originally belonged to the Benedictine abbey of St. Martin at Tournai.

First publication: First and second books published in *Iacobi de Vitriaco . . . libri dvo quorum prior orientalis sive Hierosolymitanae, alter, occidentalis historiae nomine inscribitur,* edited by Franciscus Moschus

(Douai, France: Balthazeris Belleri, 1597; republished, Farnborough, U.K.: Gregg, 1971); prologue and first book in *Gesta Dei per Francos, sive Orientalium expeditionum et regni Francorum Hierosolimitani historia,* 2 volumes, edited by Jacques Bongars (Hannover: Wechel, 1611), II: 1047–1145.

Standard edition: Second book, in *The Historia Occidentalis of Jacques de Vitry: A Critical Edition,* edited by John Frederick Hinnebusch, Spicilegium Friburgense, no. 17 (Fribourg, Switzerland: Fribourg University Press, 1972).

Edition in English: Selections from first book in *The History of Jerusalem A.D. 1180 by Jacques de Vitry,* translated by Aubrey Stewart (London: The Palestine Pilgrims' Text Society, 1896; republished, New York: AMS Press, 1971).

Sermones de tempore (circa 1229?–1240)

Manuscripts: Thirty-two manuscripts containing the complete series of 194 sermons or significant parts thereof have been identified; Jean-Thibaut Welter's edition of the prologue is based on Paris, Bibliothèque Nationale de France, nouv. acq. lat. 1537, from the thirteenth century.

First publication: In *Reverendissimi D. Iacobi de Vitriaco . . . Sermones in epistolas & evangelia dominicalia totius anni,* edited by Damianus a Ligno (Antwerp: T. Lindanus, 1575).

Standard edition: Selections from the prologue in *L'exemplum dans la littérature religieuse et didactique du Moyen Âge,* edited by Jean-Thibaut Welter (Paris & Toulouse: Occitania, 1927), pp. 119–120.

Sermones de sanctis (1229?–1240)

Manuscripts: Twelve manuscripts include the series of 143 sermons as a whole or in part.

Standard edition: Only one sermon has been edited, by Jean Longère, "Un sermon inédit de Jacques de Vitry: *Si annis multis vixerit homo,*" in *L'Église et la mémoire des morts dans la France médiévale. Communications présentées à la Table ronde du C. N. R. S., le 14 juin 1982,* edited by Jean-Loup

Lemaître (Paris: Etudes Augustiniennes, 1986), pp. 31–51.

Sermones ad status or *vulgares* (1229?–1240)

Manuscripts: The complete collection of seventy-four sermons is extant in fifteen manuscripts, of which at least seven date from the thirteenth century; parts of the collection or individual sermons have been preserved in at least eighteen manuscripts.

First publication: Selections in *Analecta nouissima Spicilegii Solesmensis. Altera continuatio,* volume 2: *Tusculana,* edited by Joannes Baptista Pitra (Paris: Roger et Cherenowitz, 1888), pp. 344–461.

Standard editions: *Sermones ad leprosos et alios informos,* edited by Nicole Bériou and François-Olivier Touati, in their *Voluntate dei leprosus: les lépreux entre conversion et exclusion aux XIIème et XIIIème siècles* (Spoleto: Centro Italiano di Studi sull'alto medioevo, 1991), pp. 101–128; *Sermones ad Fratres Minores* in "Iacobi Vitriacensis episcopi et cardinalis, 1180–1240, *Sermones ad Fratres Minores,*"edited by Hilarinus Felder, in *Analecta Ordinis Minorum Cappucinorum,* 19 (1903): 113–158; *Sermo ad virgines et iuvenculas* in "Der Ursprung des Beginenwesens: Eine Auseinandersetzung mit Godefroid Kurth," edited by Joseph Greven, *Historisches Jahrbuch,* 35 (1914): 41–49; *Ad servos et ancillas* in "Deux sermons de Jacques de Vitry (†1240) 'ad servos et ancillas,'" edited by Jean Longère, in *La femme au moyen-âge,* edited by Michel Rouche and Jean Heuclin (Maubeuge: Ville de Maubeuge, 1990), pp. 261–296; *Sermones ad canonicos* in "Quatre sermons 'ad canonicos' de Jacques de Vitry," edited by Longère, *Recherches augustiniennes,* 23 (1988): 151–212; *Sermones ad religiosas* in "Quatre sermons 'ad religiosas' de Jacques de Vitry," edited by Longère, in *Les religieuses en France au XIIIe siècle,* edited by Michel Parisse (Nancy: Presses Universitaires de Nancy, 1985), pp. 215–300; *Sermo ad agricolas et vinitores et alios operarios* in *L'exemplum dans la littérature religieuse et didactique du Moyen Age,* edited by Jean-Thibaut Welter (Paris & Toulouse: Occitania, 1927), pp. 457–467.

Sermones feriales et communes (1229?–1240)

Manuscripts: The work is preserved in the following manuscripts: Bruges, Stadsbibliotheek, 268 (circa 1300); Brussels, Bibliothèque Royale/Koninklijke Bibliotheek, 1122–1124 (dated "1450") and 9682–9699 (dated "1457"); Liège, Bibliothèque Universitaire, 347 (fifteenth century).

Standard edition: Sermon 8 in "Jacques de Vitry's *Sermones feriales et communes:* Text and Context," edited by Carolyn Muessig, in *De l'homélie*

au sermon: Histoire de la prédication médiévale, edited by Jacqueline Hamesse and Xavier Hermand (Louvain-la-Neuve, Belgium: Université Catholique de Louvain, 1993), pp. 61–82; exempla in *Die Exempla des Jakob von Vitry. Ein Beitrag zur Geschichte der Erzählungsliteratur des Mittelalters,* edited by Goswin Frenken (Munich: C. H. Beck, 1914); and *Die Exempla aus den Sermones feriales et communes des Jakob von Vitry,* edited by Joseph Greven (Heidelberg: Winter, 1914).

Jacques de Vitry was one of the most successful preachers and storytellers of his age. Although in many ways a staunch defender of traditional values in the medieval church, Jacques helped to revolutionize preaching by his attention to the needs of the audience. He was an effective listener, incorporating in his spiritual writings tales and themes alive in the popular oral tradition.

Jacques was probably born in Vitry-en-Perthois (or Vitry-le-Brulé), a small town in Champagne. Since he is known to have been a student at the Parisian cathedral school of Notre Dame in 1187 and a "master" by 1193, scholars assume Jacques de Vitry was born between 1160 and 1170. His main teacher at Paris must have been Peter the Chanter, one of the most innovative theologians of the era. At some time during his advanced studies at the nascent University of Paris, Jacques be-came acquainted with Marie, a laywoman known for her saintly life, who lived near the monastery of regular canons at Oignies in the diocese of Liège (Oignies is located a few miles east of the city of Charleroi in present-day Belgium). Ordained to the priesthood in 1210, Jacques left Paris to join the monastery of Oignies, evidently to be closer to Marie, whom he came to view as his spiritual mentor. When she died in 1213, he continued to revere her. Not only did he cut off one of her fingers which he wore around his neck as a relic for the rest of his life, but he also set out to write her life story, the *Vita Mariae Oigniacensis* (Life of Marie d'Oignies), completed in 1215.

In the *Vita Mariae Oigniacensis,* Jacques offered a vision of Christianity revitalized by the piety of laywomen in the diocese of Liège and adjacent regions. Although formally simple and lacking all literary sophistication, the story of Marie's asceticism, good works, and mystical transports served a complex agenda. Dedicated to Bishop Foulque of Toulouse, who left southern France during the crusade against the Cathar heresy and visited the north in 1211 or 1212 and again in 1213, the *Vita* was intended to demonstrate how a vigorous lay devotion would subdue the Cathar heretics. In Jacques's view, Marie's example proved that traditional Christian values could be upheld by laywomen guided by the orthodox reformed priesthood against the claims of Cathars and other heretics who revered their own *perfecti* and *perfectae,* the male and female "perfect" or "elect." Her special devotion to Christ's Passion and the extraordinary powers she was said to have acquired also supported the validity of the Eucharist as salvific in the face of Cathar denials of the redemptive power of the sacraments. Marie's *Vita* therefore provided concrete examples of orthodox virtues that could be used in anti-Cathar preaching.

The *Vita* also served another purpose, however: women like Marie, popularly known as *Beguines* (a term of derision either derived from the hypothetical old-Dutch stem *begg-,* to mumble prayers, or the name of the priest Lambert Li Bègue, an early defender), were regarded with suspicion by the more-conservative forces of the clergy, who rejected the idea that women—especially those, like Marie, who had been married—could lead virtuous lives outside a monastery. Jacques forcefully argued, on the contrary, for Marie's exemplary sanctity despite the temptations of a sinful world, all the while assuring his audience that she observed the regulations and admonitions of the clerical hierarchy. He thus launched a forceful defense of the Beguines and other lay individuals interested in leading a religious life in the secular world, unaffiliated with a monastic order, a movement that became increasingly popular in the Low Countries in the course of the thirteenth century; yet, because the *Vita Mariae Oigniacensis* placed so much emphasis upon Marie's subordination to the clergy and her retreat as a recluse, it also imposed on the Beguines strict expectations and conditions that furthered ecclesiastical control of them. Not surprisingly, the *Vita* was received well in ecclesiastical milieus, and translated into various vernacular languages for the use of the laity: versions in medieval Swedish, Norse, English, French, and Italian are known.

Shortly before Marie's death Jacques had actively joined the preaching of a crusade against the Cathars. His travels to various parts of France and the Low Countries spread his fame as a skillful and energetic preacher. News of his efforts to promote the crusading enterprise apparently reached Palestine, where canons of the cathedral of St. John of Acre elected him as the new bishop sometime between 1213 and the spring of 1216. Upon receiving word of his election, Jacques left the Low Countries for Rome to be consecrated as bishop of Acre on 31 July 1216. In October of that year he sailed from Genoa to his new post in Palestine, which he reached on 4 November 1216. For nine years he fulfilled the varied duties of a bishop in the crusader kingdom of Jerusalem, traveling widely in the area and through neighboring states.

Jacques left an account of his experiences in the Near East in at least seven letters that have been preserved and date from the first stage of his episcopate at Acre, 1216-1221. These are personal letters, mainly to friends in the diocese of Liège but also to Pope Honorius III and to masters at the University of Paris. The letters appear to have circulated only among Jacques's acquaintances, and on the whole remained little known. The letters are, nevertheless, of historical importance for their vivid description of the new religious movements in Italy of the Humiliatia (a quasi-religious order devoted to a life of mortification and care of the poor) and the Franciscans, their reports on crusader history, and for Jacques's report of a victory against the Muslims by "King David of India," purportedly the son or grandson of Prester John, the legendary ruler of a Christian kingdom in the East.

While participating in the Fifth Crusade in Egypt, Jacques witnessed the siege of Damietta (1218-1219). As Christian Cannuyer has argued, he may have started work on his *Historia Hierosolimitana Abbreviata* (Short History of Jerusalem) as early as 19 March 1219, after the capture of Damietta by the crusaders. The work consists of a prologue; the first book, known as the *Historia Orientalis,* or the History of the Orient; the second book, entitled the *Historia Occidentalis,* or History of the West. Some manuscripts also include a third book, a history of the Holy Land from the Fourth Lateran Council of 1215 to the capture of Damietta in 1219, but it is generally considered a version of Oliver of Paderborn's *Historia Damiatina* (History of [the siege of] Damietta, circa 1217-1222) and not Jacques's work.

The *Historia Orientalis,* probably completed in 1220, is usually ranked with the historical writings of William of Tyre as one of the main sources regarding Western perceptions of the Near East in the early Middle Ages. Jacques relied heavily on William's work for information about the history of Palestine and its adjacent regions from the age of Mohammed until the time of the Third Crusade, but his account of the more recent Western presence in the Near East is original. The value of the book lies primarily in Jacques's critique of contemporaneous conditions, which he depicts with verve, aided by a keen interest in the customs, daily life, and mentality of Christians in the Near East. Although Jacques's knowledge of Mohammed and the basic tenets of Islamic belief appears limited—largely because he could not read Greek and Arabic, the languages of the sources at his disposal—he has been credited with reporting accurately on Muslim customs in this age. Still, there is no doubt that Jacques wrote above all as a moralist who condemned and often overstated the moral disarray of Christians and Muslims in the East.

Shortly afterward, in 1221–1223, Jacques wrote a compendium volume on the history of the West, the *Historia Occidentalis,* for which he may have collected supplementary materials during a trip to Italy in 1222–1223. In this case, too, the book was less a history than a panorama of religious and moral conditions in the Christian commonwealth in the early thirteenth century. Jacques's account depicted a society in deep religious crisis; a crisis that could be overcome, he argued, by the forces of renewal in the church. A large part of the *Historia Occidentalis* is thus taken up by an analysis of the virtues (and, in some instances, also the flaws) of groups in the church whom Jacques regarded as the harbingers of reform: the various kinds of hermits, monks, regular canons, and the newly-established Franciscans (the *Historia Occidentalis* includes one of the first enthusiastic assessments of the Friars Minor by a major church leader). Jacques paid special attention to religious movements carried by the laity. Insofar as they obeyed the Gospels, Jacques regarded all ranks in society as social groups living by a religious rule and as members of the church, a remarkably pluralist stance that encapsulates well his vision of Christianity.

In 1225 Jacques made another voyage to the West, this time in the entourage of Queen Isabella of Jerusalem, soon to wed Holy Roman Emperor Frederick II. This trip brought him first to Italy, then to the Low Countries again, where he is attested as an auxiliary to the bishop of Liège from October 1226 until April 1228. At this time Jacques also presided over the solemn translation of Marie's remains at Oignies and dedicated the monastery's church, which he had personally endowed with jewels, silks, manuscripts, and relics from the East. He never returned to the Holy Land; at some point in 1227 or 1228 he resigned from his position in Acre, and by 29 July 1229 he had assumed duties for the Roman Curia as cardinal bishop of Tusculum. He spent the last ten years of his life as a Roman cardinal involved in the highest affairs of the church.

It was most probably during his service as a cardinal that Jacques completed his vast collection of model sermons, although they are surely based on his preaching experiences in the Low Countries and in the Near East. As he explains in the prologues to the *Sermones de tempore* (Sermons for Sundays and Feast Days) and the *Sermones ad status* (Sermons to Various Social Groups), he compiled these sermons as a practical aid to preachers involved with a variety of audiences. It was important, he thought, that a priest select carefully among these materials for items that fitted the particular audience and circumstances, and his sermon collections are therefore quite varied in their range of topics and style, allowing users to design their own sermons.

While the more conventional *Sermones de tempore* appear to have enjoyed the most widespread success in the Middle Ages, the *Sermones ad status* best reflect Jacques's innovative preaching to the laity, which greatly influenced the apostolate of the mendicant orders later in the thirteenth century. The *Sermones ad status* were tailored to the new social and professional categories that came to the fore in the early thirteenth century and marked the demise of the traditional tripartite division of early medieval society into those who pray, those who fight, and those who labor. Jacques stands out as one of the first ecclesiastics to have grasped the importance of the new social differentiation spurred by the urban revolution of the twelfth century, and to have sketched out an ecclesiastical policy to accommodate those new groups. His sermons to twenty-eight different social groupings–including monks, priests, merchants, craftsmen, widows, young boys, and adolescents–demonstrate a new sensitivity to a changing world and to the special religious needs of people differentiated by ecclesiastical status, social position, occupation, gender, and age.

In order to accommodate the traditional Christian message to the new environment, Jacques recommended the use of exempla–short, captivating, and often funny stories presented as true, which preachers should insert in their sermons to illustrate virtues, vices, or even more complex issues of Christian doctrine. Jacques employed about four hundred such stories in his sermons. They were based on classical fables, patristic hagiography, and early medieval anthologies, but also derived from personal encounters with people of different social stations and cultures during his travels in the East and the West.

Jacques died in Rome on 1 May 1240. He left to the monastery of Oignies all of his possessions, including relics and books; according to his last wishes, his body was taken to Oignies and buried there. His exempla and model sermons exerted a significant influence on thirteenth- and fourteenth-century preachers, including the mendicants Humbert de Romans, Étienne de Bourbon, and Guibert de Tournai. Few of them could match him, however, in negotiating the divide between learned theology and popular culture. Humbert de Romans, who compiled a manuscript collection of exempla between 1261 and 1277, now in the Bibliothèque Nationale de France in Paris (f. lat. 15953, ff. 188), wrote: "Jacques de Vitry's preaching and his use of exempla in sermons moved the whole of France to a degree never achieved by anyone before or after him."

In later centuries, Jacques continued to be esteemed as a prolific writer of sermons, but his historical works and exempla did not appeal to the intelligentsia of the eighteenth and early nineteenth centuries, who

Page from an early fifteenth-century manuscript for Jacques de Vitry's Historia Hierosolimitana *(from Maggs Bros.,* The Art of Writing: 2800 B.C. to 1930 A.D., *1930)* deplored his credulity and flaws as a stylist. It was only at the beginning of the twentieth century that folklorists and cultural historians began to reappraise his writings. Modern scholarship has underscored his lifelong, genuine interest in the experience of laypeople, which made him not only an astute–albeit overly moralizing–observer of contemporary society but also an important authority on popular traditions in the medieval West.

Biography:

Philipp Funk, *Jacob von Vitry. Leben und Werke* (Leipzig & Berlin: Teubner, 1909).

References:

John W. Baldwin, *Masters, Princes, and Merchants: The Social Views of Peter the Chanter and His Circle* (Princeton: Princeton University Press, 1970);

John Benton, "Qui étaient les parents de Jacques de Vitry?" *Le Moyen Age,* 19 (1964): 39–47;

Anne-Marie Bonenfant-Feytmans, "Les organisations hospitalières vues par Jacques de Vitry (1225)," *Annales de la société belge d'histoire des hôpitaux,* 18 (1980): 19–45;

Claude Brémond, Jacques Le Goff, and Jean-Claude Schmitt, *L'"Exemplum"* (Turnhout, Belgium: Brepols, 1982);

Christian Cannuyer, "La date de rédaction de l'Historia Orientalis de Jacques de Vitry (1160/1170–1240), évêque d'Acre," *Revue d'Histoire Ecclésiastique,* 78 (1983): 65–72;

Giles Constable, *Three Studies in Medieval Religious and Social Thought* (Cambridge: Cambridge University Press, 1995);

Alberto Forni, "Giacomo da Vitry, predicatore e sociologo," *La cultura,* 18 (1980): 34–89;

Forni, "La nouvelle prédication des disciples de Foulques de Neuilly: intentions, techniques et réactions," in *Faire Croire: Modalités de la diffusion et de la réception des messages religieux du XIIe au XVe siècle* (Rome: Ecole française de Rome, 1981), pp. 19–37;

Marie-Christine Gasnault, "Jacques de Vitry, 'Sermones vulgares' et 'Sermones communes,'" in *Les Exempla médiévaux. Introduction à la recherche, suivie des tables critiques de l'Index exemplorum de Frederic C. Tubach,* edited by Jacques Berlioz and Marie Anne Polo de Beaulieu (Carcasonne: Garae/Hésiode, 1992), pp. 119–134;

Iris Geyer, *Maria von Oignies: Eine hochmittelalterliche Mystikerin zwischen Ketzerei und Rechtgläubigkeit* (Frankfurt am Main, Berlin, New York & Paris: Peter Lang, 1992);

Patricia Deery Kurtz, "Mary of Oignies, Christine the Marvelous, and Medieval Heresy," *Mystics Quarterly,* 14 (1988): 186–196;

Michel Lauwers, "Expérience béguinale et récit hagiographique. A propos de la 'Vita Mariae Oigniacencis' de Jacques de Vitry (vers 1215)," *Journal des Savants* (January–June 1989): 61–103;

Lauwers, "Entre Béguinisme et Mysticisme: La Vie de Marie d' Oignies (†1213) de Jacques de Vitry ou la définition d'une sainteté féminine," *Ons Geestelijk Erf,* 66 (1992): 46–69;

Rita Lejeune, "L'évêque de Toulouse Folquet de Marseille et la principauté de Liège," in *Mélanges Félix Rousseau: Études sur l'histoire du pays mosan au moyen âge* (Brussels: La Renaissance du Livre, 1958), pp. 433–448;

Jean Longère, *La prédication médiévale* (Paris: Etudes Augustiniennes, 1983);

Longère, "Les chanoines d'àprès trois prédicateurs: Jacques de Vitry, Guibert de Tournai, Humbert de Romans," in *Le monde des chanoines (XIe–XIVe siècles)* (Toulouse: Edouard Privat, 1989), 257–283;

Ernest W. McDonnell, *The Beguines and Beghards in Medieval Culture. With Special Emphasis on the Belgian Scene* (New Brunswick, N. J.: Rutgers University Press, 1954);

Alcantara Mens, *Oorsprong en betekenis van de Nederlandse Begijnen- en Begardenbeweging: Vergelijkende studie: XIIde–XIIIde eeuw* (Antwerp: Standaard-Boekhandel, 1947);

Armando Quaglia, "Giacomo da Vitry e la regola francescana," *Miscellanea Francescana,* 78 (1978): 133–141;

Quaglia, "Sulla datazione e il valore della Historia Occidentalis di Giacomo da Vitry," *Miscellanea Francescana,* 83 (1983): 177–192;

Monica Sandor, "The Popular Preaching of Jacques of Vitry." dissertation, University of Toronto, 1993;

Johannes Baptist Schneyer, *Repertorium der lateinischen Sermones des Mittelalters,* volume 3 (Münster: Aschendorffsche Verlagsbuchhandlung, 1971), pp. 179–221;

Walter Simons, "Les Beguines au Moyen Age," in *Béguines et Béguinages,* edited by Marianne Trooskens (Brussels: Archives Générales du Royaume, 1994), pp. 7–25;

Thomas of Cantimpré, *Supplement to the Life of Marie d'Oignies,* translated, with introduction and notes, by Hugh Feiss (Toronto: Peregrina, 1990);

Gryt Anne van der Toorn-Piebenga, "De 'Vita Mariae Oigniacensis' in Scandinavië," *Ons Geestelijk Erf,* 65 (1991): 13–22;

André Vauchez, "Prosélytisme et action antihérétique en milieu féminin au XIIIe siècle: la Vie de Marie d'Oignies (†1213) par Jacques de Vitry," *Problèmes d'Histoire du Christianisme,* 17 (1987): 95–110.

John of Garland
(Jean de Garlande, Johannis de Garlandia)
(circa 1195 – circa 1272)

R. Barton Palmer
Clemson University

WORKS: *Dictionarius* (circa 1220)

Manuscripts: This work is preserved in several manuscripts, including most prominently: Paris, Bibliothèque Nationale de France, f. lat. 4120; Bibliothèque Nationale de France, f. lat. 11282; Bibliothèque Nationale de France, 7679; Lille, Bibliothèque Municipale, 369 (4); Rouen, Bibliothèque Municipale, 1026 (0.32); London, British Library, ms. Harley, 1002 (18); British Library, ms. Cotton. Titus D. xx; and Oxford, Bodleian Library, ms. G. 96.

First publication: In *Paris sous Philippe le Bel d'après des documents originaux,* edited by H. Géraud (Paris, 1837).

Standard edition and edition in English: *The Dictionarius of John de Garlande and the Author's Commentary,* edited and translated by Barbara Blatt Rubin (Lawrence, Kans.: Coronado Press, 1981).

Epithalamium Beatae Marie Virginis (circa 1229–1232)

Manuscripts: This work is preserved complete in four manuscripts: London, British Library, ms. Cotton. Claudius A. X.; Manchester, Chetham's Library, 28024, ms. 5.7.16; Oxford, Bodleian Library, ms. Digby 65; and Weimar, Landesbibliothek, Q 113.

Standard edition: *Epithalamium beate virginis Marie, Giovanni di Garlandia,* edited, and translated into Italian, by Antonio Saiani (Florence: L. S. Olschki, 1995).

Georgica Spiritualia (circa 1229–1232)

Manuscript: The only extant text consists of quotations in a florilegium, Paris, Bibliothèque Nationale de France, f. lat. 15155.

First publication and standard editions: In *Mélanges Paul Fabre: Etudes d'histoire du moyen âge,* edited by Francesco Novati (Paris: Picard, 1902; republished, Geneva: Slatkine, 1972).

Parisiana Poetria de Arte Prosaica, Metrica, and Rithmica (circa 1232–1249)

Manuscripts: The work survives in six manuscripts: Bruges, Bibliothèque Publique, 546; Cambridge, University Library, L1. 14; Munich, Bayerische Staatsbibliothek, f. lat. 6911; Oxford, Bodleian Library, lat. misc. d. 66; Paris, Bibliothèque Nationale de France, f. lat. 11867; and Vienna, Osterreichische Nationalbibliothek, lat. 3121.

First publication: Selections in *Briefsteller und Formelbücher des elften bis vierzehten Jahrhunderts,* edited by Ludwig Rockinger (Munich, 1863).

Standard edition and edition in English: *The Parisiana Poetria of John of Garland,* edited and translated by Traugott Lawler, Yale Studies in English, no. 182 (New Haven & London: Yale University Press, 1974).

Integumenta super Ovidii Metamorphosin (circa 1234)

Manuscripts: The work survives, with or without a prose commentary by Guillelmus de Thiegiis, in several manuscripts, including, most importantly: Paris, Bibliothèque Nationale de France, f. lat. 8008; Leiden, Bibliotheek der Rijksuniversiteit, Voss. 46; Oxford, Bodleian Library, Digby 104; Oxford, Bodleian Library, Canon. lat. 9; Oxford, Bodleian Library, Acut. F. 5, 16; Oxford, Merton College, ms. CCXCIX (11); Prague, University Library, IX C. 3.

First publication: *Integumenta Ovidii: poemetto inedito del secolo XIII,* edited by Fausto Ghisalberti, Testi e documenti inediti o rari no. 2 (Messina: G. Principato, 1933).

Standard edition: "The *Integumenta* on the *Metamorphoses* of Ovid by John of Garland," edited by Lester K. Born, dissertation, University of Chicago, 1929.

Compendium grammatice (circa 1234)

Clavis compendii

Manuscripts: These two works occur together in: Bruges, Bibliothèque Publique, 546; Cambridge,

Gonville & Caius College, ms. 385; and Gonville & Caius College, ms. 593.

Morale Scolarium (1241)

Manuscripts: The work survives in four manuscripts: Bruges, Bibliothèque Publique, 546; Cambridge, Gonville & Caius College, ms. 385; Lincoln, Cathedral Library, ms. 132; and Paris, Bibliothèque Nationale de France, nat. nouv. acq. lat. 1544.

First publication and standard edition: *Morale scolarium of John of Garland (Johannes de Garlandia), A Professor in the Universities of Paris and Toulouse in the Thirteenth Century,* edited by Louis J. Paetow, Memoirs of the University of California no. 2 (Berkeley: University of California Press, 1927).

De triumphis ecclesie (circa 1245)

Manuscript: The work survives in a single manuscript: London, British Library, Cotton. Claudius A. X.

First publication and standard edition: *Johannis de Garlandia: De Triumphis Ecclesiae libri octo: A Latin Poem of the Thirteenth Century,* Thomas Wright, Roxburghe Club, no. 73 (London: J. B. Nicols, 1856).

De Mysteriis Ecclesie (1245)

Manuscripts: This work survives in several manuscripts. Among the most important are: Bruges, Bibliothèque Publique, 546; London, British Library, ms. Cotton. Claudius A; Oxford, Bodleian Library, Auct. F. 5.6; Cambridge, Gonville & Caius College, ms. 385; Lincoln, Cathedral Library, ms. 132; Vienna, Österreichische Nationalbibliothek, 380; Munich, Bayerische Staatsbibliothek, 3812, Bayerische Staatsbibliothek, 4371, Bayerische Staatsbibliothek, 4710.

First publication and standard edition: In *Commentarii critici in codices Bibliothecae Academicae Gissensis graecos et latinos, philolgicos et medii aevi historicos ac geographicos,* edited by Friedrich Wilhelm Otto (Giessen: G. F. Heyeri, 1842).

Commentarius (1246)

Manuscripts: This dictionary survives in three manuscripts: Cambridge, Gonville & Caius College, ms. 385; Bruges, ms. 546; and Rome, Biblioteca Casanatense, 2052.

Miracula Beatae Marie Virginis, also known as Stella Maris (circa 1248–1249)

Manuscripts: Two extant manuscripts preserve this collection: Bruges, Bibliothèque Publique, 546 and London, British Library, Royal 8 c iv.

Standard edition: *The Stella Maris of John of Garland,* edited by Evelyn Faye Wilson (Cambridge, Mass.: Wellesley College, Medieval Academy of America, 1946).

Accentarium (circa 1249)

Manuscripts: This poem survives in several manuscripts, chiefly: Bruges, Bibliothèque Publique, 546; Cambridge, Gonville & Caius College, ms. 385; Oxford, Bodleian Library, ms. Rawl. C. 496; Lincoln, Cathedral Library, ms. 132; London, British Library, Royal 15 A xxxi (8); and British Library, Add. ms. 15832.

John of Garland, one of the first professors of grammar at the University of Paris, is one of the most important intellectual figures of the first half of the twelfth century. He produced several scholarly works, including the first dictionary, important critiques of contemporary Latin grammars, and the *Parisiana Poetria de Arte Prosaica, Metrica, et Rithmica* (Parisian Poetics Concerning the Art of Prose, Metrical, and Rhythmic Composition, circa 1232–1249), a groundbreaking attempt to impose one scheme on the common elements of rhetoric, poetry, and *dictamen* (letter writing). Unlike many of his contemporaries, John remained devoted to the duties of the *grammaticus* (instructor in grammar), which included the teaching of language, writing skills, and what is now termed literary criticism. Though he became interested in the possibilities of approaching grammatical and syntactical study through the use of logical categories, he never abandoned the study of classical literature for logic, a field suddenly reconstituted during the middle of his teaching career by the reintroduction into western Europe of the works of Aristotle.

Born in England to a non-noble family, probably around 1195, John reveals in an autobiographical passage of the *De triumphis Ecclesie* (On the Triumphs of the Church, circa 1245), that he received his university training at Oxford, where he studied under a man, otherwise unknown, named John of London. Perhaps lured by the reputation of the University of Paris, John left England about 1217 and took up residence in the Clos de Garlande, then a newly established neighborhood on the Left Bank near the ancient church of St. Julien-le-Pauvre. It is from this residence that he took the surname by which he is most often called (manuscripts and documents offer several variants, including Garlandria, Garlandius, Gerlandus, Gallandria). It is probable, though by no means proven, that the John of Garland who is the author of many grammatical, literary, theological, and other works is also the John of Garland who authored many important works on music theory (some sources consider John of Garland the music theorist a separate figure, though the evidence for this is weak, especially in light of the musical interest and knowledge John manifests in several of his grammatical works).

By his own account, John was an enthusiastic immigrant; he writes "England was my mother and France a nurse to me, and in my own mind I prefer the nurse to the mother." In Paris he began life as a *grammaticus*, teaching grammar, one of the three subjects in the trivium (rhetoric and logic being the others) that formed the basis for the first arts course in the emerging university.

Around this time he probably produced the first and most important of a series of wordbooks intended for his students, what John termed his *Dictionarius* (Dictionary, circa 1220), likely the first scholarly tool of this kind. Unlike the modern dictionary, which is normally organized alphabetically, John's wordbook groups entries topically, listing items commonly found together, such as the furnishings of a room. John also compiled a list of Latin words pertaining to noble aristocratic pursuits (perhaps for the children of a noble family) and a metrical list of difficult Latin words, treating classes such as trees, plants, animals, and parts of the body.

In 1229 his quiet career was disrupted by the carnival riot of the students in the nearby suburb of St. Marcel that resulted in the closing of the university when most of the teachers and students left Paris in protest against what they considered many injustices perpetrated against the students by both ecclesiastical and civil authorities. At the same time the university was dispersing, Count Raymond VII of Toulouse, defeated by the northern army sent against him during the Albigensian Crusade, was in Paris to draft a peace treaty with King Louis IX (eventually ratified in April of that year). One of the articles of this treaty provided for the foundation of a university in Toulouse, to be closely supervised by the bishop and the cardinal legate, one of whose functions would be to assist in the re-establishment of orthodox belief among a population just recently separated by force from its attraction to the Albigensian or Cathar heresy. By this treaty, two *grammatici* were to be hired and the salaries of all fourteen professors were to be paid by Raymond for a period of ten years. John of Garland was chosen to be one of the grammarians.

In the *De triumphis Ecclesie,* John reveals himself as an enthusiastic supporter of this enterprise; the university would be, he hoped, free from unwanted prohibitions and could offer the student a more regular, more liberal education than Paris. In reality, however, his task would be largely to aid in stamping out the last vestiges of heresy, not in providing a safe haven for disinterested learning. John entered the intellectual fray, writing books on, among other religious subjects, the relationship between hope and faith and the marriage of the Virgin Mary. He enthusiastically supported the incendiary preaching of Roland of Cremona, professor of theology (and a former colleague at Paris). The intellectual atmosphere at Toulouse, tightly monitored by the Dominican Inquisition in the area, likely proved somewhat stifling to John, especially since he was interested in rehabilitating classical authors, notably Ovid, and classical literary forms such as the epithalamion for a Christian literary culture. John's enthusiasm for pagan writers may have caused him trouble, and he was also dissatisfied by Raymond's failure to pay the promised salary. Leaving the south by a circuitous route and traveling through territory hostile to northern intellectuals, he made his way back to Paris after much hardship, arriving sometime in 1232 in a city where the university had at last reopened.

Most of his surviving works were probably written or completed after his return to Paris. John's *Epithalamium Beatae Marie Virginis* (A Marriage Hymn to the Blessed Virgin Mary) may have been begun in 1229, while he was in Toulouse, and completed soon after he returned to Paris. The *Epithalamium* is derivative, owing much to the epic treatments of similar themes in the *Anticlaudianus de Antirufino* (Against Claudian's *Against Rufinus,* circa 1181–1184) of Alan de Lille and the *Cosmographia* (Description of the Universe, circa 1150) of Bernard Sylvestris. As did his predecessors, John employs hexameter verse. An immense poem of some six thousand lines, the *Epithalamium* adapts the pagan marriage song tradition, which in its epic form had featured Venus as the heroic protagonist for a celebration of the Virgin Mary, whose chastity figures the paradoxical connection of physical barrenness yet spiritual fecundity. For John, the work had an important theological purpose; its meditations on the Incarnation were meant to influence the recently defeated Cathars of the south to return to the true faith by providing a convincing explanation of the unification of the spiritual and material in Christ. Placing the Incarnation at the center of secular and religious history, John also uses the epithalamium form as a vehicle for a universal history of the human soul. Without a reliable modern edition, not much more can be said about what John probably intended to be his most ambitious effort in using pagan content and form as vehicles for a Christian work. Similar in intent is the *Georgica Spiritualia* (Spiritual Georgics, circa 1229–1232), a work that apparently survives only in fragments, in which John offers a Christianized version of Virgil's *Georgics* (circa 37–30 B.C.) where the pagan poet's evocation of an ideal rurality is refigured as a moral study of the progress of the soul through the *hortus conclusus* (enclosed garden) that figures so prominently in the biblical Song of Songs.

The relative dating of John's published works on grammar, including study aids such as the *Dictionarius,* is extremely provisional and uncertain, and their composition undoubtedly spread over several decades. These works are devoted to a common project: easing the learning of Latin grammar and syntax for university students whose access to that language was impeded by traditional textbooks and, in John's mind, contemporary revisions that were full of errors and inaccuracies. In John's time, instruction in Latin traditionally depended on two late Latin authorities, the works of Donatus (circa A.D. 350) and Priscian (circa A.D. 500) These two treatises had been written for students whose native language was Latin, not for those approaching it as an acquired tongue. The flourishing of grammatical study at early-thirteenth-century universities had produced two contemporary Latin grammars more suited to the needs of medieval students: the *Doctrinale* (Handbook) of Alexander of Villedieu and the *Graecismus* (Greek Approach) of Eberhard of Bethune. Unlike the grammars of Priscian and Donatus, these works were composed in Latin verse (the first in leonine hexameters and the second in hexameters) in accord with the contemporary trend for versified works. Most textbooks and even more utilitarian genres of writing, including the occasional charter, were at this time written in verse. Alexander and Eberhard dealt with etymology, syntax, quantity, accent, and figures of speech in order to serve the university student, who was expected to compose Latin verses as part of his training.

Arguably, John's most important contribution to the study of grammar as he understood the discipline is his *Parisiana Poetria,* probably written between 1232 and 1249. John is here following in the tradition of fellow *grammatici* Matthew of Vendôme and Geoffrey of Vinsauf, whose respective treatises, *Ars Versificatoria* (Art of Versification, circa 1175) and *Poetria Nova* (New Poetics, circa 1200), had responded to and furthered a vogue for the teaching of Latin poetic composition. For John and these other thirteenth-century teachers, poetics is in some important senses identical with classical rhetoric, especially as transmitted by the authentic and supposed works of Cicero. John's contribution to this discipline is to extend the analogy beyond rhetoric and poetic to include *dictamen* or the writing of prose letters, the equivalent in the medieval curriculum of the modern business writing course. For John, the precepts for good writing exist in an ideal form that underlies the various genres, and his work is an attempt to stake out that common ground. Like the texts of his predecessors, his work depends on too many misunderstandings of Cicero to be ultimately satisfying as far as modern rhetorical and literary theorists are concerned. Importantly, however, John's *Parisiana Poetria* demonstrates that the study of discourse in the Middle Ages was by no means static, a mere vulgarizing and misuse of classical precepts. Instead, this work betrays an unmistakable and laudable attempt to formulate the underlying principles of human communication and enunciate usable precepts for its practice.

John follows the pattern of Cicero and the anonymous *Rhetorica ad Herennium de arte dicendi* (Rhetoric for C. Herrenius Concerning the Art of Public Speaking, 40 B.C.) a work often attributed to Cicero in the Middle Ages, but he adapts the ancient scheme to his different ends, divides his treatment of discourse into seven parts: invention (or the discovery of suitable material); selection from what has been discovered; the disposition and ornamentation of the material; the conventional structure of letters and the common errors in letter writing; rhetorical ornament; and, by way of illustration, examples of letters, metrical and rhythmical compositions (that is, the classical and medieval forms of poetic writing). In John's plan is to be discerned the Ciceronian division of a speech into three main parts: *inventio* (invention), *dispositio* (arrangement), and *elocutio* (style); however, John, like his contemporaries, ignores most of the issues associated with the discovery of appropriate material; disposition is reduced to a catalogue of stock devices for openings and closings. Elocution is the most discussed, with a long and elaborate catalogue of the *colores rhetorici* (the "colors of rhetoric" or figures of speech). John's discussion of *amplificatio* or "amplification" is particularly impressive and groundbreaking, and he discusses many devices for expanding and dilating a given theme. An important and, undoubtedly for John's student audience, useful part of the work is the series of models with which John illustrates his general precepts at every turn. For John and his contemporaries artful writing, for good or ill, was elaborate speech, and the *Parisiana Poetria* is devoted mainly to stylistic ornament rather than to questions of content and structure.

John's *Compendium grammatice* (Compendium of Grammar) and *Clavis compendii* (Key to the Compendium), both written circa 1234, enter into a sometimes unfriendly dialogue with the *Doctrinale* of Alexander of Villedieu and the *Graecismus* of Eberhard of Bethune; these two poems by John offer trenchant criticisms of authors who to John were giving currency to falsehoods and misunderstandings that he likely was forced to correct in the classroom. Extending over more than four thousand hexameters, the *Compendium* treats its subject

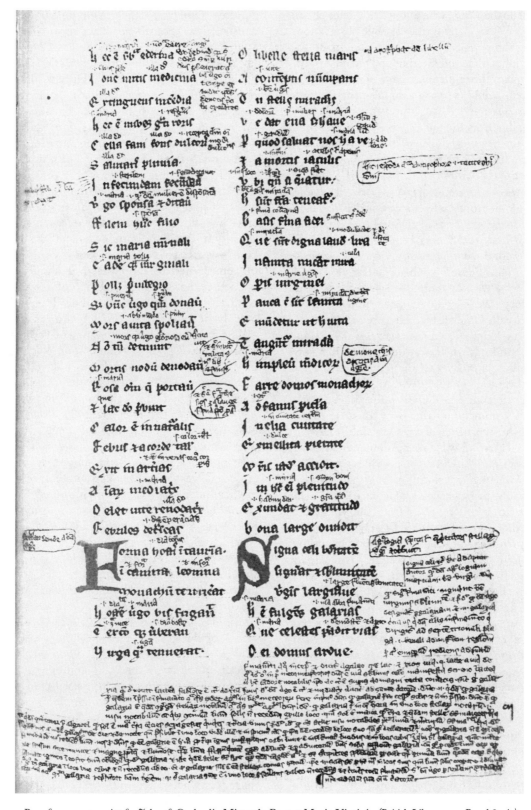

Page from a manuscript for John of Garland's Miracula Beatae Marie Virginis *(British Library, ms. Royal 8 c iv)*

in detail, while the *Clavis,* with about 2,250 lines of hexameter verse, offers many further specific observations. Recognizing the popularity of the two authors he was correcting, John undoubtedly did not intend his two works to replace theirs; he must have hoped that what he published would serve as supplementary texts. John's *Compendium* and *Clavis,* however, never became standard textbooks in the university arts curriculum, to judge from the few surviving manuscripts, as compared to the huge number of manuscripts containing the texts of Alexander and Eberhard.

John was more noteworthy as a teacher than a poet, making one foray into literary criticism: *Integumenta super Ovidii Metamorphosin* (Moral Interpretations of Ovid's *Metamorphoses,* circa 1234), his work on the *integumenta* (moral narratives) in Ovid's *Metamorphoses* (circa A.D. 1–8). These very brief narratives, which often (but not always) attempt to draw a moral from Ovidian story, are incomprehensible unless read in conjunction with Ovid; John's interpretations do not resemble the long, drawn-out exegeses—sometimes exceeding hundreds of verses—devoted to the same tales a century later by the anonymous vernacular author of the *Ovide moralisé* (Ovid Moralized). Sometimes John offers an explanation rather than an allegoresis. His comment on the story of Orpheus is: "Orpheus who scorned women is made the prey of women, by whom he was taken, mutilated, and was killed." Most times, however, he provides a generalizing and abstracting moralization, one that bypasses problematically pagan aspects of content, as in his integument on Adonis: "The life of the youth that lasts for a short time is called a flower, that quickly fades away and escapes like a shadow." In writing this work, John hoped to make reading Ovid safe for his impressionable students; this book, he says, "unknots the knotty secrets, it reveals hidden facts, it scatters the mist of obscurity." John's *Integumenta super Ovidii Metamorphosin* perhaps did not inaugurate, but certainly gave intellectual energy to the Christian reading of the hitherto most maligned of pagan authors, a movement that culminates in the fourteenth century *Ovide moralisé* and influences deeply the most important late-medieval authors from Dante and Geoffrey Chaucer to Giovanni Boccaccio and Guillaume de Machaut. Like the humanists of the early Renaissance, John was also vitally interested in recuperating classical forms for a Christian literary culture that would include what was good or useful from pagan writers and yet would demonstrate their inadequacy and incompleteness.

John followed in his own literary efforts the precepts set forth in the *Parisiana Poetria,* his treatise on discourse. As a consequence, his poetry is extremely verbose, filled with difficult and arcane constructions that often do not repay close analysis, and marred by major structural flaws. His verse does not compare favorably with the classical models—particularly Virgil, Ovid, and the satirists—that he draws upon. Most successful, perhaps, is his attempt to reproduce Roman light satire. In *Morale Scolarium* (Moral Life of Students, 1241), for example, John's gentle preachments sometimes run, with unintended amusement, from the more or less sublime to the patently ridiculous, an instability of tone that is traditional in the satire as a "mixed" form. John makes a heartfelt plea for morality in the study of the liberal arts—"we should cultivate eloquence, an active mind, chastity, fear of God, prudence, and virtues of every kind"—whose study John rightly sees threatened by the emergence of more-practical studies, law and medicine, that promise riches, not moral advancement, to their practitioners. This high-mindedness quickly descends into specifics of a less noble sort: "Wipe your nose carefully, control your gaze, suppress your cough, hide your sputum, keep good company, do not eat too much, do not act childishly." Admonitions like the latter are given full treatment in a section entitled "Table Manners," but one searches the work in vain for an extended discussion of the liberal arts, though John not surprisingly makes vitriolic comments about the *Doctrinale* and *Graecismus,* offering the advice that "the university itself should criticize unreasonable books and measures," with the implication being that his own works on grammar should be promoted above those of his more successful rivals. Sometimes John's advice is tantalizingly specific, offering rare glimpses into the material aspects of medieval life: "If a bridge is not safe, you should dismount and let the horse pick his way over the smooth parts" or "Honest professors are deceived by certain senior assistants who are worse than sailors and more unreliable than winds." His indictments of the evils of the age, however, tend to be conventionally vague and less impressive: "Poverty plucks up many by the roots and expels them from their heritage; it shamefully beats them down and deprives them of house and home."

John's long epic poem, *De triumphis Ecclesie,* which deals with the victorious aspects of church history from biblical times to the present, is a work that bears some comparison with Vincent of Beauvais's more renowned *Speculum Historiale* (Mirror of History, circa 1255). Probably completed about 1245, but written over a period of several years and reflecting John's own experiences and the current events he found significant, the work belongs to the tradition of cyclical histories most importantly represented by the works of Orosius and Vincent of Beauvais. In a Virgilian turn, John begins by announcing: "Arma crucemque cano, qua dux superatur Averni/Et qua succumbit vulgus inerme suum" (Arms and the cross I sing, by which the Lord conquered Avernus/ and by which his sinful horde was laid low), but this is a tone he is unable to maintain. Book 1, filled with digressive meditations on a variety of moral subjects, traces biblical history up to the crossing of the Red Sea and ends with the moral example of Saturn put to flight by his own son. Book 2 treats the material of medieval legend, emphasizing the founding of New Troy by Brutus, the heroic life of St. Denis, and the necessity for a renewed crusade. Succeeding books treat topics closer to John's own time. Book 3 concentrates on the Third Crusade and offers a resounding condemnation of the rivalry between the French and English leaders that compromises its success. Book 4 offers an extended history, but without much in the way of accurate detail, of the Albigensian Crusade and the heroic achievements of Simon de Montfort, whose death before the walls of Toulouse provides a serious opening for books 5 and 6, devoted to the same general series of events and containing a fair amount of autobiographical reminiscences. Books 7 and 8 are devoted to the various expeditions of St. Louis. The work was given its final form after the fall of Jerusalem in 1244, an event that lends John's treatment of ecclesiastical triumphs a somewhat bitter conclusion. The failure of contemporary rulers, however, suits John's more general theme: an indictment of the political troubles of his time that prevent a more concerted and united military effort of the Christian West against the enemies of God. Like Virgil, John had a horror of civil war, and he was particularly anguished by the conflicts between France and England that to his mind prevented the church from attaining the temporal power God intended it to possess. The work, then, has much in common with more explicitly theoretical works on crusading, especially those by Pierre Dubois and Guillaume de Nogaret.

A companion piece, also in Latin verse, is the *De Mysteriis Ecclesie* (On the Mysteries of the Church, circa 1245), which offers an elaborate allegorical explanation of church ritual and practice. *De Mysteriis Ecclesie,* a project begun and completed while John was finishing his epic, is a lesser effort, a somewhat disorganized and amorphous collection of symbolic explications in hexameter verse on church architecture, the ceremonies, prayers, and liturgical chants associated with church services, the vestments of priests, the seven sacraments, and so forth. The poem is almost entirely derivative, drawing on the more elaborate works of Guillaume d'Auvergne, Honoré d'Autun, and Hrabanus Maurus, which would soon afterward be synthesized in Guillaume Duranti's *Rational.*

As does the earlier *Epithalamium,* John's *Miracula Beatae Marie Virginis* (Miracles of the Blessed Virgin Mary), also known as *Stella Maris* (Star of the Sea), a work probably completed between 12 February 1248 and 30 March 1249, exemplifies his enthusiasm for the cult of Mary then sweeping across France in both popular and scholarly circles. This much shorter poem refers, in the brief manner of medieval quotation books or *florilegia,* to many of the prominent legends then circulating about Mary in northern Europe. In it John offers very short narrative summaries of the principal miracles that had become associated with the cult of the Virgin. The work seems to have had a devotional purpose; the summaries make little sense unless the reader is acquainted with the fuller versions of these tales found in the various compendia of such stories then circulating in northern France.

Of his later years in Paris, John is mostly silent and little is known of his activity from other sources. He does reveal that several of his works were published in 1234, and many of the surviving manuscripts indicate that some of these achieved a certain standing and popularity among university students and teachers. Some of his early and later efforts were dedicated to famous and powerful men of the age, perhaps in expectation of some preferment: Fulk Bassett, bishop of London; John Blund, chancellor of York; Guillaume d'Auvergne, bishop of Paris; and the Cardinal legate Romain Bonaventura. He made at least one trip to England, perhaps to act as tutor to a noble family. A casual reference by Roger Bacon suggests that John was still alive as late as 1272.

Though his works are uniformly characterized by a difficult, overly ornamental style distinctive for its excess even in an era given to such literary taste, John of Garland deserves more credit and attention from scholars than he has hitherto received. His works on grammar and language are important contributions to a thirteenth-century discipline whose promising development was cut short by a wholesale abandonment of grammatical study for logic, an intellectual change that John in the *Morale Scolarium* condemns as the work of the devil, who "corrupts the standard instruction in the seven liberal arts, the handmaidens of theology, and is scattering ashes instead of light." Instead of an uninspired schoolman, as he has sometimes been characterized, John was a strong supporter of the liberal arts, especially the study of the Latin language and its literature that was to flourish a century later with the first generation of humanists, whose precursor John rightfully was. He was not blind to the value of classical authors, but glimpsed the possibility of a Christianized classicism that would do justice to the undeniable claims of both traditions. If he perhaps lacked the talent to realize that vision himself, he did put his considerable energies in its service. A devoted teacher who was angered by what he saw as defective textbooks that made his job more difficult than it should be, John also spent his life devising what were to his mind better study aids and guides, hoping to improve instruction in the arts course he saw, more than most of his contemporaries, as a necessary element in the attainment of intellectual culture. It is perhaps just that he be remembered more as a hardworking professor than a writer or original thinker of limited talents.

Bibliography:

Lester K. Born. "The Manuscripts of the Major Grammatical Works of John of Garland: *Compendium Grammatice, Clavis Compendü, Ars Lectoria Ecclesie,*" *Transactions and Proceedings of the American Philosophical Association,* 69 (1938), 259–273.

References:

Lester K. Born, "An Analysis of the Quotations and Citations in the *Compendium Grammatice* of John of Garland," in *Classical, Medieval, and Renaissance Studies in Honor of Berthold Louis Ullman,*" edited by Charles Henderson Jr. (Rome: Edizioni di Storia E Letteratura, 1964), pp. 51–83;

G. L. Bursill-Hall, "Johannes de Garlandia–Forgotten Grammarian and the Manuscript Tradition," *Historiographia Linguistica,* 3 (1976): 155–177;

Louis J. Paetow, "The Crusading Ardor of John of Garland," in *The Crusades and Other Historical Essays,* edited by Paetow (New York: F. S. Crofts, 1928), pp. 206–222;

James J. Murphy, "A New Look at Chaucer and the Rhetoricians," *Review of English Studies,* new series 15, (1964): 1–20;

William G. Waite, "Johannes De Garlandia, Poet and Musician," *Speculum,* 35 (1960): 179–195;

Evelyn Faye Wilson, "A Study of the Epithalamium in the Middle Ages: An Introduction to the *Epithalamium beate Marie virginis* of John of Garland," dissertation, University of California, Berkeley, 1930.

Antoine de La Sale

(circa 1386 – 1460/1461)

Simonetta Cochis
Transylvania University

WORKS: *Le paradis de la reine Sibylle* and *L'excursion aux îles Lipari* (circa 1437–1440)

Manuscripts: One manuscript assembles these texts in a single volume, Chantilly, Musée de Condé, 653 coté XIV G.29, an illuminated gift manuscript, with two maps and fifteen miniatures, dedicated to Agnès de Bourbon. The texts are also preserved as chapters 3 and 4 of *La Salade* in Brussels, Bibliothèque Royale/Koninklijke Bibliotheek, ms. 18210–18215.

Standard edition: *Le paradis de la reine Sibylle,* edited by Fernand Desonay (Paris: Droz, 1930).

Edition in modern French: *Le paradis de la reine Sibylle,* translated by Francine Mora-Lebrun, introduction by Daniel Poirion (Paris: Stock, 1983).

La Salade (circa 1444)

Manuscript: There is one manuscript of *La Salade:* Brussels, Bibliothèque Royale/Koninklijke Bibliotheek, ms. 18210–18215. It is an unillustrated fifteenth-century copy on paper with penwork initials and red ink highlighting.

First publications: *Le Salade* (Paris: Michel Le Noir, 1521).

Standard edition: *Antoine de La Sale, Oeuvres Complètes, Tome I: La Salade,* edited by Fernand Desonay (Liège: Faculté de Philosophie et Lettres / Paris: Droz, 1935).

La Sale (20 October 1451)

Manuscripts: Two known manuscript copies are extant: the first, Brussels, Bibliothèque Royale/Koninklijke Bibliotheek, ms. 10959, is executed on paper, with penwork initials and red ink highlighting, and no illustrations; this is the autograph edition of the text, edited and revised by La Sale. The second, Brussels, Bibliothèque Royale/Koninklijke Bibliotheek, ms. 9287–9288, completed on 1 June 1461, is a gift volume executed on fine parchment, with one full-color miniature on the cover page and thirty-eight grisaille illuminations by Loÿset Liédet.

Standard edition: In *Antoine de La Sale, Oeuvres Complètes, Tome II: La Sale,* edited, with notes, by Fernand Desonay (Paris: Les Belles Lettres, 1941).

Le Petit Jehan de Saintré (6 March 1456)

Manuscripts: There are ten extant manuscripts of *Jehan de Saintré*: (A) Paris, Bibliothèque Nationale de France, f. fr. 19169; (B) Paris, Bibliothèque Nationale de France, f. fr. 24379; (C) London, British Museum, ms. Additional 11614; (D) Brussels, Bibliothèque Royale/Koninklijke Bibliotheek, ms. 9547; (E) Florence, Biblioteca Laurenziana, Med. Pal. 102; (F) Paris, Bibliothèque Nationale de France, nouv. acq. fr. 10057; (G) Vatican, Biblioteca Vaticana, Reg. Lat. 896; (H) London, British Museum, Ms. Cotton Nero D IX; (I) Paris, Bibliothèque Nationale de France, f. fr. 1506; (J) Paris, Bibliothèque Nationale de France, nouv. acq. fr. 20234. Manuscript F is an autograph tome edited and extensively revised by La Sale. D and H are illuminated; A and B include only an abridged version of the text.

First publication: *Jehan de Saintré* (Paris: Jean Trepperel, circa 1502–1511).

Standard editions: *Le Petit Jehan de Saintré,* edited by Pierre Champion and Fernand Desonay (Paris: Editions du Trianon, 1926); *Jehan de Saintré,* edited by Jean Misrahi and Charles Knudson, Textes litteraires français no. 117 (Geneva & Paris: Droz, 1965); *Jehan de Saintré, suivi de L'Adicion extraicte des Croniques de Flandres,* edited by Yorio Otaka (Tokyo: Librairi Takeuchi, 1967); *Saintré,* 2 volumes, edited by Mario Eusebi, Les classiques françaises du moyen âge nos. 114 & 115 (Paris: H. Champion, 1993, 1994).

Standard edition and edition in modern French: *Jehan de Saintré,* edited by Joël Blanchard, translated by Michel Quereuil, Lettres Gothiques no. 4544 (Paris: Librairie Générale Française, 1995).

Edition in modern French: *Saintré: Antoine de La Sale,* translated by Roger Dubois, Traductions des classiques françaises du moyen âge no. 61 (Paris: H. Champion, 1995).

Antoine de La Sale presenting a copy of Le Petit Jehan de Saintré *to Philip the Good, Duke of Burgundy*
(Brussels, Bibliothèque Royale/Koninklijke Bibliotheek)

Edition in English: *Little John of Saintré,* translated by Irvine Gray (London: Routledge, 1931).
Le réconfort de Madame de Fresne (14 December 1457)
   Manuscripts: Brussels, Bibliothèque Royale/Koninklijke Bibliotheek, ms. 10748 and Bibliothèque Royale/Koninklijke Bibliotheek, ms. II 7827.
   Standard edition: *Le réconfort de Madame de Fresne,* edited by Ian Hill, Textes littéraires, no. 34 (Exeter, U.K.: University of Exeter, 1979).
Traité des anciens tournois et faictz d'armes (4 January 1459)
   Manuscripts: Paris, Bibliothèque Nationale de France, f. fr. 5867 and Bibliothèque Nationale de France f. fr. 1997.
   Standard edition: In *Traités du duel judiciaire: Relations de pas d'armes et tournois par Olivier de la Marche, Jean de Villiers, seigneur de l'Isle-Adam, Hardouin de la Jaille, Antoine de la Sale, etc.,* edited by Bernard Prost (Paris: L. Willem, 1872).

Antoine de La Sale wrote moral and didactic works cast in a literary mold. His eclectic narrative style, intriguing choice of subjects, and distinctive sense of order converged to produce a literature that is both edifying and enjoyable. As preceptor for the prices of two of the finest courts of France in the fifteenth century, Anjou and Luxembourg, La Sale wrote to instruct and entertain the highest aristocracy. Examples of courtly performance in its largest sense, his works capture the tastes, trends, and preoccupations of that privileged milieu while fulfilling a humanistic demand for knowledge and wisdom. La Sale's writings are as multifaceted as his own life experience: he was a soldier versed in all facets of chivalric activity, but he was also a scholar of broad learning. The joy that he derived from his own studies permeates his writings: "me suis delicté a traire de mains livres, que j'ay pris plaisir a lire. . . ." (I have taken delight in drawing from many a book, which I have had the pleasure of reading), he notes in the prologue to *La Salade* (The Salad, circa 1444).

   Born about 1386 near Arles in Provence, Antoine de La Sale was the illegitimate son of a Gascon knight of noble extraction, Bernard de La Sale, known as Chicot, who fought as a mercenary for Pope Clement VII, Bertrand Du Guesclin, and the dukes of Anjou. Antoine followed in the footsteps of the father he never knew; he was taken on as a page in 1400 by Louis II of Anjou, who recognized him as legitimate heir and bestowed upon the boy the gratitude the Angevin house owed his father. Of his mother, Perinette Damendel, only the name is known. He accompanied Louis II, and later Louis III and René, contenders for the throne of Sicily and Naples, on their various military campaigns in Italy. La Sale never took the investiture of knighthood, however–he played a more intricate role, as a squire whose extensive education, both military and academic, won him appointment as tutor to Jean de Calabre, the eldest son and heir of René d'Anjou. This position required him to accompany the young prince on all his travels and educate him in the highest ideals of chivalry, virtue, and learning. While in Naples with Jean de Calabre in 1439, the fifty-three-year-old La Sale married the fifteen-year-old Lione de la Sellana de Brusa.

An unexplained event created a painful break in his life, however. When his tutorial duties were completed with Jean de Calabre, La Sale was summarily dismissed from the Angevin court in 1448, after forty-nine years of varied and devoted service. This abrupt termination was a great source of chagrin for the still-active sexagenarian. Embittered at this ingratitude, La Sale took a position with Louis of Luxembourg as tutor for his three sons. He dedicated his later years to his writing, melancholically reliving through it the poignant memories of his youth. La Sale died in 1460 or 1461.

Le paradis de la reine Sibylle (The Paradise of Queen Sibyl, circa 1437–1440), La Sale's earliest composition, is a fantastic tale about the court of Queen Sibyl, an underground paradise where an eternity of worldly pleasures awaits an adventurous knight. *Le paradis* is also a travel narrative of La Sale's visit to the cave of the Sibyl near Montemonaco, near Ancona, in the Marche region of Italy, in 1420 during his long sojourn in the kingdom of Naples with Louis III of Anjou. *Le Paradis* is followed by another fantastic tale, *L'excursion aux îles Lipari* (The Excursion to the Islands of Lipari, circa 1437–1440), a story about a mysterious giant sailor he supposedly encountered during a trip that he took in 1407 to the volcanic islands off the coast of Sicily. These two short narratives exhibit La Sale's engaging mix of storytelling and book learning, emblematic of his desire to blend recreation with education and to align his subject matter with the interests of his audience. An Edenic court setting and a good mysterious story set in an exotic locale appealed to his readers at the Angevin court.

Le paradis de la reine Sibylle begins as a travel narrative, a popular genre at the court of Anjou, which was a crossroads of different cultures because of the penchant of the dukes for travel and their territorial interests abroad. La Sale opens his tale with descriptions of his visit to the region, which he intertwines with mysterious rumors about an underground Eden, so that six distinct yet overlapping stories combine to form the narrative. He punctuates the tantalizing stories, which he refers to as "le parler des gens d'iceluy pays" (the talk of the people of this country), with his own skeptical observations, supported by citations from classical authors. La Sale writes that during his own trip he only reached the cave where the entrance to the Sibyl's paradise is located and that he went no further; however, he recounts the progress of various characters who undertake the voyage into the ominous underground passageway. As they are impeded in their journey by progressively more-frightening obstacles (a perilous bridge, a wind tunnel, slamming metal doors, figures of dragons), they also disappear, one by one, from the story line. Only one character, a German knight, reaches the Sibyl's paradise, a refined courtly setting of countless riches, eternal youth, and free love. He soon realizes, however, that this magnificent court is the work of the devil, when he discovers that all the women turn into snakes every Friday evening. Repentant, he seeks pardon from the Pope in Rome, who is reluctant to grant it; the knight despairs and returns to the Sibyl's paradise. Since he cannot save his soul, he chooses to enjoy the pleasures of the flesh.

La Sale's second work, *L'excursion aux îles Lipari,* purports to be an eyewitness account of some bizarre occurrences. While on their way from Messina to Palermo, La Sale and several other Angevin knights and squires take passage on a merchant's vessel. When they set anchor in the port of Vulcano, the crew follows a local custom of putting crosses on the mooring lines of their boat. That evening a mysterious oarsman approaches their boat in a dinghy, saying that he is a messenger from the captain of Lipari. The man, who is huge, dirty, and misshapen, tells them that his own actions had given rise to the superstitious custom of setting crosses on boat moorings: a few years ago, when Lipari was at war with several nations, he had untied enemy ships during the night in order to force the boats aground, so that he could hear the sailors' language and determine their country of origin. Assuming that demons from the nearby portals of hell (the volcanoes) had untied the ships, the locals had begun to put crosses on mooring cables. Reassured by this tale, the young sailors aboard La Sale's ship remove the crosses they had already put on their

Signature of La Sale at the foot of a manuscript page in his Le Petit Jehan de Saintré *(Bibliothèque Nationale de France, nouv. acq. fr. 10057, fol. 60)* ship's moorings. During the night, however, their ship is caught in a storm, their cables are untied, and they almost shipwreck on the reefs. When the sailors finally meet with the captain of Lipari, he tells them that he had never sent a messenger, and that they had certainly been duped by one of the local demons.

Both *Le paradis de la reine Sibylle* and *L'excursion aux îles Lipari* generate a sense of unresolved tension because these uncanny stories about mysterious demonic beings are told with the skeptical realism of a learned man, the preceptor to a prince, who mixes doubt with fascination. This inherent duality is exemplified by the two markedly different manuscript contexts where these texts are found. The Chantilly manuscript is a delicately illuminated gift book, dedicated to Agnès de Bourbon, mother-in-law of La Sale's pupil Jean de Calabre. In the Brussels manuscript these two fantastic tales are included as chapters in *La Salade,* a didactic compilation of diverse texts for moral and practical instruction. These two manuscripts point to the dual purpose of these texts and to the tensions found in the narrative: the aesthetically pleasing Chantilly manuscript, made to entertain a courtly audience, is recreational, whereas *La Salade,* didactic and moralizing, emphasizes a pedagogically correct view of inexplicable events, framing these amazing stories within the voice of reason. Although presented as tales "pour rire et passer temps" (to laugh and to pass the time), they bring up questions that were pressing during the fifteenth century: is courtly life, like the Sibyl's court, the work of the devil? if the church refuses absolution, must man despair of salvation? is the chivalric quest doomed to end in damnation? do demons periodically erupt into daily existence and wreak havoc? Perhaps the intent of these texts was twofold: to entertain while subtly raising disturbing questions and allowing readers to formulate their own conclusions.

La Salade, written about 1444, is filled with apparently disparate ingredients, mixing pleasurable narratives with pedagogy. In this work La Sale collected and organized a series of texts for the instruction of a prince, with topics ranging from a moral treatise for successful governance, strategies for military conquest, a world geography (including *Le paradis de la reine Sibylle* and *L'excursion aux îles Lipari*), the genealogies of the kingdom of Sicily, protocols for the organization of battles, the advancement of nobles in times of war and in peace, the crowning of the king of Sicily, and the Latin text of the homage that nobles must pay to the church. In his dedicatory epistle to his pupil Jean de Calabre, La Sale explains his title: these diverse texts are the "bonnes herbes" (good herbs) that compose a salad, that is, useful moral fare to nourish the mind and spirit of his prince. In *La Salade,* Antoine de La Sale creates an

educational program, one aimed at impressing in the memory of his reader important facts, quotations from classical authors, and the precepts to be learned from his narratives. Various elements combine to form this eclectic but fully integrated program of instruction. La Sale uses short narrative exempla, whose concise internal logic and brief conclusions illustrate his precepts with economy, and he uses different formats to present detailed information: he starts with a narrative, then a list, and finally organizes key items into table form. The ingredients that compose this mixed "salad" are autonomous units: each section keeps its structural integrity and can be read separately, as a lesson or as a recreational interlude.

La Sale (The Room, 1451) is also a collection of narrative units inserted in an allegorical frame, but here the works are less disparate than they are in *La Salade*. Together they form a manual of moral instruction illustrating the ethical values that make a good ruler, a *miroir des princes* (mirror for princes), an example of a didactic genre that flourished from the thirteenth century well into the Renaissance. They were founded on the notion that by providing "doctrine necessaire au gouvernement de ceste vye" (the doctrines needed to govern this life), the prince's good self-government leads to the good government of his people, as rulers that are "loyaulx et saiges a bien conseillier" (loyal and of wise counsel) insure the good of the entire society.

In *La Sale* the author again uses exempla extensively, summarizing and organizing according to topic the writings of various classical authors, mostly those of the Latin historian Valerius Maximus, writer of brief anecdotal narratives, but also Isidore of Seville, Seneca, St. Augustine, and others. The allegory framing *La Sale* is constructed on the metaphor of a room (a *sale,* which puns on the author's name, as did *La Salade*), in which La Sale places the various exempla that comprise this moral handbook. The virtues of prudence, devotion, religion, and moderation form the foundations of the allegorical room: justice, mercy, compassion, humanity, and discipline form its walls; the windows are love, happiness, abstinence, continence, modesty, and stories of different marvels; the doors are gratitude, liberality, poverty of spirit, and the interpretation of dreams; and on the floor, which gets trampled on, are the vices of sacrilege, avarice, and ingratitude. La Sale's reworking of classical material is often sprightly and his lessons incisive. His book is organized so that first come the moral precepts most related to governance, especially humility and the divine duty of the ruler, and then La Sale gives practical advice on princely obligations such as meting out justice and waging war. Next he turns to entertaining material, to mythical stories and to issues of love, marriage, and friendship; finally, he deals with

La Sale's character Jehan de Saintré depicted defeating his opponent in a duel (from a manuscript for Le Petit Jehan de Saintré, *British Library, MS. Cotton Nero D IX)*

miscellaneous exemplary material that reinforces the lessons already treated. His aim is to form the ethical fiber of the ruler, so he accords primary importance to issues of governance, then provides a pleasing respite from serious matters, and concludes by emphasizing the important moral precepts with additional exemplary stories.

In *Jehan de Saintré* (1456) La Sale combines his talents as storyteller, moralist, and man-at-arms to create a didactic chivalric romance, a manual for the perfect knight. In this work, often considered his masterpiece, La Sale combines the educational techniques he had introduced in *La Salade* and *La Sale* with a subject matter as interesting for his courtly audience as was *Le paradis de la reine Sibylle,* melding fiction with history to create a compelling narrative. *Jehan de Saintré* purports to be the biography of an historical figure, a knight whose real-life exploits had been extolled by the fourteenth-century chronicler Jean Froissart, though La Sale takes only the name of Jehan de Saintré for his hero and the general time period of the fourteenth century as a setting for his idealized chivalric milieu. *Jehan de Saintré*

opens on a courtly scene, when Jehan, a thirteen-year-old page at the court of Jean le Bon, captures the attention of Madame des Belles Cousines, a rich widow bent on becoming his benefactress. She is generous with both advice and money: her dual role as mentor and banker transforms the timid boy into a valorous and graceful knight. She instructs him in a series of harangues that constitutes the didactic portion of the text, making it a manual for the moral and amorous conduct of a knight. Coming of age, Jehan takes on the challenges of knighthood, including tournaments, battles, and a crusade. With adulthood he also becomes Madame's lover, and their trysts are executed in the strictest secrecy, in keeping with the tenets of the courtly love tradition. Here, however, the didactic chivalric romance takes a sweeping turn to fabliau as the ideal arrangement goes askew. Jehan, tired of the yoke imposed by his all-controlling mistress, engages in a chivalric enterprise on his own, without her consent. When he returns, Madame has left the court; she has retired to her estates and has taken on a new and vulgar lover, the lax abbot of a nearby monastery. When the outraged Jehan first confronts the abbot, he loses a wrestling match against his corpulent adversary, but he takes revenge by challenging the abbot to a chivalric duel, which he wins by brutally maiming his rival. He drags Madame des Belles Cousines back to the court and exposes her duplicity in public by presenting to the queen and her ladies the story of a treacherous woman who betrayed her faithful and honorable champion, and the story ends on a moralizing note.

Though seemingly disparate, the didactic disquisitions, the chivalric episodes, the fabliau-style love triangle, and the sobering finale are held together by the plot, which frames the didactic and chivalric pieces. As Jane Taylor has pointed out in "Image as Reception: Antoine de La Sale's *Le Petit Jehan de Saintré*"(1994), illustrations in the manuscripts of *Jehan de Saintré* indicate that what captivated the fifteenth-century imagination were battle scenes and heraldry, all things related to chivalric undertakings. In *Jehan de Saintré* La Sale creates a compendium of information, a permanent record of what the ideal knight should be, an account of his deeds, all within a story that holds the pieces together and provides for salutary recreation.

Although *Le réconfort de Madame de Fresne* (The Consolation for Madame de Fresne, 1457), written during the last years of La Sale's life, is also a didactic work, it is different in tone. A fine example of the *consolatio* (consolatory treatise), it follows the tradition established by Boethius in his *De Consolatione philosophiae* (On the Consolation of Philosophy, circa A.D. 520) as a narrative that emphasizes the immortality of the soul and the truths of the human condition to provide consolation to a person afflicted by grief. Addressed to La Sale's friend Katherine de Neufville, Madame de Fresne, who was grieving over the death of her first-born son, this text is more contemplative and less pragmatic than his earlier works. Although he remains faithful to the purpose of the genre, La Sale manipulates the *consolatio* in his own particular way, combining personal experiences with pseudohistorical events and mixing his own memories with classical moral precepts, to create the two central narrative units, the two exempla of which the work is comprised.

The first exemplum draws from two historical incidents, the siege of Tarfa in Spain during the late thirteenth century and an incident recounted by Froissart in which the duke of Anjou had hostages killed at Brest in 1373. La Sale's version is the story of a mother who encourages her husband to preserve his honor even if this means the death of their only son, held hostage by the Black Prince (Edward, Prince of Wales). In the second exemplum La Sale transposes an anecdote given by Valerius Maximus onto an event that he had personally witnessed, the siege of Ceuta, when as a young man in 1415 he had taken part in the expedition of the Portuguese king to Morocco. He blends history with personal memories and tells the pathetic story of a mother who represses her grief over the death of her son in order to console her prince. Both stories focus on the value of sublimating one's own sorrow in order to abide by higher principles: justice, honor, and selflessness. Here La Sale seeks to distract Madame de Fresne with vivid narratives that speak to her emotions, that redirect her grief, and provide moral instruction and sustenance.

La Sale's last work, *Traité des anciens tournois et faictz d'armes* (Treatise on the Old Tournaments and Feats of Arms, 1459), is a short manual on the conduct of tournaments and chivalric exercises. It includes an historical account of the territorial subdivisions that distinguish the different participants, the *marches* (frontier regions) established by Charlemagne, each with its own heraldry, battle cry, and alliances. In his youth La Sale had participated in such chivalric feats, the colorful and ceremonious tournaments and jousts that punctuated aristocratic life in the fifteenth century. In *Traité des anciens tournois*, La Sale relates his experiences at the tournament in Brussels in 1409 that honored the marriage of Antoine de Brabant and the tournament given at Ghent in 1414 by Philip the Good. With his customary orderliness and brevity, La Sale sets out the rules, the protocols, and the structures of these famed tournaments, comparing tournaments held at the time he is writing with those held at the beginning of the century. His tone throughout is melancholy, as he notes the decline of the chivalric code of honor.

The traditional manifestations of a virtuous life, embodied by strict adherence to the chivalric code, to Christian selflessness, and to the moral precepts of classical Scholasticism were slipping away in the last century of the feudal Middle Ages in France. In his writings La Sale tried to capture the tenets and stories that underlie and define this passing world of glory, virtue, and high ideals. His writings both reflect and serve the milieu that gave him life and purpose. As Erich Auerbach points out in his *Mimesis: The Representation of Reality in Western Literature* (1953), La Sale "lives enveloped in a class-determined atmosphere with its distinctive conception of honor, its ceremonies, and its heraldic pomp." The confines of his universe are the exigencies of the court, his social class the leisured aristocracy; however, the paradigms of virtue he so eloquently portrayed in his moralizing works were already themselves vestiges of the past and no longer appear tenable in the reality in which he lived. In his *Traité des anciens tournois* he notes that gone are the days when "dames et damoiselles . . . blasonnoient bien les armes des seigneurs . . . que aroit bien souffiz à ung roy

Page from the manuscript for La Sale's Le Petit Jehan de Saintré, *with corrections and marginal notes in La Sale's handwriting*
(Bibliothèque Nationale de France, nouv. acq. fr. 10057, fol. 60)

d'armes ou hérault" (ladies and young women . . . blazoned correctly the arms of lords . . . well enough for a king of arms or a herald). The melancholy that permeates his last work is not just the self-indulgent regrets of an aging courtier and soldier; La Sale wrote manuals of instruction and entertainment, but all of his works look back rather than forward, mourning the loss of a chivalric ideal that is already a thing of the past.

Over the centuries Antoine de La Sale's multifaceted works have baffled critics, whose criticism of his works has generally reflected the preoccupations of the times when each critic was writing. In the neoclassical seventeenth century, an anonymous critic questioned the *vraisemblance* (versimilitude) of the actions and motivations of Saintré and Madame de Belles Cousines; in the Romantic early nineteenth century, Marcel Lecourt challenged Le Sale's originality and called his compilations of classical writings plagiarism; in the early twentieth century literal-minded philologists such as Gaston Paris, Pio Rajna, and Fernand Desonay retraced La Sale's travels to seek the cave of Queen Sibyl in Italy. Later in the twentieth century La Sale's *Saintré* became a choice ground for testing semiotic, linguistic, and deconstructionist theories as in *Le texte du roman approche Sé miologique d'une structure discursive transformationnelle* (1970), in which Julia Kristeva called *Saintré* the first French prose novel. Only recently have critics such as Madeleine Jeay and Jane Taylor approached the works of Antoine de La Sale with an eye to their historical and literary contexts.

References:

Erich Auerbach, "Madame du Chastel," in his *Mimesis: The Representation of Reality in Western Literature,* translated by Willard Transk (Princeton, N. J.: Princeton University Press, 1953), pp. 232–261;

Alphonse Bronarski, *Le petit Jehan de Saintré, une énigme littéraire* (Florence: Olschki, 1922);

Anne Caillaud, "La belle dame des Belles Cousines, élément dynamique du *Petit Jehan de Saintré,*" dissertation, Michigan State University, 1992;

Elizabeth Caron, "Le Petit Jehan de Saintré dans la tradition des fabliaux," *Fifteenth Century Studies,* 15 (1989): 67–80;

Patricia Francis Cholakian, "The Two Narrative Styles of A. de La Sale," *Romance Notes,* 10 (1968): 362–372;

Alfred Coville, *Recherches sur quelques écrivains du XIVe et XVe siècle* (Paris: Droz, 1935);

Coville, *La vie intellectuelle dans les domaines d'Anjou-Provence de 1380–1435* (Geneva: Slatkine Reprints, 1974);

Pierre Demarolle, "A propos du vocabulaire d'Antoine de La Sale: nature et portée des faits de syntaxe lexicale," *Travaux de Linguistique: Revue Internationale de Linguistique Française,* 25 (November 1992): 13–24;

Jeanne Demers, "La quête de l'anti-Graal ou un récit fantastique: *Le Paradis de la reine Sibylle,*" *Le Moyen Age,* 83, 3-4 (1977): 469–492;

Fernand Desonay, *Antoine de La Sale, aventurier et pedagogue* (Liége: Bibliothèque de la faculté de philosophie et lettres de l'Université de Liége, 1940);

Desonay, "Comment un écrivain se corrigeait au quinzième siècle. Etude sur les corrections du manuscrit d'auteur du *Petit Jehan de Saintré* d'Antoine de La Sale," *Revue Belge de Philologie et d'Histoire,* 6 (1927): 81–121;

Janet Ferrier, "Antoine de La Sale and the Beginnings of Naturalism in French Prose," *French Studies,* 10 (1956): 216–223;

Ferrier, "An Experiment in Adaptation: *Le Petit Jehan de Saintré,*" in *Forerunners of the French Novel: An Essay on the Development of the Nouvelle in the late Middle Ages* (Manchester, U.K.: Manchester University Press, 1954), pp. 54–78;

Madeleine Jeay, *Donner la parole: l'histoire-cadre dans les recueils de nouvelles des XVe–XVIe siècles,* Le moyen française no. 31 (Montreal: CERES, 1992);

Jeay, "Les éléments didactiques et descriptifs de Jehan de Saintré: des lourdeurs à réconsidérer," *Fifteenth Century Studies,* 19 (1992): 85–100;

Jeay, "Une théorie du roman: le manuscrit autographe de *Jehan de Saintré,*" *Romance Philology,* 47, no. 3 (1994): 287–307;

Jeay, "Le travail du récit à la cour de Bourgogne: *Les Evangiles des quenouilles, Les Cent nouvelles nouvelles et Saintré,* in *"A l'heure encore de mon escrire": Aspects de la littérature de Bourgogne sous Philippe le Bon et Charles le Téméraire,* edited by Claude Thiry (N.p.: Les Lettres Romanes, 1998);

Allison Kelly, "Abbreviation and Amplification: *Jehan de Saintré*'s Rewriting the Artifice of History," *French Forum,* 11, no. 2 (1986): 133–150;

Kelly, "Christine de Pizan and Antoine de La Sale: The Dangers of Love in Theory and Fiction," in *Reinterpreting Christine de Pizan,* edited by Earl J. Richards (Athens: University of Georgia Press, 1992), pp. 173–186;

Kelly, "*Jehan de Saintré:* Rewriting the Artifice of History," dissertation, Princeton University, 1987;

Charles Knudson, "Une aventure d'Antoine de La Sale aux îles Lipari," *Romania,* 54 (1928): 99–109;

Knudson, "The Prussian Expedition in *Jehan de Saintré,*" in *Etudes de langue et de littérature du Moyen Age offertes à Félix Lecoy* (Paris: H. Champion, 1973), pp. 271–277;

Julia Kristeva, *Le texte du roman: approche sémiologique d'une structure discursive transformationnelle* (The Hague: Mouton, 1970);

Denis Lalande, "Le couple Saintré-Boucicaut dans le roman de *Jehan de Saintré*," *Romania*, 111 (1990): 481–494;

Marcel Lecourt, "Antoine de La Sale et Simon de Hesdin: une restitution littéraire," in *Mélanges offerts à M. Emile Chatelain* (Paris: H. Champion, 1910), pp. 341–353;

Guy Mermier, "*Jehan de Saintré*: 'Nouveau roman' médiéval," *Fifteenth Century Studies*, 8 (1979): 141–158;

Mermier, "Le message paradoxal du *Petit Jehan de Saintré* à courtoisie et à chevalerie au XVe siècle," *Studi Mediolatini e Volgari*, 26 (1978–1979): 143–159;

Mermier, "Structure et sens de la conjointure narrative et dramatique du roman *Petit Jehan de Saintré*," in *The Nature of Medieval Narrative*, edited by Minette Grunmann-Gaudet and Robin Jones (Lexington, Ky.: French Forum, 1980), pp. 191–204;

Francine Mora-Lebrun, "Métamorphoses dans *Le paradis de la reine Sibylle*: des archétypes mythiques aux jeux d'une écriture," in *Métamorphose et bestiaire fantastique au Moyen Age*, edited by Laurence Harf-Lancer (Paris: Ecole normale superieure des jeunes filles, 1985), pp. 287–315;

Joseph Nève, *Antoine de La Salle: sa vie et ses ouvrages d'après des documents inédits* (Geneva: Slatkine, 1975);

Michèle Perret, "L'invraisemblable vérité: Témoignage fantastique dans deux romans du 14e et 15e siècles," *Europe: Revue Littéraire Mensuelle*, 654 (October 1983): 25–35;

Daniel Poirion, "Ecriture et ré-écriture au Moyen Age," *Littérature*, 14 (February 1981): 109–118;

Corrado Rosso, "Un philosophe oublié: La Salle," *Studies on Voltaire and the Eighteenth Century*, 16 (1992): 303–313;

Monique Santucci, "Rire et ire dans *Jehan de Saintré*," in *Le Rire au Moyen Age dans la littérature et dans les arts: Actes du colloque international des 17, 18 et 19 novembre 1988*, edited by Thérèse Bouché and Hélène Charpentier, with the cooperation of Centre National de la Recherche Scientifique (Bordeaux: Presses Universitaires de Bordeaux, 1990);

Jane Taylor, "Courtly Patronage Subverted: *Lancelot en Prose, Petit Jehan de Saintré*," *Medioevo Romanzo*, 19 (1994): 277–292;

Taylor, "Image as Reception: Antoine de La Sale's *Le Petit Jehan de Saintré*," in *Literary Aspects of Courtly Culture: Selected Papers from the Seventh Triennial Congress of the International Courtly Literature Society, University of Massachusetts, 27 July – 1 August 1992*, edited by Donald Maddox and Sara Sturm-Maddox (Cambridge, U.K.: D. S. Brewer, 1994), pp. 265–279;

Taylor, "The Pattern of Perfection: *Jehan de Saintré* and the Chivalric Ideal," *Medium Aevum*, 53, 2 (1984): 254–262;

Karl Uitti, "Renewal and Undermining of Old French Romance: *Jehan de Saintré*," in *Romance: Generic Transformations from Chrétien de Troyes to Cervantes*, edited by Kevin Brownlee and Marina Scordilis Brownlee (Hanover, N. H. & London: Published for Dartmouth College by University Press of New England, 1985), pp. 135–154;

Thomas Vesce, "Antoine de La Sale's Fabulous Trip to the Lipari Isles," in *Jean Misrahi Memorial Volume: Studies in Medieval Literature*, edited by Hans Runte, Henri Niedzielski, and William Hendrickson (Columbia, S.C.: French Literature Publications, 1977), pp. 310–321;

Charity Cannon Willard, "Antoine de la Salle, Reader of Christine de Pizan," in *The Reception of Christine de Pizan from the 15th to the 19th Century*, edited by Glenda McLeod (Lewiston, N.Y.: Mellen Press, 1991).

Guillaume de Machaut

(circa 1300 – 13? April 1377)

Nadia Margolis
Christine de Pizan Society

WORKS: *La Louange des Dames* (circa 1324–1377)

Manuscripts: The text is represented in complete works manuscripts among others: Paris, Bibliothèque Nationale de France, f. fr. 1586 (circa 1356); New York, Wildenstein Collection, no shelfmark (circa 1370), which was formerly owned by the marquises de Vogüé; Paris, Bibliothèque Nationale de France, f. fr. 1584 (circa 1370–1377); Bibliothèque Nationale de France, f. fr. 22545–22546 (circa 1390); Bibliothèque Nationale de France, f. fr. 843.

Standard editions: *Guillaume de Machaut: Poésies lyriques. Edition complète en deux parties, avec introduction, glossaire, et fac-similés publiée sous les auspices de la Faculté d'Histoire et de Philologie de Saint-Pétersbourg,* edited by Vladimir F. Chichmaref [Shishmarev] (Paris: H. Champion, 1909; republished, Geneva: Slatkine, 1973); *La Louange des Dames by Guillaume de Machaut,* edited by Nigel Wilkins (Edinburgh: Scottish Academic Press, 1972).

Le Jugement dou Roy de Behaingne (1330s – before August 1346)

Manuscripts: Titled *Le Temps Pascour* in Paris, Bibliothèque Nationale de France, f. fr. 1586 only; the text is also found (normal title) in other complete works manuscripts, as well as Arras, Bibliothèque Municipale 897; Bern, Burgerbibliothek 218; Paris, Bibliothèque de L'Arsenal 5203; Paris, Bibliothèque Nationale de France, f. fr. 2166; Bibliothèque Nationale de France, f. fr. 2230, f. fr. 1149, f. fr. 20026, and f. fr. 1595; ex-Phillipps 6740 (last listed at H. P. Kraus, New York); Stockholm, Kungliga Biblioteket, Vu 22.

First publication: "Le jugement dou Roy de Behaigne," edited by Caron, in *Mémoires de l'Académie d'Arras,* 33 (1861): 307–366.

Standard edition and edition in English: In *Le Jugement du Roy de Behaigne and Remede de Fortune,* edited by James I. Wimsatt and William W. Kibler, music edited by Rebecca A. Baltzer (Athens: University of Georgia Press, 1988), pp. 59–165.

Edition in English: *Guillaume de Machaut: The Judgment of the King of Bohemia,* edited and translated by R. Barton Palmer (New York: Garland, 1984).

Twenty-three Motets (1330s–early 1360s)

Manuscripts: Paris, Bibliothèque Nationale de France, f. fr. 1586; New York, Wildenstein Collection, no shelfmark; Bibliothèque Nationale de France, f. fr. 843; Bibliothèque Nationale de France, f. fr. 1584; Bibliothèque Nationale de France, f. fr. 22545–22546; and Bibliothèque Nationale de France, f. fr. 9221.

Standard editions: In *Guillaume de Machaut: Musicalische Werke,* 4 volumes, edited by Friedrich Ludwig and H. Besseler (Leipzig: Breitkopf & Härtel, 1926–1943; republished, 1954); in "The Music of Guillaume de Machaut," edited by Sarah Jane Williams, dissertation, Yale University, 1952; in *The Works of Guillaume de Machaut,* 2 volumes, edited by Leo Schrade, Polyphonic Music of the Fourteenth Century nos. 2–3 (Les Remparts, Monaco: L'Oiseau-Lyre, 1956; republished, 1977); in *Guillaume de Machaut: Œuvres complètes,* 4 volumes, edited by Sylvette Leguy (Paris: Le Droict Chemin de Musique, 1977).

Le Dit dou Vergier (1330)

Manuscripts: The text is represented in complete works manuscripts: Paris, Bibliothèque Nationale de France, f. fr. 1586; Aberystwyth, National Library of Wales, 5010 C (circa 1356); New York, Wildenstein Collection, no shelfmark; Paris, Bibliothèque Nationale de France, f. fr. 1585 (circa 1370–1372); Bibliothèque Nationale de France, f. fr. 1584 (circa 1370–1377); Bibliothèque Nationale de France, f. fr. 22545; Bibliothèque Nationale de France, f. fr. 9221 (ca. 1390).

First publication: In *Les Œuvres de Guillaume de Machault,* edited by Prosper Tarbé (Reims & Paris: Techener, 1849; republished, Geneva: Slatkine, 1977), pp.11–39.

Standard edition: In *Œuvres de Guillaume de*

Guillaume de Machaut (illumination from a manuscript, Bibliothèque Nationale de France, f. fr. 1587, f. 1r.)

Machaut, 3 volumes, edited by Ernest Hoepffner (Paris: Firmin-Didot, 1908–1921; republished, New York: Johnson, 1965), I: 13–56.

Standard edition and edition in English: In *Guillaume de Machaut: The Fountain of Love (La Fonteinne Amoureuse) and Two Other Love Vision Poems,* edited and translated by R. Barton Palmer, Garland Library of Medieval Literature no. 54 (New York: Garland, 1993), pp. 22–87.

Le Dit de l'Alerion (1340s)

Manuscripts: Also known as *Le Dit des .iiii. Oiseaus,* the text is represented in several manuscripts, including the complete works manuscripts: Aberystwyth, National Library of Wales, 5010 C; Paris, Bibliothèque Nationale de France, f. fr. 1586; New York, Wildenstein Collection, no shelfmark; Paris, Bibliothèque Nationale de France, f. fr. 1584; Bibliothèque Nationale de France, f. fr. 22545–22546; and Bibliothèque Nationale de France, f. fr. 843.

First publication and standard edition: In

Œuvres de Guillaume de Machaut, 3 volumes, edited by Ernest Hoepffner (Paris: Firmin-Didot, 1908–1921; republished, New York: Johnson, 1965), II: 239–403.

Edition in English: In *Guillaume de Machaut: The Tale of the Alerion,* edited by Minette Gaudet and Constance B. Hieatt (Toronto & Buffalo: University of Toronto Press, 1994).

Le Remede de Fortune (1340 – before 1357)

Manuscripts: The best surviving manuscript is Cambridge, Magdalene College, Bibliotheca Pepysiana 1594; the text is also preserved in complete works manuscripts Paris, Bibliothèque Nationale de France, f. fr. 1586; Bibliothèque de l'Arsenal, 5203; and Bern, Burgerbibliothek, 218; fragments, without the music, are preserved in Aberystwyth, National Library of Wales 5010 C.

First publication: In *Les Œuvres de Guillaume de Machault,* edited by Prosper Tarbé (Reims & Paris: Techener, 1849; republished, Geneva: Slatkine, 1977), pp. 83–88.

Standard edition and edition in English: In *Le Jugement du Roy de Behaigne and Remede de Fortune*, edited by James I. Wimsatt and William W. Kibler, music edited by Rebecca A. Baltzer (Athens: University of Georgia Press, 1988), pp. 167–409.

Le Dit dou Lyon (1342)

Manuscripts: The text is represented in complete works manuscripts: Paris, Bibliothèque Nationale de France, f. fr. 1586; New York, Wildenstein Collection, no shelfmark; Paris, Bibliothèque Nationale de France, f. fr. 1585; Bibliothèque Nationale de France, f. fr. 1584; Bibliothèque Nationale de France, f. fr. 22545–22546; Bibliothèque Nationale de France, f. fr. 9221.

First publication and standard edition: In *Œuvres de Guillaume de Machaut,* 3 volumes, edited by Ernest Hoepffner (Paris: Firmin-Didot, 1908–1921; republished, New York: Johnson, 1965), II: 159–237.

Le Jugement dou Roy de Navarre and *Lay de Plour* (after 1349)

Manuscripts: These two attached texts are represented in complete works manuscripts: New York, Wildenstein Collection; Paris, Bibliothèque Nationale de France, f. fr. 843; Bibliothèque Nationale de France, f. fr. 1587; Bibliothèque Nationale de France, f. fr. 1585; Bibliothèque Nationale de France, f. fr. 1584; Bibliothèque Nationale de France, f. fr. 22545–22546; Bibliothèque Nationale de France, f. fr. 9221; and Pierpont Morgan Library, m. 396.

First publication: In *Œuvres de Guillaume de Machaut,* 3 volumes, edited by Ernest Hoepffner (Paris: Firmin-Didot, 1908–1921; republished, New York: Johnson, 1965), I: 137–282.

Standard edition and edition in English: *Guillaume de Machaut: The Judgment of the King of Navarre,* edited and translated by R. Barton Palmer (New York: Garland, 1988).

Le Confort d'Ami (1357)

Manuscripts: The text is represented in the complete works manuscripts: Paris, Bibliothèque Nationale de France, f. fr. 1585; Bibliothèque Nationale de France, f. fr. 1584; Bibliothèque Nationale de France, f. fr. 22545–22546; Bibliothèque Nationale de France, f. fr. 9221; New York, Wildenstein Collection, no shelfmark.

First publication: In *Œuvres de Guillaume de Machaut,* edited by Ernest Hoepffner (Paris: Firmin-Didot, 1908–1921; republished, New York: Johnson, 1965), III: 1–142.

Standard edition and edition in English: *Guillaume de Machaut: Le Confort d'Ami (Comfort for a*

Friend), edited and translated by R. Barton Palmer (New York & London: Garland, 1992).

Le Dit de la Harpe (1360s?)

Manuscripts: The text is represented in complete works manuscripts: Paris, Bibliothèque Nationale de France, f. fr. 1586; New York, Wildenstein Collection; Paris, Bibliothèque Nationale de France, f. fr. 1585; Bibliothèque Nationale de France, f. fr. 1584; Bibliothèque Nationale de France, f. fr. 22545–22546; Bibliothèque Nationale de France, f. fr. 9221.

First publication and standard edition: "The *Dit de la Harpe* of Guillaume de Machaut," edited by Karl Young, in *Essays in Honor of Albert Feuillerat,* edited by Henri M. Peyre (New Haven: Yale University Press, 1943), pp. 1–20.

Le Dit de la Fonteinne Amoureuse (1360–1361)

Manuscripts: The text is represented in the complete works manuscripts: Paris, Bibliothèque Nationale de France, f. fr. 1585; Bibliothèque Nationale de France, f. fr. 1584; Bibliothèque Nationale de France, f. fr. 22545–22546; Bibliothèque Nationale de France, f. fr. 9221; and New York, Wildenstein Collection, no shelfmark; a presentation copy made for the duke of Berry, to whom the poem is dedicated (Paris, Bibliothèque Nationale de France, f. fr. 9221), titles this work *Livre de Morpheus,* while Paris, Bibliothèque Nationale de France, f. fr. 843, labels it *Dit de la fonteinne amoureuse que l'on appelle Morpheus.*

Standard edition and edition in modern French: *Guillaume de Machaut: La Fontaine amoureuse,* edited and translated by Jacqueline Cerquiglini-Toulet (Paris: Stock, 1993).

Standard edition and edition in English: In *Guillaume de Machaut: The Fountain of Love (La Fonteinne Amoureuse) and Two Other Love Vision Poems,* edited and translated by R. Barton Palmer, Garland Library of Medieval Literature no. 54 (New York & London: Garland, 1993), pp. 90–239.

Le Livre dou Voir-Dit (1363–1365)

Manuscripts: The text is represented in complete works manuscripts: Paris, Bibliothèque Nationale de France, f. fr. 1584; Bibliothèque Nationale de France, f. fr. 22545–22546; Bibliothèque Nationale de France, f. fr. 9221.

First publication: *Le livre du voir-dit: ou sont contees les amours de Messire Guillaume de Machaut et de Peronnelle, dame d'Armentieres, avec les lettres et les reponses les ballades, lais, et rondeaux dudit Guillaume et de ladite Peronnelle,* edited by Paulin Paris (Paris: Société des Bibliophiles françois, 1875; republished, Geneva: Slatkine, 1969).

Standard edition and edition in modern

French: *Le Livre dou Voirdit,* edited by Paul Imbs and revised, annotated and translated by Jacqueline Ceruiglini-Toulet (Paris: Livre de Poche, 1999).

Standard edition and edition in English: *Le livre dou voir dit = The Book of the True Poem,* edited by Daniel Leech-Wilkinson, translated by R. Barton Palmer, Garland Library of Medieval Literature no. 106 (New York: Garland, 1998).

Messe de Nostre Dame (circa 1364)

Manuscripts: The text and music of this Latin polyphonic mass are preserved in Paris, Bibliothèque Nationale de France, f. fr. 1586; New York, Wildenstein Collection, no shelfmark; Paris, Bibliothèque Nationale de France, f. fr. 843; Bibliothèque Nationale de France, 1584; Bibliothèque Nationale de France, 22545–22546; and Bibliothèque Nationale de France, 9221.

Standard Edition: *Machaut's Mass: An Introduction,* edited by Daniel Leech-Wilkinson (Oxford: Oxford University Press, 1990); performing editions include *Guillaume de Machaut (1300–1377): Messe,* edited by Jacques Chailley (Paris: Salabert, 1948); and *La Messe à quatre voix de Guillaume de Machaut,* edited by Armand Machabey (Liège, 1953).

Le Dit de la Marguerite (1364–1369)

Manuscripts: The text is preserved in the manuscript collections Paris, Bibliothèque Nationale de France, f. fr. 1584; Bibliothèque Nationale de France, f. fr. 22545; Bibliothèque Nationale de France, f. fr. 843; and New York, Pierpont Morgan Library, M. 396.

First publication: In *Les Œuvres de Guillaume de Machault,* edited by Prosper Tarbé (Reims & Paris: Techener, 1849; republished, Geneva: Slatkine, 1977), pp. 123–129.

Standard edition: In *Jean Froissart: "Dits" et "Débats." Introduction, édition, notes, glossaire. Avec en appendice quelques poèmes de Guillaume de Machaut,* edited by Anthime Fourrier, Textes Litteraires Français no. 274 (Geneva: Droz, 1979), pp. 277–284.

Edition in English: In *Chaucer's Dream Poetry: Sources and Analogues,* translated by Barry A. Windeatt, (Cambridge: D. S. Brewer / Totowa, N.J.: Rowman & Littlefield, 1982), pp. 145–147.

Le Dit de la Fleur de lis et de la Marguerite (1369)

Manuscripts: The text is preserved in Paris, Bibliothèque Nationale de France, f. fr. 22546, ff. 71v–73v.

First Publication and standard editions: *The Marguerite Poetry of Guillaume de Machaut,* James I. Wimsatt (Chapel Hill: University of North Caro-

lina Press, 1970) in *Jean Froissart: "Dits" et "Debats". Introduction, èdition, notes, et glossaire,* edited by Authime Fourrier (Geneva: Droz, 1979), pp. 289–301.

La Prise d'Alexandrie (circa 1370–1372)

Manuscripts: The text is represented in complete works manuscripts: New York, Wildenstein Collection; Paris, Bibliothèque Nationale de France, f. fr. 1585; Bibliothèque Nationale de France, f. fr. 1584; Bibliothèque Nationale de France, f. fr. 22546, Bibliothèque Nationale de France, f. fr. 9221.

First publication and standard edition: *La Prise d'Alexandrie ou chronique du roi Pierre 1er de Lusignan par Guillaume de Machaut,* edited by Louis de Mas Latrie, Publications de la Société de l'Orient latin, série historique no. 1 (Geneva: Fick, 1877; republished, Osnabrück, Germany: Zeller, 1968).

Standard editions: "An Edition and Study of Guillaume de Machaut's *La Prise d' Alixãndre,*" Angela D. Dzelzainis, dissertation, Cambridge University, 1985.

Le Dit de la Rose (circa 1372?)

Manuscripts: The *dit* survives in two major manuscripts: Paris, Bibliothèque Nationale de France, f. fr. 1584 and f. fr. 22545.

First publication and standard edition: In *Jean Froissart: "Dits" et "Débats." Introduction, édition, notes, glossaire. Avec en appendice quelques poèmes de Guillaume de Machaut,* Anthime Fourrier, Textes Litteraires Français no. 274 (Geneva: Droz, 1979), pp. 285–288.

Vecxi les biens que ma dame me fait (circa 1372?)

Manuscripts: The text is extant in the complete works manuscripts Paris, Bibliothèque Nationale de France, f. fr. 1584; f. fr. 22545; and New York: Pierpont Morgan Library, M. 396.

First publication and standard edition: *Guillaume de Machaut: Poésies lyriques. Edition complète en deux parties, avec introduction, glossaire, et fac-similés publiée sous les auspices de la Faculté d'Histoire et de Philologie de Saint-Pétersbourg,* 2 volumes, edited by Vladimir F. Chichmaref [Shishmarev] (Paris: H. Champion, 1909; republished, Geneva: Slatkine, 1973), I: 273–275.

Prologue (1372)

Manuscripts: The text is preserved complete in Paris, Bibliothèque Nationale de France, f. fr. 1584; Bibliothèque Nationale de France, f. fr. 22545; and New York: Pierpont Morgan Library, M. 396.

First publication: In *Œuvres de Guillaume de Machaut,* 3 volumes, edited by Ernest Hoepffner (Paris: Firmin-Didot, 1908–1921; republished

New York: Johnson, 1965), I: 1–12.

Standard edition and edition in English: In *Guillaume de Machaut: The Fountain of Love* (La Fonteinne Amoureuse) *and Two Other Love Vision Poems,* edited and translated by R. Barton Palmer, Garland Library of Medieval Literature no. 54 (New York: Garland, 1993), pp. 2–19.

Hoquetus David (date unknown)

Manuscript: This isorhythmic hocket for three voices is preserved, without text, in Paris, Bibliothèque Nationale de France, f. fr. 1584.

Other Musical works (date unknown)

Manuscripts: Approximately 140 of Guillaume de Machaut's lyrics are set to music. The manuscript chronology is exceptionally important, since each manuscript adds to the previous one: Paris, Bibliothèque Nationale de France, f. fr. 1586 (part. 1: pre-1349; part 2: pre-1356); New York, Wildenstein Collection (pre-1365). Less significant manuscripts include: Paris, Bibliothèque Nationale de France, f. fr. 843; Bibliothèque Nationale de France, f. fr. 1584; Bibliothèque Nationale de France, f. fr. 22545–22546; and Bibliothèque Nationale de France, f. fr. 9221.

Standard Editions: *Guillaume de Machaut: Musicalische Werke,* 4 volumes, edited by Friedrich Ludwig and H. Besseler (Leipzig: Breitkopf & Härtel, 1926–1943; republished, 1954); "The Music of Guillaume de Machaut," edited by Sarah Jane Williams, dissertation, Yale University, 1952; *The Works of Guillaume de Machaut,* 2 volumes, edited by Leo Schrade, Polyphonic Music of the Fourteenth Century nos. 2–3 (Les Remparts, Monaco: L'Oiseau-Lyre, 1956; republished, 1977); *Guillaume de Machaut: Œuvres complètes,* 4 volumes, edited by Sylvette Leguy, (Paris: Le Droict Chemin de Musique, 1977).

Guillaume de Machaut was an innovative and extremely influential figure in French poetry and music, pioneering new genres and techniques while revitalizing old ones. He stands as the key transitional figure in forging the new (or "second") rhetoric in poetry, the movement to elevate and ennoble the French language as a linguistic equal to Latin, the language of the "first" rhetoric, while advancing the "new art" *(ars nova)* in music. His achievements extend beyond formal composition, for he subtly analyzes social mores, psychology, and philosophy as centered on the theme of love. He also interweaves poetic subjectivity and detachment, dreams and reality, to formulate a narrative persona imperceptibly fluctuating between fiction and autobiography. Machaut thus stands out as more than a mere

A court lady and her lover exchanging rings (illumination from a manuscript for Machaut's collected works, Bibliothèque Nationale de France, f. fr. 1586)

practitioner of fourteenth-century French rhetorical theory: he is the first self-conscious creator in a manner usually associated with more modern authors and artists. Machaut attracted patronage and other rewards from popes and kings as well as lesser nobles for both his artistic and his administrative talents. Despite holding many ecclesiastical offices, he wrote all of his literary works in French and on secular topics, and even his musical works were mostly in French instead of Latin. His role in the development of French as a language worthy of expressing noble sentiments and sophisticated ideas inspired the best poets and composers of the fourteenth through the fifteenth centuries.

Information on Machaut's early life is sketchy since he came from humble origins. Born to commoners in what is now the Champagne-Ardenne region of northern France, most likely in the village of Machault in the diocese of Reims in about 1300, he apparently received a thorough education in theology and letters, including a master of arts degree, although it is not known where he received this training. He did not complete his theological studies and never became a priest. According to papal bulls in 1330 offering background preliminary to granting him benefices, in about 1323 he became an almoner to John of Luxembourg, king of Bohemia, whom he would serve as clerk and personal secretary until about 1338. Machaut's duties as secretary included accompanying the king on his crusading with the Teutonic Knights in Germany and eastern Europe in 1327, venturing as far north as Lithuania in 1329, down to northern Italy in 1330, and into Austria in 1331. Early on in this period, Machaut composed his first known work, *Bone pastor Gullerme/Bone pastor qui/Bone pastor* (Good Shepherd William/Good Shepherd Who/Good Shepherd, circa 1324), a Latin motet dedicated to Guillaume de Trie upon the latter's election as new archbishop of Reims. During his sojourn in Prague, then capital of the kingdom of Bohemia, Machaut is thought to have influenced composers in that region. He composed fifteen of his motets for French texts, six for Latin texts, and two more combining Latin and French. The majority of these date from before about 1350 and celebrate some aspects of courtly love, as do Machaut's major literary works.

It is important to remember that the concept of love held by Machaut and his contemporaries was that of *fin'amors* (refined or courtly love), which might be defined as a kind of love for love's sake, in contrast with the feudal contracted marriages of the time. Because such love was either extra- or premarital, it met with social disapproval. At the same time, its transgressive tension reinforced its appeal for lovers constantly seeking to avoid the tragic consequences of scandal generated by jealous gossips (*losengiers*)–and also for poets enticed by the situation's artistic potential.

By the fourteenth century, scenarios of emotionally pure but socially illicit love had undergone so many refinements by poets and romancers that sentiment had become inextricably bound with its mode of expression. The rules for courtly love, such as those discussed in occasionally paradoxical fashion by Andreas Capellanus in his *De amore* (On Love, circa 1185), met their literary-theoretical match in the manuals of rhetoric, and both were often referred to as "arts." Gestures and words of love thus became overly stylized, and late-medieval authors set about creating new genres and styles for representing and scrutinizing the problems of true love amid social strictures and condemnation. Having exhausted the repertory of poetic styles, writers turned to rhetorical models from other disciplines, notably legal styles of advocacy and debate. Guillaume de Lorris and Jean de Meun, in their *Le Roman de la Rose* (Romance of the Rose, circa 1225–1275), had enriched and revamped the entire notion of love poetry and its philosophical underpinnings, but their innovations were

controversial. Although he only mentions the *Rose* briefly in his later *Le Livre dou Voir-Dit* (The Book of the True Tale, 1363–1365), throughout his poetry Machaut reveals himself to be one of its most perceptive and influential readers and improvisers, as modern scholars William Calin and Sylvia Huot have demonstrated.

Machaut's official duties and travels enabled him to furnish his settings with realistic detail and to probe psychologically such motifs as lordship and vassalage, warfare, and displacement beyond their conventional poetic limits. His *Le Dit dou Vergier* (The Tale of the Grove, 1330) is a dream vision comprising 1,293 verses in octosyllabic rhyming couplets, in which the narrator recounts his meeting with the God of Love within an exceptionally flowery grove. From its *locus amoenus* (pleasant place) setting onward, the *Vergier* bears the strong imprint of the *Roman de la Rose;* however, Machaut adds some touches of his own, particularly in his treatment of allegory, in that all characters except for the narrator are more abstractly personified ideas, and their fuller meaning is heightened by the addition of "satellite figures," lesser allegorical entities highlighting character facets of principal figures. As in the *Rose,* nonlyric poetic discourses are inserted into the main text, that is, three lengthy lectures by the God of Love as he instructs the naive, boyish narrator on the nature of love.

Machaut's story engages not only courtly and clerkly styles, as exemplified in the alternating love-lyric and objective lectures on love, but also what Calin in his *Poet at the Fountain: Essays in the Narrative verse of Guillaume de Machaut* (1974) distinguishes as "idyllic" and "military" erotic imagery, alternating evocations of flowering groves and singing birds with arrows and *psychomachia* (battles within the mind). Although there is a parallel between the relationship of the narrator and the God of Love and the vassal-overlord relationship of Machaut and John of Luxembourg, the reader should not assume the narrator is simply Machaut recalling his youthful innocence. His use of the first-person narrator is a medieval literary convention, one incorporated by Machaut with increasing deftness as he matured as a poet.

The *Vergier* was the first of ten *dits* (tales) composed by Machaut. A narrative genre whose free and open-ended structure constituted its major appeal for the storyteller, the *dit* lies at the opposite end of the poetic-discursive spectrum from the highly formalized lyric *formes fixes* (fixed forms): chanson royale, ballade, rondeau, lay and virelay. Machaut later would frequently insert lyric genres within his *dits,* either to highlight or provide relief from key moments within the narrative. He later set fixed-form poems to music, but the poetic text always preceded the music and was cre-

Opening page from a late fourteenth-century manuscript for La Louange des Dames *(Bibliothèque Nationale de France, f. fr. 1584, f. 177v)*

ated to stand on its own. Such lyric intervals inject textual and emotional variety while also adding psychological realism to the story. By Machaut's time, lyric forms had yielded to the *dit* as the favored personal-poetic genre because, as Michel Zink suggests, the former had become excessively stylized and wedded to music while the *dit* allowed greater freedom of expression.

Probably written at his patron's Durbuy Castle in Luxembourg, *Le Jugement dou Roy de Behaingne* (The Judgment of the King of Bohemia, circa 1330s–August 1346), a love-debate poem of 2,079 verses, reflects Machaut's expertise even at this early stage in his literary career and established him as an important poet. Machaut signals his greater self-confidence as a poet in the *Behaigne* by working his name into the lines of the poem as an anagram: a form of arcane signature traditionally used by established poets, with which Machaut would continue to stamp his *dits*. The popularity of the work is attested by the large number of extant manu-

scripts (twenty) of this work. The concatenated quatrains–with three decasyllabic and one tetrasyllabic verse linked by rhyme: *aaab, bbbc, cccd,* and so on–making up the poem's stanzas are unique to the *Behaingne*'s versification: no other *dit* by Machaut follows this pattern, though he would use stanzas somewhat like these in one of his lyric genres, the complainte.

Again concerned with the problems of love, Machaut yet again incorporates John of Luxembourg as a character, this time not disguised as the God of Love but in his actual person as king of Bohemia, arbiter in a debate on the question of who suffers more in a love relationship, the lady or the knight. The lady's lover has just died, while, in a separate case, the knight, despite his loyalty to his beloved, is betrayed by her. By incorporating glimpses of John's court and the historical figure of John of Luxembourg into an allegorical framework comprised of various discursive styles, Machaut achieves more than realism. He places rhetorical duels on love on a level equal to the diplomatic and military disputes with which John was no doubt more accustomed. Machaut also transposes his own real-life relationship to his overlord in another fashion: in the *Behaingne* the narrator serves as notary to love-debate deliberations instead of diplomatic ones. The increased importance and complexity of both topic and discussants, as R. Barton Palmer has argued, make the poet's role a more serious one as the poem unfolds: he changes from solitary, subjective sufferer to enlightened guide for others enduring similar pain, since it is the narrator who leads the debaters to the arbiter for resolution. The turning point in this transformation occurs when the narrator overhears the knight and lady arguing. He is thus neither a dreamer in a vision nor a mere foil, as is usually the narrator's function in debate poetry, but a wakeful, active witness and aide. The king, abetted by the allegorical figures of Reason, Love, Courtesy, and Youth, among others, decides in favor of the knight. This judgment both ends this tale and occasions a festive week for all at his castle to comfort the knight and lady. The verdict also invites an eventual symmetrical sequel deciding for the Lady, *Le Jugement dou Roy de Navarre* (The Judgment of the King of Navarre) of about ten years later (1349), accompanied by the *Lay de Plour* (Lay of Weeping) of about the same time. Scholars, such as Palmer, have named these narrative poems the "judgment series" because of their unifying intertextuality; that is, the connection among the three poems runs more deeply than a shared topic, as they also have in common recurrent episodic patterns, symbols, discursive modes (lyric, narrative, didactic, and so on), phrasing, and even vocabulary—all mediated by Machaut's self-representation as both protagonist and author.

Machaut received benefices from John of Luxembourg throughout his career. The king of Bohemia arranged for Pope John XXII to make Machaut a canon of Verdun in 1330, then a chaplain at Arras in 1332, and a canon of St. Quentin the following year. In 1335 John obtained from Pope Benedict XII a canonry for Machaut at the cathedral of Notre Dame of Reims, where Machaut received a prebend in 1337. John of Luxembourg also arranged for the poet's brother, Jean de Machaut, another royal almoner, to have a similar post. Despite the canonry's strict demands on their daily lives and habits when within the cloister, the two brothers were not required to live there and thus shared what seems to have been a richly furnished house in Reims at which they hosted many cultivated aristocrats. This new situation, particularly lucrative for a mere tonsured lay clerk like Guillaume, afforded him both financial security and a more sedate way of life, although on occasion he may have traveled to meet briefly with his patron. As one of seventy-two canons at Reims, Machaut's main duties involved singing in the Offices and saying a required number of Masses per year. Now able to live comfortably and mostly in one place, Machaut embarked upon the most productive phase of his career in both poetry and music, which lasted from the late 1330s until about 1370.

After about 1331 Machaut mentions John of Luxembourg less in his writing, perhaps, as Palmer has hypothesized, because the king's career was faltering, in part because of encroaching blindness caused by an unknown eye disease first contracted in 1337 when the king set forth without Machaut on a campaign against the Lithuanians. The king's complete loss of vision in 1339 earned him the epithet Jean L'Aveugle (John the Blind). Another possible reason for Machaut's increasing silence arose out of distress over the beleaguered king's looting of holy places at Prague and in Austria while trying to maintain control over his domains. It was not for John of Luxemburg, but rather for John's daughter, Gutha (gallicized to Bonne) of Luxembourg, that Machaut composed his next major poem, *Le Remede de Fortune* (The Remedy of Fortune, circa 1340 before 1357), which scholars William Kibler and Lawrence Earp have called "probably the best and most influential French love poem of the 14th century."

The narrator of the *Remede de Fortune,* secretly in love with his lady for a long time, writes lyric poems about his feelings that he anonymously circulates. One day a lay he has composed falls into his lady's possession. When she asks him about its author's identity, he is too paralyzed by fear to confess his love and he retreats to lament, through a lengthy complainte, the wickedness of Love and Fortune. Like Lady Philosophy appearing to console the imprisoned Boethius in his *De Consolatione philosophiae* (On the Consolation of Philosophy, circa A.D. 520), or the Cumaean Sibyl to comfort and instruct Christine de Pizan in her *Le Livre du Chemin de long estude* (The Book of the Road of Long Study, 1402–1403), *Dame Esperance* (Lady Hope) comes before the lover in Machaut's poem and explains the ways of Love and Fortune to him. Encouraged, he goes to his lady to declare his love and exchanges rings with her. Afraid of gossipmongers, however, the lady later ignores him in public to preserve the secrecy of their affair. Her coldness hurts him deeply, and the poem ends on a realistic if less than joyous note.

While the theme of a book as remedy to problems of love and other ills was not new, Machaut adds greater sophistication to this construct and to the author's role as both patient and healer through his art and his message. As Lady Hope tries to instruct the narrator, so Machaut provides, in addition to its apotheosis of hope, a survival manual and consolation for the courtly reader as a member—and potential victim—of a

Page from a manuscript for a collection of Machaut's works (Bibliothèque Nationale de France, f. fr. 1584, f. D)

refined yet ruthlessly stringent society. Scholars have found in the *Remede* a prototype for Geoffrey Chaucer's *Book of the Duchess* (circa 1368–1372) and *Troilus and Criseyde* (circa 1382–1386). The *Remede* is the most copiously illustrated of all Machaut's *dits*, and Sylvia Huot's analysis of the visual-textual interplay in key manuscripts in the Bibliothèque Nationale de France in Paris leads to the suggestion that it is a source for Christine de Pizan's highly successful *L'Epistre d'Othea* (The Letter of Othea, circa 1400). Huot's comparison of the oldest manuscript (Bibliothèque Nationale de France 1586) with Machaut's final version (Bibliothèque Nationale de France 1584) points toward a shift in the poet's authorial self-image: the miniatures and text portray him as more concerned with his "writerly process," as Laurence De Looze calls it, by 1370 than he was in 1340, when he first composed the *Remede*. The poet's access to scribes and illuminators of such high caliber even by the time of the first compilation of his works in the

1350s indicates the high esteem he had already garnered among the literary public as well as in official circles. In the later manuscript, Machaut updated his earlier work according to his intensified self-image as a poet—more than mere narrator or would-be lover—evidenced in his later works.

Daniel Poirion has called the *Remede* a veritable *ars poétique* or guide to writing poetry, since the *formes fixes* lyrics and nine musical pieces inserted within the narrative of the *Remede* have endured as epitomes of their art, later to be imitated by Jean Froissart, Oton de Grandson, Christine de Pizan, and Chaucer. Musicologists value the list of more than thirty instruments in the scene describing a minstrel's performance as an historical document. Like Machaut's other works, the *Remede* documents mid-fourteenth-century life but cannot be read as biography, although its multitalented narrator, communicating through text, music, and image, reflects Machaut's own multifaceted career.

Even in this period of his patron's decline, Machaut celebrated John's exploits during the brutal Lithuanian campaigns, quite uniquely by incorporating them into his *Le Dit dou Lyon* (The Tale of the Lion) of circa 1342. This 2,204-verse adventure, divided into seven segments, injects his realistic wartime recollections into this account fusing the didactic allegory of love poetry and fairy-tale elements recalling courtly romance. Its central motif of a lion befriending a man forms a distinctive variation on Chrétien de Troyes's Arthurian romance *Le Chevalier au Lion, ou, Yvain* (The Knight with the Lion, or Yvain, circa 1179–1180), which was itself derived from the Androcles story in Aulus Gellius's second-century Latin collection, the *Noctes Atticae* (Attic Nights). Machaut's narrator, venturing in a magic boat onto an enchanted isle, encounters a friendly and charming lion who leads him through a wasteland into a grove to meet a noble lady and her entourage. Whenever the lady turns her gaze from the lion as he pays court to her, he is besieged by snarling, vicious beasts. At the lady's behest, an elderly knight explains the meaning of this scene to the narrator: the lion symbolizes the faithful lover—mirroring the narrator's desire for his own lady, while the menacing beasts represent the malicious jealousy of others. There are many kinds of lovers, as the old knight elaborates in his speech with satirical flair as Machaut has him imitate various voices besides his own courtly diction: scholarly or clerkly, sermonizing, and rustic, but only true lovers are worthy to enter the garden of *fin'amors*. With this new awareness, the narrator again views the spectacle of the poor lion harassed by the beasts. The lady discourses further on the significance of the scene, mimicking learned interpolations to lend authority while also condemning this clerkly style as fundamentally limited in dealing with matters of the heart. Instead of being intimidated by these explanations, the hero seems to gain strength from them and intercedes on behalf of the lion to plead his case as devoted lover-servant to the lady and prevent further abuse from the beasts of envy. Although the lady rejects some of the requests the narrator makes, she does provide advice for warding off the beasts, which the lion follows with great success. The narrator and liberated lion part company, and the former returns to his manor in time for dinner as the tale ends. As in previous works, Machaut is extrapolating naturalistic and philosophical settings from the *Roman de la Rose*. His development of a narrative persona is more sophisticated than in predecessor texts, however, as Machaut develops the stock, disengaged narrator of the initial scenes of springtime and birdsong into a self-assured participant in the end.

Allied with King Philip VI of France against the English, John of Luxembourg met a valiant end at the decisive battle of Crécy in 1346. By now completely blind, John had himself led on horseback into the battle, where he died in combat: a demise that rivaled those of epic heroes and was celebrated by chroniclers. Machaut, for whatever reason, did not write about his patron's death. He turned to Bonne, now queen of France through her marriage to Philip's son, as his new patron. Why he did not join instead the court of her brother Charles, recently crowned Holy Roman Emperor, is uncertain, although Machaut later dedicated *La Prise d'Alexandrie* (The Capture of Alexandria, circa 1370–1372) to him. Bonne, the vivacious—some would say frivolous—wife of King John the Good of France, had two sons destined to be great rulers and bibliophiles: one as King Charles V, "le Sage" (The Wise), born in 1338; the other John, Duke of Berry, born in 1340, both of whom would also figure in Machaut's career as two of his most powerful patrons. Bonne of Luxembourg died in 1349, either of the plague, which raged during 1348–1349, or by poisoning. Machaut shut himself indoors as much as possible to avoid the epidemic, which wiped out twenty thousand inhabitants of Reims, including many of his friends. His contemporary fame is attested by the chronicler Gilles li Muisit, who mentions him in his *Méditations* (Meditations) and also in an anonymous motet, *Musicalis Scientia* (Science of Music), both written in about 1350.

Machaut then entered into the service of Charles II, King of Navarre—who became known by the epithet "Charles le Mauvais" (Charles the Bad) after the following century—though this association never bore the official stamp as had Machaut's service to the house of Luxembourg. Charles had married a daughter of John the Good and Bonne of Luxembourg, his family being related to the court of Champagne. It was for Charles the Bad that Machaut resumed his judgment theme from the *Behaingne* in his *Jugement dou Roy de Navarre,* a poem of 4,212 verses. Despite its title, Poirion convincingly suggests it was originally written for Bonne of Luxembourg, after whose death in 1349 (the year the poem was completed) Machaut rededicated it. In the *Navarre* Machaut reverses the verdict of the *Behaingne* to favor the lady. The prologue, in addition to presenting this love debate, alludes to the Black Death and its repercussions, most striking among these perhaps being the evocation of violent anti-Semitism as Jews were falsely accused of spreading the plague. Even more than in his earlier poems, Machaut anchors the *Navarre* in major historical events as in the prologue, where he attempts to infuse the background to the debate with both chronicle and apocalyptic writing. Because of this more ambitious prologue, the poet figure, while still functioning as notary, benefits from self-citation and

Machaut being presented to the daughters of Nature: Sense, Rhetoric, and Music (from a manuscript for his La Louange des Dames, *Bibliothèque Nationale de France, f. fr. 9221, f. 1r)*

modification acquired since the *Behaingne* and thereby increases his authoritative presence.

Le Dit de l'Alerion (The Tale of the Alerion, 1340s), which Machaut himself titled *Le dit des Quatre Oiseaux* (The Tale of the Four Birds), echoes the bestiary allegory of the *Lyon,* with many dream-vision aspects, recounted in 4,418 verses, making it one of Machaut's longest poems. This tale also uses traditionally fierce animals–in this case, birds of prey–to illustrate the ways of love in society, as the poet interweaves the art of falconry with the art of love. Machaut's comparison of courting and hawking, both upper-class pursuits, also echoes the opposition of gentle and militant iconography in the early *Vergier.* The songbirds serving as mellifluous catalysts in the *Lyon* are here transformed into the central image of trained raptors. The alerion, a mythical type of eagle used as a heraldic device, is the favorite in comparison to three other birds of prey described–a sparrow hawk, an eagle, and a gyrfalcon–all raised, loved, and lost by the narrator in different ways. Each bird, its habits and fate, reminds the narrator one of the four ladies he has loved as he deftly interweaves falconry terminology with that of love treatises. Calin characterizes Machaut's use of the bird/woman episodes as his first use of exempla, or moral tales. Each story relates to a principal quality of the ideal lover based on appropriate thought, speech, and action–and its deterioration, while extended avian metaphors such as that of plumage and molting to symbolize each bird's state of virtue approach the level of conceits. In the end the honorable alerion finally returns to the narrator as a reward for following Reason's teachings. This tale resembles the *Remede* in its didacticism but is more eru-

dite in its choice of illustrative examples from falconry manuals and also general history and literature. The narrator's guiding authority figures, Reason and Love, speak but remain out of sight, serving to emphasize the narrator's autonomy as a rational lover-hero worthy of true happiness in love. The influence of *Alerion* is readily visible in several of Chaucer's works, especially his *The Parliament of Fowls* (circa 1378–1381).

Charles the Bad of Navarre incarnated the hopes held by some nobles and intellectuals for the reform of the French monarchy. After Charles was taken prisoner by his father-in-law, King John II the Good, in April 1356, Machaut composed *Le Confort d'Ami* (The Comfort for a Friend) in 1357, a poem of 4,004 verses differing in style and content from the dit amoureux (amorous tale) poems preceding it. The confort is not as conventionalized a genre as are the fixed forms and belongs to the category of official poetry or poetry of circumstance. Gone is the mediating narrator: Machaut here speaks as Machaut, veteran royal notary to Charles, king of Navarre. His poem of solace includes many exempla from history and the Bible, telling of others who have suffered similar misfortunes and how they survived.

King John was captured and imprisoned by the English following his defeat at Poitiers in 1356, and Charles was released in November 1357, rewarding Machaut for his confort with the gift of a horse in 1360 or 1361. By that time, however, Machaut, who composed a musical lay mourning the French disaster at Poitiers, "En demantant" (While Sadly Contemplating, after 1356), had joined other Navarre supporters in shifting his allegiance to King John. Machaut endured the bitter winter of 1359–1360 at Reims, then under attack by the English: a situation requiring him, now aged about sixty, to serve in the military, as recalled dourly in his lyric complaint, "A Toi Henri" (To You, Henry). He accompanied the king's son, John, Duke of Berry, to Calais in October 1360, lending moral support to the duke before his departure as hostage to England to gain the king's release. The duke of Berry would reward the poet by becoming his next benefactor.

In 1360–1361, for this most generous of literary and artistic patrons in France, Machaut wrote *Le Dit de la Fonteinne amoureuse* (The Tale of the Amorous Fountain), a dream vision of 2,848 verses. As usual, Machaut sets the action of the poem against a real historical event—here, the imprisonment of the duke of Berry as a hostage in England. Machaut relates the duke's situation to that of the lover in the poem by means of an anagram and by three passages, each alluding in some way to a noble hostage. The lover is lamenting his imminent exile and consequent separation from his lady when he is overheard by the narrator. The next day, the two men stroll into a garden enclosing a magical fountain—anyone who drinks from it will fall in love. Falling asleep nearby, they are awakened by the goddess Venus and the lover's lady, who promises that she will be faithful during his exile. Reassured, the lover returns to his manor and listens to mass, whereupon he gives alms generously and, singing happily in all lyric genres, joyfully embarks upon his exile across the sea.

Whereas the comfort given in the *Confort d'Ami* addresses itself to a prince preoccupied with court and government, that provided in the *Fonteinne* returns to the arena of courtly love. The dominant image of the fountain in the garden exists not only as a pleasant place, like the groves and enclosed gardens of Machaut's other works, but also as a source of replenishment and especially as a mirror. In her 1993 book on melancholy in fourteenth-century literature, Jacqueline Cerquiglini-Toulet observes that this privileged place of solace and serene pleasure is inevitably tinged with melancholy, like all meditation on the human condition as reflected—or refracted—through *fin'amors*. Instead of provoking action as do its literary counterparts, the fountain inspires languorous contemplation, since neither man drinks from the fountain—which might have touched off a love story like that of *Tristan et Iseult* (first popularized circa 1170 by the Anglo-Norman poet Thomas)—nor do they, like Narcissus (in the episode recounted in the *Roman de la Rose*), become entranced by their faces reflected in the water so much as by their thoughts. The *Fonteinne* is a static, cerebral rewriting of the *Roman de la Rose,* Chrétien's romances, and the

romances adapted from classical antiquity. Machaut merges the clear-obscure mediating mirror with the still more surreal world of sleep—the realm of Morpheus, god of dreams; hence the alternate title of the work appearing in some manuscripts, *Le Livre de Morpheus* (The Book of Morpheus). The somnolence engaged here also implies fatigue, the helplessness one experiences when deprived of joy. With its aura of lassitude, despite its closing description of the lover's gladdened heart, this is a late-medieval evocation of elegant despair.

Le Livre dou Voir-Dit of 1363–1365, Machaut's last and longest *dit,* is considered his greatest work. In it he recounts the story of a love affair between the aged poet-narrator and a young girl, in 9,009 verses with intercalated prose letters reflecting the culmination of the poet's art in genres and techniques new and old, comprising learned poetic disquisitions and parodies on courtly love, a variety of exquisitely rendered verse and prose forms, and the innovative inclusion of strategically placed letters. There is also an abiding authorial self-awareness alternately merging and separating from the narrator's as the story pursues two principal levels: that of the love affair and that of the creation of the *Voir-Dit* as a book. Its originality thus lies in its self-consciousness as a coherent, though innately varied, whole informed by a certain notion of truth, together with the usual high standard reflected in some individual lyrics and other passages.

The *Voir-Dit* concerns the narrator, a man in his sixties—thus resembling Machaut—who falls in love with *Toute-Belle* (All Beautiful), a young admirer and aspiring poet who triggers the affair by anonymously sending the older poet a poem. Many early critics, attempting to read this tale as a roman à clef, identified *Toute-Belle* with several different women, particularly one Peronne d'Armentières, Machaut's supposed real-life beloved. This interpretation gained further support from the inserted anagram, deciphered as "Guillaume de Machaut; Peronelle d'Armentiere," but has proven inconclusive since scholars have managed to read the anagram in different ways. The correspondence and lyric pieces lend not only verisimilitude as part of the "record" but also psychological, textual, and tonal variety within the plot progression. The love affair develops from the lovers' first desires to joyous sensual discoveries, with the anguish of frequent separations, malicious gossip, and recriminations balanced by the hopefulness of each reconciliation—but ends in disaffection, rupture, and sadness. Despite two bedroom scenes, there is no true sexual consummation of their love (the lover does not place his "key" in the lock of the young woman's "treasure coffer"), and this only intensifies the erotic aspect of the poem, in a way typical of *fin'amors* relation-

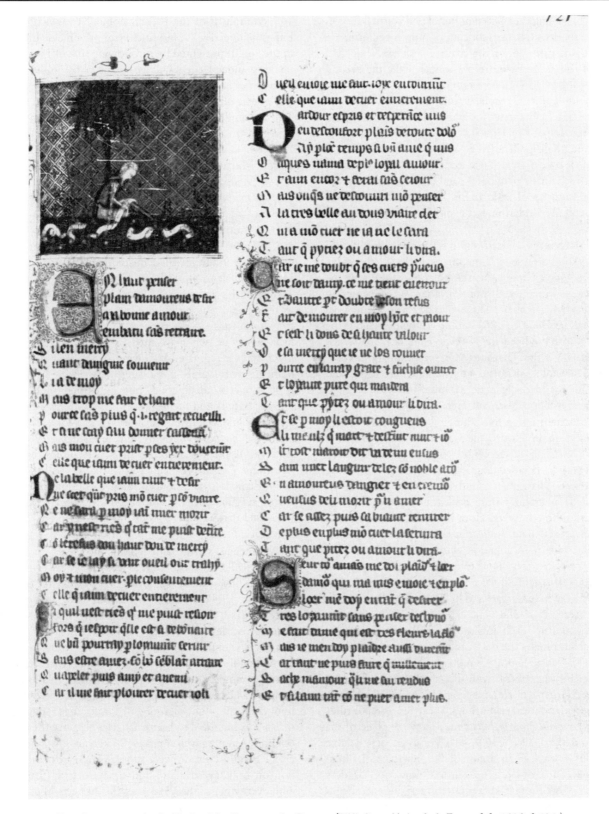

Page from a manuscript for Machaut's La Louange des Dames *(Bibliothèque Nationale de France, f. fr. 1586, f. 121r)*

ships. Balancing the tale's emotional and sensual fervor, Machaut also introduces touches of humor centering on the disparity in age of the main characters. The first half of the *dit* is the more passionate while the second portrays the dissolution of the joy of love, as the story ends with a sort of reconciliation but without any real closure, thus enhancing the verisimilitude of the work as a depiction of a real love relationship. Jane Taylor has explored the significance of the title's invocation of truth as it concerns both text and reader, demonstrating how Machaut's "poetics of the title" transcends the usual assertions of truth found in medieval narratives and playfully undermines the professed intent of the title.

Machaut is conjectured to have ended his alleged affair with Peronne d'Armentières in 1364, the same year in which Charles V, the patron he lauds in the *Voir-Dit,* assumed the throne. Another patron named in the *Voir-Dit* is Robert, Duke of Bar, whom the poet received in October 1363. Some scholars believe the *Voir-Dit* to have been the *romanzo* (romance) for which Amadeus VI, the illustrious "Green Count of Savoy," paid Machaut 300 florins at a banquet in 1368, and Machaut mentions Jean de Melun, Count of Tancarville, and Robert d'Alençon, Count of Perche.

Machaut wrote five shorter narrative love poems of uneven quality during the next five years. *Le Dit de la Harpe* (The Tale of the Harp) consists of 354 decasyllabic verses in rhymed couplets dedicated to comparing a woman's virtues to the strings on a harp, in an extended metaphor most critics have found rather tedious, although Sylvia Huot has noted that it reveals Machaut's self-identification in later life with Orpheus, as well as his preoccupation with passing from performance to book. Despite its title and topic, no portion of this poem was set to music.

Le Dit de la Marguerite (The Tale of the Daisy, after 1366), consists of 208 verses divided into thirteen sixteen-line stanzas, each governed by different rhymes. In it Machaut praises the daisy, to whom the speaker compares his lady. James I. Wimsatt has identified the speaker in the poem with Peter of Lusignan, who wooed Margaret of Flanders circa 1366. The floral metaphor, with political undertones, is carried a step farther in the *Dit de la Fleur de lis et de la Marguerite* (Tale of the Lily and the Daisy, 1369), 416 verses in octosyllabic couplets composed in honor of the marriage of Philip the Bold, Duke of Burgundy, and Margaret of Flanders in 1369. Here the speaker, after enumerating the virtues of each flower, decides to remain faithful to the daisy—a clever invocation of the bride, since *marguerite* is French for both "Margaret" and "daisy," as well as "pearl," which Machaut also evokes. With equal polyvalence, the female purity of the lily, masculine linguistic gender,

and symbolism of the French nobility to which Duke Philip belonged serves to underscore the blessedness of this union, represented by the glowing sun. While erotic imagery indeed occurs, it is balanced by noble traits such as faith and honor. Wimsatt has demonstrated that this poem, the earlier *Dit de la Marguerite* and the poet's Sixth Complainte, written between 1324–1377 (whose first stanza bears the acrostic "MARGVERITE/ PIERRE"), not only constitute an intriguing pattern within Machaut's writing and patronage history, but that they also belong to an important tradition, "marguerite poetry," to which Deschamps, Froissart and Chaucer would also contribute.

A more erotic floral evocation dominates *Le Dit de la Rose* (The Tale of the Rose, circa 1372?), but instead of his usual imitation-plus-refashioning of Guillaume de Lorris and Jean de Meun, Machaut appears to be answering his masters as he has his narrator succumb to desire and pluck the rose, receiving many wounds from the thorns in the process. These wounds quickly heal, however, when touched by the rose itself. Both lover and lady thus end up winning each other, rather than the man simply possessing the woman. In its elegant, concise, distinctive reformulation of familiar *fin'amors* motifs and themes, the *Dit de la Rose* is arguably Machaut's most impressive short work. *Veczi les biens que ma dame me fait* (Here are the Blessings My Lady Bestows upon Me, circa 1372?), resembles one of Petrarch's *Rime sparse* (Scattered Rhymes, 1330s–1350s) in its depiction of a concentrated emotional moment, whose singular focus is emphasized by a single rhyme, *-our,* used throughout. It does not belong to any of the fixed lyric forms.

Machaut's last major work is the *Prise d'Alexandrie* of 1369–1371. Never too old to attempt a new genre, he wrote his first and only historical work at the age of seventy. Like the *Confort d'Ami,* the *Prise* is a long poem (8,886 verses in octosyllabic rhyming couplets and three prose letters) but not a *dit;* it resembles more closely a versified chronicle with some romance-style reshaping of major events and their significance. Its anagram commemorates the poet-to-prince relationship between Machaut and Peter I of Lusignan, its presumed honoree, although Cerquiglini-Toulet has suggested that it was intended to honor Charles V, since the poem celebrates him as well. Because of its value as a chronicle of Peter's crusade with supplementary documentation on military strategy, diplomacy, oriental customs and even music, the *Prise* was the first of Machaut's poems to attract nineteenth-century scholars such as Louis de Mas Latrie, who noted several factual errors while commending it. In the *Prise* Machaut recounts how Peter was born under Olympian aegis: created by Jupiter, with Venus and Mars as his guardians, Minerva

Illumination of singers performing, in a manuscript for Machaut's Les Louange des Dames *(Bibliothèque Nationale de France, f. fr. 9221, f. 16r)*

and others endow him with wisdom and other talents, while Vulcan fashions his armor. Machaut of course takes care to emphasize the role of the Christian God, however invisible his physical presence, in Peter's triumphs over the pagans. Peter is depicted as a youth dreaming of this crusade and eventually taking steps to realize this vision, upon becoming king of Cyprus in 1359, by capturing the cities of Gorhigos and Adalia in Asia Minor. He and his allies then take control of Alexandria in 1365 in a glorious victory. Among the characters in this epic story are the usual good and wise councillors—as well as evil or incompetent councillors—in Peter's entourage, whose personalities are revealed as much through carefully wrought speeches as by their recounted deeds. One of Peter of Lusignan's most devoted barons, Florimond de Lesparre, disagrees with his policies and turns against him, while family discord is embodied in the treachery of Peter's brother, Prince John of Antioch. When Peter's son steals from the Gib-

lets, this proud rival family of Nicosia retaliates, creating a conflict that Peter settles not by chastising his son or offering reparations to the Giblets but by humiliating their men and torturing and molesting their women. Unconcerned by such offenses against the chivalric code and their potential consequences, Peter prepares new campaigns requiring further support from Europe and is offered the crown of Armenia. Machaut associates Peter with his old patron, John of Bohemia, praising John's son, Holy Roman Emperor Charles IV, as heir to their greatness. Although Machaut ranks Peter as a tenth among the pantheon of Nine Worthies, this able warrior and diplomat nonetheless pays for his antichivalric cruelty when he is brutally assassinated, lying naked beside his wife in bed, betrayed by disgruntled nobles, on 17 January 1369. Such are the epic and historical elements of the *Prise,* in which Machaut reveals more than his poetic sense of chivalric tragedy: his political conservatism in his approval of just war, his disapproval of tyrannicide and revolt regardless of cause, his exclusively Western viewpoint on the Crusades and Middle-Eastern cultures, and his general application of the *ubi sunt* motif: a nostalgia for the bygone Golden Age characteristic of other late-medieval poets. On the other hand, Machaut's travels did imbue him with some knowledge for Eastern culture, particularly language, as when he qualifies the Arabic of the Saracen diplomats as "their Latin." Finally, Machaut was not above skewing historical facts to portray his crusader-king as a warrior Christ, martyred by members of his own culture.

Machaut seems to have spent his final years gathering and ordering his many writings in manuscript form, as if to retain control over their future reception, a purpose signaled expressly in his *Prologue,* written circa 1372 and preserved in the collected works manuscript, Paris, Bibliothèque Nationale de France, f. fr. 1584. Unifying the totality of his non-musical fixed-form lyric poems, the collection entitled the *Louange des Dames* (Praise of Women) arranges more than two hundred poems according to their manner of praising women. Poirion has called this title analogous to the *Louange de Dieu* (Praise of God) convention in devotional literature praising God or the Virgin, here applied to extolling female beauty and virtues. Some of the more famous poems include the ballades "Puis que Desirs ne me laise durer" (Since Desire Will Not Let Me Endure), "Gais et jolis, liez, chantans et joieus" (Bright and Pretty, Happy, Singing and Joyful), and "Quant de vous departiray" (When I Leave You); and the rondeau "Blanche comme lis" (White as a lily).

Machaut took particular care to finalize the evolution of his narrative persona and technique in his *Prologue*–in reality his epilogue and summa of all his writerly experience.

Richard Hoppin's survey provides a full discussion of Machaut's musical accomplishment. Particularly noteworthy is his *Messe Nostre Dame* (Mass for Our Lady, circa 1364), which is analogous to the *Voir-Dit* since both are masterpieces of artistic breadth and daring, while retaining a subtle inner cohesiveness in their respective disciplines. Several scholars point to Machaut's merging of musical polyphony and secular lyric to formulate the literary counterpart of the *Messe* in the *Voir-Dit.* By contrast, his lays and motets are considered his most conservative pieces, although even in these, especially the motets, their musical style is more "modern" than their texts. Though long believed to have been composed for the coronation of Charles V, the *Messe* may have been conceived as part of a foundation for Guillaume and his brother Jean after their deaths and interments (Jean having predeceased him)

at Reims cathedral, where it was performed annually in their memory at least through 1411.

Machaut's monumental stature as founder of the new school of French poetic meter and versification is due to both his refining and revitalizing existing genres and his invention of new genres. His ballades, chants royaux, rondeaux, lays, and virelays outshine earlier examples of these forms; without Machaut's artistry and establishment of rules and standards for composition, these genres might have perished. Machaut invented the chanson royale (a ballade without refrain) and double ballade, among other forms, mainly by tinkering with preexisting poetic forms. Lefèvre and Becker cite among his innovations the precise definition of the lay and the differentiation of the ballade from the virelay, in keeping with an overall tendency toward complexity and "verbal acrobatics" so appealing to the late-fifteenth-century *Rhétoriqueurs.* His *Prologue* parades the more sophisticated rhymes with which he experimented: "leonine," "retrograde," "equivocal," and "serpentine." It is fitting that Deschamps rendered his famous lament on the death of Machaut, "Armes, Amours, Dames, Chevalerie" (Arms, Loves, Ladies, Chivalry), in the double ballade form that Machaut had invented.

Bibliography:

Lawrence Earp, *Guillaume de Machaut: A Guide to Research* (New York: Garland, 1995).

Biographies:

Armand Machabey, *Guillaume de Machault 130?–1377: la vie et l'œuvre musicale,* 2 volumes (Paris: Richard-Masse, 1955).

Sylvie Lefèvre and Georges Becker, "Guillaume de Machaut," in *Le Dictionnaire des lettras francaises: le Moyen Age,* edited by Geneviève Hasenohr and Michael Zink (Paris: Fayard/Lirre de Poche, 1992).

William W. Kibler and Lawrence Earp, "Machaut, Guillaume de," in *Medieval France: An Encyclopedia,* edited by William W. Kibler and Grover A. Zinn (New York: Garland, 1995).

References:

Barbara K. Altmann, "Re-opening the Case: Machaut's *Jugement* Poems as a Source in Christine de Pizan," in *Reinterpreting Christine de Pizan,* edited by Earl Jeffrey Richards and others (Athens: University of Georgia Press, 1992);

François Avril, *Manuscript Painting at the Court of France: The Fourteenth Century,* translated by Ursula Molinaro and Bruce Benderson (New York: Braziller/ London: Chatto & Windus, 1978);

Maureen Boulton, *The Song in the Story: Lyric Insertions in French Narrative Fiction, 1200–1400* (Philadelphia: University of Pennsylvania Press, 1993);

Kevin Brownlee, "Guillaume de Machaut's *Remede de Fortune:* The Lyric Anthology as Narrative Progression," in *The Ladder of High Designs: Structure and Interpretation of the French Lyric Sequence,* edited by Doranne Fenoaltea and David Lee Rubin (Charlottesville & London: University Press of Virginia, 1991);

Brownlee, "Machaut's Motet 15 and the *Roman de la Rose*: The Literary Context of *Amours qui a le pouoir/Faus Semblant m'a deceü/Vidi dominum,*" *Early Music History,* 10 (1991): 1–14;

Brownlee, *Poetic Identity in Guillaume de Machaut* (Madison: University of Wisconsin Press, 1984);

William C. Calin, "Machaut's Legacy: The Chaucerian Inheritance Reconsidered," *Studies in the Literary Imagination,* 20 (Spring 1987): 9–21;

Calin, "Medieval Intertextuality: Lyrical Inserts and Narrative in Guillaume de Machaut," *French Review,* 62 (October 1988): 1–10;

Calin, *The Poet at the Fountain: Essays in the Narrative Verse of Guillaume de Machaut* (Lexington: University Press of Kentucky, 1974);

Jacqueline Cerquiglini-Toulet, *La Couleur de la mélancolie: la fréquentation des livres au XIVe siècle, 1300–1415* (Paris: Hatier, 1993);

Cerquiglini-Toulet, *"Un Engin si soutil": Guillaume de Machaut et l'écriture au XIVe siècle* (Paris: H. Champion, 1985);

Jacques Chailley and others, eds., *Guillaume de Machaut: poète et compositeur, Colloque-table ronde organisé par l'Université de Reims (19–22 avril 1978),* Actes et Colloques no. 23 (Paris: CNRS/Klincksieck, 1982);

Madeleine Pelner Cosman and Bruce Chandler, eds., *Machaut's World: Science and Art in the Fourteenth Century,* Annals of the New York Academy of Sciences no. 314 (New York: New York Academy of Sciences, 1978);

Laurence De Looze, "Guillaume de Machaut and the Writerly Process," *French Forum,* 9(1984): 145–161;

De Looze, "Masquage et démasquage de l'auteur dans les *Jugements* de Guillaume de Machaut," in *Masques et déguisements dans la littérature médiévale,* edited by Marie-Louise Ollier (Montréal: Presses de l'Université de Montréal / Paris: J. Vrin, 1988);

De Looze, "'Mon Nom Trouveras': A New Look at the Anagrams of Guillaume de Machaut–The Enigmas, Responses and Solutions," *Romanic Review,* 79 (1988): 537–557;

De Looze, *Pseudo Autobiography in the Fourteenth Century* (Gainesville: University Press of Florida, 1998);

Lawrence M. Earp, "Machaut's Role in the Production of Manuscripts of His Works," *Journal of the American Musicological Society,* 42 (1989): 461–503;

Margaret J. Ehrhart, *The Judgment of the Trojan Prince Paris in Medieval Literature* (Philadelphia: University of Pennsylvania Press, 1987);

Jody Enders, "Music, Delivery, and Rhetoric of Memory in Guillaume de Machaut's *Remede de Fortune,*" *PMLA,* 107 (1992): 450–564;

Françoise Ferrand, "Les portraits de Guillaume de Machaut à l'entrée du Prologue à ses œuvres, signes iconiques de la nouvelle fonction de l'artiste, en France, à la fin du XIVe siècle," in *Le portrait,* edited by Jean-Marc Bailbé (Rouen: Université de Rouen, 1987), pp. 11–20;

F. Alberto Gallo, *Music of the Middle Ages II,* translated by Karen Eales (Cambridge: Cambridge University Press, 1985);

Otto Gombosi, "Machaut's *Messe Notre Dame,*" *Musical Quarterly,* 36 (1950): 204–224;

Ursula Günther, "Chronologie und Stil der Kompositionen Guillaume de Machauts," *Acta Musicologica,* 35 (1963): 96–114;

Steven R. Guthrie, "Machaut and the *Octosyllabe,*" *Studies in the Literary Imagination,* 20 (1987): 55–75;

G. B. Gybbon-Monypenny, "Guillaume de Machaut's Erotic 'Autobiography': Precedents for the Form of the *Voir-Dit,*" in *Studies in Medieval Literature and Languages in Memory of Frederick Whitehead,* edited by W. Rothwell and others (Manchester: Manchester University Press / New York: Barnes & Noble, 1973);

Richard H. Hoppin, *Medieval Music,* Norton Introductions to Music History no. 1 (New York: Norton, 1978);

Sylvia J. Huot, *From Song to Book: The Poetics of Writing in Old French Lyric and Lyrical Narrative Poetry* (Ithaca N. Y.: Cornell University Press, 1987);

Huot, *The Romance of the Rose and its Medieval Readers: Interpretation, Reception, Manuscript Transmission* (Cambridge: Cambridge University Press, 1993);

Caroline A. Jewers, *"L'art de musique et le gai sentement:* Guillaume de Machaut, Eustache Deschamps and the Medieval Poetic Tradition," in *Eustache Deschamps: Fourteenth-Century Courtier-Poet,* edited by Deborah Sinnreich-Levi (New York: AMS Press, 1997);

Leonard W. Johnson, *"Les règles du jeu:* Guillaume de Machaut and Poetic Practice," in *Poets as Players: Theme and Variation in Late Medieval French Poetry* (Stanford, Cal.: Stanford University Press, 1990);

Douglas Kelly, "The Genius of the Patron: The Prince, the Poet, and Fourteenth-Century Invention," *Studies in the Literary Imagination,* 20 (1987): 77–97;

Kelly, "Guillaume de Machaut and the Sublimation of Courtly Love in Imagination," in his *Medieval Imagination: Rhetoric and the Poetry of Courtly Love* (Madison: University of Wisconsin Press, 1978);

Daniel Leech-Wilkinson, *Machaut's Mass: An Introduction* (Oxford: Clarendon Press / New York: Oxford University Press, 1990);

Leech-Wilkinson, "*Le Voir Dit:* A Reconstruction and Guide for Musicians," *Plainsong and Medieval Music,* 2 (1993): 103–140;

Kumiko Maekawa, "New Analytical Methods for Study of Secular Illuminated Manuscripts–in the Case of Guillaume de Machaut's *Collected Works*," *Dokkyo Daigaku Furansu Bunka Kenkyu* (Studies on French Culture at Dokkyo University), 20 (1989): 20–31;

Rosemary Morris, "Machaut, Froissart, and the Fictionalization of the Self," *Modern Language Review,* 83 (1988): 545–555;

R. Barton Palmer, "Transtextuality and the Producing-I in Guillaume de Machaut's Judgment Series," *Exemplaria,* 5 (1993): 283–304;

Daniel Poirion, *Le Poète et le prince: l'évolution du lyrisme courtois de Guillaume de Machaut à Charles d'Orléans* (Paris: Presses Universitaires de France, 1965);

Poirion, "Guillaume de Machaut," in *Littérature française: Le Moyen Age II: 1300–1450* (Paris: Arthaud, 1971), pp. 191–196;

Eric M. Steinle, "'Car tu as scens, retorique et musique': Machaut's Musical Narrative of the *Remede de Fortune*," *Mediaevalia,* 11 (1985): 63–82;

Margaret L. Switten, "Guillaume de Machaut: Le *Remede de Fortune* au carrefour d'un art nouveau," *Cahiers de l'Association Internationale des Etudes Françaises,* 41 (1989): 101–116;

Jane H. M. Taylor, "Machaut's *Livre du Voir-Dit* and the Poetics of the Title," in *Et c'est la fin pour quoy sommes ensemble: Hommage à Jean Dufournet, Littérature, Histoire et Langue du Moyen Age,* 3 volumes, edited by Jean-Claude Aubailly and others (Paris: H. Champion, 1993), III: 351–362;

Nigel Wilkins, "A Pattern of Patronage: Machaut, Froissart and the Houses of Luxembourg and Bohemia in the Fourteenth Century," *French Studies,* 37 (1983): 257–284;

Sarah Jane Williams, "An Author's Role in Fourteenth-Century Book Production: Guillaume de Machaut's 'Livre ou je met toutes mes choses'," *Romania,* 90 (1969): 433–454;

James I. Wimsatt, "Machaut and His Tradition: *Troilus,* the *Legend,* and the *Tales*," in *Chaucer and His French Contemporaries: Natural Music in the Fourteenth Century* (Toronto: University of Toronto Press, 1991);

Michel Zink, "Musique et subjectivité: le passage de la chanson d'amour à la poésie personnelle au XIIe siècle," *Cahiers de civilisation médiévale,* 25 (1982): 225–232.

Marie de France

(flourished 1160 – 1178)

Matilda Tomaryn Bruckner
Boston College

WORKS: *Les Lais* (circa 1160–1190)

Manuscripts: Five manuscripts preserve one or more of Marie de France's *Lais* (Lays). H (British Library, Harley 978, folios 118z–160a, written in England in the mid-thirteenth century) offers twelve *Lais* introduced by a general prologue and signed by Marie. Four other manuscripts in Continental and Anglo-Norman dialects offer a selection of individual *Lais:* S (Bibliothèque Nationale de France, nouv. acq. f. fr. 1104, composed at the end of the thirteenth century) includes nine of Marie's lays–*Guigemar, Lanval, Yonec, Chievrefoil, Deux Amanz, Bisclavret, Milun, Le Fresne,* and *Equitan*–mixed into an anonymous collection of twenty-four Breton lays. *Guigemar, Lanval,* and *Yonec* appear in P (Paris, Bibliothèque Nationale de France, f. fr. 2168); *Lanval* appears in C (British Library, Cotton. Vesp. B. XIV); and *Yonec* appears in Q (Paris, Bibliothèque Nationale de France, f. fr. 24432). Harley 978 is thus the most important base manuscript for modern editions of the *Lais.* A manuscript closely related to H undoubtedly served as the model for the Norwegian translation of the *Lais* made for King Hákon Hákonarson, who reigned from 1217 until 1263; its nineteen extant *lais* include eleven by Marie.

First publication: *Poésies de Marie de France, poète anglo-normand du XIIIe siècle, ou recueil de lais, fables et autres productions de cette femme célèbre,* volume 1, edited by Jean-Baptiste Bonaventure de Roquefort (Paris: Chasseriau, 1820).

Standard editions: *Die Lais der Marie de France,* edited by Karl Warnke (Halle: Niemeyer, 1925); *Lais,* edited by Alfred Ewert (Oxford: Blackwell, 1944); *Les Lais de Marie de France,* edited by Jean Rychner (Paris: H. Champion, 1969).

Editions in modern French: *Les Lais de Marie de France,* edited by Harry F. Williams (Englewood Cliffs, N. J.: Prentice-Hall, 1970); *Les Lais de Marie de France,* translated by Pierre Jonin (Paris: H. Champion, 1977); *Les Lais de Marie de France,*

Marie de France (Paris, Bibliothèque de l'Arsenal, f. 3142)

translated by Laurence Harf-Lancner (Paris: Livre de Poche, Lettres Gothiques, 1990).

Editions in English: *The Lais of Marie de France,* translated by Robert Hanning and Joan Ferrante (New York: Dutton / Toronto: Clarke, Irwin, 1978); *The Lais of Marie de France,* translated by Glyn S. Burgess and Keith Busby (New York: Penguin, 1986).

Les Fables (circa 1167–1189)

Manuscripts: Marie's collection of fables survives in twenty-five manuscripts and a fragment, dating from the thirteenth to the sixteenth centuries; seven more copies date from the eighteenth and nineteenth centuries. Only two manuscripts are complete with prologue, epilogue, and 102 fables. The British Library's Harley 978, folios 40a–67b, which is identified as A among the

Fables manuscripts, has remained the basis for all modern editions since Karl Warnke's in 1898; none of these editions, however, has reexamined the entire manuscript tradition. A offers the only collection of Marie's *Fables* bound in the same codex as her *Lais*. Manuscript N (Bibliothèque Nationale de France, f. fr. 1593) is also complete with prologue, epilogue, and 102 fables. Manuscripts Q (Paris, Bibliothèque Nationale de France, f. fr. 2173), T (Paris, Bibliothèque Nationale de France, f. fr. 24428), Z (Vatican, Ottob. 3034), and a manuscript recently discovered at Cologny, Switzerland (Bodmer 113) include illuminations of the fables.

First publication: *Poésies de Marie de France, poète anglo-normand du XIIIe siècle, ou recueil de lais, fables et autres productions de cette femme célèbre,* edited by Jean-Baptiste Bonaventure de Roquefort, volume 2 (Paris: Chasseriau, 1820), pp. 59–402.

Standard edition: *Die Fabeln der Marie de France,* edited by Karl Warnke (Halle: Niemeyer, 1898).

Edition in modern French: *Les Fables: Edition critique accompagnée d'une introduction, d'une traduction, de notes et d'un glossaire,* edited and translated by Charles Brucker (Louvain: Peeters, 1991).

Editions in English: *The Fables of Marie de France: An English Translation,* translated by Mary Lou Martin (Birmingham, Ala.: Summa, 1982); *Fables: Marie de France,* translated and edited by Harriet Spiegel (Toronto: University of Toronto Press, 1987).

Espurgatoire Seint Patriz (after 1190)

Manuscript: Marie's translation of the knight Owen's voyage through purgatory survives in a single manuscript: Paris, Bibliothèque Nationale de France, f. fr. 25407.

First publication: *Poésies de Marie de France, poète anglo-normand du XIIIe siècle, ou recueil de lais, fables et autres productions de cette femme célèbre,* edited by Jean-Baptiste Bonaventure de Roquefort, volume 2 (Paris: Chasseriau, 1820), pp. 411–499.

Standard editions: *Marie de France: Espurgatoire Seint Patriz, an Old French Poem of the Twelfth Century published with an Introduction and a Study of the Language of the Author,* edited by Thomas A. Jenkins (Philadelphia, 1894; Geneva: Slatkine, 1974); *Das Buch vom Espurgatoire S. Patrice der Marie de France und seine Quelle,* edited by Karl Warnke (Halle: Niemeyer, 1938); *Marie de France: Œuvres complètes,* edited by Yorio Otaka (Tokyo: Kazama, 1987); *L'espurgatoire Seint Patriz,* edited and translated by Tolande de Pontfarcy (Paris: Peeters, 1995).

Editions in modern French: *Espurgatoire Seint*

Patriz de Marie de France édité d'après le manuscrit unique: 25407, fonds français, de la Bibliothèque Nationale, edited by Yorio Otaka (Ochayasho Nishinomiya: Université de Jeunes Filles d'Otemae, 1980);

Edition in English: *Saint Patrick's Purgatory: A Poem by Marie de France,* translated by Michael J. Curley with Warnke's Old French text on facing pages (Binghamton, N. Y.: Medieval and Renaissance Texts & Studies, 1993).

A poet, storyteller, and translator who clearly establishes her ambitions and credentials on the side of the moderns, Marie de France is one of the finest writers of the twelfth-century Renaissance and the first woman poet whose name has come down through the history of French literature. Her popularity today recalls what must have been her fame for medieval audiences. In his life of St. Edmund (after 1170, possibly 1190–1200), Denis Piramus associates "dame Marie's" renown with that of the contemporary romancer who wrote *Partonopeu de Blois.* Taking the moralist's point of view and questioning the veracity of her tales, he complains that she and her rhymed lays are much praised, appreciated by a courtly audience of counts, barons, knights, and, especially, ladies:

> E si en aiment mult l'escrit
> E lire le funt, si unt delit,
> E si les funt sovent retreire.
> Les *lais* solent as dames pleire,
> De joie les oient e de gré,
> Qu'il sunt sulun lur volenté.
>
> (And they love the written tales
> And have them read out loud, taking great delight in them,
> And they frequently have them told.
> The lays always please the ladies,
> Who willingly listen to them with joy,
> Since they are made to their wishes.)

Denis Piramus's description indicates how much Marie's art belongs to the world of aristocratic courts in which they were read aloud. She evokes the life of the court in the characters and situations portrayed in her lays, as in her dedications to a "nobles reis" (noble king) and a valorous "cunte Willame" (Count William). But identifying Marie and the works that should be attributed to her remains problematic despite intensive scholarly research. Among the works of the period signed "Marie," three are generally considered to be by the same author: the *Lais* (Lays, circa 1160–1190), the *Fables* (circa 1167–1189), and the *Espurgatoire Seint Patriz* (Purgatory of Saint Patrick, after 1190)–although some speculate that the same Marie may have composed the

Manuscript illumination for Marie's Fable 15, "The Ass Who Wanted to Play with His Master" (Bibliothèque Nationale de France, f. fr. 2448)

Anglo-Norman life of St. Audrey, as well. Claude Fauchet coined the name "Marie de France" for his *Recueil de l'origine de la langue et poésie françoise* (Collection on the Origin of French Language and Poetry, 1581), the first modern reference to Marie, who was then known primarily as the author of the *Fables;* critical attention shifted to the *Lais* in the nineteenth century. The name reflects the way she identifies herself in the epilogue to the *Fables:* "Marie ai num, si sui de France" (My name is Marie and I am from [or of] France). The phrasing seems to imply that she was a native of France but was writing elsewhere.

Efforts to identify Marie begin with an examination of her works, whose language and style place them approximately in the late-twelfth century. Several considerations point to the likelihood that Marie was writing in England: the manuscript Harley 978 in the British Library, which is the principal source for her

works, was probably copied at the Abbey of Reading; Marie claims to be translating the *Fables* from an English version; and the *Espurgatoire Seint Patriz* is a translation of a Latin text composed in England, the *Tractatus de Purgatorio Sancti Patricii* (Treatise on Saint Patrick's Purgatory, 1179–1181 or 1185/1186) of the Cistercian monk Henry of Saltrey. The geographical references in the *Lais* suggest, moreover, that Marie's knowledge of England and South Wales was more precise than her knowledge of the Continent.

Further clues to Marie's identity may be found in the dedications of the *Lais* and the *Fables,* although here again there is no certainty. Most scholars accept Henry II, who lived from 1133 to 1189, as the royal patron Marie seeks for her *Lais,* since his dates correspond best to those proposed for the *Lais*–between 1160 and 1190, and probably around 1170 to 1175, if the *Lais* were, as most scholars believe, Marie's first work. Henry's eldest son, Henry the Young King, who was crowned in 1170 and died in 1183, has also been suggested. There is no general agreement, however, as to the identity of the "cunte Willame" evoked in the epilogue to the *Fables,* since counts named William abounded in England at that period. The most likely possibilities include William de Mandeville, Earl of Essex from 1167 to 1189, a known patron of the arts and well esteemed by Henry II; William Marshall, made earl of Pembroke in 1199, first preceptor of the Young King; William Longsword, the natural son of Henry II and Rosamund Clifford, who became earl of Salisbury in 1196/1197 and died in 1226; William of Gloucester; William of Warren; and Guillaume de Dampierre.

Marie was probably a native of the Ile-de-France or nearby Normandy. She may have been a natural daughter of Geoffrey Plantagenet, Henry II's father. This Mary, the half sister of Henry II, was born in France and lived in England between 1181 and 1216 as the abbess of Shaftesbury, an abbey patronized by her nephew William Longsword. There is, however, no evidence of any literary activity on her part. Other suggestions include Marie de Boulogne, the daughter of Stephen of Blois and Matilda, who was the abbess of a Benedictine monastery at Romsey in Hampshire but was compelled by Henry II to marry Mahieu de Flandre, with whom she had a daughter (Ida, who was married in 1216) before returning to the religious life; Marie de Meulan, or de Beaumont, born around 1150 to 1155, the daughter of Waleran II, Count of Meulan, and Agnes de Montfort, the wife of Hugh Talbot, whose family held lands in southwestern England, where some of the events in *Eliduc* take place; and, finally, Mary, the abbess of Reading, an abbey with which William Marshall and William de Mandeville were closely associated and where Harley 978 may have been copied.

Although Marie de France thus remains more or less anonymous, her writing shows an easy familiarity with the rivalries, pleasures, and pursuits of courtly life. Her level of learning, unusual for anyone during this period but especially for a woman, also suggests an aristocratic background. Her translation of the *Tractatus de Purgatorio Sancti Patricii,* as well as remarks in the general prologue to the *Lais,* attest to her fluency in Latin; her works also demonstrate a good knowledge of the classics, especially Ovid. Marie refers to the Aesopic traditions in Greek and Latin in the prologue and epilogue to the *Fables,* while her claim that she has translated the fables from English indicates her knowledge of that language. She occasionally gives English and even Breton translations of the titles of her lays: in the prologue to *Laüstic,* for example, she explains the Breton word for nightingale by translating it into French and English;

she supplies *gotelef,* the contemporary English equivalent for *chievrefoil* (honeysuckle); and in *Bisclavret* she explains the meaning of the Breton term for werewolf by giving the Norman translation, *garwaf.* Since Breton storytellers circulated their tales to francophone publics on both sides of the English Channel, however, Marie could have known these words without being fluent in Breton. In any case, she demonstrates in the *Lais* her acquaintance with oral, as well as written, traditions of the "matière de Bretagne" (matter of Britain). Her knowledge of contemporary works includes Wace's *Roman de Brut* (Romance of Brutus, circa 1155), the *Roman d'Eneas* (Romance of Aeneas, circa 1160), Geoffrey's *Historia Regum Britanniae* (History of the Kings of Britain, circa 1135), Gaimar's *Estoire des Engleis* (History of the English, circa 1135), and some versions of the Tristan story. Her descriptions of beds, ships, and luxury items show Marie to be a master of the rhetorical techniques and literary traditions shared by the writers of her time.

Marie's works are quite diverse, ranging from tales of aristocratic adventures to moralizing fables and otherworldly journeys. Modern readers have concentrated most of their attention on the *Lais,* and much discussion has focused on what, exactly, constitutes a "lay." Marie appears to be the initiator of the lay as a narrative or short tale, a genre that flourished between 1170 and 1250 alongside other short narrative types such as the fabliau (ribald tale). About forty narrative lays are extant, many of them anonymous. While Harley 978 presents Marie's collection of twelve lays as a distinct entity, other manuscript collections are miscellanies into which Marie's lays are mixed. Although scholars generally accept her authorship of the twelve lays in Harley 978 and consider the anonymous lays to have been written after her time—as those with authors who identify themselves certainly were—some still question the authenticity of the collection or even the likelihood of the existence of a woman writer in this period.

Such questions elude final resolution because of the way in which the *Lais* appear in Harley 978. First, there is no epilogue to mark the end of the collection and to serve as a counterweight to the elaborate opening remarks. These remarks include the fifty-six-verse section designated by modern scholars as the general prologue and the twenty-six verses that follow, in which Marie supplies traditional topics on authorship, names herself, and evokes the atmosphere of envy that surrounds those at court—men or women—who distinguish themselves from the crowd. Modern editors generally print these verses as the prologue to the first lay, *Guigemar,* since the concluding section moves from general comments on Breton lays to the evocation of a particular adventure that occurred long ago in Brittany and that she promises to tell "El chief de ce commence-ment" (at the end of this beginning). The reprise here of her previous remarks on Breton lays has led scholars to speculate that Marie composed and circulated some of her lays individually before putting them together in a collection for which she would have written a new introduction, while retaining the prologue that precedes *Guigemar*. Various scholars have proposed chronologies of composition for the twelve lays, based on geographical references or stylistic and thematic aspects, which do not correspond to the order of presentation in Harley 978. Such speculations remain unverifiable; what is certain is that in Harley 978 no final epilogue announces the end of Marie's collection with the kind of fanfare that accompanies its opening. The epilogue to *Eliduc*—the last lay in the collection and extant only in Harley 978—briefly reiterates the motifs Marie associates with her project and her raison d'être as author.

The second problem encountered in Harley 978 concerns the gender of two rhyming adjectives that modify the author: the scribe has written them in the masculine rather than the feminine form. Modern editors and translators have generally put this anomaly down to the scribe's inadvertence and corrected the agreement with a feminine author; but some scholars have seen this scribal inconsistency as calling Marie's authorship into question. On the other hand, the testimony of Denis Piramus concerning the popularity of "Dame Marie" for twelfth-century English aristocratic and francophone audiences confirms the sense most readers of her collection of twelve lays have of a consistently female narrating voice. Some readers discern a feminine interest in the author's representation of children and their welfare (for example, in *Fresne* and *Milun*); others, such as Michelle Freeman, see a female "poetics of silence" distinguishing Marie's art from that of her clerkly male contemporaries. No reader can fail to notice the importance the author gives to female characters (with or without names), who frequently occupy the main focus of the tales or supply the motivation for their action.

The short prologues and epilogues that frame each of her stories refer to the lays performed by Breton storytellers to commemorate adventures that truly occurred in the past. Celtic and English place-names corroborate Marie's claimed sources to an extent: four lays take place in continental Brittany, three in Wales, two in both, and one in an undetermined "*Bretagne*." Marie claims to do nothing more than write down in verse tales that were circulating orally; but analysis of her work demonstrates that her versions are artfully crafted compositions combining the written traditions of Latin and vernacular writings with legendary materials from Celtic and popular tales. Is Marie simply using

a literary device in identifying her stories as Breton lays, or is there some historical truth in the process of transmission she describes? It may be impossible to unscramble literary topos from historical reference, but the stages of transmission and transformation, as indicated by Marie and other writers of the period, are clear. The process begins with an adventure being heard of by Bretons, who compose a "lay"—a musical composition sung with harp accompaniment—to commemorate it. Marie, having heard the song, writes down the narrative in octosyllabic verse with rhymed couplets—the same form she uses in the *Fables* and the *Espurgatoire Seint Patriz* and which is generally used in poetic narratives of the period. By carefully designating the original title in each case, she guarantees the authenticity of the process. Although subsequent writers refer to her written tales as lays, Marie herself generally uses the word *lay* to designate the musical compositions commemorating the adventures. The narrative genre she thus launches seems to be unrelated to the lyric lay, which flourished from the twelfth to the fifteenth centuries.

The general prologue to the twelve lays in Harley 978 opens with a traditional exordial topic on writers' obligation to share their talents and then cites the authority of Priscian to describe the relationship between ancient and modern writers:

> Costume fu as ancïens,
> Ceo testimoine Precïens,
> Es livres ke jadis feseient,
> Assez oscurement diseient
> Pur ceus ki a venir esteient
> E ki aprendre les deveient,
> K'i peüssent gloser la lettre
> E de lur sen le surplus mettre.

Glyn S. Burgess and Keith Busby give a prose translation of this passage in *The Lais of Marie de France* (1986):

> It was customary for the ancients, in the books which they wrote (Priscian testifies to this), to express themselves very obscurely so that those in later generations, who had to learn them, could provide a gloss for the text and put the finishing touches to their meaning.

Do philosopher-poets hide a surplus of meaning to be found later in the obscurities of their writing, or do later, more subtle poets add meaning to their predecessors' works? These verses raise the problem of interpretation at the very moment the subject of glossing is introduced by Marie's authorial persona. She goes on to explain the nature of her project: it will not be a translation from the Latin, which many others have done; seeking greater worth and praise, she will do

Page from a manuscript for Marie's Les Fables *(Paris, Bibliothèque de l'Arsenal, f. 3142)*

something new, demanding hard labor and sleepless nights, by writing down in rhyme the adventures commemorated in the musical lays already known to her public in their oral form. Hoping to receive great joy in return, Marie offers her collection to a noble king. She carefully names herself in the next verses before introducing the first tale.

The twelve lays of Harley 978, in order, are *Guigemar* (886 verses), *Equitan* (314 verses), *Le Fresne* (The Ash, 518 verses), *Bisclavret* (318 verses), *Lanval* (646 verses), *Deus Amanz* (Two Lovers, 254 verses), *Yonec* (558 verses), *Laüstic* (160 verses), *Milun* (534 verses), *Chaitivel* (The Wretched One, 240 verses), *Chievrefoil* (118 verses), and *Eliduc* (1,184 verses). The brevity of most of the lays limits their plots to a single anecdote or episode, although in the medium-length and longer ones, especially *Guigemar* and *Eliduc,* the characters' love develops through a series of episodes. The adventures narrated in the *Lais* differ from those of romance: there is no quest; and personal experiences lead to private fulfillment and happiness, with no special relationship between the protagonists' destiny and that of society. While some lays (for example, *Guigemar, Yonec,* and *Lanval*) offer marvelous and folktale elements that recall their Celtic sources, others (for example, *Equitan, Le Fresne, Milun,* and *Chaitivel*) are realistically placed in the courtly world of the twelfth century.

While the *Lais* offer great diversity, they are unified by the themes of love and adventure. The interplay among the lays invites exploration of an open-ended series of variations on those themes, in which Marie reveals the complexities and varieties of human experience. The process can be illustrated in the way the two short tales *Laüstic* and *Chievrefoil* play off against each other. Each involves a love triangle of married couple plus the wife's lover. *Chievrefoil* relates a secret reunion of Tristan and Iseut that takes place during Tristan's exile. King Mark remains ignorant of the lovers' tryst, but the husband in *Laüstic* discovers his wife's nocturnal meetings with her lover. Although their affair has been chaste, limited to mutual gazing through opposite windows, the angry husband traps and kills the nightingale that the lady claims as the motivation for her nightly visits to the window. The lady sends her lover the nightingale's body wrapped in an embroidered cloth. He places the body in a golden box adorned with precious stones and keeps it with him always.

The golden reliquary in *Laüstic* emblematizes the end of the lovers' meetings; but it may suggest, as well, the triumph of continued love despite separation. Optimistic and pessimistic readings of the ending are equally plausible and are characteristic of Marie's subtle art. The honeysuckle as an emblem in *Chievrefoil* testi-

fies to the enduring nature of Tristan and Iseult's love: just as the hazelwood dies (so it was thought) if the honeysuckle growing around it is cut away, so the lovers would die if separated: "Bele amie, si est de nus: ne vus sanz mei, ne jeo sanz vus" (Beautiful friend, so it is with us: neither you without me, nor me without you). Thanks to the piece of hazelwood Tristan prepared as a signal, the lovers were reunited. Whereas the emblem in *Laüstic* marks an ending, the one in *Chievrefoil* initiates a reunion and symbolizes the permanence of Tristan and Iseult's love. The pattern of repetition and variation between the two lays creates echoes and contrasts at all levels of Marie's text. Likewise, throughout the collection various combinations of the same materials invite readers to analyze and comment on their interactions, building the "surplus of meaning" anticipated by Marie. The arrangement of twelve lays in a collection thus considerably increases the potential for meanings, however elusive they may remain. This intertextual density gives her *Lais* the kind of weight and proportion normally associated with the romance tradition evoked in her general prologue.

The economy and brevity of Marie's style are enriched by the subtlety of her narrating voice. Her use of free indirect discourse, in particular, allows her to merge her voice with those of her characters, while maintaining the distinctness of each. Marie's literary art joins her work to the chain of anonymous Breton storytellers who preserved and passed on the original adventures through oral transmission. She extends, as well, the tradition of philosopher-poets whose books are worthy of glossing and interpretation.

Modern readers have accepted Marie's implicit invitation to gloss and interpret her works, as two ample volumes of bibliography attest. These readers include not only scholarly commentators and interpreters but also storytellers who continue to elaborate on the chain of transmission she transferred from oral to written form. The many translations of her *Lais* into modern vernaculars are motivated by the same impulse that led her to make these compelling stories more accessible to a French-speaking public in the twelfth century. This impulse can also be seen in creative rewritings of her tales, such as John Fowles's *Ebony Tower* (1974), which includes a translation and transformation of *Eliduc,* and Ursula K. Le Guin's "The Wife's Story," included in her *Buffalo Gals and Other Animal Presences* (1987), which retells the story of *Bisclavret* from the point of view of the werewolf's wife.

Although twentieth-century reception has recognized Marie primarily as the author of the *Lais,* the number of extant manuscripts of the *Fables*—recently increased by two, to a total of twenty-five—attests to their popularity throughout the Middle Ages and well

Illumination for Marie's Fable 21, "The Wolf and the Sow" (Bibliothèque Nationale de France, f. fr. 2173)

into the eighteenth century. Marie claims to be translating the *Fables* from King Alfred's English adaptation of a Latin collection; no such adaptation is known, however, and Marie may have invented the source. Her fables derive from the Anglo-Latin *Romulus* in combination with other traditions: some details bring her collection closer to the Greek fables than to the Latin, some may have been influenced by Arabic fable tradition, and evidence of an oral tradition is also apparent. Hers are the first known examples of Old French *Isopets,* fable collections of which several French adaptations appeared in the thirteenth and fourteenth centuries. They are generally placed between the *Lais* and the *Espurgatoire Seint Patriz* in Marie's corpus and dated around 1167 to 1189.

The collection is framed by a prologue and an epilogue in which Marie identifies the tradition in which she is writing, as well as herself and the patron who has summoned her to her task as translator. Some manuscripts give an Old French title to each fable; modern editors and translators who use Harley 978 as their base manuscript usually supply titles from the Latin tradition, since Harley 978 has no titles. Each fable has two parts: a short narrative of 8 to 124 verses and a moral lesson that follows from the narrative. The distinction between the two segments is clearly marked in most manuscripts by red and blue capitals, historiated letters (enlarged capital letters framing pictures), or illuminations, but the division between narrative and moral is not made clear in all modern editions.

The political stance revealed in the fables is basically conservative and reflects an aristocratic point of view: the social hierarchy should be maintained for the sake of harmony, and people should accept their places in the hierarchy, as well as their individual responsibilities. In fable 15, for example, an ass becomes jealous of

a dog who is playing with his master. When the ass tries to imitate the dog by jumping up, pawing his master, and braying loudly, the master is terrified. Knocked to the floor, the master shouts for his men, who rescue their lord by beating the ass so severely that it can hardly crawl back to the stable. The lesson is that those who try to rise higher than their station will achieve unhappy results.

But Marie's examples also suggest that justice should be available to all classes. In fable 88 the fox and the wolf take their quarrel to be judged at the lion's court; the moral points to a lord's duty to settle disputes among his vassals and refuse to be drawn into their mutual accusations. The need for justice between lord and vassal is demonstrated in fable 19, in which the doves choose a goshawk for their lord and find that he devours any subject who approaches him. The lesson here is that the vassals have chosen poorly. In fable 11, on the other hand, a lion king goes hunting with his seneschal, the buffalo, and his provost, the wolf, and is finally abandoned by his subjects because he repeatedly claims all the prey for himself. The moral is that danger is posed to the poor and weak by the rich and powerful. Marie's concern for mistreatment of the poor also appears in fable 2, in which a wolf invents a series of false accusations to justify killing the lamb who came to drink downstream from him. The moral targets the rich robber barons, viscounts, and judges who exploit those in their power with trumped-up charges.

Although most of the fables have animal protagonists, about a third include humans or even inanimate objects in prominent roles—for example, fable 58, in which the moon fools the fox into thinking that the moon's reflection is a morsel of cheese. Marie's treatment of animals is more flexible than that in the Latin fable tradition, as can be illustrated by her varied uses of the fox. Aesopic fables generally offer the stereotype of the sly, crafty fox who always triumphs through deceit. In Marie's fables, however, the fox's nature changes in relation to his antagonist. In fable 61 the fox plays the traditional role of "felons veizïez" (villain full of ruse) when he tries to deceive the dove. On the other hand, fable 10 narrates the plight of a fox whose cub has been carried off by an eagle; deaf to the fox's pleas, the eagle refuses to return the cub until his own nest is endangered by a fire that the fox sets at the base of his oak. The moral of the fable comments, on behalf of the fox, that such is the quality of mercy the poor can expect from the proud and the rich, unless they have some means to avenge themselves.

The *Espurgatoire Seint Patriz* is one of the earliest vernacular examples of the visionary tradition that later inspired Dante's *La Commedia* (The Divine Comedy, circa 1308–1321). Marie's faithful translation of Henry of Saltrey's *Tractatus de Purgatorio Sancti Patricii* combines in its more than two thousand verses a variety of materials—Romanesque, hagiographic, and homiletic—through which she adapts the otherworldly experiences of Saint Patrick and the knight Owen for a lay audience. Thanks to the proselytizing efforts of St. Patrick an entrance to purgatory for the living has been established in a churchyard so that belief in the afterlife might be strengthened. After suitable prayers and instructions many have descended to witness the tortures of the damned and the delights of the saved, but not all have returned from the perilous journey. The story follows in detail the preparation and descent of an Irish knight of the time of King Stephen, who reigned from 1135 to 1154. After suffering ten diabolical torments and being saved each time by invoking the name of Jesus, Owen arrives at the earthly paradise, from which he views the gates of the celestial paradise. In a passage in which Marie specifies what the Latin text merely implies, Owen, returned from purgatory, purified and dedicated to saintly pursuits, is confirmed in his knightly career by the king. This passage was particularly important for a non-Latin-speaking and, hence, nonclerical audience, since it asserts the equal value of secular and religious vocations as ways to salvation.

One of the most noteworthy aspects of the *Espurgatoire Seint Patriz* is the way Marie tones down the racial stereotypes of the Irish held by twelfth-century historians such as William of Newburgh and Gerald of Wales. The author of the *Tractatus de Purgatorio Sancti Patricii* shares the view of many influential English and Continental prelates that the Irish are barbarians given to various forms of vice. But Marie's translation—in which she adds her own first-person narrator to that of the original—undermines the stereotype by transferring to the time of St. Patrick an anecdote of an old Irishman who did not yet know that homicide is a sin, and by attributing the error to changeable custom rather than unchanging nature. This flexibility in Marie's manner of treating at least some racial views—her leniency does not extend to Jews, who are represented as deicides—recalls her varied treatment of animal types in the *Fables* and her demystification of the werewolf stereotype in *Bisclavret*.

In new editions and translations, through fiction and literary gloss, those works continue to fulfill the promise projected by Marie in one of the opening proverbs of her general prologue:

> Quant uns granz biens est mult oïz,
> Dunc a primes est il fluriz,
> E quant loëz est de plusurs,
> Dunc ad espandues ses flurs.

(When a truly beneficial thing is heard by many people, it then enjoys its first blossom, but if it is widely praised its flowers are in full bloom [translation by Burgess and Busby]).

Bibliographies:

Glyn S. Burgess, *Marie de France: An Analytical Biography* (London: Grant & Cutler, 1977);

Burgess, *Marie de France: An Analytical Biography: Supplement No. 1* (London: Grant & Cutler, 1986).

References:

Sahar Amer, Review of Marie de France, *Les Fables: Edition critique accompagnée d'une introduction, d'une traduction, de notes et d'un glossaire,* edited by Charles Brucker (1991), *Romance Philology,* 48 (1995): 306–311;

Richard Baum, *Recherches sur les œuvres attribuées à Marie de France* (Heidelberg: Winter, 1968);

Howard Bloch, "The Medieval Text—*Guigemar*—as a Provocation to the Discipline of Medieval Studies," *Romanic Review,* 79 (1988): 63–73;

Matilda Tomaryn Bruckner, "Of Men and Beasts in *Bisclavret,*" *Romanic Review,* 81 (1991): 251–269;

Bruckner, "Textual Identity and Marie de France's *Lais,*" in her *Shaping Romance: Interpretation, Truth, and Closure in Twelfth-Century French Fictions* (Philadelphia: University of Pennsylvania Press, 1993), pp. 157–206;

Paula Clifford, *Marie de France: Lais* (London: Grant & Cutler, 1982);

Mortimer J. Donovan, *The Breton Lay: A Guide to Varieties* (Notre Dame, Ind.: University of Notre Dame Press, 1969);

Roger Dragonetti, "Le Lai narratif de Marie de France 'pur quei fu fez, coment e dunt,'" in *Littérature, histoire, linguistique: Receuil d'études offert à Bernard Gag-*

nebin (Lausanne: l'Age d'homme, 1873), pp. 31–53;

Alfred Foulet and Karl D. Uitti, "The Prologue to the *Lais* of Marie de France: A Reconsideration," *Romance Philology,* 35 (1981–1982): 242–249;

Jean Frappier, "Remarques sur la structure du lai, essai de définition et de classement," in *La Littérature narrative d'imagination, des genres littéraires aux techniques d'expression* (Paris: Presses Universitaires de France, 1961), pp. 23–39;

Michelle Freeman, "Dual Natures and Subverted Glosses: Marie de France's 'Bisclavret,'" *Romance Notes,* 25 (1985): 288–301;

Freeman, "Marie de France's Poetics of Silence: The Implications for a Feminine *Translatio,*" *PMLA,* 99 (1984): 860–883;

Arnold C. Henderson, "Of Heigh or Lough Estat: Medieval Fabulists as Social Critics," *Viator,* 9 (1978): 265–290;

Jean-Charles Huchet, "Nom de femme et écriture féminine au moyen âge," *Poétique,* 12 (1981): 407–430;

Tony Hunt, "Glossing Marie de France," *Romanische Forschungen,* 86 (1974): 396–418;

Pierre Jonin, "Le *Je* de Marie de France dans les *Lais,*" *Romania,* 103 (1982): 170–196;

Don Maddox, "Triadic Structure in the *Lais* of Marie de France," *Assays: Critical Approaches to Medieval and Renaissance Texts,* 3 (1985): 19–40;

Philippe Ménard, *Les Lais de Marie de France: Contes d'amour et d'aventure du moyen âge* (Paris: Presses Universitaires de France, 1979);

Emanuel J. Mickel Jr., *Marie de France* (New York: Twayne, 1974);

Marie-Louise Ollier, "Les *Lais* de Marie de France ou le recueil comme forme," in *La Nouvelle,* edited by M. Piccone and others (Montreal: Plato, 1983), pp. 64–79;

Jean Charles Payen, "Le Lai narratif," in his *Typologie des sources du moyen âge occidental,* fascicle 13 (Turnhout, Belgium: Brepols, 1975), pp. 33–63;

Rupert T. Pickens, "History and Meaning in the *Lais* of Marie de France," in *Studies on the Seven Sages of Rome and Other Essays in Medieval Literature Dedicated to the Memory of Jean Misrahi* (Honolulu: Educational Research Associates, 1978), pp. 201–211;

Denis Piramus, *La vie seint Edmund le rei: poème anglo-normand du XIIe siècle,* edited by Hilding Kjellman (Göteborg, Sweden: Elanders, 1935);

Kurt Ringger, *Die Lais: Zur Struktur der Dichter. Einbildungskraft der Marie de France* (Tübingen: Niemeyer, 1973);

Judith Rice Rothschild, *Narrative Technique in the Lais of Marie de France: Themes and Variations* (Chapel Hill: University of North Carolina Department of Romance Languages, 1974);

Hans R. Runte, "'Alfred's Book,' Marie de France, and the Matron of Ephesus," *Romance Philology,* 36 (1982–1983): 556–564;

Edgard Sienaert, *Les Lais de Marie de France: Du conte merveilleux à la nouvelle psychologique* (Paris: H. Champion, 1978);

Leo Spitzer, "The Prologue to the *Lais* of Marie de France and Medieval Poetics," *Modern Philology,* 41 (1943–1944): 96–102;

Robert Sturges, "Texts and Readers in Marie de France's *Lais,*" *Romanic Review,* 71 (1980): 244–264.

Matthew of Vendôme

(circa 1130 – circa 1200)

Elisabeth Mitchell
Harvard University

WORKS: *Piramus et Tisbe* (before 1175?)

Manuscript: This work is preserved in a single manuscript, Cambridge, Trinity College, 895, which includes a variety of poetic and rhetorical works. The copy of *Pyramus et Tisbe* can be dated to the fourteenth or fifteenth century and appears at the end of the codex without a title. Notable among the other works in the codex is a thirteenth-century witness of Geoffrey of Vinsauf's *Poetria Nova,* a rhetorical treatise routinely compared with Matthew of Vendôme's *Ars Versificatoria.*

First publication: In *Pseudo-Antike Literatür des Mittelalters,* edited by Paul Lehmann (Leipzig-Berlin: Teubner, 1927).

Standard edition: In *Mathei Vindocinensis Opera,* volume 2: *Piramus et Tisbe, Milo, Epistule, Tobias,* edited by Franco Munari (Rome: Edizioni di Storia e Letteratura, 1982).

Milo (before circa 1175)

Manuscripts: Two manuscripts, V and W–Vienna, Österreichische Nationalbibliothek, 303 and 312, respectively–are preserved. V is the earlier, having been written circa 1250–1275. This codex brings together a wide assortment of poems, fables, and comedies, including the medieval *Miles Gloriosus,* a comic work once attributed to Matthew and now believed by many scholars to have been written by Matthew's archrival, Arnulf d'Orléans. W, dating from the fourteenth century, includes the *Miles Gloriosus* and the *Lidia,* another comedy once assigned to Matthew and now attributed to Arnulf.

First publication: In *Exempla poesis latinae medii aevi,* edited by Moriz Haupt (Vienna: C. Gerold, 1834).

Standard edition: In *Mathei Vindocinensis Opera,* volume 2: *Piramus et Tisbe, Milo, Epistule, Tobias,* edited by Munari (Rome: Edizioni di Storia e Letteratura, 1982).

Edition in modern French: Edited and trans-lated by Marcel Abraham, in *La "Comédie" latine en France au XIIe siècle,* edited by Gustave Cohen, volume 1 (Paris: Les Belles-Lettres, 1931).

Edition in Italian: Edited and translated by Paola Busdraghi as "De Afra et Milone," in *Commedie latine del XIIe XIII secolo,* volume 1, edited by Ferruccio Bertini (Genoa: Instituto di Filologia Classica e Medievale deli'Università di Genova, 1976).

Ars Versificatoria (circa 1175)

Manuscripts: The work has been handed down complete, or nearly complete, in seven manuscripts. Edmond Faral based his influential volume *Les arts poétiques du XIIe et du XIIIe siècle* (1924) on his edition of G (Glasgow, Hunterian Museum 511, circa 1225), which is generally acknowledged to be the best of the manuscripts. Faral chose not to cite variants from the other three manuscripts known to him at the time, V (Vienna, Osterreichische Nationalbibliothek, 246) and O (Oxford, Balliol College, 263 and 276), although he did make use of a late, incomplete manuscript, the *Trecensis* (Troyes, Bibliothèque Municipale, 1612), to support several corrections to the text. Recent scholarship has brought three additional manuscripts to light: D (Durham, Cathedral Library, B III 33), L (London, British Library 23892), and A (Rome, Biblioteca Angelica, 401), along with at least ten more codices containing excerpts of the treatise.

First publication: *Matthaei Vindocinensis Ars versificatoria,* edited by Louis Bourgain (Paris: Societé générale de la librairie catholique 1879), based on the fragmentary *Trecensis.*

Standard editions: In *Les arts poétiques du XIIe et du XIIIe siècle,* edited by Edmond Faral (Paris: Champion, 1924), the text on which the current English translations have been based; *Mathei Vindocinensis Opera,* volume 3: *Ars versificatoria* (Rome: Edizioni di Storia e Letteratura, 1988).

Editions in English: Excerpts translated and summarized by Ernest Gallo in "Matthew of

Vendôme: Introductory Treatise on the Art of Poetry," *Proceedings of the American Philosophical Society*, 118 (1974): 51–92; *The Art of Versification,* translated by Aubrey E. Galyon (Ames: Iowa State University Press, 1980); *Ars Versificatoria (The Art of the Versemaker),* translated by Roger P. Parr (Milwaukee: Marquette University Press, 1981).

Epistulae (circa 1175–1185)

Manuscripts: The work survives complete in a late-twelfth-century manuscript, M (Munich, Bayerische Staatsbibliothek, Clm 19.488), and in partial form in A (Admont, Austria, Stiftsbibliothek, 128), dated 1260. A fragment of the work also appears in a fifteenth-century manuscript, L (London, British Library, Harley, 3362).

First publication: Edited by Wilhelm Wattenbach, in *Sitzungsberichte der philosophisch-philologischen und historischen Classe der k.b. Akademie der Wissenschaften zu München,* 2 (1872): 561–631.

Standard edition: In *Mathei Vindocinensis Opera,* volume 2, edited by Franco Munari (Rome: Edizioni di Storia e Letteratura, 1982).

Tobias (circa 1185)

Manuscripts: Owing to its popularity as a school text, this work has been preserved in more than one hundred manuscripts. The earliest among these can be dated to circa 1200: D (Douai, Bibliothèque Municipale, 39), M (Munich, Bayerische Staatsbibliothek, Clm 14.685), and O (Oxford, Bodleian Library, Bodley, 656). Nine thirteenth-century manuscripts and three late-thirteenth- or fourteenth-century manuscripts serve as other important witnesses to the text.

First publication: In *Auctores octo cum glossa* (Lyon: Jean Du Pré, 1488); *Matthaei Vindocinensis Tobias,* edited by August Wilhelm Mueldener (Göttingen: Sumptibus Dieterichianis, 1855), the first published critical edition.

Standard edition: In *Mathei Vindocinensis Opera,* volume 2, edited by Franco Munari (Rome: Edizioni di Storia e Letteratura, 1982).

Matthew of Vendôme is recognized today primarily as the author of the *Ars Versificatoria* (Art of Versification, circa 1175), the earliest of the twelfth- and thirteenth-century rhetorical handbooks known as the "arts of poetry." Like Geoffroi of Vinsauf and John of Garland, both of whom wrote in the thirteenth century, Matthew saw himself as an innovator who departed from the tradition of Horace's *Ars Poetica* (Art of Poetry, circa 13 B.C.) to set forth a new Latin poetics. Matthew believed poetry was his true calling, and his own creative work—all of it in Latin—encompassed a variety of genres: romance, comedy, verse epistle, and biblical

epic. His final long poem, the *Tobias* (circa 1185), based on the Apocryphal Book of Tobit in the Hebrew Bible, won Matthew considerable fame and secured his work a lasting place in the medieval school curriculum.

The few extant details of Matthew's early life have been gleaned from his works. He relates in the *Epistulae* (Epistles, circa 1175–1185) that he was *"natus Vindocini"* (born at Vendôme); the exact date of his birth is not known, but it is reasonable to assume that he was born during the first third of the twelfth century, since he speaks as an old man in the epilogue to the *Tobias.* When still young, Matthew moved southwest to Tours, where he was raised by his paternal uncle. There, Matthew reports in the *Epistulae,* he came to study with the renowned Bernard Silvestris: "me docuit dictare decus Turonense magistri Silvestris, studii gemma, scolaris honor" (the glory of Tours, Silvestris the Master, jewel of scholarship, pride of the schools, taught me to compose verses). It may have been at Tours that Matthew wrote his version of the Pyramus and Thisbe story, Ovid's account of ill-fated love in book 4 of the *Metamorphoses* (circa A.D. 8). Matthew's poem, consisting of 174 verses in elegiac distich, bears all the hallmarks of a medieval school exercise. Its studied use of rhetorical figures to help dramatize the conflicts and allurements of young love parallels the application of such devices in school compositions of the period. While a few scholars question the authorship of the poem, textual evidence and Matthew's claim that he composed a work on Pyramus and Thisbe have led the majority of scholars to attribute the piece to him. If Matthew is the author, the poem must be an early work: it is less developed in technique and sophistication than his *Milo,* which was probably written during the 1160s. Moreover, it betrays a fervor to express philosophical content in keeping with the intellectual atmosphere at Tours around the middle of the century. The poem is significant both for the window it offers on medieval school instruction and for the influence it may have exerted on later writers.

Matthew faithfully recounts the major points of Ovid's story. A youth named Pyramus and a girl named Thisbe live in houses adjacent to one another in ancient Babylon. They fall in love, but their parents forbid them to marry. For a time they communicate and exchange endearments through a chink in the wall separating the two properties. When they can no longer bear the separation, they arrange an evening tryst at the mulberry tree by Ninus's tomb. Thisbe arrives first but sees a lioness approaching, fresh from a kill. She flees in terror, dropping her veil as she runs. The lioness, sated from her recent meal, mouths the veil for a few moments with her bloody jaws and then calmly departs. Pyramus arrives to find the bloody veil and the tracks of a beast leading away from it. Imagining the worst, he despairs and rashly takes his own life with his sword. Within moments, Thisbe cautiously returns. Grief stricken at the sight of her slain lover, she cries out, pronouncing herself Pyramus's wife, and kills herself with the same sword. The tragedy concludes with the ashes of the lovers laid to rest in a common urn.

Despite his faithful adherence to these points, Matthew departs from his source in some telling ways. His treatment of the material is markedly more idea driven and abstract than Ovid's, relying on general statements rather than palpable imagery and narrative action. Matthew opens the poem, for example, with a proverbial statement and then swiftly moves to establish its main idea:

Est amor ardoris species et causa cruoris,
Dum trahit insanus in sua fata manus.
Piramus et Tisbe duo sunt nec sunt duo: iungit
Ambos unus amor nec sinit esse duos.
Sunt duo nec duo sunt. . .

(Love is a form of fervor and cause of cruel violence,
When mad it draws the hands of lovers to their doom;
Pyramus and Thisbe are two and yet are not two:
One love joins two together, and won't permit them to be two;
They are two and not two. . . .)

Matthew's apparent fascination with the paradox of a love that can unite two people yet cannot overcome the real boundaries that separate them emerges several times in the poem, often highlighted by rhetorical figures expressing conjunction and antithesis. While modern readers may find Matthew's frequent use of such devices pedantic and overly subtle, their application in verse was appreciated by a medieval literary audience attuned to Latin rhetoric.

Matthew's taste for ideas also manifests itself in a tendency to moralize and explain. This fondness for exposition helps to account for his apparent fixation on the problem of love-madness in the poem. If the love of Pyramus and Thisbe were not somehow mad and excessive, why would two otherwise sensible and laudable young people rashly take their own lives? Like other medieval writers seeking to absolve lovers who transgress the bounds of forbidden love, Matthew vindicates Pyramus and Thisbe through the agency of *imperialis Amor* (imperial or all-powerful love). He is also eager to describe the psychology of his protagonists and often supplies details absent from his source, such as the erotic visions that torment Pyramus at night while the lovers are separated.

The poem appears to have had more influence than its intrinsic merit would warrant. There is evidence that Gottfried von Strassburg knew Matthew's version of the tale and that he echoes it in his *Tristan und Isolde* (circa 1210). Matthew's *Piramus et Tisbe* (before 1175?) is the first in a line of surviving Latin versions, a tradition that may have helped give rise to the Renaissance motif of "one soul in bodies twain." From the standpoint of Matthew's own development, it is notable that the poem's characteristic features—an emphasis on abstract ideas, a preference for rhetoric and description over action, and a marked interest in the psychology of human relationships—can be found to varying degrees in all of his succeeding works. If the poem is viewed as a window on Matthew as a young man and apprentice poet, it reveals a Matthew eager to demonstrate his talent and preoccupied with moral questions, not the least of which was how to deal with the powerful enticements of love and sexual desire.

Matthew eventually left Tours to study and teach in Orléans, another renowned center of learning in the Loire valley. He almost certainly wrote his *Milo* and *Ars Versificatoria* there, for he pointedly refers to the *Milo* toward the end of the latter work and then concludes with a farewell to the city: "michi dulcis alumpna tempore Primatis, Aurelianis, ave" (sweet patroness to me in the time of Primas, Orléans, farewell). It is not known precisely when the lyric poet Hugh Primas was in Orléans, but evidence points to the middle of the century. Matthew may have lived and worked there until as late as 1174 or 1175. In any case, Orléans was remarkable for its literary industry in Latin at the time, and it is not surprising that Matthew seems to have cherished his tenure there.

The *Milo* signals a clear advance in Matthew's development as an author. The poem, comprising 256 lines in elegiac couplet, can be dated to the 1160s or early 1170s. Although it has been classed as a comedy, the poem lacks indications of staging and can more accurately be described as a moral fabliau. Its tone of earnest sincerity, together with a penchant for allegory and wordplay, resonates with many elements of *Piramus et Tisbe*. By contrast, however, the *Milo* exhibits a suppleness of phrasing and a range of diction well beyond the rather limited formulations in the earlier work. The story is set in Constantinople, where the reader is introduced to the marvelously beautiful Afra; her description is strikingly similar to the account of ideal feminine beauty that Matthew sets forth as a model in the first part of his *Ars Versificatoria*. Afra is wedded to Milo, who cherishes her and works hard to scrape together a humble living for the couple. Business frequently takes Milo out of town, however, leaving his young wife unattended. In time, Afra's charms attract the notice of the king, who begins to pressure her to yield to his amorous advances. Although Afra resists the king's overtures, he exerts the persuasive power of his wealth and position until she succumbs. Milo discovers Afra's adultery, but rather than confront her, the aggrieved husband simply begins to ignore his wife. Afra complains to her relatives, who are so offended by this slight to the family honor that they appeal to the king for justice. The relatives pose their complaint in the form of an allegory. Milo, they claim, has been entrusted with a vine to cultivate—a common metaphor for feminine sexuality in medieval fabliaux—but, owing to Milo's neglect, the vine cannot flourish or bear fruit. When the king turns to Milo and demands to know whether this charge is true, Milo shrewdly explains that he cherished the vine and sought to tend it, but lately he has been scared away from it by a lion—an obvious metaphor for the king. Aware of his own guilt in the affair, the king assures Milo that the lion will never approach the vine again. Milo promises to devote himself to the vine, and so the pair will spend the rest of their days in happiness. Matthew concludes the work with a *sphragis* (seal), a brief phrase identifying himself as the author, which appears at the end of all his succeeding works.

The narrative in *Milo* shows obvious parallels with that in *Piramus et Tisbe:* a love story set in an exotic locale, a third party who threatens the couple in the form (real or symbolic) of a lion, and a crucial set of signs that the male protagonist must interpret and to which he must respond. Unlike Pyramus, however, Milo interprets the signs with a level head, and so his story ends happily. Whereas Matthew could only strive to endow the elements of *Piramus et Tisbe* with allegorical resonance, he now produces a genuine allegory and deploys it to great effect. Matthew is also more successful in his attempts to highlight the potential irony and paradox in his subject matter, as when he contrasts the king's noble rank with his ignoble behavior or observes that Afra's physical beauty has led her into moral turpitude. Perhaps the most striking feature of the poem is the author's humanity, a quality he demonstrates in his compassion for his characters and in a new willingness to acknowledge that complex realities cannot always be made to conform to preconceived rules and ideas.

Milo appears in two codices that include several other "comedies," notably the *Miles Gloriosus* (Boastful Soldier) and the *Lidia*. Although both of these works were originally attributed to Matthew, they are now believed by many scholars to be the compositions of Matthew's notorious colleague and rival, Arnulf of Orléans. The prologue to *Lidia* even has what appears to be a rebuke of Matthew as Arnulf taunts a rival poet, addressing him as "Invide" (Jealous One). Arnulf, who was a charismatic teacher and gifted poet, seems also to have provoked the ire of other contemporaries, most notably Hugh Primas. Matthew's quarrels with the red-headed scholar eventually drove him from Orléans,

but not before he completed his handbook on verse composition, *Ars Versificatoria.*

Matthew conceived the *Ars Versificatoria* as a prosimetrum (work that alternates prose with poetry) in four parts: the writing of descriptions, the elegance of diction, the quality or manner of expression, and the execution of material. The treatise represents the first critical attempt by a known author to wed Horation poetics with Ciceronian rhetoric (based on Cicero's *De Inventione* [On Invention] and on the pseudo-Ciceronian *Rhetorica ad Herennium* [Rhetoric to Herennius]). In addition to these literary-critical sources Matthew quotes a variety of others, thereby providing a good profile of his learning and education. Among the authors he cites, Lucan, Statius, Virgil, Ovid, Horace, Juvenal, Claudian, Cato, and Bernard Silvestris figure most prominently. Other notable sources include the Bible, Boethius, Isidore of Seville, and the grammarians Donatus and Priscian. While he naturally must draw on his acquired knowledge in the course of the work, Matthew also asserts the *novitas* (novelty) of his enterprise. He refers to himself and his peers as *moderni* (modern or contemporary), and he does not shy from critiquing the work of literary forbears such as Ovid, the classical poet he emulates and perhaps the one with whom he most identifies.

Matthew opens the prologue to *Ars Versificatoria* with a telling couplet: "Spiritus invidie cesset, non mordeat hostis / Introductivum Vindocinensis opus" (Let the spirit of envy cease, let no enemy satirize this introductory work of Vendôme). He then explains that he can delay no further in presenting his long-promised work to its audience, that is, to students and others who seek an introduction to the subject of writing verse. The book, therefore, is intended primarily as a handbook to be read in the schools, so it is not surprising that Matthew uses the prologue to launch his first attacks on his chief rival in that setting. Matthew bids his adversary, whom he calls Rufinus (Redhead) or Rufus, to seek the embrace of the concubine Thaïs (a typical Latin name for a whore) rather than swell with envy at Matthew's achievement and vex him as a result. *Ars Versificatoria* is peppered with lewd personal attacks on Arnulf. While the directness and obscene content of these barbs may seem uncouth to modern readers, the use of obscenity and invective was common in Matthew's cultural milieu—especially in Orléans, where satirists such as Juvenal were much read and admired.

The first part of *Ars Versificatoria* proper is by far the most extensive, comprising 118 subsections, compared with approximately 50 subsections in each of the three remaining parts. Unlike Geoffroi of Vinsauf and John of Garland, who treat description as a limited category of *amplificatio* (amplification), the process by which an author may expand on a given topic, Matthew devotes more than a third of his treatise to this subject. He opens his discussion with a definition of descriptive verse and then sets forth examples in its various categories. He will proceed in this fashion throughout the work: presenting a term, defining it, and then producing exemplary passages from various Latin authors or from his own work. From the start Matthew betrays a pointed concern for how a poet may safeguard his work from attack. He recommends, for example, that a writer begin a poem or passage with a proverbial statement, a general truth on which all readers can agree. Such a statement will protect the work from would-be critics at the outset. (The practice also happens to suit Matthew's own taste for general statements; he begins virtually all of his poetry in this fashion.) He goes on to discuss the faults and weaknesses a writer must be careful to avoid, thus continuing to express his concern for critical defense and offense. Such concern manifests itself perhaps most dramatically in the dynamic of praise and blame in his treatment of formal descriptions. Matthew argues that descriptions consist in assigning the proper attributes to persons or things and that the purpose of assigning such attributes is either to praise or to blame. For the most part, his sample descriptions break into two groups: those that laud and those that censure. This dichotomy underscores the powerful function that praise and blame served both in how students were taught in the classrooms of Matthew's day and also in how the rival members of the adult intellectual community conducted their disputes.

In the second part of *Ars Versificatoria* Matthew announces that he will discuss the elegant use of words. He opens with a dream vision, a literary device commonly employed in the Middle Ages to reveal knowledge or philosophical truth. Matthew declares that he intends to use the device so that he may convey his material in a pleasant fashion, but he is also eager to lend his treatment some of the prestige that allegorical dream visions such as Boethius's *De Consolatio Philosophiae* (On the Consolation of Philosophy, circa A.D. 524) and Alain de Lille's *De Planctu Naturae* (On the Plaint of Nature, circa 1160–1165) enjoyed during the period. Matthew uses personification allegory to portray the genres of poetry—tragedy, satire, comedy, and elegy—as the attendants of Philosophy. He reserves the most prominent position for Elegy, his own preferred genre, and has her present what he calls the "threefold elegance of versification": *verba polita* (polished diction), *dicendi color* (figurative expression), and *interior favus* (inner sentiment). In other words, Matthew explains, elegance in verse arises from three things: the exterior ornamentation of words, the manner of figurative expression, and the beauty of ideas. He devotes the

remainder of this discussion to classes of words and their grammatical functions, since grammarians and rhetoricians vied with one another throughout the Middle Ages to claim poetics as their province.

Matthew describes the rhetorical tropes and figures appropriate to poetry in the third part and concludes his treatise in the fourth part with a discussion of the common errors students are prone to make in verse composition. Matthew, who is often liveliest when finding fault, takes advantage of this closing segment to launch his final volleys at Arnulf and to reveal his rival's identity. Although he has already shot a series of attacks at his opponent, one suspects he has done so more in an attempt to disarm Arnulf than to injure him. Matthew declares that he plans to write a set of epistles in which he will even the score with his adversary: "quamvis in hoc opusculo parcius, in reciprocis epistulis plenius tibi condignam reportabo talionem" (although [I have criticized you] sparingly in this work, nevertheless, in an exchange of epistles I shall deliver the recompense you more fully deserve). He closes the treatise by announcing that he is headed for Paris. Thus Matthew departs from the Loire region, where he has spent his entire life until this point, around 1174.

Matthew spent the next ten to twelve years in Paris, where he did write a set of letters in verse, the *Epistulae.* Although these documents are written from the point of view of various fictional personae, they also supply some details about Matthew's life. The letters, comprising more than eighteen hundred lines in elegiac distich, are divided into two sets of poems, each set having its own poetic prologue. In the prologue to the first group Matthew affirms poetry as his true calling and seeks to consolidate his credentials by listing the works he has written to date. In addition to *Piramus et Tisbe, Milo,* and his *summula* (treatise) on versification, he claims to have composed a variety of works on mythological themes, such as the stories of Phaedra and Hippolytus and of Jupiter and Europa; these works, if he did compose them, are lost.

In view of Matthew's earlier promise to write a set of epistles regarding Arnulf, it is reasonable to expect to find some discussion of his rival in the *Epistulae.* None of the twenty-one "letters" can be construed, however, as addressing or referring to Arnulf. The poems can be divided into three principal categories, which, in turn, reflect Matthew's abiding interest in human relationships: correspondence between an ecclesiastical authority and his subordinate (1.1–4; 2.5–7), letters exchanged by a student and his close relatives (2.8–13), and those treating the subjects of friendship (1.5–8) and erotic love (2.1–4). While the letters are typical of the standard theoretical exchanges in such epistles, Matthew's own voice and personal preoccupations sometimes break through. For example, he appears to be speaking of himself in Epistle 1.3, in which a clerk appeals to a bishop for aid and protection by explaining that the clerk has exhausted his resources during his ten years in Paris in spite of his considerable achievements as a poet and a teacher. If these statements are autobiographical, as most scholars have concluded, the *Epistulae* seem to offer a picture of Matthew in middle age, suffering in poverty without a stable position, and reasserting his credentials as both a man of learning and an *auctor* (author or authority).

The *Epistulae,* therefore, does not offer any real information on Matthew's conflict with Arnulf, who seems, above all, to have threatened Matthew's well-being by ridiculing his work and questioning its authenticity. Although Matthew's later poems appear to say nothing else on the matter, a set of prose letters from the same period—the 1170s or early 1180s—in the correspondence of Bernard de Meung, canon of St. Lifard de Meung near Orléans, do include imagined exchanges of a character resembling Arnulf, a rival poet, and their students. While some scholars now attribute these documents to Matthew, there is as yet no consensus on the authorship of the letters, and they do not include Matthew's *sphragis*. If, on the other hand, Matthew did write the letters, perhaps soon after completing *Ars Versificatoria*, it is reasonable to view these works as an attempt to vent his resentment and discreetly play out the rivalry that consumed him in his handbook on poetics.

After Paris, Matthew returned to Tours, where he conceived *Tobias* and probably spent the remaining years of his life. With *Tobias* Matthew finally achieved the literary fame and success he had always sought and, indeed anticipated. The poem, which consists of more than twenty-one hundred elegiacs, became a standard text in the school curriculum by the thirteenth century and went on to earn a place in the so-called *Auctores octo* (Eight Classic Authors), editions of Latin texts read by students in the fifteenth and sixteenth centuries. Although *Tobias* is commonly referred to as an epic, primarily because of its length and its association with works such as Walter of Châtillon's *Alexandreid* (circa 1182) and Petrarch's *Africa* (circa 1340), it is essentially a verse retelling of a biblical narrative and is meant to edify its audience. Scholars today find the poem valuable in great part for the chronological indications it gives with respect to Matthew's life. In view of its long-standing popularity, however, the work also has importance as a document of cultural history.

The poem recounts the story told in Jerome's Vulgate of Tobias (or Tobit, as he is sometimes called), a pious Jew whose courageous efforts, despite civil bans, to bury his dead compatriots in Nineveh lead him to lose both his wealth and his eyesight. He sends his only son, also named Tobias, on a mission to collect a loan in Media. There the youth risks his life to save a relative, Sara, from the evil demon who possesses her. Young Tobias eventually succeeds not only in exorcising the demon from Sara, whom he marries, but also in curing his father's blindness and restoring the family's fortunes. At length, the father discovers that the angel Raphael has been aiding the son in the guise of his traveling companion. Such divine assistance reveals God's favor for the elder Tobias, who, despite his early trials, never expresses resentment at his hardships or loses his faith, but wisely and prudently carries on. Matthew's poem ends with the family mourning the father's death at a prosperous old age.

Throughout the poem Matthew's authorial tone displays a reserve and emotional maturity it sometimes lacked in his earlier work; on the other hand, it does not have the linguistic range and psychological subtlety of poems such as *Milo*. *Tobias* does, however, display an atmosphere of serenity and faith. Matthew's newfound peace may reflect the conditions of his life at the time the poem was written. Statements in the epilogue indicate that he had come under the protection of Bartholomew, archbishop of Tours, and Bartholomew's brother Engelbaud, dean of Saint Martin's. Matthew's rivalries now appear to be more literary than personal as he expresses his hope that *Tobias* will surpass the *Alexandreid* of Walter of Châtillon. Above all, *Tobias* signals that Matthew's piety had deepened in his later years, a development that is first exhibited in *Epistulae* and achieves its full expression in his final work. By the time of his death around 1200, Matthew was well known and highly regarded by his peers. Gervase of Melkley, who also wrote a poetic version of the Pyramus and Thisbe story and an *Ars Versificaria* [*sic*] in the early thirteenth century, places Matthew in the company of Bernard Silvestris and Alain de Lille. Writing somewhat later, Eberhard the German recommends in his *Laborintus* that students read both *Ars Versificatoria* and *Tobias*. *Ars Versificatoria* exerted considerable influence through the tradition of the "arts of poetry," and it was apparently known to a wide variety of authors that included Dante and possibly Geoffrey Chaucer. Strong echoes of Matthew's poetry have surfaced in works such as von Strassburg's *Tristan und Isolde* and Petrarch's *Africa* (1396).

Modern critics have often been less generous in their assessment of Matthew's work. In the nineteenth century Barthélemy Hauréau acknowledged that Matthew was a celebrated teacher and one of the most prolific poets of his time but disparaged his talent as "mediocre." Frederick J. E. Raby charges Matthew with treating poetry as though it were merely a "school-exercise." On the other hand, Winthrop Wetherbee and

Douglas Kelly note the important ways in which Matthew reflected the concerns of his time and contributed to the development of medieval poetics. Bruce Harbert goes further, reaffirming the value of Matthew's work in its own right and urging that critics pay closer attention to his virtues as a writer. New interest in the "arts of poetry" since the 1960s has enabled readers to develop a more thoughtful appreciation of medieval Latin poetry and the critical ways in which it interacted with vernacular literature. Matthew of Vendôme's reputation can only benefit from the greater understanding this renewed attention has helped to foster.

References:

Charles S. Baldwin, *Medieval Rhetoric and Poetic (to 1400)* (New York: Macmillan, 1928);

M. D. Chenu, *Nature, Man, and Society in the Twelfth Century,* edited and translated by Jerome Taylor and Lester K. Little (Chicago & London: University of Chicago Press, 1968);

Ernst Robert Curtius, *European Literature and the Latin Middle Ages,* translated by Willard R. Trask (Princeton, N.J.: Princeton University Press, 1952);

Karsten Friis-Jensen, "The 'Ars Poetica' in Twelfth-Century France: The Horace of Matthew of Vendôme, Geoffrey of Vinsauf, and John of Garland," *Cahiers de l'Institut du moyen-âge grec et latin,* 60 (1990): 319–388;

Robert Glendinning, "Pyramus and Thisbe in the Medieval Classroom," *Speculum,* 61 (1986): 51–78;

Bruce Harbert, "Matthew of Vendôme," *Medium Ævum,* 44 (1975): 225–237;

Douglas Kelly, *The Arts of Poetry and Prose* (Turnhout, Belgium: Brepols, 1991);

Kelly, "The Scope of the Treatment of Composition in the Twelfth- and Thirteenth-Century Arts of Poetry," *Speculum,* 41 (1966): 261–278;

J. M. Manly, "Chaucer and the Rhetoricians," in *Chaucer Criticism: The Canterbury Tales,* edited by Richard J. Schoeck and Jerome Taylor (Notre Dame, Ind.: University of Notre Dame Press, 1960);

James Jerome Murphy, *Rhetoric in the Middle Ages: A History of Rhetorical Theory from Saint Augustine to the Renaissance* (Berkeley: University of California Press, 1974);

Reginald L. Poole, *Studies in Chronology and History* (Oxford: Clarendon Press, 1934);

Frederick J. E. Raby, *A History of Secular Latin Poetry in the Middle Ages,* volume 2, second edition (Oxford: Clarendon Press, 1957);

Bruno Roy, "Arnulf of Orleans and the Latin 'Comedy,'" *Speculum,* 49 (1974): 258–266;

Walter Bradbury Sedgwick, "The Style and Vocabulary of the Latin Arts of Poetry of the Twelfth and Thirteenth Centuries," *Speculum,* 3 (1928): 349–381;

Winthrop Wetherbee, *Platonism and Poetry in the Twelfth Century* (Princeton: Princeton University Press, 1972).

Philippe de Mézières

(circa 1327 – 1405)

Joan B. Williamson
Long Island University

WORKS: *Letters, diplomatic documents, and speeches* (1365–1382)

Manuscripts: Paris, Bibliothèque de l'Arsenal, 499, fourteenth century; letter to the bishop of Amiens (1382) in Paris, Bibliothèque Nationale de France, 14454 (circa 1380–1386), probably owned by Philippe; *Epistola ad nepotem suum* (Letter to His Nephew, 1381) on the priesthood, Besançon, Bibliothèque Municipale, 1986; two spiritual treatises in his own hand, *Contemplatio hore mortis* and *Soliloquium peccatoris,* composed before 1392, precede his will in Paris, Bibliothèque de l'Arsenal 408.

First publication: Excerpts from *Epistola ad nepotem suum* published as "L'Epître de Philippe de Mézières à son neveu," edited by Nicolae Iorga, *Bulletin de l'Institut pour l'étude de l'Europe sud-orientale,* 8 (1921): 27–40.

Vita sancti Petri Thomasii (1366)

Manuscripts: Three extant fifteenth-century manuscripts include Philippe's Latin life of St. Peter Thomas: Bibliothèque de Troyes, 1106; Cambridge, Trinity College, B. 14. 31; and Brussels, Bibliothèque Royale/Koninklijke Bibliotheek, 1122476. There is also a French translation, *La Legende de saint Piere Thomas patriarche de Constantinople,* in a fifteenth-century manuscript, Brussels, Bibliothèque Royale/Koninklijke Bibliotheek II. 2243. Paris, Bibliothèque Nationale de France, f. lat. 17641 and 5615, both of the fourteenth century, include a life by Jean Carmesson that is linked with Philippe's.

First publication: In the *Acta Sanctorum, January,* volume 2, edited by Jean Bolland and Godfrey Henschen (Antwerp: Meursium, 1659; reprinted, Brussels: Culture et Civilisation, 1970), pp. 990–1023.

Standard edition: *The Life of Saint Peter Thomas by Philippe de Mézières: Edited from Hitherto Unpublished Manuscripts, with an Introduction and Notes,* edited by Joachim Smet, O. Carm., Textus et Studia Histor-

ica Carmelitana, volume 2 (Rome: Institutum Carmelitanum, 1954).

Nova religio milicie Passionis Jhesu Christi pro acquisicione sancte civitatis Jherusalem et Terre Sancte, first redaction (circa 1367–1368)

Manuscript: Paris, Bibliothèque Mazarine 1943, part 2, folios 1–44, copied no earlier than 1384.

Letter, Office and Liturgical Drama on the Feast of the Presentation of the Virgin in Latin (circa 1372–1373)

Manuscripts: This title is assigned to a letter, an office, and a liturgical drama all included in three fourteenth-century manuscripts: Paris, Bibliothèque Nationale de France, f. lat. 14511, 14454 (circa 1380–1386, probably owned by Philippe), and 17330 (circa 1370–1379, definitely owned by Philippe).

First publication: The letter was first published in *Lettres de Charles cinquième . . . et de Philippe de Mézières,* edited by Martin Meurisse, bishop of Metz (Metz, 1638); the published version was bound into the manuscripts Paris, Bibliothèque Nationale de France, Collection Dupuy, 564, folios 175–247, and Brussels, Bibliothèque Royale/Koninklijke Bibliotheek, 20614; the office and the drama were first published in *Praesentatae gloriosae virginis Mariae in templo,* edited by Daniel A. Virgine Maria, O. Carm. (Antwerp, 1666). The office, drama, and letter were first published together by Karl Young in "Philippe de Mézières' Dramatic Office of the Presentation," *PMLA,* 26 (1911): 181–234.

Standard edition: *Philippe de Mézières' Campaign for the Feast of Mary's Presentation,* edited by William E. Coleman, Toronto Medieval Latin Texts no. 11 (Toronto: Pontifical Institute of Medieval Studies, 1981).

Edition in English: *Figurative Representation of the Presentation of the Virgin Mary in the Temple,* translated and edited by Robert S. Haller (Lincoln: University of Nebraska Press, 1971);

Philippe de Mézières presenting his book to King Richard II (illumination in a manuscript for L'Epistre au roi Richart, *British Library, Royal ms. 20 B VI, fol. 2r.)*

Nova religio Passionis Jhesu Christi pro acquisicione sancte civitatis Jherusalem et Terre Sancte, second redaction (1384)

Manuscript: Paris, Bibliothèque Mazarine, f. lat. 1943, folios 45–123.

Le Livre de la vertu du sacrement de mariage (circa 1384–1389)

Manuscript: This work survives in a single autograph manuscript: Paris, Bibliothèque Nationale de France, f. fr. 1175 (circa 1384–1389). A donation scene on folio 1 representing the author offering his book to the donors was executed in the style of late-fourteenth-century Paris workshops by an important artist named the Policraticus Master by François Avril.

First publication: Excerpts in *Etude sur le "Livre de la vertu du sacrement de mariage" de Philippe de Mézières,* by Elie Golenistcheff-Koutouzoff (Belgrade: Svetlost, 1937); Philippe's French translation of Petrarch's tale of Griselda, which appears at the end of *Le Livre sur la vertu du sacrement de mariage,* in *L'Histoire de Griseldis en France au XIVe et XVe siècle,*

edited by Golenistcheff-Koutouzoff (Paris: Droz, 1933; reprinted, Geneva: Slatkine Reprints, 1975), pp. 153–191.

Standard edition: *Le Livre de la vertu du sacrement de mariage,* edited by Joan B. Williamson (Washington, D.C.: Catholic University Press of America, 1993).

Le Songe du vieil pelerin (completed in 1389)

Manuscripts: Seven manuscripts–or nine, if consecutive volumes dividing the work into two parts are counted as separate manuscripts–include this text. The most important, since they include autograph marginal corrections, are from the fourteenth century: Paris, Bibliothèque de l'Arsenal, f. fr. 2682 and 2683. The other manuscripts that include the work date from the fifteenth century: Paris, Bibliothèque Nationale de France, f. fr. 9200–9201 and 22542; Chantilly, Musée Condé, Bibliothèque de l'Institut de France, Chantilly 292; Vienna, Imperial Library, f. fr. 2251; Cleveland, Public Library, John G. White Collection

W4091.94. M579s; and Geneva, Bibliothèque Public et Universitaire, f. fr. 183 (circa 1460). Bibliothèque de l'Arsenal, f. fr. 2682 has an incomplete miniature of Charles VI as a leaping stag on folio 1v, suggesting that 2682 and 2683 were intended for the king but were not actually presented to him. Bibliothèque Nationale de France, f. fr. 22542 has three elaborately executed miniatures (folios 1, 102, and 202), as does the Vienna manuscript, while the Geneva manuscript has finely executed colored pen drawings. The Chantilly manuscript has a notation on folio 337 that it belonged to the "Duc de Nemours, conte de la Marche." In the sixteenth century a miniature was added on folio 1, and the arms of the house of Chateaubriant were added on folios 1 and 5. The Vienna manuscript was owned by Tanneguy du Chastel, counselor and chamberlain to King Charles VII of France. The Geneva manuscript appears, from the arms of the Créquy family inscribed in the belly of the first decorated initial in Book I, to have been executed for a member of that family. It was executed around 1460 in the workshop of the master of Jean de Wavrin, a Picard nobleman who was later counselor and chamberlain to Philip the Good.

First publication: *Le Songe du vieil pelerin,* 2 volumes, edited by George W. Coopland (Cambridge: Cambridge University Press, 1969). This edition is based on Paris, Bibliothèque Nationale de France, f. fr. 22542 because of restrictions on the editor's movements, although the Arsenal manuscripts would have been the better choice; there are, however, no serious differences between the texts.

Oratio tragedica seu declamatoria Passionis Domini nostri Christi (circa 1389–1390)
   Manuscript: Paris, Bibliothèque Mazarine, 1651, with additions in Philippe's hand.

La Sustance de la Chevalerie de la Passion de Jhesu Crist en françois (circa 1389–1394)
   Manuscripts: Oxford, Bodleian Library, Ashmole 813, executed in the fourteenth century; there is also a seventeenth-century copy made by Elias Ashmole himself, Ashmole 865. Six colored drawings illustrating various garments of the order, including one for women, form part of Ashmole 813.
   First publication: "La Sustance de la Chevalerie de la Passion de Jhesu Crist en françois," edited by Abdel Hamid Hamdy, *Bulletin of the Faculty of Arts, Alexandria University,* 18 (1964); republished as part 3 of *Philippe de Mézières and the New Order of*

the Passion (Alexandria: Alexandria University Press, 1965).

Le Testament (1392)
   Manuscript: This work survives in a fourteenth-century autograph manuscript, Paris, Bibliothèque de l'Arsenal, f. fr. 408, folios 240–287, of which there is a seventeenth-century copy in Paris, Bibliothèque Nationale de France, f. fr. 15077.
   First publication: "Le 'Testament' de Philippe de Mézières (1392)," edited by Alice Guillemain, in *Mélanges Jeanne Lods: Du moyen âge au XXe siècle,* volume 1, Collection de l'Ecole Normale Supérieure de Jeunes Filles no. 10 (Paris: Ecole Normale Supérieure de Jeunes Filles, 1978), pp. 297–322.

L'Epistre au roi Richart (1395)
   Manuscript: The text is found in the fourteenth-century donation copy, London, British Library, Royal, B VI. Flawlessly copied, the text is introduced by two artistically accomplished miniatures on folios 1v and 2. The miniature on folio 1v shows Christ's crown of thorns shedding drops of blood equally on the crowns of England and France–hence, on Charles VI and Richard II–and thus symbolically uniting them. The illumination on folio 2 shows the donation scene, with the author offering the letter to the English king.
   First publication and edition in English: *Letter to King Richard II: A Plea Made in 1395 for Peace between England and France,* edited and translated by George W. Coopland (Liverpool: Liverpool University Press, 1975; New York: Barnes & Noble, 1976).

De la Chevallerie de la Passion de Jhesu Crist (1396)
   Manuscript: The text survives in a single fourteenth-century manuscript, Paris, Bibliothèque de l'Arsenal, f. fr. 2251.
   First publication and standard edition: "Philippe de Mézières' Order of the Passion: An Annotated Edition," edited by Muriel Anderson Brown, dissertation, University of Nebraska, 1971.

Epistre lamentable et consolatoire sur le fait de la desconfiture lacrimable du noble et vaillant roy de Honguerie par les turcs devant la ville de Nicopoli (circa 1396–1397)
   Manuscript: This text survives in a single fourteenth-century manuscript, which is probably the one sent to the duke of Burgundy: Brussels, Bibliothèque Royale/Koninklijke Bibliotheek 10486.
   First publication: Excerpts published in *Œuvres de Froissart: Chroniques,* volume 16, edited by Henri Marie Bruno Joseph Léon Kervyn de Lettenhove (Brussels: Devaux, 1872), pp. 414–523.

Testamentum (1370)

> **Manuscript:** Philippe's legal will, which is accompanied by a codicil, is Raffain Caresini Dossier 483, document 33, Venice Archives.
>
> **First publication:** Excerpts published as "Le Testament de Philippe de Mézières," edited by Nicolae Iorga, *Bulletin de l'Institut pour l'Etude de l'Europe sud-orientale,* 10–12 (1921): 119–140.

Book of Prayers (undated)

> **Manuscript:** Paris, Bibliothèque Mazarine 516, assembled by Philippe himself.

One of the seminal figures of the late fourteenth century, Philippe de Mézières was born around 1327 as the twelfth and youngest son in a family of impoverished Picard nobility. He was schooled by the canons at the Cathedral of Notre Dame school in Amiens before taking up a career in arms under Luchino Visconti in 1345. He rose rapidly to serve six kings in various capacities: Andrew of Sicily; Alphonse XI of Castile; Hugh IV, Peter I, and Peter II of Cyprus; and Charles V of France, for whom he was not only royal counselor but also tutor to the future Charles VI. Two of the rulers he served—Andrew and Peter I—were assassinated during his tenure. A diplomat, Philippe represented the court of Cyprus at the papal court in Avignon, was a friend of Petrarch, and was given the keys to the city of Venice. This honor was probably accorded him because of his donation of the fragment of the True Cross to the Confraternity of St. John in Venice; the fragment had been bequeathed to him by his friend St. Peter Thomas, the papal legate of Jerusalem. Philippe is immutably connected to the city by enormous canvasses celebrating the miracles performed by the relic, which were painted just before and after 1500 by some of the greatest Venetian artists of the time: Gentile Bellini, Vittore Carpaccio, Giovanni Mansueti, and Lazzaro Bastiani. A large room in the Accademia in Venice is reserved for the paintings of these fifteenth-century masters that celebrate the relic of the True Cross donated by "Filippo Masserii" and the miracles associated with it.

Philippe's first composition, *Vita sancti Petri Thomasii* (Life of St. Peter Thomas, 1366), narrates the birth, career, and death of his friend, who, like Philippe and the prince Philippe served, King Peter I of Cyprus, was deeply interested in the organization of a new crusade. Philippe emphasizes the legate's efforts on behalf of the crusade and gives an extensive account of the fiasco of the siege of Alexandria; the city was held for five days in 1365, then sacked and abandoned because the Western knights feared a Saracen attack. Descriptions of miracles attributed to the corpse of Peter Thomas and of Peter I's petition for Peter Thomas's canonization conclude the text. Constructed as a formal

hagiography, Philippe's text was used for Peter Thomas's inclusion in the Bollandists' *Acta sanctorum* (Lives of the Saints, 1643). Jean Carmesson, a Carmelite who preached at Peter Thomas's funeral in 1366, wrote a life of the saint that was influenced by Philippe's text; Philippe, in turn, rewrote his own work to incorporate material from Jean's narrative. To this day, Philippe's text remains the chief record of Peter Thomas's career.

Philippe's next composition marks the initiation of his lifelong endeavor to transform Western society into the ideal Christian state. He had journeyed to Jerusalem in 1347, and he claimed that in the Church of the Holy Sepulchre he received a vision instructing him to found a new religious-military order to win back the East for Christianity. His *Nova religio milicie Passionis Jhesu Christi pro acquisicione sancte civitatis Jherusalem et Terre Sancte* (New Order of the Passion of Jesus Christ for Claiming the Holy City of Jerusalem and the Holy Land, circa 1367–1368) is a preliminary draft for the rule of his Order of the Knighthood of the Passion of Jesus Christ. The document is a fragmented, partial text, including spiritual meditations on the necessity of crusade and minutely detailed descriptions of the garments the members of the order are to wear on various occasions.

Philippe's next project was a campaign for the celebration in the West of the Eastern Feast of the Presentation of the Virgin. He organized celebrations of the feast in Avignon in 1372 and in Paris in 1373, then persuaded Charles V of France to write letters to various ecclesiastics supporting the feast. In a collection of documents that bear no collective title Philippe begins with a sermon on the Presentation, followed by a letter explaining the benefits to be derived from such a celebration. He next narrates the miraculous conversion of two Jews by the power of the Virgin. Next is the office, a series of antiphons alternating with psalm readings for each of the canonical hours. A mass for the feast and a liturgical drama enacting the Presentation of the Virgin in the Temple are also included. While the feast had occasionally been celebrated in the West before, Philippe's persuasiveness led to its inclusion in the Western calendar.

When Charles V died in 1380, Philippe withdrew to the Celestine convent in Paris, but he did not withdraw from the world. The Celestine convent housed the confraternity of the king's notaries and secretaries, which celebrated a daily mass. Further, the king's brother, Louis, Duke of Orléans, was a frequent visitor, and it is probable that other notables of the court also frequented the monks' austere dwelling place. It was at this convent that Philippe composed most of his works.

The second redaction of the *Nova religio Passionis Jhesu Christi pro acquisicione sancte civitatis Jherusalem et Terre*

Opening page from a manuscript for Phillippe's Le Livre de la vertu du sacrement de mariage
(Bibliothèque Nationale de France, f. fr. 1175, fol. 1)

Sancte (1384) is, like the first, seriously incomplete. There is a further rumination on the ills that make crusade a necessity, as well as inspirational meditations drawn from the Bible and history to exhort Philippe's readers to military zeal. In the prologue he reviews his earlier career, his travels to the East, his regrets over Alexandria, his friendship with Charles V, and his withdrawal to the Celestines on his monarch's death. He conceives of himself as a new Moses who has received the laws and rules of his order from God on two tablets. Turning to practical matters, he lists the titles of the chapters of thirty books he intends to write.

Between 1384 and 1389 Philippe wrote his first work in French: *Le Livre de la vertu du sacrement de mariage* (The Book on the Virtue of the Sacrament of Marriage) was composed for Jehanne de Chastillon in gratitude for a good deed her husband, Pierre de Craon, had done for him. While he wrote the work in French because the lady might not have known Latin, it marks a change in his language of composition: he seems to have written only one later work, the *Oratio tragedica seu declamatoria Passionis Domini nostri Christi* (Tragic or Declamatory Oration on the Passion of Our Lord Jesus Christ). This work, however, has only a putative date of 1389–1390; it may, in fact, have been written earlier than *Livre de la vertu du sacrement de mariage*. If he did compose the *Oratio tragedica* after the *Livre de la vertu du sacrement de mariage,* he may have varied the language to reach a different audience, since the two books deal with some of the same material. It is noteworthy, in any case, that this change of language occurred so late in Philippe's career: Charles V, who allegedly knew no Latin, had vigorously encouraged translation into French at his court. It comes, therefore, as a surprise that Philippe should first write in French nine years after his king's death.

The *Livre de la vertu du sacrement de mariage* marks the beginning of a progression in Philippe's works from specifically spiritual themes to treatment of the same themes allied with political and social concerns. The work is a vulgarization of a Latin genre, a religious meditation, in keeping with the fourteenth-century movement toward popular piety. The meditation, on the passion and death of Christ, takes the form of an allegorical marriage of Christ and the Virgin Mary, representing the church, which is at the same time the marriage of the mystical ruby and the diamond. Philippe's evocations, though stylized, nevertheless pull at the heartstrings and can bring tears to the eyes. He continues with examples of holy wives and anecdotes of wicked ones, explaining that his words apply not only to the relationship of the soul to Christ but also to that of the physical woman to her earthly spouse. He compares the various sins to which a woman is subject to

the effect of metals and the planets on her and uses imagery of precious stones and diseases and medicines to present her sins to her in more vivid tones. After citing Hugh of St. Victor on the reasons why the soul should love God, he closes the work with his translation of Petrarch's Latin tale of the patient Griselda, who allowed her husband to test her by taking her daughter and then her son from her, supposedly to be killed, and then repudiating her. This, according to Philippe, is not only the way a soul should obey Christ but also the way a wife should obey her husband, given that human marriage is to be seen as the mirror of the divine.

To enable Christians to go on crusade, Philippe worked for the reform of society. The age of crusade was past; nevertheless, he exerted considerable influence, particularly in France, with works such as *Le Songe du vieil pelerin* (The Dream of the Old Pilgrim, 1389), a long, complex web of multiple layers of allegory. Within the framework of a dream voyage, his characters evaluate all states and communes and the social hierarchies of all peoples. The biblical talents, a latter-day Moses, the minting of money, the sixty-four squares of the chessboard, a royal chariot, precious stones, exotic peoples and customs, and animals and monsters appear in this moral, social, and political critique. Through this vast, intricately woven tapestry of allegories, Philippe offers a blueprint for a model society and instructs the future Charles VI how to govern himself and his realm. In this respect it constitutes an *enseignement aux princes* (instruction of princes). He writes eloquently against abuses by the powerful and the military, against injustices in the legal system, and against the onerous taxation that burdened the people of inflationary late-fourteenth-century France. He includes descriptions of exotica such as the marvels of India and the armies of the Great Khan from the *Romance of Alexander* and the *Travels of Marco Polo* but also from accounts given to him personally by travelers. One reads of processions through the streets of Rome by people disguised in animal headdresses, celebrating myths such as that of the Wild Hunt led by Mesnie Hellequin. There is a lively picture of the autumn herring catch in the North Sea, on which the poor of Europe survive during Lent, and of the belief in sea monsters lurking at the outer extremes of the sea. Philippe's vivid imagery and prolific use of proverbs and items of popular wisdom, together with his minute depiction of a fourteenth-century Europe wracked by wars and pestilence, provide a mirror of his time. The expensively executed manuscripts containing this work were obviously intended for powerful recipients. Vienna 2551, for example, was owned by Tanneguy du Chastel, counselor and chamberlain to King Charles VII of France, who reigned from 1422 to 1461, indicating that Philippe's advice on kingship was appreciated by this later royal adviser. The vastness of the undertaking, the literary quality of Phil-

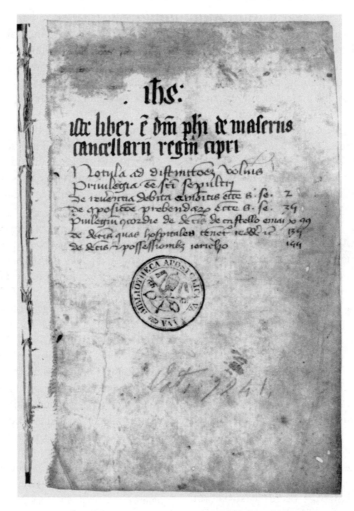

Manuscript for the Assize of Jerusalem, *with Philippe's ownership inscription (Vatican, Biblioteca Apostolica Vaticana, 7241)*

ippe's writing, the perspicacity of his criticism, and the cogency of his recommendations make *Le Songe du vieil pelerin* a chef d'œuvre that is deserving of attention even today.

At some point between finishing *Le Songe du vieil pelerin* in 1389 and the end of 1390 Philippe composed the *Oratio tragedica seu Declamatoria passionis Domini nostri Christi.* Composed in his cell at the convent of the Celestines, this rather melancholy meditation exudes regret that the author's active days are over and general pessimism about the future. After the obligatory prologue he intended his text to have six parts; the sixth part, however, which was to have treated of charity, and particularly the burning Charity of the Crucified, he omitted—because, he admits in the margin, of his crass negligence. The first part is a contemplation of the wrongs suffered by Christ in his Passion and death. Comparing Christ to the elephant in his salvific aspects as was traditional in medieval bestiaries and to the phoenix in his resurrection, Philippe invokes the help of the Holy Spirit and the intercession of the blessed Mother of God. The second part assigns mystical attributes to the crusader's arms and

uses imagery of the culture of the vine, the roles of physician and patient, the treasure of the merchant, the mystical qualities of precious stones, the kinds of wood named in the Bible, and ointments and aromatics to call forth associations with the divine. In the third part Philippe praises God and loses himself in a dissolution of his natural senses as he contemplates the divine. The fourth part is more grounded in earthly reality as he reviews the events of his life; in the fifth he raises his petitions to God and confesses his faults and inadequacies. This is a highly personal intellectual and spiritual voyage, but other meditators can readily trace its itinerary.

In 1392 Philippe composed a spiritual will in French, *Le Testament,* as a penance, leaving a unique manuscript written in his own hand. After a short prologue in which he tries to put himself in a fit frame of mind to meet his maker, he makes precise stipulations as to the humiliations to be visited upon his corpse and the humble burial that is to be accorded him. He hopes for the grace of the Eucharist and the company of brothers who will pray with and for him in case he is no longer able to do so for himself. The work is an *ars moriendi* (art of dying), a genre popular in France and Italy from 1350 to 1450. Philippe presents his vision of human destiny with a macabre realism, particularly in the details he gives for the funeral preparations, making him a participant in the movement of the later Middle Ages toward more-vivid portrayals of the horrors of death and decay.

Between 1389 and 1394 Philippe wrote *La Sustance de la Chevalerie de la Passion de Jhesu Crist en françois* (The Substance of the Chivalry of the Passion of Jesus Christ in French), aimed at inducing in his readers pity for the holy places under non-Christian rule and a zeal for crusade. He lists twenty reasons why his order of chivalry is necessary, followed by a prologue to the knights, both of which are written in a rhetoric that is designed to excite and persuade. Then follows a practical enumeration of officials, councils, chapters, buildings, habit, vestments, arms, schools, and rules and regulations for the governing of the order. The text closes with a prayer in French followed by one in Latin. Six colored drawings form part of the Bodleian Library manuscript, illustrating the banner and the various garments of the order. The illustrations include a habit for women since it was expected that if a married man joined the order his wife would also join; such couples would not be required to take vows of chastity.

In 1395 Philippe wrote *L'Epistre au roi Richart* (*Letter to King Richard II: A Plea Made in 1395 for Peace between England and France*, 1975) at the behest of Charles VI, urging the twenty-eight-year-old king of England, recently bereft of his queen, Anne of Bohemia, to marry Charles's eight-year-old daughter Isabel. Philippe's argument is couched in allegorical terms. Medicines, wounds and healing, animals, the idyllic garden of peace as opposed to the loathsome garden of war, and, particularly, precious stones are used to urge peace between the two nations so that they can jointly turn to a new crusade. While the crusade did not come about, the royal marriage did and was, by all accounts, a happy one.

In 1396 Philippe produced the fourth redaction of his plan for his order, *De la Chevallerie de la Passion de Jhesu Crist* (Concerning the Chivalry of the Passion of Jesus Christ). In this text he outlines his plans for the five works he proposes to write for his order. The first, the "Livre de seint Regle" (Book of Holy Rule), is to consist of thirty books on the laws, decrees, and regulations necessary for governing the order in the East and will not be made widely available. The second, the "Sustance abregie de la Passion de Jhesu Crist" (The Abbreviated Substance of the Passion of Jesus Christ), an abridgment of the first, will circulate throughout the Christian world. A third work, the "Livre du secret de la sainte chevalerie" (Book of the Secret of the Holy Chivalry), will deal with the finances of the order. The fourth will be a summary of the third and

will, like the second, circulate widely. The last work, the "Livre du commencement de la sainte chevalerie de nostre Seigneur Jhesu Crist" (Book of the Beginning of the Holy Chivalry of Our Lord Jesus Christ), is to explain the government of the order and set out the rules for the members' way of life, the procedure for joining the order, and the behavior expected of the troops during the voyage to the East. From this detailed plan it appears that the *Nova religio milicie Passionis Jhesu Christi pro acquisicione sancte civitatis Jherusalem et Terre Sancte* of 1367–1368 and that of 1384 together form the kernel of the Latin form of the first of these works, which was never written. *La Sustance de la Chevalerie de la Passion de Jhesu Crist en françois* in the Bodley manuscript and the "Substance abregie de la Passion de Jhesu Crist" incorporated within the Arsenal manuscript form two variants of the French version of Philippe's second text. There are no known copies of the third and fourth texts, the "Livre du Secret de la sainte chevalerie" and its summary form, neither of which was, perhaps, ever written. The Arsenal text includes the prologue to the "Livre du Commencement de la sainte chevalerie de nostre Seigneur Jhesu Crist," followed by what appears to be material appropriate for the fifth work.

In *De la Chevallerie de la Passion de Jhesu Crist* Philippe lays blame for the failure of previous crusades on the three cardinal vices—pride, lust, and avarice—as had the earlier crusade chroniclers; St. Augustine, in his *De civitate Dei* (The City of God, 413–426), had cited the same vices as the cause of the downfall of imperial Rome. Philippe proposes his chivalry as an antidote, claiming that he has structured his order so as to drive these vices from the army. He offers material drawn from the Bible and from history to provide exempla for his readers to emulate as he encourages them to crusade. He then inserts "Substance abregie de la Chevalerie" (Abbreviated Substance of the Chivalry), followed by the prologue to the "Livre du commencement de la sainte chevalerie de nostre Seigneur Jhesu Crist," a further plea for the necessity of crusade. He continues by saying that his knights should be drawn from seven languages and four social estates and that his militia should consist of certain numbers of members belonging to various categories, such as knights, brothers, squires, nobles, bourgeois, and sergeants. This contingent would be twenty-one-thousand strong; to them Philippe adds ten thousand warriors of the fleet. He specifies how much each knight must pay, according to category of membership and personal fortune; what each will receive in return; and the length of the initial term of service for each. He discusses the vessels that will make up the fleet and how many men and horses shall travel in each ship. There follows an extensive list of the various job specialties that will be required by the order. The manuscript closes with the names of men who have joined the order and of those who have promised their support.

Illumination from a manuscript for Philippe's Le Songe du vieil pelerin *(Paris, Bibliothèque de l'Arsenal, f. 2682–3, fol. 34r)*

Philippe's last known work, *Epistre lamentable et consolatoire sur le fait de la desconfiture lacrimable du noble et vaillant roy de Honguerie par les turcs devant la ville de Nicopoli* (Epistle of Lamentation and Consolation on the Fact of the Woeful Defeat of the Noble and Valiant King of Hungary by the Turks before the City of Nicopolis, circa 1396–1397), addressed to the duke of Burgundy, is a last unheeded plea for the organization of a new crusade and for the implementation of his Order of Chivalry as a way of curing the ills of the Western soldiery, thus enabling them to achieve victory. He again seeks to move his readers to pity by a description of the condition of the places where Christ walked and suffered and of the miseries endured by Christians under Muslim rule. He seeks to launch a rescue of the unfortunate comrades captured at Nicopolis by narrating a dream in which one of the captives, his friend Jehan de Blaisy, came to him to ask for help. At the end he notes that in his old age he can do no more and describes how he let his pen slip from his fingers to bury his face in his hands. Nothing more is heard from him or about him until his death in 1405.

The manuscript tradition shows the social milieu in which Philippe de Mézières functioned and the importance and power of the people to whom he addressed his writings. It also reveals a shift from Latin to the vernacular that followed by a few years the influence exerted in this direction by Charles V of France, which, in turn, was part of a trend that accelerated in the following century. Philippe's calls for a new crusade were echoed by other fourteenth-century propagandists, but all went unheeded. As a diplomat and statesman, however, he was second to none, and as a social, moral, and political critic he remains without peer. As such he provides a window onto a world long gone, and his works are precious as witnesses to the medieval mentality. His writing, in both Latin and French, tends to long, compound sentences in the style of the end of the fourteenth century. As modern readers become accustomed to this style, which is so different from the terse usage of today, they increasingly appreciate the harmonious balance and beauty of Philippe's rhythms. They feel the force of his imagery, from the poignant comparison of the fragility of human life to a spider's web torn by the wind to the biting critique of fashions so abbreviated that they not only offend against decency but also fail to keep the wearer warm in winter and the savage portrayal of the sins of pride, lust, and avarice as triple-headed hybrid monsters. Philippe is an artist worthy of attention, one whose vast, airy canvasses of words come close to matching those immortalizing him in oil in the Accademia in Venice.

References:

Olivier Caudron, "Philippe de Mézières," in *Dictionnaire de spiritualité ascétique et mystique, doctrine et histoire,* edited by Marcel Viller, S.J., and others, volume 12, part 1 (Paris: Beauchesne, 1983), cols. 1309–1316;

Bernard Gagnebin, *L'Enluminure de Charlemagne à François Ier: Les Mansucrits à peinture de la bibliothèque public et universitaire de Genève* (Geneva: Bibliothèque publique et universitaire et Musée d'art et d'histoire 1976), pp. 153–154;

Elie Golenistcheff-Koutouzoff, *Etude sur le "Livre de la vertu du sacrement de mariage" de Philippe de Mézières* (Belgrade: Svetlost, 1937);

Golenistcheff-Koutouzoff, *L'Histoire de Griseldis en France au XIVe et XVe siècle* (Paris: Droz, 1933; Geneva: Slatkine Reprints, 1975);

Abdel Hamid Hamdy, *Philippe de Mézières and the New Order of the Passion,* 3 volumes (Alexandria: Alexandria University Press, 1964–1965);

Nicolae Iorga, *Philippe de Mézières, 1327–1405, et la croisade au XIVe siècle,* Bibliothèque de l'Ecole des Hautes Etudes, Sciences philologiques et historiques, fascicle 110 (Paris: Bouillon, 1896; Geneva: Slatkine Reprints, 1976);

Auguste Molinier, "Description de deux manuscrits, contenant la règle de la Militia Passionis Jhesu Christi de Philippe de Mézières," *Archives de l'Orient Latin*, 1 (1881): 335–364;

Otto Pächt and Dagmar Thoss, *Die illuminierten Handschriften und Inkunabeln der Österreichischen Nationalbibliothek: Französische Schule 1*, volume 1 of text and plates (Vienna: Osterreichischen Akademie der Wissenschaften, 1974), pp. 89–91;

Jean-Louis G. Picherit, *La métaphore pathologique et thérapeutique à la fin du Moyen Age* (Tübingen: Niemeyer, 1994);

Joan B. Williamson, "Allegory in the Work of Philippe de Mézières," in *Allegory Revisited: Ideals of Mankind*, edited by Anna-Teresa Tymzieniecka, Analecta Husserliana no. 41 (Dordrecht: Kluwer Academic Publishers, 1994), pp. 107–121;

Williamson, "Animal Imagery in Philippe de Mézières' *Livre de la vertu du sacrement de mariage*," in *Europäische Literaturen im Mittelalter, Mélanges en l'honneur de Wolfgang Spiewok*, edited by Danielle Buschinger (Greifswald: Reineke, 1994), pp. 439–448;

Williamson, "The *Chevalerie de la Passion Jhesu Crist*: Philippe de Mézières' Utopia," in *Gesellschaftsutopien in Mittelalter: Discours et figures de l'Utopie au moyen âge*, edited by Buschinger and Wolfgang Spiewok, Etudes médiévales de Greifswald no. 45 (Greifswald: Reineke, 1994), pp. 165–173;

Williamson, "The French-Italian World of Philippe de Mézières," in *Romance Languages Annual 1991*, volume 3, edited by Jeanette Beer, Charles Ganelin, and Anthony Julian Tamburri (West Lafayette, Ind.: Purdue Research Foundation, 1992), pp. 140–145;

Williamson, "L'Idée de bonheur dans l'oeuvre de Philippe de Mézières," in *Actes du Colloque d'Amiens de mars 1984*, edited by Buschinger, Göppinger Arbeiten sur Germanistik no. 414 (Göppingen: Kümmerle, 1990), pp. 439–456;

Williamson, "The Image of the Book in the Works of Philippe de Mézières," in *Romance Languages Annual 1992*, volume 4, edited by Beer, Ganelin, and Tamburri (West Lafayette, Ind.: Purdue Research Foundation, 1993), pp. 175–183;

Williamson, "The Image of the Horse in the Work of Philippe de Mézières," in *Reindardus: Yearbook of the International Reynard Society*, volume 5 (Amsterdam: Benjamins, 1992), pp. 217–229;

Williamson, "Jerusalem: The Poetics of Space in the Works of Philippe de Mézières," in *The Elemental Passion for Place in the Ontopoiesis of Life: Passions of the Soul in the Imaginatio creatrix*, edited by Tymzieniecka, Analecta Husserliana no. 44 (Dordrecht: Kluwer Academic Publishers, 1995), pp. 339–352;

Williamson, "The Lady with the Unicorn and the Mirror," in *Reinardus: Yearbook of the International Reynard Society*, volume 3 (Amsterdam: Benjamins, 1990), pp. 213–225;

Williamson, "Paris B.N. MS. fr. 1175: A Collaboration between Author and Artist," in *Text and Image*, ACTA, no. 10, edited by the David W. Burchmore Center for Medieval and Early Renaissance Studies (Binghamton: State University of New York at Binghamton, 1986), pp. 77–92;

Williamson, "Philippe de Mézières' Book for Married Ladies: A Book from the Entourage of the Court of Charles VI," in *The Spirit of the Court: Selected Proceedings of the 4th Congress of the International Courtly Literature Society, Toronto, 1983*, edited by Robert Taylor and Glynn Burgess (Woodbridge, U.K.: Boydell & Brewer, 1985), pp. 393–407;

Williamson, "Philippe de Mézières and the Idea of Crusade," in *The Military Orders: Fighting for the Faith and Caring for the Sick*, edited by Malcolm Barber (Aldershot, U.K.: Variorum, 1994), pp. 358–364;

Williamson, "Philippe de Mézières et l'influence du Cycle de la Croisade au 14e siècle," in *Les Epopées et la Croisade*, edited by Karl-Heinz Bender, Zeitschrift für französische Sprache und Literatur no. 11 (Stuttgart: Steiner, 1984), pp. 163–169;

Williamson, "La Première Traduction française de l'histoire de Griseldis de Pétrarque: Pour qui et pourquoi fut-elle faite?" in *Amour, mariage et transgressions au moyen âge*, Actes du Colloque du Centre d'Etudes Médiévales de l'Université de Picardie, March 1983, edited by Buschinger and André Crépin, Göppinger Arbeiten zur Germanistik no. 420 (Göppingen: Kümmerle, 1984), pp. 447–456;

Williamson, "Les Rapports culturels de Philippe de Mézières avec l'Italie," in *Die Kulturellen Beziehungen zwischen Italien und den Anderen Ländern Europas im Mittelalter*, edited by Buschinger and Spiewok, Jahrestagung der Reineke Gesellschaft no. 4 (Greifswald: Reineke, 1993), pp. 187–196;

Williamson, "*Le Songe du vieil pelerin*: Philippe de Mézières' Discovery of the New World," in *La Découverte du Monde â la fin du Moyen Age: La Grande Aventure de la découverte du monde au moyen âge*, edited by Buschinger and Spiewok, Annales de la Société Reineke no 6 (Greifswald: Reineke, 1995), pp. 159–166;

Williamson, "Ysangrin and Hellequin's Horde in *Le Songe du vieil pelerin*," in *Reinardus: Yearbook of the International Reynard Society*, volume 1 (Grave: Alfa, 1988), pp. 75–88.

Na Prous Boneta

(circa 1296 – 1328)

Claudia Rattazzi Papka
Columbia University

WORK: *Confession* (1325)

Manuscript: The confession is preserved only in one late-seventeenth-century copy: Paris, Bibliothèque Nationale de France, Collection Doat, vol. XXVII, f. fr. 51r–79v.

Standard edition: "The Confession of Prous Boneta: Heretic and Heresiarch," edited by William Harold May, in *Essays in Medieval Life and Thought,* edited by John Mundy (New York: Columbia University Press, 1955), pp. 3–30.

Edition in English: Partial translation in *Medieval Women's Visionary Literature,* by Elizabeth Alvida Petroff (New York & Oxford: Oxford University Press, 1986), pp. 284–290.

On a November morning in 1328, in Carcassone, the inquisitors Henri Chamayou and Pierre Brun delivered sentences upon twenty-two men and women of southern France accused of the heresies of the Béguins and Spiritual Franciscans, against which Pope John XXII had been battling vehemently for ten years. What had begun as an ideological debate over poverty within the Franciscan order in the previous century had become, in the early years of the fourteenth, an eschatologically charged and socially and geographically dispersed battle between authority and heresy, from one perspective, or between the forces of the Antichrist and the True Church, from the other. The trial of November 1328 marked the end of the phase of this battle that had been fought in Provence, and it marked also the end of the life of Na Prous Boneta, one of the twenty-two tried, who was declared a heretic and heresiarch, unrepentant despite all efforts to convert her, and turned over to the secular arm to be burnt at the stake.

Three years earlier, Na (for *domina,* lady) Prous, daughter of Durandus Bonetus of the diocese of Nîmes, had been arrested at Montpellier, where she had lived since about the age of seven, and had been brought before the Inquisition at Carcassone. On 6 August 1325 she gave her confession in her native Occitan, answering the charges of heresy. Recorded in the Latin translation of the inquisitorial scribe, the confession is an extraordinary document that combines visionary autobiography with apocalyptic interpretations of current events and conflates the two in Na Prous's declaration of her own role in a dawning millennial age. The confession stands out from those of the others accused at this time, not only in the extremity of the vision it presents and the rhetoric it employs but also for the way in which Na Prous constructs her narrative independently of the *interrogatoria* prescribed to ferret out heretics of her particular ilk. The questions devised by Bernard Gui, chief inquisitor for the region, do not dominate Na Prous's confession as they do those of others tried in the years around 1325, although Na Prous does clearly show herself to partake of those beliefs the Inquisition had labeled heretical. The scribe who recorded her confession asserts that it was made "gratis et sponte et sine interrogatione" (freely, willingly, and without interrogation), and this willingness suggests Na Prous's desire to tell her story and control her narrative–a desire that renders the text more nearly a manifesto than a confession. It is, furthermore, not so much a manifesto of the beliefs of the Spiritual Franciscans and their lay followers, the Béguins, as a manifesto of a new religion, centered on herself.

Na Prous's conviction that her own impending death on the pyre would be a martyrdom paralleling Christ's passion and initiating the millennial age of the Holy Spirit is based in her interpretation of the exegetical prophesies of the abbot Joachim of Fiore. Over a century before, Joachim had derived from the Scriptures, and particularly the Apocalypse, a model of human history divided into three ages, or *statūs,* corresponding to the three persons of the Trinity and in "concordance" with one another through the parallel unfolding of events. The first *statūs,* corresponding to the Old Testament, was that of the Father; the second, corresponding to the New Testament, was that of the Son; and the third *statūs,* still to come, would be that of the Holy Spirit, characterized in Joachim's conception by monastic perfection and a spiritual knowledge emanating from the *concordia* (harmony) of the two Testaments together. In southern France at the end of the thirteenth century, Joachim's exegetical principles were adopted by a Franciscan friar, Pierre Jean Olivi, who, in his *Lectura super apocalypsim* (Commentary of the Apocalypse), extrapolated from Joachim's three ages the notion that there would thus be three advents of Christ: the first had been in the flesh; the second would be in the spirit of evangelical reform and would bring about a perfected new church (corresponding to Joachim's third *status*); and the third would be at the end of time, in final judgment.

The reformist ecclesiology of Olivi's version of Joachim's millennium was seized upon by Franciscans who wished, in the face of opposition within their order and eventually by the Pope, to maintain a strict observance of poverty, and was used to give apocalyptic authorization to their dissent and eschatological significance to their persecution. The system of historical concordances that Olivi had adopted from Joachim of Fiore as exegetical tools became for his followers among the Spirituals and Béguins the means for interpreting not biblical text but rather the events of their own lives and deaths. What was for Olivi imminent becomes actual; what was elusive symbol is pinned down and named. Olivi himself becomes the angel with the face like the sun who holds a book in the tenth chapter of the Apocalypse; he is venerated as a saint without the Church's authorization, and his own book is translated into the vernacular and treated like a sacred text.

In the specifics of her interpretation of Olivi's role, of her vision of history as a series of Joachite concordances, and of her equation of John XXII with the Antichrist, as well as in the vision of her own role as "donatrix Spiritus Sancti" (the bearer of the Holy Spirit), Na Prous goes beyond even the most radical of the Béguins' claims. Her confession is also distinguished from those of her Beguine contemporaries in its use of a visionary framework, which sets forth her spiritual autobiography in terms similar to those of some of the women mystics of the era. After this gradual buildup of mystical credentials—in an astonishingly controlled and essentially "orthodox" rhetorical performance—Na Prous launches into the second part of her confession, where no holds are barred in the denunciation of the ecclesiastical oppressors or in the assertion of her own role in the Apocalypse. While it is tempting to see Na Prous's visionary autobiography as an attempt on her part to render her opinions more acceptable in some way, it soon becomes clear that she neither hopes nor desires that she should be spared the flames of the heretic's stake. Indeed, she uses images that specifically incorporate consumption by fire—the element par excel-

lence of the Holy Spirit—and her theology of history is predicated, in many ways, on her own impending "Passion," suggesting once more that she sees her confession as a manifesto, not as an opportunity for exculpation or reconciliation.

Na Prous begins her narrative with a flashback to four years earlier, on Good Friday in 1321, when she was in the Franciscan church at Montpellier, lingering after the service, and was rapt to the first heaven by Christ. There she saw Christ in his human and divine forms, and he offered to her his heart, which was perforated like a lantern, through the holes of which shone splendid rays of light that allowed her to see the divinity of God "clare et aperte" (clearly and openly). These rays reappeared and enveloped her as she left the church and walked through the cemetery, as they did again when she was at home, and once again when she returned to the church for the *tenebrae* service. The elements of rapture, physical proximity to Christ, and Christ's body as lacerated and permeable are found frequently in much of the female spirituality of the period. Although individual women did, given the appropriate context, pursue such mystical intimacy with Christ as Na Prous experiences in this vision, when this intimacy provided the basis for more radical theological or political claims, as it did in Na Prous's case, religious women could be persecuted with uncompromising vigor. For the moment, however, Na Prous's position in the confession remains within the bounds of mystical orthodoxy. The emanating rays, enveloping first Christ and then Na Prous, are not explicitly connected to the image of the Holy Spirit as light, but do suggest the bestowal of the Holy Spirit on Na Prous, which will become explicit later in the text (corroborated, as it were, by this earlier incident). The image of the sacred heart (eventually to become a theme of female devotion) in Na Prous's vision emanates light from its wounds and may allude to the controversial Olivian assertion that the heart wound was received before Christ's death. More importantly, it is an image of the perforated body of Christ as the passageway for the emanation of the Holy Spirit, an image of the wounded flesh as a pathway for power that may have had particular resonance in the inquisitorial context of torture and death.

The next day, during the Holy Saturday Mass, God the Father appears to her in the first of many visits during which he often tells her cryptically, "memet ipsum dedi tibi sicut vergine, et memet ipsum retinui" (I myself have given him to you, as to the Virgin, and I have kept him with me). The Lord may simply be explaining to Na Prous the miracle of the Eucharist, by which Christ is given in the flesh for the sacrifice of the altar that replays his Incarnation and Passion; but while

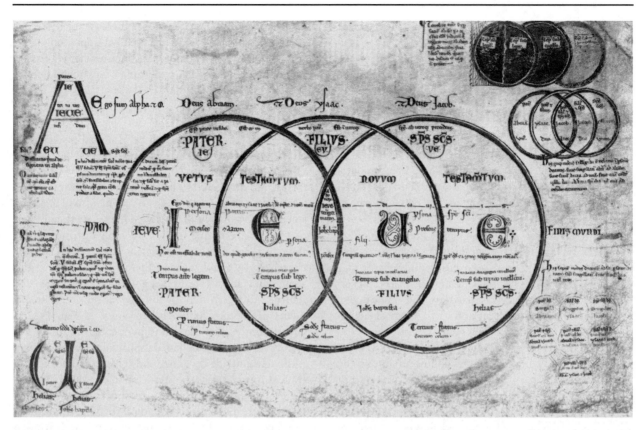

Illuminated page from a manuscript for Joachim de Fiore's Liber Figurarum, *diagramming the three stages of the world; Na Prous Boneta believed his prophesy of the Apocalypse (Oxford, Bodleian Library)*

the nature of the Eucharist is clearly at issue here, the significance of these words for Na Prous goes far beyond the mass itself. That God's statement is not a general theological one but a personal message for Na Prous—and thus decidedly beyond the bounds of ortho-doxy—becomes clearer when the Lord soon declares, "Sanctus Joannes Baptista fuit praeco adventus baptismi sacri Jesu Christi, et tu es praeco adventus Spiritus Sancti" (Saint John the Baptist was the herald of the advent of Jesus Christ's holy baptism, and you are the herald of the advent of the Holy Spirit). With the decla-ration of an imminent advent of the Holy Spirit, Na Prous tips her hand, and one can imagine the notary pricking up his ears at the first real hint of a Joachite, and Béguin, worldview.

Na Prous claims, with the requisite visionary humil-ity, that she resisted this double call to be bearer and herald, protesting that she was nothing but a sinner. But the Lord responded by showing her a fire and saying: "Vides hunc ignem; qualiter totam materiam et substan-tiam lignorum convertit in suam naturam, eodem modo natura divinitatits convertit in se animas quas sibi vult" (See this fire; just as it converts the whole matter and substance of the wood into its nature, in the same way the nature of divinity converts to itself the souls it wishes for itself). Thus Na Prous reports the subtle authorization given her by God for her own transfor-mation or deification, not by her will but by that of God, in a new incarnation of divinity that makes Na Prous like Christ himself. The result of this transforma-tion will be the consumption of Na Prous's own human flesh by the flames, not of divinity, but of the heretic's pyre. The details of her heresy emerge as she continues to relate her visionary experience, always aware, it seems, of her inexorable movement toward those flames and intent on figuring that movement as a divinely ordained progression to the most glorious mar-tyrdom in the fire of the Holy Spirit.

Na Prous goes on to report that God had told her "in te sumpsi et feci cameram meam" (In you I have been clothed and made my chamber), suggesting again her typological link to the Virgin Mary, which is made explicit and explicitly autobiographical, as Christ explains to Na Prous that "quando tu fecisti votum virginitatis, tunc indulsi omnia peccata tua, ita complete sicut indulsi matri meae virgini in ventre sui matris" (when you made your vow of virginity, I forgave all your sins as fully as I absolved my virgin mother in her mother's womb). The connection to Mary becomes fully apoca-lyptic shortly afterwards, when Na Prous reports the

Lord's proclamation that "beata virgo Maria fuit donatrix Filii Dei et tu eris donatrix Spiritus Sancti" (the blessed virgin Mary was the bestower of the Son of God, and you will be the bestower of the Holy Spirit). This incredibly audacious assertion, replete with Joachite and Olivian resonances, is prefaced by another instance of mystical autobiography, in which Na Prous's life is linked to the divine unfolding of history, with Pierre Jean Olivi as the mediating presence and with impregnation and gestation as the dominant images. Returning to the day, twenty years before, when she had made her vow of virginity, Na Prous recounts how Christ explained to her that on that day the Lord "conceptit ipsam Naprous in spiritu" (conceived Na Prous in the spirit) and that nine months later, on the day of the feast of brother Olivi, at his very tomb in Narbonne, "ipse dominus peperit eam in spiritu" (the Lord had given birth to her in the spirit). These images of birth and rebirth, conception and transformation, conflate Na Prous's own spiritual rebirth with her giving birth to the Holy Spirit and to the new age, whose significance is ultimately transcendent, as her body has become.

God has given birth to Na Prous–significantly, at Olivi's very tomb–but her birth is transformed into her own impregnation as she parallels herself to Mary, claiming that God gave the divinity to her as entirely as he had given it to Mary and her Son. This claim then shades into a Joachite vision of history and millennial epistemology as Na Prous assumes the voice of the prophet/exegete and identifies herself with the type of Mary in the twelfth chapter of the Book of Revelations: the "mulier amicta sole" (woman clothed with the sun), who is pursued by the seven-headed dragon identified in Joachite interpretations with the Antichrist, and by Na Prous, in an exegetical tour-de-force, with her own persecutor and that of the Béguins and Spiritual Franciscans, Pope John XXII.

Na Prous begins to elaborate this apocalyptic vision of her world and her role in it only after God has unequivocally stated that she is the "donatrix Spiritus Sancti," at the conclusion of the first part of the confession, and thus authorized her, as the bearer of the third age, to speak in his name. She speaks prophetically and exegetically, and often about herself, for just as Mary's role in the history of salvation is predicated upon a loss that must be repaired, so Na Prous sees her own election as redemptive. She follows Mary as Ave follows Eva (Eve), as Na Prous makes clear in a brilliant passage of concordances that takes as its point of departure the identification of John XXII with Adam. This concordance informs Na Prous's whole vision of the state of the Church and of salvation at the beginning of the fourteenth century, which is intricately bound up not only with Na Prous's life but with that of Pierre Jean Olivi and his followers among the Spirituals and Beguines of Provence.

The seven-point concordance between John XXII and Adam begins with the betrayal of the Franciscans and the condemnation of the gospel by the Pope, which, according to Na Prous, corresponds to the eating of the apple and its tasting by Adam, in greed and in knowledge of wrongdoing. These two moments clearly refer to two of the infamous papal bulls promulgated by John XXII in his battle against the Spiritual Franciscans and their claims about poverty. The first, *Ad conditorem canonum* (1322), revoked the privilege granted to the Franciscans of holding property in the name of the Church and abolished their ability to use clothing, food, and shelter without owning anything. John XXII thus "betrayed" the most basic condition of the Franciscan Order by rendering impossible its observance of the founding rule, as well as betraying the Friars Minor and the papacy itself by reversing the previous papal decree. The death of which Na Prous speaks is both figurative and literal, in that the Order as it had been was no more, and to adhere to its previous condition was tantamount to seeking death. The "condemnation of the Gospel" that is the second part of John XXII's transgression is a reference to the next papal bull he issued in his increasingly vehement battle against the Franciscan Spirituals and their lay counterparts: *Cum inter nonnullos* (1323), which declared heretical the belief in the poverty of Christ and the apostles. In Na Prous's eyes, this was a declaration that only greed could explain, and in which the betrayal of the gospel was so patent that the Pope's knowledge of his own wrongdoing was inevitable–as were the apocalyptic consequences of such corruption at the head of Christ's Church.

When Na Prous declares that John XXII's sin in condemning Olivi's *scriptura* was as great as Adam's when he ate the apple and blamed Eve, she makes clear that the problem is the abuse of power: just as Adam ought to have ruled Eve rather than blamed her (since the man is the head of the woman), so the Pope should have ruled the Church as a good shepherd rather than persecuting his flock. Olivi is a scapegoat, Na Prous is saying, just as Eve was. Because of these abuses of his power, John XXII has lost the grace given him by God, just as Adam did; and because God is just, the punishment fits the crime: he who abuses power loses power. It is not his position that John XXII has lost, but that which gives his position power in the mediation between the earthly and the divine: that is, the power of the sacraments. In saying this, Na Prous goes much farther than her Béguin contemporaries were willing to go. John XXII's sin has not just made him a heretic, or temporarily powerless, it has spiritually killed the whole of Christianity and barred the doors to salvation, just as Adam's Fall did—until, of course, the coming of Christ. This is the basis of the elaborate theology she goes on to expound in the remainder of her testimony, explaining how this second Fall necessitates another advent of Christ (the second of three).

By asserting the identity of John XXII with Adam, Na Prous is positing a recommencement of history, a third beginning; but she is also elaborating other aspects of the concordance in order to gain greater insight into the present by looking at the biblical past. As for Joachim and Olivi, there is for Na Prous not just one "setting" at which the three circles of history interlock, but many; this multiplicity of significance is multiply enforcing. John XXII is thus not only Adam but also Cain, Herod, Caiphas, Simon Magus, Lucifer, and, last but not least, the Antichrist. These seven transgressors recall the seven tyrannical persecutors with which Joachim glossed the seven-headed dragon of Apocalypse 12: Herod, Nero, Constantine, Muhammed, Mesemoth, Saladin, and an unnamed seventh who is called Antichrist and who is followed by the final tyrant, symbolized by the dragon's tail, who will be the final Antichrist. The correlation of a pope with the Antichrist was suggested by Olivi's apocalypse commentary and taken up by the Spirituals and their sympathizers when John XXII began his vehement persecutions. And indeed there were others who, under interrogation, confessed to having heard John XXII referred to as Antichrist, but Na Prous is unique in spelling out the associations and elaborating them in her confession: John XXII is another Caiphas, who crucified Christ; another Herod, for just as Herod procured the deaths of innocent children, so has John XXII burned innocent Béguins and lepers; another Cain, who killed his brother, just as this Pope killed all of human nature, which is the Pope's "brother"; another Simon Magus, who, like this Pope, wanted to be worshiped by all the world; another Adam, because he too causes an irreparable Fall; and another Lucifer, who was given the most beautiful name, Lucibel, and then the most hideous. Finally, he is the Antichrist, "the sum total of all evil," and it is as such that he is all of these other evil men.

As these identifications emerge, they unequivocally assert the identification of John XXII with the "draco magnus e rufus" (great red dragon) of Apocalypse 12. This *concordia* takes on profound significance as the associations proliferate and shift, and as they begin to revolve around a female figure who turns out to be Na Prous herself, as she claims she appears prefigured in the Apocalypse. In the biblical text the dragon is the second great sign that appears in the sky after the seventh trumpet of the seventh seal has been blown and

voices have been heard in heaven announcing the imminent arrival of the kingdom of God. The first great sign, which marks the beginning of the end of the world—its transition into the "kingdom of God"—is the woman clothed with the sun, who gives birth to the end of the world in Apocalypse 12:21: "et in utero habens et clamat parturiens et cruciatur ut pariat" (and her womb was full and she cried out while giving birth and was in torment that she should be delivered). The image and the text itself are central to Na Prous's entire apocalyptic theology, linking her mystical experience to her eschatological vision while at the same time authorizing that vision with biblical authority.

After Na Prous has elaborated her judgment of John XXII as the Antichrist, annuller of the sacraments, persecutor of the gospel, and betrayer of Christ (in the diatribe that constitutes the central section of her confession), Christ shows her a serpent, which she crushes beneath her foot, and says:

> de caetero non oportet vos timere de isto serpente; asserens quod Dominus sibi dixit quod ille serpens erat draco ille quem beatus Joannes vidit in libro revelationum, qui persequebatur illam dominam quam non nominavit. Item dixit quod semel Deus dixit sibi quod duae foeminae sunt nominatae seu recitatae in sancta scriptura, et quod uni earum debebat dari Filius Dei, et alteri debebat dari Spiritus Sanctus; et dixit illi Deus quod ipsamet Naprous erat illa cui debebat dari Spiritus Sanctus....

> (from now on you need not fear this serpent; and she asserted that the Lord told her that this serpent was the dragon that the blessed John saw in the book of revelations, who persecuted that woman who was not named. Again, she said that once God told her that two women are named or described in Holy Scripture, and that one of them was to be given the Son of God, and to the other was to be given the Holy Spirit; and God told her that it was she herself, Na Prous, to whom the Holy Spirit would be given. . . .)

It is impossible to know where the inception of Na Prous's apocalyptic vision of herself as "mulier amicta sole" and "donatrix Spiritus Sancti" is to be found, for the image brings together a whole matrix of spiritual, historical, and exegetical concerns so tightly intertwined that it is difficult to unravel them. It is certain that the text of the Apocalypse was central in Na Prous's mind, as it was in the mind of Olivi and of many of his followers for whom it became the script of their lives. In Na Prous's case, the imagery of the *mulier* and the dragon's defeat lends a specifically threatening resonance to the images of conception and parturition in her confession: the birth of the third age is a violent one. It is also, however, the beginning of a new dispensation.

The second Fall by the second Adam (John XXII) necessitates a second Incarnation and a second Passion, which is taking place in her own persecution by the Inquisition, which is the Passion of the Holy Spirit. Thus Na Prous's biblical visions, her eschatological interpretations of history, her veneration of Olivi, and her own impending death are brought together, and as the confession nears its conclusion, these elements converge in the articulation of what can only be called a new religion, in which Na Prous and Olivi are alternately the new, spiritual versions of Mary and Christ, and the two aspects of the new, spiritual Word. The "texts" of Na Prous and Olivi (her spoken words and his written ones) are together figured as the Testament of the Holy Spirit—the dispensation for the Third Age—and thus Na Prous emphatically characterizes her own words as having evangelical status, enforcing the reading of her confession as self-consciously constructed to a remarkable degree.

It is with a complex series of Joachite concordances that Na Prous ends her confession, saying that the Lord has told her that she is the one who opens the seven seals of the book seen by John XXII in his Apocalypse vision, that she holds the arc of God (the rainbow) so tightly over her head that she bends it into a circle, and that she is the white horse ridden by Jesus Christ. Finally, she claims that the Lord has told her "quod abyssus erit cantata et clausa illis qui credent verbis suis . . . et illis qui non credent verbis suis erit abyssus aperta" (that the abyss will be shut and closed for those who believe her words . . . and for those who do not believe her words, it shall be opened). As her testimony before the Inquisition ends, Na Prous asserts her authority and the authority of the "text" of her confession absolutely and thus proclaims her heresy unequivocally. She figures herself as the angel with the keys of the abyss from Apocalypse 20, therefore claiming to initiate the millennium, as if her words could bind the Satan she sees in John XXII and his inquisitorial min-

ions. But in the end it is she who is bound and brought to the stake to be burned "asserens in praedictis, tamquam in veritate se velle vivere atque mori" (claiming that in the aforesaid [beliefs], as in the truth, she wishes to live and die).

Na Prous was unrepentant and apparently died firm in her beliefs, which in many ways allowed her to come to terms with her impending death by transforming it into a glorious new beginning rather than a fiery end. But the Inquisition's condemnation of her as both a heretic and a heresiarch suggests that her vision of history and her own role in it was shared by others, who would have been her followers. Though the inquisitorial records show no one tried at the time to have been willing to jeopardize his or her own life by confessing to be a believer in Na Prous's apocalyptic religion, it is certainly possible that Na Prous's rhetorical skills, exegetical prowess, and visionary credentials had earned her a following in and around Montpellier. Although her death may have put an end to her influence and silenced the voice that resounds in her confession, renewed interest in medieval women's writings, in heresy, and in the apocalyptic mentality have led scholars back to Na Prous's confession and let her voice be heard once again.

References:

David Burr, "Olivi, Apocalyptic Expectation, and Visionary Experience," *Traditio,* 41 (1985): 273–288;

Gordon Leff, *Heresy in the Later Middle Ages* (Manchester & New York: Manchester University Press, 1967);

Raoul Manselli, *Spirituali e Begghini in Provenza* (Rome: Istituto Storico Italiano per il Medio Evo, 1959);

Barbara Newman, *From Virile Woman to Woman Christ* (Philadelphia: University of Pennsylvania Press, 1995);

Marjorie Reeves, *The Influence of Prophecy in the Later Middle Ages: A Study of Joachimism* (Oxford: Clarendon Press, 1969).

Nicolas de Clamanges

(circa 1363 – 1437)

Nadia Margolis
Christine de Pizan Society

WORKS: *Ecloga* (1394)

Manuscripts: Paris, Bibliothèque Nationale de France, f. lat. 16403 (circa 1410), a collection of works by Jean Gerson and Clamanges, fols. 89–96.

Standard edition: "Un'egloga inedita di Nicolas de Clamanges," edited by Dario Cecchetti, in *Miscellanea di studi e ricerche sul Quattrocento francese,* edited by Franco Simone (Turin: Giappichelli, 1967), pp. 25–57.

Epistolae (1394–1424)

Manuscripts: The most important, complete texts of the 150 known letters are in Montpellier, Bibliothèque de la Faculté de Médecine, H 87 (post-1422); Troyes, Bibliothèque Municipale, 1497 (circa 1450) and 915; Orléans, Bibliothèque Municipale, 311. Other letters are in Paris, Bibliothèque Nationale de France, f. lat. 3127, Bibliothèque Nationale de France, f. lat. 3128 (dated 1448), Bibliothèque Nationale de France, f. lat. 13061, Bibliothèque Nationale de France, f. lat. 14920, Bibliothèque Nationale de France, f. lat. 16403 (circa 1410); and Reims, Bibliothèque Municipale, 628 (circa 1425–1429). The Montpellier, Bibliothèque de la Faculté de Médecine, H 87; Reims, Bibliothèque Municipale, 628; and Paris, Bibliothèque Nationale de France, f. lat. 16403 manuscripts were revised by Clamanges and are thus deemed superior.

First publication and standard edition: 137 letters in volume 2 of *Nicolai de Clemangiis Catalaunensis, Archidiaconi Baiocesis, Opera omnia quae partim ex antiquissimis Editionibus, partim ex MS. V. CL. Theodori Canteri, descripsit, Coniecturis Notisque,* edited by Johannes Lydius (Leiden: Printed by Louis Elzevier & Hendrick Laurenz for Johannes Balduinum, 1613).

Standard editions: "L'Epistolario di Nicolas de Clamanges," edited by Dario Cecchetti, thesis, University of Turin, 1959–1960; "Letter to Clement VII," edited by André Combes, in his *Jean de Montreuil et le chancelier Gerson* (Paris: J. Vrin, 1973), pp. 629–633; "Five Letters to Gontier Col," edited by Alfred Coville, in his *Recherches sur quelques écrivains du XIVe et du XVe siècle* (Paris: Droz, 1935), pp. 301–313; "Six Letters to Jean de Montreuil," edited by Coville, in his *Recherches sur quelques écrivains du XIVe et du XVe siècle* (Paris: Droz, 1935), pp. 287–301; "Seven Letters to Gérard Machet," in "Nicolas de Clamanges e Gérard Machet: Contributo allo studio dell'epistolario di Nicolas de Clamanges," edited by Cecchetti, in *Atti della Accademia delle scienze di Torino* (Turin: Giappichelli, 1965–1966), pp. 113–190; "Letters to Pierre d'Ailly," edited by Combes, in his "Sur les 'lettres de consolation' de Nicolas de Clamanges à Pierre d'Ailly," *Archives d'Histoire doctrinale et littéraire du Moyen Age,* 15–17 (1942): 359–389; "Letters on the Pietramala Affair," edited by Cecchetti, in his *Petrarca, Pietramala e Clamanges: Storia di una "querelle" inventata* (Paris: CEMI, 1982), pp. 129–201; *Quanquam majorum nostrorum,* edited by C. E. Du Boulay, in his *Historia universitatis Parisiensis,* volume 4 (Paris, 1668), pp. 687–696; "Two Letters to Simon de Bergères," edited by Coville, in his *Recherches sur quelques écrivains du XIVe et du XVe siècle* (Paris: Droz, 1935), pp. 314–317; "Complaint on Depredations of the Soldiery," in Jean Gerson's *Œuvres complètes,* volume 2, edited by Palémon Glorieux (Paris: Desclée, 1960), pp. 116–123; "Letter to Renaud des Fontaines" (1423), edited by Cecchetti, in his "Sulla fortuna di Petrarca in Francia: un testo dimenticato di Nicolas de Clamanges," *Studi francesi,* 32 (1967): 201–222.

De ruina et reparatione Ecclesiæ (circa 1401)

Manuscripts: Paris, Bibliothèque Nationale de France, f. lat. 3128 and 3625; Paris, Bibliothèque Mazarine, 1652 and 3884; Bibliothèque de l'Université de Paris, 633; Wolfenbüttel, Herzog August Bibliothek, 347 and 411.

First publication: In *Opera,* by Jean Gerson, volume 2 (Cologne: Johann Koelhoff, 1483–1484), pp. 174–187.

Standard edition: In *Le Traité de la ruine de l'Eglise de Nicolas de Clamanges et la traduction française de 1564,* edited by Alfred Coville (Paris: Droz, 1936), pp. 109–156.

Floridan et Elvide, or *Descriptio cuiusdam rei mirabilis que in Galliis accidisse ferebatur* (circa 1403–1410)

Manuscripts: The oldest known copy (circa 1410) is Paris, Bibliothèque Nationale de France, f. lat. 16403. The standard editions, published before this manuscript was discovered, use Paris, Bibliothèque Nationale de France, f. lat. 3128 (dated 1448) as their base. Others are Paris, Bibliothèque Nationale de France, f. lat. 3127 and 13061, and Bibliothèque de l'Université de Paris, 633.

First published: As "Historia de raptoris raptaeque virginis lametabili exitu," in *Supplementum patrum,* edited by Jacques Hommey (Paris: Pierre de Laulne, 1684).

Standard edition: In *Floridan et Elvide,* by Rasse de Brunhamel, edited by H. P. Clive (Oxford: Blackwell, 1959), pp. 1–29.

Edition in English: In "The Middle French nouvelle *Floridan et Elvide,*" translated by John Roscoe Finn, dissertation, University of Illinois, 1959.

Deploratio calamitatis ecclesiastice per scisma (circa 1408)

Manuscript: Montpellier, Bibliothèque de la Faculté de Médecine, H 87 (dated circa 1430), fols. 232v–233r; Reims, Bibliothèque Municipale, 628 (circa 1425–1429).

Descriptio et laus urbis Janue (1408)

Manuscripts: Montpellier, Bibliothèque de la Faculté de Médecine, H 87; Reims, Bibliothèque Municipale, 628 (circa 1425–1429) f. f. 233v–234v.

Standard edition: In *Recherches sur quelques écrivains du XIVe et du XVe siècle,* edited by Alfred Coville (Paris: Droz, 1935), pp. 254–259.

Orationes (1408–1417)

Manuscripts: Bayeux, Bibliothèque du Chapitre, 4, fols. 90v–95v; El Escorial, Real Biblioteca Monast., Q. III.6, fols. 106–112; Oxford, Hatton, 36, fols. 113v–119v; Paris, Bibliothèque Nationale de France, f. lat. 3129, fols. 288–291; Paris, Bibliothèque Nationale de France, f. lat. 3132A, fols. 91–95v.

Standard edition: "Les prières inédites de Nicolas de Clamanges," edited by Jean Leclercq, *Revue d'ascétique et de mystique,* 23 (1947): 171–183.

De filio prodigo, De fructu eremiti, De fructu rerum adversarum, De novis festivitatibus, De studio theologico, and *Contra prelatos simoniacos* (1408–1417)

Manuscripts: *De filio prodigo:* Paris, Bibliothèque Nationale de France, f. lat. 16403; Oxford, New College, 128. *De filio prodigio* and all others: Bibliothèque Nationale de France, f. lat. 3625, fols. 1–87; Paris, Bibliothèque de l'Université 633, fols. 93–158.

Standard edition: In *Nicolai de Clemangiis Catalaunensis, Archidiaconi Baiocesis, Opera omnia quae partim ex antiquissimis Editionibus, partim ex MS.V.CL.Theodori Canteri, descripsit, Coniecturis Notisque,* edited by Johannes Lydius (Leiden: Printed by Louis Elzevier & Hendrick Laurenz for Johannes Balduinum, 1613), pp. 109–125.

Ad Gerardum Macheti, ad sui visitationem incitatio (1409–1411?)

Manuscript: Montpellier, Bibliothèque de la Faculté de Médecine, H 87, fols. 194v–195v.

Standard edition: In *Recherches sur quelques écrivains du XIVe et du XVe siècle,* edited by Alfred Coville (Paris: Droz, 1935), pp. 272–273.

Disputatio habita super materia concilii generalis cum quodam scholastico Parisiensi (1409–1418)

Manuscripts: Bayeux, Bibliothèque du Chapitre 4; El Escorial, Real Biblioteca Monast. Q. III. 6; and Oxford, Hatton 36.

Standard edition: In volume 1 of *Nicolai de Clemangiis Catalaunensis, Archidiaconi Baiocesis, Opera omnia quae partim ex antiquissimis Editionibus, partim ex MS.V.CL.Theodori Canteri, descripsit, Coniecturis Notisque,* edited by Johannes Lydius (Leiden: Printed by Louis Elzevier & Hendrick Laurenz for Johannes Balduinum, 1613), pp. 65–80.

Deploratio elegiaca (1411)

Manuscript: Montpellier, Bibliothèque de la Faculté de Médecine, H 87, fol. 112.

Standard edition: In *Recherches sur quelques écrivains du XIVe et du XVe siècle,* edited by Alfred Coville (Paris: Droz, 1935), pp. 265–269.

De lapsu et reparatione iustitie (late 1419–early 1420)

Manuscript: Paris, Bibliothèque Nationale de France, f. lat. 3625.

Standard edition: In volume 1 of *Nicolai de Clemangiis Catalaunensis, Archidiaconi Baiocesis, Opera omnia quae partim ex antiquissimis Editionibus, partim ex MS. V. CL.Theodori Canteri, descripsit, Coniecturis Notisque,* edited by Johannes Lydius (Leiden: Printed by Louis Elzevier & Hendrick Laurenz for Johannes Balduinum, 1613), pp. 41ff.

Expositio super quadraginta septem capitula Isaie (1413–1426)

Manuscript: Paris, Bibliothèque de l'Arsenal, 137.

Standard edition: Excerpts in *Le Traité de la ruine de l'Eglise de Nicolas de Clamanges et la traduction française de 1564,* edited by Alfred Coville (Paris: Droz, 1936), pp. 91–106.

Descriptio vite rustice and *Descriptio vite tirannice* (before 1425)

> **Manuscripts:** Montpellier, Bibliothèque de la Faculté de Médecine, H 87, ff. 224–225v.; Reims, Bibliothèque Municipale, 628 (circa 1425–1429); Reims, Bibliothèque Municipale, 565, fols. 36r–36v.
>
> **First publication:** Paris: Anthoine Caillaut, 1490.
>
> **Standard edition:** In *Recherches sur quelques écrivains du XIVe et du XVe siècle,* edited by Alfred Coville (Paris: Droz, 1935), pp. 273–281.

Nicolas de Clamanges (also spelled Clémanges, Clemangis, or Clemangiis), in both his writings and his political career, promoted the study and imitation of classical Roman and Greek authors in their original form—bypassing the medieval commentators—as models for understanding and enriching both secular and Christian life. Because of such figures as Clamanges, scholars have come to realize that the cultural renewal known as the Renaissance flourished in France well before the sixteenth century, thus bringing the French into more favorable chronological proximity to the Italian-based humanist movement of the fourteenth century. While several of Clamanges's contemporaries may be judged equal or superior to him in certain areas—such as polemical effectiveness, textual criticism, and philology, or Latin literary style—none achieved his scope and eloquence in political tracts, devotional works and commentary, letters, and poetry. His long lifetime encompassed the political and spiritual upheaval wrought by the Great Schism, the Hundred Years' War, and the Armagnac-Burgundian civil war. Clamanges also played a major role in the passionate cultural competition between Italy and France, as he championed his country's claim to be the more legitimate heir to the learning and virtue of classical antiquity against no less than Petrarch and his disciples. Through his political and religious treatises, epistles, poetry, and discovery and transmission of manuscripts of important classical authors, Clamanges, like his fellow humanists, sought to remedy France's problems and lead his country into a golden age. He thus helped to forge its nascent national self-image into what it is today. However, as patriotic as he was, Clamanges never wrote in French, but in classical-style Latin (imitating the refined language of Cicero, Pliny the Younger or Clamanges's favorite, Seneca, as opposed to medieval-scholastic Latin), since this was a prerequisite to capturing the *clergie* (Old French for wisdom) of ancient Rome for the good of France.

He was born Nicolas Poilevilain in Clamanges, near Chalons-sur-Marne in Champagne, in about 1363. Having won a scholarship to the Collège de Navarre in Paris, he studied there from 1375 to 1381, taking his master's degree. One mentor was Pierre d'Ailly, who was later the royal chaplain and chancellor of the University of Paris; another teacher may have been the mathematician Nicolas Oresme. Among Clamanges's fellow students to achieve distinction were Jean Gerson, d'Ailly's successor at Paris, and the brilliant orator and successor to Gerson, Jean Courtecuisse. Clamanges's letters from these years also reveal formative intellectual friendships with such future powerful officials as Jean de Montreuil, Jean Muret, Gontier Col, Réginald des Fontaines, Gérard Machet, and, somewhat later, his student Jacques de Nouvion. The circle of humanists that had first convened at the Collège de Navarre maintained its unity for many years, thriving not only as the diplomatic-administrative brain trust of various courts within France but also as the national intellectual and literary avant-garde. This elite group revered Clamanges as its principal luminary because of his character, learning, and rhetorical talent. Although he never acquired more than a bachelor's degree in theology (1394), whereas Gerson, Courtecuisse, and others advanced to master's ranking in theology, Clamanges's lesser certification neither prevented him from teaching in the *Faculté des arts* (College of Arts and Letters) at the University of Paris from 1381 to 1394, since he already held a master of arts, nor hindered his active career as an ecclesiastical official. Although he became a priest, the date of his ordination is unknown.

The scholar Remigio Sabbadini has divided Clamanges's career into several phases, as dictated by his travels: first as a cleric in Paris, then as papal secretary at Avignon, followed by retreats to Langres and southern France, gradually moving through monasteries nearer to Paris, and finally back to Paris itself, at the "second Athens," the Collège de Navarre. During his first phase, as a cleric in Paris, Clamanges taught at the university alongside d'Ailly from 1381 to 1397. Already recognized for his excellence in *ars dictaminis* (official letter-writing), Clamanges composed epistles enunciating the university's stand on several pressing issues. Chief among these issues was the Great Schism of 1378–1417 that followed the French domination of the papacy known as the Babylonian Captivity (1309–1378). Because the Schism brought about the elections of as many as three rival popes, it sundered not only papal unity but also affected the moral atmosphere of both the church and the French public. For Clamanges and his contemporaries, the Schism loomed as more than an ecclesiastical-administrative problem; it shaped their entire careers. As traditional feudal-governmental structures crumbled along with a self-destructive nobility and church hierarchy, this rising class of lawyers from modest backgrounds—experts in using rhetoric as an instrument of power–gained enormous influence. The university strove to end the conflict with as little damage as possible to its interests, and those of France, through the so-called way of cession (*via cessionis*). They enunciated this plan in a letter cowritten by Clamanges, d'Ailly, and Gilles Deschamps to Charles VI, dated 6 June 1394 and known by its opening words, *Quanquam majorum nostrorum:* both popes should abdicate and their colleges should elect a new pope together. Furthermore, if either pope refused this mandate, he should be driven from office and executed as a heretic. They also lamented the "destroyed liberties" of the Gallican, or French-centered, church, as opposed to the Roman Catholic Church. Later in 1394 Clamanges also wrote on the university's behalf to the college of cardinals as well as to the newly elected Pope Benedict XIII; at least one of these missives was altered by Avignonese "correctors." Clamanges maintained a nuanced approach because of the complexity of the situation: though he first openly supported the university's position favoring cession, he later opposed it, deferring more to Benedict, the chief proponent of the Avignon claim to the papacy. He also wrote personally to Benedict deploring the schismatic Popes' desertion of their duty as "good shepherds" to the faithful. As of 1395 Clamanges–like d'Ailly, who had also shifted to an anticession position–had thus fallen from favor at the university and become deacon and canon of St. Cloud in the Parisian diocese. In November 1397 Clamanges's growing support of the Pope and the influential Avignonese cardinal Pietramala's admiration for his epistolary style culminated in his being named pontifical secretary, whereupon he moved to Avignon.

In these early years he produced works of literary as well as political controversy. Though more aesthetically oriented, his works of this type are as argumentative and as rooted in a sense of French cultural patrimony as his official letters. Just as the Schism involved a political rivalry between Avignon and Rome, so his epistolary exchanges with figures such as Cardinal Pietramala and friends and colleagues such as Montreuil, Col, d'Ailly, Jacques de Nouvion, and Gérard Machet fixed on another Franco-Italian contest: that informed by the concept of *translatio studii* (transmission of learning) from Greek and Roman antiquity. Earlier in that century, Petrarch had promulgated Italy's exclusive entitlement as heir to this glorious construct. Various French apologists rose to refute his position, later echoed by admirers (some of whom were French, such as Montreuil and Laurent de Premierfait), but no one could match the subtlety of Petrarch's style and arguments–until Clamanges. His role in the debate surfaces during 1394–1395, beginning with Cardinal Pietramala's letter to Clamanges, *Sepe alias* (2 December

1394), praising the latter's Latin and expressing surprise that a Frenchman could attain such a high degree of Ciceronian eloquence. Incensed at this slight to his countrymen, Clamanges answered within days with his epistles 4 and 5, since then esteemed as monuments of neo-Latin polemical style, the apotheosis of contemporary French culture. He also composed a series of letters to his friends–who, like Montreuil, would support him–continuing to defend and promote the excellence of French eloquence as worthy of that of Cicero and Quintilian. Pietramala eventually conceded the argument, to some extent, before his death in 1397. As with all important affairs, this debate elicited outwardly trivial developments reappearing in other controversies: for example, the use of the familiar second-person singular (*tu*) as a fraternal sign among these humanists even in their formal epistles as first espoused by Salutati. During the famous first debate on women, the quarrel of the *Roman de la Rose* (1401–1404), Christine de Pizan chastised Col when he addressed her in an insulting way, thereby necessitating a lengthy defense by Col of his use of *tu*. If, unlike his friends the Cols and Montreuil, Clamanges managed to stay out of the *Rose* debate–although he most probably, like d'Ailly, saw at least some of the epistles involved–he nonetheless had to answer attacks from more potent detractors concerning his *tutoiement* (use of the familiar *tu*) of the Pope in epistle 3. Entranced by its literary and ideological intensity, scholars have assessed and reassessed the reality of the Pietramala affair. Dario Cecchetti contends that much of it, particularly its anti-Petrarchist component, was reinvented by Clamanges decades later when editing his own letters; nevertheless, this exchange and its context remain a significant case in the history of ideas. Another, more heated, humanistic quarrel (1397–1400) involving Clamanges was ignited by Ambrogio dei Migli, a Milanese adventurer and would-be humanist who had befriended Col and Montreuil, the latter having helped Migli become secretary to the duke of Orléans. Once the Italian pronounced the Parisian humanists' noble Cicero inferior to Ovid (whom the humanists held to be clever but "degenerate"), the epistolary battle was on. It raged most dangerously on a personal level in that it threatened the longstanding bond between Col and Montreuil, since Col was torn between his new affection for the "godless" (in Montreuil's words) Migli and his older one for Montreuil and Cicero. In an effort to counterbalance Migli's pitting Col against Montreuil, Clamanges acted as intermediary spokesperson between them, as evidenced in his epistles 6 and 7. Though the participants never resolved the literary debate, they eventually patched things up personally; the details of this reconciliation remain conjectural.

Like his letters on the Schism, the tone and scope of his and other participants' letters in the Pietramala, the *Roman de la Rose* (tangentially), and Migli affairs reflect how seriously these philosophical and rhetorical controversies resounded at that time, as either patriotic or morally defining enterprises. Their epistolary style also reveals their indebtedness to Petrarch as a model whom Clamanges used, but whom he could never bring himself to acknowledge in the way he did Seneca: to name the first-century Roman enhanced his and France's link with a glorious civilization, whereas to invoke the Italian amounted to cultural treason. Clamanges practiced his anti-Petrarchism more tenaciously than did other pro-French humanists.

Clamanges's pre-Avignon writing is also marked by attempts to supplant Petrarch and other Italian humanists in Latin verse composition during this time, as is the work of his later career. His *Ecloga* (Eclogue, late 1394), inspired by his desire to compete with Petrarch's *Bucolicum carmen* (Rustic song), echoes passages and themes from the latter and alludes to the works of Virgil, Ovid, Horace, Terence, and others. As he did in the Pietramala affair, Clamanges modeled his effort here on Petrarch's example as the epitome of a vernacular author mastering a standard classical Latin genre. Clamanges's eclogue, an elegant 189-verse dialogue between two shepherds, Alexis and Philarus (whom some have equated with Clamanges and Montreuil), discusses more than sheep and nymphs. He deploys the motif of the good and bad shepherds and their flocks, enhanced by classical and biblical citations, to voice his ideas on the recurrent theme of the ruination of the Church—here in a more poetic mode than in his treatises and epistles on that subject. Ironically his Latin style, especially in poetry, is often inferior to Petrarch's and even to that of his "bilingual" (that is, writing in both French and Latin) compatriot, Gerson. An exception is the forty-hexameter poem, *Ad Gerardum Macheti, ad sui visitationem incitatio* (To Gérard Machet, to Entice His Visit, 1409–1411?) appended to one of the letters to his good friend and fellow humanist (epistle 116). Alfred Coville judged this as Clamanges's most delicate work in its balancing of pastoral setting, mythological allusions, and development of the classical theme of *visitatio amici* (visit of a friend) without ever lapsing into clichés.

The final dimension in Clamanges's rivalry with Italian humanists, the discovery and dissemination—through collecting and copying—of manuscripts of Latin authors, also blossomed during these years. Although the noted Italian humanist Poggio Bracciolini had been credited with first having found a complete manuscript of a set of Cicero's speeches in 1415, Gilbert Ouy discovered that the lacunae of the manuscript had been annotated in Clamanges's deliberately distinctive handwriting, thus making him, a Frenchman, the first to have collated this document (now Paris Bibliothèque Nationale de France f. lat. 14749, circa 1400) as well as one of the first philologists to have dealt with manuscripts of Virgil and Macrobius. Clamanges also copied Cicero's Verrine orations in Paris Bibliothèque Nationale de France f. lat. 7823. Both Italian and French humanists pursued and preserved these treasures not merely as random exotic collectibles for the learned but as a science in itself, defined in Gerson's manual *De laude scriptorum* (In praise of scribes, circa 1400?) and Clamanges's epistle 109, to accelerate *translatio studii,* for the benefit of the cultural heritage of their respective countries.

During Clamanges's second career phase, at Avignon, he nearly died in 1398 from the plague, which did in fact claim his uncle, a doctor in Chalons, the following year. He also received several benefices while remaining attached to the papal court until 1408: Benedict named him canon of Langres in 1398, treasurer of that chapter the following year, and then cantor of Bayeux in about 1403. During this period, Clamanges inveighed against and proposed remedies to the Schism in his treatise *De ruina et reparatione Ecclesiæ* (On the Ruin and Repair of the Church, 1401), which would be translated into French and transformed into pro-Protestant propaganda by 1564, and in the poetic exhortation to the Pope the *Deploratio calamitatis ecclesiastice per scisma* (Lamentation on the Church's Misfortunes Wrought by the Schism, circa 1408), comprising 129 verses in dactylic hexameter. Meanwhile, Charles VI, suffering bouts of insanity since 1392, succumbed to left-wing influence, and a royal ordinance of July 1398 announced his first "subtraction of obedience": France's refusal to pay taxes and recognize Benedict's authority in other functions. This rebellious mandate, criticized by Clamanges (in epistles 13 and 17), was overturned by proclamations of submission, then compromise, and another subtraction in 1407. When the Pope finally issued a bull in May 1407 excommunicating King Charles VI, Clamanges left Avignon, passed through Nice and Savona, and stopped at Genoa—then under French governance—where Benedict XIII was due to meet with the Roman Pope Gregory XII in December 1408. This situation inspired his ninety-eight-line dactylic-hexameter poem *Descriptio et laus urbis Janue* (Description and Praise of the City of Genoa, 1408) and epistles 132 and 135 to Renaut de Fontaine and Jacques de Nouvion, respectively. His poetic panegyric to Genoa glorifies that city's beauty and might as a great seaport, invoking various classical myths. The last third especially resembles a classical-rhetorical prayer to that city when, having recalled all of her qualities, he

Title page for the first edition of Nicolas de Clamanges's collected works, published in Leiden in 1613

then pleads for her to end the Schism by becoming the site of reconciliation between the two pontiffs, "Et tandem grex unus erit pastore sub uno" (And at last there will be one flock under one shepherd). At around this point, in 1408 he decided to take his leave of the court of Benedict XIII permanently.

His decision came none too soon, for upon his return to France from Italy in May 1408, Clamanges faced disgrace and even peril when he was accused of having written, as pontifical secretary, the 1407 decree excommunicating King Charles VI, which his enemies labeled an act of treason. He first tried to defend himself with several epistles addressed either directly to the university (epistle 42) or to various colleagues (epistles 43–56), carefully averring that, even when pontifical secretary, he was also a loyal French subject.

Clamanges spent the third phase of his career, 1408–1417, mostly in solitude and religious contemplation, first at Langres, then at the Carthusian monastery in Valprofonde, near Auxerre, and later the Augustinian monastery at Fontaine-au-Bois, near Provins, from 1409 to 1417. As his first type of literary escape from political chaos during this period, however, Clamanges experimented with genres beyond the Latin poems of his second phase. Most intriguing of all is the work first known as "Historia cuiusdam rei mirabilis" (Story of a Wonderous Event, circa 1403–1410), a tale that he claims to have based on an actual event about which he had heard in his travels from Langres to Avignon (epistle 112). The story takes place in France. The greedy father of the beautiful young Elvide wants to marry her to an older man because of his wealth, while the girl loves the young war hero Floridan, who loves her in return. To escape her father, who refuses to permit their marriage, the lovers elope. The fleeing couple stop for the night at an inn during a village festival. Thinking that Elvide is a prostitute, four peasant revelers storm into the inn to take her. Attempting to protect his beloved, Floridan is killed by the brigands, who then advance toward Elvide. She pleads with them to spare her virtue, and when they ignore her pleas, she kills herself. Clamanges elevates this story from simple exemplum to poignant, romantic tale, using the pleas of both imperilled lovers as a chance to insert oratorical eloquence. He also glosses in clerkly style the underlying humanistic questions of female virtue and justifiable suicide. In this commentary he justifies the suicides of both Elvide and her legendary counterpart Lucretia against ecclesiastical condemnation. Clamanges continues in this humanistic vein by praising Elvide over Lucretia because she killed herself before allowing the rape to corrupt her. This story became popular and resurfaced in several French and Italian versions over the next two centuries. Most notably in France, Rasse

de Brunhamel's version, entitled *Floridan et Elvide,* after Clamanges's two protagonists, formed a sequel to Antoine de La Sale's *Petit Jehan de Saintré* (Little John of Saintré, 1456), figuring later, in a more dramatic rendition, as number ninety-eight of the anonymous *Cent nouvelles nouvelles* (One Hundred New Novels, 1456–1461).

At Fontaine-au-Bois, Clamanges also wrote on conventional religious themes in *De filio prodigo* (On the Prodigal Son), *De fructu eremiti* (On the Fruits of the Reclusive Life), *De fructu rerum adversarum* (On the Fruits of Adversity), and probably also *De festivitatibus* (On New Religious Feasts), *De studio theologico* (On the Study of Theology), and *Contra prelatos simoniacos* (Against Simoniac Priests). Modern scholars have interpreted his professed renunciation of pagan classical authors in favor of Christian ones as a new development in his humanism rather than his abandonment of it. François Bérier has argued that Clamanges's ten prayers, the *Orationes* (1408–1417), are a humanistic reworking of a conventional penitential genre, here structured according to the seven canonical hours merged with the seven gifts of the Holy Spirit, to whom he addresses his prayers. Still retaining contact with affairs of church and state, Clamanges openly reacted to the councils of Pisa (1409) and Constance (1414–1418) in epistles 1, 71, and 79; in letters addressed to the Council Fathers (epistles 112, 113); and via his *Disputatio habita super materia concilii generalis cum quodam scholastico Parisiensi* (A Disputation Held on the Matter of the General Council with a Certain Parisian Scholastic, 1409–1418). By 1418 the English menace during the Hundred Years' War was a greater source of concern than even the Schism. Clamanges dared to communicate his concerns over the church and civil unrest in France to King Henry V of England in epistle 137 (1417–1418). After the Burgundian massacre of the Armagnacs in Paris in 1418, Clamanges learned of the tragic deaths of three of his humanist friends and associates, Montreuil, Col, and Premierfait. Persevering nevertheless, he lamented and proposed reform for the decline of justice due to the civil war in *De lapsu et reparatione iustitie* (On the Fall and Repair of Justice, 1419–1420), dedicated to Duke Philip the Good of Burgundy, ally of the English cause.

After returning to the Collège de Navarre in or around 1423, Clamanges turned his moral-didactic efforts toward prophecy in his lengthy commentary on the Book of Isaiah, *Expositio super quadraginta septem capitula Isaie* (Exposition on Forty-seven Chapters of Isaiah, 1423–1425), the Old Testament book that had served as the guiding visionary source for his later political works. Having maintained contact with the Pope while in seclusion, Clamanges aspired to rejoin the papal court, but this plan never bore fruit. He stayed in Paris through 1425, to resume theological studies with his former student and friend Pierre de Dierrey at the Collège de Navarre, where he died in 1437. A humanist to the end, Clamanges evokes his geographical and educational identities and aspirations by way of this epitaph in elegiac couplets miming Virgil's: "Belga fui, Catalaunus eram, Clemangius ortu. / Hic humus ossa tenet, spiritus astra petit." (I was a Belgian, I used to be a Catalan, a Clamangian by birth. / Here the earth holds my bones, my spirit seeks the stars.)

Nicolas de Clamanges successfully challenged Petrarch in all ways but one in his highly varied productivity and authorial personality: he lacked the confidence in his native language to attempt anything like Petrarch's *Canzoniere* (Songs, 1330–1374). It was this paradoxical refusal to recognize the cultural value of his own country's vernacular that diminished his direct influence for posterity. On the other hand because of his relentless efforts and personal example, his successors and even contemporaries felt encouraged to continue developing French language, literature, and character into a worthy culture all its own. While Col and others tried to imitate Clamanges's Latin style, his most interesting contemporary emulator in French was arguably Christine de Pizan, whose breadth of erudition and political concern in both lyric and prose genres and her later turn to devotional works have usually been attributed to the influence of Gerson, Petrarch, and others, neglecting the closer parallels her work has with that of Clamanges. In a larger sense, however, Clamanges's Gallic-humanistic spirit would find its true apotheosis in the works of such sixteenth-century humanists as François Rabelais, Marguerite de Navarre, and Michel de Montaigne.

Bibliography:

Sylvie Lefèvre, "Nicolas de Clamanges," in *Dictionnaire des lettres françaises: Le Moyen Age,* edited by G. Hasenohr and Michel Zink (Paris: Livre de Poche/Fayard, 1992), pp. 1063–1065.

Biographies:

Remigio Sabbadini, "Nicola de Clemangis," *Le Scoperte dei codici latini e greci ne' secoli XIV e XV: nuove ricerche* (Florence: Sansoni, 1914): 74–87.

Palémon Glorieux, "Notations biographiques sur Nicolas de Clémanges," in *Mélanges offerts à M. D. Chenu, maître en théologie* (Paris: J. Vrin, 1967), pp. 291–310.

References:

Pierre-Yves Badel, *Le Roman de la Rose au XIVe siècle: étude de la réception de l'œuvre* (Geneva: Droz, 1980);

Evencio Beltran, "L'Humanisme français au temps de Charles VII et Louis XI," in *Préludes à la Renais*

sance: Aspects de la vie intellectuelle en France au XVe siècle, edited by Carla Bozzolo and Ezio Ornato (Paris: CNRS, 1992), pp. 123–162;

François Bérier, "Note sur la datation, la tradition manuscrite et le contenu des dix oraisons de l'humaniste Nicolas de Clamanges," in *La Prière au Moyen-Age: Littérature et civilisation, Senefiance,* no. 10 (Aix-en-Provence: Centre universitaire d'études et de recherches médiévales d'Aix, 1981);

Bérier, "Remarques sur le *De lapsu et reparatione iustitiae* de Nicolas de Clamanges (vers 1360-1437) et sa traduction en français par François Juret (1553-1626)," in *Travaux de littérature offerts à Noémi Hepp,* Travaux de littérature, no. 3. (Boulogne: ADIREL, 1990), pp. 25–39;

Bérier, "Remarques sur l'évolution des idées politiques de Nicolas de Clamanges," in *Pratiques de la culture écrite en France au XVe siècle,* edited by Monique Ornato and Nicole Pons (Turnhout, Louvain-la-neuve: FIDEM, 1995), pp. 109–125;

Bérier, "Remarques sur l'*Expositio super quadraginta septem capitula Isaie* de Nicolas de Clamanges," in *L'Hostellerie de pensée: études sur l'art littéraire au Moyen Age offertes à Daniel Poirion,* edited by Michel Zink, Danielle Bohler, Eric Hicks, and Manuela Python (Paris: Presses de l'Université de Paris-Sorbonne, 1995), pp. 41–50;

Dario Cecchetti, "L'elogio delle arti liberali nel primo Umanesimo francese," *Studi francesi,* 28 (1966): 1–14;

Cecchetti, *L'Evoluzione del latino umanistico in Francia* (Paris: CEMI, 1986);

Cecchetti, *Il Primo Umanesimo Francese* (Torino: Albert Meynier, 1987);

Cecchetti, "'Sic me Cicero laudare docuerat': la retorica nel primo umanesimo francese," in *Préludes à la Renaissance: Aspects de la vie intellectuelle en France au XVe siècle,* edited by Carla Bozzolo and Ezio Ornato (Paris: CNRS, 1992);

Cecchetti, "Temi umanistici nell'opera di Jean de Montreuil," *Le Moyen français,* 8–9 (1981): 37–110;

Alfred Coville, *Gontier et Pierre Col et l'Humanisme en France au temps de Charles VI* (Paris: Droz, 1934);

Coville, *Recherches sur quelques écrivains du XIVe et du XVe siècle* (Paris: Droz, 1935);

Grover C. Furr III, "France vs. Italy: French Literary Nationalism in 'Petrarch's Last Controversy' and a Humanist Dispute of circa 1395," *Proceedings of the Patristics, Mediaeval and Renaissance Conference,* 4 (1979): 115–125;

Colette Jeudy, "La Bibliothèque cathédrale de Reims, témoin de l'humanisme en France au XVe siècle," in *Pratiques de la culture écrite en France au XVe siècle,* edited by Monique Ornato and Nicole Pons (Louvain-la-neuve: FIDEM, 1995), pp. 75–92;

Howard Kaminsky, *Simon de Cramaud and the Great Schism* (New Brunswick, N.J.: Rutgers University Press, 1983);

Nicholas Mann, "Humanisme et patriotisme en France au XVe siècle," *Cahiers de l'Association Internationale des études françaises,* 23 (May 1971): 51–66;

Ezio Ornato, "Les humanistes français à la redécouverte des classiques," in *Préludes à la Renaissance: Aspects de la vie intellectuelle en France au XVe siècle,* edited by Carla Bozzolo and Ezio Ornato (Paris: CNRS, 1992), pp. 1–46;

Ornato, *Jean Muret et ses amis Nicolas de Clamanges et Jean de Montreuil: étude des rapports entre les humanistes de Paris et ceux d'Avignon (1394–1420)* (Geneva & Paris: Droz, 1969);

Ornato, "La redécouverte des discours de Cicéron en Italie et en France à la fin du XIVe et au début du XVe siècle," in *Acta conventus Neo-Latini Bononiensis (1979),* edited by R. J. Schoeck (Binghamton, N.Y.: CEMERS, 1985), pp. 564–576;

Gilbert Ouy, "Le Collège de Navarre, berceau de l'humanisme français," in *Actes du 95e Congrès national des Sociétés Savantes (Reims, 1970),* volume 1 (Paris, 1973), pp. 275–299;

Ouy, "La Dialectique des rapports intellectuels franco-italiens et l'Humanisme en France aux XIVe et XVe siècles," in *Rapporti culturali ed economici fra Italia e Francia nei secoli dal XIV al XVI. Atti del Colloquio italo-francese (Roma 18–20 febbraio 1978),* (Rome: Giunta Centrale per gli Studi Storici, 1979), pp. 137–155;

Ouy, "In Search of the Earliest Traces of French Humanism: the Evidence from Codicology," *Library Chronicle, University of Pennsylvania,* 53 (Spring 1978): 3–38;

Ouy, "Nicolas de Clamanges (circa 1360–1437) philologue et calligraphe. Imitation d'Italie et réaction anti-italienne dans l'écriture d'un humanisme français du début du XVe siècle," in *Akten des Colloquium über Renaissance- und Humanistenhandschriften,* edited by J. Autenrieth (Munich: Oldenbourg, 1988), pp. 31–50;

Ouy, "Paris, l'un des principaux foyers de l'Humanisme en Europe au début du XVe siècle," *Bulletin de la Société de l'Histoire de Paris et de l'Iles-de-france: 1967–1968* (1970): 71–98;

Ouy, "Le Thème du 'tædium scriptorum gentilium' chez les humanistes, particulièrement en France au début du XVe siècle," *Cahiers de l'Association Internationale des Etudes Françaises,* 23 (May 1971): 9–26;

Franco Simone, *Il rinascimento francese* (Turin: Società d'edizione internazionale, 1961);

Simone, *The French Renaissance: Medieval Tradition and Italian Influence in Shaping the Renaissance in France,* translated and abridged by H. Gaston Hall (New York: Macmillan, 1969);

Lionello Sozzi, "La Nouvelle française au XVe siècle," *Cahiers de l'Association Internationale des études françaises,* 23 (May 1971): 67–84;

François Suard, "*Floridan et Elvide* aux XVe et XVIe siècles," in *La Nouvelle: définitions, transformations,* volume 1, edited by Bernard Alluin and François Suard (Lille: Presses Universitaires de Lille, 1990), pp. 163–179;

Georg Voigt, *Die Wiederbelebung des classischen Altertums, oder das erste Jahrhundert des Humanismus,* 2 volumes (Berlin: G. Reimer, 1882).

Marguerite Porete
(? – 31 May 1310)

Miren Lacassagne
Université de Paris, XVII

WORK: *Le Miroir des simples âmes anéanties et qui seulement demourent en vouloir et desir d'amour* (before 1306)

Manuscripts: A Latin version dating prior to 1310 is Vatican, Biblioteca Apostolica, Chigiano B IV 41. The text in Old French preserved in Chantilly, Musée Condé, Ms F XIV 26 was written at a later date.

First publication and standard edition: In *Il Movimento del Libero Spirito. Testi e Documenti,* edited by Romana Guarnieri, Archivio Italiano per la Storia della Pietà, IV no. 23 (Roma: Edizioni di Storia e Letteratura, 1965), pp. 513–635; republished in *Speculum simplicium animarum Margaretae Porete,* with a fourteenth-century Latin translation, edited by Paul Verdeyen, Corpus Christianorum Continuatio Medievalis no. 69 (Turnhout, Belgium: Brepols, 1986).

Editions in modern French: *Le Miroir des âmes simples et anéanties,* edited and translated by Max Huot de Longchamp (Paris: Albin Michel, 1984); *Le miroir des simples âmes anéanties et qui seulement demeurent en vouloir et desir d'amour,* edited by Emilie Zunn Brunn, translated by Claude Louis-Combet (Grenoble: Jérôme Millon, 1991).

Editions in English: *The Mirror of Simple Souls, by an Unknown French Mystic of the Thirteenth Century; Translated into English by M. N.: Now First Edited from the Mss.,* by Clara Kirchberger (London: Burns, Oates & Washbourne, 1927); *An Appendix to Margaret Porete, "The Mirror of Simple Souls." A Middle English Translation,* edited by M. Doiron (Roma: Edizioni di Storia e Letteratura, 1968); *A Mirror for Simple Souls: By a French Mystic of the Thirteenth Century,* edited, translated, and abridged by Charles Crawford (Dublin: Gill & Macmillan, 1981; New York: Crossroad, 1981); *The Mirror of Simple Souls,* translated, with an introduction, Ellen L. Babinsky (New York: Paulist Press, 1993).

Marguerite Porete, also referred to as Marguerite Poiret, Porret, or as Marguerite de Hainaut, is the author of what is now considered a major spiritual text of French literature. For a long time, however, she was no more than a name, and her book was unknown. Her importance was recognized in 1946 when Romana Guarnieri conclusively identified the book that caused all her misfortunes: *Le Miroir des simples âmes anéanties et qui seulement demourent en vouloir et desir d'amour* (The Mirror of Simple Annihilated Souls Who Only Live in Hope and Desire of Love, before 1306), an anonymous treatise of mysticism widely known in several English, Italian, and Latin versions, which had been discovered in 1867 by Francesco Töldi, who mistakenly attributed it to St. Marguerite of Hungary.

Marguerite Porete's own story is mingled with the fortune of her book. What is known about her is drawn from the records of the French Inquisition during the reign of King Philippe le Bel (1285–1314) and from the few indications scattered in the *Miroir*. Marguerite was a Beguine, a member of a community of pious women who had not taken religious vows. It is likely that she belonged to the beguinage of Valencienne, (founded in 1239), since her book was burned publicly in her presence in Valencienne between 1296 and 1306, during the episcopate of Gui de Colmieu, Bishop of Cambrai, who forbade circulation of the book under threat of excommunication. Marguerite continued to preach and to circulate her work, however, and this activity led to her persecution, first by Philippe de Marigny, Colmieu's successor, then by the Inquisitor of Haute Lorraine. Her subsequent imprisonment in Paris lasted a year and a half. During this period she refused to appear before an ecclesiastical court, to swear the truth to the Inquisitor, or to recant when faced with the threat of being burned alive at the stake. The book was tried a second time in 1310 by the Inquisitor Guillaume de Paris in the presence of twenty-one theologians from the Sorbonne (half of whom had sat at the trial of the Knights Templars). Marguerite's case was treated together with that of Guiard de Cressonessart, a *beghard* (male Beguine) who had expressed his support for her and was suspected of heresy. Guiard recanted, however, after hearing his death sentence, and Marguerite alone was condemned as a heretic and a backslider and was executed 31 May 1310 on the Place de Grève. The editor of the *Grandes Chroniques de France* (Great Chronicles of France) designating her as a "béguine clergesse" (a cleric Beguine), witnessed that her courage aroused great emotion among the large crowd attending the public punishment.

Marguerite's refusal to bow before the ecclesiastical hierarchy and power reflects a personal commitment, but it also partakes of the spiritual and historical context in which she lived.

Her mystical conception of the church is evident in the *Miroir,* where she expresses a clear distinction between "Sainte Eglise la Petite" (The Little Holy Church) designating individuals holding religious authority, and "Sainte Eglise la Grande" (The Great Holy Church), an elite of souls called to a life of contemplation, as were the members of the Beguine community to which she belonged. The devotion of these women presented a threat to Christian orthodoxy, which feared the spread of mystical practices. In modern Christian terminology, religious mysticism implies the direct and passive experience of the presence of God. A Christian establishes his relation to the divinity without intermediaries, thus ignoring the mediation established by the structures of the worldly church. The term "mystic," however, was used from the time of the Church Fathers to refer to the mysteries of faith and of the Church, such as the sacraments. The High Middle Ages did not exclude the modern definition, but what is called mystic today was then called contemplation.

It remains difficult to draw a historical picture of medieval mysticism. An interest in mysticism spread from the cloisters in the wake of the reforms of St. Bernard of Clairvaux and became common in devout communities for whom the intimate affective union with Jesus introduces the soul to the spiritual union with its divinity. This mysticism of intimacy with the incarnated Word is contemporary, however, with the development of a new theology that, under the influence of the Greco-Arab philosophy, exalts divine transcendence so much that it threatens to lead all religious thought to fideism, a reliance on faith, rather than on reason, in determining questions of ultimate truth. This fideism confronted the Christians with the option of a divided interior life: on the one side, intelligence asserting that God is and will ever be unknowable; on the other, faith in the promises of the Gospel. Devotion took the form of a more affective piety. The clergy had to face the personal inner conflict of the best and most gifted of its members. When men trained in the established scholarly systems could not cope with the challenge of thinking of faith in new terms, women dared to develop an

original alternative, which corresponded more to experience and was corroborated by the Scripture.

The intellectual emergence of these women derives from the extraordinary cultural development of Western bourgeoisie after the rise of the new and powerful towns. The aristocracy kept its rural lifestyle while the bourgeoisie of the towns controlled international exchange and the promotion of art and education. The daughters of the urban bourgeoisie were received in the old monasteries on an equal basis with the daughters of the aristocracy, although they were better educated. This social change accounts for the creation of new foundations, first in Cîteaux (the Cistercians), then in the mendicant orders, which attracted a large number of followers who intended to join in their spirituality while living the evangelical life in the world. Contemplative women such as Hildegard of Bingen or Claire of Assis took up the spiritual management of all matters concerning the life of prayers. Their criticism of clergy, hierarchy, and papacy did not tarnish their authority and influence; nevertheless, just as St. Catherine of Sienna had to prove her orthodoxy to the general chapter of the Dominicans of Florence, Beguines like Marguerite Porete sometimes faced lethal accusations.

According to the Cistercian monk Gilles d'Orval, these women were called Beguines after their first defender, the priest Lambert li Bègue from Liège, who died in 1177; a more recent conjecture is that the term is derived from the hypothetical old-Dutch stem *begg,* to mumble prayers. Although the Cistercians seemed to hold these devout women (many of whom were their benefactors) in great veneration, most members of the clergy and of the religious orders accused them of pantheist heresy and of despising the sacraments; however, the real reason for persecuting these women was related to influence and spiritual domination: they represented a threat to the authority of the orthodoxy.

The historical background of Marguerite's persecution is thus marked by quarrels over spiritual and temporal questions. There is an obvious contradiction between the judgment of the *Miroir* by the theologians representing the University of Paris and the approval she obtained from three highly competent clerics before the first condemnation of the book: according to the prologue to the late fourteenth-century Middle English translation, one was a Franciscan named Jean de Querayn; the second, a Cistercian monk called Franc, from the abbey of Villers in Brabant; while the third was a prominent theologian from Flanders, Godefroi de Fontaines, a renowned scholar and former regent of the University of Paris. The assortment could not be more appropriate nor more complete, since all three belonged to different scholarly traditions: the first to the monastic, the second to more advanced and modern trends,

A thirteenth-century beguinage in Bruges, Belgium, similar to the one in which Marguerite Porete lived

and the third to the university and the secular clergy. Their attestations display the existing divisions on the subject of mysticism, as the views of these three men were not unanimous. While the Cistercian expressed no reservation, Godefroi and the Franciscan praised the subtlety of the author, but they feared the broad diffusion of a work that was meant for a spiritual elite and that could dangerously undermine traditional ecclasiastic authority.

After Marguerite's death, the doctrine of the *Miroir* was condemned again by the Council of Vienna (1311–1312) along with the works of the Rheno-Flemish mystics, particularly those of Meister Eckhart. The book was seen as the breviary of a vast current of thought in which some *beghards* and Beguines were involved: the Free Spirit movement, which spread at the end of the thirteenth century and during the fourteenth century in the north of France, in Belgium, the Netherlands, Rhenany, Silesia, south Germany, and in central

and northern Italy, reaching all of the German-speaking countries by the end of the fifteenth century. Although its manifestations were occasional and the number of its followers always limited, scholars are inclined to consider the *Miroir* as its book of initiation and popularization, the most coherent expression of its doctrine.

The records of prosecutions give evidence of the influence of the work, and its popularity throughout all of Europe is attested by various translations. There is no evidence as to the original language in which the book was written. It is likely that Marguerite composed it in the Old French vernacular, as did the other Beguines who narrated their personal experiences. The original has probably been lost, as have all the copies circulating during her lifetime. A Latin translation was made before 1310, perhaps originally for the Inquisition. Several other texts are recorded: two Italian versions in the late fourteenth and early fifteenth centuries; then, in the second half of the fourteenth century, a

Middle English translation was made by the bishop of London, Michael of Northbrook, which was in turn translated into Latin by Richard Methley. A German text probably existed, but it has left no trace.

Campaigns organized in Italy by influential preachers from Venice and Padua led to another condemnation of the *Miroir* by the Council of Basel in 1439. Thereafter, despite the hostile attitude of the Church hierarchy and its constant opposition, the *Miroir* remained in favor in some Italian monasteries, such as Subiaco, where the manuscript now in the Vatican Library was completed in 1521. This persistence testifies to the success of the Free Spirit doctrine in Italy. Its audience in France and England is difficult to determine, but it must have been wider than the single surviving late vernacular manuscript seems to indicate. In France, Jean Gerson praised the subtlety of the author but warned the unprepared reader against it.

Marguerite's doctrine is informed by the spirituality of the Greek Fathers and especially by the teachings of the Pseudo-Denys, which she might have known through Guillaume de Saint-Thierry: there are many points of convergence between his *Lettre aux frères du Mont-Dieu* (Letter to the Brothers of Mont-Dieu, 1444–1445) and her *Miroir*. She also read St. Bonaventure and St. Augustine. She has many themes and expressions in common with the Flemish Beguines, and particularly Beatrice de Nazareth. Therefore, it is within the frame of orthodox mysticism that the *Miroir* must be considered.

The symbolism of the *miroir* (mirror) is based on the principle of analogy, which seeks to pass from what is visible to what is invisible, from what is known to what is unknown. The *miroir* thus evokes the manifestation of transcendence into immanence. This function takes different aspects and is represented with a remarkable continuity within the philosophical and theological traditions. Scholasticism used the topos of the flawlessness of the *miroir,* referring to the fact that God is unattainable. In the *Miroir des simples âmes anéanties,* the *miroir* is an ascetic and mystical means to show a suprarational truth that, once it is perceived, will make the soul simple. Thus the central theme is the emancipation of the soul.

The book begins with a table of contents noting 139 chapters or divisions, which is directly followed by a 4-stanza poem that warns theologians and clerics not to apply their reason uselessly in reading the book, for love and faith are the only keys to understanding it.

The prologue introduces the subject matter by means of a literary topos, that of *l'amor de lonh* (distant love), a topos that originated in Occitan poetry and then became common in Old French poetry as well. The tone is thus set for a comparison of worldly and divine love, and the book is a dialogue in rhymed prose, using courtly terminology, between allegorical characters: *Ame* (Soul) and *Dame Amour* (Lady Love), surrounded by *Courtoisie* (Courtesy) and *Entendement d'Amour* (Understanding of Love), and confronted by *Raison* (Reason), *Entendement de Raison* (Understanding of Reason) and the *Vertus* (Virtues). The *Miroir* was intended to be read aloud and lyricism pervades from the beginning to the end, and formal parallels have been drawn with Mechtild of Magdebourg's *Das Fliessende Licht der Gottheit* (The Flowing Light of the Divinity, circa 1250–1282). The dialogic form confers spontaneity and warmth on the most abstract and scholarly formulations which are woven into a discourse soliciting as much affect as intelligence. Courtly characters shift from the literary to the spiritual scene, as *Dame Amour,* representing God, is substituted for the worldly *Fine Amour* (courtly love):

> Love: I am God, because Love is God and God is Love, and this Soul is God by the condition of Love; I am God by divine nature, and this soul is [God] by the justice of love, and so my precious friend is taught and guided by me without herself, because she is transformed into me.

Dame Amour is henceforth totally passive under the guidance of the divine will that operates in her. The Soul and Love try to explain these truths to Reason. She is shocked by such paradoxes and dies theatrically while a higher understanding of God prevails, and the Soul, representing the traditional courtly knight, dismisses the Virtues to elevate herself higher in the supreme freedom of Love.

Peter Dronke has underlined the originality of this treatise of speculative mysticism which narrates in her own terms Marguerite's personal experience: the emancipation of the soul. The *Miroir* describes it as a seven-stage process by which the soul rises from the valley of humility up to the peak of the mountain of contemplation.

The first degrees of purification are classical. The soul observes the commandments (first stage), then the advices (second stage), and it forces itself to obedience (third stage). Therefore, it reaches contemplation, exaltation, and spiritual rapture (fourth stage). Blinded by the great light of Love, the soul believes itself to be at the summit of life in union, when it is still in the state of the *marris,* a term that designates those involved in a self-centered quest for virtues. From the fifth degree onward, the soul reaches a state of perfect identity of its will with that of God: in a sudden illumination by the Holy Spirit, the soul sees itself as nothing, forming a single being with sin. It is thus pushed to carry its will in God to unite the former with divine will, which is the state of freedom. At the sixth stage, the soul is absorbed, ontologically annihilated within the "deity." The soul has thus reached a stage of perfect freedom and peace. It is flawless and indifferent even to its own salvation. This produces insights of the beatitude reserved for those who enter Paradise. To summarize, the main idea of the *Miroir* is clearly expressed in the title of chapter twelve: "Ce livre dit que l'Ame adnientie n'a point de voulenté" (This book says that the annihilated soul has no will). The soul united with God is annihilated in love to the point of losing all proper being: personal will ceases to exist and disappears before the will of the Beloved. Its nature is no longer human, but completely divine.

Marguerite felt the necessity to deliver her personal spiritual experience as a didactic testimony to the quest of human Soul. Emily Zum Brunn writes that an autobiographical extract of the *Miroir* explains the contradiction existing in all mystical authors, between the impossibility of speaking of God and the fact of writing abundantly on the subject. For Marguerite the composition of her book was a necessity anterior to liberation:

> Indeed I am convinced it must be done before one comes to the state of freedom. However, the Soul who wrote this book says, I was so foolish at the time I did it, or rather at the time Love did it for me according to my request, that I granted a great price to something that could neither be done, nor thought, nor said: as if one wished to keep the sea confined into one's eye, to carry the world at the end of a reed, or to illuminate the sun with a lantern or a torch. Yes, I was more foolish than he who wanted to do that when I granted price to what cannot be said, and burdened myself with these words I had to write. But in this manner I went my way, and that was for my rescue, to reach the highest grade of the state we talk about, which is perfected when the Soul remains in pure nothingness and thoughtless, and not before.

Marguerite Porete's book is a major work of French spiritual literature. The many reproductions and varied translations of the text, despite the condemnation of the church, attest to its importance and to the scope of its influence. The *Miroir des simples âmes* must not, however, be viewed only as a treatise on mysticism. It appeals to secular readers for a treatment of love that resumes the aesthetical elements of courtly literature, and records the emergence of a feminine medieval voice.

Bibliography:

F. Vieillard and J. Monfrin, *Manuel bibliographique de la littérature française du Moyen Age de Robert Bossuat,* third supplement, 2 volumes (Paris: Editions du CNRS , 1986 , 1991), II: nos. 7821–7826.

References:

J. Dagens, "Le 'Miroir des simples âmes' et Marguerite de Navarre," *Revue de l'histoire des religions,* 88 (1969): 35–60;

Peter Dronke, *Women Writers of the Middle Ages. A Critical Study of Texts from Perpetua (203) to Marguerite Porete (1310)* (Cambridge: Cambridge University Press, 1984);

Georges Duby and Michelle Perrot, eds., *Histoire des femmes en Occident. Le Moyen Age* (Paris: Plon, 1990);

G. Epiney-Burgard and Emily Zum Brunn, "Marguerite Porete," in their *Femmes troubadours de Dieu* (Turnhout, Belgium: Brepols, 1988), pp. 174–213;

Amy Hollywood, *The Soul as Virgin Wife : Mechthild of Magdeburg, Marguerite Porete, and Meister Eckhart* Studies in Spirituality and Theology no. 1 (Notre Dame & London: University of Notre Dame Press, 1995);

Bernard McGinn, ed., *Meister Eckhart and the Beguine Mystics: Hadewijch of Brabant, Mechthild of Magdeburg, and Marguerite Porete* (New York: Continuum, 1994);

Catherine M. Müller, *Marguerite Porete et Marguerite d'Oingt de l'autre côté du miroir,* Currents in Comparative Romance Languages and Literatures no. 72 (New York: Peter Lang, 1999);

J. Orcibal, "Le 'Miroir des simples âmes' et la 'secte' du Libre Esprit," in *Revue de l'histoire des religions,* 88 (1969): 35–60;

K. Ruh, "Beginnenmystik. Hadewijch, Mechthild von Magdeburg, Marguerite Porete," *Zeitschrift für deutsches Altertum und deutsche Literatur,* 106 (1977): 268;

P. Skarup, "La Langue du miroir des simples âmes," in *Studia Neophilologica,* 60 (1988): 231–236;

Paul Verdeyen, "Le Procès d'inquisition contre Marguerite Porete,'" in *Revue d'histoire ecclésiastique,* 81 (1986): 47–94.

Rashi

(circa 1040 – 1105)

Sheila J. Rabin
St. Peter's College

WORKS: *Commentaries on the Bible*

Manuscripts: There are several manuscripts of commentaries on various books of the Bible, over 200 on the Torah portion alone. The best version of the Torah commentary is Oxford, Bodleian Library, 2440. No one has yet tried to collate the manuscripts of all the commentaries.

First publication: *Perush 'al ha-Torah,* Reggio di Calabria, Italy: Abraham bar Yitzhaq ben-Garton, 1475; facsimile edition (Jerusalem: Makor, 1969).

Standard editions: *RaSHI 'al ha-Torah,* edited by Abraham Berliner (Frankfurt-am-Main: Kauffmann, 1905; revised edition, edited by Hayyim Dov Chavel, Jerusalem: Ne'emanah, 1961 or 1962; republished, Jerusalem & New York: Feldheim, 1969); *Perushe i Rashi 'al ha-Torah,* edited by Chavel (Jerusalem: Mossad ha-rav Kuk, 1982); commentaries on the minor prophets, Isaiah, and Psalms in *Parshan-data: ve-hu perush Rashi 'al nevi'im u-ketuvim, 'al pi defusim ve-kitve yad shonim im mavo, he'arot u-haghot,* 3 volumes, edited by Isaiah Maarsen (Amsterdam: Menno Hertzberger, 1930; Jerusalem: Merkaz, 1933, 1936).

Standard edition and edition in English: *Perush Rashi 'al ha-Torah: The Torah with Rashi's Commentary. The Sapirstein Edition,* edited by Yisrael Isser Zvi Herczeg, Yakov Petroff, and Yoseph Kameneysky (Brooklyn: Mesorah Publications, 1994–); in *The Megilloth and Rashi's Commentaries with Linear Translation: Esther, Song of Songs, Ruth,* translated by Avraham Schwartz and Yisroel Schwartz (New York: Hebrew Linear Classics, 1983).

Commentaries on the Talmud

Manuscripts: There are almost 300 extant manuscripts of various tractates. Commentaries of complete tractates without variant readings are present in the following manuscripts: Cambridge, University Library, Add. 478.8 (Bava Kamma) and 494 (Rosh ha-Shanah); Madrid, Real Biblioteca del Monasterio de San Lorenzo, G-II-4 (Yoma and Sukkah) Hamburg, Staatsbibliothek, Cod. Heb. 228 (Rosh ha-Shanah); Innsbruck, Üniversitätsbibliothek, Cod. 291 (Niddah); Jerusalem, Jewish National and University Library, 4013 (Zevahim, Me'ilah, Temurah); Leipzig, Üniversitätsbibliothek, Nr. 1105 (Pesahim); London, British Library Or. 5975 (Berakhot), ms. Harley 5585, ms. Add. 27,196 (Bava Kamma), and ms. Add. 27,196 (Bava Mezia); Moscow, Lenin State Library, 594 (Yevamot); Munich, Bayerische Staatsbibliothek, Cod. Hebr. 216 (Eruvin, Megillah, and Hagigah); New York, Jewish Theological Seminary, Rab. 718 (Shabbat), Rab. 840 (Rosh ha-Shanah, Bezah, Hagigah), Rab. 832 (Sukkah), Rab. 841 (Bezah); Oxford, Bodleian Library, Opp. Add. 4023 (Bezah), Opp. 97 (Yevamot), and Lyell Empt. 62 (Shevu'ot); Paris, Bibliothèque Nationale de France, Heb. 324 (Shabbat and Eruvin), and Heb. 325 (Zevahim); Parma, Biblioteca Palatina, 2589 (Berakhot), 2087 (Shabbat), 2244 (Rosh ha-Shanah, Bezah, and Hagigah), 2903 (Yoma, Bezah, Kiddushin, and Shevu'ot), 3155 (Makkot and Avodah Zara), 3151 (Shevu'ot), and 2756 (Hullin); Vatican, Biblioteca Apostolica, Ebr. 138 (Shabbat), Ebr. 135 (Gittin), Ebr. 158 (Kiddushin), Ebr. 157 (Bava Kamma), Ebr. 131 (Bava Mezia), Ebr. 140 (Shevu'ot), and Ebr. 139 (Hullin).

First publication: *Talmud Bavli,* 30 volumes (Venice: Daniel Bomberg, 1520–1526).

Standard edition: *Rashi le-mikra be-perusho le-Talmud,* three volumes, edited by Yoel Florsheim (Jerusalem: Reuven Maas, 1981–1989).

Responsa

Manuscripts: There are no separate manuscripts of Rashi's responsa, although 350 of Rashi's letters can be found in the twenty-nine extant manuscripts of *Teshuvot hakhmei Tsarfat ve-Lothir* (Responsa of the sages of France and Lorraine). The most important manuscripts are in the Jewish Theological Seminary of New York, one in the Adler Collection and ms. 443.

Standard edition: *Teshuvot Rashi,* edited by Israel Elfenbein (New York: Shulsinger, 1943; republished, Jerusalem: Yahadut, 1980).

Rabbi Shlomo Yitshaki (in English, Solomon ben Isaac) is known, following the customary way of referring to great medieval Jewish scholars, as Rashi, the Hebrew acronym for his name. He wrote what continue to be the most important and extensive commentaries in Hebrew on the Hebrew Bible and the Babylonian Talmud. The Bible commentaries have been a major part of biblical studies among Jews, and more than two hundred commentaries were written on his Torah commentaries, some by famous Jewish scholars in their own right. Rashi's Torah commentaries were also used by important Christian medieval Bible scholars, such as Hugh of St. Victor, Andrew of St. Victor, Peter Comestor, Roger Bacon, and Nicolas de Lyra.

Little is known of Rashi's early life. Most scholars accept 1040 as the year of his birth, although some maintain that no one could have accomplished all that he did in only sixty-five years, and these follow a tradition—that arose much later—that he was born in 1030, the year Rabbenu Gershom, the influential talmudist from Mainz whose disciples were Rashi's teachers, died.

Rashi was born and lived most of his life in the capital of the county of Champagne, Troyes, a major commercial center on the main trade route between Italy and the North Sea. Twice a year trade fairs were held in Troyes (which is close to the Rhineland), fairs that attracted merchants from all over the Holy Roman Empire and from England and Italy as well. The Jews of Troyes were primarily merchants, and many owned land. At this time, they were protected by the counts of Champagne, and there was little persecution by their Christian neighbors. Rashi was a vintner (a rabbi was an unpaid position), and he used his knowledge about worldly affairs in his commentaries. He was familiar with different standards of currency, banking, and commerce; he knew about agriculture and animal husbandry; he was also conversant with such trades as soldering, engraving, weaving, embroidery, and even laundering.

Little is known about Rashi's father Isaac. There is one reference to him that indicates he was a martyr; however, there is no mention of how he was martyred, and it seems unlikely that Rashi would have written so little about him had he died a martyr. Rashi does mention in a Talmud commentary having been taught by his father, so presumably he was a learned man. On his mother's side, Rashi's uncle was Rabbi Simeon ben Isaac the Elder, an author of liturgical poetry. Rashi married at about seventeen or eighteen and had three

daughters, two of whom married disciples of his: Miriam married Judah ben Nathan, and Jochebed married Meir ben Samuel. Two of Jochebed's sons, Samuel (Rashbam) and Jacob (Rabbenu Tam) became important scholars in their own right and may have helped disseminate Rashi's Bible commentaries among Christian scholars, as Rashbam knew Latin and Rabbenu Tam frequented the court of Champagne.

Before Rashi became the leading Jewish scholar of medieval Europe, Jewish scholarship had its greatest schools in the Rhineland where they focused exclusively on the Bible and Talmud, without the intense concentration on philosophy and secular poetry that was characteristic of Jewish scholarship in Islamic areas, such as Spain. Rashi's earliest education was in Worms, where he studied with Isaac Halevi. A small chapel in that city has been venerated as Rashi's Chapel, the place where he studied, but it was actually built many years after his death. Destroyed by the Nazis in World War II, it was later rebuilt. Although Worms was a recognized center of biblical and talmudic studies, it paled beside Mainz, so Rashi went there for further studies at about the time he was married. In Mainz he was the student of Jacob ben Yakar and Isaac ben Judah, disciples of Rabbi Gershom of Mainz, who founded the noted talmudic academy there. Rabbi Gershom was the greatest northern European rabbinic leader before Rashi. His rulings—the most famous are those prohibiting polygamy and requiring the woman as well as the man to agree to a divorce—were accepted as binding on all European Jews, and his text of the Bible was considered accurate to the last detail of the Masorah, the traditional body of notes on the Hebrew Bible accepted by all Jews. Perhaps most importantly, he compiled a manuscript of the Talmud that was accepted as authentic by northern European Jews and that was the text used by Rashi in his commentaries.

In about 1070 Rashi returned to Troyes where he spent the rest of his life. In Troyes he set up his own school for biblical and talmudic studies, and because of his fame, the schools of Champagne and northern France eventually supplanted those of the Rhineland. While teaching, Rashi also wrote his commentaries, which may have developed out of the explanations he had to make for his students. As he worked simultaneously on his commentaries on the Bible and the Talmud, editing them continuously, it is impossible to date them precisely.

Rashi's main goal in both commentaries was to give the literal meaning of the text—in Hebrew, *peshat.* He used various means to explain difficult words and phrases. One was to simply give a more common Hebrew expression. For example, in Genesis 3:13 where Eve blames the snake, she uses the word *hishi'ani*

Twelfth-century French Jews depicted in scenes from the life of St. Anne (Paris, Notre Dame Cathedral)

(he beguiled me), which is very rare; as a substitute, Rashi suggests the better known word *hiti'ani* (he led me astray). He used the second-century Aramaic translation by Onkelus—the *Targum*—to help him with difficult words. His knowledge of commerce and various trades gave him the ability to explain in depth such aspects of the text as the description of the building of the tabernacle in Exodus. He even drew diagrams to illustrate shapes or details, but these were dropped from the printed editions of his works and were subsequently lost. His commentaries at times not only give plausible—albeit not necessarily correct—explanations of strange concepts in the Bible or Talmud but also shed light on contemporary practices. For example, in the tractate *Ketubot* (Marriage Contracts), while discussing the right of a woman to divorce a man whose profession was to collect dog excrement, his knowledge of contemporary methods of laundering leads him to remark that he had observed the practice in German lands of soaking clothes for a day or two in dog droppings, although he adds that he does not know why the Germans do so. He also translated words into the vernacular—what Rashi called *la'azim,* an acronym for *lashon am zar,* language of the foreign people. He gave about one thousand such words in the Bible commentaries and two thousand in the Talmud commentaries. These expressions give modern researchers clues to difficult

words in Old French and their pronunciation, since the French word is transcribed into the phonetic Hebrew letters. He understood how the accent marks that indicate the cantillation of a biblical text are a clue to its correct reading and therefore its correct meaning. For example, he notes that the accent on the first syllable of *ba'ah* in Genesis 29:6 indicates that Rachel was in the process of coming to the well, whereas three sentences lower, the accent on the second syllable indicates the past tense of the same word. Without openly questioning the accuracy of the biblical text, he would suggest a different word order so that it made better sense. For example, in Genesis 41:57 a literal reading of the text is "all the countries came into Egypt to buy corn to Joseph." Rashi suggests that it should be understood to read "they came to Joseph to buy corn." Since there was no canonical version of the Talmud, he could more easily suggest such rewritings, and he made important corrections to the text that have been accepted and introduced into all standard editions.

Rashi's commentaries on the Bible were written in the order in which the books appear in the Hebrew canon. Apparently he died before he could complete the task. He did not write a commentary on Chronicles, the last two books, and some scholars question whether the commentaries on Job from 40:25, Ezra, and Nehemiah are entirely his. The literal interpretations in

במדבר

וַיְדַבֵּר יְדֹוָד אֶל־מֹשֶׁה
בְּמִדְבַּר סִינַי בְּאֹהֶל
מוֹעֵד בְּאֶחָד לַחֹדֶשׁ
הַשֵּׁנִי בַּשָּׁנָה הַשֵּׁנִית
לְצֵאתָם מֵאֶרֶץ מִצְרַיִם לֵאמֹר׃
שְׂאוּ אֶת־רֹאשׁ כָּל־עֲדַת בְּנֵי
יִשְׂרָאֵל לְמִשְׁפְּחֹתָם לְבֵית
אֲבֹתָם בְּמִסְפַּר שֵׁמוֹת כָּל־זָכָר
לְגֻלְגְּלֹתָם׃ מִבֶּן עֶשְׂרִים שָׁנָה
וָמַעְלָה כָּל־יֹצֵא צָבָא בְּיִשְׂרָאֵל
תִּפְקְדוּ אֹתָם לְצִבְאֹתָם אַתָּה
וְאַהֲרֹן׃ וְאִתְּכֶם יִהְיוּ אִישׁ אִישׁ
לַמַּטֶּה אִישׁ רֹאשׁ לְבֵית־אֲבֹתָיו
הוּא׃ וְאֵלֶּה שְׁמוֹת הָאֲנָשִׁים אֲשֶׁר
יַעַמְדוּ אִתְּכֶם לִרְאוּבֵן אֱלִיצוּר
בֶּן־שְׁדֵיאוּר׃ לְשִׁמְעוֹן שְׁלֻמִיאֵל
בֶּן־צוּרִישַׁדָּי׃ לִיהוּדָה נַחְשׁוֹן
בֶּן־עַמִּינָדָב׃ לְיִשָּׂשכָר נְתַנְאֵל
בֶּן־צוּעָר׃ לִזְבוּלֻן אֱלִיאָב בֶּן־חֵלֹן׃
לִבְנֵי יוֹסֵף לְאֶפְרַיִם אֱלִישָׁמָע
בֶּן־עַמִּיהוּד לִמְנַשֶּׁה גַּמְלִיאֵל בֶּן־
פְּדָהצוּר׃ לְבִנְיָמִן אֲבִידָן בֶּן־
גִּדְעֹנִי׃ לְדָן אֲחִיעֶזֶר בֶּן־עַמִּישַׁדָּי׃

פרשת

Rashi's commentary at the foot of a page from the 1547 edition of the Torah printed in Istanbul by Eliezar Soncino

Rashi's biblical commentaries were mostly his original work, although he also included much homiletic interpretation–*derash* in Hebrew–derived from the body of rabbinic exegesis and legend known as midrash. Rashi claimed that he was using midrash to explain a text only when the literal interpretation fell short, not just for the sake of telling a good story. He does not quote a midrash literally but alters it to make it more easily comprehensible and to adapt the language of the midrash to the text, making for a smooth, clear, uniform style. Generally, he preferred the midrash when it both elucidated a text and gave what he considered a useful lesson. Thus, he remarks on the use of the plural in Genesis 1:26, "Let us make man in our image," that "The great teacher [Moses] comments that God consulted the angels although they did not assist in the Creation. This teaches us the value of proper and modest conduct, in that the leader should have enough respect for his subordinates as to consult them." In addition to the lesson about leadership, Rashi's commentary may have been intended to counter the Christian interpretation that the use of the plural referred to the Trinity. Such homiletic interpretations give his commentaries human interest and made them more popular than such commentaries as those of his grandson Rashbam, which rely entirely on literal interpretation and seem dry and boring in comparison. Rashi's use of the rabbinic literature popularized the legends among Jewish scholars. While Christian commentators were also attracted by his use of the midrash and his accessible style, they may also have preferred his commentaries because they seemed to give story instead of theology.

Rashi's commentaries on the Bible were so popular among Jews that the first book printed in Hebrew was his commentary on the Torah. It was published in Reggio di Calabria, Italy, in February 1475, by Abraham bar Yitzhaq ben-Garton, a Spanish Jew, and then again in Spain the following year. The difficult lettering that has come to be known as "Rashi script" was not used by Rashi, but is actually a cursive script from Spain, brought from there by the original printer. It has been used to represent Rashi's writings in Hebrew ever since. The Torah itself was only first printed in 1482–in an edition that included Rashi's commentary.

The Babylonian Talmud is a much more difficult text than the Bible, as it was composed in two parts. The first part, the Mishnah, is in Hebrew and consists of rabbinic commentary on the Torah that had originally been passed down orally, presumably so that it would not compete with the Torah. The second part, the Gemara, is in Aramaic and consists of commentary on the Mishnah. The compilers of the Talmud had wanted to preserve its oral character, resulting in several problems. As there was no canonical text of the Talmud, as there was of the Bible, questions of textual authenticity arose. Furthermore, there is no punctuation so that it is difficult to know where one sentence ends and another begins, or whether it is a question or a statement. In the attempt to maintain the sense of the reader's presence at a live discussion, the compilers gave no clue as to who is speaking or when a speaker is interrupted and another interjects his comments. An additional problem arose from the fact that Aramaic, unlike Hebrew, was no longer commonly spoken by European Jews. These difficulties all had to be dealt with before the basic text could be intelligible to its students. Therefore, Rashi's Talmud commentaries stick to literal explanation–the *peshat*–and lack the stories that gave the Bible commentaries their popular appeal.

Rashi commented on most of the tractates of the Babylonian Talmud although he did not seem to do so in any order. He did not comment on the three tractates that lack Gemara–*Eduyot* (Testimonies), *Middot* (Measurements), and *Tamid* (Daily Sacrifice)–nor did he comment on the last part of *Bava Batra* (Last Gate), and he died before completing his commentary on *Makkot* (Stripes). Some scholars contend that the commentaries on *Ta'anit* (Fast), *Nedarim* (Vows), *Nazir* (Ascetic), and *Horayot* (Teachings) are not his. The commentary on *Mo'ed Qatan* (Minor Festival) traditionally ascribed to him is not in fact his; the authentic one was first published in 1961 by Ephraim Kupfer.

The Talmud has two basic concerns. There are the legal sections, which establish laws of Jewish ritual (the Halakhah) and there are the legends (the Haggadah). In the legal sections, Rashi acts as a guide to the student through the most difficult passages, seemingly projecting himself into the scene as an observer so that he knows who was speaking and the tone and sense of the argument. He delineates the underlying principles and ideas, removing any obstacles to a basic understanding of the text, and thus revealing to the reader exactly what the law is. In treating the legends, however, Rashi confines himself to explaining the text. In fact, a modern reader may find Rashi naive in his uncritical acceptance of rabbinic folklore and his failure to distinguish between history and legend. But as an explication of a difficult, at times seemingly impossible text, Rashi's commentary is incomparable. His students continued his work as commentators on the text, and they were the first generation of what has come to be known as *tosaphists*, supplementers. The first complete Babylonian Talmud was printed in Venice in 1520–1526, and it formed the model for the more than one hundred editions produced since: the Mishnah and

Gemara in the center column, the commentaries by Rashi on the inside column, and the *Tosafot* (literally "additions": the work of the tosaphists) in the outer column of each page.

Rashi's responsa, which were not published separately until 1943, when they were culled from a collection of letters of medieval French and German rabbis, are less known than are his commentaries. When a rabbi became famous, individuals and communities would write to him to request advice on a point of law or custom, often with a question on a specific, ephemeral issue. Rashi's replies to such queries include little theology and no insights about the methodology for his commentaries, but they shed light on his personality—he was rarely dogmatic and would readily acknowledge if he had made a mistake—and provide knowledge about Jews in northern Europe in the eleventh century. He understood that the economic and social situation of the Jews in Europe required a different relationship to gentile neighbors than that of the Jews in pre-Diaspora Palestine. Thus, although the Talmud prohibits cattle dealing with non-Jews lest such trade involve the Jew in promoting pagan practices, Rashi argues that the prohibition was promulgated at a time when all Jews lived together and could easily trade only with each other; but at a time when Jews were a minority among gentile neighbors such a practice would cause economic disaster and could not be followed. In another letter, he states that the prohibition against handling pagan wine should not be applied to Christian wine, as Christians are not pagans and therefore their wine could not have been used for idolatrous purposes; however, he still prohibits drinking Christian wine.

Rashi lived during the First Crusade when there were terrible acts of violence against Jews in the Rhineland, including massacres. Some Jews converted to Christianity to avoid harm, but after the danger passed, they wished to return to their faith, often only to find themselves rejected as apostates by other Jews. With his characteristic generosity and understanding, Rashi denied that conversion under such circumstances was true apostasy and urged that they be welcomed back into the Jewish community.

Few individuals within the Jewish scholarly tradition have had the effect of Rashi. His fame made northern France the most important center of Jewish studies within Christian Europe during the High Middle Ages, and since the medieval period, only the works of Maimonides are as famous and as frequently consulted. His responsa have helped shape Jewish tradition since the Middle Ages; his commentaries are still used by all Jewish students of the Bible and the Talmud, and scholars of the Hebrew Bible

Rashi Chapel in Worms, France (from Maurice Liber, Rashi, *1906)*

from all faiths still rely on his insights. Since the beginning of the thirteenth century, almost every talmudic scholar has referred to Rashi's commentaries, and they have been included in every edition of the Babylonian Talmud since the advent of printing in the West. He made the language of the Hebrew Bible and the Talmud more accessible to readers, and his use of story made his commentaries appealing. Indeed, the Babylonian Talmud was so difficult for students in the Middle Ages to decipher that, without Rashi's commentaries, the Babylonian Talmud might not have maintained its central position in the Jewish religion. Perhaps no other religious scholar has ever approached his popularity or influence.

Bibliographies:

Aron Freimann, "Manuscript Supercommentaries on Rashi's Commentary on the Pentateuch," *Rashi Anniversary Volume* (New York: American Academy for Jewish Research, 1941), pp. 73–114;

Shlomo Pick and Sarah Munitz, *A Tentative Catalogue of Manuscripts of the Rashi Commentary to the Talmud* (Ramat-Gan, Israel: Bar-Ilan University, 1988).

Biographies:

Maurice Liber, *Rashi,* translated by Adele Szold (Philadelphia: Jewish Publication Society of America, 1906; republished, New York: Hermon Press, 1970);

Samuel M. Blumenfield, *Master of Troyes: A Study of Rashi, the Educator* (New York: Behrman House, 1946);

Esra Shereshevsky, *Rashi: The Man and His World* (New York: Sepher-Hermon Press, 1982);

Chaim Pearl, *Rashi* (London: Halban, 1988);

Simon Schwarzfuchs, *Rachi de Troyes,* Présences du judaïsme no. 3 (Paris: Albin Michel, 1991).

References:

Abraham Berliner, *Kuntrus ha-be-la'azin: Die Altfranzösischen ausdrücke im Pentateuch-Commentar Raschis Alphabetisch geordnet und erklärt* (Cracow: Josef Fischer, 1905);

Menahem Banitt, *Rashi, Interpreter of the Biblical Letter* (Tel Aviv: Chaim Rosenberg School of Jewish Studies, Tel Aviv University, 1985);

Mochè Catane, *Otsar ha-le'azim* (Jerusalem & Tel Aviv: Gitler, 1984);

Robert Chazan, *Medieval Jewry in Northern France* (Baltimore & London: Johns Hopkins University Press, 1973);

Pinhas Doron, *Be'ur setumot be-Rashi,* 4 volumes (Hoboken: Ketav, 1985; New York & Jerusalem: Moznayim, 1989; New York: Sepher-Hermon Press, 1990, 1994);

Doron, *The Mystery of Creation According to Rashi* (New York: Moznayim, 1982);

Yoel Florsheim, *Rashi la-Mikra be-ferusho la-Talmud* (Jerusalem: Reuven Maas, 1981);

Benjamin J. Gelles, *Peshat and Derash in the Exegesis of Rashi*, Etudes sur le judaïsme médiéval no. 9 (Leiden: E. J. Brill, 1981);

Emanuel Gottlieb, *Mafteah nos'im le-Rashi al ha-Torah* (Jerusalem: Akademon, 1977);

Herman Hailperin, *Rashi and the Christian Scholars* (Pittsburgh, Pa.: University of Pittsburgh Press, 1963);

Sampson A. Isseroff, *An Introduction to Rashi's Grammatical Explanations in the Book of Genesis* (Jerusalem: World Zionist Organization, 1985);

Joel Müller, ed., *Teshuvot hakhme Tsarfat ve-Loter* (Vienna: Loewy & Alkalay, 1881);

Pinhas Ne'eman, *Rashi mefaresh ha-Torah* (Jerusalem: Massada, 1945);

Joseph Pereira-Mendoza, *Rashi as Philologist* (Manchester, U.K.: Manchester University Press, 1940);

Beryl Smalley, *The Study of the Bible in the Middle Ages* (Oxford: Clarendon Press, 1941);

Emily Taitz, *The Jews of Medieval France: The Community of Champagne* (Westport, Conn.: Greenwood Press, 1994).

Richard de Fournival

(10 October 1201 – 1 March 1259 or 1260)

Jeanette Beer
Purdue University

WORKS: *Chansons*

Manuscripts: Twenty-one poems are attributed with varying degrees of certainty to Richard de Fournival. They are in Arras, Bibliothèque Municipale, 1139 (anc. 657); Bern, Bürgerbibliothek, 389; Modena, Biblioteca Estense, etr. 45, R. 4, 4; Paris, Bibliothèque de l'Arsenal, 5198; Paris, Bibliothèque Nationale de France, f. fr. 844, 845, 846, 847, 1591, 12615, 20050, nouv. acq. 1050; and Vatican, Biblioteca Apostolica Vaticana, Reg. Lat. 1522.

Editions: *Kritischer Text der Lieder Richards de Fournival,* edited by Paul Zarifopol (Halle, Germany: Karras, 1904); *L'Oeuvre lyrique de Richard de Fournival: Edition critique,* edited by Yvan G. Lepage (Ottawa: Editions de l'Université d'Ottawa, 1981).

Nativitas (before 22 October 1239)

Manuscripts: Vatican, Palantine Library, Vat. Reg. Suec. 1261, ff. 59r–60v; Oxford University, Hertford College, no. 4, ff. 159r–160r; London, British Library, Sloane 3281, ff. 14r to 15v.

Biblionomia (circa 1250)

Manuscript: Paris, Sorbonne, 636.

Editions: "Biblionomia," in *Cabinet des manuscrits de la Bibliothèque Nationale,* volume 2, edited by Leopold Delisle (Paris: Imprimerie Imperiale, 1874), pp. 518–535; "La 'Biblionomia' de Richard de Fournival du manuscrit 636 de la Sorbonne, textes et facsimilé avec la transcription de L. Delisle," edited by H. J. De Vleeschauwer, *Mousarion,* 6 (1965).

Le Bestiaire d'amour (circa 1250–1259)

Manuscripts: More than fifty manuscripts are extant in libraries throughout the world.

Editions: *Le Bestiaire d'amour, suivi de, La reponse de la dame, enrichi de 48 dessins graves sur bois: Publies pour la premiere fois d'apres le manuscrit de la Bibliotheque Imperiale,* edited by C. Hippeau (Paris: Aubry, 1860; Geneva: Slatkine Reprints, 1968); *Eine mittelniederfrankische ubertragung des Bestiaire d'amour, sprachelich untersucht und mit altfranzosischem paralleltext,* edited by John Holmberg (Uppsala, Sweden: Uppsala Universitets Arsskrift, 1925); in S. Vitte-Clémencet, "Richard de Fournival: Etude sur sa vie et ses oeuvres, suivie de l'édition di Bestiaire d'amour, de la réponse de la dame et des chansons," dissertation, l'Ecole des Chartes, 1929; *Li Bestiaires d'amours di Maistre Richart de Fornival e li Response du Bestiaire,* edited by Cesare Segre (Milan: Ricciardi, 1957); *Il Bestiario d'Amore e la Riposta al Bestiario,* edited by Francesco Zambon (Parma, Italy: Pratich, 1987).

Edition in English: *Master Richard's Bestiary of Love and Response,* translated by Jeanette Beer (Berkeley, Los Angeles & London: University of California Press, 1986); reprinted with new introduction by Beer (West Lafayette, Ind.: Purdue University Press, 1999).

Le Bestiaire d'amour en vers (circa 1259–1260)

Manuscript: Paris, Bibliothèque Nationale de France, f. fr. 25.545 (anc. fonds Notre Dame 274 bis), folios 207v–218 (fourteenth century).

Edition: "Bestiaire d'amour en vers," edited by A. Långfors, *Mémoires de la Société néophilologique de Helsingfors,* 7 (1924): 291–317.

De arte alchemica

Manuscripts: Oxford C.C.C. 124, folios 91–94; Condover Hall, Shropshire, Library R. Cholmondeley, folios 54–60; Florence, Biblioteca Laurenziana, XXX cod. 29, folios 73–79; Klagenfurt, Bischoffs Bibliothek, XXIX d. 24 (1421.23), folios 278–291.

Commens d'amours (attributed to Richard)

Manuscript: Dijon, Bibliothèque Municipale, 526, folios 4–10.

Edition: "Commens d'amour," edited by Antoinette Saly, *Travaux de Linguistique et de Littérature,* 10, no. 2 (1972): 21–55.

Consaus d'amours (attributed to Richard)

Manuscript: Paris, Bibliothèque Nationale de France, f. fr. 25.566, folios 207v–218.

First publication: "Consaus d'amours," edited by W. M. McCleod, *Studies in Philology*, 32 (1935): 1–21.

Standard edition: "Il *Consaus d'amours*, di Richard de Fournival," edited by G. B. Speroni, *Medioevo Romanzo*, 1/2 (1974): 217–278.

De Vetula (attributed to Richard)

Editions: *La Vieille: Ou, les dernières amours d'Ovide. Poème français du XIVe siècle, traduit du latin de Richard de Fournival par Jean Lefèvre; publié pour la première fois et précédé de recherches sur l'auteur du Vetula,* edited by Hippolyte Cocheris (Paris: Aubry, 1861); *Pseudo-Ovidius De Vetula: Untersuchungen und Text,* edited by Paul Klopsch (Leiden & Cologne: E. J. Brill, 1967); *The Pseudo-Ovidian De vetula,* edited by Dorothy M. Robathan (Amsterdam: Hakkert, 1968 [i.e., 1969]); *La Poissance d'amours dello Pseudo-Richard de Fournival: Edizione critica,* edited by Gian Battista Speroni (Florence: La Nuovo Italia, 1975).

Richard de Fournival was a churchman, author, licensed surgeon, mathematician, musician, astronomer—in sum, a scholar of extraordinary erudition and versatility. In the astrological treatise *Nativitas* (Nativity) written some time before 22 October 1239, Richard plotted the positions of the stars and planets for the date of his birth in Amiens on 10 October 1201. Parish records from the Chapter of Notre Dame in Amiens reveal that Richard's parents were Roger de Fournival, the king's physician, and Elisabeth de le Pierre, who is also called Elisabeth de Paix and Elisabeth de la Perche. A half brother, Arnoul, Elisabeth's son by a previous marriage, was bishop of Amiens from 1236 to 1246. A papal bull issued by Innocent IV in 1246 records that Richard was authorized to practice surgery by Pope Gregory IX and was reconfirmed as a licensed surgeon by Innocent. The document also notes that Richard was a canon by 1240, a deacon by 1246, and was elevated to the rank of chancellor of the Chapter of Notre-Dame in Amiens. An obituary for Cardinal Robert de Somercote in the bull mentions that Richard was the cardinal's chaplain until the latter's death in 1241. Church records from Notre Dame in Amiens show that Richard died on 1 March 1259 or 1260. His contribution to French culture continues not only through his own works but also through his library of manuscripts, which was posthumously transferred, through Gérard d'Abbeville, to the College de Sorbonne. This rich collection, indexed by Richard around 1250 in a catalogue that he called *Biblionomia,* is indicative of the range of his intellectual interests. After a brief introduction, *Biblionomia* describes 162 philosophical, mathematical, astro-nomical, and medical manuscripts; these descriptions are followed by a list of legal and theological texts. *Biblionomia* is an invaluable record of the scientific texts, many of which are no longer extant, that were circulating in Richard's century.

Richard composed lyric poetry; the editor of the 1981 critical edition of his chansons, Yvan G. Lepage, attributes eighteen poems to Richard. The majority are *chansons courtoises,* one of which (III in Lepage's edition) is constructed as a *débat* over the relative merits of loving a *dame* (woman) or a *pucele* (girl), while two (XVII and XVIII) are *jeux-partis* (games of two parties) in which Richard debates about love with a contemporary Picard poet, Gautier de Dargiés. Vernacular topoi of love are abundant, and classical references are restricted to a brief mention of Echo and Narcissus in IX and of Daedalus and Theseus in XV. The names of Theophilus, Jesus, and the Virgin Mary occur in XIX, which is of disputed authorship, and there is a passing reference to Arthurian material—"Mais je ne sui pas rois Artus" (But I am not King Arthur)—in I. The Lepage edition lists XIX, XX, and XXI (a *chanson pieuse,* a *chanson de croisade,* and a *chanson de femme,* respectively) as "*chansons douteuses.*"

The language and versification of the chansons show some Picard features, but, like most vernacular poets, Richard draws mainly on the koine of love that had been developed by previous troubadours and trouvères. Agonized prayers for the *joie d'amours* (joy of love) and for his lady's mercy bring little relief from love's *dangier* (domination) or from its *torment* (suffering). Slander from *felons* increases the poet's *duel* (anguish) without diminishing his *devocion.* Several lyrics begin with a mention of the season or with birdsong. For all the topoi, however, Richard's chansons are unconventional, and many have a cryptic brilliance. Formally, no two chansons are identical, although *unissonans,* in which the order of rhymes is identical in every strophe, is the favored rhyme scheme. The poems have musical accompaniments, for which there has as yet been no complete musicological analysis.

Richard wrote what the rubrics in some manuscripts call *Le Bestiaire d'amour* (The Bestiary of Love, circa 1250–1259)—more properly known as *Li Arierebans d'amours* (The Arrière-ban of Love), since that was the name given to it by its author—in the middle of the century. He explains the function of the "arrière-ban":

Ausi comme uns rois, quant il va guerroier fors de son roialme, il en maine de ses melleurs hommes une partie, et s'en lasse encore une gringor partie a sa terre garder; mais quant il voit qu'il ne se puet soufire a tant de gent com il a mené, si parmande tous chiax qu'il a laissiés et fait son ariereban: ausi me covient il faire.

meuri le teste 7 enmena
le vache a sen peire.

quel recourer ypoet il auoir.
la vite si est. calucun recourer
il poet il auoir. mais iou ne
sai quels li recouriers est
uient plus lie de laronde.
Car on a esproue. ke quo
on le emble ses peris aron
deaus. son los crieue les iols.
7 on les remec el ni ia p
chu ne demorra. kil ne noiet.
Ains quil soient pareru 7
pense on bien ke laronde
les garist. mais on ne set
p quel medicine.

Le por chu di iou. ke puis
ke argus sendormi aforce de
uois ia soie. kil eust au tat
te ieus. co il a en le keue
del paon. ki senefie porue
ance. ke che nest pas mer
ueille. se iou p mi toute
me porueance men dormi
aforce de uois. ne se ien
morue. car tout dis sieut
la mors aps lendormi daus.
Si co il a este dit 7 del hõ
me ki sen doit ale seraine.
7 ale unicorne ki sen dorz
ale pucele. Se cil meismes
argus.

Dont sui ie mors che
    vous. ia il point del
recourir. 7 se sai mais ke

tieus en tele maniere est
il de la mostoile. ke se on
li ocist ses falons. 7 on lui
rent tout mors. elle set de
se nature une medicine

Page from a manuscript for Richard de Fournival's Le Bestiaire d'amour *(Bibliothèque Sainte-Geneviève, 2200, f. 183a)*

(As a king who goes to wage war outside his kingdom will take with him a group of his best men, leaving an even greater part behind to guard his territory, but when he sees the number he has taken cannot suffice for his needs, he summons all of those he left behind and makes his arrière-ban, so I must do. For if I have spoken and sent you many fine words and they have not served me as much as I needed, I must now assemble my resources in the arrière-ban of this last composition).

This mingling of love and war imagery had many precedents, from Ovid's *Amores* onward, but Ovid is the only author named in the work. Other poets who are vaguely cited but not named are "uns poitevins" (a Poitevin), "li poitevins qui en sievi Ovide" (the Poitevin who followed Ovid in this), and "li autres" (the other).

Another unacknowledged intellectual influence on the *Bestiaire d'amour* is Aristotle. In the middle of the thirteenth century Aristotle's scientific treatises had come into favor in the Faculty of Arts of the University of Paris, which had just reversed several papal proscriptions against Aristotle's works of natural philosophy. Consequently, the intellectual climate of the time was becoming naturalistic, and Richard's opening sentence, "Toutes gens desirent par nature a savoir" (All men naturally desire knowledge), is a translation of the first sentence of Aristotle's *Metaphysics,* book 1. Although Richard never expatiates on nor even names Aristotle, Aristotelian themes such as memory and sense perception are woven into the introduction. These are not so much popularizations of Aristotelian science as personalizations of scientific catchwords on which Richard chooses to hang his declarations of love. For example, he notes that there are two pathways to memory, *painture* and *parole*. His arrière-ban will, he says, use both of these pathways to ensure that he remains in his lady's memory.

Richard's main source is Pierre de Beauvais's early thirteenth-century translation of the *Physiologus* (Naturalist), the work compiled by an unknown author before the middle of the second century B.C. that served as a model for the many medieval bestiaries. Richard borrows many of his descriptions of animal properties from the translation and explains their relevance to the human love condition. It was customary for bestiaries to begin with the lion, symbol of the Lion of Judah and, hence, of divine domination and majesty, but Richard gives pride of place to the cock, which had figured either insignificantly or not at all in earlier bestiaries. Using this domesticated fowl as a parodic symbol for himself as poet/lover, Richard explains to his lady that his previous writings had resembled the cock's crowing at dawn. Now, however,

in the despairing midnight of his love, he must pour all of his desperate efforts into this arrière-ban of love. Other similes of self-mockery follow: he is as desperate as the ravenous wild ass that expends its last energies in braying and as speechless as the wolf transfixed by a man's gaze. He must not emulate the cricket, which pours out its life in song, or the swan, which sings most exquisitely when it is dying. Terminating these images of futility with an image of revulsion, he wishes that he could call back the lyric words of love that had "volee des dens" (flown out through his teeth) like the dog that eats its own vomit. By this graphically brutal transition he shifts the symbolism from his own love to feminine love. Woman's lubricity, inconsistency, and cruelty, already commonplaces in the love literature of his age, are among the defects Richard criticizes in women in general, if not specifically in his lady. Thus, for all his ostensible homage to "la plus bele rien ke jou onques eüse veü a mon jugement" (the loveliest creature that, in my judgment, I had ever seen), the lexicon of love is profoundly ambivalent in *Le Bestiaire d'amour*. Richard ends it with a plea for mercy from the lady.

Le Bestiaire d'amour en vers is a fragment of rhyming octosyllabic couplets that has survived in a fourteenth-century manuscript now in the Bibliothèque Nationale de France in Paris. It begins by saying that "Maistre Richars ha, por miex plaire, / Mis en rime le Bestiaire" (Master Richard, to give more pleasure, / has put the bestiary into rhyme). This statement would put the date of composition of *Le Bestiaire d'amour en vers* around 1259 or 1260, near the end of Richard's life. Substantively, it is completely faithful to its predecessor, while stylistic alterations occur primarily because of repetitive expansions; there are no innovations in vocabulary. There is little formal resemblance between Richard's early lyric poetry and the versified bestiary's explicit didacticism. His renunciation of lyricism in *Le Bestiaire d'amour* continues into *Le Bestiaire en vers,* even when the former's statement of intent, "Car le canter doi jou bien avoir perdu" (For I am bound to have lost my singing), is versified into "Car je le chanter avoir doi / Perdu." The fragmentary nature of the work indicates that the author may have abandoned the new enterprise as unworkable—or it may have been interrupted by his death.

Richard de Fournival's bestiary of love was translated into many European vernaculars and was frequently adapted—for example, in the anonymous thirteenth-century *Bestiaire d'amour rimé* and in Nicole de Margival's *Le Dit de la Panthère d'amours*. Today the multifaceted sophistication of the thirteenth-century chancellor's works is being rediscovered anew.

References:

Jeanette Beer, "*Le Bestiaire d'amour en vers,*" in *Medieval Translators and their Craft,* edited by Beer (Kalamazoo, Mich.: Medieval Institute Publications, 1990), pp. 285–296;

Beer, "Duel of Bestiaries," in *Beasts and Birds of the Middle Ages: The Bestiary and Its Legacy,* edited by Willene B. Clark and Meradith McMunn (Philadelphia: University of Pennsylvania Press, 1989), pp. 96–105;

Beer, "A Fourteenth-Century *Bestiaire d'amour,*" *Reinardus: Yearbook of the International Reynard Society,* 4 (1991): 19–26;

Beer, "The New Naturalism of *Le Bestiaire d'amour,*" *Reinardus: Yearbook of the International Reynard Society,* 1 (1988): 16-21;

Beer, "The *Response* to Richard de Fournival's *Bestiaire d'amour,*" *Teaching Language through Literature,* 25, no. 1 (1985): 3–11;

Beer, "Richard de Fournival's Anonymous Lady: The Character of the Response to the *Bestiaire d'amour,*" *Romance Philology,* 42 (February 1989): 267–273;

Gabriel Biancotto and Michel Salvat, eds., *Epopée animal, fable, fabliau* (Paris: Presses Universitaires de France, 1984), pp. 107–119;

Alexandre Birkenmajer, "La Bibliothèque de Richard de Fournival, poète et érudit français du début du XIIIe siècle et son sort ultérieur," *Etudes d'histoire des sciences et de la philosophie du Moyen Age: Studia copernica,* 1 (1970): 117–215;

Birkenmajer, "Pierre de Limoges commentateur de Richard de Fournival," *Isis,* 40 (1949): 18–31;

Birkenmajer, "Robert Grosseteste and Richard de Fournival," *Medievalia et Humanistica,* 5 (1948): 36–41;

M. Bormans, "Notice sur deux fragments manuscrits de poésies thyoises de la fin du XIIIe siècle (*le Bestiaire d'amours* et *l'Art d'aimer* d'Ovide)," *Bulletin de l'Académie Royale des sciences, des lettres et des beaux-arts de Belgique I,* second series, 27 (1864): 488–506;

Roberto Crespo, *Una versione pisana inedita del "Bestiaire d'Amours"* (Leiden: Universitaire Pers, 1972);

Nicole Deschamps and Roy Bruno, "L'Univers des bestiaires: Dossier bibliographique et choix de textes," *Etudes françaises,* 10 (August 1974): 231–282;

P. Glorieux, "La bibliothèque de Gérard d'Abbeville," *Recherches de Théologie ancienne et médiévale,* 36 (1969): 48–83;

Glorieux, "Etudes sur la 'Biblionomia' de Richard de Fournival," *Recherches de théologie ancienne et médiévale,* 30 (1963): 205–231;

Glorieux, "Quelques œvres de Richard de Fournival," *Bibliothèque de l'Ecole des Chartes,* 65 (1904): 101–115;

Ch.-V. Langlois, "Un document relatif à Richard de Fournival," *Mélanges d'archéologie et d'histoire,* 10 (1890): 123–125;

G. Lozinski, "Un fragment du *Bestiaire d'amour* de Richard de Fournival," *Romania,* 51 (1925): 561–568;

Christopher Lucken, "Du ban du coq à *l'Ariereban,*" *Reinardus: Yearbook of the International Reynard Society,* 5 (1992): 109–124;

Lucken, "Les Portes de la mémoire: Richard de Fournival et 'l'ariereban' de l'amour," dissertation, University of Geneva, 1994;

Paulin Paris, "Notice sur la vie et les ouvrages de Richard de Fournival," *Bibliothèque de l'Ecole des Chartes,* 2 (1840–1841): 32–56;

C. F. Pickford, "The *Roman de la rose* and a Treatise Attributed to Richard de Fournival: Two Manuscripts in the John Rylands Library," *Bulletin of the John Rylands Library,* 34 (1952): 333–365;

Richard Rouse, "The Early Library of the Sorbonne," *Scriptorium,* 21 (1967): 42–71, 227–251;

Rouse, "Manuscripts Belonging to Richard de Fournival," *Revue d'histoire des textes,* 3 (1973): 253–269;

E. Seidler, "Die Medizin in der 'Biblionomia' des Richard de Fournival," *Sudhoff's Archiv,* 51 (1967): 44–54;

Helen Solterer, *The Master and Minerva* (Berkeley & Los Angeles: University of California Press, 1993).

Rutebeuf

(flourished 1249 – 1277)

Leslie Dunton-Downer

WORKS: *Poems* (1249–1277)

Manuscripts: Rutebeuf's remaining fifty-five pieces survive in fourteen manuscripts, the most important of which, A and C, respectively serve as textual bases for the two current standard editions. Paris, Bibliothèque Nationale de France, f. fr. 1593 (B), a fifteenth-century collection of stories and fabliaux, a curious collation of three thirteenth-century manuscripts, includes twenty-six pieces by Rutebeuf. Paris, Bibliothèque Nationale de France, f. fr. 24.432 (D), copied in 1345, contains eighty-two *dits* and fabliaux; five are by Rutebeuf. Paris, Bibliothèque Nationale de France, f. fr. 12.483 (G) includes three pieces by Rutebeuf and dates from after 1328. The thirteenth-century manuscript Chantilly, Condé Museum, 1578 (I) includes two of Rutebeuf's fabliaux; this manuscript once belonged to a jongleur. Royal Belgian Library, 9411–26 (R), from after 1277, comprises forty-three moral and religious works, of which five (two illustrated with miniatures) are by Rutebeuf. Lost to a fire in 1904 was the thirteenth-century Turin, University Library, L.V.32 (T), which included two pieces by Rutebeuf. Six remaining manuscripts include only one piece by Rutebeuf, and in only three of these is the attribution sound: Paris, Bibliothèque Nationale de France, f. fr. 12.786 (H), from after the late thirteenth century, includes *Le Dit d'Aristote;* fifteenth-century Paris, Bibliothèque Nationale de France, f. fr. 1634 (P) includes *La Voie de Paradis;* and Reims, Municipal Library, 1275 (S), which dates from after 1278, also includes *La Voie de Paradis.*

First publication: In *Œuvres complètes de Rutebeuf,* 4 volumes, edited by Achille Jubinal (Paris: Eduard Pannier, 1839).

Standard editions: *Onze poèmes de Rutebeuf concernant la croisade,* edited by Julia Bastin and Edmond Faral (Paris: P. Geuthner, 1946); *Rutebeuf, I Fabliaux,* edited by Alberto Limentani (Venice: Corbo and Fiore, 1976); *Œuvres complètes de Rutebeuf,* 2 volumes, edited by Faral and Bastin (Paris: Picard, 1977).

Standard editions and editions in modern French: *Rutebeuf, Poèmes de l'infortune et autres poèmes,* edited and translated by Jean Dufournet (Paris: Gallimard, 1986); *Rutebeuf: Œuvres complètes,* edited and translated by Michel Zink (Paris: Classiques Garnier, 1989–1990).

Le Miracle de Théophile (circa 1276)

Manuscripts: This play survives in two manuscripts containing the most complete collections of compositions attributed to Rutebeuf: Paris, Bibliothèque Nationale de France, f. fr. 837(A) and Paris, Bibliothèque Nationale de France, f. fr. 1635 (C). Dating from the end of the thirteenth century, A includes what may be the entire text of the work. Thirty-three of Rutebeuf's works are copied in this manuscript, which belonged to the Royal Library at Fontainebleau by the time of François I. Copied after 1285, C comprises fifty of fifty-six pieces attributed to the author, including two extracts of the play. C employs a dialect from an area of France encompassing Rutebeuf's native Champagne.

First publication: In *Œuvres complètes de Rutebeuf,* 4 volumes, edited by Achille Jubinal (Paris: Eduard Pannier, 1839).

Standard editions: *Le Miracle de Théophile,* second edition, edited by Grace Frank, Classiques Français du Moyen Age 49 (Paris: Champion, 1949); *Rutebeuf: Le Miracle de Théophile,* edited and translated into modern French by Jean Dufournet (Paris: Flammarion, 1987); *Œuvres complètes de Rutebeuf,* 2 volumes, edited by Edmond Faral and Julia Bastin (Paris: Picard, 1977).

Standard edition and edition in modern French: In *Rutebeuf: Œuvres complètes,* 2 volumes, edited and translated by Michel Zink (Paris: Classiques Garnier, 1989, 1990).

The writer known only as Rutebeuf composed some of the most important works written in Old

French during the thirteenth century. His *Le Miracle de Théophile* (The Miracle of Theophile, circa 1276) exerted a strong influence on the development of medieval religious drama. In lyrical poems, his autobiographical voice is so unusual for its time that he has come to be seen as the founder of the modern French lyrical voice. Furthermore, representations of urban, Parisian themes and voices–along with the absence of courtly literature–in Rutebeuf's work have prompted literary historians to characterize Rutebeuf as the first French author of *la littérature bourgeoise* (bourgeois literature).

There is no surviving historical or literary attestation of the individual known as "Rutebeuf." This is not to say that the work went unnoticed: the number and variety of manuscripts in which Rutebeuf's works have survived indicate that his compositions circulated broadly. Furthermore, some of Rutebeuf's polemical pieces may have prompted a papal bull (*Quasi lignum vitae*) condemning booklets offensive to the church politics of Pope Alexander IV. If this was indeed the case, Rutebeuf was possibly too well known for his own good: other authors of tracts condemned by this bull were excommunicated and exiled.

Rutebeuf could be a surname, although no attestation of such a name or any credible variation of it is known to exist. Most likely, "Rutebeuf" is a pseudonym. In four pieces Rutebeuf observes that his name is composed of two words: *rude* (rustic or rude) and *beuf* (ox). Animal names of this kind were exchanged as nicknames among school boys during the Middle Ages. Since Rutebeuf's writings indicate that he received a clerical education, "Rutebeuf" could have been a school nickname the author preserved as a pen name.

Rutebeuf names himself in fifteen of his surviving fifty-six pieces, and sometimes puns on his name or explains formulaically that he is "Rutebeuf qui rudement oeuvre," best translated as "Rutebeuf, whose work is crude." Whoever Rutebeuf was, he worked in many literary genres, including political poetry, fabliau, dream allegory, prose monologue, hagiography, confessional poetry, and religious drama. One may conclude from the absence of love poetry in the surviving works of Rutebeuf that his commissions were earned idiosyncratically and piecemeal. Poets such as Jean de Meun or Guillaume de Lorris took up grand projects designed for courtly consumption, but Rutebeuf did not rely upon the continued support of any single patron. Instead, he was a medieval freelance writer working in an urban environment where he was commissioned within different communities, each with its particular ideological and aesthetic discriminations. For this reason, generalizing about Rutebeuf's views is problematic: he may have been espousing the views of those who paid him. The polemical nature of Rutebeuf's

commissions and the problem of distinguishing the poet's voice from the experiences of the composer complicate attempts to correlate neatly Rutebeuf's literary output with his biography. Postmedieval prejudices have also confused assessments of Rutebeuf's career. Some of Rutebeuf's fabliaux, for example, have been considered especially puerile; *Le dit du pet au vilain* (The Tale of the Peasant's Fart), is one such tale often attributed to the younger Rutebeuf. As a writer always looking for a commission, however, Rutebeuf would have had good reason to produce a remunerated fabliau at almost any stage in his career.

While it is impossible to simplify the evolution of Rutebeuf's career of more than thirty colorful and troubled years, it is helpful to understand his writings as belonging to three periods. During the first, from 1249 to 1260, Rutebeuf was predominantly concerned with the *querelle universitaire* (university quarrel), a famous antagonism pitting mendicant professors against secular masters at the University of Paris. In the second period, from 1261 to 1264, Rutebeuf passed through a time of reflection and conversion; during this time he began to compose *poésies personnelles* (personal poems) and wrote his dramatic opus, *Le Miracle de Théophile*. During the third period, from 1265 to 1277, Rutebeuf promoted crusades planned in the purported interest of Latin Christendom.

The first work known to be by Rutebeuf is *Le Dit des cordeliers* (A Word about the Cordeliers, 1249), which situates the author in Troyes and the county of his probable origin, Champagne. This dit addresses inhabitants of Troyes regarding a conflict between parish leaders within the walled city and friars of the Franciscan Order, who attempted to move their residence from beyond the walls into the center of town. Rutebeuf's poem favors the Franciscans, who he claims will save Troyes from God's disfavor. Here, poetic language exhibits what will become signature elements of Rutebeuf's nonsense-sounding style. For example, Rutebeuf manipulates relentlessly the word *cordeliers,* meaning Franciscans and referring to the *corde* (rope) they wore as a belt. The poem features the rhetorical figure *annominatio,* which Rutebeuf exploited peerlessly in later works. *Annominatio* involves the repetition of units of sound, as in this verse using *corde:* "En la corde s'encordent cordee a trois cordons" (They tie themselves with the rope knotted with three knots). *Annominatio* has annoyed readers who think it merely produces tongue twisters. However, Rutebeuf's acoustic patternings argue that language carries intrinsic truths that can, with poetic effort, be teased out for the social and spiritual edification of his audience.

Throughout his career Rutebeuf used wordplay with a zeal less mischievous than religious. According

Rutebeuf praying to the Virgin Mary and Jesus (illumination from a manuscript in the Bibliothèque Nationale de France)

to Rutebeuf's poetics, language no longer works as God intended. Hypocrites are particularly responsible for the decay of language because their actions and words conflict, thereby debasing all areas of life touched by linguistic exchange. When a friar claims he serves humility yet lives the life of an avaricious glutton, he twists all sense out of the word "humility" and thereby offends God. This view of language, marginal yet moral, characterizes much of Rutebeuf's writing.

By the time he composed *La Discorde des jacobins et de l'université* (The Discord between the Jacobins and the University, 1255), which addresses the antagonism between mendicants and secular masters at the University of Paris, Rutebeuf had moved to Paris, possibly to further his education. *La Discorde,* accusing Jacobins of destroying the university, captures the turbulent atmosphere in which Rutebeuf composed. By 1255 Rutebeuf appears to have executed an ideological volte-face: in

Troyes he supported mendicants, but in Paris he attacked them. It is unclear as to whether these were Rutebeuf's own views or if he adopted the opinions of those who commissioned him. Whatever his initial convictions, Rutebeuf eventually develops an aversion for mendicants. He rarely fails, throughout the remainder of his career, to exploit opportunities to ridicule or criticize them.

To understand the phase of Rutebeuf's career heralded by *La Discorde,* one needs to know that anti-mendicantism has historical roots in the University of Paris. By 1217 both Jacobins (or Dominicans, also referred to as Friars Preacher) and Franciscans (or Friars Minor) had established themselves in Paris with papal support. Soon thereafter, convents of these orders developed theological schools incorporated into the university. Problems arose when secular masters in the faculty of theology had to compete for students, for whom mendicants provided excellent instruction free of charge. When the Jacobins, allotted a single chair in the faculty of theology, appointed in September 1252 to a second chair their rising star, Thomas Aquinas, the campus mood grew hostile. Chance events further divided the mendicant and secular camps when, in March 1253, Paris guards assaulted four clerks, killing one. The university was prevented from responding unanimously (and therefore effectively) to this incident by its mendicant professors. Animosity then escalated to such an extent that Pope Innocent IV, deeming intervention necessary, called the feuding parties to Rome. With the papal bull known by its opening Latin words as *Etsi animarum,* Innocent IV favored the secular camp, which was led by Guillaume de Saint-Amour. However, this triumph was short-lived. A new pope, Alexander IV, overturned *Etsi animarum* with his own bull, *Quasi lignum vitae,* which gave the mendicants everything they sought. Infuriated, Guillaume de Saint-Amour responded with a tract arguing that mendicants signaled the coming of the Antichrist; he was excommunicated and exiled. The new leader of the secular group, Gérard d'Abbeville, probably kept Rutebeuf busy advancing the secular cause, eulogizing its heroes, and assailing mendicants.

Rutebeuf may have been a student of secular masters during the *querelle universitaire;* in any case, members of the entourage around Guillaume de Saint-Amour, whether actively recruiting the poet or discovering the talented pamphleteer already in their midst, commissioned from him polemical pieces serving as propaganda for their camp. Pieces dating from this period attack the mendicants and Alexander IV: *C'est d'Hypocrisie* (On Hypocrisy, 1257); *Le Dit de maître Guillaume de Saint-Amour* (A Word about Master Guillaume of Saint-Amour, 1257); *La Complainte de maître Guillaume de Saint-Amour* (The Lament for Master Guillaume of Saint-Amour, 1258), which, with its hagiographical overtones, brazenly likens the activist leader to Christ; *Des Règles* (On Rules, 1259); *De sainte Eglise* (On the Holy Church, 1259); *Le Dit du mensonge* (A Word about Lying, 1260), alternatively titled *La Bataille des Vices contre les Vertus* (The Battle of the Vices against the Virtues); *Des Jacobins* (On the Jacobins, 1260); and *Les Ordres de Paris* (On the Orders of Paris, 1260). These short but often virulent poems are composed in tones of anger, satire, and sometimes despair. Rutebeuf remains convinced, however, that justice will ultimately triumph. In *De sainte Eglise,* for example, he reminds mendicants and their supporters that they will answer for their sins on Judgment Day: "Se Diex vous het, il n'en puet mais." (If it Turns out God hates you, it's not as though he had a choice).

Probably during the same period Rutebeuf composed two often-anthologized pieces characterized by the fresh voice of personal crisis returning later in confessional poems. These are *La Griesche d'hiver* (The Winter Greek) and *La Griesche d'été* (The Summer Greek), both probably dating from the late 1250s. The titles refer to what was thought to be a Greek, or *Griesche,* game of chance. Here the speaker presents himself in typed poses of defeat explained by the twin evils of gambling and drinking. But Rutebeuf handles these *topoi* with such flair that they seem to be written by a truly destitute medieval gambler. The first poem begins:

> Contre le tenz qu'aubres deffuelle,
> Qu'il ne remaint en branche fuelle
> Qui n'aut a terre.

> (During the time when the tree drops its leaves,
> until there remains not a leaf on the branch
> that has not gone to the ground.)

Rhythmic verses capture the gradual loss of leaves until, with the short third verse, the reader learns that every leaf has dropped. Having missed the bittersweet image and cadence of the last gliding leaf, the poem shifts into the universe of a gambler who has set all hopes on a final roll of the dice, only to discover that the game is over; he has lost. Rutebeuf's leaf, *fuelle,* is also Old French for a leaf of paper, so that disappearing fruits of nature suggest Rutebeuf's labor. *La Griesche d'été* engages the same theme from the safe distance warm weather provides.

By 1260 the affair of Guillaume de Saint-Amour had long been settled, and Rutebeuf no longer had cause to write about it. The few surviving antimendicant pieces of 1260 (*Du mensonge* and *Des Jacobins*) bear no marks of the commissioned work, inviting some scholars to ask whether Rutebeuf continued composing antimendicant pieces for his own satisfaction. Perhaps the loss of his role as propagandist led Rutebeuf to a turning point in 1261: he began to compose works now known as "personal poems." Rutebeuf appears in these poems to reveal himself with such autobiographical transparence that readers have been quick to take them at face value. Whether they reveal Rutebeuf's genuine self or not, the poems attest to a dramatic moment in the poet's development. *Le Mariage de Rutebeuf* (The Marriage of Rutebeuf) tells of the speaker's marriage to a poor, old, unattractive woman with whom he lives in dire poverty and daily anguish. The poem concludes with a prayer for the transformation of these trials into penitence that will bring the speaker closer to God. Composed between 1 January and the beginning of

Lent in 1261, the poem may represent Lenten austerity with carnivalesque playfulness, but most prefer to read it as an earnest display of personal crisis.

Before the end of the year 1261, Rutebeuf turned his attention to two historical events. The satirical *Renart le Bestourné* (Renard the False) employs stock characters from fable literature to malign the stinginess of Louis IX in barring poets and minstrels from court in order to save funds and set the mood for a new crusade. A ban on court entertainment would discourage a professional poet whose livelihood depended on the vitality of court festivities. From 1261 to 1265, while the ban was in effect, no fees were to be earned for such works as fabliaux or secular songs. Another work, *La Leçon d'hypocrisie et d'humilité* (A Lesson on Hypocrisy and Humility, 1261), known in manuscript A as *Du Pharisien* (About the Pharisee), celebrates the departure of the enemy of Guillaume de Saint-Amour, Pope Alexander IV, and the election of Pope Urban IV. It is a dream allegory produced, Rutebeuf explains, after he drank wine and passed out on the floor. The first personified figure Rutebeuf meets on his dream journey is *Courtois*, Old French for the Latin *urbanus* (courteous), indicating that *Courtois* stands for Urban IV. The piece presents an exchange in which *Courtois*, having learned that his guest is none other than the poet Rutebeuf, explains that cowards listen to Rutebeuf's poetry in private, while those who fear hypocrites less than they fear God read Rutebeuf openly. Rutebeuf was anxious about championing the secular masters' cause–in the closing verses of *Le Dit sur l'exil de maître Guillaume de Saint-Amour* (The Tale of the Exile of Master Guillaume de Saint-Amour), for instance, he claims he may be executed for his writings–and audiences may indeed have consumed his controversial works at notable risk.

In late 1261 or early 1262 Rutebeuf wrote what has become his best-known poem: *La Complainte Rutebeuf* (Rutebeuf's Lament), a sequel to the *Mariage Rutebeuf*. The situation at the speaker's home has, incredibly, worsened. He claims that God is turning him into a second Job: he has lost an eye (the better one); his horse has broken a foot; the house is cold; the landlord is owed rent; and his wife, still charmless, has delivered a baby the poet cannot afford to feed. These verses ponder the loss of friendship in difficult times:

> Que sunt mi ami devenu
> Que j'avoie si pres tenu
> Et tant amei?
> Je cuit qu'il sun trop cleir semei;
> Il ne furent pas bien femei,
> Si sun failli.

> (Whatever has become of my friends?
> They were so close to me.

> And I loved them so.
> I think they are as seeds, too few sown
> and not well tended.
> And now they're gone.)

With exasperation reaching comical heights in this poem, some readers have taken it to be satirical, while others deem it a literal outpouring of pathetic autobiographical information. The best reading negotiates these two extremes, however. The piece concludes with a plea to Alphonse, Count of Poitiers, brother of King Louis IX, for help. There is no reason to doubt that Rutebeuf was in dire need of support, in part because commissions were, after the *querelle* and during the regal proscription of court entertainment, probably harder than ever to attain. Furthermore, Rutebeuf's role as controversial polemicist may have tarnished his reputation, and Alphonse, regent of the university when the *querelle* reached its fever pitch in 1253, would have been aware of the poet's predicament. The authenticity of Rutebeuf's appeal to a benefactor does not, however, authenticate each detail describing his unfortunate condition. It is not known whether Rutebeuf's poem moved the count to help him, but later compositions suggest that Alphonse was a supportive benefactor. The fabliau entitled *Charlot le juif qui chia dans la peau du lièvre* (Charlie the Jew who Shat in the Hide of a Hare) was commissioned by Alphonse in the mid 1260s, and *La complainte du comte de Poitiers* (Lament for the Count of Poitiers), composed following the count's death in 1271, praises his generosity, loyalty, and piety. In any case, by 1262 Rutebeuf's situation had improved.

This change of fortune coincides with Rutebeuf's conversion. It is not that Rutebeuf did not believe in God before. On the contrary, virtually all of his previous work is marked by his conviction that his opponents are offensive to him precisely because they offend God. But by 1262 Rutebeuf had reevaluated himself, his former writings, and his relationship with God. In *La Repentance de Rutebeuf* (The Repentance of Rutebeuf, alternately titled *La Mort Rutebeuf*, The Death of Rutebeuf), which has been dated around the winter of 1261–1262, he announces this change. In seven strophes of twelve octosyllabic verses, the speaker repents of his former way of life, in which he failed to serve God and cared only for amusements. Many elements of the poem, indeed the genre of the repentance itself, are conventional, but the unusual circumstances of Rutebeuf's career as a polemical writer make his voice unique: "J'ai fait rimes et s'ai chantei / Sus les uns por aux autres plaire" (I've composed verses and, yes, sung / about some to please others).

By late winter in 1262 Rutebeuf undertook a spiritual rehabilitation. He wrote *La Voie d'humilité* (The

Path of Humility), a dream allegory in which the dreamer follows a path leading to Paradise. During the same year, other pieces attest to the survival, by now significantly softened, of his animosities toward mendicants and Louis IX. *La Chanson des Ordres* (The Song about the Mendicant Orders), scripted for a veritable *chanson* (song), tours Parisian orders strophe by strophe, lightly teasing each one. *Le Dit de Frère Denise Le Cordelier* (The Tale of Brother Denise the Franciscan) takes a good swipe at mendicants, but, couched as it is in the genre of the irreverent fabliau, it can hardly have been offensive. The tale tells of Denise, a young woman persuaded by Brother Simon that she can best serve God by cross-dressing so she can secretly join his order. Simon teaches Denise how to love God and, at the same time, how to make love to him. The piece abounds with double entendres.

Rutebeuf's conversion period produced four religious works, composed between 1263 and 1265, dealing with conversion aided by the intercession of the Virgin. These works feature protagonists whose spiritual paths resemble the one Rutebeuf describes in confessional poems as his own. *La Vie De Sainte Marie l'Egyptienne* (The Life of Saint Mary the Egyptian), based on a Greek narrative translated during the middle ages into Latin and vernacular languages, tells the story of a good-for-nothing girl hellbent on being as wanton as possible. She offers her body to an entire crew of sailors in exchange for passage on a ship that leads her to a church where miraculous events prompt her conversion. The Virgin instructs her to take refuge in the wilderness beyond the River Jordan, where she is later discovered by a pious abbot, Zozimas. He witnesses her perform miracles, learns from her the wisdom of humility and self-denial, and eventually buries her with the help of an intelligent lion. Another hagiographical work from this period, *La Vie de Sainte Elysabel* (The Life of Saint Elysabel), recounts the life of Elizabeth, the daughter of King Andrew II of Hungary, who had been canonized in 1235. The commission suggests that Rutebeuf was finding favor in ecclesiastical and courtly society: the piece was requested by the canon of Auxerre (and great-grandson of Geoffroy de Villehardouin), for Isabelle, daughter of King Louis and wife of Thibaut V (son of troubadour Thibaut of Champagne), count of Champagne and king of Navarre. Rutebeuf later memorialized Thibaut, who died returning from the ill-fated crusade to Tunis, in his *Complainte du roi de Navarre* (Lament for the King of Navarre, 1270). A third religious work from this period, *Le Miracle du Sacristain et d'une dame accompli par Notre Dame* (Our Lady's Miracle of the Sexton and a Woman), is a delightful narrative pitting courtly love against the love of God. A virtuous sexton falls hopelessly in love with the equally virtuous

wife of a knight; she returns the sexton's love. Having stolen treasures from the church and made off with belongings from home, they run away together and are on the brink of becoming sinners when they seek and gain help from the Virgin, who performs miracles restoring them without blemish to their lives of virtue.

The most important religious work is Rutebeuf's celebrated dramatic rendering of the legend of Théophile, *Le Miracle de Théophile* (The Miracle of Théophile). The legend had been translated from Greek into Latin by Paul Diacre and circulated widely in collections of miracles, legends, and sermons as well as in sacred iconography. Rutebeuf's work has earned special attention because little dramatic literature from before the end of the thirteenth century survives in Old French. The text was possibly completed in time to be performed on the day of the Virgin's nativity, 8 September 1263.

Whether the play survives only in fragmented form is also open to debate. In the most complete surviving manuscript (A), the action opens with Théophile, a clerk whose bishop has inexplicably dishonored him, distraught and convinced God has mocked him. Enter Salatin, modeled on the figure of the Jew in the Théophile tradition, who proposes that Théophile reject God to become Satan's vassal. Théophile is initially ready to do whatever it takes to set things straight, but once alone he despairs about his decision. It is too late, however: in a nonsense tongue with touches of pseudo-Hebrew, Salatin conjures the devil, who settles Théophile's score in exchange for a letter, written in blood, in which the clerk promises never to invoke Jesus. The bishop, realizing his mistake, attempts to repair the damage he has done, but Théophile merely wisecracks with him. As hotheaded as ever, Théophile then runs into fellow clerks and addresses them with cruel taunts. Alone again, Théophile is horrified by his rash behavior. He enters a chapel, where he undergoes a kind of spiritual breakdown before composing himself to pray. Appearing miraculously, the Virgin agrees to deliver the clerk from his bond with Satan, who is made to surrender the charter after a lively debate with her. Théophile reports these events to his bishop, who reads the charter to the audience and explains how the Virgin rescued Théophile from this crisis. In the final verses the bishop invites the audience to join in the "Te Deum laudamus," a hymn in praise of God.

Parallels between Rutebeuf and Théophile can be argued on the basis of their related spiritual trajectories. Both believe they have been righteous, build expectations that are dashed, undergo crises yielding to introspection, and turn to the Virgin Mary for spiritual guidance. *La Repentance de Rutebeuf* provides an example of Rutebeuf's investment in her powers of spiritual healing, as do three other pieces from around 1265: *Un dit de Notre Dame* (A Word about Our Lady), *L' Ave Maria de Rutebeuf* (Rutebeuf's Ave Maria), and *C'est de Notre Dame* (About Our Lady). Both Rutebeuf and Théophile finally emerge from self-examination to repent and serve God. The formal possibilities of the dramatic mode (allowing impersonated juxtapositions in soliloquy, dialogue, confession, and prayer) permit Rutebeuf to render Théophile's interior fluctuations with unusual clarity and sophistication.

During the final phase of Rutebeuf's career, he wrote commissioned crusade poems. He had produced one crusade poem while embroiled in the *querelle: La Complainte de Monseigneur Geoffroy de Sergines* (Lament for Sir Geoffroy of Sergines, 1255) extols the memory of the Champagnois noble whose military leadership excelled in Egypt. Six years later Rutebeuf composed *La Complainte de Constantinople* (The Lament for Constantinople) in response to Michael Paleologue's invasion of July 1261. The ten remaining poems dealing with crusades date from circa 1265 to 1277. Always ready for controversy, Rutebeuf became a crusade propagandist at a time when religious motivations were used to conceal political ambitions. Urban IV conceived a "crusade" to replace Manfred, son of Emperor Frederic II, on the throne of Sicily with Charles of Anjou, King Louis's brother. The legitimacy of this mission was debated, but Charles took up the cross. Rutebeuf championed the mission in *La Chanson de Pouille* (The Song of Apulia) and *Le Dit de Pouille* (A Word about Apulia), both dating from around 1265. In 1266 Charles conquered Sicily and killed Manfred. With Sicily taken, Pope Clément IV launched another crusade to the Holy Land. Rutebeuf, warming to the genre of the propagandistic crusade poem, composed *La Complainte d'Outremer* (The Complaint for the Crusade Overseas, 1266). When Count Eudes de Nevers died in Acre in the same year, his executor, Gérard de Valeri of Champagne, probably commissioned the eulogy *La Complainte du comte Eudes de Nevers* (Lament for Count Eudes of Nevers, 1266).

In 1267 King Louis and his three sons took up the cross, as did Thibaut of Champagne. *La Voie de Tunis* (The Crusade to Tunis, circa 1267) exhorts others to follow their example. *Le Débat du croisé et du décroisé* (The Debate Between the Crusader and the Non-Crusader, circa 1267), offers an amusing dialogue between knights that Rutebeuf claims to have overheard. One knight has already joined the king in taking up the cross, but the other has different plans: "Je wel entre mes voisins estre / Et moi deduire et solacier" (I prefer to stay among my neighbors and to amuse myself and have fun.) The piece ends with the carousing knight transformed into an exemplary crusader.

As the tone of this piece conveys, Rutebeuf did not consider crusade propaganda and humor incompatible, and he continued to be a satirist during this phase of his career. His satiric depiction of the fast-talking *herbier,* a medieval herbalist akin to a modern confidence man, was also probably composed after 1265. *Le Dit de l'herberie* (A Word about Herbs), part verse and part prose monologue, portrays the charlatan who will say anything, no matter how indecorous or absurd, to make a sale:

> Ce n'est mie freperie
> Mais granz noblesce.
> J'ai l'erbe qui les veiz redresce
> Et cele qui les cons estresce
> A pou de painne.
>
> (This is no thrift shop here.
> These are high class items.
> I have the herb that makes cocks stiff
> plus the one that makes cunts tight with no pain
>   whatsoever.)

The herbalist claims to be able to cure every ailment from hemorrhoids to sudden death. Tuned to the pitch of the marketplace, this work demonstrates Rutebeuf's talent for capturing voices not only of the lettered but also of those in the streets of his Paris.

Rutebeuf's remaining compositions suggest that at the end of his career he had once again fallen on hard times. St. Louis died in Tunis in 1270, leaving the young Philippe III king. *Le dit d'Aristote* (The Tale of Aristotle, circa 1270), adapted from a section of Gautier de Châtillon's *Alexandréide,* purporting to reproduce Aristotle's teachings for prince Alexander, was probably intended for the young king Rutebeuf hoped would become his benefactor. Most of Rutebeuf's supporters died on the crusades, and he would have been eager to replace them, but prospects for new commissions were apparently grim. In the epigram *De Brichemer* (On Brichemer, circa 1270), Rutebeuf complains that someone in the court has made false promises to him of generosity. *La Paix de Rutebeuf* (Rutebeuf's Peace) also implies the loss of a supporter; the poet hopes none of his friends ever achieves high social standing lest he fall in with flatterers and lose true friendship. In *La pauvreté Rutebeuf* (The Poverty of Rutebeuf, circa 1277), Rutebeuf implores Philippe III for help: "Sire, je vos fais a savoir, / Je n'ai de quoi do pain avoir . . ." (Sire, I inform you that / I have nothing with which to buy bread.)

The only subsequent work whose authorship is certain, however, is *La Nouvelle complainte d'outremer* (The New Complaint for a Crusade Overseas, circa 1277). In 1277 Pope Jean XXI tried to revive interest in a stale plan for a crusade to the Holy Land, but the mission never got off the ground. Rutebeuf wrote when there was a flicker of hope for the enterprise, seizing on the potential of his youthful addressees to live up to the memories of great crusaders the poet had known.

Critical reception of Rutebeuf begins with Legrand d'Aussy, who noted on the eve of the French Revolution of 1789 that Rutebeuf was a poet for whom nothing was sacred; he asked how Rutebeuf could even have existed under a king as pious as Louis IX. During the Romantic period, when readers assumed he was a miraculously literate peasant genius, Rutebeuf was considered to be a noble savage expressing the disillusionment of downtrodden medieval masses. Following the Revolution of 1848, Rutebeuf was seen as the original French bourgeois individual, a brilliant exposer of papal and regal shams, the fearless confronter of ugly truths about the self and society.

Rutebeuf's poetry is the product of conflicts, whether of grand scale (wars waged in the name of Christendom), of local scale (the fractious corporation of the university), or within the individual. Railing against citizens, mendicants, or himself, Rutebeuf believed he is the champion of God, even as his relationship to God evolved. Rutebeuf had his eyes and ears unusually open to his cosmopolitan environment as well as his own combative identity.

Rutebeuf's legacy is twofold. For one, *Le Miracle de Théophile* was the first dramatization of the narrative miracle. This play opened an important chapter in the story of the development of the medieval religious drama because the miracle play went on to gain immense popularity during the fourteenth century. Secondly, Rutebeuf's poetic innovation, the voice of the urban individual, has earned him a distinction as the earliest delineator of the modern voice in the French lyrical tradition. Not until the arrival of François Villon would the sound of Rutebeuf's voice be heard again. Clear reverberations of Rutebeuf's Paris survive, too, in the language of the bohemian poets of the late nineteenth century known as the *poètes maudits* (accursed poets).

References:

Jean-Pierre Bordier, "L'Antéchrist au quartier latin selon Rutebeuf," *Milieux universitaires et mentalité urbaine au Moyen Age* (Paris: Presses de l'Université de Paris-Sorbonne, 1987), pp. 9–21;

Léon Clédat, *Rutebeuf* (Paris: Hachette, 1891);

Anne-Lise Cohen, "Exploration of Sounds in Rutebeuf's Poetry," *French Review,* 40 (1966–1967): 658–667;

Gustave Cohen, "Rutebeuf: L'Ancêtre des poètes maudits," *Etudes classiques,* 21 (1953): 1–18;

Roger Dragonetti, "Rutebeuf. Les poèmes de la 'griesche,'" *Présent à Henri Maldiney* (Lausanne: L'Age d'Homme, 1973), pp. 83–110;

Jean Dufournet, "Rutebeuf et les moines mendiants," *Neuphilologische Mitteilungen,* 85 (1984): 152–168;

Dufournet and François de la Breteque, "L'univers poétique et moral de Rutebeuf," *Revue des Langues Romanes,* 87 (1984): 39–78;

Leslie Dunton-Downer, "Poetic Language and the Obscene," in *Obscenity: Social Control and Artistic Creation in the European Middle Ages,* edited by Jan M. Ziolkowski (Leiden: Brill, 1998);

Dunton-Downer, "Treasures in the Body: An Old French Acrostic," *Medievalia et Humanistica,* 18 (1992): 67–78;

Edmond Faral, *La Vie quotidienne au temps de saint Louis* (Paris: Hachette, 1942);

Jean Frappier, "Rutebeuf, poète du jeu, du guignon, et de la misère," *Du Moyen Age à la Renaissance* (Paris: Champion, 1976), pp. 123–132;

Omer Jodogne, "L'anticléricalisme de Rutebeuf," *Lettres Romanes,* 23 (1969): 219–244;

Albert Junker, "Über dem Gebrauch des Stilmittels der 'Annominatio' bei Rutebeuf," *Zeitschrift für Romanische Philologie,* 11 (1957–1958): 226–239;

Gordon Leff, *Paris and Oxford Universities in the Thirteenth and Fourteenth Centuries* (New York: John Wiley, 1968);

Jacques Le Goff, *Les intellectuels au Moyen Age* (Paris: Seuil, 1957);

Per Nykrog, *Les fabliaux: Etude d'histoire littéraire et de stylistique médiévale,* second edition (Geneva: Droz, 1973);

L. G. Pesce, "Le portrait de Rutebeuf," *Revue de l'Université d'Ottowa,* 28 (1958): 55–118;

G. Post, "Parisian Masters as a Corporation: 1200–1246," *Speculum,* 7 (1934): 421–445;

Nancy Freeman Regalado, *Poetic Patterns in Rutebeuf. A Study in Noncourtly Poetic Modes of the XIIIth Century* (New Haven: Yale University Press, 1970);

Michel Rousse, "Le Mariage Rutebeuf et la fête des fous," *Le Moyen Age,* 88 (1982): 435–449;

Michel Zink, "De la *Repentance Rutebeuf* à la *Repentance de Théophile*," *Littératures,* 15 (1986): 19–24;

Zink, "Rutebeuf et le cours du poème," *Romania,* 107 (1986): 546–551;

Zink, *La subjectivité littéraire. Autour du siècle de Saint Louis* (Paris: Presses Universitaire de France, 1985);

Paul Zumthor, *La lettre et la voix. De la 'littérature' médiévale* (Paris: Seuil, 1987).

Geoffroi de Villehardouin

(circa 1150 – circa 1215)

Jeanette Beer
Purdue University

WORK: *La Conquête de Constantinople*

Manuscripts: This work is preserved in six manuscripts: Oxford, Bodleian Library, Laud. misc. 587; Paris, Bibliothèque Nationale de France, f. fr. 4972 (anc. 9644); Bibliothèque Nationale de France, f. fr. 2137 (anc. 7974); Bibliothèque Nationale de France, f. fr. 12204 (anc. Suppl. 207); Bibliothèque Nationale de France, f. fr. 12203 (anc. Suppl. 455); Bibliothèque Nationale de France, f. fr. 24210 (Sorbonne 397).

Editions: The "Premier cahier" of Villehardouin's text was published in Venice in 1572 from the now-lost Contarini manuscript. No known copies of this edition remain. *Histoire de Geoffroy de Villehardouyn, mareschal de Champagne et de Romenie, de la Conqueste de Constantinople par le barons françois associez aux Venitiens, l'an 1204; d'un costé en son vieil langage, et de l'autre en un plus moderne et intelligible,* edited by Blaise de Vigenère (Paris: Abel Langelier, 1585) from the now-lost Zacco manuscript; *L'Histoire ou Chronique du seigneur Geoffroy de Villehardouin, mareschal de Champaigne et de Romanie, representee de mot a mot en ancienne langue françoise, d'un vieil exemplaire escrit a la main, qui se trouve dans les anciens archives de la serenissime republique de Venise, contenant la conqueste de l'empire de Constantinople, faicte par des barons françois confederés et unis avec les seigneurs venitiens, l'an 1204. Ensemble la description de la prinse de Constantinople, extraicte de la fin des Annales de Nicete Coniates, historien grec et chancelier des empereurs constantinopolitains, de nouveau mise en françois* (Lyon: Les Héritiers de Guillaume Rouille, 1601) from the now-lost Contarini manuscript in conjunction with the Paradin manuscript and the Zacco manuscript (or, possibly, the Vigenère edition of the Zacco manuscript); C. Du Fresne, Seigneur Du Cange, ed., H*istoire de l'empire de Constantinople sous les empereurs françois,* part 1: *Histoire de la conqueste de la ville de Constantinople par les François et les Venitiens,* by Geoffroy de Villehardouin, from the Bibliothèque du Roy manuscript, with historical notes and a glossary (Paris: Imprimerie royale, 1657); a second edition was produced in Venice (B. Javarina, 1729) from the 1601 Lyon edition, including variants from the Paris, Bibliothèque Nationale de France, f. fr. 4972 (anc. 9644) manuscript; Petitot, ed., *Collection complète des mémoires relatifs à l'histoire de Franc,* volume 1: Villehardouin, *Mémoires* (Paris: Foucault, 1819) from Du Cange. Dom Brial, ed., *Recueil des historiens des Gaules et de la France* XVIII: 431–514 (Paris: Imprimerie royale, 1822); *De la conquête de Constantinople,* by Villehardouin, from Du Cange including variants from Paris, Bibliothèque Nationale de France, f. fr. 2137 (anc. 7974) and Bibliothèque Nationale de France, f. fr. 12204 (anc. Suppl. 207); J.-A. Buchon, ed., *Collection des chroniques nationales francaises écrites en langue vulgaire du XIIIe au XVIe siècle,* volumes 1–2: *Chronique,* by Villehardouin, reedited from Du Cange's second edition (Paris: Verdières, 1826); Michaud and Poujoulat, eds., *Nouvelle collection de mémoires pour servir à l'histoire de France, depuis le XIIIe siècle,* series 1, volume 1: *Villehardouin* (Paris: l'Editeur du Commentaire analytique du Code civil, 1836) from Du Cange; Paulin Paris, ed., *De la conqueste de Constantinople* by Geoffroi de Villehardouin, (Paris: J. Renouard, 1838) from Paris, Bibliothèque Nationale de France, f. fr. 4972, 2137, 12203, 12204, and 15100; J.-A. Buchon, *Recherches et matériaux pour servir à une histoire de la domination française aux XIIIe, XIVe et XVe siècles dans les provinces démembrées de l'empire grec,* 2 parts (Paris: A. Desrez, 1840); Part 2: *Chroniques des empereurs Baudouin et Henri de Constantinople,* p. 33 (from Paris, Bibliothèque Nationale de France, f. fr. 12204); Natalis de Wailly, ed., *Conquête de Constantinople,* by Ville-Hardouin, (Paris: Firmin-Didot, 1872, reprinted 1874; new edition, 1882) from Paris, Bibliothèque Nationale de France, 4972, 2137, 12203, 12204, 24210, and 15100; Emile Bouchet, ed., *La Conquête de Constantinople,* by Villehardouin, text and new translation (Paris: A. Lemerre, 1891) from N. de Wailly; Gaston Paris and A. Jeanroy, eds. *Extraits des Chroniqueurs français–Villehardouin, Joinville, Froissart, Comines,* (Paris: Hachette, 1927); Edmond Faral. ed., *La Conquête de*

Constantinople, by Villehardouin, (Paris: Belles Lettres, 1938), 2 volumes; A. Pauphilet and E. Pognon, eds., *Historiens et Chroniqueurs du Moyen Age* (Paris: Gallimard, 1952). Sir Frank T. Marzials, trans., *Memoirs of the Crusades* (New York: E. P. Dutton, 1958). Margaret Shaw, ed. and trans., *Chronicles of the Crusades* (Harmondsworth, U.K.: Penguin, 1963; reprinted 1986). J. E. White, ed., Geoffroy de Villehardouin, *La Conqueste de Constantinople* (New York: Appleton-Century-Crofts, 1968) from the Bodleian, Laud. misc. 587 with readings from Faral. Jean Dufournet, *Villehardouin, "La Conquête de Constantinople"* (Paris: Garnier-Flammarion, 1969).

Geoffroi de Villehardouin, Maréchal de Champagne and cousin to Thibaut and Louis de Champagne, enlisted as a crusader with his brother Stephen at Perche in 1199, and his role as planner, provisioner, diplomat, and leader was of supreme importance in the Fourth Crusade (1202–1204). Ranking just below the counts of Flanders, Champagne, and Blois and trusted by them for his diplomatic skill and absolute dependability, he was selected to be one of six envoys who met with the doge of Venice to secure transportation for the crusade. He was also privy to, and influential upon, all negotiations and decisions that determined the course of the crusade, working to hold the controversial expedition together when it foundered and personally participating in all its hazards through to its eventual outcome: the parceling out of feudal domains and the defense of the new "Romania." By the breadth of his experience and his professional familiarity with legal and administrative prose, Villehardouin was ideally qualified to record the events of the Fourth Crusade. Thus, *La Conquête de Constantinople* (The Conquest of Constantinople), although one of the earliest chronicles in the French vernacular, is perhaps the richest and most cogent source of information extant concerning the Fourth Crusade.

Geoffroi de Villehardouin was born circa 1150– the name, "Gofridus de Ville Hardoin," appears in a list of vassals of the count of Champagne in 1172, a listing that would not have been valid if he had been still been a minor. He succeeded to the title of "maréchal de Champagne" (marshal of Champagne) in 1185 and was married twice. He was related by birth or marriage to many of Champagne's noble houses, among them the Villemaur, Lezinnes, Chappes, and Monbar families. He was often called upon to arbitrate serious disputes between local and church authorities: for example, Countess Marie de Champagne asked him to mediate between the abbey of Pontigny and Sir Engobran de Saint-Chéron (1195); the monks of Montieramey requested him as their arbitrator in 1198; and in the same year he mediated

Fulk of Neuilly preaching in favor of the Fourth Crusade (illuminated initial in a manuscript for Geoffroi de Villehardouin's La Conquête de Constantinople, *Oxford, Bodleian Library, ms. Laud Misc. 587, fol. 1)*

between Count Thibaut de Champagne and the cathedral chapter of Troyes. The remaining events of his life as crusader and negotiator are narrated with clarity in the third-person narrative of *La Conquête de Constantinople.* The work begins with the formality of a proclamation:

> Sachiez que .M. et .C. et quatre vinz et .XVII. anz aprés l'incarnation Nostre Sengnor Jesu Crist, al tens Innocent, apostoille de Rome, et Phelippe, roy de France, et Ricchart, roy d'Engleterre, ot un saint home en France, qui ot nom Folques de Nuilli (cil Nuillis si est entre Ligni sor Marne e Paris) et il ere prestres et tenoit la parroiche de la ville. Et cil Folques dont je vos di comença a parler de Dieu par France et par les autres terres entor; et Nostre Sire fist maintes miracles por lui.

> (Be it known that eleven hundred and ninety-seven years after the Incarnation of Our Lord Jesus Christ, in the time of Innocent, Pope of Rome, and Philip, King of France, and Richard, King of England, there was in France a holy man called Fulk of Neuilly [which Neuilly is between Ligny-sor-Marne and Paris], and he was a priest and held the town's parish. And this said Fulk began to speak of God throughout the Ile-de-France and the other regions around; and Our Lord did many miracles on his account.)

Without flowery preamble, Villehardouin has engaged his public with the command to be informed—"sachiez"—and be persuaded (an element of self-justification cannot be ruled out of Villehardouin's self-avowed "testimony"). Documentary preoccupations declare themselves immediately in the formal dating, the hierarchical presentation of monarchs spiritual and temporal, and the legal hyper-explicitness of Villehardouin's precision. He moves swiftly from the popular preaching of Fulk and the papal promise of indulgences for a crusading pilgrimage to the details that, as leader and administrator, only he knew so completely. Enlistment for the crusade began at a tournament arranged at Ecry by Thibaut de Champagne "at the beginning of Advent" (that is, 28 November 1199). Hierarchically again, Villehardouin names those who committed themselves to the enterprise, including "Joffrois de Vilehardoin li mareschaus de Campaingne" (Geoffrey de Villehardouin, the marshal of Champagne) and "Joffrois ses niers" (Geoffrey his nephew), who were among those who took the cross with their overlord, Thibaut de Champagne.

At the end of 1200, Villehardouin was chosen to be one of six envoys to secure transport for the Fourth Crusade. The six arrived in Venice in February 1201 and delivered to the doge letters of credence that gave them full powers to negotiate for the crusading barons. Villehardouin stresses the authority of the envoys meticulously, giving their letters of credence as much prominence as the ambassadors themselves, and mentioning that "Jofrois de Vilehardoin li mareschaus de Campaigne moustra la parole par l'acort et la volenté as autres messages" (Geoffroi of Villehardouin, the marshal of Champagne, was spokesman by the will and agreement of the other envoys). Not surprisingly, he finds high drama in the formal reception of the envoys, which included a solemn mass in the Basilica of St. Mark's, emotional pleas for assistance from the weeping envoys on their knees, and thunderous acclamation from the Venetians, which was so great that "the very ground seemed to tremble." Few scenes in *La Conquête de Constantinople* elicit such explicit emotion from the army negotiator, statesman, and advocate as these preliminary negotiations with Venice.

The six were granted an audience with the doge's Small Council on the fourth day, but the decision-making process required several stages, including ratification by the Great Council. After much debate, it was agreed that for the sum of eighty-five thousand marks, to be delivered by the French in four installments by April 1202, the Venetians would supply transport and provisions for the crusading army. The fleet would then be able to depart on 29 June of that year. Before returning to France, the envoys borrowed two thousand marks to enable the Venetians to begin construction of the crusading fleet. It remained only to obtain the Pope's confirmation of the enterprise, which was given early in May.

From the beginning of the crusade, therefore, Villehardouin was a leading figure in its planning, and this role continued through its various vicissitudes. For example, difficulties arose over the choice of a leader, Thibaut de Champagne having died on 24 May. After two refusals—from Duke Eudes of Burgundy and Count Thibaud de Bar-le-Duc—Villehardouin proposed Boniface de Montferrat, "mult prodom et uns des plus proisiez qui hui cest jor vive" (a fine man, one of the most esteemed of our time), who became the new leader. Other problems included defectors, who reneged on the Crusade, and a scarcity of money so that the crusading leaders could not meet their commitments to the Venetians. The latter used the opportunity to obtain a diversion of the Fourth Crusade to Zara in return for extending the time of the crusading loan. That decision was not universally approved by all the crusaders, many of whom feared that they would be excommunicated if they attacked a Christian city. Villehardouin lists the early defectors, among whom was the important Count Louis de Blois, and records that Hugh, Count of St. Pol, and he were personally sent "pour les exhorter et pour les supplier d'avoir pitié de la terre d'outremer et [leur montrer] qu'aucun autre passage ne pouvait être de profit que celui de Venise" (to exhort them and beg them to have pity on the Holy Land overseas and [show them] that no other route could be of profit except that from Venice). Zara was then besieged and captured, and the fears of some of the crusaders proved to be justified when they received a letter from the Pope forbidding any attack upon a Christian city on pain of excommunication. An embassy was despatched to the Pope, arguing for his absolution of the crusaders on the grounds that their attack upon Zara was an inevitable means toward the end of rescuing Jerusalem. Villehardouin takes care to report that the Pope granted this request, "Car il savoit bien que sans cele ost ne pooit li servises Dieu estre fais" (For he knew that the service of God could not be achieved without the services of this expedition).

The army remained split, and Villehardouin lists among the new defectors "Symons de Montfort . . . , Guys de Monfort ses freres, Symons de Neafle, et Roberz Malvoisins, et Drius de Cressonessart, et l'abés de Vals, qui ere moine de l'ordre de Cistiaus, et maint autre . . . et Engelranz de Bove, et Hues ses freres." His own point of view is made very clear when he castigates these defectors and their many followers: "molt fu granz domages a l'ost, et honte a cels qui le firent" (it was a very great loss to the army and shame upon those who did this).

Illumination depicting the assault on Constantinople (from a manuscript for Villehardouin's La Conquête de Constantinople, *Oxford, Bodleian Library, ms. Laud Misc. 587, fol. 1)*

Meanwhile, talks had been going on between the crusaders and the young Byzantine prince Alexius, who was trying to acquire the throne of Constantinople that had been seized from his father, Isaac, by his uncle, Alexius III. The crusading leaders undertook this new mission in return for aid promised to the Jerusalem expedition by the young pretender. Defections continued, but the leaders managed to persuade many of the dissidents to stay with them until the feast of St. Michael (29 September 1203), when they would be entitled to request ships to travel onward to Jerusalem, if they so wished. The sobriety of Villehardouin's controlled narrative style cannot totally obscure his pride of achievement on the proud day when he saw the crusading fleet leave Corfu for Scutari:

Ensi se partirent del port de Corfol la veille de Pentecoste, qui fu .M. et .CC. anz et trois aprés l'incarnation Nostre Seignor Jesu Crist; et enqui furent totes les nés ensemble et tuit li uissier et totes les galies de l'ost et assez d'autres nés de marcheans qui avec s'erent aroutees. Et li jors fu bels et clers, et li venz dolz et soés. Et il laissent aler les voilles al vent.

Et bien testimoigne Joffrois li mareschaus de Champaigne, qui ceste oevre dita, que ainc n'i menti de mot a son escient, si com cil qui a toz les conseils fu, que onc si bele chose ne fu veüe; et bien sembloit estoire qui terre deüst conquerre: que, tant que om pooit veoir a oil, ne pooit on veoir se voilles non de nés et de vaissiaus, si que li cuer des hommes s'enjoïssoient mult.

(And so they left the port of Corfu on the eve of Pentecost, which was twelve hundred and three years after the Incarnation of Our Lord Jesus Christ; all the ships were assembled there, and all the transports and all the army's galleys, and many other merchant ships that had joined them. The day was fine and clear, and the gentle wind was favorable. They unfurl their sails to the wind.

Geoffrey, the Marshal of Champagne who dictated this work and never to his knowledge lied in it with a single word, having been present at all the councils, bears witness that there never was such a beautiful sight. It certainly looked like a fleet destined to conquer territory for, as far as the eye could see, there was nothing but sails of ships and vessels, and men's hearts rejoiced.)

The fleet of crusaders did indeed achieve the conquest of Constantinople after they had attacked the city by land and by sea. Villehardouin records the various stages of the capture, listing the crusading divisions, the distinguished names and their acts of heroism (or cowardice), the tactics and weapons, and a variety of other details that were available uniquely to him as marshal of the army.

His exhilaration at the brilliant, if expensive, victory, at the dazzling wonders of Constantinople, and at the coronation of the young Alexius as the city's new emperor soon give way to reality, however, and to an ominous situation that was pending. The newly crowned emperor had conveniently forgotten his obligations to the crusading expedition and was refusing to supply them with the promised funds to leave Constantinople for Jerusalem. After many futile requests to obtain what they considered to be their dues, the crusaders sent six envoys, among them Villehardouin, to present their demands personally, a mission that was not without its hazards. In his usual understated manner, Villehardouin reports:

Mult tindrent li Greu a grant mervoille et a grant oltrage ceste desfiance, et distrent que onques mais nus n'avoit esté si ardiz qui ossast l'empereor de Costantinople desfier en sa chambre. Mult fist as messages malvais semblant l'empereres Alexis et tuit li autre, qui mainte foiz lor avoient fait mult bel.

(The Greeks were very amazed and very outraged at this challenge, saying that no one had ever been so bold as to defy the emperor of Constantinople in his own palace. The envoys were now given evil looks by the Emperor Alexis and all the rest who had often regarded them very favorably.)

The mission to Alexius was unsuccessful, and the uneasy alliance between him and the crusaders came to an end. Next, however, the anti-Latin agitator Alexius Ducas, called Mourtzuphle, usurped the throne of Constantinople, causing another attack upon the city and a second conquest by the crusaders. The subsequent occupation of Constantinople, the army's acquisition of booty, the wedding of Boniface de Montferrat to Margaret, widowed empress of Isaac III, and the election of Baldwin of Flanders to be emperor of the new empire called "Romanie" (Romania or Thrace) are among the events narrated by Villehardouin for the years 1204–1205.

The impermanent nature of the crusading achievement becomes clear in the second half of *La Conquête de Constantinople,* which records the partition of the new empire among the victorious barons and their painful struggles to defend it. After endless skirmishes and petty victories and defeats, Villehardouin's chronicle ends inconclusively with the death of Boniface de Montferrat from wounds received in an ambush. "Et ceste mesaventure avint en l'an de l'incarnation Jhesu Crist .MCC. et .VI. anz" (And this misadventure took place in the year twelve hundred and six after the Incarnation of Jesus Christ). As for Villehardouin himself, little beyond what he has written is known of his activities after he went to occupy his large fief in Romania. It is not even known where or how the newly titled "mareschaus de Romenie" met his death. His nephew, Geoffroi I de Villehardouin, who with Guillaume de Champlitte had subdued the Greeks in Morea, succeeded the latter as prince of Achaia in 1210 and there founded a Villehardouin dynasty, which ended with the death of Guillaume de Villehardouin in 1278.

Although Villehardouin was one of the earliest chroniclers in the vernacular, *La Conquête de Constantinople* is a sophisticated and professional account of the Fourth Crusade. It combines the eyewitness authority that any crusader possessed by virtue of participation with the privileged information of a leader, planner, negotiator, and provisioner. Inevitably, those official

roles molded Villehardouin's point of view, causing him to highlight certain events and personalities while downplaying others, but a charge of dishonest reporting is difficult to sustain. It is useful to make a comparison of his *La Conquête de Constantinople* with the contemporary *La Conquête de Constantinople* of Robert de Clari. Robert was a lowly Picard knight without political savvy. His account of the Fourth Crusade was reliable only in its reports of what Robert had personally experienced: a common soldier's awe at the richness of the fleet in Venice and the exoticism of marvelous Constantinople, a common soldier's disgruntlement at being shortchanged at the time of booty distribution, and a common soldier's hearsay reports of the leaders' strategies. Villehardouin, on the other hand, commanded an overview of the whole enterprise from its ambitious beginnings to its challenging, some would say pathetic, end. His orderly mind and his gift for systematic narration make this as informed a history as any modern general's memoirs.

Villehardouin's *La Conquête de Constantinople* is a rare stylistic achievement, reflecting the professionalism of a prose that had been honed over five centuries in palaces, churches, chanceries, and political embassies for just such purposes. By the thirteenth century, French vernacular prose was the ideal medium for the "testimony" of an administrator who preferred to dispense with flowery preambles. Villehardouin chose to begin with the formality of a proclamation and to sign the record off just as formally ("Et ceste mesaventure avint en l'an de l'Incarnation Jhesu Crist .MCC. et .VI. anz"). His manner of narration was also unelaborate. Composition by dictation encouraged the use of communication techniques borrowed from oral narrative (repetition, exclamation, direct apostrophe of the public, formulae of recapitulation, anticipation, and summary), giving *La Conquête de Constantinople* directness and clarity. The chansons de geste also supplied inspiration and fervor: Villehardouin imbues the doge of Venice with the heroic qualities of a Charlemagne and vilifies "the others" (whether pagans, Greeks, or even French defectors). Nourished in heroic traditions and cognizant also of the monumental efforts that had been expended on its planning, it was inevitable that even such a sober adminstrator as Villehardouin would see the Fourth Crusade as an event of epic proportions: "Onques si grant affaires ne fu empris de tant de gent puis que li monz fu estorez" (No greater enterprise was ever undertaken since the world began).

Modern readers no longer share Villehardouin's convictions about the rightness of the Fourth Crusade, and modern historians attempt to tangle out hidden complexities that might lurk between the lines of his straightforward narration. Yet *La Conquête de Constantino-*

ple continues to be one of the most reliable resources for the crusading years 1202–1204 and their aftermath. The marshal's leading role in the events he describes, his absolute command of their every detail, and his skillful ordering of the privileged information in a diplomatic prose that is simple yet authoritative make his chronicle unique. It is one of the ironies of history that the most dubious of the crusading enterprises should have been gifted with the ablest of the vernacular chroniclers.

References:

Jeanette Beer, *Early Prose in France* (Kalamazoo, Mich.: Medieval Institute Publications, 1992), pp. 127–140;

Beer, *Villehardouin, Epic Historian* (Geneva: Droz, 1968);

Beer, "Villehardouin and the Oral Style," *Studies in Philology,* 67, no. 3 (1970): 267–277;

Beer, "Author-Formulae and the Differentiation of Material in Villehardouin's *La Conquête de Constantinople,*" *Studies in Philology,* 32, no. 3 (1979): 298–303;

Beer, "The Notion of Temporality in Early Vernacular History," *New Zealand Journal of French Studies,* 8, no. 1 (1987): 5–15;

F. M. Bonhard, "A Critical Study of the Archaisms in the Vocabulary of Villehardouin," dissertation, University of Southern California, 1947;

Louis Burgener, *L'Art militaire chez Villehardouin et chez Froissart* (Bienne: Les Editions du Chandelier, 1948);

Jean Dufournet, *Villehardouin et Clari,* 2 volumes (Paris: Société d'Enseignement Supérieur, 1973);

Dufournet, "Villehardouin et Clari, juges de Boniface de Montferrat," *Revue des langues romanes,* 79 (1969): 29–58;

Dufournet, "Villehardouin et les Vénitiens," *L'Information littéraire,* 1 (1969): 7–19;

Edmond Faral, "Geoffroy de Villehardouin: la question de sa sincérité," *Revue historique,* 177 (1936): 530–582;

Jean Frappier, "Les discours dans la chronique de Villehardouin," in *Etudes romanes dédiées à Mario Roques* (Paris: Droz, 1946);

Frappier, "Le style de Villehardouin dans le style de sa chronique," *Bulletin of the John Rylands Library,* 30 (1946): 57–70;

John Godfrey, *1204, The Unholy Crusade* (Oxford & New York: Oxford University Press, 1980);

G. Gougenheim, "Notes sur le vocabulaire de Clari et de Villehardouin," *Romania,* 68 (1944–1945): 401–421;

Bernhard Greving, *Studien über die Nebensätze bei Villehardouin: ein Beitrag zur historischen Syntax der französischen Sprache* (Kiel: Vollbehr & Riepen, 1903);

A. Haase, *Syntaktische Untersuchungen zu Villehardouin und Joinville* (Oppeln: Wilhelm Gronau, 1884);

Richard Hartman, *La Quête et la croisade: Villehardouin, Clari et le Lancelot en prose* (New York: Postillion Press, 1977);

Arbois de Jubainville, "Nouvelles Recherches sur le chroniqueur Geoffroi de Villehardouin," *Revue des Sociétés Savantes,* series 3, 1 (1863): 364–373;

Adolf Kressner, "Über des epischen Charakter der Sprache Villehardouins," *Archiv für neuere Sprachen,* 57 (1877): 1–16;

G. Landertinger, 'Der kriegstechnische Wortschatz bei Villehardouin und Robert de Clari," dissertation, University of Vienna, 1937;

Jean Larmat, 'Sur quelques aspects de la religion chrétienne dans les Chroniques de Villehardouin et de Clari," *Moyen Age,* 80 (1974): 403–427;

Jean Longnon, *Les Compagnons de Villehardouin: recherches sur les croisés de la quatrième croisade* (Geneva: Droz, 1978);

Longnon, *Recherches sur la vie de Geoffroy de Villehardouin suivies du Catalogue des actes des Villehardouin* (Paris: H. Champion, 1939);

Colin Morris, "Geoffroy de Villehardouin and the Conquest of Constantinople," *History,* 53 (1968): 24–34;

Albert Pauphilet, "Robert de Clari et Villehardouin," *Mélanges de linguistique et de littérature offerts à M. Alfred Jeanroy,* (Paris: Droz, 1928);

P. J. Penwarden, "A Linguistic and Stylistic Comparison of the Chronicles by Villehardouin and Robert de Clari of 'La Conquête de Constantinople,'" dissertation, University of London, 1953;

Ernest Petit, *Les Sires de Villehardouin* (Troyes: J.-L. Paton, 1913);

Donald E. Queller, *The Fourth Crusade* (Philadelphia: University of Pennsylvania Press, 1977);

Queller, *Medieval Dipomacy and the Fourth Crusade* (London: Variorum Reprints, 1980);

P. M. Schon, *Studien zum Stil der frühen französischen Prosa (Robert de Clari, Geoffroy de Villehardouin, Henri de Valenciennes), Analecta Romanica; Beihefte zu den Romanischen Forschungen,* 8 (Frankfurt-am-Main: V. Klostermann, 1960);

Elise Siepmann, "Die Wortstellung in der Conquête de Constantinople von Ville-Hardouin," dissertation, University of Münster, 1937;

Cornelis J. Starrenburg, "L'ordonnance de la phrase chez Villehardouin," dissertation, University of Leiden, 1939;

Robert Lee Wolff and Harry W. Hazard, eds., *The Later Crusades,* volume 2 of *A History of the Crusades,* edited by Kenneth M. Setton (Madison: University of Wisconsin Press, 1969).

François Villon

(1431 – circa 1463?)

Judy Kem
Wake Forest University

WORKS: *Ballades en jargon* (circa 1450)

Manuscripts: These eleven ballades appear in Brussels, Bibliothèque Royale/Koninklijke Bibliotheek, VI 541, copied in 1568, includes ballades 1, 2, 5, and 6; and Stockholm, Kungliga Biblioteket, V.u. 22, fifteenth century, after 1477, includes ballades 7–11.

First publication: Ballades 1–6 in *Le Grant Testament Villon et le petit. Son codicille. Le jargon & ses ballades* (Paris: Pierre Levet, 1489); ballades 1–11 in *Oeuvres complètes de François Villon, publiées d'après les manuscrits et les plus anciennes éditions,* edited by Auguste Longnon (Paris: Lemerre, 1892), pp. 148–158.

Standard edition: In *François Villon: Oeuvres,* 2 volumes, edited by Auguste Longnon and Lucien Foulet, fourth edition (Paris: H. Champion, 1970).

Editions in modern French: *François Villon: Ballades en jargon (y compris celles du manuscrit de Stockholm),* translated by André Lanly (Paris: H. Champion, 1971); *Les Onze "Ballades du jargon et jobelin," traduites en français moderne,* translated by Ionela Manolesco (Montreal: Guérin, 1980); in *François Villon: Poésies,* edited and translated into prose by Jean Dufournet (Paris: Imprimerie Nationale, 1984), pp. 229–240.

Editions in English: Ballades 1–6 in *The Complete Works of François Villon,* translated by Anthony Bonner (New York: Bantam, 1960), pp. 170–181; ballades 1–11 in *François Villon: Complete Poems,* translated by Barbara Nelson Sargent-Baur (Toronto: University of Toronto Press, 1994), pp. 300–321.

Poèmes variés (also known as *Poésies diverses* and *Le Codicille,* circa 1450?–1463)

Manuscripts: These sixteen poems appear in a great number of manuscripts, often in a different order and interspersed with verses from *Le Lais* and *Le Testament:* poem 12 appears in A (Paris, Bibliothèque de l'Arsenal 3523, last quarter of the fifteenth century); poems 1, 2, 10, and 13–16 in Br. Brussels, Bibliothèque Royale/Koninklijke Bibliotheek, VI 541, copied in 1568; poems 11–12 and 14–16 in C. (Paris, Bibliothèque Nationale de France, f. fr. 20041, copied in the fifteenth century, after 1463); poem 5 in Chantilly, Musée Condé, Cc. 723, 1482 or after; poems 2–4, 11, and 13–16 in F. (Stockholm, Kungliga Biblioteket, V.u. 22, fifteenth century, after 1477); poems 5 and 10 in H. (Berlin, Kupferstichkabinett, Signatur 78 B 17, circa 1475); poem 5 in N. (Paris, Bibliothèque Nationale de France, f. fr. 2206, sixteenth century, after 1562); poems 3 and 7–8 in O/1 (Paris, Bibliothèque Nationale de France, f. fr. 25485, last poem dated 14 February 1458) and in O/2 (Paris, Bibliothèque Nationale de France, f. fr. 1104, between 1458 and 1465); poems 2, 3, 10–12, and 14–16 in P. (Paris, Bibliothèque Nationale de France, f. fr. 1719, end of the fifteenth century or beginning of the sixteenth); poem 1 in Pa. (Paris, Bibliothèque Nationale de France, f. fr. 833, late fifteenth or early sixteenth century); poems 2, 3, 5, 10, 11, and 13–16 in R. (Paris, Bibliothèque Nationale de France, f. fr. 12490, sixteenth century, after 1514); poem 5 in S. (Paris, Bibliothèque Nationale de France, f. fr. 2375, late fifteenth or early sixteenth century), and 5 and 14 in T. (Paris, Bibliothèque Nationale de France, f. fr. 24315, sixteenth century, after 1560).

First publication: In *Le Grant Testament Villon et le petit. Son codicille. Le jargon & ses ballades* (Paris: Pierre Levet, 1489), omits poems 1, 4–9, and 12; in *Œuvres completes de François Villon, publiées d'après les manuscrits et les plus anciennes éditions,* edited by Auguste Longnon (Paris: Lemerre, 1892), pp. 129–142, omits poem 3; in *Le Lais Villon et les poèmes variés,* 2 volumes, edited by Jean Rychner and Albert Henry, Textes Littéraires Français no. 239 (Geneva: Droz, 1977), pp. 40–77, omits poem 6.

Edition in modern French: In *François Villon: Œuvres,* two volumes, translated by André Lanley (Paris: H. Champion, 1969), II: 310–381.

Editions in English: In *The Complete Works of François Villon,* translated by Anthony Bonner (New York: Bantam, 1960), pp. 132–167; in *The Poems of François Villon,* translated by Galway Kinnel (Boston: Houghton Mifflin, 1965), pp. 158–217; in *The Legacy, The Testament, and Other Poems,* translated by Peter Dale (London: Macmillan, 1973; New York: St. Martin's Press, 1973), pp. 138–145; In *François Villon: Selected Poems* (Harmondsworth, U.K.: Penguin, 1978), pp. 202–227; in *François Villon: Complete Poems,* edited and translated by Barbara Nelson Sargent-Baur (Toronto: University of Toronto Press, 1994).

Le Lais (also known as *Le Petit Testament* or *Le Premier Testament,* 1456)

Manuscripts: This work appears in four late-fifteenth-century manuscripts: A (Paris, Bibliothèque de l'Arsenal 3523, last quarter of the fifteenth century, omits verses 167–184); B (Paris, Bibliothèque Nationale de France, f. fr. 1661, after 1464, omits verses 177–184); C (Paris, Bibliothèque Nationale de France, f. fr. 20041, after 1463, omits verses 25–72 and 281–312); and F (Stockholm, Kungliga Biblioteket, V.u. 22, after 1477, omits verses 225–232), and one sixteenth-century manuscript, Br. (Brussels, Bibliothèque Royale/Koninklijke Bibliotheek VI 541, copied in 1568, omits verses 25–72, 177–184, 197, and 281–320).

First publication: "Le Petit Testament," in *Le Grant Testament Villon et le petit. Son codicille. Le iargon & ses ballades* (Paris: Pierre Levet, 1489).

Standard editions: In *François Villon: Œuvres,* edited by Auguste Longnon and Lucien Foulet, fourth edition (Paris: H. Champion, 1970); "Le Lais," in *Le Lais Villon et les poèmes variés,* 2 volumes, edited by Jean Rychner and Albert Henry, Textes Littéraires Français nos. 239 and 240 (Geneva: Droz, 1977), I: 11–30.

Edition in modern French: In *François Villon: Œuvres,* 2 volumes, translated by André Lanley (Paris: H. Champion, 1969), I: 5–46.

Editions in English: "The Legacy," in *The Poems of François Villon,* translated by Galway Kinnell (Boston: Houghton Mifflin, 1965), pp. 2–23; "The Legacy," in *The Legacy, The Testament, and Other Poems,* translated by Peter Dale (London: Macmillan, 1973; New York: St. Martin's Press, 1973); in *François Villon: Selected Poems* (Harmondsworth, U.K.: Penguin, 1978), pp. 12–39; in *François Villon: Complete Poems,* edited and translated

by Barbara Nelson Sargent-Baur (Toronto: University of Toronto Press, 1994), pp. 18–41.

Le Testament (also known as *Le Grand Testament or le testament second,* 1461)

Manuscripts: Parts of *Le Testament*–sometimes only a single poem–appear in several fifteenth- and sixteenth-century manuscripts: A (Paris, Bibliothèque de l'Arsenal 3523, last quarter of the fifteenth century); C (Paris, Bibliothèque Nationale de France, f. fr. 20041, fifteenth century, after 1463); Dm (Dijon, Bibliothèque Municipale 517, between 1470 and 1480); F (Stockholm, Kungliga Biblioteket, V.u. 22, fifteenth century, after 1477); H (Berlin, Kupferstichkabinett, Signatur 78 B 17, circa 1475); Hk (The Hague, Koninklijke Bibliotheek, 124 G 20, fifteenth century); O/2 (Paris, Bibliothèque Nationale de France, f. fr. 1719, end of fifteenth century or beginning of sixteenth); Br (Brussels, Bibliothèque Royale/Koninklijke Bibliotheek, Vi 541, copied in 1568); K (Copenhagen, Kongelige Bibliotek, fonds de Thott 59, copied in 1522 or after); and R (Paris, Bibliothèque Nationale de France, f. fr. 12490, copied in the sixteenth century after 1514). The poem "Mort jappelle de ta rigueur" appears with music in Dm. and Wc. C. omits only verses 305–312 of *Le Testament* and is, thus, the most complete manuscript.

First publication: "Le Grant Testament," in *Le Grant Testament Villon et le petit. Son codicille. le jargon & ses ballades* (Paris: Pierre Levet, 1489); omits verses 1006–1013, 1551–1558, 1623, 1768–1775, 1784–1803, and 2004–2023).

Standard editions: In *François Villon: Œuvres,* edited by Auguste Longnon and Lucien Foulet, fourth edition (Paris: H. Champion, 1970); *Le Testament Villon,* 2 volumes, edited by Jean Rychner and Albert Henry, Textes Littéraires Français nos. 207–208 (Geneva: Droz, 1977); "Le Testament," in *Le Testament Villon, le lais Villon et les poèmes variés,* edited by Rychner and Henry, Textes Littéraires Français no. 335 (Geneva: Droz, 1985).

Edition in modern French: In *François Villon: Œuvres,* 2 volumes, translated by André Lanly (Paris: H. Champion, 1969).

Editions in English: In *The Poems of François Villon,* translated by Galway Kinnell (Boston: Houghton Mifflin, 1965); "The Testament," in *The Legacy, The Testament, and Other Poems,* translated by Peter Dale (London: Macmillan, 1973; New York: St. Martin's Press, 1973); in *François Villon: Complete Poems,* edited and translated by Barbara Nelson

François Villon (woodcut from Le Grant Testament Villon et le
petit. Son codicille. Le jargon
& ses ballades, *1489)*

it "avecques l'ayde de bons vieillards qui en savent par cueur" (with the aid of good old men who know it by heart). That old men had learned Villon's work by heart and that Marot's edition went through fifteen reprintings from 1533 to 1542 attest to the poet's popularity. François Rabelais mentions Villon in *Les horribles et épouvantables faits et prouesses du très renommé Pantagruel, roy des Dipsodes* (The Horrible and Terrifying Deeds and Words of the Renowned Pantagruel, King of the Dipsodes, 1532) and quotes from his poetry in the *Quart livre* (Fourth Book, 1548). Over the next five hundred years such widely different authors as the classical French critic Nicolas Boileau, the English poet A. C. Swinburne, and the American poet Ezra Pound praised Villon. Villon's life has been romanticized in novels, plays, and motion pictures, and many modern literary anthologies cite him as the best of the late medieval poets in France.

Much of Villon's popularity arises from sympathy for the difficult life he led, which is described with both humor and poignancy and at great length in his largely autobiographical poetry. In fact, little is known for certain of Villon's life beyond what he relates. In two court documents dated January 1456 he is referred to as "François des Loges, autrement dit de Villon" (François des Loges, otherwise called de Villon) and "François de Montcorbier." Most scholars agree that Montcorbier and Villon were one and the same.

From a remark in the first line of *Le Testament*, which he wrote in 1461 at the age of thirty, one can surmise that Villon was born of poor parents in 1431:

> Povre je suis de ma jeunesse
> De povre et de petite extrasse;
> Mon pere n'eust oncq grant richesse,
> Ne son ayeul, nommé Orace;
> Povreté tous nous suit et trece.
> Sur les tumbeaux de mes ancestres,
> Les ames desquelz dieu embrasse!
> On n'y voit couronnes ne ceptres.

> (Poor I am, and from my youth,
> Born of a poor and humble stock.
> My father never had much wealth
> Nor yet his grandfather, Orace.
> Poverty tracks us, every one.
> Upon the tombs of my ancestors,
> The souls of whom may God embrace!
> Sceptres and crowns aren't to be seen.)

Villon apparently knew little about his father, but in *Le Testament* he refers to his mother as still living. He spent his early years as a student at the University of Paris in the home of Guillaume de Villon, a respected lawyer, whom he calls in *Le Testament* his "plus que pere . . . / Qui esté m'a plus doulx que mere" (more than father . . . /

Sargent-Baur (Toronto: University of Toronto Press, 1994), pp. 52–193.

Although his verse gained him little or no financial success during his life, François Villon is today perhaps the best-known French poet of the Middle Ages. His works surfaced in several manuscripts shortly after his disappearance in 1463, and the first printed collection of his poetry—the Levet edition—came out as early as 1489. More than one hundred printed editions followed, and Villon's poetry has been translated into more than twenty-five languages. At the request of King Francis I, the poet Clément Marot prepared the first critical edition of Villon's work in 1533. Basing his edition on previous printed editions, Marot supplemented

Who's been to me kinder than a mother), and he later adopted Guillaume's surname, at least for his poetry.

By his own admission Villon was not a serious student. During his university years he either took part in or observed an incident in which, as a prank, students stole a stone called "*le Pet au diable*" (the Devil's Fart) from the property of a Mademoiselle de Bruyères and were dealt with harshly. In *Le Testament* Villon says that he wishes to bequeath a work that he wrote, titled *Le romaunt du Pet au deable* (The Romance of the Devil's Fart), to Guillaume; but the work, if it ever existed, has been lost. Villon participated in many other pranks and brawls during his student years that brought him into conflict with the authorities, but he earned a baccalaureate in 1449 and a master of arts in 1452.

Three years later, a much more serious affair led to Villon's abrupt departure from Paris. In June 1455 he was attacked by a priest, Philippe Sermoise, who cut his lip with a large dagger; in self-defense, Villon wounded Sermoise in the groin with a small dagger he kept under his cloak. When the priest did not desist from the attack, Villon hit him in the head with a rock. Villon went to a barber to have his wound dressed, giving the false name Michel Mouton. Before Sermoise died, he named Villon as his assailant, and Villon fled. Through the intervention of his friends and, no doubt, his adoptive father, Guillaume, he was granted a full pardon for an act of justifiable homicide, and he returned to Paris in January 1456.

Shortly before Christmas, however, Villon was in trouble with the authorities again: he and three others stole five hundred écus from the Collège de Navarre, and one of his accomplices, Guy Tabarie, named Villon as the ringleader. Villon fled Paris a second time. Before his departure he wrote *Le Lais* (The Legacy, 1456), bequeathing his possessions, both real and imaginary, to his friends.

The next four years of wanderings are ill documented. Villon may have spent some time at the court of Duke Charles d'Orléans at Blois; three of his poems appear in the duke's personal album. He wrote one of them in praise of the duke's daughter, Marie d'Orléans, either at her birth on 19 December 1457 or at her entry into Orléans on 17 July 1460. In any case, what protection he may have found at the duke's court was short-lived. According to *Le Testament,* he was imprisoned at Meung-sur-Loire in the summer of 1461 for an unnamed, and perhaps minor, offense by order of the bishop of Orléans, Thibaut d'Aussigny. There, again according to *Le Testament,* he was starved and possibly tortured; but when the new king, Louis XI, traveled through Meung-sur-Loire on 2 October 1461, Villon was liberated along with other prisoners.

Back in Paris, Villon was again imprisoned for a minor offense. While in custody he was recognized as a participant in the Collège de Navarre robbery. He was released after being sentenced to pay 120 écus over the next three years for the crime. A few months later he was arrested for a trivial role he played in a street brawl, taken to the Châtelet, subjected to water torture, and condemned to death. He appealed to Parlement, and his sentence was commuted on 5 January 1463 to ten years' exile from the city. After this third and, apparently, last departure from Paris, Villon disappears from history. Most critics surmise that he died shortly thereafter because he says in *Le Testament* and in some of his *Poèmes variés* (Miscellaneous Poems, 1450?–1463) that he is a broken man, both physically and financially, who feels that he can no longer count on his friends.

If Villon had died in the prison of Meung-sur-Loire in the summer of 1461, he would probably have vanished poetically as well as personally. Up to that time he had only written *Le Lais,* which is for the most part an immature work. Written in 1456, according to the first stanza, the poem consists of approximately three hundred verses grouped into octaves. Adopting the mock-testamentary form that he later used with greater skill in *Le Testament,* Villon says that he is about to leave Paris because he has been unhappy in love—a stock poetic commonplace:

> Me vint le vouloir de briser
> La tres amoureuse prison
> Qui faisoit mon cueur debriser.
>
> (The longing came on me to break
> Away from love's imprisonment,
> Which had my heart at breaking point.)

Villon makes no mention of his legal problems, which most critics cite as the real reason for his departure. Before leaving, he bequeaths his nonexistent or valueless property to his friends and relatives. For instance, he wills his "renown," which could not have been great at that point, to Guillaume de Villon; his heart, enclosed in a shrine, to his faithless lover; and several tavern signs, such as Le Beuf Couronné (The Crowned Ox), to various friends and acquaintances. To the poorhouses he leaves his window frames draped with cobwebs and to his barber, his hair clippings. Villon signs *Le Lais* in the last stanza.

Although *Le Lais* is hardly a great work of art, the poem provides a glimpse at the poetic genius that Villon later revealed in *Le Testament.* Pierre Champion points to Villon's wanderings and hardships during his exile from Paris and the time he spent in the Meung-sur-Loire prison as the major contributing factors to the more mature style of *Le Testament,* written only five years later. The

Illustration and opening lines for "La ballade des pendus" (in Le Grant Testament Villon et le petit. Son codicille. Le jargon & ses ballades, *1489)*

Je plains le temps de ma jeunesse
(Ouquel j'ay plus qu'autre gallé
Jusqu'à l'entrée de viellesse)

(I mourn the season of my youth
[When, more than most, I lived it up
Until old age came upon me]).

The mood in this work is much darker than in the earlier *Lais;* Villon freely vents his hatred not only for d'Aussigny but also for others who have left him poor and friendless.

Le Testament, however, is not simply a long litany of complaints and regrets. In stanza 29 Villon begins the *ubi sunt* (where are . . . ?) theme that takes up a large part of the poem. In one highly lyrical and poignant passage he asks where all the young men he once knew have gone:

Ou sont les gracieux galans
Que je suivoye ou temps jadiz
Si bien chantans, si bien parlans,
Sy plaisans en faiz et en diz?

(Where are they, all the fine young men
I went about with formerly?
So good in song, so good in speech,
So pleasing in word and in deed?)

All will one day die; both rich and poor, "Mort saisit sans excepcïon" (Death seizes them without exception). Two ballades continue the *ubi sunt* theme. In his 1533 edition Marot titled the first "La Ballade des dames du temps jadis" (The Ballade of the Ladies of Bygone Days) and the second "La Ballade des seigneurs du temps jadis" (The Ballade of the Lords of Bygone Days). In these two poems Villon asks what has become of the famous women and men of classical antiquity and the recent past. Where are Flora, Héloïse, Blanche de Castille, and Joan of Arc? Where are Charlemagne, King Arthur, and Charles VII? One of Villon's most celebrated ballades, "La Ballade des dames du temps jadis" ends with the poignant and much-quoted refrain "Mais ou sont les neiges d'anten?" (But where are the snows of yesteryear?).

Another recurring theme is that of unrequited love and women's faithlessness and cruelty. In stanzas 46–56 Villon describes the lost beauty of an aged and ugly woman and then inserts a ballade Marot titles "La belle Heaulmière aux filles de joie" (The Beautiful Helmet-Maker's Wife Speaks to the Prostitutes), in which a once lovely and lustful woman gives advice to younger "working girls." In stanza 63 Villon asks, "What drives women to love so freely and so many?" and answers "C'est nature femeninne" (It is feminine nature). In the double ballade that follows he advises men to avoid

complete poem consists of 2,023 verses; the octaves that form the will proper are interspersed with ballades that may have been written at an earlier date and inserted into the work.

Le Testament begins with a tirade against Villon's jailer at Meung-sur-Loire, Thibaut d'Aussigny: "Mon seigneur n'est ne mon evesque" (My lord he's not, my bishop not). He goes on to praise Louis XI and thank the king for his release: may Louis live as long as Methuselah, produce twelve male heirs, and one day see paradise as his reward. Because of the harsh conditions of his imprisonment, Villon says, his mental and physical health is poor. In stanza 22 he says that he now regrets his misspent youth:

such women: "Bien eureux est qui rien n'y a!" (Happy the man who keeps away!).

After listing his personal misfortunes in love, he begins to bequeath his possessions. To his mother he leaves a ballade written in her own narrative voice: "Femme je suis povrecte et ancïenne" (A woman I am, a poor and ancient one). In the dramatic monologue that follows, Villon's mother addresses the Virgin and repeats the refrain: "En ceste foy je vueil vivre et mourir" (In this faith I desire to live and die). Villon also leaves ballades and other poems to his faithless lover, his friends, and his enemies. To Ythier Merchant—a possible love rival, according to Jean Dufournet—he leaves the poem that begins, "Mort j'appelle de ta rigueur" (Death, I appeal your harsh decree), challenging Merchant to set the poem to music. (It later appeared with musical accompaniment in two manuscripts.) To others Villon leaves various real and imaginary possessions. Ironic asides and plays on words, the meaning of some of which can now only be surmised, abound, as do bitter attacks on his enemies. In one such attack he lists vile liquids and other substances as the ingredients for a recipe, ending with the refrain: "Soient frictes ces langues ennuyeuses!" (In all this may those spiteful tongues be fried!). Other ballades, such as the one Marot titles "Ballade de Villon et de la Grosse Margot" (Ballade of Villon and Fat Margot) are, as Barbara Nelson Sargent-Baur says, "deliberately coarse and disgusting." Although they show a human side of Villon and are far from atypical of the period, these are not the poems for which he is best remembered.

The ballade that ends *Le Testament* is an example of the latter. In this poem Villon switches narrative voice again and writes in the third person, directly appealing to the reader as though the testator were already dead and, thus, the will can now be executed:

Icy se clost le testament
Et finist du povre Villon.
Venez a son enterrement,
Quant vous orrez le carillon

(Here closes and comes to an end
The testament of poor Villon.
Come to attend his burial
When you will hear the carillon).

Villon also alternates among the past, the present, and the future and between written and oral discourse.

The most studied and debated of Villon's works, *Le Testament* has been characterized by Champion as "la plus pathétique des poésies" (the most moving of poems) as well as the most complex and ambiguous. Throughout the work Villon often changes not only his narrative

voice but also his audience. Sargent-Baur studies Villon's "multifarious audience" in her "Communication and Implied Audience(s) in Villon's *Testament*" (1992) and finds that he addresses not only his friends and enemies but also an "ideal reader," humanity in general, and himself or his "divided psyche." In "Oral Textuality–Textual Orality: Patterns of Ambiguity in François Villon's *Testament*" (1990) Robert D. Peckham says that Villon has created an ambiguity in the text by alternating between oral and written discourse. David Fein studies Villon's use of time in his "Time and Timelessness in Villon's Testament" (1987). All praise the work as the most complex and ambiguous of Villon's oeuvre.

The sixteen works in *Poèmes variés* were written at various times during Villon's life, beginning around 1450; fifteen of them were published for the first time as a group in the 1892 edition of his works by Auguste Longnon. Most are ballades with three stanzas of eight to ten lines, each stanza ending with a refrain, and the whole ballade concluding with a short envoy with the same refrain. Three were included in Charles d'Orléans's personal album. The first of these, written in praise of Marie d'Orléans, was written during Villon's exile from Paris and ends "Vostre povre escolier Françoys" (Your poor scholar François). Villon apparently based the second, "Je meurs de seuf auprés de la fontaine" (I die of thirst at the fountain's edge), on a theme proposed by the duke; the poem includes the name VILLON in acrostic. The third, written in macaronic style (in French and Latin), has been attributed to Villon but is unsigned. A fourth signed ballade was not included in the duke's album but is an urgent request for a loan addressed to him.

Although most of the other works in *Poèmes variés* include an acrostic of VILLON or FRANCOYS, it is not certain that Villon wrote all of them. The best known of the poems with an acrostic for his name, however, titled in most editions "Epitaphe" or "Epitaphe Villon" and commonly called "La Ballade des pendus" (The Ballade of the Hanged Men), is universally attributed to him. Apparently written in late 1462, when Villon was in the Châtelet prison under sentence of death, it is, perhaps, his most poignant poem. He adopts a collective narrative voice, writing from the point of view of hanged men who urge their brothers to pray for them and to shun their example. He vividly describes the hanged men's bodies swinging in the wind:

La pluye nous a debuez et lavez
Et le soulail deceschez et noirciz.
Pies, corbeaux nous ont les yeulx cavez
Et araché la barbe et les courcilz.
Jamais nul temps nous ne sommes assis;

a groſſe margot
Mais adonc il ya grant deḣait
Quāt ſās argēt ſeḃa coucher margot
Deoir ne ſa puis mō cuer mort ſa ḣait
Sa roḃe prent/chaperon et ſurcot
Si ſuy iure quil tiendra pour ſeſcot
Par ſes couſtes:ſi ſe prent ſantecriſt
Crie et iure par ſa mort ieſucriſt
Que nō fera:ſors iēpongne ḃng eſcſat
Deſſus ſō nez ſuy en fais ḃng eſcript
En ce ḃordeau ou tenons noſtre eſtat

Page from the 1489 edition of Villon's poetry, with an illustration and the opening lines of his "Ballade de Villon et de la Grosse Margot"

Puis ça, puis la, comme le vent varie,
A son plaisir sans cess nous charie,
Plus becquetés d'oiseaux que dex a couldre.

(The rain has soaked us and has washed us clean
And the sun dried us up and turned us black.
Magpies and crows have hollowed out our eyes
And plucked away our beards and eyebrows too.
Never at any time are we at rest;
This way and that, as the wind may vary,
It pushes us about just as it likes,
More pecked by birds than any sewing thimble.)

Each stanza is followed by the haunting refrain "Mais priez Dieu que tous nous vueille absouldre" (But pray to God He may absolve us all).

Villon's *Ballades en jargon* are written in the language of the *Coquillards* (thieves and counterfeiters).

Critics have attempted to decipher these poems, but with limited success. The most complete study is Pierre Guiraud's *Le Jargon de Villon et le gai savoir de la Coquille* (The Jargon of Villon and the Merry Learning of the Coquille, 1968). Most English translations of Villon's work do not include *Le Ballades en jargon,* but Sargent-Baur has attempted an approximate translation of the poems in her *François Villon: Complete Poems* (1994).

One of the poems serves as an illustration of the type of poetry that Villon wrote in jargon as well as the debate on the meaning of the jargon poems. The first stanza reads:

> Ioncheurs ionchans en ioncherie
> Rebignez bien ou ioncherez
> Quostac nembroue vostre arerie
> Ou accolles sont voz ainsnez
> Poussez de la quille et brouez
> Car tost seriez rouppieux
> Eschec quacollez ne soies
> Par la poe du marieux.

Sargent-Baur translates the stanza:

> Tricksters tricking in trickery,
> Take a good look at where you play your tricks
> Lest Ostac send your behind
> Where your elders were taken by the neck.
> Shake a leg and speed away
> For you'd soon be sorry.
> Take care not to let your neck be grabbed
> By the hangman's paw.

Sargent-Baur interprets this poem and other jargon poems as warnings to the *Coquillards* to watch out for the hangman, while Guiraud, who has translated the poem into modern French, refers to it as one of the "Ballades des tireurs de cartes" (Ballades of the Card Players) and sees it as advice to players who cheat. Interpretations and translations of the poems vary widely, and the debate promises to continue. While some have declared the poems hardly worth the effort to translate, others claim that they provide valuable insight into Middle French and the argot or slang of fifteenth-century France.

Villon used fixed forms, such as the ballade and the rondeau, even in the jargon poems. The stanza form he adopted for *Le Lais* and *Le Testament* is eight octosyllabic lines rhyming *ababbcbc,* which was used by Alain Chartier in *La Belle Dame sans mercy* (The Beautiful Lady without Mercy, 1424). The mock testamentary form was not new, either. Jean de Meun's thirteenth-century *Testament,* Eustache Deschamps's fourteenth-century *Testament par esbatement,* and Philippe de Hauteville's early-fifteenth-century *Confession et testament de l'amant trespassé de deuil* (Confessions and Testament of the Lover Destroyed by Grief) are earlier examples of the genre. Although Villon was not an innovator of forms or genres, the deeply personal nature of his poetry and his artistry ensure his place in the French literary canon, while the ambiguities inherent in his work and the resultant widely divergent interpretations ensure that his poetry will remain the subject of lively and continued critical debate.

Bibliographies:

Robert D. Peckham, *François Villon: A Bibliography* (New York & London: Garland, 1990);

Rudolf Sturm, *François Villon: Bibliographie und Materialien, 1489–1988* (Munich: Saur, 1990).

Biographies:

Auguste Longnon, *Etude biographique sur François Villon d'après les documents inédits conservés aux Archives Nationales* (Paris: Henri Menu, 1877);

Pierre Champion, *François Villon: Sa Vie et son temps,* 2 volumes (Paris: H. Champion, 1913; Geneva & Paris: Slatkine Reprints, 1984).

References:

Jean Dufournet, *Nouvelles Recherches sur Villon* (Paris: H. Champion, 1980);

Dufournet, *Recherches sur le Testament de François Villon,* 2 volumes, revised edition (Paris: SEDES, 1971);

Dufournet, *Villon: Ambiguïté et carnaval* (Geneva: Slatkine, 1992);

Dufournet, *Villon et sa fortune littéraire* (Bordeaux: Ducros, 1970);

David Fein, *François Villon and His Reader* (Detroit: Wayne State University Press, 1989);

Fein, *François Villon Revisited* (New York: Twayne, 1995);

Fein, "Time and Timelessness in Villon's *Testament,*" *Neophilologus,* 71 (1987): 470–473;

John Fox, *The Poetry of Villon* (London: Nelson, 1962);

Pierre Guiraud, *Le Jargon de Villon ou le gai savoir de las Coquille* (Paris: Gallimard, 1968);

David Kuhn, *La Poétique de François Villon* (Paris: Colin, 1967);

Gaston Paris, *François Villon* (Paris: Hachette, 1901);

Robert D. Peckham, "Oral Textuality–Textual Orality: Patterns of Ambiguity in François Villon's *Testament,*" *Fifteenth-Century Studies,* 17 (1990): 291–298;

Odette Petit-Morphy, *François Villon et la scolastique* (Paris: H. Champion, 1975);

Barbara Nelson Sargent-Baur, *Brothers of Dragons: Job Dolens and François Villon* (New York & London: Garland, 1990);

Sargent-Baur, "Communication and Implied Audience(s) in Villon's *Testament,*" *Neophilologus,* 76 (1992): 35–40;

Italo Siciliano, *François Villon et les thèmes poétiques du moyen-âge* (Paris: Nizet, 1934);

Mary B. Speer, "The Editorial Tradition of Villon's *Testament:* from Marot to Rychner and Henry," *Romance Philology,* 31 (1977–1978): 344–361;

Jacques T. E. Thomas, *Lecture du Testament Villon* (Geneva: Droz, 1992);

Louis Thuasne, *Rabelais et Villon* (Paris: H. Champion, 1969);

A. J. A. van Zoest, *Structures de deux testaments fictionnels: Le Lais et le Testament de François Villon* (The Hague & Paris: Mouton, 1974)

Philippe de Vitry

(31 October 1291 – 9 June 1361)

Andrew Tomasello
City University of New York

WORKS: *Motets* (circa 1314–1343)

Manuscripts: The early works are found in Paris, Bibliothèque Nationale de France, f. fr. 146 (*Fauvel*), and the later compositions have been copied in Ivrea, Biblioteca Capitolare 115 (*IV*).

First publications: "Studien zur Musik des Mittelalters, I: Neue Quellen des XIV. Und beginnenden XV. Jahrunderts," edited by Heinrich Besseler, in *Archiv für Musikwissenschaft,* 7 (1925): 167–252; "Studien zur Musik des Mittelalters, II: Die Mottete von Franco von Köln bis Phillippe von Vitry," edited by Besseler, in *Archiv für Musikwissenschaft,* 8 (1926): 137–258.

Standard edition: *The Works of Philippe de Vitry,* edited by Leo Schrade (Monaco: L'Oiseau-Lyre, 1956).

Ars nova (circa 1320)

Manuscripts: The most important manuscripts are: London, British Museum, Add. 21455 (circa 1400), fols. 1–6; Paris, Bibliothèque Nationale de France, f. lat. 14741 (fifteenth century), fols. 4–5; Paris, Bibliothèque Nationale de France, f. lat. 7378A (fourteenth century), fols. 61v–62; Vatican, Biblioteca Vaticana, Barberini 307 (circa 1400), fols. 17–20v; and Siena, Biblioteca Communale L.V.30, fols. 129–129v.

First publication: In *Scriptorum de Musica Medii Aevi,* new series, 3, edited by Edmond de Coussemaker (Paris: A. Durand & Pedone-Lauriel, 1869), pp. 15–46.

Standard edition: *Philippi de Vitriaco Ars nova,* Corpus scriptorum de musica 8, edited by Gilbert Reaney, André Gilles, and Jean Maillard (N.p.: American Institute of Musicology, 1964).

Edition in English: "Philippe de Vitry's Ars Nova: A Translation," translated by Leon B. Plantinga, *Journal of Music Theory,* 5 (1961): 204–223.

Le Chapel des trois fleurs de lis (1332–1335)

Manuscripts: Paris, Bibliothèque Nationale de France, f. fr. 926, fols. 317–326; Berne, Schweizerische Landesbibliothek, ms. 217, fols. 71 ff.; Paris, Bibliothèque Nationale de France, f. fr. 12787, fols. 9 ff.; London, British Library, Old Roy.19.C.IX; London, British Library, Harley 4878.

Standard edition: "*Le Chapel des fleurs de lis* par Philippe de Vitri," edited by Arthur Piaget, *Romania,* 27 (1898): 72–92.

De terre o grec Gaule appellee (circa 1337–1338)

Manuscripts: Paris, Bibliothèque Nationale de France, f. lat. 3343, fols. 109–111v; Philadelphia, University of Pennsylvania, MS French 15, fols. 23–23v.

First publication and standard edition: "Ballades mythologiques de Jean de la Mote, Philippe de Vitri, Jean Campion," edited by E. Pognon, *Humanisme et Renaissance,* 5 (1938): 385–417.

Edition in English: "The Poetic Exchange between Philippe de Vitry and Jean de Le Mote: A New Edition," edited by F. N. M. Diekstra, *Neophilologus,* 70 (1986): 504–519.

Dit de Franc Gontier

Manuscript: Paris, Bibliothèque Nationale de France, Rés. Ye 169.

Standard edition: "*Le Chapel des fleurs de lis* par Philippe de Vitri," edited by Arthur Piaget, *Romania,* 27 (1898): 63–64.

Carissimi, cum diligencia (1350)

Manuscript: Paris, Bibliothèque Nationale de France, f. lat. 3343, fols. 111v–112.

First publication and standard edition: "Ballades mythologiques de Jean de la Mote, Philippe de Vitri, Jean Campion," edited by E. Pognon, *Humanisme et Renaissance,* 5 (1938): 54.

Philippe de Vitry, early humanist scholar, poet, composer, and prelate, was held in high regard by intellectuals and literary figures of his day. Gace de la Buigne wrote that Philippe "made better motets than any man." The anonymous author of *Les règles de la seconde rhétorique* (The Rules of the Second Rhetoric) asserts that Philippe "invented the way of composing motets, ballades, lais, and simple rondeaux, and in music invented the four prolations, red notes, and new proportions." Pierre Bersuire called him "an extraordinary lover of moral philosophy, history, and antiquity, and learned in all the mathematical disciplines." The Provençal mathematician Levi ben Gershon (Leo Hebraeus) referred to Philippe as "the pre-eminent *magister* of the science of music." Modern scholarship has credited the poet-composer with some of the most important innovations in musical style and notation. The passage of more than six hundred years, however, has obscured a good deal of his work.

According to marginal notes added to a copy of the *Grande chronique* (Great Chronicle) of Guillaume de Nangis, a "Philippe de Vitry," presumably the owner of the manuscript, was born on 31 October 1291. Recent research points to the town of Vitry-en-Artois (Pas-de-Calais) as his most likely place of birth, though Eustache Deschamps indicated he was *champaynois* (from Champagne). Phillipe lived in Paris, ostensibly as a student, during the 1320s, perhaps as early as the 1310s. He might have resided at the Collège des bons enfans d'Arras, though he has traditionally been linked to the Collège de Navarre. Philippe traveled in university circles, but it is still unclear whether or not he received the *magister artium* from Paris before this time as has sometimes been asserted. Subsequent fourteenth-century writers often refer to him as *magister* and at least one bestows on him the title of *doctor in musica*.

The first evidence of his work comes from the revised *Roman de Fauvel* (Romance of Fauvel), compiled in Paris during the days of Philippe's residence. Among the 169 musical works (34 of them polyphonic) added to the satiric poem by Chaillou de Pesstain, several motets are believed to be Philippe's. Since the *Fauvel* manuscript was compiled by someone conversant with the musical innovations taking place in Paris at the time Chaillou was reworking it, the notion that Philippe played an integral role in its preparation and in the composition of some heretofore unascribed works, both polyphonic and monophonic, seems plausible.

Perhaps the earliest of the motets credited to Philippe is *Firmissime/Adesto/Alleluya* (circa 1314–1316), whose *triplum* (highest voice), as a confession of faith, represents an appeal to God by those who sing the motet. The middle part, the motetus (*Adesto*), employs a popular hymn to the Holy Trinity. The melody of the chant tenor (*Alleluya*) has been drawn from the repertory of the diocese of Arras (Benedictine abbey of Saint-Vaast). In this work the composer stays true to his theme as he fashions an overall musical structure reflecting the three-in-one aspect of the Trinity. The motet, considered an early work, has been putatively linked to his diocese of origin.

Three motets from *Fauvel* attributed to Philippe are concerned with the political intrigues surrounding the financial councillor to Philippe le bel, Enguerrand de Marigny. In the motet of *Floret/Florens/Neuma,* the abuses of Enguerrand are enumerated as the text draws the analogy between the supporters of the minister and those from the Book of Esther who bent their knee before Haman, humiliating Mordecai, and thereby preparing their ruin. This work seems technically less advanced than the previous motet, but, because of its subject matter, it has been assigned a date as early as fall 1314. Since only the triplum with its more abstract text appears in *Fauvel*, the question arises whether the motetus text was composed after Enguerrand's death.

Garrit gallus/In nova fert/N[euma] also protests the minister's abuse of power and has sometimes been dated before his fall from grace and subsequent imprisonment, which occurred after the king's death (29 November 1314). Beginning with passages excerpted from Ovid's *Metamorphoses,* the text tells how St. Michael the Archangel will conquer the evil dragon through the power of the Cross, and how Christ himself will judge the dragon. The fox eats the chickens and sucks the blood of the sheep. The cock (*gallus*) and the French (*Galli*) mourn. The poet refers to Jacob, Absalom, and Ulysses. It is the earliest known motet with red notation altering the mensuration, and it possesses a more advanced phrase structure than some later motets. These observations call into question the traditional dating of the *Fauvel* pieces to conform with historical events since the uncertainty remains whether the works predict the fall of Enguerrand or report it.

Tribum/Quoniam secta/Merito surely dates from after Enguerrand's execution at the public gallows of Paris at Montfaucon on 30 April 1315 and has been dated from as early May 1315 to the end of 1316. The text proclaims that the fox who gnawed the cocks has fallen, and generations to come are told to remember this event. The text again quotes Ovid (*Epistulae ex Ponto*), and the final couplet of the triplum is drawn from Joseph of Exeter (*De bello troiano*). Recent research points to these last three *Fauvel* motets as having been composed in late 1316 as an admonition to the future generation (Philip V and England's Edward II, who represented a serious threat to the throne of France). New evidence has shown that during this time, Philippe was serving a band of French nobles led by Charles de Valois, a group committed to preserving the French crown. The revised *Fauvel* may therefore have been compiled around 1317 to conform to the nationalist political motives of this faction.

What is believed to be Philippe's only French motet, *Douce playsence/Garison/[Neuma],* has been dated 1317–1320. It is quoted by Gace de la Bigne in his "Deduis de la Chasse" with attribution to Philippe and cited by the music theorist Pseudo-Theodoricus de Campo. The text stylistically approximates many motets from the previous century. Its musical structure relies on the repetition of the tenor melody (color) in the second section of the piece with halved rhythmic values.

Philippe became an exponent of a new approach to notation for which he is well known in musical circles. His thought, as all musical-theoretical work, must have followed practice, in that it was a codification of what was becoming the style at the time. Certain aspects of these innovative concepts had already been introduced in the writings of others. For example, Philippe no doubt met the music theorist Jehan des Murs, who was a student in Paris in 1318 and who spent time at the Sorbonne during the next seven years. Jehan's most important writing on music, *Notitia artis musice* (Notation of the Art of Music), or *Ars nove musice* (Art of New Music, 1321), sketches the new ideas that were circulating at the time. Philippe's contribution to this novel musical and notational style, titled *Ars nova* (New Art), was generated around the same year. Several manuscripts of the treatise are extant and, because of their disparate and fragmented quality, might represent the notes of students and disciples. Whether Philippe ever composed a definitive exposition of *Ars nova* is in serious doubt. Nonetheless, even if the work is removed from his canon, the consensus is that the treatise accurately reflects innovations Philippe promulgated during his lifetime and that it includes what appears to be his earliest composition. That is, many of the attributions of his motets are inferred from their being excerpted in the treatise as examples of the new style.

By 1321 Philippe had entered Holy Orders. The first church records of his presence are the papal letters dated 20 January 1321 and 2 August 1322, which granted him benefices at Cambrai and Soissons respectively. By January 1323 he received a prebend at Clermont and later one at Verdun. Like countless educated and talented chaplains employed in the households of fourteenth-century nobility and ecclesiastics, Philippe began his career as a notary. Sometimes in the case of important clerics, service to the court went beyond the bounds of being limited to one employer. A few bureaucrats seemed to have been shared by those linked by blood and politics, so it may be futile to establish a linear career history for Philippe. Modern scholars are confident that he served Louis, Duke of Bourbon, before 1328, but he may have already worked for Louis when he was count of Clermont as early as 1317–1318. Although historians are unclear whether Philippe served at the royal court during the early part of the decade, he did function as notary for Philip VI in 1328.

Philippe's knowledge of the court no doubt engendered a distaste for some of the aspects of the job and its environment. The motet *Colla iugo/Bona Condit/Libera* (circa 1320), protests against *vita curialis* (clerical life) and its intrigue and is a paean to the spiritual pleasures of a simple country life. It cries out for limits to clerical excesses and for the rejection of sin. Its overall design reflects the tradition of sevenfold exegesis drawn from virtues and vices literature through its seven pairs of lines in the triplum text and seven repeated statements of the tenor *talea*, the melody of which is adopted from Lauds of Wednesday in Holy Week.

Tuba sacre/In arboris/Virgo (circa 1320) deals with faith and virginity. It is an early work that employs black and red notation. *Cum statua/Hugo/Magister* has been given a date ranging from circa 1320 to circa 1330. The work is a counterattack on a personal enemy of Philippe's named Hugo. The poet casts the man as a liar, false prophet, hypocrite, and prince of envy.

During October 1327, while in the city of Avignon to present letters of the count of Clermont to the Pope, Philippe began a lifelong friendship with Petrarch, whom he met a second time in Paris in 1333. Philippe was included in a list of twenty *maistres . . . notaires* (master notaries) from the king's household in 1329–1330 and regularly thereafter as *clericus, notarius Regis* (clerk, notary to the king).

Philippe composed his poem "Le Chapel des trois Fleurs de Lis" to promote the Valois crusade planned for 1335, announced on 25 July 1332. The allegorical text describes the three indispensable virtues–knowledge, faith, and chivalry–combining to reconquer the Holy Land. The knowledge of good and evil allows one to know God and to find the source of all good. Chivalry is the incarnation of all human virtues. The poet quotes translated passages of the well-known treatise *Epitome rei militaris* (Epitome of Warfare, fourth century A.D.) of Vegetius.

The next group of motets belong together stylistically and might date from the same decade. Thought to be from the early 1320s to the 1330s, the four-voice motet *O canenda/Rex quem/Contratenor/Rex regum* concerns Robert of Anjou, King of Naples. The motet is eight lines of dactylic hexameter, spelling out in acrostic "Robertus" and alluding to classical and Old Testament figures as it addresses Robert as king, soldier, scholar, and judge. *Vos quid/Gratissima/Contratenor/Gaude,* another four-voice motet thought to date from the 1330s, concerns Mary but also recalls the Song of Songs. The triplum of this allegory of divine love compares the perfection of the virgin to the imperfection of all others. *Impudenter/Virtutibus/Contratenor/Tenor,* perhaps the latest of this group of four-voice motets, appears to date from the 1330s (also dated before 1355) and presents texts of a mature man who catalogues the sufferings of his youth, a period in which he was dominated by lust. The composer contrasts this experience with the absolute joys derived from love for the Mother of God.

Philippe's *De terre o grec Gaule appellee*–variously dated before 1340, 1328–1339, after 1348, or the 1350s–is a denunciation of the poet Jean de Le Mote for his rejection of France in favor of England. Philippe calls Jean a beaver, an animal that, when pursued, will bite off its own testicles, and compares him to Actaeon, promising that he will meet his judges in the underworld. The Frenchman tells Jean he cannot make Pegasus fly in Albion, which is cursed by God.

During the 1340s Philippe continued in service to the French monarchs as *maître des requêtes* (master of petitions). Probably not long after the conclave of 1342, he wrote a motet specifically honoring the accession of Pierre Roger to the throne of St. Peter. Pierre was a scholar at the Sorbonne from 1303 to 1323 and, like Philippe, went on to prominence at the French court, preaching the crusade to the court on 1 October 1333. The text of *Petre Clemens/ Lugentium/Non est* specifically refers to the pontiff, punning not only on the names Pierre and that of the first Pope, Petrus or Cephas (Aramaic for "rock"), but also on his chosen name, Clement, and his outstanding personal attribute (clemency). Philippe draws on their mutual experience in Paris, extolling Pierre's exhortations to wage the crusade. The work is enormous in scale, almost three times the length of the earliest motets. No doubt as a reward for his friendship and service to both king and pope, on 18 July 1343 Philippe was cited as one of the *capellani commensales pape,* the higher level ecclesiastics who sometimes acted as emissaries for the Curia but who served no real function as household chaplains. While in Avignon during 1342–1343, the poet renewed his relationship with Petrarch.

Around this time, Philippe seemed to stimulate the productivity of other mathematicians. Jehan des Murs dedicated his *Opus quadripartitum numerorum* (Four-Part Work in Music, 1343) to Philippe as "the one person in the world more estimable than this work." That same year, Philippe requested that Levi ben Gershon write *De numeris harmonicis* (Concerning Musical Harmony) a treatise that solved some of the problems of the notation of musical rhythm. His influence on mathematical writings extends to Nicholas Oresme (circa 1325–1382), a savant from the Collège de Navarre who dedicated the *Algorismus* to him.

By March 1345 Philippe was no longer listed as *maître des requêtes* at the royal palace, but in May of the following year he held the titles of *maître de l'hôtel* and *concillarius*. His duties included appearing in Parliament and traveling as a royal diplomat. Conceivably after this date, he created the motet *Phi millies/O creator/Iacet/Quam sufflabit,* the music for which has not been discovered. In a similar fashion to the attack on Jehan de le Mote, the text rails against an unnamed French musician who betrayed his country for England, a force that has devastated his homeland. The poet hopes France will rise again. The fifteenth-century manuscript source for this text gives the heading "Meldensis Episcopus Philipus de Vitriaco et ultimus fratrum suorum," perhaps a reference to his brother Adam, a canon at St. Donatien of Bruges. Philippe accompanied John of Normandy to the siege of Aiguillon, arriving on 20 May 1346. For his service he was to be paid two hundred livres during the fall of that year. Besides serving the king, Philippe was in John's retinue as his *maître des requêtes de l'hôtel* from 1346 to 1350. In November 1349 Philippe was granted a canonicate at Notre Dame of Paris by King Philip VI. He resided in Paris and was a regular participant at chapter meetings until February 1350.

By mid century, Philippe had attained the height of his fame. Petrarch made him his interlocutor in the fourth eclogue of the *Bucolicum carmen* (Country Songs, 1346–1348). Philippe continued a correspondence with Petrarch through 1350, when the Italian humanist designated him as the *"poeta nunc unicus Galliarum"* (poet unique among the French). At the end of August, Petrarch mentions a letter sent to their mutual patron Cardinal Gui de Boulogne and alludes to certain texts sent him. In the early fall of the same year, after the death of the king, Philippe once again was sent to Avignon, no doubt to make arrangements for the visit to the Curia of the new monarch. At the time, he stayed at Villeneuve-lès-Avignon, a town in French royal territory that accommodated the suburban residences of many cardinals. Pope Clement also lived there at the time of Philippe's residence. After a brief return to Paris, Philippe was again in Villeneuve from about 23 December 1350 until February 1351. Within that period, the poet-musician is first designated *electus Meldensis* (3 January 1351) in a papal document, and he was consecrated bishop of Meaux near this time. A letter from Petrarch (23 October) congratulates him on his appointment to the see.

During his remaining years Philippe passed time at his two episcopal residences at Meaux and at nearby Paris. In early December of 1356 two servants of Pierre Bersuire and two sergeants of the Châtelet broke into his Paris residence and attempted to arrest his manservant for rape. The controversy that arose from the bloody altercation involving Pierre's men, Philippe's two bodyguards, and his sister's husband was resolved through the bishop's intervention.

On 3 March 1357 the Estates General established the Grand Council of Reformers of the Kingdom of France, of which the bishop of Meaux was a member. At the end of 1360 Petrarch once more visited Paris and yet again may have encountered his colleague. Philippe died in Paris 9 June 1361. Upon learning of Philippe's death, Petrarch on 22 August wrote in his copy of Virgil, "Dissimulabam et credere recusabam. Heu mihi! Nimis crebrescunt Fortune vulnera."

Philippe de Vitry's motet texts are filled with biblical and classical quotations and subtle allusions to contemporary events. The skillfully structured music of his pieces often symbolically corresponds to the significance of the words. Petrarch and his contemporaries reckoned Philippe among the greatest talents of their day. Through the influence of the Italian author, Philippe's posthumous reputation as a humanist began to flourish, initiating a trend to preserve and attribute his works. Francesco Piendibeni da Montepulciano, chancellor of Perugia, wrote a commentary on Petrarch's *Bucolicum carmen* (1394) identifying Philippe as Gallus of the fourth eclogue, thereby prolonging Philippe's reputation. The incunabulum containing the first edition of "Le Chapel" incorporates the response of Pierre d'Ailly and a Latin translation by Nicolas de Clémanges, both intellectuals associated with the Collège de Navarre. The *Dit de Franc Gontier* was known to François Villon and ridiculed by him in his *Contra Dit*. Philippe's reputation traveled from France into north Italy and then into Germany. Aeneas Silvius Piccolomini (*De misera curialium sacerdotium*, 1444) and later northern humanists based writings on *Colla iugo*, and German sources well into the fifteenth century include Philippe's texts in a more rigorous form than do the early ones. Despite all the vagaries surrounding both the ascription of works to Philippe and what he actually wrote in the *Ars nova* treatises, Philippe was a musical innovator and a paragon of poetic and musical style.

References:

Margaret Bent, "Polyphony of Texts and Music in the Fourteenth-Century Motet: *Tribum que non abhorruit/Quoniam secta latronum/Merito hec patimur* and its Quotations," in *Hearing the Motet: Essays on the Motet of the Middle Ages and Renaissance,* edited by Dolores Pesce (Oxford: Oxford University Press, 1997), pp. 82–103;

Heinrich Besseler, "Studien zur Musik des Mittelalters, I: Neue Quellen des XIV. und beginnenden XV. Jahrhunderts," *Archiv für Musikwissenschaft,* 7 (1925): 167–252;

Besseler, "Studien zur Musik des Mittelalters, II: Die Motette von Franco von Köln bis Philippe von Vitry," *Archiv für Musikwissenschaft,* 8 (1926): 137–258;

A. Coville, "Philippe de Vitri: Notes biographiques," *Romania,* 59 (1933): 520–547;

F. N. M. Diekstra, "The Poetic Exchange between Philippe de Vitry and Jean de Le Mote: A New Edition," *Neophilologus,* 70 (1986): 504–519;

Kurt von Fischer, "Philippe de Vitry in Italy and an Homage of Landini to Philippe," in *Kurt von Fischer: Essays in Musicology,* edited by Tamara S. Evans, Pro Helvetia Swiss Lectureship 6 (New York: The Graduate School and University Center, City University of New York, 1989), pp. 66–75;

Sarah Fuller, "A Phantom Treatise of the Fourteenth Century?" *Journal of Musicology,* 4 (1985–86): 23–50;

Mildred Jane Johnson, "The Motets of the Codex Ivrea," dissertation, Indiana University, 1955;

Karl Kügle, *The Manuscript Ivrea, Biblioteca capitolare 115: Studies in the Transmission and Composition of Ars nova Polyphony,* Wissenschaftliche Abhandlungen Bd. 69 (Ottawa, Canada: Institute of Mediaeval Music, 1997);

Ernst Langlois, *Recueil d'arts de seconde rhétorique* (Paris: Imprimerie nationale, 1902);

Daniel Leech-Wilkinson, *Compositional Techniques in the Four-Part Isorhythmic Motets of Philippe de Vitry and His Contemporaries,* 2 volumes (New York: Garland, 1989);

Leech-Wilkinson, "The Emergence of *ars nova,*" *Journal of Musicology,* 13 (1995): 285–317;

Leech-Wilkinson, "Related Motets from Fourteenth-Century France," *Proceedings of the Royal Music Association,* 109 (1982–83), pp. 1–22;

Arthur Piaget, "*Le Chapel des fleurs de lis* par Philippe de Vitri," *Romania,* 27 (1898): 55–92;

E. Pognon, "Ballades mythologiques de Jean de la Mote, Philippe de Vitri, Jean Campion," *Humanisme et Renaissance,* 5 (1938): 385–417;

Pognon, "Du nouveau sur Philippe de Vitri et ses amis," *Humanisme et Renaissance,* 6 (1939): 48–55;

Susan Rankin, "The Divine Truth of Scripture: Chant in the *Roman de Fauvel,*" *Journal of the American Musicological Society,* 47 (1994): 203–243;

Anne Walters Robertson, "Which Vitry?: The Witness of the Trinity Motet from the *Roman de Fauvel,*" in *Hearing the Motet: Essays on the Motet of the Middle Ages and Renaissance,* edited by Dolores Pesce (Oxford: Oxford University Press, 1997), pp. 52–81;

Edward H. Roesner, introduction to *Philippe de Vitry: Complete Works* (Monaco: L'Oiseau-Lyre, 1984);

Roesner, introduction to *Le Roman de Fauvel* (Monaco: L'Oiseau-Lyre, 1984);

Roesner, François Avril, and Nancy Freeman Regalado, *Le Roman de Fauvel in the Edition of Mesire Chaillou de Pesstain: A Reproduction in Facsimile of the Complete Manuscript, Paris, Bibliothèque Nationale, f. fr. 146* (New York: Broude Brothers, 1990);

Ernest H. Sanders, "The Early Motets of Philippe de Vitry," *Journal of the American Musicological Society,* 28 (1975): 24–45;

Leo Schrade, "Philippe de Vitry: Some New Discoveries," *Musical Quarterly,* 42 (1956): 330–354;

Andrew Wathey, "The Motets of Philippe de Vitry and the Fourteenth-Century Renaissance," *Early Music History,* 12 (1993): 119–150;

G. Zwick, "Deux motets inédits de Philippe de Vitry et de Guillaume de Machaut," *Revue de musicologie,* 30 (1948): 28–57.

Epic and Beast Epic

Sahar Amer
University of North Carolina, Chapel Hill

EPICS (circa 1095 – after 1390)

La Chanson de Roland (circa 1100)

Manuscripts: The oldest extant version is Oxford, Bodleian Library, ms. Digby 23. It is used for all standard editions of the poem.

First publication: *La Chanson de Roland,* edited by Francisque Michel (Paris: Silvestre Librairie, 1837).

Standard edition: *La Chanson de Roland,* edited by Joseph Bédier (Paris: L'Edition d'Art, H. Piazza, 1922).

Editions in modern French: *La Chanson de Roland,* translated by Gérard Moignet (Paris: Bordas, 1969); *La Chanson de Roland. Texte,* translated by Joseph Bédier (Paris: Union générale d'éditions, 1982); *La Chanson de Roland,* edited and translated by Ian Short (Paris: Librairie Générale Française, 1990).

Editions in English: *The Song of Roland: The Oxford Text,* translated by D. D. R. Owen (London: Allen & Unwin, 1972); *The Song of Roland: An Analytical Edition,* edited by Gerard J. Brault (University Park: Pennsylvania State University Press, 1978); *The Song of Roland,* translated by Frederick Goldin (New York: Norton, 1978).

Le Charroi de Nîmes (circa 1100–1130)

Manuscripts: Eight manuscripts of the *Charroi* exist in four groups, A, B, C, and D. The four manuscripts in the A group render the best edition of the poem. The best manuscript, upon which the standard edition is based, is A^1, held in Paris at the Bibliothèque Nationale de France.

First publication: In *Guillaume d'Orange, chansons de geste des XIe et XIIe siècles,* edited by W. J. A. Jonckbloet, volume 1 (La Haye, France: M. Nyhoff, 1854), pp. 73–111.

Standard editions: *Le Charroi de Nîmes,* edited by Duncan McMillan (Paris: Klincksieck, 1972); *Le Charroi de Nîmes,* edited by J.-L. Perrier (Paris: H. Champion, 1982).

Edition in modern French: *Le Charroi de Nîmes,* edited and translated by Fabienne Gégou (Paris: Champion, 1971).

Edition in English: *Le Charroi de Nîmes,* edited and translated by H. J. Godin (Oxford: Blackwell, 1936).

Le Voyage de Charlemagne à Jérusalem et à Constantinople (circa 1109–after 1205)

Manuscript: The poem was preserved in a single manuscript in the British Museum until 1879 or 1880, when it disappeared.

First publication: *Charlemagne: An Anglo-Norman Poem of the Twelfth Century,* edited by Francisque Michel (London: Pickering, 1836).

Standard edition: *Karls des Grossen Reise nach Jerusalem und Constantinopel: ein altfranzösisches Heldengedicht,* edited by Eduard Koschwitz (Leipzig: Reisland, 1923).

Editions in modern French: In *Le Pèlerinage de Charlemagne,* translated by Anna J. Cooper (Paris: A. Lahure, 1925); *Le Voyage de Charlemagne à Jérusalem et à Constantinople,* translated, with an introduction, by Paul Aebischer (Geneva: Droz, 1965); *Le Voyage de Charlemagne à Jérsalem et à Constantinople,* edited and translated by Madeleine Thyssens (Ghent, Belgium: E. Story-Scientia, 1978).

Editions in English: Selection in *The Merry Pilgrimage,* translated by Merriam Sherwood (New York: Macmillan, 1927); *The Journey of Charlemagne to Jerusalem and Constantinople,* translated and edited by Jean-Louis G. Picherit (Birmingham, Ala.: Summa, 1984); *The Pilgrimage of Charlemagne,* edited and translated by Glyn S. Burgess (New York: Garland, 1988).

Gormont et Isembart (circa 1130)

Manuscript: This fragment, written in a thirteenth century hand, is preserved only at the Bibliothèque Royale/Koninklijke Bibliotheek of Belgium, folder 11.101.

First publication: In *Les Bulletins de la commission royale d'histoire de Belgique,* edited by Reifenberg (séance du 7 Mai 1837), pp. 265–269.

Standard edition: *Gormont et Isembart: fragment de chanson de geste du XIIe siècle,* edited by Alphonse Bayot (Paris: H. Champion, 1914).

Edition in English: "The *Gormont et Isembart:* A Translation with Critical Commentary," translated and edited by Salvatore Federico, dissertation, University of Utah, 1990.

Le Couronnement de Louis (circa 1130)

Manuscripts: Nine manuscripts or fragments are extant. The standard edition is based on the A group, which consists of four mss. They are held at the Bibliothèque Nationale de France, f. fr. 774, fols. 18–33; f. fr. 1449, fols. 23–38; f. fr. 368, fols. 161–162 (mss. A^1, A^2, A^4) and at the Biblioteca Trivulzienne in Milan, fols. 22–38 (ms. A^3).

First publication: In *Guillaume d'Orange, chansons de geste des XIe et XIIe siècles,* edited by W. J. A. Jonckbloet (La Haye, France: M. Nyhoff, 1854).

Standard editions: *Le Couronnement de Louis,* edited by Ernest Langlois (Paris: Firmin-Didot, 1888); second revised edition (Paris: H. Champion, 1920); *Les Rédactions en vers du couronnement de Louis,* edited by Yvan G. Lepage (Geneva: Droz, 1978).

Edition in modern French: *Le Couronnement de Louis, chanson de geste du douzième siècle,* translated by André Lanly (Paris: H. Champion, 1969).

Edition in English: *The Coronation of Louis,* in *Guillaume d'Orange: Four Twelfth-Century Epics,* translated by Joan Ferrante (New York: Columbia University Press, 1974).

La Chanson de Guillaume (circa 1150)

Manuscript: This text exists by itself and in only one version, an Anglo-Norman manuscript of the thirteenth century, London, British Library, Ms. Additional 38663.

First publication: *La Chançun de Willame,* edited by George Dunn (London: Chiswick, 1903).

Standard editions: *La Chanson de Guillaume,* 2 volumes, edited by Duncan McMillan, Société des anciens textes français (Paris: Picard, 1949–1950); *La chançun de Willame,* edited by Nancy V. Iseley (Chapel Hill: University of North Carolina Press, 1961).

Edition in modern French: *La Chanson de Guillaume,* edited by François Suard (Paris: Bordas, 1991).

Edition in English: *The Song of William (La Chançun de Guillelme),* translated into verse by Edward Noble Stone (Seattle: University of Washington Press, 1951).

La Prise d'Orange (circa 1160–1165)

Manuscripts: The verse version of this work is preserved in nine manuscripts of the cycle of Guillaume and is presented as a continuation of the *Charroi de Nîmes;* manuscripts include Paris,

Bibliothèque Nationale de France, f. fr. 774, fols. 41–52; f. fr. 1449, fols. 47–60; f. fr. 368, fols. 167–173; and Milan, Biblioteca Trivulzenne, 1025, fols. 47–58.

First publication: In *Guillaume d'Orange, Chansons de geste des XIe et XIIe siècles,* edited by W. J. A. Jonckbloet (La Haye, France: M. Nyhoff, 1854).

Standard editions: *Les Rédactions en vers de la "Prise d'Orange,"* edited by Claude Régnier (Paris: Klincksieck, 1966); *La Prise d'Orange: Chanson de geste de la fin du XIIe siècle,* edited by Claude Régnier (Paris: Klincksieck, 1967).

Edition in modern French: *La Prise d'Orange: Chanson de geste de la fin du XIIe siècle,* translated by Claude Lachet and Jean-Pierre Tusseau (Paris: Klincksieck, 1972).

Edition in English: *The Conquest of Orange,* in *Guillaume d'Orange: Four Twelfth-century Epics,* translated by Joan Ferrante (New York: Columbia University Press, 1974).

Raoul de Cambrai (circa 1180–1190)

Manuscripts: The poem exists in three major manuscripts: Paris, Bibliothèque Nationale de France, f. fr. 2493 (fullest version with 150 folios); Claude Fauchet's manuscript copy, Paris, Bibliothèque Nationale de France, f. fr. 24726 (contains quotations from Raoul between ff. 71a and 72b); and the Brussels fragment, Brussels, Bibliothèque Royale / Koninklijke Bibliotheek, f. fr. IV 621 (consists of two fragments).

First publication: *Li romans de Raoul de Cambrai et de Bernier,* edited by Edward Le Glay (Paris: Techener, 1840; republished, Geneva: Slatkine, 1969).

Standard edition: *Raoul de Cambrai: Chanson de geste,* edited by Paul Meyer & A. Longnon (Paris: Firmin-Didot, 1882).

Editions in modern French: *Histoire de Raoul de Cambrai et de Bernier, le bon chevalier,* translated by R. Berger and F. Suard, with an introduction by M. Rouche (Troesnes, France: Corps 9, 1986); *Raoul de Cambrai: Chanson de geste du XIIe siècle,* translated by William Kibler and edited by Sarah Kay (Paris: Livre de Poche, 1996).

Standard edition and edition in English: *Raoul de Cambrai,* translated and edited by Sarah Kay (Oxford: Clarendon Press, 1992).

Edition in English: *Raoul de Cambrai: An Old French Feudal Epic,* translated by Jessie Crosland (London: Chatto & Windus, 1926).

La Geste de Guillaume d'Orange ou de Monglane (circa 1350)

Manuscripts: The work is extant in two major manuscripts: the Cheltenham manuscript (circa 1490), held at the University of Oregon, consists of rhymed alexandrines and is divided into laisses of varying length; and in prose, a manuscript from circa 1467: Paris, Bibliothèque de l'Arsenal, f. 3351.

First publication: One verse poem in *Ausgaben und Abhandlungen, aus der gebiete des Romanischen Philologie,* no. 84, edited by Edmund Stengel (Marburg, Germany: N. G. Elwert, 1890).

Standard editions: *La Geste de Monglane,* edited by David M. Dougherty and E. B. Barnes, from the Cheltenham Manuscript (Eugene: University of Oregon Books, 1966); *La Geste de Guillaume d'Orange,* edited by Madeleine Thyssens (Paris: Belles Lettres, 1967); *La Geste de Garin de Monglane en prose,* edited by Hans-Erich Keller, from the Arsenal MS. 3351 (Aix-en-Provence, France: Centre universitaire d'études et de recherches médiévales d'Aix, 1994).

BEAST EPICS (1170–1342)

Le Roman de Renart (circa 1174–1250)

Manuscripts: The different branches of the *Roman de Renart* are preserved in fourteen mostly complete manuscripts and sixteen incomplete, partial, and fragmented manuscripts; they include Paris, Bibliothèque Nationale de France, f. fr. 20043; fr. 371 (also known as Ms. de Cangé); f. fr. 1579; and Turin: Biblioteca Nazionale Universitaria, varia 151.

First publication: In *Le Roman du Renart, publié d'après les manuscrits de la Bibliothèque du Roi des XIIIe, XIVe et XVe siècles,* 4 volumes, edited by Dominique M. Méon (Paris: Treuttel et Würtz, 1826).

Standard editions: *Le Roman de Renart,* 3 volumes, edited by Ernest Martin (Strasbourg, France: Trübner, 1882–1887); *Le Roman de Renart, édité d'après le manuscrit de Cangé,* 6 volumes, edited by Mario Roques (Paris: H. Champion, 1948–1963); *Le Roman de Renart, d'après les manuscrits C et M,* 2 volumes, edited by Naoyuki Fukumoto, Noboru Harano, and Satoru Suzuki (Tokyo: France Tosho, 1983).

Editions in modern French: *Le Roman de Renart,* edited by Micheline de Combarieu du Grès and Jean Subrenat (Paris: Union Générale d'Editions, 1981); *Le Roman de Renart,* 2 volumes, edited and translated by Jean Dufournet and Andrée Méline (Paris: Flammarion, 1985).

Editions in English: *Renard the Fox,* translated by Patricia A. Terry (Boston: Northeastern University Press, 1983); *The Romance of Reynard the Fox,* translated by D. D. R. Owen (Oxford: Oxford University Press, 1994).

Renart le Bestourné (1261)

Manuscripts: This poem is extant in three manuscripts, preserved at the Bibliothèque Nationale de France in Paris: A (f. fr. 837); B (f. fr. 1593); C (fr. 1635). Manuscripts A and C serve as the base manuscripts for any edition of Rutebeuf's work.

First publication: In *Rutebuef's Gedichte, nach den Handschriften der Pariser National-Bibliothek,* edited by Adolf Kressner (Wolfenbüttel: J. Zwissler, 1885).

Standard edition: In *Œuvres complètes de Rutebeuf,* volume 1, edited by Edmond Faral and Julia Bastin (Paris: Picard, 1959), pp. 532–544.

Editions in modern French: In *Rutebeuf: Poésies,* translated by Serge Wellens (Paris: Librairie Saint-Germain-des-Prés, 1969); in *Rutebeuf: Poésies traduites en français moderne,* translated by Jean Dufournet (Paris: H. Champion, 1977), pp. 20–23; in *Rutebeuf: Œuvres complètes,* volume 1, edited and translated by Michel Zink (Paris: Bordas, 1989), pp. 253–263.

Edition in English: In *Rutebeuf and Louis IX,* edited by Edward Billings Ham (Chapel Hill: University of North Carolina Press, 1962), pp. 35–49.

Le Couronnement de Renart (circa 1263–1270)

Manuscript: This poem is preserved in a single manuscript, Paris, Bibliothèque Nationale de France, f. fr. 1446, ff. 71a–88d.

First publication: In *Le Couronnement du Renard, publié d'après les manuscrits de la Bibliothèque du Roi des XIIIe, XIVe et XVe siècles,* volume 5, edited by Dominique M. Méon (Paris: Treuttel et Würtz, 1826).

Standard edition: *Le Couronnement de Renard: Poème du treizième siècle,* edited by Alfred Foulet (Princeton: Princeton University Press, 1929).

Renart le Nouvel (circa 1288–1292)

Manuscripts: The poem is preserved in four manuscripts: Paris, Bibliothèque Nationale de France, f. fr. 372 and Bibliothèque Nationale de France, f. fr. 1581 contain only *Renart le Nouvel,* while Bibliothèque Nationale de France, f. fr. 1593, and Bibliothèque Nationale de France, f. fr. 25566 include other poems and fragments. The musical/lyrical sections of this text change place from one manuscript to the next.

First publication: In *Le Couronnement du Renart, publié d'après les manuscrits de la Bibliothèque du Roi des XIIIe, XIVe et XVe siècles,* volume 5, edited by Dominique M. Méon (Paris: Treuttel et Würtz, 1826).

Standard edition: *Renart le Nouvel par Jacquemart Gielée, publié d'après le manuscrit la Vallieère (Biblio-*

thèque Nationale de France fr. 25566), edited by Henri Roussel (Paris: Picard, 1961).

Le Roman de Renart Le Contrefait   (circa 1319–before 1342)

Manuscripts: This work, consisting of two parts, is preserved in two manuscripts. Manuscript A (Paris, Bibliothèque Nationale de France, f. fr. 1630) contains thirty-two thousand verse lines; Manuscript B is divided into two volumes (B^1: Vienna 2562 with a copy in Paris, Bibliothèque Nationale de France, f. fr. 369; B^2: fr. 370). B^1 contains 41,150 verse lines and over sixty folios of prose.

First publication: Extracts of MS. Vienna 2562 published at the end of the eighteenth century by Legrand d'Aussy as "Le roman de Renart le Contrefait," in *Notices et extraits des mss.,* volume 5, pp. 330–357.

Standard edition: *Le Roman de Renart le Contrefait,* edited by Gaston Raynaud and Henri Lemaître (Paris: Champion, 1914).

Along with saints' lives and lyric poetry, the Old French epic poem or chanson de geste (song of deeds) is among the earliest surviving genres in the vernacular. Chansons de geste were very popular between the eleventh and fourteenth centuries, and more than 120 survive. The anonymous *La Chanson de Roland* (Song of Roland) is the oldest known example of the genre, dating from circa 1100. Due to their popularity many chansons de geste were quickly translated from Old French into other vernacular languages of western Europe. The most noteworthy examples of adaptations of the *Chanson de Roland* are the fourteenth century Norse saga *Karlamagnus* (The Epic of Charlemagne), and the Italian *Reali di Francia* (The Royal Family of France) by Andrea de Barberino. The most popular stories were reworked in prose in the fourteenth and fifteenth centuries and were among the first books to be printed at the end of the fifteenth century. Finally, chansons de geste were included in popular collections until the end of the nineteenth century, such as the inexpensive, blue-covered booklets called the *Bibliothèque bleue,* and are still being read today.

Various theories of the origins of the chansons de geste have been advanced. The first one, formulated by Gaston Paris in the nineteenth century, claims that the chansons de geste were mythologized instantly in the wake of important historical events. These lyric epics or cantilenas were transmitted orally through the centuries and were put into writing later by inspired poets. In the early twentieth century, Joseph Bédier instead claimed that the chansons de geste had literary and clerical sources. This view, known as the "individualist theory," postulates that the chansons de geste were created along pilgrimage routes during the eleventh and twelfth centuries and were the fruit of collaboration between monks who kept the local legends and jongleurs (itinerant public performers). This view, rejected today, has been superseded by the neotraditionalist theory developed by Ramón Menendez Pidal. Echoing Paris's theory, though more rigorously, Pidal maintains that the epic exists only through its variants. In other words, the epic, because of its essentially oral nature, is in continual becoming.

Using a formulaic style and drawing from a standard repertoire of scenes, the jongleurs reproduced—sometimes faithfully, more often with great variations—chansons they had previously heard performed by others. Recited with the accompaniment of stringed instruments such as the *vielle* (a medieval ancestor of the fiddle) or the *rote* (a boxlike lyre or harp), chansons de geste were performed in front of noble audiences in castles or in front of crowds at fairs or marketplaces. The texts retain traces of this oral delivery since they are punctuated with exhortations to the public (such as "listen!" "be quiet," and so on) and are permeated with repetitions that appear to summarize the action of the prior scenes performed.

The chansons de geste are divided into *laisses* (strophes of varying lengths), with each unit having the same assonance or rhyme. The lines may be comprised of eight syllables (the only example is *Gormont et Isembart*), ten syllables (as in *Chanson de Roland, Enfances Ogier, Anseïs of Carthage,* and others), or even twelve (as in *Le Pèlerinage de Charlemagne, Fierabras, Gui of Bourgogne,* and others), with a caesura usually after the fourth or sixth syllable.

At the end of the twelfth century the poet Bertrand de Bar-sur-Aube, author of *Girart of Vienne,* grouped the existing chansons de geste into three main cycles. First, the cycle of Charlemagne (or the kings of France) celebrates the king and his son Louis and includes texts such as the *Chanson de Roland, Le Pèlerinage de Charlemagne* (The Pilgrimage of Charlemagne, circa 1150), *Aspremont* (1190), and Renaud of Montauban's *Quatre fils Aymon* (Four Brothers of Aymon, 1200). Second, the cycle of Guillaume d'Orange (or Garin of Monglane, Guillaume's ancestor), which recounts Guillaume's exploits from youth to his saintly death as well as the deeds of his forebears and nephews. Twenty-four epic poems from this cycle survive including such well-known examples as *Le Couronnement de Louis* (The Coronation of Louis, circa 1130); *La Prise d'Orange* (The Conquest of Orange, circa 1160–1165); *Le Charroi de Nîmes* (circa 1100–1130); *Aimeri of Narbonne, Aliscans,* and *Moniage Guillaume.* Third, the cycle of Doon de Mayence

fin et esmer faute en bonne wine. En la
destre main tient une clef. la face tornee de
uers midi. Si ont sorti les sarrasins que
telle clef li doit ekoou de la main en tele an
nee que vns rois de france sera nes en firan

la cite dara et la cite de sait iehan de logres :
sour le demin as pelerins. Et la .v. aussi de
saint iaque en la cite de paris : entre le fluu
de saine et mont martre. Et eglises + autres
q il estora et fora sain nôbre parmi le monde.

Roland defending a city (illumination from a late fourteenth-century manuscript for Les Grandes Chroniques de France, *British Library, Ms. Royal
16 G VI, fol. 167)*

develops the theme of rebellious vassals supposedly belonging to the same lineage and includes *Gormont et Isembart* (1130), *Girard et Roussillon* (1150), *Raoul de Cambrai* (circa 1180–1190), *Le Chevalier Ogier* (The Knight Ogier, 1200) and *Huon de Bordeaux* (1220). Apart from Bertrand's classification there also exists the cycle of the Crusade, which claims to recount events from the First Crusade but which is entirely fictitious (except for the *Chanson d'Antioche* or Song of Antioch), and another minor cycle, the cycle of "Relics," most of whose texts are lost but whose existence is attested in *Mort Aymeri de Narbonne* (Death of Aymeri of Narbonne).

The chansons de geste are tales about a hero's exploits conceived on a genealogical model: the word "geste" (a hybrid word from the Latin noun *gesta* and the verb *gero*) means both deeds and lineage. Every great hero is thus the object of a song: Roland, Guillaume, Raoul of Cambrai, Renaud of Montauban, and Girart of Roussillon. The composition in cycles leads to songs that describe the adventures of heroes in their *enfances* (childhoods), their youth, their *chevalerie* (knightly exploits), their conversion to *moniage* (monastic life), and finally their saintly deaths. The cycle of Guillaume, for example, shows how after a heroic childhood (*Enfances Guillaume*) Guillaume becomes the king's

protector (*Couronnement de Louis*). The king treats him with ingratitude, however, and Guillaume, rather than accepting land offered to him by the king as compensation, vows to keep only land he will conquer in his own right from the Saracens. He overtakes Nîmes by ruse (*Charroi de Nîmes*), and then Orange with the help of Queen Orable with whom he falls in love (*Prise d'Orange*). He then settles down in this city which becomes the center of his exploits against the infidels (*Chevalerie Vivien, Aliscans*) and leaves it only to enter into monastic life (*Moniage Guillaume*). A cycle is not confined only to a hero's own life, however, but also includes epics recounting the hero's illustrious ancestry and complete lineage. The success of the *Chanson de Roland* thus led to the composition of various epics about Charlemagne himself such as *Berte aux grans pies* (Berte with the Large Feet) and *Le Voyage de Charlemagne à Jérusalem et à Constantinople* (The Voyage of Charlemagne to Jerusalem and Constantinople).

In the Middle Ages chansons de geste were considered a popular form of historiography and were often taken at face value by noble families who vicariously enjoyed the fame of a putative ancestor's achievements; at the end of the twelfth century, for instance, the viscounts of Narbonne began to call their heirs

Renart escaping the noose; illumination from a manuscript for Le Roman de Renart *(Bibliothèque Nationale de France)*

"Aimeri" in honor and memory of Aimeri de Narbonne of the Guillaume cycle. Despite both the *jongleurs'* claim of telling the truth and the recounting of contemporary events during performances, the chansons de geste nevertheless have only a tenuous basis in history; rather, they express the values and structure of eleventh- and twelfth-century society anchored in Christianity and feudalism. Moreover, while many of the more famous chansons de geste are based upon an actual historical event, such elements are consistently subordinated to both the dramatic and mythical aspects of the genre as well as to the poet's own manipulations (personal, professional, or even propagandistic).

If Old French epic poems are not in direct accordance with historical facts, they nonetheless were used as tools of persuasion in the shaping of a French past and in the promotion of a unified Christian identity. The role of the *Chanson de Roland* in the First Crusade is an excellent illustration of this premise. Serving as an ideal precedent, the *Chanson de Roland* was sung not only at the battle of Hastings, as Guillaume of Malmesbury reported in 1125, but it was also evoked by Pope Urban II in order to convince French knights to fight in the First Crusade. The power of the chansons, whose prevalent theme was precisely the struggles of Christianity against paganism, was used to unite listeners in order to foster a common mentality that made the crusades pos-

sible. It mattered little that the very Charlemagne being heralded as a Christian hero, who had destroyed pagan kingdoms and extended the boundaries of the Holy Church, had actually failed during his expedition to Spain in 778, events supposedly recounted in the *Chanson de Roland*. Indeed, the silencing of Charlemagne's defeat in favor of the idealized and mythic epic character demonstrates the extent to which the chansons de geste furthered a sense of heroism in the people and provided them with models to emulate.

The use of the chansons de geste in the distortion of historical events to fit a specific sociopolitical and religious agenda works similarly in other contexts as well. For just as Charlemagne's defeat was masked by his symbolization as the Christian struggle against enemies of the faith, so was Roland's lineage (as Charlemagne's son from an incestuous relationship with his sister) obscured by his depiction as an innocent martyr. As the medieval audience, alongside the *jongleur,* elevated the image of Roland–the victim and dutiful knight who had burst his temples as he blew his horn to alert the emperor of the impending disaster–they failed to see in his death a possible punishment for Charlemagne's transgressive act.

While the chansons de geste worked toward creating French mythical figures on the one hand, they also worked toward presenting a totalizing view of the "enemy" on the other. Through the chansons de geste, French crusaders were led to perceive Islam and the Arabs as they did the Saracens of the epic tales. The word "Saracen" in the chansons de geste, rather than designating a specific enemy (Arabs from Spain and North Africa), referred to all pagan forces perceived as an exterior threat. This included not only Arabs, Persians, and Turks but also Germanic, Scandinavian, and Slavic pagans as well. Conditioned by ecclesiastical and political manipulation of the blurring of history and fiction in the chansons de geste, crusaders of the twelfth century felt threatened by an omnipresent enemy that had to be crushed. This flight from history and the coexistence of historical actualities with both epic legend and artistic realities allowed for the constitution of a specifically French contribution to Christian identity by creating a solid foundation myth which empowered the crusaders to fight the Saracens in the east.

Epic texts, because of their link to history (however tenuous) and their genealogical content, arouse heated debate about their meaning. Many scholars continue to investigate the complex relationship between epics and history, as well as the process governing the transformation of history into literature. Other approaches to the chansons de geste are also flourishing, ranging from philological studies to gender studies; for example, the relative absence of women in the chansons de geste is no longer perceived as proof that the chansons de geste were primarily concerned with male, chivalric exploits, but rather as an indication that the epic tradition inscribes itself within the medieval courtly and misogynistic traditions of France. Furthermore, the chansons de geste hold great potential for cultural studies and promise to reveal much about the perceptions of the "Other" in the Middle Ages and about the forces that contributed to what would later become a fixed opposition between Occidental and Oriental cultures in the early years of Europe's formation. The continuous interest in the chansons de geste is further evident in the growing body of scholarship devoted to the topic. The chansons de geste are at the very heart of medieval studies and will undoubtedly continue to intrigue scholars in the future.

The beast epic rewrites the epic world of heroes into an anti-epic of animals. As a true representative of medieval intertextuality, the beast epic is a hybrid genre, at the crossroads not only of the epic, but also of the Aesopian fable. The beast epic appropriates the style and formal structure of the chanson de geste and also borrows many of its themes and episodes from the animal fable. In parallel to the structure of the epic, the beast epic presents itself as a series of encounters and confrontations between a fox (Renart) and other animals. As a text that is reducible neither to the epic nor

to the animal fable, the beast epic is highly consistent in its characterization of animals, even across several centuries (from the twelfth to the fifteenth century) and languages. The Old French beast epic, like the chansons de geste, enjoyed immense popularity in the Middle Ages; however, unlike the epic, the French versions of the beast epic fell into oblivion by the middle of the thirteenth century. The tradition of Renart nevertheless remained popular, particularly in the Low Countries where it underwent many adaptations and modernizations, including Johann Wolfgang von Goethe's *Reinecke Fuchs* (Reynard the Fox), composed in 1794.

The first example of a beast epic in French is *Le Roman de Renart* (The Romance of Renart), a title given in the twelfth century to a collection of stories (called branches) in which the same animal characters regularly appear. Apart from branches 2–5a by Pierre de Saint-Cloud, branch 9 by the priest of Croix-en-Brie, and branch 12 by Richard of Lison, these stories were composed between 1170 and 1250 by some twenty anonymous authors of varying talent, taste, and intent. The *Roman de Renart* is thus not a unified composition; rather, it is a collection of independent stories linked essentially by the presence of the cunning Renart. (In later branches the fox often does not appear but is replaced by either Isengrin the wolf, as in branches 18, 14, 20, or by Tibert the cat, as in branch 15). Like the epic cycles, every new branch of the *Roman de Renart* was written in response to the great popularity of the *matière de Renart* (Renart's stories) and recounted yet another episode of Renart's tricks. The numbering of the branches in modern editions is thus anachronistic and represents an attempt to order the various episodes in a logical, linear fashion. The manuscripts, on the other hand, which had started to gather the various branches together in the thirteenth century, remain original in their selection and relative ordering.

The question of the origins of the French beast epic remains unresolved. Nineteenth-century scholarship emphasized a Germanic influence because the name Renart evoked a Germanic Reginhart or Reinhart and thus suggested an oral tradition imported into France. While emphasizing the talent of individual poets, more recent scholars have considered the *Roman de Renart* to be a fusion of various Latin sources: The most important ones are the *Romulus,* a collection of Aesopic fables; the *Disciplina Clericalis* (Discipline of the Clergy) by Petrus Alfonsi which is the source material of branches 4 and 9; and the *Ecbasis captivi per tropologiam* (Escape of a Captive Treated Allegorically), a tenth century beast epic composed by a German monk at the monastery of St. Evre in Toul, which recounts the farm animals' deliverance of a calf the wolf had stolen. The importance granted to the story of the sick lion in this

Illuminated initial from a thirteenth-century manuscript for Chronique de l'Anonyme de Bethune, *showing Roland with horse and horn*
(Bibliothèque Nationale de France, nouv. acq. fr. 6295, fol. 29 r)

Latin text seems to have influenced branch 9 of the *Roman de Renart*. The French beast epic also appears to be heavily indebted to the *Ysengrimus,* a complicated poem composed in the middle of the twelfth century by the monk Nivard, in which the fox is already dubbed Reinardus and his companion, Ysengrimus.

The branch that marked the birth of this immensely popular new French epic genre (in its most complete state the *Roman de Renart* comprises more than twenty-five thousand lines) is branch 2, composed circa 1175 by Pierre de Saint-Cloud. After describing several encounters between Renart and Chantecler the cock, the *mésenge* (the titmouse), Tibert the cat, and Tiécelin the crow, this branch tells the story of the rape of the wolf's wife, Dame Hersent, by her lover, Renart. This event marks the source of the long enmity between Renart and Isengrin the wolf, which thus became the guiding theme of the various other branches that make up the French beast epic. Isengrin is always Renart's chief victim, being no match for Renart's cunning. A good example of their hostility can be found in branch 10, which is based on the well-known Greek version of the ailing king lion. Here Renart, disguised as a doctor, takes revenge on Isengrin by recommending that he be flayed so that his skin may be used to cure the lion, King Noble. Branch 3 provides another illustration of the animosity between Renart and Isengrin; this time, Renart uses boiling water to administer a tonsure to Isengrin under the premise of admitting him to the monastic order of Tiron. He then has him fish in a freezing pond where Isengrin loses his tail and is severely beaten by the villagers.

Isengrin is not Renart's only enemy, however, and some branches do not deal directly with their relation. Yet, every branch does underline Renart's crafty nature. Renart's judgment at Noble's court in branch 1, perhaps the most well-known branch of all, is a good example. Though condemned to be hanged, Renart is able to escape because he promises to make a pilgrimage to the Holy Land to atone for his many crimes. Renart's pervasively cunning nature and the everlasting threat of his tricks are presented even more strongly in branch 17, in which Renart, believed to be dead, is given a funeral before all the animals in the kingdom.

At the last minute, however, he regains consciousness and flees. Renart is thus able to outwit even death itself; not only does he remain undefeated, but one can never predict when he will appear in another branch.

The ostensible comic dimension of the *Roman de Renart* stems primarily from the continual movement between the animal world and the human world. It is further manifest in the verbal explosions and wordplay that are a distinguishing trait of the genre. This trait is seen, for example, in the multiple words that refer to cunning, lies, and tricks: *laz, broion, trape, guiche, barat, boidie, voidie*. Renart's vocabulary, moreover, turns around trickster language: *favele, fauvele, falorde, frecele, losenge, treslue* (all having the connotation, "to deceive," "to lie," to trick"). Since language is used only to deceive, it is often deformed as though it were being reduced to pure sounds in order to emphasize its function as the mere play of signifiers without signifieds.

Though the various authors of the branches insist on the comic element of the Renart episodes and deny any serious intent, both a pervasive social and literary parody as well as a religious and judiciary satire are easily identifiable in the *Roman de Renart*. Unlike the anonymous world of the fable tradition, but like that of the epic, all the characters in the beast epic have names; in fact, the entire epic world of the *Roman de Renart* is modeled on the feudal world of late-twelfth-century France. All classes of society are represented: the monarchy (Noble the Lion evokes the weakness of King Louis VII); the nobility (Renart, Brun the bear, Tibert and Chantecler are all barons, Isengrin is the king's constable, and Brichemer the stag is the jurist and seneschal of the realm); the clergy (Monseigneur the Camel of Lombardy is probably a parody of Cardinal Pietro di Pavia, Louis VII's counselor); and finally the peasantry (the wealthy farmer Constant des Noes in branch 2 and the peasant Liétard in branch 9). Not only do the characters behave in ways strongly reminiscent of a feudal society, but they are also judged in conformity with the judicial procedures and customary laws of northern France, as in the case of Renart's judgment at Noble's court in branch 1. The *Roman de Renart* also strongly parodies the most famous literary genres of the late twelfth century: the epic and the romance. In Noble presiding over his animal kingdom one can discern the image of King Arthur or even of Charlemagne holding court; the barons of the beast epic evoke the Knights of the Round Table, and their pursuit of Renart at the end of branch 1 is an obvious travesty of an epic attack; Renart's adulterous relation with Dame Hersent recalls Tristan and Isolde or Lancelot and Guinevere, while Isengrin stands out as an image of King Mark. Finally, anticlerical sentiment and a violent satire of the religious establishment are pervasive in the *Roman de Renart*, particularly in branches 12 and 14 where Renart irreverently parodies the religious offices, or in branch 4 where the Black Monks and White Monks (respectively, the Benedictines and the Cistercians) are accused of laziness, cupidity, and wickedness.

The last branches of the *Roman de Renart* betray an evident moralizing tendency. Renart's primarily entertaining character transforms into a true allegory of ruse and hypocrisy. In fact, the word *renardie* was coined to illustrate this semantic displacement and acted as a supplement to the linguistic change instituted by the *Roman de Renart* for the word *fox:* although once *goupil* stood for fox, *renard* has replaced it in modern French.

Although no new branches appear after 1250 in France, the character of Renart was appropriated by a slightly different tradition, that of the satirical and moralistic allegorical poem. Philippe de Novare, for example, most famous for his practical manual for lawyers and his moral-didactic treatise on the four ages of man, inserted several elements of the *Roman de Renart* into his *Mémoires* (circa 1250), a satire in which he portrays contemporary political issues. In 1261, the poet Rutebeuf wrote *Renart le Bestourné*, a satire against the mendicant order that had been accused of leading Louis XI and the entire kingdom to destruction. Other works featuring the character Renart include the *Le Couronnement de Renart* (The Coronation of Renart, circa 1263–1270), a political allegory of the struggle of the counts of Flanders against the growing power of wealthy patricians; and *Renart le Nouvel*, a moral treatise composed between 1288 and 1292 by Jacquemart Gielée of Lille, in which the decadence of feudalism, chivalry, and Christian morality is examined. Finally, sometime before 1342 appeared *Le Roman de Renart le Contrefait* (Renart the Counterfeit), an encyclopedic compilation of Renart tales interspersed with chapters on world history and contemporary politics and morality. In each of these texts Renart is no longer a character but has rather become a true allegory of evil, hypocrisy, and vice.

While attention has often been called to how the *Roman de Renart* reflects the social, political, and religious aspects of medieval society, its importance to the construction and expansion of medieval literary genres cannot be overestimated. While attacking the feudal and judicial systems, religion, or the casuistry of courtly love, beast epics such as the *Roman de Renart* also parodied and played with well-established literary genres (most notably the epic, the fable, the romance, and the storytelling traditions). Through its complex intertextuality and hybrid forms the Old French beast epic explodes all generic boundaries as

Renart in King Noble's court; illumination from a manuscript for
Le Roman de Renart *(Bibliothèque Nationale de France)*

it situates itself beyond genre; it thus demonstrates the extent to which medieval literature, far from being reduced to social commentary, was indeed a highly innovative and self-conscious practice.

References–Epics:

Paul Bancourt, *Les Musulmans dans les chansons de geste du cycle du Roi,* 2 volumes (Aix-en-Provence: Université de Provence, 1982);

Joseph Bédier, *Les Légendes épiques,* 4 volumes (Paris, 1908–1913 and 1914–1921);

Norman Daniel, *Islam and the West. The Making of an Image* (Edinburgh: Edinburgh University Press, 1960);

Joseph Duggan, "The Epic," in *A New History of French Literature,* edited by Denis Hollier (Cambridge, Mass.: Harvard University Press, 1982), pp. 18–23;

Duggan, *The Song of Roland: Formulaic Style and Poetic Craft* (Berkeley: University of California Press, 1973);

B. Guidot, *Recherches sur la chanson de geste au 13e siècle, d'après certaines œuvres du cycle de Guillaume d'Orange,* 2 volumes (Aix-en-Provence: Université de Provence, 1986);

James Kritzeck, *Peter the Venerable and Islam,* Princeton Oriental Studies no. 23. (Princeton, N.J.: Princeton University Press, 1964);

Pierre LeGentil, *La Chanson de Roland* (Paris: Hatier, 1955);

Stephen G. Nichols, *Romanesque Signs: Early Medieval Narrative and Iconography* (New Haven: Yale University Press, 1983);

Gaston Paris, *Histoire poétique de Charlemagne* (Paris: E. Bouillon, 1865 and 1905);

Ramon Menendez Pidal, *La Chanson de Roland et la tradition épique des Francs,* translated by I.-M. Cluzel (Paris: Picard, 1960);

Daniel Poirion, "Chansons de geste ou épopée? Remarques sur la définition d'un genre," *Travaux de linguistique et de littérature,* 10 (1972): 7–20;

Jean Rychner, *La Chanson de Roland: Essai sur l'art épique des jongleurs* (Geneva: Droz, 1955);

R. W. Southern, *Western Views of Islam in the Middle Ages* (Cambridge, Mass.: Harvard University Press, 1962);

Eugene Vance, *Reading the Song of Roland* (Englewood Cliffs, N.J.: Prentice-Hall, 1970);

References–Beast epics:

Jean Batany, *Scènes et coulisses du Roman de Renart* (Paris: Société d'édition d'enseignement supérieur, 1989);

G. Bianciotto and M. Salvat, *Epopé animale, fable, fabliau. Actes du IVe colloque de la société internationale renardienne (Evreux 7–11 Septembre 1981)* (Paris: Presses Universitaires de France, 1984);

Jean Bichon, *L'Animal dans la littérature française aux douzième et treizième siècles,* 2 volumes (Lille, France: Service de reproduction des thèses, 1976);

Robert Bossuat, *Le Roman de Renart* (Paris: Hatier-Boivin, 1957);

Ecbasis cuiusdam captivi per tropologiam, edited and translated by Edwin Zeydel (Chapel Hill: University of North Carolina Press, 1964);

John Flinn, *Le Roman de Renart dans la littérature française et dans les littératures étrangères au Moyen Age* (Toronto: University of Toronto Press, 1963);

Lucien Foulet, *Le Roman de Renart* (Paris: H. Champion, 1914);

Jan Goosens and Timothy Sodmann, eds., *Third International Beast Epic, Fable and Fabliau Colloquium, Münster 1979* (Cologne: Bohlau, 1981);

Kathryn Gravdal, *Ravishing Maidens: Writing Rape in Medieval French Literature and Law* (Philadelphia: University of Pennsylvania Press, 1991), pp. 72–103;

Hans-Robert Jauss, *Untersuchungen zur mittelalterlichen Tierdichtung* (Tübingen, Germany: Niemeyer, 1959);

Nancy Freeman Regalado, *Poetic Patterns in Rutebeuf: A Study in Noncourtly Poetic Modes of the Thirteenth Century* (New Haven: Yale University Press, 1970);

Jean R. Scheidegger, *Le Roman de Renart ou le texte de la dérision* (Geneva: Droz, 1989);

Richard Edwin Smith, *Type-Index and Motif-Index of the Roman de Renard* (Uppsala, Sweden: Etnologiska Institutionen, 1980);

Armand Strubel, *La Rose, Renart et le Graal* (Geneva: Slatkine, 1982).

French Arthurian Literature

Norris J. Lacy
Pennsylvania State Univesity

WORKS: Béroul, *Tristran* (circa 1180)

Manuscript: Béroul's romance is preserved in a single manuscript, Paris, Bibliothèque Nationale de France, f. fr. 2171, which dates from the second half of the thirteenth century.

Standard editions: *Le roman de Tristan: poème du XIIe siècle,* edited by Ernest Muret; fourth edition revised by L. M. Defourques, Lucien Foulet and Mario Roques (Paris: H. Champion, 1947); *The Romance of Tristran by Beroul,* edited and translated by Stewart Gregory (Amsterdam: Rodopi, 1992).

Editions in English: *The Romance of Tristan by Beroul,* translated by Alan S. Fedrick (Harmondsworth, U.K.: Penguin, 1970); in *The Romance of Tristran,* edited and translated by Norris J. Lacy (New York: Garland, 1989); *The Romance of Tristran by Beroul,* edited and translated by Stewart Gregory (Amsterdam: Rodopi, 1992).

Chrétien de Troyes, *Romances* (circa 1165–1190)

Manuscripts: There are forty-five manuscripts or fragments preserving some or all of Chrétien's works. Dates range from the end of the twelfth or the beginning of the thirteenth century (Tours, Bibliothèque Municipale, 942) to the early sixteenth century (Paris, Bibliothèque Nationale de France, f. fr. 1638). The best-known and most frequently used manuscript–though not necessarily the most reliable–is Bibliothèque Nationale de France, f. fr. 794, known as the Guiot copy (after the name of the scribe who executed the codex shortly before the middle of the thirteenth century).

Standard editions: *Erec et Enide,* edited by Mario Roques (Paris: H. Champion, 1973); *Erec et Enide,* edited and translated by Carleton W. Carroll (New York: Garland, 1987); *Cligés,* edited by Claude Luttrell and Stewart Gregory (Cambridge: D. S. Brewer, 1993); *Lancelot (Le Chevalier de la Charrete),* edited by Mario Roques (Paris: H. Champion, 1970); *Lancelot,* edited and translated by Alfred Foulet and Karl D. Uitti (Paris: Bordas, 1989); *Yvain (Le chevalier au lion),* edited by Mario

Roques (Paris: H. Champion, 1971); *The Knight with the Lion, or Yvain (Le chevalier au lion),* edited and translated by William W. Kibler (New York: Garland, 1985); *Le Roman de Perceval,* edited by Keith Busby (Tübingen: Niemeyer, 1993).

Editions in English: *Arthurian Romances,* translated by D. D. R. Owen (London: Dent, 1987); in *Complete Romances,* translated by David Staines (Bloomington: Indiana University Press, 1990).

The Prose Lancelot (also known as *The Vulgate Cycle, The Lancelot-Grail Cycle,* or *The Pseudo-Map Cycle,* circa 1215–1235)

Manuscripts: The *Prose Lancelot* is extant, in part or in its entirety, in some one hundred manuscripts; two of the most important are British Library, Add. 10292, 10293, and 10294 (late thirteenth century); and Cambridge, Corpus Christi College Library, Ms. 45 (second half of the thirteenth century).

Standard editions: *The Vulgate Version of the Arthurian Romances,* 7 volumes, edited by H. Oskar Sommer (Washington, D.C.: The Carnegie Institute, 1908–1916); *Le Saint Graal,* 3 volumes, edited by Eugène Hucher (Le Mans: E. Monnoyer, 1875); *Estoire del saint Graal,* edited by Jean-Paul Ponceau, doctoral thesis, Paris IV-Sorbonne, 1989; *Merlin: Roman du XIIIe siècle,* edited by Alexandre Micha (Geneva: Droz, 1979); *Lancelot: roman en prose du XIIIe siècle,* 8 volumes, edited by Alexandre Micha (Geneva: Droz, 1978–1982); *Lancelot do Lac: The Non-Cyclic Old French Prose Romance,* 2 volumes, edited by Elspeth Kennedy (Oxford: Clarendon Press, 1980); *La Queste del saint Graal,* edited by Albert Pauphilet (Paris: H. Champion, 1921); *La Mort le roi Artu,* edited by Jean Frappier (Geneva: Droz, 1964).

Editions in English: *Lancelot-Grail: The Old French Vulgate and Post-vulgate in Translation,* 5 volumes, edited by Norris J. Lacy, translated by Lacy and others (New York: Garland, 1993–1996); *The Quest of the Holy Grail,* translated by Pauline Matarasso (Harmondsworth, U.K.: Penguin, 1969);

The Death of King Arthur, translated by James Cable (Harmondsworth, U.K.: Penguin, 1971); *From Camelot to Joyous Guard: The Old French "La Mort le roi Artu,"* translated by J. Neale Carman (Lawrence: University Press of Kansas, 1974).

Marie de France, *The Lais* (circa 1175)

Manuscripts: The *Lais* are preserved in five manuscripts, although only one–British Library, Harley 978 (thirteenth century)–is a full and satisfactory collection of the twelve lays. Nine of them are contained, though not all of them in their entirety, in Paris, Bibliothèque Nationale de France, nouv. acq. fr. 1104, whereas three other manuscripts offer one to three lays each.

Standard editions: *Die Lais der Marie de France,* edited by Karl Warnke (Halle: Niemeyer, 1885); *The Lais of Marie de France,* edited by Alfred Ewert (Oxford: Blackwell, 1944); *Les Lais de Marie de France,* edited by Jean Rychner (Paris: H. Champion, 1966).

Editions in English: *The Lais of Marie de France,* translated by Robert Hanning and Joan Ferrante (New York: Dutton, 1978); *The Lais of Marie de France,* translated by Glyn S. Burgess and Keith Busby (Harmondsworth, U.K.: Penguin, 1986).

Prose Tristan (first version, second quarter of the thirteenth century; second version, third quarter of the thirteenth century)

Manuscripts: At least eighty manuscripts and fragments preserve the *Prose Tristan;* they include Vienna, Österreichische Nationalbibliothek, 2542, dating from circa 1300; and Paris, Bibliothèque Nationale de France, f. fr. 335 (1400).

Standard editions: *Le Roman de Tristan en prose,* 3 volumes, edited by Renée L. Curtis (Woodbridge, U.K.: Brewer, 1985); *Le Roman de Tristan en prose,* 9 volumes to date, edited by Philippe Ménard and others (Geneva: Droz, 1987–).

Edition in English: *Romance of Tristan: The Thirteenth-Century Old French "Prose Tristan,"* translated by Renée L. Curtis (Oxford: Oxford University Press, 1994).

Thomas of Britain, *Tristan* (circa 1180)

Manuscripts: The most extensive manuscripts are Oxford, Bodleian, Ms. Douce d. 6 (mid-thirteenth century), known as the Douce fragment; and Oxford, Bodleian, Ms. Fr. d. 16 (beginning of the thirteenth century), known as the Sneyd fragments.

Standard editions: *Thomas. Les Fragments du roman de Tristan, poème du XIIe siècle. Edités avec un commentaire,* edited by Bartina H. Wind (Geneva: Droz, 1960); *Thomas of Britain: Tristan,* edited and translated by Stewart Gregory (New York: Garland, 1991).

Editions in English: *Gottfried von Strassburg: Tristan, with the Surviving Fragments of the Tristan of Thomas,* translated by A. T. Hatto (Harmondsworth, U.K.: Penguin, 1960); *Thomas of Britain: Tristran,* edited and translated by Stewart Gregory (New York: Garland, 1991).

It may be thought odd that King Arthur, a pseudohistorical British king, should be the most popular figure in the literature of medieval France. Yet, from the birth of the romance form in France in the mid-twelfth century to the end of the Middle Ages, Arthur and his knights were the subject of at least one hundred romances, cycles, chronicles, and lays. Moreover, the influence of these French texts was enormous: not only did they directly inspire the Arthurian literatures of other countries, but many of the French romances were translated or adapted into other languages. Even Sir Thomas Malory, the late-medieval English author whose work is most directly responsible for the veritable explosion of modern Arthurian literature in English, counted French romances among his principal sources.

Arthurian literature came to France in 1155, one of the few dates surrounding the genre that is firm. That year saw the composition of the *Roman de Brut* (Romance of Brutus) by Wace, a writer born around 1110 on the isle of Jersey and later patronized by Eleanor of Aquitaine. His Anglo-Norman chronicle-romance is a comparatively free adaptation of Geoffrey of Monmouth's important Latin chronicle *Historia regum Britanniae* (History of the Kings of Britain, circa 1137 or 1138). Wace's composition, like Geoffrey's, tells of Arthur's conception and birth, his military exploits, and the uncertainty about his death, that is, about the possibility that he will eventually return to save Britain. Wace departs from his model in several innovations, the most momentous of which is the first reference ever made to the Round Table.

With the exception of a few chronicles and lays, as well as some lyrics that are Arthurian only by virtue of allusions to characters drawn from the legend of Arthur, French Arthurian literature during the Middle Ages is preserved in romances. The romance takes three basic forms: episodic, biographical, and dynastic.

Episodic romance deals with a limited number of adventures occurring over a limited period, although that period can be several years long. In most instances, the protagonist is an Arthurian knight whose chivalric career is already established when the story begins. The romance becomes biographical when it narrates the youth and much of the later adventures of a knight; and it is dynastic if it presents his life and that of his ancestors and/or descendants.

King Arthur listening as his knights tell him of their quests (illumination from a manuscript for the Vulgate Lancelot, *Manchester, John Rylands Library, French 1 ff. 114)*

Chrétien de Troyes and the Continuations

All of these forms are present in the works of Chrétien de Troyes, although the dynastic is represented in a rudimentary way in the presentation of the story of Cligés after that of his father, Alexandre. Although Chrétien was clearly influenced by Old French romances of antiquity and perhaps by classical models directly, Chrétien is the creator of Arthurian romance in three areas—thematic, structural, and rhetorical.

He also made a crucial innovation in the character and presentation of King Arthur. Most notably, Arthur is not the primary focus of any of Chrétien's romances—or indeed of most of those to come during the following two centuries. His prestige is unchallenged, and knights regularly come from throughout the world to seek their chivalric fortune at his court. Yet, Arthur no longer participates in tourneys and rarely seeks adventures. He is a revered patriarch, but his function is to endorse a chivalric ethic and to provide a site for the gathering of knights and dramatization of intrigues. Moreover, in some of Chrétien's work the king is shown as ineffectual, doddering, and almost foolish; yet even then, his prestige remains intact.

Little is known about the life of Chrétien de Troyes. Presumably he was from Troyes or at least spent some time there. He wrote under the patronage of at least two persons, first Marie of Champagne (daughter of Eleanor of Aquitaine) and later Philip of Flanders. Uncertainty about his biography extends even to the approximate dates of his life and of his works. He certainly wrote during the second half of the twelfth century, but beyond that there is little agreement. It may be that his literary production began in the late 1150s or soon thereafter, but other scholars date his major activity to the 1180s. It is also possible that he continued to work as late as 1191: his final romance is dedicated to his patron Philip, who died in that year.

Chrétien wrote some non-Arthurian texts and may have written other works, such as the romance entitled *Guillaume d'Angleterre* (William of England, attributed to a Chrétien, but not with certainty). He is known in particular for his authorship of five Arthurian romances, all of them composed in octosyllabic verse, during the second half of the twelfth century.

His first composition, *Erec et Enide,* can also be considered the first Arthurian romance. Following his marginally Arthurian *Cligés,* Chrétien wrote the romances *Le Chevalier de la Charrete ou, Lancelot* (The Knight of the Cart or, Lancelot) and *Le Chevalier au lion ou, Yvain* (The Knight with the Lion or, Yvain). It is unclear which of these came first; most likely their composition overlapped to some extent, since allusions to events recounted in *Lancelot* are found in *Yvain. Lancelot* is one of the pivotal romances of the Middle Ages, for it is in that text that Chrétien introduced Lancelot into world literature and presented the story of his love affair with Guinevere. This romance also includes the first mention of Camelot.

No less important and influential is Chrétien's last romance, *Perceval, ou, Le Conte del Graal* (Perceval, or the Story of the Grail). In this unfinished work, Perceval witnesses the Grail procession several times. The Grail itself is a marvelous platter or dish from which a great light emanates. The reader later learns that it contains a single communion wafer capable of sustaining a human life. It is eventually described as a "very holy thing," but it is clearly not yet the "Holy Grail" as it is now known, that is, the Chalice of the Last Supper. Perceval's moral deficiency prevents him from asking about the Grail; he will eventually learn that his question, had he posed it, would have healed the maimed Fisher King. Later, he sets out to seek the Grail and remedy his earlier failing, but the text breaks off before he can succeed in his quest. Chrétien may have died before completing the work.

The romance was not destined to remain incomplete, however. Between 1200 and about 1230, four authors, two of them anonymous, added lengthy verse continuations in a successful effort to supply a conclusion to the Grail story. Together, these additions to Chrétien's romance added some sixty thousand lines to Chrétien's ninety-two hundred lines. The first continuation advances Gawain's adventures, which in Chrétien's romance had been interlaced with the romance of Perceval. The second elaborates on Perceval's quest, as does the third, by Manessier, who dramatizes the hero's triumph when he becomes the Grail King. There was a fourth continuation, by Gerbert de Montreuil; this text, sometimes interposed between the second and the third continuations, prepared the way for that triumph and for the conclusion of the quest.

Early Tristan Texts

Chrétien was without a doubt the finest writer of his generation, but several others, writing near the same time, merit discussion alongside him. The most notable are Béroul, Thomas (known as Thomas of Britain or of England), and Marie de France.

Béroul and Thomas are authors of Tristan romances, drawn from a tradition that was originally independent of the Arthurian legend. By 1170–1190, when they were writing, stories of Arthur and his knights were tangentially linked to that of the lovers Tristan and Iseut and to their inevitable conflict with King Mark, who is Tristan's uncle and Iseut's husband.

The texts of both Béroul (composed between 1175 and 1191) and Thomas (circa 1180) are preserved in fragmentary form, but the early and late portions of Thomas's text survive in several fragments, as does the central section (nearly five thousand lines) of Béroul's text. Yet, if these texts mesh nicely in terms of narrative content, they differ markedly in tone. Scholars have explained that distinction by identifying two traditions or branches, called the primitive, or common, and the courtly. Béroul's, belonging to the former, is presumably closer to the original form of the legend; it is vigorous, direct, and unflinching in its realistic treatment of the story (such as when, for punishment, Iseut is delivered to a leper colony to permit the lepers to satisfy their physical urges). Thomas's romance, in the extant fragments, shows instead the influence of courtly culture and literature: his characters are given to introspection and analysis of their love, and both the sentiments and the language are more refined, though less vigorous.

The love of Tristan and Iseut springs from a potion the lovers drink by mistake. From that moment on, they are irrevocably bound by passion to each other, although also by loyalty and love to King Mark. They are repeatedly threatened and exposed by their enemies at court, including a despicable dwarf and three barons who are jealous of Tristan. The story is episodic in that the lovers periodically vow to leave each other (or are required to do so by fear or by discovery) and inevitably fall again into their sin. Eventually, separated from Iseut and suffering from jealousy, Tristan marries another woman, in large part because of the resemblance of her name (Iseut of the White Hands) to that of the woman he loves. Finally, he dies while waiting for the first Iseut to come to him; finding his body, she dies beside him.

Both the popularity and the nature of the lovers' story made it virtually inevitable that other writers would construct additional episodes in which Tristan and Iseut might be temporarily reunited and again separated. Two such texts are known as the *Folie Tristan* (Tristan's Madness), and are distinguished by the location of the manuscripts (Bern and Oxford). They recount how Tristan, banished from court, disguises himself as a fool and returns to see the queen. Another brief episode, known as the *Tristan Menestrel* (Tristan the Minstrel, inserted into the fourth continuation of Chrétien's *Perceval*), has Tristan assume the role indicated by the title. In *Tristan Rossignol* (Tristan the Nightingale), he imitates birdcalls in order to give Iseut a pretext for joining him outside the castle. Of all the brief episodic texts devoted to the lovers' story, however, the most effective and best known is Marie de France's lay entitled *Le Chievrefueil* (The Honeysuckle).

Marie de France

Marie was France's first woman of letters. She apparently lived or worked in England, writing about the same time as Chrétien, Béroul, and Thomas. She dedicated her *Lais* to a king presumed to be Henry II.

Le Chievrefueil tells of the exiled Tristan sending a message to Iseut, indicating that he awaits her in the forest. She meets him for a brief passionate encounter and then goes on her way. The short text (120 lines) is distinguished by the symbol of honeysuckle entwined around a hazel branch, representing the unity of their lives and fates: neither of them can live without the other.

Of the twelve lays composed by Marie, only *Chievrefueil* and one other are Arthurian. The other is *Lanval,* which tells in some seven hundred lines about a knight who finds love with a fairy being, a lady of the otherworld, who swears him to secrecy. Of particular interest is the fact that Guinevere makes advances to Lanval and is rebuffed. To defend himself, Lanval must reveal his love, justifying his rejection of the queen by praising his lady's beauty as greater than the queen's. Despite his betrayal, the lady eventually comes to court,

Illumination from a manuscript for Roman de Lancelot du Lac *(Pierpont Morgan Library, M. 805-6)*

where her beauty is acknowledged and praised by all, thereby vindicating Lanval.

Early Grail Romances

The first indentification of the Grail as the chalice of the Last Supper and the vessel in which Christ's blood was collected was made by Robert de Boron in his verse *Roman du Graal* (Romance of the Grail), or *Joseph d'Arimathie* (Joseph of Arimathea), a romance that dates from around 1200. A writer of limited talent but great vision, Robert sets the Grail story in the larger context of Christian history and emphasizes Trinitarian symbolism throughout, especially by integrating the Grail Table into a series of three, preceded by the table of the Last Supper and followed by the Round Table. A bleeding lance, which had also remained mysterious in Chrétien's *Perceval,* is here interpreted as the spear that pierced Christ's side at the Crucifixion. Although Robert's text lacks the enigmatic quality of Chrétien's, his innovations have proved to be enormously productive, for henceforth the equivalence of Grail and chalice would be forever established in the popular and literary imagination.

Robert also composed a *Merlin* romance in verse, only a small fragment of which has survived; he may also have been the author of a *Perceval,* now lost. Soon, prose redactions of all three were prepared by an anonymous adapter, and they were to be crucial in the formation of the Vulgate Cycle of Arthurian romance.

About the same time, and perhaps as early as 1200–1210, another anonymous author composed *Perlesvaus, ou, Li Hauz Livres du Graal* (Perlesvaus, or, The High History of the Grail), which may be the first prose Arthurian romance. Perlesvaus is a refashioned version of Perceval. The text, conceived as a kind of sequel to Chrétien's *Perceval,* suggests that Britain in general and King Arthur in particular suffer as a result of Perceval's earlier failure, as recounted by Chrétien. *Perlesvaus* narrates failed Grail quests by Gawain and Lancelot before the hero successfully liberates the Grail Castle.

An additional romance dealing with Perceval, dating from around 1220 or 1230, is a short prose composition most often known as the *Didot Perceval* (after a former owner of the two manuscripts that preserve it). The anonymous work probably derives from Robert de Boron's lost *Perceval* romance. Perceval, like the other knights, undertakes the Grail quest, but he is distracted by other quests and tasks before finally achieving the Grail. Following his success, the story turns to Arthur, to his wound at the hand of Mordred, and to his departure for Avalon.

The Vulgate and Post-Vulgate Cycles

One of the great monuments of medieval literature is the cycle of five romances known variously as the Lancelot-Grail, the Prose Lancelot, the Vulgate Cycle of Arthurian Romance, or the Pseudo-Map Cycle (dating from circa 1215–1235). The last of those designations reflects the cycle's attribution, within the text itself, to Walter Map. A native of England, though educated in Paris, Walter held various posts in the court of Henry II and in the Church, eventually becoming archdeacon of Oxford.

Walter is known to have been a writer, although the work definitely attributed to him does not inspire confidence that he could have produced the Vulgate Cycle; moreover, there is also a far more serious complication, which is that he died around 1208, that is, nearly a decade before the cycle could have been undertaken. The attribution to Walter having been dis-

Gawain and Hector in the Perilous Cemetery (illumination from Pierpont Morgan Library, MS. 806)

counted, scholars have proposed several possible authors for the cycle, but none of the suggestions has been widely accepted.

The cycle appears to have grown out of a non-cyclic romance, that is, a text that does not obviously imply a continuation. That romance is a long and narratively complex *Lancelot* composition, which deals with Lancelot's origins, his chivalric career, and his love for Guinevere. There is no Grail quest, but references are made to Perceval (not to Galahad) as the Grail winner. This text has come to be known, following the scholarly work done by Elspeth Kennedy, as the Non-Cyclic *Lancelot*.

This romance was soon integrated into a cycle, with modifications that open it to further developments, the principal among them being a reinterpretation of the love of Lancelot and Guinevere as destructive and the introduction of Lancelot's son, Galahad, as the Grail hero. The core of the cycle, begun around 1215, comprises three romances. Following the *Lancelot* is *La Queste del saint Graal* (The Quest for the Holy Grail); the author of that romance, an anonymous Cistercian monk, traces the moral imperfection of other knights, including Perceval and especially Lancelot, in order to contrast them to the purity and perfection of Galahad, the only one worthy of achieving the final Grail vision. The cycle was completed by *La Mort le Roi Artu* (The Death of King Arthur), attributing the dissolution of the Arthurian world to moral deficiency in general and to the adultery of Lancelot and Guinevere in particular.

Soon after, two additional romances were composed and added to the cycle—but at the beginning, where they provide a prehistory of the Grail and an account of Arthurian origins. These two are *L'Estoire del saint Graal* (The History of the Holy Grail) and *Merlin*, which traces the magician's role in bringing about Arthur's birth (by transforming his father-to-be, Uther Pendragon, into the likeness of a man whose wife he desires) and in later advising and assisting the young man as he assumes his royal duties.

Even though the cycle is enormous and complex (and obviously the product of several authors), it gives the impression of having been carefully planned and meticulously organized. Through a technique known as *entrelacement* (interlacing), several separate though related narratives can be simultaneously advanced, with each one regularly interrupted and eventually resumed. Furthermore, the authors frequently insert references (for example, "as the story will tell later") that foreshadow or recall narrative developments. So frequent are such references—though their technique and function vary from romance to romance—that most scholars concur with Jean Frappier's contention that the cycle, or at least the original three romances, must have had an "architect." Frappier's suggestion is that one person set out the general plan of the cycle and may have written part or all of the *Lancelot* romance. The remaining material was added by others in accord with that plan. There have been some attempts to identify the architect, but no such attempt has gained broad scholarly acceptance.It is possible to discern two large thematic concerns in the cycle. First, there is a sort of dialectic of courtly love, with the *Lancelot* advancing the relationship of Lancelot and Guinevere (and without any obvious censure of its adulterous nature), while the *Queste* condemns that love and illustrates its disastrous effects on the lovers and the kingdom alike. (That disaster is played out fully and starkly in *La Mort le Roi Artu*.) The second thematic focus is on chivalry, as the *Queste* endorses an uncompromisingly rigorous morality, a "celestial chivalry" that supplants the "earthly chivalry" practiced at court. The chivalric and the amorous are interrelated in that even the slightest taint of sin–or even the experiencing of carnal desire–will limit a knight's potential. Lancelot's sin, in fact, will disqualify him entirely from the Grail quest.

Soon after the Vulgate romances were completed, they were reworked in a cycle known as the Post-Vulgate or the Pseudo-Robert de Boron cycle, the latter because of its spurious attribution to Robert. In this cycle, the *Merlin* romance and perhaps the *Estoire*–it is uncertain whether the latter was included–were simply taken over intact from the Vulgate. Thereafter, the differences are striking. A *Merlin suite* (Merlin Continuation) provides a transition from the *Merlin* to later romances, and the material from the enormous Vulgate *Lancelot Proper* is reduced significantly. Then the *Queste* is greatly expanded and is followed by a dramatically truncated *Mort le Roi Artu*.

These changes are by no means a simple matter of physical dimensions. The diminution of the *Lancelot* and the expansion of the *Queste* reflect a change in the adapter's interest and focus. In the Post-Vulgate, the human dimension of the Arthurian story (including the love affair of Lancelot and Guinevere) is de-emphasized in favor of the sacred material presented in the *Queste*. The result is a more sharply focused cycle characterized by an extraordinarily rigorous moral and religious emphasis. The Post-Vulgate does not survive intact, but it has been largely reconstructed from fragments in French and in medieval Spanish and Portuguese translations.

Gauvain Romances

Parallel with the thirteenth-century development of Grail romances and cycles are many episodic romances, most of them anonymous, most of them significantly shorter than the Grail texts, and a good many of them centered on the adventures of Gauvain (Gawain). Chrétien's *Perceval* stands at the head of this tradition, as it does at the head of the Grail tradition in French: the second half of his final, uncompleted, romance is devoted largely to the adventures of Gauvain, set in contrast to those of Perceval.

One of the earliest texts ostensibly inspired by Chrétien is a composition entitled *Le Bel Inconnu* (The Fair Unknown, circa 1190), by Renaud de Bâgé, Lord of Saint-Trivier, circa 1165–circa 1230. The story concerns not Gauvain but his son Guinglain, who is torn between his love for two women, a fact that some have taken as evidence not only that he shares his father's amorous proclivities, but even that the story may originally have been about Gauvain.

Indeed, in the Gallic tradition, Gauvain is a fascinating character. He is often described as the greatest of knights, indomitable in battle, unparalleled in prowess and strength. And yet, French authors, clearly fascinated with Gauvain throughout the thirteenth century, most often contrasted his physical perfection with his personal foibles (especially frivolity, vanity, and an eye for any attractive lady) or his moral failings. He thus serves as a flawed model of chivalry, but criticism of him, if expressed at all, is generally implicit in narrative development rather than explicitly communicated by authorial commentary. It would be misleading, however, to suggest that the view of Gauvain is constant from one text to another: whereas many works emphasize his flaws, they rarely do so in the same way or to the same extent.

La Vengeance Raguidel (The Vengeance of Raguidel, circa 1220), by a writer named Raoul, is clearly an anti-Gauvain romance, concentrating on Gauvain's reputation with the ladies. Here, in burlesque fashion, he is rejected by women, one of whom leaves him for a man who is sexually superior to him. A similar event occurs in a short romance entitled *Le Chevalier à l'épée* (The Knight with the Sword, early thirteenth century), and this text offers further evidence of Gauvain's inconstancy. So, ironically, does *La Mule sans frein* (The Mule without a Bridle, early thirteenth century), by presenting, through a comical series of events, a Gauvain uncharacteristically single-minded in his devotion to duty. The last of these romances is composed by one "Paien de Maisières," which may be a pseudonym parodying Chrétien de Troyes.

Gliglois (early thirteenth century) contrasts its hero with Gauvain. Both love the same woman, and Gliglois eventually wins her because he serves her more faithfully and selflessly. *Hunbaut* (circa 1250) also emphasizes the unreasonable behavior of Gauvain and the superiority of Hunbaut, whereas *Meriadeuc,* also known as *Le Chevalier aux deux épées* (The Knight with Two Swords, between 1230 and 1250) presents Gauvain as a genuinely great knight who must be surpassed by the hero. In a few romances, such as *L'Atre perilleux* (The Perilous Cemetery, circa 1250), Gauvain is no longer presented as a figure whose function is to highlight the finer qualities of the principal hero; he is instead returned to the central role in the romance.

The Raoul who composed *La Vengeance Raguidel* may be the same as Raoul de Houdenc, author of *Mer-*

Page from a manuscript for La Queste del saint Graal *(Bibliothèque Nationale de France, f. fr. 343)*

augis de Portlesguez (circa 1215). The presentation of Gauvain is considerably more subtle here, and it is not clear that there is more than the mildest indictment of him. Several other romances present Gauvain as either the central figure or as a character whose exploits present a dramatic contrast to the hero's; most of them, in one way or another, highlight the duality of a Gauvain who is both a consummate knight and a flawed human being.

The Prose Tristan

Rivaling the Vulgate Cycle both in dimensions and in influence is the vast *Prose Tristan,* which dates from the second and third quarters of the thirteenth century. One of the most important and influential of all Arthurian compositions, the *Prose Tristan* is preserved in more than eighty manuscripts (some of them fragmentary) and about the same number of early printed editions.

The *Prose Tristan* is extant in two forms, each of them attributed to an author (Luces de Gat and Hélie de Borron, respectively) who is otherwise unknown. Many scholars have concluded that both attributions are false.

The earlier Tristan romances had been only marginally Arthurian: the king is the subject of an anecdote recounted in one fragment of Thomas's work, and he and his court play a significant role in a single major episode of Béroul's romance. In the Post-Vulgate Cycle, Tristan, Iseut, and Mark figure prominently in the Arthurian story, with Mark presented as a villain who detests Arthur and is responsible for the final destruction of Camelot after the king's death.

The *Prose Tristan* completes the integration of Tristan, his lady, and his uncle into the Arthurian narrative. It presents Tristan as a knight of the Round Table and as a close friend of Lancelot—appropriately so, since they are the two best and most valorous of knights. Their pairing is natural in another sense as well: each is part of a famous love triangle. The cycle presents Tristan's ancestry before recounting his birth, his early life, and a long series of adventures. Gradually, though, Tristan, Iseut, and Mark cease to be the dominant characters, and the focus shifts to Arthur and his court.

The author or authors appear in general to be less concerned with the analysis of love and emotions than with the presentation of exploits and adventures, tourneys and battles. The structure of the work is considerably looser than that of the Vulgate cycle, and in many instances the relationship of episodes to one another or to the central thematic development of the work is unclear. A rudimentary system of interlace is apparent, but narrative threads that are dropped are not always resumed, and some quests are begun but never completed. As a result, the modern reader may be left with an impression of formlessness or even narrative chaos, but it is amply clear either that medieval readers perceived elements of form that escape the modern eye, or that by the middle of the thirteenth century, a tightly knit structure was not a necessary precondition to literary appreciation.

Late French Romance

Beyond the thirteenth century, Arthurian romances were no longer composed in verse, with one notable exception: *Meliador,* by Jean Froissart (1337–after 1404), who was also an important chronicler of the Hundred Years' War. Froissart composed an initial version of the romance between 1359 and 1361, a period during which he was in England, in the service of Philippa of Hainaut, the queen of Edward III. He revised it in the period 1383–1388, following the death of his patron, Wenceslas of Brabant. The result is a long romance (more than thirty thousand lines) set in the early days of Arthur's reign. It recounts a series of tournaments—the last of them at Camelot—fought to gain the hand of Hermondine of Scotland; the victor, predictably, is Meliador.

All other romances of the period are in prose, and it may be noted that all are in some way responses to a need to renew Arthurian romance. Those responses move in two diametrically different directions, with some authors opting for the extension of textual borders, sometimes to phenomenal limits, whereas others move toward a new concision and brevity.

Several writers, such as Rusticiano da Pisa (or Rusticien de Pise), Jehan Vaillant, and Michot Gonnot, are responsible for Arthurian "compilations" (circa 1290, 1391, and 1470, respectively); these are long and complex texts that result from the combination of material from earlier romances with some newly composed episodes. In some cases, the result achieved such proportions that scribes and redactors might eventually redivide a compilation into separate and largely independent romances.

This tendency toward impressive expansion of textual boundaries also produced the anonymous *Perceforest* (1314–1340), a romance of a length that most readers find numbing: it is longer than either the Vulgate or the *Prose Tristan* (only a partial modern edition has appeared; a full one might well run to some seven thousand pages). Not only is it impressive for its length, but it also significantly extends the temporal framework of romance, by having Perceforest placed on the British throne by Alexander the Great, only to have the civili-

Knights of the Round Table seeing the Holy Grail in a vision (illumination from a fourteenth-century manuscript for Le livre de messire Lancelot du lac, *Bibliothèque Nationale de France, f. fr. 120, f. 544v)*

zation founded by him ultimately destroyed by Julius Caesar.

From the late fourteenth century, *Ysaïe le Triste* (Ysaïe the Sad) also extends across generational lines and creates new characters, recounting the story of Tristan's son, Ysaïe, and of the latter's son, Marc, who are potent forces in the restoration of order after Arthur's death. The contrary tendency, toward brevity and greater simplicity, resulted in several noteworthy texts between the late fourteenth and the mid sixteenth centuries. They include prose adaptations of Chrétien's *Erec* and *Cligés,* prepared by anonymous redactors for the Burgundian court (mid-fifteenth century), as well as an anonymous *Prose Yvain* that has but a single episode that relates it to Chrétien's romance. Between 1525 and 1529, Pierre Sala composed a short *Tristan* romance that emphasizes further the close friendship between Lancelot and Tristan; he had earlier prepared an updated verse version of Chrétien's *Yvain.* In 1554 Jean Maugin wrote a *Nouveau Tristan* (New Tristan), in which he updated the love potion (here a simple aphrodisiac) and other themes in an effort to appeal to more modern tastes.

Owing to the fascination Arthur and his court held for medieval writers and readers, Arthurian elements were often added to texts that were fundamentally non-Arthurian. Béroul and Thomas offer early examples of this phenomenon, and later cases include *Claris et Laris* (1268), which is Arthurian only because the second half of the narrative has the title characters

joined by Gauvain and Yvain, with Merlin prominent only in the denouement. A similar situation is presented by Heldris de Cornuälle's *Roman de Silence* (Romance of Silence, second half of the thirteenth century), a fascinating romance in which the protagonist, a young woman named Silence, is brought up as a man and succeeds as a knight; there is little in the text that is Arthurian beyond Merlin's role in revealing her sex in the final episode.

Thus, the boundaries between the Arthurian and the non-Arthurian are sometimes indistinct, and in some instances, such as in Robert de Blois's *Floris et Lyriopé* (second half of the thirteenth century), the only connection is an episode in which a character spends a brief period at the court or simply passes through. For present purposes, the principal value of such works is to demonstrate the magnetic appeal of the Arthurian story, which attracts to itself compositions that must originally have been independent. The strong implication is that the process of adding at least marginally Arthurian elements to a story was considered a way to ensure its popularity and success: apparently, Arthurian romances were more likely than others to become medieval "best-sellers." Moreover, little has changed in that regard, even in the late twentieth century. Postmedieval Arthurian literature remained popular in France, though never to the extent that it did in the English-speaking world. During the seventeenth century, Arthurian ideals were held up as guides to proper conduct by nobles. The eighteenth century represents something of a hiatus: Arthurian characters were rarely the subjects of original literary compositions, but the continued currency of the legend is demonstrated by children's stories and popular songs about the king. The nineteenth century rediscovered Arthur and embraced the legend with enthusiasm, and thereafter many dozens of poets and novelists, as well as movie-makers and songwriters, have either retold the stories or used them as productive sources of artistic inspiration.

Bibliographies:

Edmund Reiss, Louise Horner Reiss, and Beverly Taylor, *Arthurian Legend and Literature: An Annotated Bibliography,* volume 1: *The Middle Ages* (New York: Garland, 1984);

Keith Busby and Karen A. Grossweiner, "France," in *Medieval Arthurian Literature: A Guide to Recent Research,* edited by Norris J. Lacy (New York: Garland, 1996), pp. 121–209;

References:

Emmanuèle Baumgartner, *L'Arbre et le pain: essai sur "La Queste del saint graal"* (Paris: CDU et SEDES, 1981);

Baumgartner, *Le "Tristan en prose": essai d'interprétation d'un roman médiéval* (Geneva: Droz, 1975);

Merritt R. Blakeslee, *Love's Masks: Identity, Intertextuality and Meaning in the Old French Tristan Poems* (Cambridge: D. S. Brewer, 1989);

Fanni Bogdanow, *The Romance of the Grail: A Study of the Structure and Genesis of a Thirteenth Century Arthurian Prose Romance* (Manchester: University of Manchester Press, 1966);

Matilda Tomaryn Bruckner, *Shaping Romance: Interpretation, Truth, and Closure in Twelfth-Century French Fictions* (Philadelphia: University of Pennsylvania Press, 1993);

Glyn S. Burgess, *The Lais of Marie de France: Text and Context* (Athens: University of Georgia Press, 1987);

E. Jane Burns, *Arthurian Fictions: Re-reading the Vulgate Cycle* (Columbus: Ohio State University Press, 1985);

Keith Busby, *Gauvain in Old French Literature* (Amsterdam: Rodopi, 1980);

Jean Frappier, *Chrétien de Troyes: The Man and His Work,* translated by Raymond J. Cormier (Athens: Ohio University Press, 1982);

Frappier and Reinhold R. Grimm, eds., *Grundriss der romanischen Literaturen des Mittelalters,* vol. IV: *Le Roman jusqu'à la fin du XIIIe siècle* (Heidelberg: Carl Winter, 1978), pp. 503–625;

Joan Tasker Grimbert, ed. *Tristan and Isolde: A Casebook* (New York: Garland, 1995);

Douglas Kelly, *The Art of Medieval French Romance* (Madison: University of Wisconsin Press, 1992);

Kelly, *Medieval French Romance* (New York: Twayne, 1993);

Kelly, ed., *The Romances of Chrétien de Troyes: A Symposium* (Lexington, Ky.: French Forum, 1985);

Elspeth Kennedy, *Lancelot and the Grail: A Study of the Prose Lancelot* (Oxford: Clarendon Press, 1986);

William W. Kibler, ed., *The Lancelot-Grail Cycle: Text and Transformations* (Austin: University of Texas Press, 1994);

Norris J. Lacy and Geoffrey Ashe, *The Arthurian Handbook* (New York: Garland, 1988);

Lacy and others, eds., *The New Arthurian Encyclopedia, Updated Edition* (New York: Garland, 1995);

Alexandre Leupin, *Le Graal et la littérature* (Lausanne, Switzerland: L'Age d'Homme, 1982);

Roger Sherman Loomis, ed., *Arthurian Literature in the Middle Ages: A Collaborative History* (Oxford: Clarendon Press, 1959);

Donald Maddox, *The Arthurian Romances of Chrétien de Troyes: Once and Future Fictions* (Cambridge: Cambridge University Press, 1991);

Alexandre Micha, *Essais sur le cycle du Lancelot-Graal* (Geneva: Droz, 1987);

Micha, *Etudes sur le Merlin de Robert de Boron: roman du XIIIe siècle* (Geneva: Droz, 1980);

Emanuel J. Mickel Jr., *Marie de France* (New York: Twayne, 1974);

Beate Schmolke-Hasselmann, *Der arthurische Versroman von Chrestien bis Froissart* (Tübingen: Niemeyer, 1980);

Jane H. M. Taylor, "The Fourteenth Century: Context, Text and Intertext," in *The Legacy of Chrétien de Troyes,* 2 volumes, edited by Norris J. Lacy, Douglas Kelly, and Keith Busby (Amsterdam: Rodopi, 1987–88), I: 267–332;

Colette-Anne Van Coolput, *Aventures querant et le sens du monde: aspects de la réception productive des premiers romans du Graal cycliques dans le "Tristan en prose"* (Leuven, Belgium: Leuven University Press, 1986).

Medieval French Drama

(circa 1200 – circa 1500)

Leslie Abend Callahan
University of Pennsylvania

and

Robert L. A. Clark
Kansas State University

LATIN WORKS: The Fleury *Playbook*
Manuscript: Orléans, Bibliothèque Municipale, 201.
Standard edition: In *The Drama of the Medieval Church,* 2 volumes, edited by Karl Young (Oxford: Clarendon Press, 1933).
Edition in English: *Visizacio sepulchri, Ordo ad repraesentandum Herodem, [Ordo] ao reprae sentandum Beati Apostoli Gentonis* in *Medieval Drama,* edited and translated by David Bevington (Boston: Houghton Mifflin, 1975).

Hilarius
Manuscript: Paris, Bibliothèque Nationale de France, f. lat. 11331.
Standard edition: *Hilarii versus et ludi,* edited by John Bernard Fuller (New York: Holt, 1927).
Edition in English: *Suscitacio Lazari,* in *Medieval Drama,* edited and translated by David Bevington (Boston: Houghton Mifflin, 1975).

Beauvais, Danielis ludus, and *Peregrinus*
Manuscripts: London, British Library, Egerton 2615 (*Danielis ludus*); Paris, Bibliothèque Nationale de France, nouv. acq. lat. 1064 (*Peregrinus*).
Standard edition: In *The Drama of the Medieval Church,* 2 volumes, edited by Karl Young (Oxford: Clarendon Press, 1933).
Edition in English: In *Medieval Drama,* edited and translated by David Bevington (Boston: Houghton Mifflin, 1975).

Philippe de Mézières, *Officium presentacionis Beate Marie Virginis in templo*
Manuscript: Paris, Bibliothèque Nationale de France, f. lat. 17330.
Standard edition: In *The Drama of the Medieval Church,* 2 volumes, edited by Karl Young (Oxford: Clarendon Press, 1933).
Edition in English: *Figurative Representation of the Presentation of the Virgin Mary in the Temple,* edited and translated by Robert S. Haller (Lincoln: University of Nebraska Press, 1971).

FRENCH WORKS: *Ordo representacionis Ade (Le Jeu d'Adam)*
Manuscript: Tours, Bibliothèque Municipale, 927.
Standard edition: *Le Jeu d'Adam (Ordo representacionis Ade),* edited by Willem Noomen (Paris: H. Champion, 1971).
Edition in English: In *Medieval Drama,* edited and translated by David Bevington (Boston: Houghton-Mifflin, 1975).

Seinte Resureccion
Manuscripts: Paris, Bibliothèque Nationale de France, f. fr. 902; London, British Museum, add. 45103.
Standard edition: *La Seinte Resureccion,* edited by T. Atkinson Jenkins, J. M. Manly, and others, Anglo-Norman Texts 4 (Oxford: Blackwell, 1943).
Edition in English: In *Medieval Drama,* edited and translated by David Bevington (Boston: Houghton-Mifflin, 1975).

Jean Bodel, *Jeu de saint Nicolas*
Manuscript: Paris, Bibliothèque Nationale de France, f. fr. 25566.
Standard editions: *Le Jeu de saint Nicolas de Jehan Bodel,* third edition, edited and translated by Albert Henry (Brussels: Palais des Académies, 1981); *Le Jeu de saint Nicolas,* edited by Albert Henry (Geneva: Droz, 1981); *Le Jeu de saint Nicolas,* edited by F. J. Warne (Oxford: Blackwell, 1972).
Edition in English: In *Medieval French Plays,* trans-

lated by Richard Axton and John Stevens (Oxford: Blackwell, 1971).

Courtois d'Arras

Manuscripts: Paris, Bibliothèque Nationale de France, f. fr. 1553, f. fr. 837, and f. fr. 19152; Pavia, University Library, CXXX. E. 5.

Edition in English: In *Medieval French Plays,* translated by Richard Axton and John Stevens (Oxford: Blackwell, 1971).

Adam de la Halle, *Jeu de la Feuillée*

Manuscript: Paris, Bibliothèque Nationale de France, f. fr. 25566.

Standard edition: *Le Jeu de la Feuillée,* edited by Ernest Langlois (Paris: H. Champion, 1923).

Edition in English: In *Medieval French Plays,* translated by Richard Axton and John Stevens (Oxford: Blackwell, 1971).

Adam de la Halle, *Jeu de Robin et Marion*

Manuscripts: Paris, Bibliothèque Nationale de France, f. fr. 1569; f. fr. 25566; Aix-en-Provence, Bibliothèque Méjanes, 572.

Standard edition: *Le Jeu de Robin et Marion,* edited by Ernest Langlois (Paris: H. Champion, 1924).

Editions in English: In *Medieval French Plays,* translated by Richard Axton and John Stevens (Oxford: Blackwell, 1971); *Le Jeu de Robin et Marion,* edited and translated by Shira I. Schwam-Baird (New York: Garland, 1994).

Garçon et l'Aveugle

Manuscript: Paris, Bibliothèque Nationale de France, f. fr. 24366.

Standard edition: Le Garçon et l'Aveugle, second edition, edited by Mario Roques (Paris: H. Champion, 1921).

Edition in English: In *Medieval French Plays,* translated by Richard Axton and John Stevens (Oxford: Blackwell, 1971).

Rutebeuf, *Miracle de Théophile, Dit de l'herberie*

Manuscripts: *Théophile:* Paris, Bibliothèque Nationale de France, f. fr. 837, and f. fr. 1635 (lines 384–539); *Herberie:* Paris, Bibliothèque Nationale de France, f. fr. 1635, and f. fr. 24432.

Standard editions: Rutebeuf, *Œuvres complètes,* 2 volumes, edited by Edmond Faral and Julia Bastin, (Paris: Picard, 1959, 1960); *Le Miracle de Théophile,* second edition, edited by Grace Frank (Paris: H. Champion, 1949).

Edition in English: *Miracle de Théophile* in *Medieval French Plays,* translated by Richard Axton and John Stevens (Oxford: Blackwell, 1971).

Passion du Palatinus

Manuscript: Vatican, Palatinus Latinus, 969.

Standard edition: La Passion du Palatinus,

edited by Grace Frank (Paris: H. Champion, 1922).

Miracles de Nostre Dame par personnages

Manuscript: Paris, Bibliothèque Nationale de France, f. fr. 819–820.

Standard edition: *Les Miracles de Nostre Dame par personnages,* 7 volumes, edited by Gaston Paris and Ulysse Robert (Paris: Société des Anciens Textes Français, 1876–1883); *Glossaire et Tables,* edited by François Bonnardot (Paris: Firmin-Didot, 1893).

Nativité Nostre Seigneur, Jeu des trois rois, Résurrection Nostre Seigneur, Vie monseigneur saint Fiacre, Passion Nostre Seigneur, Martyre saint Estienne, Conversion saint Pol, Conversion saint Denis, Comment saint Pere et saint Pol alerent a Romme, Jeu saint Denis, Miracles madame sainte Genevieve

Manuscript: Paris, Bibliothèque Sainte-Geneviève, 1131.

Standard editions: *La Nativité et le Geu des Trois Rois: Two Plays from Manuscript 1131 of the Bibliothèque Sainte-Geneviève, Paris,* edited by Ruth Whittredge (Bryn Mawr, 1944); "La Résurrection Nostre Seigneur Jhesucrist, from Manuscript 1131 of the Saint Geneviève Library in Paris, a Critical Edition," edited by James F. Burks, dissertation, Indiana University, 1957; *La Vie de monseigneur saint Fiacre,* edited by James F. Burks and others (Lawrence: University of Kansas Press, 1960); *Le Mystère de la Passion Nostre Seigneur du manuscrit 1131 de la Bibliothèque Sainte-Geneviève,* edited by Graham A. Runnalls (Geneva: Droz, 1974); Edward J. Gallagher, *A Critical Edition of La Passion Nostre Seigneur from Manuscript 1131 from the Bibliothèque Sainte-Geneviève* (Chapel Hill: University of North Carolina Press, 1976); *Le Geu saint Denis,* edited by Bernard J. Seubert (Geneva: Droz, 1974); *Le cycle de Mystères des premiers martyrs,* edited by Graham A. Runnalls (Geneva: Droz, 1976); *Les Miracles de Sainte Genevieve,* edited by C. Sennewaldt, Frankfurter Quellen und Forschungen 17 (Frankfort: Moritz Dieterweg, 1937).

Passion d'Autun

Manuscript: Paris, Bibliothèque Nationale de France, f. fr. 4356; f. fr. 4085.

Standard edition: *La Passion d'Autun,* edited by Grace Frank (Paris: Société des Anciens Textes Français, 1934).

Passion de Semur

Manuscript: Paris, Bibliothèque Nationale de France, f. fr. 904.

Standard edition: *The Passion de Semur,* edited by Lynette Muir and Peter T. Durbin (Leeds: University of Leeds, 1981).

Eustache Marcadé, *Mystère de la Passion d'Arras, Vengance Jhesucrist*

Manuscript: Arras, Bibliothèque Municipale, 597.

Standard editions: *Le Mystère de la Passion: Texte du manuscrit 697 de la Bibliothèque d'Arras,* edited by Jules-Marie Richard (Arras: Imprimerie de la Société du Pas-de-Calais, 1891); Andrée Marcelle Fourcade Kail, "Edition de *La Vengance Jesucrist* by Eustache Marcadé: Ière et IIIème journées," dissertation, Tulane University, 1955; Adèle Cornay, "Edition of *La Vengance Jesucrist* by Eustache Marcadé: 2nde journée," dissertation, Tulane University, 1957.

Arnoul Gréban, *Mystère de la Passion*

Manuscripts: Paris, Bibliothèque Nationale de France, f. fr. 815; f. fr. 816; f. fr. 1550; f. fr. 15064; f. fr. 15065; Bibliothèque de l'Arsenal, B.L. f. fr. 270; Rome, Biblioteca Corsini.

Standard edition: *Le Mystère de la Passion,* 2 volumes, edited by Omer Jodogne (Brussels: Palais des Académies, 1965, 1983).

Edition in English: *The Mystery of the Passion: The Third Day,* translated by Paula Giuliano (Asheville, N.C.: Pegasus, 1996).

Jean du Prier, *Mystère du roi Advenir*

Manuscript: Paris, Bibliothèque Nationale de France, f. fr 1042.

Standard edition: *Le Mystère du roy Advenir,* edited by A. Meiller (Geneva: Droz, 1970).

Jean Michel, *Mystère de la Passion*

Standard edition: *Le Mystère de la Passion (Angers 1486),* edited by Omer Jodogne (Gembloux: Duculot, 1959).

Passion d'Auvergne

Manuscript: Paris, Bibliothèque Nationale de France, nouv. acq. fr. 462.

Standard edition: La Passion d'Auvergne, edited by Graham A. Runnalls (Geneva: Droz, 1982).

André de La Vigne, *Mystère de saint Martin*

Manuscript: Paris, Bibliothèque Nationale de France, f. fr. 24332.

Standard edition: *Le Mystère de saint Martin,* edited by A. Duplat (Geneva: Droz, 1979).

Simon and Arnoul (?) Gréban, *Mystère des Actes des Apôtres*

Manuscripts: Paris, Bibliothèque Nationale de France, f. fr. 1528-29; British Library, add. 17425-8; Paris, Bibliothèque de l'Arsenal, f. fr. 3360-3.

Mystère du Viel Testament

Early edition: *Mistère du Viel Testament* (Paris: Pierre Le Dreu, [circa 1500]).

Standard edition: *Le Mistere du Viel Testament,* 6

volumes, edited by Baron James de Rothschild (Paris: Firmin-Didot, 1878-1891).

Pacience de Job

Manuscript: Paris, Bibliothèque Nationale de France, f. fr. 1774.

Standard edition: *La Pacience de Job,* edited by Albert Meiller (Paris: Klinckseick, 1971).

Mystère du siège d'Orléans

Manuscript: Vatican Library, Vat. Reg. 1022.

Standard edition: *Le Mistere du Siège d'Orléans,* edited by François Guessard and Eugène de Certain (Paris: Imprimerie Impériale, 1862).

Jacques Milet, *Istoire de la destruction de Troye la grant*

Manuscripts: Paris, Bibliothèque Nationale de France, f. fr. 1415, f. fr. 1625, f. fr. 1626, f. fr. 24333, and supp. f. fr. 431; Oxford, Bodleian Library, Douce 356.

Standard edition: *L'Istoire de le Destruction de Troye la Grant,* edited by E. Stengel (Marburg & Leipzig: Elwert & Le Soudier, 1883).

Mystère de saint Louis

Manuscript: Paris, Bibliothèque Nationale de France, f. fr. 24331.

Standard edition: *Le Mystère de saint Louis, roi de France,* edited by Francisque Michel (Westminster, U.K.: Nichols, 1871).

Passion of Leiden

Manuscript: Leiden, University of Leiden, LTK 1055.

Standard edition: Graham A. Runnalls, "The French Passion Play Fragment of the University of Leiden," *Romania,* 105 (1984): 88-110.

Passion de Troyes

Manuscript: Troyes, Bibliothèque Municipale, 2282.

Standard edition: *Le Mystère de la Passion de Troyes,* 2 volumes, edited by Jean-Claude Bibolet (Geneva: Droz, 1987).

Mystère de l'Incarnation et Nativité

Early edition: *Mystère de l'Incarnation et Nativité* ([Paris or Rouen]: Baptiste Bourguet, [late fifteenth century]).

Standard edition: *Mystère de l'incarnation et nativité de Nostre Saveur et Rédempteur Jésus-Christ, représenté à Rouen en 1474,* 3 volumes, edited by Pierre Le Verdier (Rouen: Société des Bibliophiles Normands, 1884-1886).

Mystère de l'Advocacie Nostre Dame

Manuscript: Angers, Bibliothèque Municipale, 572 [536].

Standard edition: Graham A. Runnalls, "The *Mystère de l'Advocacie Nostre Dame:* A Recently Discovered Fragment," *Zeitschrift für romanische Philologie,* 100 (1984): 41-77.

OCCITAN WORKS: *Sponsus*

Manuscript: Paris, Bibliothèque Nationale de France, f. lat. 1139.

Standard edition: *Le Sponsus, mystère des vierges sages et des vierges folles,* edited by Lucien-Paul Thomas (Paris: Presses Universitaires de France, 1951).

Passion Didot

Manuscript: Paris, Bibliothèque Nationale de France, nouv. acq. fr. 4232.

Standard edition: *La Passion Provençale du manuscrit Didot, mystère du XIVe siècle,* edited by William P. Shepard (Paris: H. Champion, 1928).

Mystères rouergats

Manuscript: Paris, Bibliothèque Nationale de France, nouv. acq. fr. 6252.

Standard edition: *Mystères provençaux du quinzième siècle,* edited by Alfred Jeanroy and Henri Teulié (Toulouse: Privat, 1893).

FARCES, MORALITIES, AND SOTTIES: André de La Vigne, *Farce du meunier de qui le diable emporte l'âme en enfer*

Manuscript: Paris, Bibliothèque Nationale de France, f. fr. 24332.

Standard edition: In *Recueil de farces (1450–1550),* 12 volumes, edited by André Tissier (Geneva: Droz, 1986–1998), IV: 167–191.

Farce de Maistre Pierre Pathelin

Manuscript: Paris, Bibliothèque Nationale de France, f. fr. 24341 (Recueil La Vallière).

Standard editions: *Recueil de farces (1450–1550),* volume 7: *Maître Pathelin,* edited by André Tissier (Geneva: Droz, 1993); Jean-Claude Aubailly, *La Farce de Maistre Pathelin et ses continuations,* edited by André Tissier (Paris: Société d'Education et d'Enseignement Supérieur, 1979); in *Four Farces,* edited by Barbara C. Bowen (Oxford: Blackwell, 1967), pp. 53–124.

Farce du cuvier

Early edition: *British Museum Collection.*

Standard editions: In *Four Farces,* edited by Barbara C. Bowen (Oxford: Blackwell, 1967), pp. 15–34; in *Recueil de farces (1450–1550),* 12 volumes, edited by André Tissier (Geneva: Droz, 1986–1998), III: 15–78.

André de La Vigne, *Moralité de l'Aveugle et du Boiteux*

Manuscript: Paris, Bibliothèque Nationale de France, f. fr. 24332.

Standard edition: In *Le théâtre français avant la Renaissance,* edited by Edouard Fournier (Paris: Laplace & Sanchez, 1872), pp. 155–161.

Moralité de Bien advisé, Mal advisé

Early edition: *Moralité de Bien advisé, Mal advisé*

(Paris: Pierre le Caron for Anthoine Verard, [circa 1494]).

Standard edition: In *Moralités françaises: Réimpression de 22 pièces allégoriques imprimées aux XVe et XVIe siècles,* 3 volumes, edited by Werner Helmich (Geneva: Slatkine, 1980), I: 1–110.

Moralité de l'homme pécheur

Early edition: *Moralité de l'homme pécheur* (Paris: Anthoine Vérard [circa 1494]).

Standard edition: In *Moralités françaises: Réimpression de 22 pièces allégoriques imprimées aux XVe et XVIe siècles,* 3 volumes, edited by Werner Helmich (Geneva: Slatkine, 1980), I: 113–421.

Simon Bourgouin, *Moralité de l'homme juste et de l'homme mondain*

Early edition: *Moralité de l'homme juste et de l'homme mondain* (Paris: Anthoine Vérard, 1508).

Standard edition: In *Moralités françaises: Réimpression de 22 pièces allégoriques imprimées aux XVe et XVIe siècles,* 3 volumes, edited by Werner Helmich (Geneva: Slatkine, 1980), I: 423–81.

Nicole de la Chesnaye, *Condamnation de Banquet*

Early edition: *Condamnation de Banquet* (Paris: Anthoine Vérard, [1508]).

Standard edition: *La Condamnation de Banquet,* edited by Jelle Koopmans and Paul Verhuyck (Geneva: Droz, 1991).

Michault Taillevent (or Michault Le Caron), *Moralité du Povre Commun*

Manuscripts: Valenciennes, Bibliothèque Municipale, 776; Ghent, Bibliothèque Universitaire, 4389.

Standard edition: In *Un poète bourguignon du XVe siècle,* edited by Robert Deschaux (Geneva: Droz, 1975), pp. 87–110.

Le Franc archer de Bagnolet

Early editions: Paris: Galliot du Pre, 1532; Paris: Antoine Bonnemere, 1532.

Standard edition: *Le Franc Archier de Baignollet suivi de deux autres monologues dramatiques: Le Franc-Archier de Cherré, le Pionnier de Seurdre,* edited by Lucie Polak (Geneva: Droz, 1966).

EARLY COLLECTIONS: *Recueil Trepperel*

Early edition: *Le Recueil Trepperel* (Paris: Jehan Trepperel, [circa 1501–1521]; facsimile edition, Geneva: Slatkine, 1966).

Standard editions: *Le Recueil Trepperel: Les sotties,* edited by Eugénie Droz (Paris: Droz, 1935); *Le Recueil Trepperel: Les farces,* edited by Eugénie Droz et Halina Lewicka (Geneva: Droz, 1961); "Le Recueil Trepperel: Edition critique des sept moralités inédites," edited by William Edward Walton, dissertation, Pennsylvania State University, 1978.

British Museum Collection

Facsimile edition: *Le Recueuil du British Museum,* introduction by Halina Lewicka (Geneva: Slatkine, 1970).

Standard edition: *Ancien théâtre françois,* 3 volumes, edited by Anatole de Montaiglon (Paris: P. Jannet, 1854–1857).

Recueil Cohen

Standard edition: *Recueil des farces françaises inédites du XVe siècle,* edited by Gustave Cohen (Cambridge, Mass.: Medieval Academy of America, 1949).

Recueil La Vallière

Manuscript: Paris, Bibliothèque Nationale de France, f. fr. 24341.

Facsimile edition: *Manuscript La Vallière* (Geneva: Slatkine, 1977).

Standard edition: *Receuil de farces, moralités et sermons joyeux,* edited by A. Leroux de Lincy and Francisque Michel (Paris: Techener, 1837).

ANTHOLOGIES: *Le théâtre français avant la Renaissance,* edited by Edouard Fournier (Paris: Laplace & Sanchez, 1872).

Four Farces, edited by Barbara C. Bowen (Oxford: Blackwell, 1967).

Recueil de farces (1450–1550), 12 volumes, edited by André Tissier (Geneva: Droz, 1986–1998).

Moralités françaises: Réimpression de 22 pièces allégoriques imprimées aux XVe et XVIe siècles, 3 volumes, edited by Werner Helmich (Geneva: Slatkine, 1980).

Recueil de sermons joyeux, edited by Jelle Koopmans (Geneva: Droz, 1988).

The drama of the French and Occitan Middle Ages was an extremely varied phenomenon encompassing both Latin church drama and vernacular plays produced for a wide range of religious and lay communities in an equally wide range of venues. Whether religious or profane, it typically involved the broad participation of the community for which it was performed, enacting that community's central beliefs or representing its deepest preoccupations. An impermanent and nonprofessional theater until the end of the period in question, its performances were tied to specific religious observances or to one-time secular events or purposes. With a few, primarily late, exceptions, all parts were played by boys or men. Despite the large body of texts and other evidence of dramatic activity that have survived, only a small fraction of the corpus of this widespread and popular medium is extant, espe-

cially that from before the fourteenth century; and while a number of authors are known—some quite early—the majority of extant works are anonymous.

Scholars have long sought the origins of the medieval drama in the liturgy of the Church and especially in troping, a practice that became common in the ninth century in which musical and textual embellishments, called tropes, were added to liturgical chants in order to expand or explain their meaning. The *Quem quaeritis* (Whom do you seek?) trope of the Easter liturgy—expanding on the central moment in the Easter story when the visitors to Christ's tomb encounter an angel who tells them that he has risen—was sung either as a trope to the introit of the Easter Mass (or during the procession before it) or at the end of Easter Matins just before the *Te Deum.* The latter was the practice in northern Europe, including northern France and England, and the less circumscribed context of Matins allowed for the dramatic amplification of the trope in the *ordo* (office or service) of the *Visitacio sepulchri* (Visit to the Sepulchre), the more elaborate versions of which include, in addition to the dialogue between the Angel and the Three Marys, the race between Peter and Paul to the tomb and Mary Magdalene's encounter with the risen Christ disguised as a gardener. The long-accepted hypothesis of a linear evolution from the simplest form of the trope into ever-more-elaborate dramatic forms has not withstood the scrutiny of more recent scholarship, most notably in O. B. Hardison's work. Still, it remains clear that the Easter and, to a lesser extent, Christmas liturgies were the site of dramatic experiments and developments to which the reemergence of a formal dramatic mimesis in western Europe is closely related.

In the case of liturgical offices and services, one cannot properly speak of a "play" in the modern sense. Rather than representing a dramatic action, they re-present, or make present, the central moments of Christian sacred history. Such a distinction does not, however, minimize the truly dramatic aspect of offices such as the *Visitacio sepulchri.* Indeed, a version of the latter figures among nine other twelfth-century music dramas in the first "anthology" of medieval drama, the Fleury *Playbook,* named for its former home, the Benedictine monastery of Saint-Benoît-sur-Loire at Fleury. Five of these other dramas are essentially liturgical services: *Ordo ad repraesentandum Herodem* (Service for Representing Herod), also referred to as *Officium stellae* (Office of the Star); *[Ordo] ad Interfectionem Puerorum* (Slaughter of the Innocents), also referred to as *Ordo Rachelis* (Service of Rachel); *Peregrinus* (the "Pilgrim" Christ's Appearance to his Disciples after the Resurrection); *[Ordo] ad repraesentandum Beati Pauli Apostoli* (Conversion of Saint Paul); and *Versus ad Resuscitationem Lazari*

Adam de la Halle (illumination from a thirteenth-century manuscript, Bibliothèque Municipale de Arras, ms. 697)

(Raising of Lazarus). The first four plays in the *Playbook* are St. Nicholas miracle plays: *Tres Filie* (Three Daughters); *Tres Clerici* (Three Scholars); *De Sancte Nicolao et de Iudeo* (Saint Nicholas and the Jew), also referred to as *Iconia* (Image [of Saint Nicholas]); and *Filius Getronis* (Son of Getron). St. Nicholas was the patron saint of students, and these plays were probably written and performed in cathedral or monastic schools on his feast day, 6 December. It is not known for what community the Fleury *Playbook* was intended, but the *Playbook* demonstrates that dramas of different types and of different inspiration were recognized as such when they were transcribed with musical notation in this thirteenth-century manuscript.

The Church, through its liturgical services and its schools, thus served as the setting in which twelfth-century music-drama developed. Secular Latin comedy, which flourished in the schools between circa 1130 and 1180, may have contributed to the emergent conscious-

ness of the dramatic genre, although such classically inspired comedies as *Geta* and *Aulularia* by Vitalis of Blois seem to be more literary than truly theatrical works. The three plays of Hilarius (second quarter of the twelfth century), a self-professed wandering scholar and student of Peter Abelard, are also highly accomplished literary creations from the milieu of the schools. His *Suscitacio Lazari* (Raising of Lazarus), *Historia de Daniel representanda* (Play of Daniel), and St. Nicholas *Iconia* plays figure in an anthology of his poetic works along with student songs, a nun's life, and letters of friendship or love to boys. Hilarius's plays suggest performance in a liturgical context, and, like their counterparts in the Fleury *Playbook,* they have been recorded in a nonliturgical manuscript, this time without musical notation. His *Lazarus* and *Iconia* plays skillfully integrate lines in the vernacular for heightened emotional effect. Musical dramas have also survived from the cathedral school of Beauvais: *Ordo ad Peregrinum* (Service for [Representing] the Pilgrim) and *Danielis ludus* (Play of Daniel). The latter, which incorporates lines or half lines in the vernacular in a refrainlike pattern, consists largely of a splendid series of processions for the liturgical celebration for the feast of the Circumcision, 1 January.

Some two centuries later, Philippe de Mézières (1327–1405) composed his *Officium presentacionis Beate Marie Virginis in Templo* (Presentation of the Blessed Virgin Mary in the Temple), a Latin drama with elaborate stage directions. Philippe, who had encountered this feast during his travels in the Christian East as a soldier-diplomat, campaigned vigorously for its introduction in the West, winning the support of the papacy and of Charles V of France, whom he served as counselor. The feast was introduced at Avignon on 21 November 1372, although the play may not have been performed there until 1385. Philippe intended for his play to be performed before mass on the day of the feast but allowed that it could be performed in the vernacular for the benefit of the common people.

The earliest extant vernacular dramas appear in the twelfth century alongside the Latin liturgical drama, which continued to flourish throughout the Middle Ages. Two anonymous Anglo-Norman works have survived from this period, as well as the Latin-Occitan *Sponsus.* The earliest extant drama in French is the 944-line *Ordo representacionis Ade* (Service for Representing Adam), or *Jeu d'Adan* (Play of Adam), remarkable for its detailed stage directions and the subtlety of its characterizations. Showing close ties to the liturgy, its skillful dramatization of episodes from Genesis is punctuated by seven choral responsaries drawn from the Matins office of Septuagesima (ninth Sunday before Easter). The Adam and Eve episode, by far the most developed, includes the placing of Adam and Eve in Paradise, the unusual double temptation of Adam and Eve by Satan, and the Expulsion. After the more briefly treated Cain and Abel episode, the play concludes with the semiliturgical *Ordo Prophetarum* (Procession of Prophets) announcing the advent of Christ, itself a dramatization of the Pseudo-Augustinian *Sermo contra Judeos, Paganos, et Arianos de Symbolo* (Sermon on the Creed against the Jews, Pagans, and Arians).

Fragments of the *Seinte Resureccion* (Holy Resurrection) survive in two different manuscripts, highly unusual for such an early dramatic work. Like the later mystery plays, the *Seinte Resureccion* makes free use of both the Gospels and apocryphal accounts. The extant material includes the interview between Pilate and Joseph of Arimathea, the piercing of Christ's side by Longinus, the deposition and burial, and, in the more extended fragment, the boasting of the soldiers as they set up watch at the tomb and Joseph's arrest and appearance before

Caiaphas. The prologue, with its description of the necessary playing stations, indicates that the original play almost certainly included the visit of the Three Marys to the tomb and Christ's appearance to his disciples at Emmaus. Although performance in a church seems likely, the text is not specific on this point and contains no liturgical chants.

Four early vernacular plays have survived from the city of Arras: Jean Bodel's *Jeu de saint Nicolas,* the anonymous *Courtois d'Arras,* and Adam de la Halle's *Jeu de la Feuillée* and *Jeu de Robin et Marion.* A major center for the production and marketing of woolen cloth since the early eleventh century, Arras fostered through its civic institutions a remarkable literary period.

What little is known of Jean Bodel's life has been gleaned from the *Congés,* his poetic farewell to public life written after he contracted leprosy. In the service of the town government of Arras before his forced retirement, Bodel was a versatile poet who produced lyric, narrative, and dramatic texts: five pastourelles, among the earliest in *langue d'oïl;* nine fabliaux, characterized by their sharp observation of peasant and urban life; the *Chanson des Saisnes* (Song of the Saxons), an unfinished epic poem; the *Congés;* and the 1,530-line *Jeu de saint Nicolas,* the earliest French saint's play. Its prologue indicates that the first performance was on St. Nicholas's Eve (5 December), while other indices allow a date between 1191 and 1202. Bodel's immediate source is unknown, but he may have known the saint's life by Wace and earlier dramatic treatments of the *Iconia* legend. Bodel's version is not in any case a slavish adaptation of the legend but a highly original fusion of hagiographic and epic elements, with keen depictions of the everyday life of the tavern that would influence his successors, Adam de la Halle and the anonymous author of *Courtois d'Arras.* Bodel's treatment of the story is played on several registers: the epic, the comic, the popular, and the devotional. In connection with the epic spirit of the play, it has often been noted that Bodel took the cross but was prevented by his illness from departing on the fourth crusade. The prevalence of the tavern scenes (roughly half the play) has led some critics to view the entire piece as a comedy, but such a judgment fails to do justice to Bodel's accomplishment of inscribing religious matter within a frame that also depicts everyday preoccupations and material concerns.

The 664-line *Courtois d'Arras,* which survives in four manuscripts, is a dramatization of the biblical parable of the prodigal son in a twelfth-century setting. The play's style is, for the most part, comic and lively, especially in the tavern scene, but Courtois's misadventures issue in a moving lament of more than one hundred lines. The inclusion of six lines of nondramatic narration has led some to suggest that the piece may have been performed as a dramatic monologue, a genre cultivated by the jongleurs of the time, but one cannot exclude the possibility of performance by a small troupe of actors.

Adam de la Halle (circa 1240–circa 1285) was one of the great innovators of medieval French theater. Also called "Adam le Bossu" (Adam the Hunchback)–although there is no evidence that the name referred to an actual physical deformity–Adam studied in Paris and bore the title "Master" but spent most of his life in his native city of Arras, marrying there in the 1270s. In addition to being a dramatist, Adam was a prolific poet and musician whose creative output included thirty-six chansons, forty-six caroles, fourteen polyphonic rondeaux, and several motets. He also participated in eighteen *jeux-partis* (poetic debates), composed a *Dit d'amour* (Tale of Love), and began an epic poem, the *Roi de Sicile* (King of Sicily), to commemorate Charles of Anjou, at whose court he had lived. In 1276 or 1277 Adam wrote his *Congé,* or poem of farewell, as he prepared to leave Arras to continue his studies in Paris (as he also does in the *Jeu de la Feuillée*). Whether he actually did leave is one of the many mysteries surrounding his life, as is the date of his death, believed to have occurred between 1285, the year Charles of Anjou died, and 2 February 1289, when Adam's death is noted in a copy of the *Roman de Troie* (Romance of Troy) transcribed by his nephew, Jean Madot.

Much debate has centered around the meaning of the title of Adam's 1,099-line play, the *Jeu de la Feuillée* (circa 1276–1277), the first known secular drama in French. It has been argued that "feuillée" refers to the leafy shelter constructed to protect the statue of the Virgin at Pentecost and referred to at the end of the play, perhaps an indication of the occasion for which the play was composed; but others see in the word a reference to the "folie," or madness, that is an integral part of the play. A semiepisodic piece that satirizes such character types as doctors and itinerant monks peddling pardons, the *Jeu de la Feuillée* can be considered a drama à clef because it satirizes individual inhabitants of the town of Arras while also dramatizing aspects of Adam's own life. Adam's 780-line *Jeu de Robin et Marion* is a dramatized pastourelle and *bergerie* (shepherds' play) in which the audience witnesses an encounter between a knight and a shepherdess and the consequences of her refusal of his advances. The action unfolds in a mixture of dialogue and song, including the use of musical refrains known from other thirteenth-century sources.

The anonymous thirteenth-century *Garçon et l'Aveugle* (The Blind Man and His Boy) also originates from the north, from the city of Tournai. Although not designated as such in the manuscript, it has often been considered the earliest farce for its rather cruel and physical humor, predicated on the mistreatment and duping of the blind man by the boy whom he takes as servant. This simple, two-person play was probably in the repertory of a small traveling company and incorporates into the dramatic action a direct appeal to the audience for alms.

The tremendous development of the cult of the Virgin Mary in the thirteenth century brought with it a new dramatic genre, the Marian miracle play, the earliest example of which is the *Miracle de Théophile* by Rutebeuf (died circa 1285). Nothing is known of the life of this prolific poet except what can be gleaned from his work, which comprises some fourteen thousand lines of verse. The range of his work is quite broad: fabliaux, religious narratives, polemical pieces, and autobiographical texts (of dubious veracity). He was doubtless a clerk, a staunch defender of the masters of the University of Paris and self-declared enemy of the mendicant orders. Of Greek origin, the Theophilus legend was extremely popular in the Christian West (no fewer than twenty-five Latin versions are extant). Rutebeuf's dramatization of the story of the once-powerful cleric who makes a pact with the devil and then begs the Virgin Mary for forgiveness is noteworthy for its sharp characterizations and its richly varied poetic meters. Rutebeuf is also the author of the dramatic monologue *Dit de l'herberie* (Herbseller's Harangue), marked by comic boastfulness and colorful language, including a scatological cure for toothache.

The most important dramatic corpus of the fourteenth century is the *Miracles de Nostre Dame par personnages,* comprising forty plays performed on a yearly basis (circa 1340–1382) for a confraternity of Parisian goldsmiths. The subject matter of the collection is broader than its title might suggest: fewer than half the plays actually derive from Marian legends, the others drawing on epic, romance, and hagiographic sources. Another large corpus of plays has recently come to light: seventy-two fifteenth-century processional pageant plays from the northern city of Lille. The plays were performed by rhetorical societies and neighborhood groups at an annual procession under church and civic sponsorship, and the best plays competed for prizes in a dramatic contest organized by the bishop of Fools. The collection includes forty-three plays drawn from the Old Testament, twenty-one from the New Testament, five from Roman history, one saint play, one miracle play, and one morality play.

The mystères, however, were the dominant force in the theatrical landscape of late medieval France. The term *mystère* (mystery) was commonly used as a descriptive term in the titles of plays written in French or Occitan from the thirteenth through the sixteenth centuries, but as a generic marker the term is vague and may refer to any large-scale dramatic work. Four subcategories emerge: mystères de la Passion, or plays representing the Passion of Christ; mystères hagiographiques, or mysteries representing the lives of the saints; mysteries on Old Testament themes; and historical mysteries on nonsacred themes.

The Passion cycles, which trace the life, death, and resurrection of Christ, may be wide in scope, reaching back in time to the Creation and projecting forward to the Resurrection, or more narrowly focused on the events of Holy Week. The Passion plays have various Latin sources: the canonic Gospels of the Bible, the apocryphal gospels such as the *Gospel of Nicodemus* and the *Acts of Pilate,* the *Legenda aurea* (Golden Legend), devotional texts such as the Pseudo-Bonaventure *Meditationes beatae Mariae* (Meditations of the Virgin) and Ludolphus of Saxony's *Vita Jesu Christi* (Life of Christ), and the biblical commentaries of Nicolas of Lyra. An important vernacular source for several Passion plays is the *Passion des jongleurs* (Minstrels' Passion), an anonymous narrative poem with many passages in dialogue (late twelfth or early thirteenth century).

Only seven complete Passion cycles survive, along with roughly another half dozen fragments and incomplete versions, ranging in length from around two thousand to thirty-five thousand lines. The longer plays were divided into *journées,* or days of performance, and called for the participation of hundreds of individuals in various capacities. The production of a Passion play was a community event, involving the town's inhabitants or else staged by a confraternal organization. The performance was generally held in a public space—a town square or marketplace—to permit the attendance of the largest possible number.

The earliest surviving Passion play, the *Passion du Palatinus* (Palatine Passion; late thirteenth or early fourteenth century) is also the briefest, less than two thousand lines. Drawing on the *Passion des jongleurs,* its focus is limited mainly to the events of Holy Week. The belief that the *Passion du Palatinus* was the single source for all subsequent Passions has largely been discounted in view of recent fragments that have come to light, such as the late-thirteenth-century fragment of a Passion found at the University of Leiden, which presents a different version of events from the *Palatinus.* The *Palatinus* bears some resemblance to the later *Passion d'Autun* (Autun Passion), the two versions of which include none of the comic elements associated with other late-medieval Passion plays.

The *Mystère de la Passion Nostre Seigneur* (circa 1380), of the important manuscript 1131 of the Bibliothèque Sainte-Geneviève in Paris, is based on the Bible and the *Gospel of Nicodemus.* Less than 4,500 lines long, it dramatizes, like the *Passion du Palatinus,* the events of Holy

Week, beginning with the supper at the house of Simon the Leper and ending with the Centurion's invitation to the audience to join him in singing the *Te Deum* and *Benedicamus.* Because of its inclusion in a manuscript of plays found at Sainte-Geneviève, the play is believed to have been performed by the Confraternity of Sainte-Geneviève-du-Mont.

The *Passion de Semur* believed to have been performed in Semur-en-Auxois (Burgundy), survives in one manuscript, dated 1488, although the text is thought to be from the first thirty years of the century. The *Passion* of nearly ninety-six hundred lines was performed over two days with the participation of more than one-hundred ninety individuals. The action of the play spans the life and death of Christ from the Nativity through the Resurrection.

The *Passion d'Arras,* the first of the great medieval French mystery plays to extend the representation of the life of Christ over four days, is also the first Passion play to be associated with a named author. The presumed author, Eustache Marcadé (circa 1390–1440) also wrote another mystery play, the *Vengance Jhesucrist* (Vengeance of Jesus Christ), which survives in the same manuscript. Marcadé, who studied theology at the University of Paris and held various ecclesiastical offices, was appointed dean of the faculty of Canon Law of the University of Paris in 1439. His training and experience in ecclesiastical law can be seen in his innovative addition to the Passion cycle of the *Procès de Paradis* (Trial in Paradise), a debate in Heaven among the Four Daughters of God. Justice and Truth debate Mercy and Peace before God the Father, who decides to send his Son to the world to redeem the human race. The twenty-five-thousand-line Passion play has its sources in the canonic and apocryphal Gospels, Bible commentary, St. Thomas's *Summa,* and Guillaume de Digulleville's *Pèlerinage de Jésus-Christ* (Pilgrimage of Jesus Christ) and includes scenes from the life and Passion of Christ, sermons, and many comic scenes, including playful devils, haranguing merchants, and wise-cracking executioners.

The best-known of all the Passion plays is the thirty-five-thousand-line *Mystère de la Passion* (circa 1450) by Arnoul Gréban, preserved complete in three similar manuscripts and incomplete in several others. Born in Le Mans around 1425, Gréban was a student of theology at the University of Paris in the 1450s. He lived in the cloister of the cathedral of Notre-Dame in Paris, where, from 1450 to 1455, he was organist, master of grammar, and master of the choirboys. Gréban is generally believed to have died sometime after 1473, the date of the death of his patron, the comte du Maine, but some biographers claim that he spent his final years in Italy and died circa 1495. Gréban's *Mystère* employs the four-day structure introduced by Marcadé as well as a greatly expanded *Procès de Paradis*. For many critics, Gréban's *Passion* marks the highpoint of the genre, with its huge dimensions, its variety of metrical forms, and its vivid characterizations of the holy and the profane, the serious and the comic, the solemn and the joyous.

Gréban's *Passion* provided inspiration and material for two subsequent cycles: the *Passion* of Jean Michel, performed in Angers in 1486 and then in Paris in 1490, 1498, and 1507; and the incomplete *Mystère de la Passion de Troyes* (Troyes Passion). Jean Michel (died 1501) was a doctor who practiced medicine in Angers. Taking Gréban's second and third days as his point of departure, he transposed the text almost verbatim and expanded upon it, focusing action on the adult life of Jesus from baptism to death. The cycle's thirty thousand lines are divided among four days. Michel's aim was to move his audience to empathize with the events, and thus he emphasized the role of the Virgin Mary and the more "human" side of the characters, expanding the roles of Mary Magdalene, Lazarus, and Judas and placing increased emphasis on the activity of preaching within the dramatic context of the play.

The manuscript of the *Passion de Troyes* shows evidence of many reworkings and thus can serve as an example of how such a mystery changes and develops. The beginning is based on the *Mystère du Vieil Testament* (Mystery of the Old Testament), and the rest is a version of Gréban's *Passion*. Each day, comprising roughly eight thousand lines, is found in a single notebook, although the third day, presenting the Passion of Christ, has been lost. The play includes 212 speaking roles and was frequently performed from 1482 to 1490, in 1496, 1505, and 1531.

Unlike Jean Michel's *Passion* and the *Passion de Troyes,* the *Passion d'Auvergne* (Auvergne Passion), performed in 1452, 1477, and in the early sixteenth century, shows no affinities with the *Passions* of Marcadé and Gréban. Only three days of this cycle, which was performed on Whitmonday and the six Sundays that preceded it, survive. Each journée comprises between fifteen hundred and two thousand lines. The play has many distinctive features, including several violent and vulgar scenes, especially during the Crucifixion, and a comic episode using the lower Auvergne dialect. Most important and unusual are the scenes that conclude each surviving day, in which Jesus and his mother meet, regardless of whether the traditional sources allow for such a scene.

Other mysteries representing episodes from the life of Christ are extant, including three of the plays found in the manuscript Sainte-Geneviève 1131: the *Mystère de la Nativité* (Mystery of the Nativity), the *Geu des Trois Roys* (Play of The Three Kings), and the *Mystère de la Résurrection* (Mystery of the Resurrection). Another Nativity play, the *Mystère de l'Incarnation et Nativité* (Mystery of the Incarnation and Nativity) was performed over two days of Christmas 1474 on the Place du Neuf-Marché of Rouen. Plays representing events after the Resurrection have also survived: a fourteenth-century play of the Last Judgment and fragments of a fifteenth-century play on the same theme, both of which dramatize the battle between God and the Antichrist, and the enormous *Mystère des Actes des Apôtres* (Mystery of the Acts of the Apostles), at least partially written by Simon Gréban (died 1473), canon at Le Mans, perhaps in collaboration with his brother Arnoul. Commissioned by King René of Anjou and written between 1460 and 1470, the *Mystère des Actes des Apôtres* is the longest dramatic piece from medieval France. Comprising sixty-two-thousand lines and employing five hundred characters, it is based on the Book of Acts and traces the history and itineraries of the Apostles upon their departure from Jerusalem, culminating in Rome with the history of the Roman emperors from Tiberius to Nero and the martyrdoms of St. Peter and St. Paul. The play caters to the taste of the late-medieval audience in its juxtaposition of serious, comic, magical, and edifying elements as well as in the violence that it presents.

Several plays exist on Old Testament themes, most of which are found within the compilation known as the *Mystère du Vieil Testament*. This roughly fifty-thousand-line compendium of Old Testament material comprises one large, episodic historical play, beginning at the Creation and ending with the Queen of Sheba's visit to Solomon, followed by six shorter plays: Job, Tobit, Susannah, Daniel, Judith, Esther, and Octavian and the Sibyls. Much legendary material is mixed in with the biblical stories. Also extant are the anonymous fifteenth-century play the *Pacience de Job* (Patience of Job) and, in the Lille collection, forty-three plays on Old Testament themes, including seventeen episodes not found in the *Mystère du Vieil Testament.*

Three "historical" mystery plays are extant. In the 20,529 lines of the *Mystère du siège d'Orléans* (Mystery of the Siege of Orleans; second half of the fifteenth century) that city's defense against the English, under the leadership of Joan of Arc, is represented. Jacques Milet's *Istoire de la destruction de Troye la grant* (History of the Destruction of Troy the Great), is rooted in the French myth of Trojan origins. Milet (1425–1466), who had studied law at the University of Orléans and was also the author of an allegorical poem, "La Forest de tristesse" (The Forest of Sadness), dedicated his twenty-seven-thousand-line play to Charles VII. Its survival in thirteen manuscripts and in several early printed editions attests to its popularity. Finally, the *Mystère de saint Louis* (1470) also can be considered a hagiographical

Frontispiece for the 1493 edition of the works of the Roman playwright Terence, published by Jean Trechsel, depicting a contemporary theater

mystery and presents, in 19,197 lines to be presented over the course of three days, events from the life of the saint-king, including his coronation, marriage, and death. The sole manuscript belonged to the Parisian Confrérie de la Passion and provides abundant stage directions for the 232 performers it required.

Among the earliest and most popular of dramatic genres, dramatized hagiographic material from saints' lives and other sources was, if anything, even more popular in the later Middle Ages. Approximately one hundred French or Occitan saints' plays are extant, and another forty are attested to in documents. Noteworthy examples from the later period include several of the plays in manuscript 1131 of the Bibliothèque Sainte Geneviève in Paris, which includes, in addition to *Vie monseigneur saint Fiacre* (Life of My Lord Saint Fiacre), a cycle of hagiographic plays that were intended for performance together or individually: *Le Martyre saint Estienne* (Martyrdom of Saint Stephen), *La Conversion saint Pol* (Conversion of Saint Paul), *La Conversion saint Denis* (Conversion of Saint Denis), *Comment saint Pere et saint Pol alerent a Romme* (How Saint Peter and Saint Paul went to Rome), *Le Jeu saint Denis* (Play of Saint Denis), and the *Miracles madame sainte Genevieve* (Miracles of My Lady Saint Genevieve), the last being a series of eleven short plays.

The *Mystère du roi Advenir* (Mystery of King Avenir, circa 1455) by Jean du Prier, valet de chambre in the household of René d'Anjou from 1451 to 1480, was typical of the mammoth proportions and elaborate staging of the late mystery plays. A rendering of the legend of Barlaam and Josaphat staged in three days with a cast of 115 characters, it includes martyrdom scenes remarkable for their elaborate *feintes* (stage tricks), which were popular with the public of the time.

Many towns or religious associations, such as confraternities, used drama to honor their patron saints or to invoke the protection of other saints in time of need (for example, plague or war). The Parisian shoemakers of Paris and Rouen staged plays in honor of their patrons, St. Crispin and St. Cripinian, while the citizens of Lengres staged a play in 1474 in honor of their local saint, St. Didier. St. Sebastian was widely venerated as a protector against plague, which may explain the relative popularity of plays dramatizing his life and martyrdom, two examples of which have survived. Plays of such popular saints as Nicholas and, of course, the Virgin Mary, continued to be performed in the late Middle Ages. Late Marian plays include two late-fourteenth-century fragments of the *Mystère de l'Advocacie Nostre Dame* (Mystery of the Advocacy of Our Lady), a dramatization of the work of the same name by Jean Justice, and the *Mystère de l'Assomption de la Vierge* (Mystery of the Assumption of the Virgin), a play of approximately three thousand lines for 39 characters.

Evidence survives of a rich theatrical tradition in *langue d'oc,* or Occitan. The most important examples are the late-eleventh- or early-twelfth-century liturgical drama, the *Sponsus* (Bridegroom), which relates in forty-seven Latin and forty Occitan lines the biblical parable of the Wise and Foolish Virgins; a Passion play, known as the *Passion Didot,* after the manuscript in which it is found; and a late-fifteenth-century cycle of a dozen mysteries totaling approximately nine thousand lines known as the *mystères rouergats* for their place of origin in south-central France. The *Passion Didot* represents a somewhat different tradition than the northern cycles and includes material not found therein, such as a more developed lament of the Virgin and the representation of the legend of Judas.

As with medieval religious and profane drama, no clear separation exists in the medieval French theatrical tradition between comic and serious drama. Comic elements certainly appear in the mystery plays, and likewise, plays that are not considered strictly religious in their subject matter may be serious in their intention. The medieval French moralité, or morality play, is illustrative of the difficulties in making generic distinctions. The aim of the moralité–a form that reached its height in the century or so after the staging in 1427 of the first such play for which a text is extant– is to instruct, to teach a "moral" lesson, but it often uses comic elements to do so. Moralités, which can range from less than two hundred to more than thirty thousand lines, have been described as allegorical dramas in which the protagonist must choose between good and evil. Representative examples include the anonymous eight-thousand-line *Moralité de Bien advisé, Mal advisé* (Morality of the Wise Man and the Foolish Man, before 1439), which involves fifty-nine characters, and the *Moralité de l'homme pécheur* (Morality of the Sinful Man, circa 1494), whose twenty-two thousand lines are distributed among sixty-two characters and which includes the allegorical *Procès de Paradis,* found in many mystery plays.

Perhaps the best-known morality play by a known author is the *Moralité de l'Aveugle et du Boiteux* (Morality of the Blindman and the Lame Man, 1496) by André (or Andrieu) de La Vigne. André was born in La Rochelle, but little else is known about his activities before 1494. He is the author of works in many genres, including the *Ressource de la Chrestienté* (Consolation of Christianity), an allegorized *prosimetrum* (work of alternating prose and verse), and the narrative *Voyage de Naples* written for Charles VII, whom he accompanied on his campaign to Naples. André is also the author of *Farce du meunier de qui le diable emporte l'âme en enfer* (Farce of the Miller whose Soul Was Carried off to Hell by the Devil), and both this play and his *Moralité* were inserted as comic interludes into his massive *Mystère de saint Martin,* performed at Seurre over three days in 1496. In 1504 André was at the French court, where he was employed as a secretary to Anne of Brittany.

Other authors of morality plays include Michault Taillevent, or Michault Le Caron (circa 1390–circa 1458). Born in Saint-Omer, he worked from 1426 to 1448 at the court of Burgundy as valet to Duke Philip the Good and acted in farces presented at the court. In 1435 he wrote a morality play, *La Moralité du Povre Commun* (Morality of the Common Lot), and went on to write many other important works. Simon Bourgouin, valet at the court of Louis XII, wrote a thirty-thousand-line *Moralité de l'Homme Juste et de l'Homme Mondain* (Morality of the Just Man and of the Worldly Man). Performed at Tarascon in 1476, it combines the three popular themes of the *Procès de Paradis,* the allegorical combat of vices and virtues, and the Last Judgment. Nicole de la Chesnaye is the author of a late-fourteenth-century morality play, the 3,650-line *Condamnation de Banquet* (The Condemnation of Feasting), which illustrates the joys of the table and its abuses.

In contrast to the morality play, which is intended to instruct and educate, the sole purpose of the farce is to entertain. The majority of the approximately two hundred extant farces, most of which are anonymous, have survived in three sixteenth-century printed editions, which also include other types of plays: the *Recueil Trepperel* (five farces), the collection of the British Museum (forty-seven farces), and the *Recueil Cohen* (fifty-three farces). Only one significant manuscript containing farces survives, the sixteenth-century *Recueil La Vallière,* a copyist's manuscript.

Farces generally take easily recognizable types– the henpecked husband, the swaggering soldier, the sensual priest, the apothecary who attempts to hawk his wares, the dishonest lawyer–and put them into comic situations. The prevalence of courtroom scenes and judicial language can be attributed to the influence of the members of the Basoche, or guild of law clerks, renowned for their theatrical activities. Farce employs a broad range of techniques, including disguise, false confession, hiding (often in sacks, barrels, armoires, or tubs), and sudden reversals of action. Typical themes include the challenging of authority (either between master and servant or husband and wife), the satire of bodily functions (eating and drinking, elimination, and sexual activity), the mockery of physical infirmity, and the actions of the ever popular character of the trickster.

The *Farce du cuvier* (Farce of the Tub) presents the theme of marital discord by exploiting verbal and physical comedic techniques. The domineering wife makes her husband sign a paper listing the household chores for which he agrees to be responsible. When she falls into a tub, he justifies his refusal to come to her aid on the grounds that it was not included on his list. The sixteen-hundred-line *Farce de Maistre Pierre Pathelin,* written during the 1460s, is much longer and more complicated than the typical farce, presenting an unusually elaborate variation on the theme of the "trickster tricked in return," one of the most popular of the genre. From its combination of three types of comedy–gesture, situation, and language–emerge characters who go beyond type and who are the ancestors of the comic personages of Molière.

The problem of distinguishing among genres is particularly difficult when it comes to the farce and the sottie, which share many characteristics and whose titles often do not indicate their genre. Like the farce, the primary goal of the sottie, of which approximately sixty survive, is to amuse, with the difference that satire in the sottie may be more political in nature. The genre takes its name from the word *sot* (fool), a stock figure omnipresent in medieval life and culture easily recognizable by his costume. Many sotties were written and performed by semiprofessional *sociétés* or *compagnies joyeuses,* or societies of fools, such as the Parisian Enfants-sans-souci. The nameless fools were sometimes joined by the *Prince des Sots* (Prince of Fools) and the *Mère Sotte* (Mother of Fools), characters who often served an allegorical purpose.

Like the farce and the sottie, the remaining genres that can be considered comic–the *sermons joyeux* (mock sermons), monologues, and dialogues–have many elements in common and are sometimes difficult to distinguish. Limited to one or two characters, they are most often satirical in intent. The mostly anonymous *sermons joyeux,* of which approximately thirty have survived, are essentially sermon parodies. Often opening his sermon in macaronic Latin, the preacher addresses the public on wide-ranging topics such as politics, religion, vice and virtue, and the eternal favorites: the changeability of women and the unpleasantness of the married state. Other sermons trace the life, martyrdom, and miracles of a fictitious saint. The dramatic monologue elicits laughter by representing characters who, like the braggart soldier, also figure prominently in farce. Other types satirized in this form are the valet for hire who will go to any length to serve his master, the charlatan, and the ridiculous lover. The best-known monologue is the anonymous *Franc archer de Bagnolet,* in which one of the members of Charles VII's guard of franc-archers, a braggart, is shown to be a coward. There is some speculation as to whether the dialogue, a comic conversation between two people, originated in a fractured monologue, in which one performer acted out the part of two interlocutors. All three of these short comic forms can be incorporated into the more lengthy genres, such as the farce.

This overview of the drama of medieval France can but suggest the diversity and richness of a genre that was popular with all levels of society. The popularity of the mystery plays and various comic genres continued unabated throughout the sixteenth century; indeed, mystery plays continued to be performed in the provinces in some cases into the eighteenth century. But the heyday of the sacred mystery play indubitably had passed once it had been banished from the center of French cultural and theatrical life by a 1548 decree of the Parliament of Paris. Discord at that time between the proponents of Church reform and their orthodox opponents over the proper use of religious and sacred texts hastened the demise of the mystery play, and changing literary tastes contributed to the general disfavor into which the other dramatic genres fell. Yet, despite its passing from favor, one can see the distant descendants of the medieval religious theater in Corneille's *Polyeucte* (1641), while the early plays of Molière and the perennial popularity of *Pathelin,* performed at the Comédie-Française in an early eighteenth-century adaptation until the mid nineteenth century, attest to the longevity of the comic tradition of the medieval theater. The theater of medieval France, after having been the preserve of antiquarians, found several noted historians in the nineteenth century. The literary canon celebrated especially the twelfth- and thirteenth-century plays, while the theater of the later centuries has only recently shed the label of decadence that had first been attached to it by the literary theorists of the mid sixteenth century.

References:

Maurice Accarie, *Le théâtre sacré à la fin du moyen âge: Etude sur le sens de la 'Passion' de Jean Michel* (Geneva: Droz, 1979);

Heather Arden, *Fools' Plays: A Study of Satire in the Sottie* (Cambridge: Cambridge University Press, 1980);

Jean-Claude Aubailly, *Le monologue, le dialogue et la sottie* (Paris: H. Champion, 1984);

Aubailly, *Le théâtre médiéval profane et comique* (Paris: Larousse, 1975);

David A. Bjork, "On the Dissemination of the *Quem quaeritis* and the *Visitacio sepulchri* and the Chronology of Their Early Sources," *Comparative Drama*, 14 (1980): 46–69;

Jean-Pierre Bordier, *Le Jeu de la Passion: Le message chrétien et le théâtre français (XIIIe-XVIe s.)* (Paris: H. Champion, 1998);

Thomas P. Campbell and Clifford Davidson, eds., *The Fleury Playbook: Essays and Studies* (Kalamazoo: Medieval Institute, 1985);

Normand Cartier, *Le Bossu désenchanté: Etude sur le 'Jeu de la Feuillée'* (Geneva: Droz, 1971);

Gustave Cohen, *Le théâtre en France au Moyen Age*, 2 volumes (Paris: Rieder, 1928–1931);

Jean Dufournet, *Adam de la Halle à la recherche de lui-même* (Paris: Société d'Edition d'Enseignement Supérieur, 1974);

C. Clifford Flanigan, "The Liturgical Drama and Its Tradition: A Review of Scholarship 1965–1975," *Research Opportunities in Renaissance Drama*, 18 (1975): 81–102; 19 (1976): 109–136;

Flanigan, "Medieval Latin Music-Drama," in *The Theatre of Medieval Europe: New Research in Early Drama*, edited by Eckehard Simon (Cambridge: Cambridge University Press, 1991), pp. 21–41;

Grace Frank, *The Medieval French Drama*, second edition (Oxford: Clarendon Press, 1960);

Jean Frappier, *Le théâtre profane en France au Moyen Age* (Paris: Centre National pour la Recherche Scientifique, 1960);

O. B. Hardison, *Christian Rite and Christian Drama in the Middle Ages: Essays in the Origin and Early History of the Modern Drama* (Baltimore: Johns Hopkins University Press, 1965);

Alan E. Knight, *Aspects of Genre in Late Medieval French Drama* (Manchester: Manchester University Press, 1983);

Knight, "France," in *The Theatre of Medieval Europe: New Research in Early Drama*, edited by Eckehard Simon

(Cambridge: Cambridge University Press, 1991), pp. 151–168;

Jelle Koopmans, *Le théâtre des exclus au Moyen Age: Hérétiques, sorcières et marginaux* (Paris: Imago, 1997);

Halina Lewicka, *Etudes sur l'ancienne farce française* (Paris: Klincksieck, 1974);

Lewicka, *La langue et le style du théâtre comique français des XVe et XVIe siècles*, 2 volumes (Paris: Klincksieck, 1960–1968);

Charles Mazour, *Le théâtré français du Moyen Age* (Paris: Société d'Edition d'Enseignement Supérieur, 1998);

Donald Maddox, *Semiotics of Deceit: The Pathelin Era* (Lewisburg, Pa.: Bucknell University Press, 1984);

Lynette R. Muir, *The Biblical Drama of Medieval Europe* (Cambridge: Cambridge University Press, 1995);

Muir, *Liturgy and Drama in the Anglo-Norman Adam*, Medium Aevum Monographs, new series 3 (Oxford: Blackwell, 1973);

Muir, "The Saint Play in Medieval France," in *The Saint Play in Medieval Europe*, edited by Clifford Davidson, Early Drama, Art, Music no. 8 (Kalamazoo: Medieval Institute Publications, 1986), pp. 123–180;

Anne Joubert Amari Perry, ed., *La Passion des jongleurs* (Paris: Beauchesne, 1981);

Louis Petit de Julleville, *Histoire du théâtre en France: Les Mystères*, 2 volumes (Paris: Hachette, 1880);

Petit de Julleville, *Histoire du théâtre en France Répertoire du théâtre comique en France au Moyen Age* (Paris: Cerf, 1886);

Bernadette Rey-Flaud, *La farce ou la machine à rire: Théorie d'un genre dramatique, 1450–1550* (Geneva: Droz, 1984);

Henri Rey-Flaud, *Le cercle magique* (Paris: Gallimard, 1973);

Emile Roy, *Le Mystère de la Passion en France* (Paris: H. Champion, 1904);

Graham A. Runnalls, *Etudes sur les Mystéres* (Paris: H. Champion, 1998);

Runnalls, "Medieval French Drama: A Review of Recent Scholarship," *Research Opportunities in Renaissance Drama*, 21 (1978): 83–90; 22 (1979): 111–136.

Roman de la Rose

Guillaume de Lorris
(1200 to 1205 – circa 1230)

Jean de Meun
(1235 to 1240 – circa 1305)

Patricia E. Black
California State University at Chico

GUILLAUME DE LORRIS
WORK: *Le Roman de la Rose* (1225–1230)

Manuscripts: The earliest extant version of Guillaume de Lorris's text independent of any other author's continuation work is known as R1, and apparently survives in a single manuscript of the late thirteenth century (Paris, Bibliothèque Nationale de France, f. fr. 1573) where Guillaume's section of the *Rose* is copied by one scribal hand and followed by Jean de Meun's continuation in a different hand. The last line of Guillaume's text is followed by the rest of a folio (now numbered "34") that was left blank, while Jean's continuation starts on the next folio (now numbered "35"). There is also a single manuscript of Guillaume's work with an anonymous ending attached (the latter known as R2), independent of Jean de Meun's continuation (Paris, Bibliothèque Nationale de France, f. fr. 12786). This manuscript, from the late thirteenth or early fourteenth century, includes *Le Roman de la Poire* and the prose redaction of the *Bestiaire d'Amours* by Richard de Fournival as well as other poems and lays.

Editions: "Li Romanz de la Rose, première partie par Guillaume de Lorris," edited by Robert Püschel in *Friedrichs-Gymnasium Jahresbericht für das Schuljahr von Ostern 1871 bis Ostern 1872* (Berlin: Gustav Lange [Otto Lange], 1872); *Guillaume de Lorris, Li romanz de la Rose,* edited by Robert White Linker (Chapel Hill, N.C., 1937); *Le roman de la Rose par Guillaume de Lorris,* edited by Stephen G. Nichols Jr. (New York: Appleton-Century-Crofts, 1967).

Edition in modern French: *Le Roman de la Rose d'après Guillaume de Lorris,* translated by Juliette Goublet (Paris: J. Carvo, 1963).

JEAN DE MEUN
WORKS: *Le Roman de la Rose ou Li Miroër aus Amoreus* (1269–1278?)

Manuscripts: There are more than 300 manuscripts that include the dually authored *Roman de la Rose,* in the text known as R3. They date from the thirteenth to the sixteenth centuries and are held chiefly by the Bibliothèque Nationale de France in Paris (73 mss.), the Bibliothèque de l'Arsenal in Paris (8 mss.), the British Library in London (16 mss.), and the Bodleian Library at Oxford University (9 mss.). These manuscripts frequently contain glosses and miniatures. The manuscript tradition of Jean de Meun's continuation is very stable, however, especially in comparison with Guillaume de Lorris's *Rose.* Despite the relatively intact manuscript transmission of the joint text of the *Rose,* especially its second part, there are other versions, like the adaptation and revision by Gui de Mori in the thirteenth century. The base manuscript used by the first two important modern editors is Paris, Bibliothèque Nationale de France, f. fr. 1573.

First publication: In folio, without title, printer's name, place, or date [Lyon: Ortuin & Schenck, circa 1481].

First modern edition: *Le Roman de la Rose par Guillaume de Lorris et Jehan de Meung: nouvelle édition, revue et corrigée sur les meilleurs et plus anciens manuscrits,* in 4 volumes, edited by Dominique Martin Méon

Jean de Meun (illumination from a manuscript for Roman de la Rose, *Paris, Bibliothèque de l'Arsenal, ms. 5209)*

(Paris: P. N. F. Didot l'aîné, 1814).

Standard editions: *Le roman de la Rose par Guillaume de Lorris et Jean de Meun, publié d'après les manuscrits,* 5 volumes, edited by Ernest Langlois, Société des Anciens Textes Français (Paris: Firmin-Didot, 1914–1924; republished, New York: Johnson Reprints, 1965); *Le Roman de la Rose par Guillaume de Lorris and Jean de Meun,* 3 volumes, edited by Félix Lecoy, Classiques français du moyen âge nos. 92, 95, and 98 (Paris: H. Champion, 1965–1975).

Editions in modern French: *Le Roman de la Rose de Guillaume de Lorris and Jean de Meun,* translated by André Mary (Paris: Payot, 1928; revised edition, 1949; republished, Paris: Gallimard, 1969; republished, 1984); *Guillaume de Lorris et Jean de Meun, Le Roman de la Rose,* 2 volumes in 5, translated by André Lanly, Classiques français du moyen âge, traductions no. 12 (Paris: H. Champion, 1971–1976); *Guillaume de Lorris et Jean de Meun, Le Roman de la Rose,* translated and edited by Armand Strubel (Paris: Le Livre de Poche, 1992).

Editions in English: *The Romance of the Rose by Guillaume de Lorris and Jean de Meun,* translated by Harry W. Robbins, with an introduction by Charles W. Dunn (New York: Dutton, 1962); *The Romance of the Rose by Guillaume de Lorris and Jean de*
Meun, translated by Charles Dahlberg (Hanover, N. H. & London: University Presses of New England, 1986).

L'Art de chevalerie (1284)

Manuscripts: Paris, Bibliothèque Nationale de France, f. fr. 2063; Carpentras, Bibliothèque Inguimbertine, 332, both of the fourteenth century are the basis respectively of the two editions of the work. There are also six other manuscripts with the complete text. The translation is dedicated to John of Brienne, count of Eu.

Editions: In *L'Art de chevalerie: traduction du "De rei militari" de Végèce par Jean de Meun,* edited by Ulysse Robert, Société des Anciens Textes Français (Paris: Firmin Didot, 1897); in *Li abregemenz noble honme Vegesce Flave René des establissemenz apartenanz a chevalerie: traduction par Jean de Meun de Flavii Vegeti Renati viri illustris Epitoma institutorum rei militaris,* edited by Leena Lofstedt (Helsinki: Suomalainen Tiedeakatemia, 1977).

Li Livres de confort (circa 1300?)

Manuscripts: There are approximately seventeen manuscripts of this translation of Boethius's *De consolatione philosophiae,* among them Bibliothèque Nationale de France, f. fr. 1097, used by Dedeck-Héry for his edition. This translation is dedicated to King Phillip IV the Fair.

Standard editions: "Un fragment inédit de la traduction de la *Consolation* de Boèce par Jean de Meun" edited by Venceslas Dedeck-Héry in *Romanic Review,* 27 (1936): pp. 110-124; "Boethius' *De Consolatione* by Jean de Meun" by Dedeck-Héry, with an introduction by Alex J. Denomy, in *Mediaeval Studies,* 14 (1952): 165–275.

La vie et les epistres de maistre Pierre Abelart et Heloïs sa fame (date unknown)

Manuscript: Jean de Meun's translation of the letters of Peter Abelard and Héloïse survives in a single extant manuscript, Bibliothèque Nationale de France, f. fr. 920. There are Jean's versions of Abelard's *Historia Calamitatum Meum,* seven of the eight letters, and three other texts attributed to Jean, but probably not his, which concern the story of Abelard and Héloïse, such as the letter written to Héloïse and now identified as being by Peter the Venerable.

First publication: "Première lettre d'Abailard, traduction inédite de Jean de Meung," edited by François Génin in the *Bulletin du Comité historique des monuments écrits de l'histoire de France; histoire, sciences, lettres,* 2 (1850): 175–191, 265–292.

Standard editions: *Jean de Meun, traduction de la première épitre de Pierre Abélard (Historia Calamitatum),* edited by Charlotte Charrier (Paris: H. Champion, 1934); "Traduction française attribuée à Jean de Meun de la lettre de Pierre le Vénérable à Héloïse," edited by Michel Zink in *Pierre Abélard– Pierre le Vénérable: les courants* philosophiques, littéraires et artistiques en occident au milieu du XIIe siècle (Abbaye *de Cluny, 2 au 9 juillet 1992),* edited by René Louis and Jean Jolivet in Colloques internationales du Centre National de la Recherche Scientifique no. 546 (Paris: CNRS, 1975); *La vie et les epistres Pierres Abaelart et Heloys sa fame: traduction du XIIIe siècle attribuée à Jean de Meun,* 2 volumes edited by Eric Hicks, Nouvelle Bibliothèque du Moyen Age no. 16 (Geneva: Slatkine/ Paris: H. Champion, 1991).

The *Roman de la Rose* stands out as the pre-eminent work of the later Middle Ages and is the only major medieval work in French to have maintained an audience virtually from then until now. The prodigious number of manuscripts produced during a span of over two centuries, then the twenty printed editions of the work produced between 1481 and 1538 in France alone, as well as the adaptations and translations of the poem abroad, all attest to its great popularity. Conversely, though the literary history of the poem is well documented, the biography of the author of the first half of the work, Guillaume de Lorris, remains largely unknown. In one of his only personal statements at the beginning of the *Rose,* the narrator says that he was twenty-five when he started to write the *Rose* and scholars have generally treated this statement as representing Guillaume de Lorris's age when he started to compose the poem. Other aspects of the author's life have to be inferred from the narrative as well; the pitfall in this method lies in treating a conventional narrator as an historical person. By contrast, scholars have unearthed certain facts about Jean de Meun that have supplanted the apocryphal stories once told about his life.

Thoroughly permeated as the poem is with courtly literary and social values, most scholars have assumed that Guillaume de Lorris was either of noble background or a bourgeois writer who aspired to the nobility. The town of Lorris was a royal possession, and scholars have conjectured that the writer may have been one of several thirteenth-century Guillaumes known to have lived there and who had connections to the French royal court. Which, if any, of these Guillaumes was the writer of the *Roman de la Rose* will probably never be known. In fact, if it were not that Jean de Meun named Guillaume de Lorris as the writer of lines 1–4,028, the first part of the *Roman de la Rose* would be simply another anonymous medieval French text. Guillaume's references to classical texts show him to be an educated person, although probably not a clerk, in the opinion of Félix Lecoy, who saw him as a man of the world.

Most readers will be struck, not long into this narrative, by the fact that abstract qualities are personified. Such personification is a common characteristic of medieval allegory. As a genre, allegory intends figurative meanings although what those meanings are may not be clear. Although there may be realistic details in it, an allegory also unfolds with characters and settings that are clearly not realistic. It takes a higher reality and concretizes it while individual characters become generalized: in the *Roman de la Rose,* this higher reality is love and the generalized character is the young man who becomes the Lover. Scholars have extensively studied the allegorical significance of this work. C. S. Lewis first proposed reading R1, the common designation for Guillaume's part of the *Rose,* as an account of the psychology of falling in love. Another important minority view developed by D. W. Robertson, John R. Fleming, and others sees the *Rose* as a recounting of the Fall from Paradise. Other scholars, such as W. T. H. Jackson, have concentrated on the framing of the allegory, focusing on the literary context in which the personifications operate: in Guillaume de Lorris, a mixture of romance and lyric; in Jean de Meun, several different genres, including fabliau, epic, and satiric monologue. Hans Robert Jauss has written several studies detailing the

Page from a manuscript for Roman de la Rose *(Bibliothèque Nationale de France, f. fr. 1565, fol. 1)*

use made in the *Roman de la Rose* of the previous religious allegorical tradition, arguing that the *Roman de la Rose* introduced allegory into secular literature.

Lecoy's edition provides a convenient and standard approach for summarizing Guillaume's *Rose*. R1 opens with a prologue that serves to orient the audience to the narrative about to unfold. Such prologues are typical of the courtly narratives forming part of the tradition out of which the *Rose* develops. Characteristically, the prologue stresses the importance of the story which will be told, its truth, and the technical skills of its author or presenter. However, the prologue of R1 launches directly into a discussion of dreams and how to analyze them based on their capacity for truth or prophecy. Thus, as is the case throughout the first part of the *Rose,* the traditional format and themes of the courtly narrative are varied and recombined to create a fresh look for a long-standing literary genre; however, Guillaume retains the standard, octosyllabic rhyming couplet as his verse form, used by Chrétien de Troyes and other writers of romances as early as the twelfth century.

The reason behind the narrator's preoccupation with dreams soon becomes evident: at about the age of twenty, he had a dream which subsequently came true in his waking life. This event marked him profoundly, to the extent of impelling him to write down this dream that he had had five years earlier. As David Hult and Emanuèle Baumgartner have noted, this tactic creates a sense of atemporality or omnitemporality as the narrator is simultaneously situated in past, present, and future. In fulfillment of Love's commandments, the narrator creates his romance which he calls *Li Romanz de la Rose* (The Romance of the Rose) in which the whole art of love is enclosed. He undertakes the project in hopes of gaining the approval of a lady who is so worthy to be loved that she should be called Rose. In dedicating this poem to her, the narrator inserts into the complex of ideas and associations he is creating the image of the lady of courtly lyric, distant but the object of the poet's creations. Thus in an introduction of some didactic import, the type of discussions the audience might expect veers into an entirely different subject matter and literary genre at the end of the prologue: as Hult points out, when the narrator claims that "l'art d'Amors est tote enclose"(the art of Love is totally enclosed) in verse 38 of his poem, he is declaring that his romance of the rose "has replaced (or subsumed)" Ovid's *Ars amatoria* (Art of Love, 1 B.C.), which he is citing.

Many questions can be and have been raised about this prologue. First, scholars have investigated thoroughly the sources and implications of the dream theories cited by the narrator, namely Macrobius's commentary on Cicero's *Somnium Scipiosis* (Dream of Scipio).

For instance, beginning with Ernest Langlois, critics have realized that the prologue refers to its source incorrectly. Second, however one understands an "art of love," by the end of R1, most readers are uncertain as to whether the goal of creating one has been realized. Third, the romance tradition entails traditional characters, legendary material, and narration in the third person whereas the *Roman de la Rose* opens with a first-person narrator who recounts a personal experience.

After the prologue the narrator begins to recount how he dreamed that he awoke one May morning eager to be outdoors, thus obeying an impulse common to courtly narrative. The medieval reader would recognize in this conventional opening that his desire will lead him to love and adventure. As he wanders, he walks along a stream and hears birds singing, a setting which derives from lyric poetry. Typically found at the beginning of poems, these elements are known collectively as the *Natureingang* (nature introduction). The adventure or quest element is also signaled by the stream since quite often in courtly narratives the presence of bodies of water means that the hero is passing into a realm where marvelous events occur.

Suddenly the narrator finds himself in front of a wall painted with all manner of portraits. They bear names, and the narrator finds that their likeness illustrates their name. They all share one characteristic, being banished to the outside of the wall because, as the narrator learns, they are the antithesis of the values shared by those who dwell within the walls. These are the portraits of the courtly vices. The narrator describes some of these pictures in terms of stories which their names (such as *Covoitise,* or Envy) suggest and thus, Eric Hicks has argued, maintains a narrative focus where description might be expected. The opportunity which the text affords here for illustrations did not escape medieval scribes who frequently created miniatures depicting these vices; in fact, there are approximately one hundred illuminated manuscripts of the *Rose*.

The narrator, who is a young man of about twenty, decides to look for a way through the walls. Upon his knocking on the door, *Oiseuse* (Idleness) opens the gate and allows the young man to enter the garden of *Deduit* (Delight). Scholars have given careful attention to the meaning of *Oiseuse,* the etymology of which derives from the Latin *otium* and causes her to be associated primarily with the life of leisure. Some scholars also see her as a Venus figure, *Luxuria* (Lust). Furthermore, there are many interpretations of this garden, read variously as modeled on the walled gardens of Tafalla in Spain, as Justin Edouard Mathieu Cénac-Moncaut has argued, or, as many scholars have noted, as modeled on the Garden of Eden.

The young man is charmed to hear the songs of countless birds within the garden. He soon meets Delight and his friends who are listening to songs and dancing to the music. He is introduced to the *dex d'Amors* (God of Love) who has two sets of bows and arrows: gold ones named *Biautez* (Beauty), *Simpleice* (Simplicity), *Franchise* (Openness), *Compaignie* (Company), and *Bel Samblant* (Fair Seeming); and black ones named *Orguelz* (Pride), *Vilennie* (Villainy), *Honte* (Shame), *Deseperance* (Despair), and *Noviaus Pensers* (New Thought). When the dance is over, the couples leave to pursue their lovemaking elsewhere in the garden.

Meanwhile, the young man makes his way alone to a fountain below a pine tree, but the God of Love keeps him in sight. A sign proclaims this spot a *miroërs perilleus* (a dangerous mirror) and the *fontaine d'amors* (fountain of love), for it is the place where Narcissus died by falling in love with his reflection in the water. A third-person narration interrupts the first-person recollection of the dream in order to tell the Ovidean-inspired stories of Narcissus and Echo. Besides ending with a curious moral instructing ladies to be more welcoming of their lovers' advances, the Narcissus episode varies from Ovid's tale in other ways, including the fact that Echo, not a male admirer, utters the curse which will cause Narcissus's death. The narrative frame, the fact that it is the only classical myth fully recounted in R1, and its coincidence with the young man's falling in love make the Narcissus story important for understanding Guillaume's *Rose,* as Hult notes. Jean de Meun recognized as much when he included the story of Pygmalion in his continuation as a counterpoint to that of Narcissus. Moreover, every aspect of the Narcissus account in R1 has attracted commentary from modern scholars. Alan M. F. Gunn was one of the first to recognize the importance of the "Narcissus digression," as it has often been called; subsequently, Frederick Goldin wrote an entire study reinterpreting the *Rose* in light of the Narcissus myth. Daniel Poirion, Thomas D. Hill, and Roger Dragonetti have each written studies which elucidate how the two myths of Narcissus and Pygmalion relate to each other. The garden setting, reminiscent of Eden, led Erich Köhler to describe the fountain as the source of life and knowledge while Robertson and Fleming consider the Narcissus story a version of the biblical account of the Fall.

On approaching the fountain the young man sees two crystals at the bottom of the pool. Unwittingly, the young man has put himself in Love's power, for no one can look in this fountain without falling madly in love because Cupid has set his traps here. The crystals (or crystal, the manuscripts differ on this point) reflect a rose garden that the narrator feels impelled to visit. The enigmatic nature of the crystals in the fountain has engaged critics at least since Lewis first proposed that they represent the Lady's eyes. Among others, Paule Demats has argued that they represent the Lover's eyes. Robertson interpreted them as the eyes of the flesh; Köhler as the reflection of the Lover's eyes in the Lady's eyes. Hult has theorized that the two episodes, the Narcissus story and the young man's account of viewing the crystals, relate metaphorically and give accounts of individuals who gazed into the fountain's mirror and then through it to the bottom so that they saw both themselves and into themselves. For Hult this image suggests the fundamental nature of fiction, an imperfect reflection of the world which emanates from the subjective experience of the individual.

However, these proposals do not take into consideration the concreteness of the anecdote which relates the young man and Narcissus, thus explaining another aspect of the meaning of these crystals. First, both these characters are represented as young and immature in the *Rose.* If one considers related works, one notices that in Chrétien's romances a young knight who encounters a magic pool or fountain finds himself not only in the midst of an otherworldly experience, but this encounter also initiates his own process of maturation. As he matures, the young knight shows his lack of experience and judgment at crucial moments; the poor results he obtains serve as lessons to him. Similarly, in the *Rose,* the young man's first gaze into the reflecting pool of the fountain inaugurates a series of lessons that lead to his mental and social growth, although, like Chrétien's young knights, he initially reacts by scoffing at danger, here illustrated by Narcissus's story. He rejects the notion that ill luck could result just from looking. In an equally childish reaction, the young man notices in particular the biggest mass of roses in the nearby rose garden. Once he examines them more closely, he wants to pick one of the rosebuds, but then he has cause to regret his act for the God of Love begins attacking him with arrows. Just when he thinks he cannot endure any more pain, the arrow of Fair Seeming brings him balm. Just as Chrétien's young knights lack foresight and knowledge of themselves, so too does the young man in the *Rose:* he will spend many moments during the rest of his adventure lamenting his unforeseen suffering.

Now the young man is the God of Love's vassal; he has become the Lover. He must keep Love's commandments: avoid villainy and slander; respect women and defend them; avoid pride; care for his appearance and dress as elegantly as possible; be clean; be happy; use his natural gifts; and avoid avarice. The young man cannot imagine how he will manage, but the God of Love tells him that *Esperance* (Hope), *Douz Pensers* (Sweet Thought), *Douz Parlers* (Sweet Talk), and *Douz Regart*

(Sweet Looks) will help him. Then the God of Love vanishes.

The young man decides to visit his rosebud. *Bel Acueil* (Fair Welcome) greets him and holds back the hedge for him. But *Dangier* (whose meaning as a woman's refusal or resistance was first proposed by Langlois) is lurking among the bushes and has helpers with her: *Male Bouche* (Foul Mouth), *Honte* (Shame), and *Peor* (Fear). *Chasteez* (Chastity) asked Shame to come and *Jalousie* (Jealousy) invited Fear. When the young man asks Fair Welcome to give him the rosebud, *Dangier* blames Fair Welcome for being so gullible, and Fair Welcome runs away. The young man now despairs and does not know to whom to turn.

Now *Reson* (Reason) notices him and tries to persuade him to abandon his quest, to leave Love's company, and thus to avoid sorrow. However, the young man refuses. He seeks an *Ami* (Friend) in whom he can confide. There is such a person in the garden, and he advises the young man to make friends with *Dangier*. Having done so, the young man can again approach the rosebud. The bud has grown, but not fully opened. The young man asks Fair Welcome for a kiss, but he (masculine because *Bel Acueil*'s grammatical gender is masculine) refuses for fear of Chastity. Waving a burning torch, Venus appears and is able to change Fair Welcome's mind. The young man kisses the rose. Immediately, Foul Mouth spreads the news and Jealousy upbraids Fair Welcome. Both Fair Welcome and the young man flee. Jealousy decides to build a walled fortress around the roses with a tower in its midst in which to keep Fair Welcome imprisoned. A *Veille* (Old Woman) will be the keeper of Fair Welcome. The young man's despair is deep and his only consolation is the thought of Fortune and her wheel. He hopes that Fair Welcome will not suffer in captivity and will continue to think kindly of him.

Thus does Guillaume de Lorris's poem end enigmatically at verse 4,028. Does the poem have the final form its author intended or, as Jean de Meun's continuation claims, did death interrupt the work before its time? Even as early as the end of the thirteenth century, Gui de Mori, author of an adaptation first of Guillaume's *Rose,* then of Jean's continuation, hypothesized that Jean removed the original ending (what is now known as the anonymous ending, R2) and substituted his own, vastly longer ending. Manuscript Ter, now lost but partially transcribed by Langlois and Dominique Méon, a previous editor of the *Rose,* included these statements by Mori. Whatever the case may be, scholars remain divided on the subject, although insofar as there is a new emphasis on manuscript study, the concern that there is really a definitive first version is perhaps less troublesome than it was before. In scholarship on the *Rose* since the 1980s, critics like Sylvia Huot have studied its many individual manuscript versions as examples of how medieval audiences reacted to the texts they knew, whether that "audience" was also reworking a given text by writing it or whether an adapter, scribe, or continuator was reacting to the audience's expectations; for although Jean de Meun's continuation has a particularly stable manuscript transmission, there is nevertheless a host of variations in the continuation from one manuscript to the other.

Jean de Meun (also known as Jean Chopinel) could have been a compatriot of Guillaume de Lorris, since the towns of Meun and Lorris are both in the Orléanais, the region around the city of Orléans. Jean de Meun was a student at the University of Paris during a time of intellectual ferment, and some of these issues are reflected in his continuation of the *Rose*. He was almost certainly a master of arts and is referred to as a *maistre* (master) in certain manuscripts. His wide familiarity with classical authors is impressive and the *Rose* highlights other issues which must reflect his interests and concerns. The location of a house in Paris where he lived at least from 1292 is commemorated by a plaque at the end of the Rue Saint-Jacques.

Besides the approximately seventeen thousand lines of his continuation of the *Rose,* Jean de Meun translated several works from Latin to French: *L'Art de chevalerie* (The Art of Chivalry, 1284), a translation of the *Epitoma rei militari* (Epitome of Warfare, fourth century A.D.) of Vegetius; *La vie et les epistres de maistre Pierre Abelart et Héloïs sa fame* (The Life and Letters of Master Peter Abelard and Heloise His Wife); and *Li Livres de confort* (The Book of Comfort, circa 1300?), a translation of *De Consolatione philosophiae* (On the Consolation of Philosophy, circa A.D. 520) of Boethius. Jean de Meun mentions two other translations in a list of his works that he gives in *Li Livres de confort:* between the Vegetius and Abelard's letters he includes *Les Merveilles d'Irlande* (*De mirabilibus Hiberniae* or The Marvels of Ireland) of Giraud de Barri; between the letters and Boethius is a work he calls *Aelred de espirituelle amitié* (*De spirituali amicitia* or On Spiritual Friendship) of Aelred de Rievaux. These works are lost, but Lecoy notes that the library of Charles V held Jean's translation of Aelred's work. There are also some other works which have been attributed to Jean de Meun. They include works on alchemy, a *Testament,* and a *Codicile* that were edited by Méon. However, their attribution remains uncertain. In particular, various alchemical works were once attributed to Jean de Meun on the basis of discussions about alchemy between two of the characters of the *Rose,* but this evidence is no longer generally accepted as valid.

In the *Roman de la Rose,* Jean de Meun begins his portion of the narrative after the lines "Ja mes n'iert rien qui me confort / se je pert vostre bienveillance, / car je

Narcissus at the well (illumination from a manuscript for Roman de la Rose, *Cambridge, University Library, ms. Gg. IV 6, fol. 14)*

n'ai mes aillors fiance" (Never will there be a thing to comfort me / if I lose your goodwill / for I no longer have trust elsewhere), a statement directed by the Lover to Fair Welcome (lines 4,026–4,028 in Lecoy's edition). As Jean has it, the Lover laments his bad fortune a good deal more until Reason reappears to converse with him. In fact, though this continuation is much longer than R1, it essentially elaborates on and digresses from the major narrative elements already introduced in Guillaume's section.

Between lines 4,192 and 7,200 Reason and the Lover spar over his choices. Reason would like to convince the Lover that he would be better off not following Love's commandments. Love is a sickness and leads to the desire for carnal union, a pleasure which is contrary to Nature's plan. Love is for procreation and the continuation of the species. To do otherwise is to be addicted to pleasure and to ruin one's life. She wants the Lover to distinguish between *fole amor* (foolish love) and *bone amor* (good love). Naturally, the Lover is not

happy to be admonished in this way and asks sarcastically if she could explain the good ways of loving so that he might learn.

In reply she defines friendship, fortune, and wealth. True friendship is unselfish and unchanged by Fortune. In adversity one finds one's true friends. Too great a reliance on wealth makes us slaves. Only what we possess within us is reliable, for Fortune can take away her gifts. When the Lover remarks that he does not think that he can attain this love, that of friendship, Reason replies that he should try to love all persons, to treat them according to the Golden Rule. Growing out of charity, this love would replace justice, which is often too harsh. To prove her point, she recites Jupiter's castration of Saturn whose testicles, cast into the sea, created Venus; at the same time Justice's reign was usurped. Now there are also corrupt judges, and as an example Reason tells a famous story of justice miscarried, that of Appius and Virginia from Livy.

Now follows a famous passage concerning the word Reason used for testicles, that is *couilles,* an inexcusable term, according to the Lover. She puts off explaining why she used this word because she wants to finish her exposition of the varieties of love. The last is that of the love of parents for their children. If the Lover is inclined to love, he should take her, Reason, as his beloved. However, he must not follow the God of Love, nor believe in Fortune whose characteristics and actions Reason explains in detail. As examples of the whims of Fortune, Reason recites the stories of Nero, his atrocities, and his death (according to Suetonius); Croesus whose ignoble end was predicted by his daughter Phanie on the basis of a dream; and Charles of Anjou's conquest of Sicily against three rivals who met grim fates in 1268, one of the references that allows Jean de Meun's work on the *Rose* to be dated. With Reason, the Lover would discover that he is truly fortunate, in other words, impervious to Fortune.

The Lover immediately rejects this proposal; he would certainly not give up his Rose for her. What is more, Reason is discourteous for using the word *couilles;* she should use a euphemism. Reason explains that using correct language is not a sin and, anyway, God has left the question of names to her. She argues for the notion that in school one learns to read beyond literal meanings. In the tale of Saturn, she did not intend these words with the meaning that the Lover wanted to assign to them. True understanding of words would lead to seeing their real meaning. Moreover, allegorical interpretation would allow the Lover to understand that poets incorporate many of the secrets of philosophy in seemingly frivolous works, a medieval version of the seventeenth century maxim of *plaire et instruire.* The Lover should pay attention to these lessons if he wishes to find meaning in texts; however, she ends her argument by saying that when she used the words the second time they were to be taken literally, properly, without the glossing the Lover provided.

In fact, Reason only intended to mention testicles briefly, but the Lover made a big issue out of her use of the word. Reason's arguments about school-learned interpretation and the truths hidden in poetry make it almost impossible to interpret this section of the poem about *couillons* without falling into repeated double meanings. For instance, two aspects of this "proper" term for testicles have to be mentioned: its etymology shows that it too is a euphemism since its Latin root means "sheath" or "small bag"; in addition, *couillon* is also a slang term for "knucklehead." Critics have explained some of the further considerable wordplay involved in this passage and those where the lover criticizes Reason.

Aside from the wordplay, Reason elaborates a manner of reading the *Rose* in particular: that is, many secrets will be imparted by this ostensibly entertainment-oriented narrative, defined as such by its rhyming octosyllables and subject matter, but it will also be necessary to know when to take words at face value. This apparent paradox resolves itself if one considers the role of another character, *Faus Semblant* (False Seeming), introduced later in the story. False Seeming appears as a mendicant friar though he has no vocation to support his wearing of the cloth. Despite the fact that Fleming's view of the *Rose* as a moralistic work does not have many adherents, he cites a boast False Seeming makes about adopting only the trappings of religion for personal gain, leaving the grain and taking the chaff, of staying to the letter and not the spirit. Fleming relates this image to the Lover's dispute with Reason over her use of the word *couilles.* She tried to show that her use of the word did not mean what he thought; properly used words designate both reality and a higher reality; however, the Lover is not interested in interpreting the allegories of poets until he has the Rose and can then gloss what suits him, as shown in the final scenes of the narrative. In other words, the Lover's personal gain, not reason, motivates him to use words improperly. He also hews to the letter and not the spirit of words; like False Seeming, he does not eschew euphemism that gains him some advantage.

First, the Lover raises this possibility in his discussion with Reason; then Friend openly suggests hypocrisy in his conversation with the Lover. Finally, the personification of hypocrisy, False Seeming, creates the opportunity for the Lover to possess the Rose. Both the Lover and False Seeming gloss over activities which would invite censure otherwise. Both abuse the faith placed in them: False Seeming commits crimes under the cloak of religion and the Lover seduces Fair Welcome into allowing him to pick the Rose. Further underlining the similarities between the two characters, Fleming cites illustrations in some manuscripts which even show False Seeming doing homage to the God of Love, like the Lover. Ironically, False Seeming's attack on the fortress consists of excising Fair Welcome's critical verbal defense, Bad Mouth. Having perjured himself, False Seeming leaves the scene. Meanwhile, the Lover seduces his way to the Rose in the disguise of a religious pilgrim so that, in essence, at the end of the narrative, the Lover has taken the place of False Seeming. Tellingly among his final words at the end of the narrative, the Lover insults Reason and again puts her out of his mind.

Though the Lover rejects Reason, this personification has intrigued critics because her character is drawn from identifiable sources. One of these is Boethius, but another is Alain de Lille. Scholars are divided to some extent on the basis of whether they see primarily Alain's *De planctu Natura* (On the Plaint of Nature, circa 1160–1165) or the writings of Augustine of Hippo as Jean's source for the allegorical figure of Reason. They are thus also divided over whether Reason has limits in a postlapsarian world or whether she represents wisdom of divine origin.

With Reason's departure, the Lover begins to think of how Friend had counseled and consoled him before. Friend arrives immediately and begins, in his turn, a long speech telling the Lover how to go about obtaining his Rose: act with more reserve, try to make friends with the guardians, give them presents, ask them for favors, be discreet, watch out for rivals, choose the right time, and, if possible, pluck the Rose even if Fear, Shame, and *Dangier* make a show of resistance. In fact, some people want to be obliged to do what they dare not do on their own initiative. However, if this resistance is real, do not insist. Finally, always follow the lead of Fair Welcome. In the end the Lover follows this advice to be hypocritical. There is also another way to obtain what the Lover wants, but those who do not have the financial means cannot use it: the path of *Trop Doner* (Give-Too-Much). This way is treacherous but could lead to complete surrender of the castle in which Fair Welcome is imprisoned. Friend has already tried this way and ruined himself. Poverty is one's lot afterward and it is not a pretty sight, even though there are false beggars who keep their wealth hidden. Therefore, he advises, one should give only small gifts, fruits and flowers.

This seemingly gratuitous comment about false beggars is the first in a series of references to mendicant friars that Jean de Meun carefully sows in the text. These references come to be embodied in False Seeming, the character who uses the disguise of religion to attain whatever end he desires and who is willing and able to help the Lover. There is also Nature's priest, Genius, who Heather Arden has suggested represents the popular preacher (often a mendicant friar) of the thirteenth century, a demagogue who "has covered [ideas] with religious trappings in order to distort, to violate, them." Genius's contribution to the campaign to possess the Rose entails a promise of a heavenly abode to those who honor Nature by procreating. By implication, the Lover will have this recompense for his impregnation of the Rose. Thus, Jean de Meun draws a series of analogies that link mendicant friars to courtly lovers as mercenary, deceitful, and dishonorable perverters of those conventions designed, in the case of the friars, to reach out to the mass of the faithful, and in the case of courtly lovers, to elevate women's status.

Friend's advice continues with comments on married life, the successful outcome of pressing one's suit. He says that, generally, what women want from a man is not good looks or a fine mind but money. In the Golden Age, when property did not exist, love was free from this constraint. Now, men too have in mind their property rights when they deal with their wives. Here Friend draws a picture of the *Jaloux* (Jealous Husband) for the Lover and recites the sort of reproaches the Jealous Husband makes to his wife. She cares only for his money and at night complains of headaches when he wants to hold her close. He is sure that she does not treat certain young men that way. The Jealous Husband can do nothing to drive them away, for they are too strong. His wife and they ridicule him, yet such young men want only his wife's riches themselves. Then the Jealous Husband beats his wife and disturbs the neighborhood. Friend says that love cannot exist in such a household. Even if the wife seems to forgive her husband, he can never be sure that she is not planning revenge. No man can be master of his wife. The spouses must be equal. Often, in his wooing, the lover vows complete service to his lady. Once married, he wishes to dominate and the woman resists. In the Golden Age, people lived together in complete freedom and contentment, and riches were shared. However, one day *Tromperie* (Fraud), *Péché* (Sin), *Malheur* (Misfortune), and all the other vices appeared. People abandoned their former lives and embraced ownership and property, necessitating a ruler to keep the peace.

Friend ends this digression and returns to the rules the Lover should follow: improve himself intellectually; never accuse his beloved of wanting to leave him; give her her freedom; never mention her faults or beat her. These rules of conduct and mores are those which should govern the lover of limited means. If, on the other hand, the Lover wishes to dally with another woman, he is told to simply make sure that the relationship is kept a secret. If a virtuous woman comes the way of the Lover, Friend tells him to take advantage of the opportunity.

The Lover knows that he cannot go near the tower where Fair Welcome is imprisoned and finds himself walking toward a fountain. Wealth takes her ease there and guards the path of Give-Too-Much. She refuses to let the Lover enter it. When the Lover insists, she tells him that she already realizes that he despises her, and he is a fool anyway. He should have listened to Reason. The Lover then remembers the idea of trying to make friends with his enemies, especially Foul Mouth. The Lover reflects on the long penitence he will have; at his point in the poem, however, the God of Love decides to put an end to the Lover's trials, and he reappears to the Lover to ask the young man if he kept the faith with Love. The Lover admits that he was shaken by Reason's arguments, but when he can still recite all ten commandments, the God of Love promises to help free Fair Welcome.

The God of Love explains the difficulty of breaching the fortress and helping Guillaume de Lorris, the Lover. Thus, Jean de Meun identifies at the midpoint of the romance who wrote the first part of the *Rose,* which lines were his last, and why he stopped. He also claims that the *Rose* lacks an ending. Then, the God of Love introduces Jean as the poet who recommenced the narrative forty years after it was stopped and who wants it called the *Miroër aus Amoureus* (Mirror for Lovers). Therefore, only when Jean de Meun wrote his continuation did Guillaume de Lorris's name and the information that he came from the province of Orléans become attached to R1. The fact that the few surviving pieces of information about this writer are found mostly in the continuation and are provided in the context of conventional themes and characterizations led Hult and Dragonetti to hypothesize that Guillaume de Lorris is the literary creation of Jean de Meun. Jean takes over from Guillaume and therefore learns how to overcome Jealousy and her obstacles in his role as the Lover.

Love's vassals arrive to provide counsel on the way to attack the fortress where Fair Welcome is imprisoned. They advise the God of Love to send for Venus. They know that Wealth will not help the moneyless Lover. However, the God of Love realizes that Venus's help is not forthcoming. In fact, the only other strategy the council can imagine involves using the help of *Abstinence contrainte* (Constrained Abstinence) and False Seeming, who accompanied her as her guest. False Seeming is not sure that he is welcome, but Love reassures him that he can stay with them if he promises to help and to let them know how to recognize him despite his disguises.

This strange character's favorite camouflage is that of the religious man because the cloister and the habit provide the best hiding places. Indeed, False Seeming personifies Jean de Meun's criticism of mendicant friars. Although this character praises those who have a sincere vocation, he finds the habit very convenient for what the false religious do, preach humility and poverty while enriching themselves. Though he could be taken for a holy hermit, he is a hypocrite. As for mendicants, it is certain that Jesus and the Apostles never begged, and the masters of divinity in Paris used to agree on that point. Moreover, there are monastic orders, like the White Monks (Cistercians), the Black Monks (Benedictines), the canons regular, the Hospitalers, and the Templars who have possessions and thus allow their members to spend all their time in prayer. Earlier, Guillaume de Saint-Amour established limits to the practice of begging, limits accepted by the University of Paris; this Guillaume had even written a book against mendicant friars and said that they should work. False Seeming will never work because he prefers to use the appearance of religion to cover his ruses.

False Seeming does not fear God and he lives the easy life. Those who would unmask him—and the Gospel shows how he can be revealed—he ruins with calumny. He and his kind are the troops of the Antichrist. A book, *L'Evangile éternel* (The Eternal Gospel) has even appeared to usurp the place of the Gospels; however, the University of Paris has succeeded in nipping its influence in the bud. In any case, False Seeming's father, *Barat* (Fraud), is the emperor of the world; his mother, *Hypocrisie* (Hypocrisy), is the empress. Those who know the true nature of this family are afraid to combat them. Why should one esteem nobles and knights whose words match their deeds and who refuse hypocrisy? Beguines like Constrained Abstinence should govern (it should be noted that in the medieval period, Beguines had a reputation for taking friars as lovers). Such avowals make the God of Love hesitate to enlist False Seeming into his ranks; however, the supposed friar has not dared lie to the God of Love and promises fidelity. Constrained Abstinence, his lady, and he will deal with the Lover's problem. This assurance is given in line 11,979 and ends False Seeming's explanations.

Scholars have studied not only the subjects raised in this speech—often termed a confession—from the mendicant friar controversy mentioned by False Seeming to the importance of this hypocrite to Molière's characterization of his sanctimonious scoundrel Tartuffe, but also its narrative techniques. In keeping with his character, False Seeming adopts a multiplicity of voices in his monologue and provides many examples of the poetic use of language mentioned earlier by Reason. Though his linguistic brilliance supposedly reveals his nature, his public (Love's council) remains uncertain whether to believe him. The central dilemma posed by Reason presents itself anew: must one gloss or take False Seeming at his word? Thus, the narrator positions this character as the central personification, both literally and figuratively, of the *Rose* and the embodiment of the divorce between language and reality, according to Susan Stakel.

As part of the God of Love's forces, False Seeming and Constrained Abstinence play their part in the assault on the fortress which begins after line 12,003. They wear the disguise of pilgrims and ask Foul Mouth for hospitality and the chance to give him a sermon. Their pious dress fools Fair Welcome's jailer. In their sermon they admonish him for sinning in keeping to his post, and he is shaken enough to let down his guard. As he kneels to False Seeming in order to confess, the

Page from a manuscript for Roman de la Rose *(British Library, ms. Stowe 947, fol. 1r)*

latter strangles Foul Mouth and cuts out his tongue. Courtesy and Generosity now join in and the four of them seize the *Vieille* (Old Woman), the guardian of Fair Welcome. She is willing to be bought and to bring the Lover into Fair Welcome's presence. She approaches Fair Welcome with the chaplet of flowers offered by the Lover and offers reassurance that all will be well. In fact, she can offer advice out of long experience.

Unfortunately, she herself learned too late in life everything that would have helped her. There are indeed Love's ten commandments, but Fair Welcome should not be generous and faithful to just one. He (masculine because of the grammatical gender of *Bel Acueil*) should always think of his advantage because men cheat on women. Women are born free and despite the institution of marriage, they try to recover their lost freedom because Nature impels them. Nature is stronger than training. The law wants a single part-

ner, and Nature wants many. Once Vulcan found them out, Venus was more brazen with Mars than before. This lesson is for jealous men. If a woman's lover tries to make her jealous, she should just say that she will do the same. However, no woman should give expensive gifts to her lover. The gifts he gives her should be put away as an insurance policy against old age, though the Old Woman learned this lesson too late and, to boot, loved a man who beat her and ruined her. She was left with no money and no husband; thus, she came to Fair Welcome's tower. She concludes between lines 14,510 to 14,516 that she hopes her life's story will be a lesson to him.

Fair Welcome thanks the Old Woman and tells her that he really is not interested in love, needs no rich gifts, but since he has taken the Lover's offering he is willing to have a meeting as long as Jealousy does not know. This is no sooner said than done: the Old

Woman goes to the Lover, who promises her a fine recompense that he has no intention of giving, following Friend's advice; she tells him to go to a hidden door where she will let him inside the walls. The God of Love and his men are already inside. Fair Welcome and the Lover exchange courtesies, and it seems the moment to pluck the Rose. Suddenly, *Dangier* bars the Lover's way; Fear, Shame and *Dangier* heap scorn on the Lover for saying one thing and doing another. The three guardians seize Fair Welcome, beat him, and lock him under triple locks. The Lover would like to do penance in the same prison as Fair Welcome. Naturally, the guardians reject that request. The Lover thinks it unjust to imprison Fair Welcome, but the three only reply by preparing to throw him out of the rose garden. The Lover calls for the God of Love, and both sides prepare for battle in the epic manner.

The battle rages between lines 15,273 and 15,860 and begins with individual duels between the fortress guardians and Love's men, before the fight becomes general. The tide turns against the God of Love and he asks for a truce during which he sends for Venus, his mother. She decides to come immediately and swears to destroy Jealousy's fortress. She also swears to destroy Chastity in the hearts of all women and asks Love to do the same for men.

Meanwhile Nature is at her forge. She is busy forging the individuals destined to continue the species even though Death follows close behind. Death can take individuals but cannot overcome the species. This law controls the sublunary world. Nature works without ceasing, she laments. Hearing the oath sworn by Venus and the God of Love, she feels somewhat comforted, but the thought of an error arising in her work torments her, and she has her chaplain, Genius, come to give her confession. He agrees and remarks that women are quick to think only of their troubles. Besides that characteristic, women have other vices. They cannot keep a secret either. Nevertheless, men should not avoid women and should respect them, but as is indicated in Scripture, with examples like that of the story of Samson and Delilah, men should not let women have authority over them. However, Genius says that he does not direct these remarks to Nature, who is wise and loyal.

When Nature finally confesses to the priest Genius as she intended to do, her monologue fills 2,700 lines. She explains how she came to govern the world and how the world follows her laws, with the exception of one creature, the human being. So the planets move in their spheres and create a harmony which is the basis of our music. These planets control the combination and balance of the four elements, cold, hot, dry, and humid. This balance is delicate, and yet some people die even before the disequilibrium of elements kills them. These premature deaths prevent Nature from fulfilling her plan. People say that these deaths are fate. Perhaps a combination of the planets did lead them to act in certain, deleterious ways, but science, education, good examples, remedies, and judgment should counterbalance such a disposition of the stars. The planets do not control reason.

It is difficult to say how predestination and free will coexist. God knows everything that will happen; thus arises the problem of free will. God is just and good and therefore recompenses or punishes everyone according to the individual's merits. Thus, free will exists. Another argument for predestination and necessity is that anyone who believes that fate cannot be altered would maintain that there is no use in taking advice, working, or learning, but this belief is absurd. Nevertheless, there are many other objections to the doctrine of free will.

Nature would not bring up all these matters except that she wishes to argue against mankind, her enemy, who would say that he could not help himself with respect to these sins, that fate wanted them. This reasoning is false, for God does not lead man to sin. Humankind is responsible for its own problems. Only animals are not. Man has reason and has to use his free will; if he does not, then he is responsible for his own vice.

Her real subject, however, is the celestial bodies and how they fulfill their task, whether for ill, in the case of storms, or good, as in good weather. The sign of the return of calm is the rainbow, an explanation of whose colors requires a good teacher. The books of Aristotle on nature and the treatise on optics by Alhazen are required reading for the understanding of rainbows. In this treatise, one will find the explanation of the properties of mirrors, those which enlarge the image and those which bring far objects near. With one of these mirrors, Mars and Venus would have seen the net Vulcan spread for them. Nature describes many types of mirrors. Optical illusions are also well documented, whether because of illness, distance, or poor eyesight. She then digresses to talk about visions, waking ones and sleeping ones, and the illusions they cause. Dreams also offer the most varied images, but what truth do dreams hold?

Contrary to common belief, comets affect rich and poor alike. What is more, kings are no richer than the people; happiness is wealth and poverty results from covetousness. Actually, all are equal at birth. Fortune creates differences; yet, true nobility comes from the heart, the mind, and virtue. In fact, noble birth imposes duties. Though riches in goods can be bequeathed, riches of education cannot. Really, the only natural, noble qualities in man are natural freedom, which is the gift of Nature, and reason, which is God's gift. These two qualities make man the equal of God and angels, except for the fact of death, and man must use them to shape his own merit.

Nor does Nature complain of the elements, the plants, the birds, the fish, nor other animals. All of them follow her laws and reproduce in order to procreate. Only man refuses and yet he has received every gift from her. However, she did not give him the faculty of understanding because everything she creates perishes. God gave understanding to man who then deceived him so that God had to undergo death.

Thus, man refuses to respect the rules and Nature is obliged to complain about him to God. Hell will be man's payment. God will take care of man's sins, but one fault concerns the God of Love: how man refuses the tribute due Nature for the tools she gave him. Nature tells Genius to go to the God of Love, Venus, and their troops and give them her greetings, except to False Seeming and Constrained Abstinence, who are only there if they can be useful to the cause of lovers. She tells Genius to excommunicate all the enemies of Love. As for Nature's friends, as long as they love well and multiply, she grants them a full pardon for their sins if they confess.

Both Nature and Genius have long literary and mythological histories behind them, but Jean transforms both of them. In the *Rose,* Nature argues for the integration of the spiritual and the natural worlds, but she also emphasizes procreation without necessarily putting it in the context of marriage. Since she clearly indicates her subordination to God, probably the view of sexuality she expresses remains within the range of what medieval Christian theology could accept. Clothed as a bishop by the God of Love, Genius will enthusiastically promulgate Nature's message to procreate, yet also describe a beautiful park, with many Christian motifs, which awaits those who hear Nature's message.

Genius draws up the pardon and proclamation that he will read and goes to Love's camp. False Seeming has already left and Constrained Abstinence is on her way out. Everyone is glad to see Genius. The God of Love gives him a chasuble, ring, crosier, and miter; Venus puts a candle, not made of virgin wax, in his hand. Genius proclaims that all those who despise the means by which the continuing of the world is assured will be excommunicated and paradise will be opened to those who loyally practice love. Ill fortune shall come to those who have the tools, but do not use them. God does not want some to be continent and others not as he loves all equally. Those who do not use their tools or who use them incorrectly, in an infertile earth, turn the plow around, plow crookedly, or use their tablets and styluses upside down and take them backward, they shall be deprived of their instruments. The others need to work harder, and they must think of perpetuating their lineages against Atropos, the Fury who cuts the threads of life. Genius urges his audience to avoid the sins that are listed in the *Roman de la Rose,* to memorize his sermon, and to recite it often because Nature needs preachers.

By following his lessons, Genius assures his public that they will enter the wonderful park where the son of the virgin ewe leads his flock of little sheep. The good shepherd of the place does not sell the products of the animals. All is enjoyment here, in an eternal present, an eternal spring, with a sun which never sets. The weather is better than in the Golden Age under Saturn. This Saturn is the same that his son, Jupiter, castrated. Jupiter took power and invited people to get enjoyment out of life. He himself showed them the example of his own pleasures. According to Virgil's *Georgics* and *Bucolics,* Jupiter put an end to the happiness of the Golden Age and ushered in the successive ages of silver, bronze, and iron. Men became worse and worse, to the great joy of the gods of dark places, who keep sorrowful, black sheep tied up in dim rooms.

Genius wants to compare this park to the garden of Delight, to show how the first is better than the second. Ugly images ring Delight's garden; the park is surrounded by all the good and bad of the earth. Delight's people dance beautifully, but death awaits them. In the park, there is complete happiness because its inhabitants drink from the fountain of life, not Narcissus's fountain. The fountain of the park is fed by three canals closely placed almost as if they were one, and they water not a pine tree but an olive tree whose branches shelter the sheep and give the fruit of life. In the fountain shines a carbuncle with three facets. The brilliance of this gem creates a beautiful light in the park, brighter than that of the sun. This light insures an eternal day and illuminates the hearts of those who look in the fountain and makes them stronger. In short, in one place one finds death; in the other, life. To go to the latter place, people must honor Nature, not keep the possessions of others, not murder, not soil hands or mouth, and remain loyal and generous.

Finally, Genius throws his firebrand in the air in line 20,640 and disappears. Love's forces decide to attack the tower. Venus offers the defenders of the fortress a last chance before she sends an arrow into a small opening in front between two pillars, where Nature had placed it. These two pillars hold up a sculpted image that contains a reliquary, an image that is more beautiful than the statue of Pygmalion, transformed for him into a woman of flesh and blood. This story is extensively developed before the narrative presents Venus actually firing her flaming arrow into the opening, whereupon the fortress catches fire and all flee. Courtesy advises Fair Welcome to give the Lover the Rose.

Then, in a lengthy passage fraught with sexual metaphors, the Lover envisions himself as a pilgrim at the end of his journey. He particularly likes his pilgrim's stick. On his journey he prefers narrow paths although rich trade routes are more profitable. It is true that a rich, old woman can help in succeeding in life, as Juvenal and Ovid say, but the Lover prefers youth, although in love all experiences count. The Lover wishes to touch the relics inside the two pillars with his equipment. After some difficulty, he manages to get his stick at least halfway inside. The passage is narrow, and he believes that he is the first to go down it. At last, the Lover approaches the rosebush, and Fair Welcome begs him to do no violence. The Lover promises to do only Fair Welcome's will and his own. He seizes the rosebush and shakes the rosebud. In gathering it he sheds some seed, then mixes the seeds together as he looks down inside it. He has made the whole rosebud grow and he should not have done so. Fair Welcome scolds him for his pressing on, but allows him to take, caress, and pluck the bush, the stem, the flower, and the leaf, and so the Lover arrives at the end of his tribulations, thanks to Love, Venus, and the army. He forgets Reason. Despite his enemies, especially Jealousy, he plucks the beautiful red Rose. Then day breaks and he wakes up.

It would not be much of an exaggeration to say that virtually all medieval European literature after the *Roman de la Rose* was influenced by it. Its influence continued through the sixteenth century, although its popularity waned, with the last edition before the eighteenth century coming in 1538 in Clément Marot's modernization. Among the many French authors who either knew of the *Roman de la Rose* or may have been influenced by it are Guillaume de Machaut, François Villon, Clément Marot, Rabelais, and Pierre Ronsard. Foreign authors who may have been influenced by the *Rose* include the anonymous poet of *Piers Plowman*, Geoffrey Chaucer, John Gower, John Lydgate, John Milton, William Shakespeare, and Dante. There also exists a branch of study of reminiscences of the *Rose* in the eighteenth century French *Philosophes* (philosophers).

One of the important manifestations of the power of the *Rose* to engage writers is the *Querelle de la Rose* (Quarrel of the Rose) around 1400, an early instance of a literary debate. Admirers of the poem, Jean de Montreuil, Gontier Col, and Pierre Col, wrote texts in which they argued their views against those of Christine de Pizan and Jean Gerson. The former cite

the moral lessons to be learned from it and praise Jean de Meun as a philosopher and Christian thinker. Pierre Col also excuses the offensiveness of some of the pages of the work because of the difference between a literary character and the author, the former not necessarily voicing the opinions of the latter. Christine and Gerson attack the immorality of the work and the harm it can do to unsophisticated readers who cannot distinguish the author's intent in its figurative language. Christine further attacks the *Rose* for its obscenities, its misogyny, and its negative view of marriage. She gathered some of the letters with a preface and sent them to the queen. Thus, this exchange had public resonance and engaged even broader public interest.

Many modern critics view the two parts of the *Rose* as radically different from one another. This perspective echoes another aspect of the resounding *Querelle de la Rose,* namely that the two parts of the *Rose* have different characteristics. In particular, C. S. Lewis held a negative opinion of Jean de Meun's continuation which he saw as disorderly and digressive, but this viewpoint began to change with the publication of Gunn's landmark study, *The Mirror of Love: A Reinterpretation of "The Romance of the Rose"* (1951), in which he was the first to assert the unity, coherence, and poetic vision of the *Rose.* Gunn also replaced the *Rose* in its previous tradition of reception by its readership. Subsequent critics follow one or the other stances to some degree.

Jean seems to have anticipated this kind of debate over his work. Between lines 15,105 and 15,272, the narrator directly addresses several groups, loyal lovers first. Because the narrator promises to these lovers to explain the dream and gloss the written text, he reconnects with the discussion between Reason and the Lover over dirty words. Therefore, it is not surprising to learn that the three aspects of the narrative which require excusing are its ribald talk about love, its criticism of women, and the portrayal of False Seeming. These three issues are also broached in different contexts while Reason and the Lover talk. The narrator's first defense is the authority of a Roman historian, Sallust, who wrote that words and deeds must match in order to describe the truth. If one takes the narrator at his word, then one is obliged to admit that courtly love is a sham covering the reality of a brutal seduction. The second defense brought to bear on his description of women's behavior is similar, that is derived from the writing of the ancients. However, the narrator is more subtle on how these parts of the text should be viewed. One needs to ask if the ancients might have been mistaken; one also needs to understand that the narrator is proceeding like a poet and adding lessons as well as pleasure to what he takes from his sources. In light of Reason's explanations of how poets write, it would be reasonable to assume that the narrator's criticism of women requires interpretation. Third, the way the narrator defends himself on the subject of the hypocrite is to borrow an image from warfare, that of the archer unleashing volleys of arrows at the beginning of a battle. If some people feel the sting from that arrow, it is not because the narrator had any living person in mind. He is speaking only in general.

Importantly, this apology for the apparent import of certain aspects of the work is actually the key to understanding it. While one may wait for the dream to be explained retrospectively, one finds that there is no after-the-fact explanation. Unlike R1, however, R3 provides metaphoric as well as explicit examples of interpreting itself. This difference lies in the dissimilarity of the two narrators: the narrator in R3 is ironic and distinct from the Lover who is also a first person narrator; the narrator in R1 is the first person character of the Lover. Self-interpretation in R3 is also signaled by its much vaster development. The laconic character of R1 does indeed lend itself to hesitation over its import; much like a lyric poem, it requires a type of hermeneutical reading which calls upon knowledge of a prior tradition. The verbosity in R3 lends room for interpretations from a myriad of critical orientations; yet, it contains signposts which point out how the text could best be understood, that is, as a critique of the literature of courtly love and its singular esthetic as represented by R1.

Whether one considers the text of R3 morally repugnant or instructive, disorderly or coherent, as Arden has noted, "The profoundest influence that Jean de Meun exercised on subsequent French literature, and European literature generally, was to offer a new understanding of the potential of vernacular literature to treat a wide range of topics." Before Jean de Meun, as witness the beginning of the *Rose,* such wide-ranging, serious discussions had never found their way into a romance, just as novels later were not taken as a serious art form until Gustave Flaubert.

One of the more specific contributions of the *Rose* is its use of the first-person narrator, and thereby the conflation of lyric and narrative forms. Machaut adopts this narrative stance in his works and gradually expands its identification with the courtly lover to include that of the clerkly writer, that is, a persona like Machaut himself. Taking the long view, the injection of the personality of the writer into his works provided much of the impetus for Romantic literature; although in the medieval period, autobiography as literature remained a very dim shadow on the horizon. It would be impossible to detail all the ways in which the *Roman de la Rose* affected and altered the course of European literature. Though inevitably other literary forms superceded that of allegory and the *Rose* declined in favor, it represents the apogee of medieval literature.

Bibliography:
Heather M. Arden, *The Roman de la Rose: An Annotated Bibliography* (New York & London: Garland, 1993).

References:
Heather M. Arden, *The Romance of the Rose* (Boston: Twayne, 1987);

Pierre-Yves Badel, "Raison 'fille de Dieu' et le rationalisme de Jean de Meun" in *Mélanges de langue et de littérature du Moyen Age et de la Renaissance offerts à Jean Frappier par ses collègues, ses élèves et ses amis,* 2 volumes, Publications Romanes et Françaises no. 153, (Geneva: Droz, 1970), I: 41–52;

Emmanuèle Baumgartner, "The Play of Temporalities; or, The Reported Dream of Guillaume de Lorris" in *Rethinking the Romance of the Rose: Text, Image, Reception,* edited by Kevin Brownlee and Sylvia Huot (Philadelphia: University of Pennsylvania Press, 1992), pp. 22–38;

Justin Edouard Mathieu Cénac-Moncaut, "Les jardins du *Roman de la rose* comparés avec ceux des Romains et ceux du Moyen Age," *L'investigateur,* 8 (1868): 225–242;

Charles Dahlberg, *The Literature of Unlikeness* (Hanover, N. H. & London: University Presses of New England, 1988);

Paule Demats, "D'Amoenitas à Deduit: André le Chapelain et Guillaume de Lorris" in *Mélanges de langue et de littérature du Moyen Age et de la Renaissance offerts à Jean Frappier par ses collègues, ses élèves et ses amis,* 2 volumes, Publications romanes et françaises no. 153 (Geneva: Droz, 1970), I: 217–233;

Roger Dragonetti, *Le mirage des sources: l'art du faux dans le roman médiéval* (Paris: Editions du Seuil, 1987);

John V. Fleming, *Reason and the Lover* (Princeton: Princeton University Press, 1984);

Fleming, *The "Roman de la Rose": A Study in Allegory and Iconography* (Princeton: Princeton University Press, 1969);

Frederick Goldin, *The Mirror of Narcissus in the Courtly Love Lyric* (Ithaca: Cornell University Press, 1967);

Alan M. F. Gunn, *The Mirror of Love: A Reinterpretation of "The Romance of the Rose"* (Lubbock: Texas Tech Press, 1951);

Eric Hicks, "La mise en roman des formes allégoriques: hypostase et récit chez Guillaume de Lorris" in *Etudes sur le "Roman de la rose" de Guillaume de Lorris,* edited by Jean Dufournet, Collection Unichamp no. 4 (Paris: H. Champion, 1984);

Thomas D. Hill, "Narcissus, Pygmalion, and the Castration of Saturn: Two Mythographical Themes in the *Roman de la Rose*," *Studies in Philology*, 71 (1974): 404–426;

Larry H. Hillman, "Another Look into the Mirror Perilous: The Role of the Crystals in the *Roman de la Rose*," *Romania*, 101 (1980): 225–238;

Sylvia Huot, *The Romance of the Rose and Its Medieval Readers: Interpretation, Reception, Manuscript Transmission*, Cambridge Studies in Medieval Literature no. 16 (Cambridge: Cambridge University Press, 1993);

W. T. H. Jackson, "Allegory and Allegorization," *Research Studies*, 32 (1964): 161–175;

Hans Robert Jauss, *Genèse de la poésie française au moyen-âge (de 1180–1240)* (Heidelberg: Carl Winter, 1962);

Erich Köhler, "Narcisse, la fontaine d'amour et Guillaume de Lorris" in *L'humanisme médiéval dans les littératures romanes du XIIe au XIVe siècle, Colloque organisé par le Centre de Philologie et de Littératures Romanes de l'Université de Strasbourg du 29 janvier au 2 février 1962,* edited by Anthime Fourrier, Actes et Colloques no. 3 (Paris: Klincksieck, 1964), pp. 147–166;

C. S. Lewis, *The Allegory of Love: A Study in Medieval Tradition* (Oxford: Oxford University Press, 1978);

Dominique Martin Méon, ed., *Le Roman de la Rose par Guillaume de Lorris et Jehan de Meung: nouvelle édition, revue et corrigée sur les meilleurs et plus anciens manuscrits,* 4 volumes (Paris: P. N. F. Didot l'aîné, 1814);

D. W. Robertson, *A Preface to Chaucer: Studies in Medieval Perspectives* (Princeton, N. J.: Princeton University Press, 1962);

Susan L. Stakel, *False Roses: Structures of Duality and Deceit in Jean de Meun's "Roman de la Rose,"* Stanford French and Italian Studies no. 69 (Saratoga, N. Y. & Stanford, Cal.: Anma Libri and Department of French and Italian, Stanford University, 1991);

Winthrop Wetherbee, "The Literal and the Allegorical: Jean de Meun and the *De planctu Naturae*," *Medieval Studies*, 33 (1971): 264–291.

Saints' Lives

Michael Meckler
Ohio State University

WORKS AND WRITERS: *Sequence on Saint Eulalia* (circa 881–882)

Editions: *Les plus anciens monuments de la langue française,* sixth edition, edited by Edouard Koschwitz (Leipzig: O. R. Reisland, 1902), pp. 4–7; *A Medieval French Reader,* edited by C. W. Aspland (Oxford: Clarendon Press, 1979), pp. 4–6; *Mille et cent ans de poésie française,* edited by Bernard Delvaille, translated into modern French by Charles Oulmont (Paris: Robert Laffont, 1991), pp. 2–3.

Miracula sancti Genulfi (circa 1030)

Edition: In *Catalogus codicum hagiographicorum latinorum,* volume 3 (Brussels: Société des Bollandistes, 1893), pp. 186–191.

Odilo, abbot of Cluny, *Vita sancti Maioli* (1031 or 1033)

Edition: In *Patrologia Latina,* volume 142 (Paris: J.-P. Migne, 1853), coll. 943–962; also in *Acta Sanctorum,* second edition, May, volume 2 (Paris: Victor Palmé, 1866), pp. 683–688.

Vie de Saint Alexis (the Hildesheim manuscript version, manuscript copied circa 1120, text dated to circa 1040)

Editions: *La vie de saint Alexis,* edited by Gaston Paris and Léopold Pannier, (Paris: A. Franck, 1872); *La vie de saint Alexis: texte du manuscrit de Hildesheim,* edited by Christopher Storey (Geneva: Droz; Paris: Minard, 1968); *The Life of St. Alexius,* edited and translated into English by Carl J. Oldenkirchen (Brookline, Mass.: Classical Folia Editions / Leyden E. J. Brill, 1978);

Marbod, bishop of Rennes (fl. 1060–1123)

Edition: Collected works in *Patrologia Latina,* volume 171 (Paris: J.-P. Migne, 1854), coll. 1465–1782, especially coll. 1625–1630 (*Passio sancti Mauritii et sociorum eius*); coll. 1629–1634 (*Vita sanctae Thaidis*); coll. 1633–1636 (*Passio sanctorum Felicis et Adaucti*); and coll. 1635–1648 (*Vita beati Maurilii*). The *Vita sancti Victoris,* coll. 1615–1626, is now attributed to Hugh of Langres.

Hildebert of Lavardin, bishop of Le Mans, later archbishop of Tours (fl. 1080–1133)

Edition: Collected works in *Patrologia Latina,* volume 171 (Paris: J.-P. Migne, 1854), coll. 135–1458, especially coll. 1321–1340 (*Vita beatae Mariae Aegyptiaca*). The *Versus de sancto Vincentio,* coll. 1301–1308, and the *Passio sanctae Agnetis,* coll. 1307–1314, are no longer considered to have been written by Hildebert.

Adam of St. Victor (fl. 1140–1192)

Editions: In *Lateinische Sequenzen des Mittelalters,* edited by Joseph Kehrein (Mainz: Florian Kupferberg, 1873), pp. 481–482 (no. 714, on St. Stephen) and pp. 554–555 (no. 812, on St. Catherine); *The Liturgical Poetry of Adam of St. Victor,* 3 volumes, edited and translated into English by Digby S. Wrangham, in (London: Kegan Paul, Trench, 1881), especially volume 1, pp. 176–183 (no. 29, on St. Stephen) and volume 3, pp. 76–83 (no. 88, on St. Catherine); Sequences in *Analecta Hymnica,* volumes 54 and 55, edited by Clemens Blume (Leipzig: O. R. Reisland, 1915–1922), especially volume 55, pp. 236–238 (no. 209, on St. Catherine of Alexandria, attribution questioned) and pp. 341–343 (no. 310, on St. Stephen).

William, abbot of St. Thierry; Ernauld, abbot of Bonneval; and Geoffrey of Auxerre, abbot of Clairvaux, *Vita prima sancti Bernardi* (circa 1147–1156, revised 1163–1165)

Edition: In *Patrologia Latina,* volume 185 (Paris: J.-P. Migne, 1855), coll. 225–368.

Edition in English: Selections in *Saint Bernard of Clairvaux,* translated by Geoffrey Webb and Adrian Walker (London: A. R. Mowbray, 1960).

Gautier de Coincy, *Miracles de Nostre Dame* (circa 1218–1231)

Edition: *Miracles de Nostre Dame,* 4 volumes, edited by V. Frederic Koenig (Geneva: Droz, 1955–1970).

Edition in English: Selections in *Of the Tumbler of Our Lady and Other Miracles,* translated by Alice Kemp-Welch (London: Chatto & Windus, 1909).

Jean de Mailly, *Abbreviatio in gestis et miraculis sanctorum* (circa 1225–1230; revised, 1243)

Edition in modern French: *Abrégé des gestes et miracles des saints,* translated by Antoine Dondaine (Paris: Éditions du Cerf, 1947).

Jacobus de Voragine, *Legenda aurea* (circa 1261–1266)

Edition: *Legenda aurea, vulgo Historica lombardica dicta,* third edition, edited by Theodor Graesse (Bratislava: Koebner, 1890); *Legenda aurea,* edited by Giovanni Pãolo Maggiori (Florence: SISMEL/G);

Editions in English: *The Golden Legend or Lives of the Saints as Englished by William Caxton,* 7 volumes (London: Dent, 1931); *The Golden Legend,* 2 volumes, translated by William Granger Ryan (Princeton, N. J.: Princeton University Press, 1993).

Vida de la benaurada sancta Doucelina (circa 1297, revised circa 1315)

Edition: *La vie de sainte Douceline,* edited and translated into modern French by Raoul Gout (Paris: Bloud et Gay, 1927).

Jean de Joinville, *Vie de saint Louis* (1309)

Editions: *Joinville, Histoire de saint Louis,* edited by Natalis de Wailly (Paris: Hachette, 1881); *Vie de saint Louis,* edited by Noel L. Corbett (Sherbrooke, Québec: Naaman, 1977); *Vie de Saint Louis,* edited and translated into modern French by Jacques Monfrin (Paris: Dunod, 1995).

Editions in English: In *Chronicles of the Crusades,* translated by Margaret R. B. Shaw (Harmondsworth, U.K.: Penguin, 1963), pp. 163–353; *Life of Saint Louis,* translated by René Hague (London: Sheed & Ward, 1955); *History of Saint Louis, by Jean, sire de Joinville, seneschal of Champagne,* translated by Joan Evans (Oxford: Oxford University Press, 1938).

Jean de Vignay, *Légende dorée* (circa 1334, translation into French of Jacobus de Voragine's *Legenda aurea*)

Edition: Selections in *Les plus belles fleurs de la légende dorée de Jacques de Voragine* (Paris: La Sirène, 1920).

Vita beati Petri de Luxemburgo (circa 1387)

Edition: In *Acta Sanctorum,* second edition, July, volume 1 (Paris: Victor Palmé, 1867), pp. 448–454.

Saints' lives were a popular form of literature in France during the Middle Ages. The writing of saints' lives, or hagiography (from the Greek *hagios,* "holy," and *graphe,* "writing"), appeared not only in the learned language of Latin, but also in the vernacular languages of Old French and Occitan. The authors of these hagiographic texts were predominantly officials of the Catholic Church, whether in the secular clergy (such as bishops and priests) or in monastic orders (such as abbots and monks). Most of their writings are in Latin. In the later Middle Ages, however, writers from outside the church also became prominent producers of hagiographic literature in the vernacular languages.

It is difficult to make further generalizations about these authors. Many are unknown because the texts they wrote were handed down anonymously, and many others are known only by the names attached to the titles of their work. Some authors are extremely well known, but their fame may have less to do with the hagiographic texts they wrote than from other writings or other activities in their lives.

The relative lack of notoriety for hagiographic authors is due to the traditional nature of this literary genre. Saints' lives were expected to conform to patterns of presentation that were centuries old. In many instances, the stories themselves were centuries old, and the episodes were already well known to a medieval audience. Since so many features of a hagiographic text were fixed in advance, the author's role in transmitting a saint's life was often not perceived as being particularly prominent. The saint, not the author, was supposed to be the center of attention.

Although it is often difficult to say much about who the authors of saints' lives were, the reasons why these authors wrote of saints' lives are much more apparent. Men and women with reputations for sanctity were felt to be particularly close to God. This closeness was made manifest through miracles that occurred both during these individuals' lives and after their deaths. Miracle workers then became objects of attention and devotion because their closeness to God allowed them to act as intercessors for the requests of the pious. That devotion included ensuring that the lives of these holy men and women be remembered, and one way to do so was through the writing of saints' lives.

While the devotional nature of hagiography is paramount, these texts also served a didactic purpose. A saint's behavior provided an example to others on how to conduct their own lives. Hagiography, then, was also seen as a practical guide to ethics, a working out in one individual's life of the moral teachings of the Bible.

In trying to understand how medieval authors wrote of saints' lives, it is important to examine first the traditions that molded and constrained these authors' works. Many of the conventions of medieval hagiography in France may be found in some of the earliest saints' lives from late antiquity, such as the well-known *Vita Sancti Martin* (Life of Saint Martin), written in Latin at the end of the fourth century by Sulpicius Severus. Sulpicius was an aristocrat from Gaul, that part of the Roman Empire which was to become modern France. Most of the events described in this biography take place in Gaul, and the text was written while Martin was still alive. The narrative is arranged in a rough chronological order, from Martin's birth in Pannonia (modern Hungary) and early service in the Roman army, to his association with Hilary, bishop of Poitiers, and finally to Martin's own years as bishop of Tours.

Influenced by stories in the Gospels on the humility of Jesus, early Christian authors developed an aesthetic in which actions that were humbling or humiliating were understood as praiseworthy and were exalted. Sulpicius uses this type of role reversal in his descriptions of Martin. For example, when Martin was a soldier he had a slave to assist him, a situation that was not uncommon at the time. Instead of the slave serving the master, however, Sulpicius describes Martin as the servant—since he prepares his slave's meals and cleans his slave's boots. The most famous example of Martin gaining praise through humiliation involves another event from his days in the Roman army. The soldiers were passing through Amiens during the winter and along the way was a poor man freezing in the cold. Martin cut his cloak in half and gave half to the pauper. Although the saint looked ridiculous in half a cloak, he won favor from God because of this act of charity.

Sulpicius also describes Martin as a miracle worker. Individuals who suddenly die are quickly restored to life; violent attacks by angry pagans against the saint are thwarted; madmen possessed by the devil are cured. These stories often contain elements of folklore, but they are also colored by miracle accounts in the Bible. For example, when Martin is in Paris, he sees a leper. The saint blesses the man and cures him in a manner reminiscent of Jesus' curing a man of leprosy in the Gospels.

Sulpicius wrote his *Life of Saint Martin* in prose, yet hagiography was also from its earliest days capable of adapting to various literary forms. In the early fifth century, the Spanish poet Prudentius used the lives of martyrs as the inspiration for a series of Latin hymns known as the *Peristephanon*. The fourteen poems in the collection are written in a variety of classically inspired quantitative meters, the patterns of the lines being determined by the lengths of the vowels and not, as in English poetry, by the accented syllables of the words. Classical poetry like Virgil's *Aeneid* and Horace's *Odes* also provided much of the vocabulary and turns of phrase, with the result that Prudentius was creating poetry reminiscent of the epic and lyric of pagan antiquity but with Christian themes.

As the centuries passed and the culture of medieval France was taking shape, the stories of the saints came to combine the elements of history, folklore, epic and romance in attempts to motivate an audience to religious devotion and moral behavior. Hagiography became a rich source for a variety of forms of Latin lit-

erature, both in poetry and in prose, and saints' lives also inspired much of the developing literature in the vernacular languages of Old French and Occitan.

Saints of the early church, such as Martin, continued to be venerated in the France of the High Middle Ages, but the texts commemorating them did not remain static documents. As these texts were recopied in medieval monasteries and cathedrals, sometimes they were revised or rewritten. These revisions served to address contemporary concerns in a more immediate fashion, usually including recent miracles brought about by prayers to the saint or through acquisition of the saint's relics. An example from the eleventh century is the text described as the *Miracula sancti Genulfi* (Miracles of St. Genou) in the manuscript Paris, Bibliothèque Nationale de France, f. lat. 13320. Genou was a saint from the days of the Roman Empire, and the text, which appears to have been written in Cahors around the year 1030, may have been composed as an addition to the tenth-century *Life of Saint Genou* with which it was later bound. This version of the *Miracula sancti Genulfi* is especially interesting because it seems not to have been a finished work but rather a work in progress. The saint's name is often spelled only with the initial "G." On one page several lines remain blank, where the author has left incomplete a list of cities and their evangelists. This text provides a glimpse into how saints' lives were revised.

The anonymous author begins by claiming that out of reverence for Genou, he will describe the miracles that have taken place from the saint's death to the author's own day. The author hopes that through this act he might deserve to be received with Genou in the college of saints.

The two miracles that follow reveal the predominantly rustic character of medieval France. Some boys are swimming in a river to gain relief from the summer heat when one of them is caught by the current and saved from drowning only by a promise to the saint. A poor man is ashamed to have nothing to offer before Genou's tomb at the festival held to commemorate the translation of the saint's relics; he prays to the saint, and two turtle doves land at his feet, the birds being so tame that they let the pauper place them as an offering on the altar.

The rest of the text, does not discuss miracles but rather contains several extended parallels between the evangelization efforts in the Berry region of France by Genou and his saintly father, Genitus, and stories about biblical preaching, such as that of the prophet Jeremiah. What form the author eventually intended the *Miracula sancti Genulfi* to take is difficult to say, but it is worth noting that the revision of Genou's life included not only discussions of contemporary forms of veneration and

uiri dextera in pedef confiftit. atq;

ita cum eo ufq; adueftibulum domuf.

turba omnia infpectante proceffit.

S V BEODEM FERE

tempore MARTINVS adepifco

patum turonicae aecclf petebat;

St. Martin reviving a slave, from a manuscript for Vita Sancti Martin *(Tours, Bibliothèque Municipale, MS. 1018, fol. 18r)*

recent miracles, but also a reexamination of the saint's own actions with connections to biblical passages that may have resonated with the concerns of the author's own era.

Saints in the Middle Ages were not seen as having existed just in the remote past. Contemporary holy men and women could also be considered worthy of veneration and worthy of a saintly biography. One such biography is Odilo's *Vita sancti Maioli* (Life of St. Mayeul), written in 1031 or 1033. Mayeul, who died in 994, was abbot of the famous monastery at Cluny, and Odilo was Mayeul's successor as abbot.

The purpose of this biography is directly liturgical. A service would be held to remember a saint on the anniversary of the holy individual's death, because, through death, the saint is believed to have moved closer to God and, consequently, to have become more effective in assisting those who send the saint their prayers. Odilo states in the preface that there was no

suitable reading available for the annual service commemorating Mayeul. It was as a result of this need that Odilo became inspired to write a biography.

Odilo begins the work proper with a long digression on the importance of monks and of Cluny. He mentions that monks take the fourth place in the Christian hierarchy of human achievement, after the apostles, martyrs, and doctors of the church. The origins of monasticism are traced to the prophet Elijah and to John the Baptist, continuing to St. Benedict, through whose disciple St. Maur monasticism was brought to France. Odilo then gives a brief history of Cluny, founded early in the tenth century to reform the monastic movement, and lists Mayeul's three predecessors as abbot.

Mayeul is described as coming from a noble family and having been a serious child. The motif of the youth who behaves with remarkable maturity, called by the Latin term a *puer senex,* a "young boy/old man," is extremely common in saints' lives, and the motif is another example of the sort of role reversal characteristic of the genre. Odilo, however, takes this role reversal one step further by writing that because Mayeul remained chaste during his adolescence, the saint retained his boyish looks throughout the rest of his life.

Odilo then discusses Mayeul's education in Lyon, his ordination and appointment as archdeacon in Mâcon, and his abandonment of the secular clergy to join Cluny, which is located but a few miles from Mâcon. After six years in the monastery Mayeul was chosen as abbot.

When Odilo mentions the saint's miracles, the author describes a few minor healings and concedes that Mayeul never resuscitated the dead. It might seem that Mayeul failed to fulfill the expectation that saints must perform powerful miracles to demonstrate their great holiness, but Odilo handles the situation skillfully. If, as Odilo writes, the soul is greater than the body, then Mayeul's conversions of so many souls to leading more religious and ethical lives gave those individuals eternal life, and thus giving people eternal life should be reckoned a greater miracle than giving them merely bodily existence.

The saint's association with dukes, emperors, and kings is related, and it is while on a journey to meet with the French king Hugh Capet that the aged Mayeul dies. Finally, Odilo discusses Mayeul's capture by a band of Muslim marauders from Spain and how the saint had to be ransomed by Cluny's monasteries. Shortly thereafter, the Muslims were finally expelled from the French Mediterranean. Two comparisons are then made. The first derives from biblical and ancient history, comparing Mayeul's capture and the subsequent expulsion of the Muslims to Jesus' crucifixion and the forced exile of Jews after the destruction of the Second Temple in Jerusalem. The second comparison is more intriguing, for Odilo allegorizes the killing of a vicious wolf by Mayeul's father with the destruction of the Muslim raiders who would, many years later, kidnap this man's son. Both comparisons demonstrate Odilo's understanding of recent history as the fulfillment of events from the more remote past.

In addition to the standard characteristics of hagiography, such as role reversals, miracle stories, and biblical allusions, Odilo's *Vita sancti Maioli* (1031 or 1033) indicates another important aspect in lives written about contemporary saints: the growth of religious organizations such as monastic orders. By glorifying Mayeul, Odilo was also glorifying Cluny and the Cluniac family of monasteries. Other religious movements would be started and developed in succeeding centuries, and followers of those newer movements wanted to ensure the fame and glory of their leaders through

the writing of saints' lives. Often these hagiographic texts have a corporate nature, with multiple authors, official sponsorship, and promotion by a particular religious movement. Such was the case for the *Vita prima sancti Bernardi* (First Life of St. Bernard, circa 1147–1156).

Bernard, abbot of the monastery of Clairvaux and one of the leaders of the Cistercian order, was a controversial figure. The *Vita prima sancti Bernardi*, a composite work in five books by three different authors, was an attempt to gain acceptance of Bernard as a saint and to overcome the reluctance of many in the church who had been offended by Bernard's strident actions. The first book was written during Bernard's lifetime by his friend and ally William of St. Thierry to promote Bernard as a holy figure. After William's death in 1148 and Bernard's death five years later, continuation of the task was shared between Ernauld of Bonneval (who wrote book 2) and Bernard's assistant Geoffrey of Auxerre (who wrote the final three books).

Geoffrey, like Bernard, was a Cistercian who would himself soon become abbot of Clairvaux, and while both William and Ernauld had been abbots of Benedictine (that is to say, traditional) monasteries, William had retired to a Cistercian house. Books were circulated in advance to prominent church officials, and the entire work was presented to Pope Adrian IV in 1155 or 1156 in a request to have Bernard's saintly status confirmed. Adrian failed to act on the request, which was resubmitted to his successor Alexander III in 1163. Alexander wanted to delay the matter, and Geoffrey used the delay to revise the text further. The request was again submitted to Alexander in 1173, and the Pope officially approved Bernard's sainthood the following year.

By the time of Bernard's death, it was becoming common for one of the goals of a saint's life to be the gaining of the Pope's approval for the saint. Starting late in the tenth century, bishops began to make requests of the Pope for confirmation of sainthood, and they would send a biography of the prospective saint as evidence. In subsequent centuries, the papacy became more and more involved in determining whether or not recently deceased men and women with reputations for holiness really deserved veneration as saints. Procedures for canonization—the acceptance of new saints—developed alongside other reforms of the Catholic Church in the High Middle Ages, including the greater use of legal and philosophical reasoning in formulating doctrine, as well as the growing influence and authority of the popes. In the early thirteenth century it became officially part of church law that veneration of a deceased individual as a saint required authorization from the

Pope. This authorization came only after an official investigation, called a *processus*. The records from many of these investigations have survived to the present day and represent their own documentary subgenre of hagiographic texts.

The changes in how saints were made also affected how their lives were written. In the later Middle Ages, not only did saintly biographies need to inspire and edify the faithful, but these texts also had to address the concerns and requirements of the Holy See, which during much of the fourteenth century was based in the south of France at Avignon. Certain characteristics of sainthood, characteristics that may well have reflected papal interests, came to the fore in these later lives: noble birth, especially connections to royalty; intellectual activity; extraordinary, even excessive religious observance; and self-control when facing death. Although these biographies were affected by the growing mysticism and spirituality of the period, popular ideals of holiness had to be balanced with official views of sainthood when these lives were written.

An example of this balance may be found in the *Vita beati Petri de Luxemburgo* (Life of St. Peter of Luxembourg, circa 1387). Peter, who was not yet eighteen years old when he died in 1387, was never officially canonized, perhaps in large part due to the schism between rival popes in Avignon and in Rome during the end of the fourteenth and the beginning of the fifteenth centuries. But shortly after his death, a biography for the unsuccessful canonization procedure was prepared by an anonymous writer and addressed to the Avignonese pope Clement VII.

Peter's background fulfilled official understandings of sainthood in this period. His father was a count with lands in the territories of Artois and Bar, and his mother was a countess related to the Holy Roman Emperor Charles IV. Peter was well educated, having studied in Paris, and he was given important positions in the Church at an extremely young age, becoming bishop of Metz when only fourteen years old and not long thereafter a cardinal in Avignon. The author of Peter's biography treats this background in a conventional way. Peter is described as being noble in birth and even more noble in character, as well as beautiful in appearance yet even more beautiful in faith, characterizations that represent another example of the *puer senex* theme.

Peter was also a child of the second half of the fourteenth century, when the devastations of the plague and the Hundred Years' War with England led many of the French to seek more mystical and ecstatic religious experiences. In Peter, this desire was manifest through severe asceticism and mortification. The young cardinal regularly starved himself and practiced self-flagellation.

The Antipope Clement VII found this behavior so disturbing that Peter was ordered to mollify his routine, an order complied with out of obedience rather than desire. By this point, Peter's health had already begun to fail, and after his death, the fascinated residents of Avignon began to report miracles at his tomb.

It is interesting to see how the author handles these popular notions of holiness. Any following Peter had among the Avignonese is reduced to a one-paragraph discussion of his extensive gifts of charity to the poor. Miracles are not specified in this text but left to a subsequent document, as is any popular devotion to Peter. His attempts at mortification, however, are described in detail, even to the point of mentioning that they resulted in nearly constant stomach pain and an inability to stand on his feet. His asceticism is connected to the theme of *contemptus mundi,* or despise of this world because of a desire for the next. In this way, Peter's life of self-torture is painted as a wondrous example of self-control because the young cardinal was never tempted by the pleasures of earthly existence to avoid moving on to the heavenly realm. That the common people of Avignon who would venerate Peter hardly appear in this biography should not be surprising. First of all, Peter probably had little personal contact with them during his year in their midst. More importantly, however, the audience for this text was Clement VII and his court, and the purpose was primarily to gain official sanction for an already existing popular devotion.

The nature of the intended audience must be kept in mind when trying to understand saints' lives. Since knowledge of Latin required an education that was available only in monasteries or through the school operated by the local cathedral, Latin hagiography by its very nature had a restricted audience made up almost entirely of individuals who were in some official capacity part of the Church. This also meant that the audience was predominantly male, and the hierarchical structure of the Church created an audience predisposed to the biases of the aristocratic milieu from which the Church took its leaders.

When a saint's life came to be copied into a manuscript, it was generally not the only hagiographic text there. Usually a manuscript included lives of several saints. These collections, called legendaries (collections made up only of martyrs' lives are called passionals), were often organized according to the calendar in marking each saint's commemoration day, though collections might also have a particular geographic or thematic focus.

Collections could be revised by the editor and transformed into an original work. In the thirteenth and fourteenth centuries, members of the Order of Preachers, the Dominicans, began making such collections to provide parish priests with stories to encourage the faithful. One of the earliest was the *Abbreviatio in gestis et miraculis sanctorum* (Summary on the Deeds and Miracles of the Saints) by Jean de Mailly, first written around the years 1225 to 1230 and revised in 1243. But Jean de Mailly's work would be overshadowed even in his native France by a later collection prepared by the northern Italian Dominican Jacobus de Voragine. Jacobus composed what became known as the *Legenda aurea* (Golden Readings) between 1261 and 1266. The *Legenda aurea* were widely copied and translated during the next two centuries and became influential throughout European literature.

In addition to prose, the poetry of the period was also suffused with hagiography. Some of this poetry, especially that coming from the cathedral schools, was influenced by classical Latin models. The cathedral schools began to overtake monasteries as the primary centers of French intellectual life at the close of the eleventh century, and often the cathedrals were home to bishops involved in extensive literary activities. The most renowned of these author-bishops were Hildebert of Lavardin, bishop of Le Mans and later, archbishop of Tours; and Marbod, bishop of Rennes. Included in the writings of Hildebert and Marbod were saints' lives both in prose and in poetry. The poems were meant to be read in the way that classical poetry was read, appreciated as much for their literary technique as for any didactic message.

Most hagiographic poetry, however, was monastic and liturgical. One important form of that poetry was the sequence. The sequence developed in the early Middle Ages as a continuation of the *alleluia* sung to conclude a psalm during the service. Initially a series of pairs of rhythmical prose sentences sung by a choir in alternate parts, or antiphonally, the sequence experienced its greatest formal and expressive development in twelfth-century France, specifically at the Augustinian monastery of St. Victor in Paris.

The Victorine sequence has these general characteristics: meter is determined by stress accent and never, as in classical Latin poetry, by quantity; stanzas are composed of from one to three octosyllabic lines ending in a trochee (what modern scholars call paroxytone line, followed by a seven-syllable line ending in a dactyl (called a proparoxytone line); stanzas come in pairs, the second repeating exactly the rhythm of the first; octosyllabic lines within a stanza have an end rhyme of at least two syllables, while the end of the heptasyllabic line of a stanza rhymes with the end of the corresponding line in the pair; finally, a word appearing in one line often reappears, or an etymologically related word appears, in a different context in the following line.

These characteristics are better illustrated by examining poems attributed to Adam of St. Victor, the twelfth-century cleric acknowledged as the greatest composer of sequences. Adam's sequence on St. Stephen, sung on the saint's commemoration day of 26 December, the day after Christmas, begins with these four stanzas:

Heri mundus exsultavi   Heri chorus angelorum
Et exsultans celebravit   Prosecutus est caelorum
Christi natalitia.   Regem cum laetitia.

Protomartyr et Levita   Sub hac luce triumphavit
Clarus fide, clarus vita,   Et triumphans insultavit
Clarus et miraculis   Stephanus incredulis

(Yesterday the world rejoiced Yesterday the angelic chorus
And rejoicing celebrated   Attended the heavenly
The birthday of Christ.   King with joy.

Protomartyr and Levite,   He triumphed under this light
Renowned in faith,   And triumphing, Stephen
   renowned in life   Taunted the nonbelievers.)
And renowned in miracles,

The two stanzas on the left would have been sung by one side of the choir, in alternation with the two stanzas on the right by the other half. Adam has both sides of the choir begin by uttering the same word, *heri* (yesterday). One side sings the stanza beginning *Heri mundus exsultavit,* to be answered by the other side beginning *Heri chorus angelorum.* Adam takes the verbs *exsultavit* (rejoiced) and *triumphavit* (triumphed) and transforms them into the participles *exsultans* (rejoicing) and *triumphans* (triumphing) to use on the following lines. There is also the multiple repetition of the word *clarus* (renowned) in describing Stephen in the third stanza.

Thematically, a sequence for a saint's day will mention events in the saint's life, but it will not provide a fully elaborated narrative, instead the sequence uses poetic language to highlight certain key events. Listeners would already be expected to know the story of the saint, and in any event, they would probably hear a prose life read to them during the service. The purpose of the sequence is to glorify the saint through song.

Another example is the sequence on St. Catherine of Alexandria, a sequence whose attribution to Adam has been questioned but whose Victorine character is beyond doubt. Nearly every stanza succinctly refers to a different episode in Catherine's life, from her noble parentage to her debate with the fifty wise men to her torture and martyrdom and to the health-giving oil that flows miraculously from her tomb. The poem delights in the inversions characteristic of saints' lives: because of her courage and intelligence Catherine is described as a woman of unwomanly character (the stereotypes

All Saints Feast illumination (from the Fulda Sacramentary, *Gottingen, Niedersachsische Staats- und Üniversitätsbibliothek, Cod. Theol. 231, fol. IIIr)*

connecting femininity with weakness and masculinity with strength are common throughout medieval literature); although tortured, Catherine overcomes the torturer through her endurance; in death, she reaches the true joys of life.

Already in Adam's day many sequences were being written about Mary, the mother of Jesus. Several church festivals directly concern Mary, but devotion to her was not limited. Mary was becoming especially popular, not only among those few individuals with a literary education, but also among the population at large. By the later Middle Ages, devotion to Mary was a feature common to European culture, a feature that would leave its mark on Latin literature as well as in the literature of the vernacular languages.

Hagiography is one of the foundations for the literature of those vernacular languages. The *Sequence on Saint Eulalia,* written around 881–882 at the monastery of St. Amand near Valenciennes, is considered the earliest French poem. The poem, like Latin sequences of that early date, is quite primitive in form and contains fourteen pairs of phrases, whose lengths vary from eight to thirteen syllables. The end of each phrase in a pair has shared assonance and, sometimes, rhyme. The poem concludes with a final short line of seven syllables.

Eulalia was a young Spanish girl who was martyred in the days of the Roman Empire, and medieval interest in her grew after the announced rediscovery of her tomb in Barcelona in the year 878. The language of the sequence seems to be based on the speech of the area around the St. Amand monastery (what is now the northeast corner of France along the Belgian border), but there are linguistic elements that appear to come from the center of France (the upper Seine and Loire valleys).

In the early Middle Ages, French was developing as a spoken language out of Latin, which remained the language of writing. Yet, this situation did not mean that there was no literature in the emerging language. Undoubtedly, songs were sung and stories told, but these compositions were spread by word of mouth rather than by pen and ink. As this oral literature circulated, certain turns of phrase originating in one region's dialect would have been picked up and used in another. Such a process may explain the linguistic elements from central France found in the *Sequence on Saint Eulalia*.

Recognizing that features of a text may have been transmitted orally is important to understanding early French literature. Poetry, with its regular patterns of sound and phrase length, is easier to remember than prose and so is more easily repeated from one listener to another and from one village to the next. Not surprisingly, almost all of the earliest French literature is poetry, and in this poetry, saints' lives figure prominently.

The *Vie de Saint Alexis* (Life of St. Alexis) is a well-known example. The earliest written version of the story seems to be that of the Hildesheim manuscript, which was copied around the year 1120. Linguistically the Hildesheim text, a poem written in decasyllabic lines ending always in assonance and often in rhyme, is even earlier, usually dated to the mid-eleventh century.

Although the story is set during the days of the Roman Empire, Alexis was a relatively new saint when the Hildesheim manuscript was written. During the early Middle Ages, his tale was known in Greek and Syriac traditions but unknown in France and the West until late in the tenth century when Syrian refugees to Rome may have brought the story with them. The *Vie de Saint Alexis* of the Hildesheim manuscript, however, differs somewhat from eastern versions of the tale, and the relationships among the extant texts from the various traditions are difficult to determine.

In the Hildesheim text, Alexis is the only child of a Roman nobleman and as a young man is married to an equally noble young woman. Alexis, however, fears that by having sex and settling down he will no longer desire to serve God. On his wedding night, Alexis flees the bedroom and gains passage on a ship sailing at once for the East. He eventually ends up a beggar in the city of Alsis. (The city is identified as Edessa in other traditions; the name *Alsis* has not been adequately explained.) Alexis's father sends servants far and wide to search for his son. The servants arrive in Alsis, where they see Alexis sitting as a beggar. They give him money but do not recognize him, although the silent Alexis recognizes them. The servants return to Rome and report Alexis is nowhere to be found, a report that leads to grieving by Alexis's parents and wife.

Seventeen years later in a church in Alsis, a talking statue calls for the Man of God. When it is discovered that the statue is talking about Alexis, the saint finds himself the center of the city's attention. Alexis flees yet again, and eventually ends up on a ship that arrives in Rome. Alexis sees his father and addresses

him without revealing his identity. The saint asks for shelter underneath the staircase of his father's house and for some bread, and the father complies. For another seventeen years, Alexis lives in the same house with his parents and his wife, but they do not recognize him. The saint must also put up with harassment from household servants.

Finally Alexis realizes his death is near and asks for parchment, pen, and ink. The saint secretly writes his life story. That week voices are heard in Rome calling on the people to seek out the Man of God in order to save the city. The people ask the Pope for advice, and the entire city makes a public prayer. A voice then tells them to search the house of Alexis's father. When the Pope arrives, Alexis dies, clutching in his fist the parchment with his life story.

News of the beggar's death is brought to his unwitting father, who then realizes that this was the Man of God. The father is unable to take the parchment out of the dead man's hand, but the Pope can. The document is then read by a chancellor, and Alexis's family and all of Rome discover the identity of the beggar. After expressions of grief by the parents and wife, Alexis's body is moved to the church of Saint Boniface, where after a week of public mourning it is buried.

Humility is the main virtue promoted by the *Vie de Saint Alexis*. Wealth, position, beauty—these are all illusory and fleeting. The true rewards of life are found through contemplation of God. The spare style and preachy tone of the poem fit nicely with the severe asceticism described in the plot.

Yet, elements of romance are also quite prominent in the tale. There are sea voyages and exotic locales, a young couple separated on their wedding night and years of hidden identity. These elements, paralleled in other Old French verse romances, reinforce the fundamentally popular nature of vernacular saints' lives. Even though the origin of a story may go back to a Latin text, and the writing down of that story must have been made by someone with a literary education, these vernacular verse lives were mediated through an oral tradition of French storytelling.

The increasing devotion to Mary and the interest in recent miracles—features prominent in Latin hagiography—are also evident in French texts. A work that displays both features is the *Miracles de Nostre Dame* (Miracles of Our Lady) of Gautier de Coincy. Gautier, prior of Vic-sur-Aisne near Soissons, composed this collection between 1218 and 1231. He used various sources to compile the stories in his poems, most of which are written in pairs of rhyming octosyllabic lines and concern miracles not of the ancient past but of more recent ages, miracles effected by Mary that often involve her images.

Reflective of an age in which the Holy Lands captured by the crusaders were falling once again under Muslim control and Jews were beginning to face increasing hostility and discrimination, Gautier shows particular interest in the interaction of Christians and non-Christians, especially when his miracle stories result in conversion. For example, in "De l'enfant a un gïu qui se crestïena" (The Jewish Child Who Became a Christian, book 1, miracle 12) Gautier tells of the Jewish boy of Bourges who became a favorite of the clerics at the cathedral school and one day took communion. When the boy tells his father, a glassmaker, about taking communion, the father becomes enraged and throws his son into the furnace. The boy's mother runs screaming into the street and gathers a crowd, who recover the boy, miraculously unharmed. The boy proclaims that he had been protected from the flames by the statue of Mary in the church, a statue that had smiled at him that morning. Soon thereafter he, his mother, and many of the Jews of Bourges convert to Christianity.

In a similar vein is "De l'ymage Nostre Dame" (The Statue of Our Lady, book 1, miracle 32), the tale of the statue of Mary that came into the possession of a Muslim. The Muslim preserves the statue but for a long time will not go near it. One day, however, he approaches the image, studying it extensively. In examining the statue he comes to accept Jesus as Christ and Mary as his Virgin Mother. The Muslim decides to convert to Christianity, and he and his entire household are baptized.

The medieval world of the village craftsman and the itinerant merchant of the peasant and the lord, of monasteries and pilgrimage, this world is quite prominent in the *Miracles de Nostre Dame*. One of the best-known tales from the collection, "Dou cierge qui descendi au jougleour" (The Candle That Fell Towards the Jongleur," book 2, miracle 21), concerns the wandering minstrel, or jongleur, at the pilgrimage church of Rocadamour, north of Cahors. The jongleur, Pierre de Sygelar, sings a song of praise to Mary while he accompanies himself on the viol. When he finishes, he prays before her image that a sign be given if she approves of his song, and right away a candle falls from high on the shrine and lands on the viol. One of the monks guarding the shrine, Gérard, does not consider this event a miracle, and after calling the jongleur a sorcerer, he puts the candle back.

Pierre does not become angry at this insult. Instead he sings another song to Mary—and to an ever increasing audience within the church. When the jongleur finishes, the candle again falls onto his viol. Gérard grows ever more irritated as he pushes through the crowd to retrieve the candle, all the while accusing

Pierre of magic. With the candle yet again fixed in its holder, Pierre sings a third time with a crowd watching and listening. When the song is over, the candle falls yet again, and the onlookers shout that it was a miracle and call for the church bells to be rung. A festival is declared, and Pierre places the candle on the altar as an offering. Every year thereafter for the rest of his life, Pierre offers a candle in thanks. Gautier concludes the poem with a long discussion of the lessons clerics should learn from this jongleur.

Hagiography was important in other forms of writing as well. Early drama found saints' lives a fertile source of subject matter. Saints' lives were also increasingly written in prose. Since prose was seen as representing its subject matter more truthfully than poetry, prose became the favored medium for religious and historical texts—including saints' lives, which combined aspects of both history and religion.

An example of a prose biography of a contemporary saint is Jean de Joinville's *Vie de saint Louis* (Life of St. Louis). Joinville completed his account of the saintly French king Louis IX in 1309, only twenty-nine years after Louis's death and a dozen years after his canonization. Joinville had known the king well, having served him in the unsuccessful Seventh Crusade of 1248–1254.

The *Vie de saint Louis* comprises two books. The first book presents wise and witty remarks of the king, often made in conversation with Joinville. The sayings are folksy, preachy and not particularly tolerant, such as when Louis tells the story of an elderly and disabled knight who prematurely ends a disputation at Cluny between a monk and a rabbi. The old knight attacks the rabbi with his crutch after the Jew refuses to acknowledge Mary as the Mother of God. When the abbot tells the knight that his action is an outrage, the knight replies that trying to hold such a disputation is an even greater outrage. Louis ends the story by saying that only the most clever of clerics can enter into a disputation with those who criticize Christian doctrine. The rest should defend the faith by thrusting a sword into the enemy's stomach, as far as the weapon will go.

Several of the sayings of the first book reappear in the lengthier narrative of book two. Joinville tells the story of Louis's life in chronological order, from his early years of attachment to his widowed mother, Blanche of Castile, to his death in Tunis during the Eighth Crusade. Most of this narrative concerns Joinville's own involvement with the king, and special emphasis is given to the period when the author knew Louis best, during the Seventh Crusade. The language is unadorned and conversational, with Joinville often emphasizing that he was an eyewitness to events.

The Crusade narrative has garnered the most attention from modern scholars, and there has been debate as to whether the *Vie de saint Louis* is fundamentally a work of history or of hagiography. Some have wanted to see the Crusade narrative in book 2 as the original work that was later adapted into a hagiographic biography because of Louis's canonization. Here Joinville provides interesting ethnographic studies of Middle Eastern peoples; there is a strong autobiographical tone to the Crusade narrative; and many of the lords and other knights mentioned by Joinville are kinsmen or fellow comrades from Champagne.

Neither ethnographic digressions nor autobiographical touches nor promotion of particular families, regions, or social organizations is alien to the writing of saints' lives. In these aspects, the *Vie de saint Louis* has been compared to the lives of Cluny abbots such as Odilo's *Vita sancti Maioli.* Moreover, both in Joinville's preface and in repeated instances when digressions are curtailed does the author indicate that the primary purpose of his text is hagiographic, to promote Louis's life as an example to others.

Just as the case with Latin hagiographic texts, so too were French texts generally grouped together when a manuscript was written. Also there were established collections of saints' lives, the most renowned being Jean de Vignay's translation into French of Jacobus de Voragine's *Legenda aurea.* Vignay had been commissioned by the French queen Jane of Burgundy, the wife of Philip VI, to render the popular Latin collection into French, a task completed around the year 1334. Vignay's translation, which was titled the *Légende dorée,* proved quite popular among the French aristocracy. After Vignay's death the text was revised on two occasions: in 1402 the lives of forty-two additional saints were added to the original 183 readings for saints' days and other religious festivals; and sometime in the last quarter of the fifteenth century the order of the lives was changed and thirteen lives were added. Thirty-four manuscripts of the *Légende dorée* survive from the fourteenth and fifteenth centuries, and there are other legendaries based on Vignay's translation but which had been heavily altered.

Modern scholars have been almost universal in their condemnation of Vignay's language and style. He practiced a fixed, word-for-word translation using the same French word for every occurrence of its Latin counterpart, even when the Latin word had a different meaning. Vignay also closely followed the word order and syntax of the original Latin. This method at times make his text unintelligible.

It cannot be denied that Vignay's translation was popular, and so to some degree he must have hit the right tone. Moreover, while the heavily Latinate style of Vignay's translation may not have made for the most coherent French, such Latinisms would gain popularity in the subsequent era, when the Renaissance would bring a greater use of classical Latin models to the writing of French literature.

Many features of hagiographic literature in Old French also appear in texts written in Occitan, the language of the south of France. There are saints' lives in verse and saints' lives in prose. There are Occitan hagiographic plays; and, of course, Jacobus de Voragine's *Legenda aurea* were translated into the language.

The religious atmosphere of the south, however, was far more unsettled than that of the north. Popular religious movements that posed challenges to the hierarchy of the Catholic Church found fertile ground in the region. The Waldensians sought a Christianity unencumbered by centuries of Catholic tradition. The Cathars preached a dualistic view of a fundamentally corrupt physical world in conflict with the purity of a spiritual realm. Both movements were labeled heretical and thus were mercilessly crushed. The veneration of established saints was disapproved of by these movements, and saints' lives do not figure in what little literature has survived.

Another popular religious movement, but one that gained official church sanction, was that of the Friars Minor organized by St. Francis of Assisi. The Franciscans gained many followers in the south of France, and Franciscan writings, including Bonaventure's biography of Francis, were translated into Occitan.

One Franciscan text of special note is the *Vida de la benaurada sancta Doucelina* (Life of the Blessed Saint Doucelina). The text dates from the early fourteenth century and is preserved in the manuscript Paris, Bibliothèque Nationale de France, f. fr. 13503. Doucelina, the daughter of a merchant from Digne, was introduced to the Franciscan movement through her brother, Hugh, and both siblings would become quite prominent in the religious life of Provence. Yet, unlike those saints' lives meant to be read by men serving in important church positions, the *Vida de la benaurada sancta Doucelina* was, as shown by the early ownership of its manuscript, written for a female audience. A woman may have composed the text, so this biography may provide a rare glimpse on medieval women's views of sanctity, views that are all too often missing from most hagiographic texts, which were written by men.

The text describes a world centered on the convents for women founded by Doucelina in Hyères and Marseilles. While the saint is occasionally seen meeting with the important and powerful, most of the stories find her comforting the sick, helping the poor, and mentoring her convent companions. Doucelina did not receive a literary education, and she is portrayed several times as promoting her illiteracy as a sign of humility.

Doucelina's behavior shares many characteristics with that of the Beguines, a popular women's religious movement in the Low Countries that would eventually be suppressed by the Church. In her biography Doucelina calls herself a Beguine and says that Mary was the first Beguine. Doucelina also understands herself through the theme of the *sponsa Christi,* the "bride of Christ."

One day the saint hears a woman on the streets outside crying because her husband died. "Ah, poor me!" Doucelina exclaims. "Through my sins I have lost my Lord, and yet I am not weeping or mourning as this woman does for a mere mortal." The saint then begins to wail bitterly.

Doucelina also engages in asceticism and mortifications—wearing a hairshirt, wrapping herself tightly with a knotted rope, fasting extensively. During these fasts, the saint might have ecstatic experiences in which she visits Mary.

Yet, Doucelina always remains closely connected to the Franciscan view that the physical world must be respected and appreciated as part of God's Creation. Doucelina enjoys watching birds and shows a tenderness toward nature. Among the saint's medical miracles is the healing of a horse.

The *Vida de la benaurada sancta Doucelina* provides a somewhat different aspect from that seen in Latin saints' lives directed to the church leadership, and Doucelina has never officially been canonized. The Occitan biography shows a saint who, because of her nonaristocratic background, her lack of formal education and her gender, had a humility that, for the society of her day, was as much real as it was spiritual.

At the close of the fifteenth century, saints' lives remained a popular literary genre, but this situation was about to change. The demands of the Protestant Reformation for a simpler, more direct Christianity eliminated the need for the veneration of saints. The rationalism and empiricism of the Renaissance cast ever more skeptical views over claims of the supernatural. Under these onslaughts the Catholic Church provided only tepid support for traditional hagiography, as the Counter Reformation fashioned a more critical understanding of miracles, and changes in liturgy removed opportunities for devotion.

The High and later Middle Ages marked the apogee for hagiographic literature in France. Literature took many disparate forms and reflected many disparate concerns, all the while united in its attempts to promote religious practice and ethical behavior. The widespread popularity and influence of the genre make saints' lives of fundamental importance in any understanding of the culture of medieval France.

Bibliographies:

Christopher Storey, *An Annotated Bibliography and Guide to Alexis Studies* (Geneva: Droz, 1987);

Jacques Dubois and Jean-Louis Lemaitre, *Sources et méthodes de l'hagiographie médiévale* (Paris: Éditions du Cerf, 1993).

References:

Bibliotheca Hagiographica Latina, Subsidia Hagiographica 6 (Brussels: Société des Bollandistes, 1898–1899); supplement, edited by Henryk Fros, Subsidia Hagiographica 70 (Brussels: Société des Bollandistes, 1986);

Alain Boreau, *La Légende dorée* (Paris: Éditions du Cerf, 1984);

Adriaan H. Bredero, *Études sur la* Vita prima *de Saint Bernard* (Rome: Editiones Cistercienses, 1960);

Bredero, "The Canonization of Saint Bernard," in *Saint Bernard of Clairvaux: Studies Commemorating the Eighth Century of His Canonization* (Kalamazoo, Mich.: Cistercian Publication, 1977), pp. 63–100;

Rachel Bullington, *The* Alexis *in the Saint Albans Psalter,* Garland Studies in Medieval Literature 4 (New York: Garland, 1991);

La Cantilène de sainte Eulalie: Actes du colloque de Valenciennes, 21 mars 1989 (Lille: ACCES, 1990);

Brigitte Cazelles, *La faiblesse chez Gautier de Coinci,* Stanford French and Italian Studies 14 (Saratoga, Cal.: Anma Libri, 1978);

Hippolyte Delehaye, *The Legends of the Saints,* translated by V. M. Crawford (Notre Dame, Ind.: University of Notre Dame Press, 1961);

Peter F. Dembowski, "Literary Problems of Hagiography in Old French," *Medievalia et Humanistica* 7 (1976): 117–130;

François Dolbeau, "Les hagiographes au travail," in *Manuscrits hagiogaphiques et travail des hagiographes,* Beihefte der Francia 24 (Sigmaringen: Jan Thorbecke, 1992), pp. 49–76;

Alison Goddard Elliot, *Roads to Paradise: Reading the Lives of the Early Saints* (Hanover, N.H.: University Press of New England, 1987);

Margot Fassler, *Gothic Song: Victorine Sequence and Augustinian Reform in Twelfth-Century Paris* (Cambridge: Cambridge University Press, 1993);

Robert Garnier, *Joinville* (Paris: Perrin, 1983);

Pamela Gehrke, *Saints and Scribes: Medieval Hagiography in Its Manuscript Context,* University of California Publication in Modern Philology 126 (Berkeley & Los Angeles: University of California Press, 1993);

Antonella degl'Innocenti, *L'opera agiographica di Marbodo di Rennes* (Spoleto: Centro Italiano di studi sull'alto medioevo, 1990);

Dominique Iogna-Prat, *Agni immaculati: recherches sur les sources hagiographiques relatives à Saint Maieul de Cluny* (Paris: Éditions du Cerf, 1988);

Phyllis Johnson and Brigitte Cazelles, *Le Vain Siècle Guerpir: A Literary Approach to Sainthood Through Old French Hagiography of the Twelfth Century,* North Carolina Studies in the Romance Languages and Literatures 205 (Chapel Hill: University of North Carolina Department of Romance Languages, 1979);

Richard Kieckhefer, *Unquiet Souls: Fourteenth-Century Saints and Their Religious Milieu* (Chicago: University of Chicago Press, 1984);

Christine Knowles, "Jean de Vignay," *Romania* 75 (1954): 353–383;

Jean Leclercq, *Nouveau visage de Bernard de Clairvaux* (Paris: Éditions du Cerf, 1976); translated into English by Marie-Bernard Saïd as *A Second Look at Bernard of Clairvaux* (Kalamazoo, Mich.: Cistercian Publications, 1990);

Paul Meyer, "Légendes hagiographiques en français," in *Histoire littéraire de la France,* volume 33 (Paris: Imprimerie Nationale, 1904), pp. 328–458;

Guy Oury, "Les documents hagiographiques et l'histoire des monastères dépourvus d'archives: le cas de Saint-Genou de l'Estrée," *Revue Mabillon* 59 (1978): 289–316;

F. J. E. Raby, *A History of Christian-Latin Poetry from the Beginnings to the Close of the Middle Ages,* second edition (Oxford: Clarendon Press, 1953);

Sherry L. Reames, *The Legenda aurea* (Madison: University of Wisconsin Press, 1985);

Vida Russell, "Evidence for a Stemma for the De Vignay MSS," in *Legenda aurea: sept siècles de diffusion* (Montréal: Bellarmin; and Paris: J. Vrin, 1986), pp. 131–154;

Maureen Slattery, *Myth Man and Sovereign Saint: King Louis IX in Jean de Joinville's Sources,* American University Studies, series 2: Romance Languages and Literatures no. 11 (New York: Peter Lang, 1985);

Karl D. Uitti, *Story, Myth and Celebration in Old French Narrative Poetry* (Princeton: Princeton University Press, 1973);

André Vauchez, *Sainthood in the Later Middle Ages,* translated by Jean Birrell (Cambridge: Cambridge University Press, 1996).

Troubadours, *Trobairitz,* and Trouvères

Gale Sigal
Wake Forest University

Manuscripts: There are ninety-five principal *chansonniers* (manuscript collections) containing Occitan lyric poetry that were put together between the thirteenth and sixteenth centuries; nineteen were compiled in the Occitan region, fourteen in northern France, ten in Catalonia, and fifty-two in Italy. Manuscript R (Paris, Bibliothèque Nationale de France, f. fr. 22543) is a principal source of troubadour poems, with 1,165 texts and 160 melodies and *vidas* (biographical sketches of the poets); manuscript C (Paris, Bibliothèque Nationale de France, f. fr. 856) includes 1,206 poems; manuscript A (Rome, Biblioteca Apostolica Vaticana, latini 5232) has 626 lyrics; manuscripts G (Milan, Biblioteca Ambrosiana, R 71 superiore), R (Paris, Bibliothèque Nationale de France, f. fr. 22543), and W (Paris, Bibliothèque Nationale de France, f. fr. 844) provide transcriptions of some melodies. Trouvère manuscript K (Paris, Bibliothèque de l'Arsenal, the channsonnier de l'Arsenal) contains more than five hundred songs with musical notation; manuscript O (Paris, Bibliothèque Nationale de France, f. fr. 846) has four hundred songs, most with music.

Standard editions–Troubadours:
Poésies complètes du troubadour Marcabru, edited by J. M. L. Dejeanne (Toulouse: Privat, 1909; New York: Johnson Reprints, 1971); *The Life and Works of the Troubadour Raimbaut d'Orange,* edited by Walter T. Pattison (Minneapolis: University of Minnesota Press, 1952); *Peire d'Alvernha: Liriche,* edited and translated by Alberto Del Monte, Collezione di "Filologia romanza" no. 1 (Turin: Loescher-Chiantore, 1955); *Poésies complètes du troubadour Peire Cardenal (1180–1278),* edited by René Lavaud, Bibliothèque Méridinonale, second series volume 34 (Toulouse: Privat, 1957); *Arnaut Daniel: Canzoni,* edited by Gialuigi Toja (Florence: Sansoni, 1960); Peire Vidal, *Poésie,* 2 volumes, edited by D'Arco Silvio Avalle (Milan: Ricciardi, 1960); *The Songs of Bernart de Ventadorn: Complete Texts, Transla-*

tions, Notes, and Glossary, edited by Stephen G. Nichols Jr. and others (Chapel Hill: University of North Carolina Press, 1962); *The Poems of the Troubadour, Raimbaut de Vaqueiras,* edited by Joseph Linskill (The Hague: Mouton, 1964); *Les Poèmes de Gaucelm Faidit,* edited by Jean Mouzat (Paris: Nizet, 1965); *Bernart de Ventadour, troubadour du XIIe siècle: Chansons d'amour,* edited and translated by Moshé Lazar, Bibliothèque Française et Romane: Series B, Editions critiques de textes no. 5 (Paris: Klincksieck, 1966); *Les poésies du troubadour Raimon de Miraval,* edited by Leslie T. Topsfield, Les Classiques d'Oc no. 4 (Paris: Nizet, 1971); *Le canzoni di Arnaut Daniel,* 2 volumes, edited by Maurizio Perugi (Milan: Ricciardi, 1978); *The Songs of Jaufré Rudel,* edited by Rupert T. Pickens (Toronto: Pontifical Institute of Medieval Studies, 1978); *The Poetry of Arnaut Daniel,* edited and translated by James J. Wilhelm (New York: Garland, 1981); *The Poetry of William VII, Count of Poitiers, IX Duke of Aquitaine,* edited and translated by Gerald A. Bond (New York: Garland, 1982); *The Poetry of Cercamon and Jaufré Rudel,* edited and translated by George Wolf and Roy Rosenstein (New York & London: Garland, 1983); *Arnaut Daniel: Il sirventese e le canzoni,* edited by Mario Eusebi (Milan: All'Insegna del Pesce d'Oro, 1984); *The Poems of the Troubadour Bertran de Born,* edited by William D. Paden Jr., Tilde Sankovitch, and Patricia H. Stäblein (Berkeley: University of California Press, 1986); *The Cansos and Sirventes of the Troubadour Giraut de Borneil: A Critical Edition,* edited and translated by Ruth Verity Sharman (Cambridge: Cambridge University Press, 1989).

Standard editions–*Trobairitz*:
La Comtesse de Die: Sa vie, ses œuvres complètes, les fêtes données en son honneur, avec tous les documents, edited by Sernin Santy (Paris: Picard, 1893); *The Women Troubadours,* edited by Meg Bogin (New York & London: Paddington Press, 1976); *Trobairitz: Der*

Beitrag der Frau in der altokzitanischen höfischen Lyrik. Edition des Gesamptkorpus, edited by Angelica Rieger, Beihefte zur Zeitschrift für romanische Philologie, volume 233 (Tübingen: Niemeyer, 1991); *The Songs of the Women Troubadours,* edited and translated by Matilda Tomaryn Bruckner, Laurie Shepard, and Sarah White (New York & London: Garland, 1995).

Standard editions–Trouvéres:

Canchons und Partures des altfranzöisischen Trouvère Adan de la Hale le bochu d'Aras, edited by Rudolf Berger, Romanische Bibliothek, volume 17 (Halle: Niemeyer, 1900); *Die Lieder des Blondel de Nesle,* edited by Leo Wiese, Gesellschaft für romanische Literatur no. 5 (Dresden: Printed for the Gesellschaft für romanische Literatur, 1904); *Les Chansons de Conon de Béthune,* edited by Axel Wallensköld (Paris: H. Champion, 1921; reprinted, 1968); *Les Chansons de Colin Muset,* edited by Joseph Bédier, second edition (Paris: H. Champion, 1938); *Chansons attribuées au Chastelain de Couci: fin du XIIe–debut du XIIIe siècle,* edited by Alain Lerond, Publications de la Faculté des lettres et sciences humaines de Rennes no. 7 (Paris: Presses Universitaires de France, 1964); *The Chansons of Adam de la Halle,* edited by J. H. Marshall (Manchester: Manchester University Press, 1971); *The Lyrics and Melodies of Gace Brulé,* edited and translated by Samuel N. Rosenberg and Samuel Danon, music edited by Hendrik van der Werf (New York & London: Garland, 1985); *The Poetry of Thibaut de Champagne,* edited and translated by Kathleen J. Brahney (New York: Garland, 1989).

The troubadours, the earliest self-consciously distinct group of poets to compose in a European language, created the first great literary movement of the Romance languages. Circulating their songs in the south of France at the end of the eleventh century, the troubadours made lyric the preeminent verbal art of their time. In their themes and forms of expression the troubadours diverged from the established traditions of Latin poetry, popularizing secular subject matter, circulating increasingly inventive forms of versification, and composing accompanying melodies. They introduced fresh themes to a newly conceived audience of aristocratic men and women and entertained that courtly milieu with a flamboyant display of virtuoso stylistics, complemented by original musical and poetic forms. They endowed vernacular poetry with rhyme, tempo, and the vitality of flowing and flexible rhythm. The achievement was so significant that vernacular lyricists

in northern France, Italy, the Iberian peninsula, and Germany adopted the troubadour style.

The troubadours were literally inventors: the word *trobador* comes from the Occitan *trobar* (to find or discover). Linguistic variants among the Romance languages resulted in analogous terms for composers of vernacular song: in the north of France they were called *trouvères* (from *trouver,* to find); in Italy, *trovatores* (from *trovare,* to find). Theirs was a true lyric poetry; every poet composed both words and music. The troubadours were artists, not mere jongleurs or *joglars* (performers), although some did perform their own songs. In modern usage, Occitania (rather than Provence) refers to the region of southern France where the troubadours and *trobairitz* (women troubadours) flourished; their language is designated Occitan (rather than Provençal) .

Scholars can say little with certainty about how troubadour poetry evolved although several theories have been proposed. What is incontrovertible is that troubadour art was an art of the court. The court functioned as the center of eleventh- and twelfth-century political power and social life. The evolving conflicts and prevailing ideologies of the courts were reflected in the troubadours' verse, which, besides voicing the real dilemmas and issues of the day, also indulged–even reveled–in the personal and subjective aspect of experience. Such new subject matter fostered the creation of a panoply of lyric voices. Embedded in these narrative personae were the seeds of a literary, as well as a social, revolution, for the impact of the lyric was felt not only on literary forms but also on social life: personal relationships, especially between men and women, were described and prescribed in song so influentially that, according to some scholars, the social code the troubadours' songs initiated is still in use today.

Troubadour poetry began to be composed around 1100 and flourished until around 1270, continuing in an increasingly ossifying form until 1350. During that time a small poetic circle produced a language of devotion that has become customary ever since; both poetry and love were permanently altered by the troubadours. The troubadours' songs of passion–real or imagined, adulterous or licit–engendered a discourse in which the women who inspired love, and love itself, were idealized. The courtly mode promoted the iconoclastic idea that the beloved lady was also the lover's *domna* (from the Latin *domina,* mistress of a household), that is, his feudal sovereign. The courtly lover's explicit desire was to serve this feminine "master," to merit the favors that she, from her superior position, could freely grant or refuse. Pleasing her required courteous comportment and a particular set of virtues: nobility of heart (rather than of birth), generosity, eloquence, and etiquette. The art of conversation; skill in other expressive arts, such as the composition of song; and public celebration of the beloved's beauty and virtue were newly valued among the members of the knightly class. The troubadours called this kind of love *fin'amor* (refined love).

Love was an essential component of an individual's claim to courtliness; *fin'amor* multiplied the lover's good qualities and endowed him with those he formerly lacked. Requital on the part of the beloved, who was not necessarily free to respond, was irrelevant: love was conceived as a service, regardless of whether it was returned, and the generosity and self-sacrificing nature of such love were thought to ennoble the lover. The lady's lack of response left the singer free to contemplate an array of possible responses and to consider his own reaction to each. The rhetorical renunciation of carnal desire for the lady or of any need for response on her part was often the greatest proof of a lover's nobility of spirit and sincerity.

Although they are difficult to trace, the troubadours' social backgrounds seem to have varied widely. Reliable documentary evidence exists for only a few—mostly noble—poets; for the majority, only obscure or unreliable sources are available. Near the end of the thirteenth century, long after the heyday of troubadour lyric, *chansonniers* (manuscript collections; literally, "songbooks") began to be compiled, complete with *vidas* (biographical sketches of the poets) and *razos* (explanations of the composition, social setting, and allusions of the poems). Because the compilers generally had little to guide them unless the poet was a significant public figure, vidas and razos, although presented as factual, are frequently fanciful elaborations drawn from the lyrics; they are more valued by modern readers as fascinating tales than as accurate histories.

Because of the allusions poets make to other singers and courts, scholars divide troubadours into generations. The first generation consists of two poets, Guillem de Peiteus (1071–1127) and his vassal and legendary rival, the Viscount Eble de Ventadour, about whom little is known other than that he lived between 1096 and 1147 and whose poetry has not survived. Guillem de Peiteus was variously called Guillem IX, William IX, or Guillaume IX (referring to his status as ninth duke of Aquitaine); Guillem VII (designating his status as seventh Count of Poitiers); and "Lo Coms de Peiteus" (the count of Poitiers). One of the most powerful feudal lords of the time and commanding more territory than the kings of France, Guillem is considered "the first troubadour." Although his surviving corpus consists of only twelve lyrics and a fragment of a single melody, his poetry is the earliest known verse in the troubadour repertory. Guillem was once regarded as

the originator of the courtly love lyric; modern scholars, however, believe that he was responding to conventions that were already in vogue rather than creating his poetry, as he once boasted, *de dreyt nien* (out of completely nothing). Nevertheless, he was a master of the basic metrical forms and essential themes that would remain staples of the troubadour corpus. His multifaceted voice and extensive repertory are striking in so small a corpus: his lyrics range from crude salacious songs to subtle, poignant, and refined love lyrics. He perfected poetic techniques for performance before an audience, a cornerstone of troubadour verse. Despite the varied nature of Guillem's verse his bawdy side has dominated the reception of his works, leading to his condemnation by early critics who, failing to distinguish between the poet himself and the braggart he impersonated in his *gaps* (boasting songs), considered him carnal, crude, and brutal. Guillem took part in a failed crusade into the Holy Land in 1101–1102 and led a successful skirmish against the Moors in Spain from 1120 to 1123. Depicted by contemporary chroniclers as witty, boisterous, and sacrilegious, he had many disputes with the Catholic Church and was excommunicated more than once for usurping church lands.

Guillem's granddaughter was the legendary Eleanor of Aquitaine (1122?–1204). Married to King Louis VII of France in 1137, Eleanor became a leading patroness of courtly verse, creating a literary circle whose influence pervaded all the great francophone courts. One of her two daughters from this marriage, Marie, became countess of Champagne and continued her mother's practice of patronizing the arts. Repudiating her marriage to Louis in 1152, Eleanor married Henry Plantagenet the same year. Henry became king of England as Henry II in 1154.

Once Guillem's verse began to circulate, poetic successors and emulators proliferated throughout southern France. The second generation, reflecting an expansion into southwestern France, put the basic poetic framework in place. Generic divisions took shape: the *canso* (love song of five or six stanzas with an envoy) was differentiated from the sirventes, a satirical lyric structurally similar to a canso but dealing with moral, political, personal, or didactic subjects. Jaufré Rudel's *amor de lonh* (love from afar) defines one type of love within the canso. *Tornadas*—half-strophes used to conclude a lyric—began to be used to commend the song to its addressee.

Cercamon (flourished 1130–1149), an itinerant singer whose name can be translated as "Search-the-world" or "He who travels the world over," was a Gascon whose surviving repertory consists of only seven songs. These include melancholy cansos on the sorrows of love, sirventes, and a *planh* (lament) on

Musician playing a vielle, *an early violin, illumination from a manuscript for* Coffret de Mariage bois peint *(Vanne Cathedral, ms. 003. P. 426)*

Marcabru was also a great innovator. His brilliant handling of the *pastorela,* a short narrative poem in which a knight recounts his attempt to seduce a shepherdess, and a genre he may have invented, is evinced in a comic encounter between a shepherdess and a knight in which Marcabru calls the idea of courtliness into question while displaying his genius for creating memorable comic characters. Marcabru's corpus includes the first instance of *trobar clus* (the hermetic or closed style), and he was the earliest singer to mention the *fals amadors* (false lovers) who would constitute the addressees—along with the flatterers, slanderers, spies, and envious, vulgar, and true lovers—of the songs of future troubadours. With Uc Catola, of whom nothing else is known, Marcabru co-authored the first extant *tenso* (debate poem), wherein the two poets discuss the uses and misuses of love. Despite his many royal patrons, Marcabru is alleged in a vida to have been murdered by some lords of Guyenne because of his wicked tongue. Of his forty-five surviving poems, four are preserved with their music.

Jaufré Rudel (flourished 1125–1148), Prince of Blaye (Blaie), was the expositor of an ethereal, mystical, obsessive, and unrequited kind of love he termed *amor de lonh*. Only six or seven poems are usually attributed to him, four with melodies. Jaufré announced his intention of joining a crusade in at least one lyric, and it is generally believed that he took part in the Second Crusade in 1147, never to return. Jaufré's vida, inspired by his songs, gave rise to a well-known legend that is retold by Petrarch, Edmond Rostand, Heinrich Heine, Robert Browning, and Ezra Pound: Jaufré fell in love, sight unseen, with the countess of Tripoli and composed lyrics about her; he crossed the sea in search of her, fell sick, recovered sufficiently to feel her hold him in her arms, and died; after burying him ceremoniously, she entered a convent.

By the mid twelfth century, troubadour poetry had reached its maturity, attaining harmony among its varied elements and fostering a large number of great poets. The terms *vers* (verse) and *canso* recur continually conjoined with adjectives such as *leu* (light or easy), *greu* (heavy), *plan* (plain, smooth, or polished), *entier* (whole), *clus* (closed, hidden, or obscure), and *natural* (authentic), indicating that the poets were creating various stylistic trends. During the last quarter of the twelfth century, poets experimented further with form and style, and songs began to combine subjects that had formerly been kept in distinct genres.

Bernart de Ventadorn (also called Bernard de Ventadour, flourished 1140–1180) left a large corpus of poems (forty-one are attributed to him) and melodies. The many manuscript copies of his songs and the allusions made to him by other poets show him to have

the pilgrimage death in 1137 of Duke Guillem X of Aquitaine. Marcabru (flourished 1130–1150) was a Gascon orphan who, according to his vida, became Cercamon's pupil; some critics, however, believe that Cercamon was Marcabru's pupil. Like Cercamon's name, Marcabru's—which means "Dark spot"—signifies a person of humble and unsettled position. A clever name-caller and coiner of neologisms, Marcabru deplored the decadence of contemporary sexual mores and lashed out against the egoism, deceit, and insincerity prevalent during his time. His denunciations of the effeminacy and depravity of courtly life were perfected in his sirventes, which set the standard for political and social satire. Although he disparaged *fin'amor,* he extolled his own vision of true love, a love in harmony with, rather than rebellion against, the community.

been one of the most eminent troubadours. With the exception of three tensos, his corpus consists entirely of cansos that are considered by many to be the best in the Occitan corpus. Written in the *trobar leu* style, Bernart's verse is distinguished by sincere, simple, sensual, and delicate language. He made the canso a sophisticated, flexible form. His inconsistent and sometimes contradictory attitudes, for which he was criticized in the thirteenth-century handbook *Las razos de trobar* (Commentaries on Composition), are actually his most outstanding innovation: the clash of perspectives he dramatizes in his lyrics reflects the varieties and modulations of desire. His works epitomize the intensity, elegance, imagery, and music of the troubadour style.

Although Bernart's output represents one of the summits of Occitan love song, his life is obscure. The vidas recount that he was of low birth, the son of a furnace tender of Eble II or III of Ventadorn. His humble birth is corroborated by rival poet Peire d'Alvernhe (flourished 1149–1180) in a satirical poem. After alleged misadventures with Eble's wife he was befriended by Henry II of England, whose wife, the famed Eleanor, was said to have been another of his loves. Nothing is known of him after he stopped composing lyrics around 1180, although one biographer recounts that he entered the Cistercian monastery at Dalon, where he died.

Peire d'Alvernhe wrote love songs, sirventes, and religious lyrics; composed an enigmatic manifesto of *trobar clus;* debated with Bernart Marti in a poem on the subject of integrity (a genre known as *vers entiers*); and may have been the "Peire" with whom Bernart de Ventadorn debates the arts of love and song in the tenso "Amics Bernartz de Ventadorn" (Friend Bernart of Ventadorn). In his best-known poem, "Cantarai d'aquestz trobadors," he created a gallery of poets, some of whom he lampooned, while mocking the obscurity of his own verse. This lyric portrays the troubadours as a self-critical literary circle in which each poet achieved a recognizable idiosyncratic stamp. Peire wrote the first surviving religious lyrics in the troubadour corpus. Dante, in *De vulgari eloquentia* (On the Eloquence of the Vernacular, circa 1304–1307), called him venerable and learned. A contemporary poet recounts that Peire violated his vows as a canon of the church to take up his pen, but little is known of his life.

Guiraut de Bornelh (or Borneil or Borneill, circa 1155 – circa 1210), born in the Dordogne region, is said in his vida to have had humble origins but to have been "maestre dels trobadors" (the master of the troubadours), known for his wisdom, his learning, and his subtle, finely arranged words. He seems to have had a close relationship with his feudal overlord, Adémar V, Viscount of Limoges, but he also traveled widely, taking two jongleurs along to perform his songs. A bachelor, he donated everything he earned to poor relatives or to the church of Saint-Gervais in his native village. Dante praises him as a poet who composed on the theme of moral rectitude.

The eighty poems Guiraut left vary widely in form: there are thirty-nine cansos, twelve canso-sirventes, twenty-four sirventes, and an alba (song lamenting the arrival of dawn that separates two lovers). He composed in *trobar ric,* the rich style, which displayed sumptuous language and complex versification, as well as many other styles: *trobar clus, trobar plan,* and *trobar leu.* Four of his melodies survive. He theorized about the nature of love in satirical verses that portray the courtly life as overwhelmed by hypocrisy and vice. Many of his songs are dramatic, reflecting lively performance before an audience. In a celebrated alba the secret lovers' dawn parting is evoked not through their own lament but through the haunting song of a friend who stands guard. With its measured, stately melody and its subtlety of expression, this poem remains a concert favorite today. In a well-known tenso Guiraut and another poet debate the relative merits of *trobar clus* and *trobar leu;* Guiraut defends the accessible style and his opponent the obscure, although Guiraut defends *trobar clus* in other poems. His works demonstrate that he was equally adept at both light and closed verse.

Arnaut Daniel (flourished 1170–1210) was probably of noble birth and a native of Ribérac near Périgueux (Dordogne). An exponent of *trobar clus* and *trobar ric,* he has a style that is characterized by brilliant ornamentation, elaborate rhyme patterns, a firm sense of order and control, and the use of rare words chosen for their sounds. He sang of idealized erotic love in cansos but wrote satiric songs as well. He is most celebrated for his inventive and rich rhyme schemes, especially in his sestinas, a form he may have created. Dante, who tried his hand at composing sestinas, praises Arnaut several times in *De vulgari eloquentia;* he also cites Arnaut in *Purgatorio* XXVI.115 of *The Divine Comedy* (circa 1308–1321) as "miglior fabbro del parlar materno" (the better craftsman of the mother tongue). Eighteen of Arnaut's poems survive, seventeen of them cansos.

Peire Vidal (flourished 1170–1205) was a popular troubadour who composed in a simple style that, along with his originality, liveliness, and variety, makes him the most accessible of the troubadours to the modern reader. He expresses his originality and surprises his audience by intertwining the conventions of several genres in individual songs. He created an intimacy with his audience, before whom he took a variety of poses, mocking and praising himself in turn. Forty-five of his poems are extant, twelve with melodies. Personal references in his songs portray a man who traveled widely and served many patrons, including Count Raimon V of his native city, Toulouse; King Alfonso II of Aragon; and Vicomte Barral of Marseille. Peire Vidal's vida, which says that he was the son of a furrier, paints some extraordinary adventures for him, including having his tongue cut out by a jealous husband.

The poet and soldier Raimbaut de Vaqueiras is said in his vida to have been born around 1155 to a poor knight in a castle near Orange. His wanderings as a minstrel took him to Spain and to Italy; in the latter country he became companion in arms to Boniface I, who was made marquis of Montferrat in 1192. In recognition of Raimbaut's service on expeditions to Sicily, Constantinople, and Greece, Boniface knighted him; although Raimbaut recounts that he earned his knighthood through his songs, he is known to have fought courageously and to have saved his patron's life during the successful Sicilian campaign. The privileged position Raimbaut enjoyed at the court was unparalleled in the literary patronage of the time. He probably died at Boniface's side in 1207 during the Fourth Crusade.

Boniface's court was a literary center, welcoming such notable poets as Peire Vidal, Gaucelm Faidit, and, possibly, Cadenet and the trouvère Conon de Béthune; but Raimbaut, who was among the first to be patronized there, is reputed to have had the greatest impact of any troubadour on the course of Italian literature. He initiated the use of the Italian vernacular in lyric and introduced into Italy the poetic tradition of the collective panegyric. For his realism, vigor, sincerity, liveliness of presentation, skill in energizing and individualizing popular genres and themes, and formative influence on Italian lyric he is considered one of the most important troubadours.

The more than forty poems of Raimbaut's that survive display formal and linguistic versatility, as do the seven extant melodies. The lyrics are richly allusive, evoking legendary, historical, and contemporary heroes. His simple and direct style combine clarity and ease of expression with a gift for description and humor. Raimbaut's virtuosity is revealed in the variety of his tone, style, and theme: some of his songs assume a cosmopolitan character, while others attempt to capture the spirit of folk song. He wrote a love song in five Romance languages; a tenso in which a narrator woos in Occitan a girl who refuses him in Genoese; and one haunting love lament of his has a female narrator. His sparkling *estampida* (dance or "stamping" song), "Kalenda maia" (May Day), with its rapid rhythm and insistent rhymes, is one of the finest and most original verbal and melodic conjurings and remains a staple of early-music concerts. He wrote cansos, *partimens* (songs in which two speakers debate a point of amorous casu-

istry), tensos, and poems in other genres; his epic letter, a poem of more than two hundred lines in decasyllabic epic *laisses* (stanzas), provides a glimpse not only into the personal experiences of a poet-warrior but also into the lives, manners, and sensibility of the feudal nobility at the turn of the twelfth century.

Bertran de Born (circa 1140–circa 1214), master of the witty, satiric sirventes, was a minor nobleman, lord of the castle of Hautefort (Altafort) in Périgord. Forty-eight of his poems survive. His lyrics depict political and military action with a vividness that critics have attributed to personal experience rather than to skilled artistry. The world he portrays is dominated by lineage, territorial conflict, and war. A poetic innovator, he juxtaposes this "real" world of action to the "illusory" sphere of *fin'amor,* idealizing war rather than love. As a singer of battles, he spoke for the interests of noble mercenaries, reflecting the vavasors' conception of war as a source of profit and honor. His sirventes communicate not only the anguish of living in a land torn by dissension but the further plight of mercenaries whose property was confiscated whenever they fought on the losing side. Peacetime offered still fewer opportunities, creating poverty and suffering among the knights.

Bertran's songs were considered a major incitement to an unsuccessful revolt against Henry II by his eldest son, Henry, in 1173; son battled father, and brother fought brother. Bertran's castle was burned and he was imprisoned by Henry II's son Richard Cœur de Lion; but, he obtained a pardon from Richard, along with restoration of his land. Like Bernart de Ventadorn, Bertran de Born lived out his final days in the Cistercian monastery of Dalon. Condemned by Dante as a sower of discord, Bertran is depicted with his head separated from his body in *Inferno* XVIII.113–142 of *The Divine Comedy.* The attribution of responsibility for causing a civil war may not be accurate, but it attests to the power of Bertran's poetry. Dante also refers to Bertran in *De vulgari eloquentia,* this time as a master of martial poetry. Pound re-creates Bertran in his *Personae* (1909).

Raimbaut d'Aurenga (circa 1144–1173), Lord of Orange and Courthézon, is said to have squandered most of his patrimony, but his court patronized several troubadours and *trobairitz.* Thirty-nine of his poems, characterized by intellectual brilliance, humor, and the playful use of hyperbole, conceit, irony, and paradox, survive; most are in the *trobar clus* style.

During the last part of the twelfth century and the early thirteenth century Occitan poetry reached its fullest flower, especially in Toulouse, Narbonne, Montpellier, and Provence, regions devastated by the Albigensian Crusade (1208–1229). Launched by Innocent III against the Albigenses, or Cathars, a heretical Manichaean sect that flourished in southern France, the crusade served as pretext for northern armies to invade the south. As they swept through southern France, the crusaders wiped out many courts, decimating the region's flourishing culture. When the crusade was over, the king of France had possession of Toulouse.

With the loss of their patrons and audience, the troubadours were compelled to shift their theme and focus. The subjects of poetry, especially love, were deprived of their courtly setting, and troubadour art made its way into urban bourgeois society. Political and religious themes were given greater centrality; the Virgin Mary often replaced the beloved lady. Many poets, persuaded by the inquisition that Folquet de Marseille (1150–1231) helped establish, followed Folquet's lead and returned to hymns and sacred verse.

Folquet de Marseille, the son of a successful Genoese merchant, is reputed to have dissipated his patrimony in riotous living. He began composing around 1180, earning a reputation as a love poet, but around 1200 he renounced the secular life, repenting of his amorous poetic themes, and entered a Cistercian monastery. He soon became abbot of Le Thoronet and by 1205 was bishop of Toulouse. As bishop he played a harsh role in persecuting heretics at the inquisitions he instituted during the Albigensian Crusade. According to a contemporary poem, this "Antichrist" sent hundreds of people to their deaths. Reviled by most southern Frenchmen, he died in seclusion. Despite his contemporary disrepute, stories of his miracles were common. Nineteen of his poems survive.

Peire Cardenal (circa 1180–1275) was the greatest poet of the Albigensian period; around seventy of his songs survive, mostly moral sirventes. His bitterest sirventes revolve around the Albigensian Crusade. Born of a noble family in Puy Nôtre-Dame, he was educated for an ecclesiastical career; but, when he reached his majority, he abandoned that career to take up the art of composing. He attached himself to the courts of the counts of Toulouse as well as to that of James I of Aragon and Alfonso X of Castile.

Raimon de Miraval (flourished 1185–1213) had a substantial output. Favoring the *trobar leu* style, he composed thirty-seven cansos, five sirventes, and one partimen; twenty-two of his works survive with music. His vida recounts that he was a poor knight from the region of Carcasonne who traveled throughout the courts of southern France and Spain and acquired fame through song. His property, situated in the central area of the Cathar heresy, was taken by Simon de Montfort in 1209 or 1210 during the Albigensian Crusade. Raimon seems to have fled to Spain and to have remained there for the rest of his life.

Gaucelm Faidit (flourished 1170–1205) left at least sixty-five poems, fourteen with melodies. He was patronized at the courts of Raimon d'Agout and Marie de Ventadorn and thrived at the court of Boniface of Montferrat. He took part in the Third and Fourth Crusades and composed one song in Old French, perhaps for northern crusaders. His most celebrated lyric is a planh on the death in 1199 of Richard Cœur de Lion. According to his vida, Gaucelm was the son of a bourgeois family from Uzerche (Limousin). His razos praise his songs but disparage his singing; they are full of colorful, primarily unflattering, and probably fictitious details: they say that he gambled away his money, was a glutton, had affairs with many great ladies, and had a disreputable son. Other notable poets of this generation include Peirol (flourished 1188–1222), who left thirty poems, and the Monge (Monk) de Montaudan (flourished 1193–1210), who composed a "literary gallery" (1195) in which sixteen poets are mentioned.

Sordello (circa 1215–1270), a lower nobleman from Goito, near Mantua, was the most famous Italian who wrote in Occitan. His forty extant lyrics are mainly sirventes and partimen, but he also composed twelve cansos. He traveled to Spain and then to Provence, where he was patronized by Blacatz, Lord of Aups, and Raimon Bérenger IV, Count of Provence. Sordello returned to Italy in 1266 with Charles of Anjou. As a reward for service in the battle of Benevento and in Sicily, Sordello was granted some land and castles in the Abruzzi region, where he died. Sordello's fame was bolstered by his appearance as a prophetic figure in Dante's *Purgatorio* (VI and VII). Browning and Pound found his lyrics appealing for their intensity, energy, and scorn of corruption.

Guiraut Riquier (circa 1233–1292), "the last troubadour," adhered to the troubadour style after the Albigensian Crusade. Born in Narbonne he moved to Spain in 1270, remaining for ten years at the court of Alfonso X of Castile. He returned to Narbonne under the patronage of Vicomte Amalric IV and lived there for the greater part of his life.

A prolific poet, Guiraut left more poems than any other troubadour, although scholars disagree as to the precise number, there are more than one hundred, forty-eight with melodies. Atypically, his songs seem to have been preserved, grouped, and dated by his own hand. The eighty-nine lyrics in his œuvre include tensos, sirventes, cansos, pastorelas, an alba, and fifteen rhymed epistles. He is best known for a series of six pastorelas in which the same knight and peasant woman engage in a changing repartee during a span of twenty years.

Guiraut's verse reflects the dispersion of troubadour song brought about by the Albigensian Crusade. He laments the scarcity of an audience capable of appreciating what by then was an old tradition. In what would become the new trend, he gives greater prominence to religious themes; his later love songs are addressed to the Virgin Mary.

Before the devastations of the crusade, Occitania was characterized by an openness that made it possible for women to play public and political roles. This social visibility helps explain not only the centrality of women in courtly life and poetry but also the existence of *trobairitz* (literally, "women who compose"; the only medieval usage of the term *trobairitz* is in the thirteenth-century Occitan romance *Flamenca*).

The chansonniers that include their songs do not segregate female poets into a separate or subordinate group; women poets seem to have been integrated into the fabric of twelfth- and thirteenth-century Occitan culture. The lyrics, vidas, and razos use the same adjectives and commonplaces to describe male and female narrators, lovers, and poets. There is no indication that female poets feared rejection or were regarded as anomalous. The tendency to treat the *trobairitz* as a separate subgroup begins in some thirteenth- and fourteenth-century Italian and Catalan manuscripts. Modern scholars include the *trobairitz* as part of a long but disrupted tradition of female authorship.

Of the approximately one hundred poets whose biographies appear in vidas and razos, thirteen are women whose names are given. Five *trobairitz* have vidas of their own, all of them quite short: the Comtessa de Dia, Azalais de Procairagues, Castelloza, Tibors, and Lombarda. Garsenda, Countess of Provence, is mentioned in the vidas of Eliazs de Barjols and Gui de Cavaillon; Clara d'Anduza appears in a razo to one of Uc de Saint-Circ's songs; and Gaudairenca (none of whose work survives) is mentioned in Raimon de Miraval's razo as his poet wife. There are razos for four tensos between female and male narrators.

The number of *trobairitz* is a matter of speculation: estimates vary from fewer than twenty to more than forty, while tallies of the poems they wrote range from twenty-three to forty-nine. In addition there is the presumption that the extant work of known female poets represents only a portion of their actual writings and that there were *trobairitz* whose work has not yet been recovered. Further, few of the scores of anonymous vernacular poems give any hint as to the gender of their author. When a tenso between a man and a woman appears in a manuscript, it is not always clear whether the lady is a living respondent or a fictionalized poetic voice created by the male poet. Some critics assume that when the lady is identified by name in the tenso her authorship is genuine—especially if some record of her existence or her composition of songs can be found. The trobairitz about whom biographical information

can be gleaned from vidas and razos were aristocrats; three were countesses: the Comtessa de Dia; Garsenda, Comtessa de Proensa; and Maria de Ventadorn, the wife of Count Eble V.

Compared with the 2,500 troubadour lyrics that survive, the number of identifiable *trobairitz* poems is minuscule. With the exception of the Comtessa de Dia and Castelloza, each *trobairitz* left a single song; of these, only one has survived with music. The manuscripts that include *trobairitz* lyrics date from the end of the twelfth century and the beginning of the thirteenth, and the songs were probably not composed much earlier.

The *trobairitz* were the first women in western Europe to create, in their own tongue, songs of emotion and desire. They adopted the conventions of the troubadours, composing love poetry for single voices and in dialogues; but there are also examples of the *planh*, the *salut d'amor* (a love letter not in strophic form), and the *balada* (dance song). The *trobairitz* skillfully fashioned a subject for themselves out of a rhetoric that inherently objectified women. In the work of the *trobairitz*, the troubadours' silent *domna* becomes the singer.

The best-known and perhaps earliest *trobairitz* is the Comtessa de Dia (Countess of Die, 1150–1215?). Because there is no historical evidence of a countess of Die who wrote poetry, scholars have not been able to validate such claims as that she was the wife of Guillem de Peiteus and was in love with Raimbaut d'Aurenga; or that she was Beatritz, wife of Count William of Valentinois (1158–1189), a contemporary of Raimbaut's; or that she was Isoarde, daughter of the count of Die and wife of Raimon d'Agout, who lived a generation later than Raimbaut and William. Four or five cansos are attributed to her, two in fragmentary form and two that are preserved in many manuscripts. Her best-known song, "A chantar m'er de so qu'ieu no volria" (I must sing of what I would not), is the only *trobairitz* lyric to survive with music besides a tenso between Giraut de Bornelh and Alamanda; it is preserved in fifteen manuscripts, more than any other *trobairitz* song. The lyric adapts the troubadour convention of the rejected lover to a female viewpoint. In another of her lyrics the countess's narrator expresses openly erotic desires, inviting her beloved to take the place of her husband. She beckons all women who love to sing out. The tenso "Amics, en gran consirier" (Friend, in great distress) between Raimbaut d'Aurenga and an anonymous woman is sometimes considered to have been co-authored by the countess because the initial line of the poem echoes the initial line of her "Estat ai en greu cossirier" (I have been sorely grieved) and because her vida alleges that she fell in love with Raimbaut and wrote cansos about him.

Bertran de Born, Lady Castelloza, Jaufre Rudel, and Marcabru (illuminations from a manuscript, Bibliothèque Nationale de France, f. fr. 12473, fol. 160r, fol. 110v, fol. 107v, fol. 102r)

Azalais of Porcairagues (flourished circa 1173), probably a contemporary of the Comtessa de Dia, composed one poem that survives in eight manuscripts. Her vida says that she was a well-educated noblewoman from Montpellier whose love songs were written for Gui Guerrejat, a cousin of Raimbaut d'Aurenga. Various threads of evidence have led scholars to associate her with Raimbaut's court.

Garsenda de Forcalquier, Comtessa de Proensa, belonged to the powerful southern French family of her grandfather Guilhem IV, the last count of Forcalquier. She became countess of Provence when she married Count Alphonse II in 1193. After his death in 1209 her title and authority were usurped by her brother-in-law Pedro II. Garsenda reclaimed her authority in Aix in 1216 and held it until her son's majority and marriage to Beatrice of Savoy in 1219 or 1220. A patron of troubadours, she is praised by Raimon Vidal and is the object of love and song in the vidas of Eliazs de Barjols and the knight Gui de Cavaillon. An exchange of *coblas* (stanzas) between Garsenda and Gui is preserved in two chansonniers. In 1225 Garsenda took vows at the abbey of La Celle.

Tibors, situated by her vida in Sarenom (Séranon), composed a canso of which only part of one strophe survives in one manuscript. She is also named judge in a tenso between Bertran de Saint-Felix and Uc de la Bacalaria and may have been the "Na Tibortz de Proensa" mentioned in a dansa by Guiraut d'Espanha. Tibors may have been Raimbaut d'Aurenga's mother or sister; if she was related to Raimbaut she would have lived in the second half of the twelfth century, making her one of the earliest of the *trobairitz.*

Maria de Ventadorn (died 1226?) was the daughter of Raimon II of Torena (circa 1143–1191) and the second wife of Eble V, Count of Ventadorn. Maria's beauty is praised by Bertran de Born, and her name appears in Gaucelm Faidit's razo as his unrequited love. She debated with Gui d'Uisel in a tenso preserved in nine manuscripts. The Ventadorn court's long association with the troubadours continued with Maria, who patronized Gaucelm and many other poets. No named lady receives as much praise in the extant troubadour corpus as Maria. She is said to have entered the monastery of Grandmont with her husband in 1221.

Clara d'Anduza, who lived in the early thirteenth century, is credited as the author of the lyric "En greu esmay et en greu pessamen" (In grave distress and in grave trouble), which survives in one manuscript. She may have been of the house of Anduza, a court known for patronizing troubadours. She plays a large role in a lengthy razo for a canso of Uc de Saint Circ, who is known to have performed at Anduza.

Gaudairenca is mentioned in two razos as the beautiful wife of the troubadour Raimon de Miraval and as a woman who knew how to compose coblas and dansas, none of which has survived. Possibly from Auvergne, another *trobairitz,* Castelloza, was the wife of Turc de Mairona. She may have been associated with the court of Dalfin d'Alvernha, Count of Clermont (circa 1155–1235?), because her husband is named in the count's sirventes. Three or four songs can be attributed to her. Lombarda, who, according to her vida, came from Toulouse, wrote an exchange with Bernart Arnaut, Count of Armagnac, in the *trobar clus* style; the stanzas are preserved in one manuscript, along with a miniature.

Gormonda de Monpeslier (Montpellier) wrote on political and religious matters. One sirventes she presumably composed in 1229, toward the end of the Albigensian Crusade, is a response to Guilhem Figuerias's sirventes against Rome and the Pope (circa 1228) in which she vigorously defends church orthodoxy and wishes misfortune on the inhabitants of Toulouse. The poem reflects the political and spiritual crisis of Occitania in the aftermath of the Albigensian Crusade.

Azalais d'Altier, an early-thirteenth-century *trobairitz,* identifies herself as the author of a *salut d'amor,* an epistolary love poem to someone named Clara, possibly Clara d'Anduza, in which she intercedes on behalf of a lover who has quarreled with his lady. Azalais is addressed in the tornada of a canso by Uc de Saint-Circ, which may have been a response to her *salut.*

The *trobairitz* dared to speak on behalf of the silent lady. Recent scholarship has shed light not only on their individual talents but also on how particular poets demonstrated a consciousness of their place as women in the game of *fin'amor.* Their voices range from confident and assertive to combative and subversive of the social and linguistic structures that constrained them. Whatever genre they took up, the *trobairitz* engaged in dialogue with their fellow poets, displaying mastery of troubadour conventions.

Why the songs of the *trobairitz* emerged has been a subject of speculation. Historical circumstances seem to have been favorable to noblewomen during the period known as "the golden interlude" (circa 1180–1230) in southern France: women of aristocratic birth held a relatively privileged position, and there was a high degree of literacy among them; men were absent from their fiefdoms during crusades; women's property holdings were extensive; and inheritance laws worked in women's interests. These advantages may have encouraged noblewomen to provide the vocal counterpoint to the troubadours' mute female. It is also possible that the *trobairitz* sang out in reaction to the increasing constraints on Occitan women as their strong political and social positions began to erode.

Traveling troubadours, pilgrims, and crusaders brought the troubadour poetry to the attention of northern French courts, where it was taken up by northern poets, called trouvères, from about 1150. Eleanor of Aquitaine most likely brought north with her the troubadour sensibilities that had been cultivated in Aquitaine. By the end of the twelfth century Eleanor's daughter Marie, Countess of Champagne, had formed a brilliant court at Troyes that attracted the finest poets, including the troubadour Bernart de Ventadorn and the trouvères Gace Brulé and Thibaut de Champagne. Andreas Capallanus, author of the enigmatic *De amore* (On Love, circa 1185), and the master poet Chrétien de Troyes, who introduced Lancelot, Perceval, and the Holy Grail in his famed Arthurian romances, flourished under Marie's patronage.

The northern French had long had a lively tradition of popular song, including *chansons de toile* (sewing or spinning songs), *reverdies* (spring dances), and *chansons de la malmariée* (songs of the unhappily married woman). Although the emphasis on everyday life was a mainstay of northern French literature from its earliest songs through the fifteenth-century poetry of François Villon, by the second half of the twelfth century trouvères began imitating the formal court poetry of the troubadours. After the Albigensian Crusade stifled troubadour song in the south the trouvères became the dominant lyric artists.

The trouvères adopted the troubadour cast of characters and the theme of the suffering unrequited lover. But their emulation of the troubadours was limited: they refrained from addressing a specific audience in their songs and from striking the recognizable performative gestures of their models; instead, they adapted the precourtly chansons de toile, chansons de la malmariée, reverdies, and rondeaux to the more formal structures invented by the troubadours. They showed no interest in the *trobar clus* style; their *grand chant courtois* (great courtly song), although analogous to the troubadour canso, is more reserved, less explicit. Absent is the spirituality of troubadour verse and its mysticism of love; the trouvères replaced the troubadours' idealizing overtones, the metaphysical and transcendent aspects of *fin'amor,* with worldliness. Because trouvère poetry was self-enclosed, removed from the context of the court, the troubadour's dialogue with the courtly audience became the trouvère's exploration of his inner life or of language itself.

Northern poets preferred the narrative and dialogic genres relating amorous adventures, turning primarily to the *pastourelle* (short narrative poem that is equivalent to the Occitan *pastorela*) and *jeu parti* (debate

on love between two poets). Many trouvère songs had refrains. Crusade songs were particularly favored among the trouvères, who divided them into subgenres. Inventive and graceful melodies were the trouvères' strength, and most of the approximately 2,100 trouvère songs are preserved with their melodies–many more than for the troubadours. The overall poetic production of the northern and southern poets was roughly equal, but the names of about 450 troubadours are known whereas the names of only about 200 trouvères survive. Furthermore, compilers of trouvère manuscripts wrote no vidas or razos.

Gace Brulé (flourished 1159–1213), a nobleman, probably from Champagne, belonged to an elite poetic circle patronized by Louis VIII, Blanche of Castille, and Marie de Champagne and was welcomed, as well, at the courts of Blois and Brittany. He seems to have had contact with the highest French nobility. Like some of his fellow poets, he may have participated in the Third and Fourth Crusades. More than eighty poems are attributed to him, more than to any other trouvère, and most of their melodies are preserved. The many copies of his poems and the place of prominence they are given in chansonniers demonstrate his wide popularity. In such a large corpus Gace's homogeneity is the more striking: his songs, with the exception of three, are all chansons modeled on the troubadour canso; they incorporate the suffering lover, the unresponsive lady, and the jealous husband; they are filled with the same detractors who make up the audience of troubadour verse; and they involve the theme of a lover's submission to love and his acceptance of the inevitable torments of passion even in the absence of requital. Gace also imitated troubadour techniques, especially those of Jaufré Rudel, Gaucelm Faidit, and Bernart de Ventadorn.

In mastering and reshaping troubadour song Gace was a model for other poets. Strophes of his lyrics were incorporated into four thirteenth-century romances as well as into the verse of the thirteenth-century trouvères Guillaume le Vinier and Oede de la Couroierie and into Jehan Renart's *Guillaume de Dole.* German minnesingers used Gace's lyrics as thematic and formal models. Dante cites him in *De Vulgari eloquentia* as one of the *cantiones illustres* (exalted singers).

Guy, Chastelain de Couci (died 1203), was castle governor and regional justice of Coucy in Vermandois, southern Picardy, one of the most powerful and well-known castellanies. Guy's death at sea during the Fourth Crusade is the subject of a thirteenth-century romance in which his heart is fed to his beloved by her jealous husband; the work increased his fame measurably. Nine of his songs survive.

Modeling his lyrics on troubadour themes Guy also experimented with rhyme schemes and strophic orders. Of the many crusade farewell poems composed by trouvères, Guy's "A vous, amant" (To you, beloved) displays unparalleled stylistic sophistication and penetrating insight. His love songs are renowned, as well.

Conon de Béthune (circa 1150–1219), a nobleman from Artois, served as a negotiator in the Third and Fourth Crusades. He was related to the first French emperor of Constantinople, Baudouin IX; in 1219 he became regent of Constantinople, where he died. Composing in the troubadour mode, Conon de Béthune took up a variety of styles. His adroit, vivacious, linguistically playful, and often witty lyrics demonstrate that he had a fine sense of colloquial dialogue and a talent for playing on the themes of more straightforward love songs. His songs, of which only twelve survive, were highly regarded during his lifetime and continue to be so.

Colin Muset (flourished 1230) was probably born around 1210 in humble circumstances. He sings knowingly of the vicissitudes of the jongleur's profession, denouncing stingy patrons and praising generous ones. His overriding theme is the good life, a popular subject with trouvères. His twenty-one songs, seven with melodies, gave him the reputation of being one of the most innovative trouvères.

Richard Cœur-de-Lion (1157–1199; known in English as Richard the Lionhearted) was king of England from 1189 to 1199 but spent only six months there during his reign. He composed a small number of lyrics. The son of Henry II of England and Eleanor of Acquitane, he was active in many martial exploits and played a dramatic role in the Third Crusade. While returning home from the Crusade, he was taken captive by King Leopold of Austria and imprisoned from 1192 to 1194 in a castle at Dürrenstein, where he was held hostage until the enormous sum of two hundred thousand silver marks was paid. While imprisoned, he composed songs. Upon being ransomed from King Leopold, Richard returned to rule England for a brief time, but soon left to pursue a military campaign on the Continent. He was killed during a minor raid on a French castle at Chalus.

Although his own contribution to poetry was minor, Richard I was idealized for his courage by several troubadours in their verse and glorified for his exploits as leader of the Third Crusade in the anonymous metrical romance *Richard Cœur de Lion* (circa 1300). Later British writers such as Sir Walter Scott and Maurice Hewlett also celebrated Richard's heroism, but in reality Richard neglected his responsibilities and impoverished his country by indulging in his taste for warfare. Richard's long imprisonment in Austria, during which he composed songs, led to the legend that connected his name to that of Blondel de Nesle.

Blondel de Nesle (died 1241) may have been Jean II, Lord of Nesle (near Amiens). He participated in the Fourth Crusade in 1202 and in the Albigensian Crusade in 1209 and 1226. Twenty-four of his songs survive. A story (probably apocryphal) circulated about Blondel: when Richard Cœur de Lion was imprisoned by King Leopold of Austria in the castle at Dürrenstein, Blondel, a minstrel in his retinue, loyally sought for him for a year and a half. Recognizing the voice of the imprisoned Richard singing a song they had composed together, Blondel returned to England, gathered the huge ransom, and delivered Richard.

Thibaut de Champagne (1201–1253) was the fourth count of Champagne and Brie and king of Navarre. The grandson of Marie de Champagne, the great-grandson of Eleanor of Aquitaine and Louis VII, and a direct descendent of Guillem de Peiteus, he inherited his kingdom through his mother, Blanche de Navarre, in 1234. He fought against the English with Louis VIII and led an unsuccessful crusade in 1239–1240. He is said to have been generous to his nobles, but he lacked skill as a politician and was unpopular among his people. Sordello castigates Thibaut in a lament for Blacatz.

Thibaut inherited poetic gifts as well as property. This subtle poet purportedly sent many poems to Blanche of Castile, whom he was rumored to love. In fact, however, Thibaut participated in a revolt against Blanche on the death of her husband, Louis VIII, in 1226. Blanche forced the rebels to capitulate in 1236, bringing Champagne under the control of the French crown. Thibaut's capitulation was reported in a contemporary chronicle as a lover's submission to his lady. A late-thirteenth-century literary legend had it that Thibaut took up music to overcome the sorrow engendered by his love for Blanche.

Troubadour influence can be felt in Thibaut's strophic forms, vocabulary, singer's postures, cast of characters, and celebration of love as a refined and elite experience. The variety of voices, roles, and genres in his corpus is great. Thibaut is the only trouvère Dante singles out for praise in *De Vulgari eloquentia*. About sixty of his works survive, almost all with music.

Rutebeuf (circa 1230–circa 1285), a jongleur from Champagne, left more than fifty works. Northern France's moralist, Rutebeuf stands out for his vigorous outspokenness. His work centers on two political and intellectual quarrels of the day: the crusades and the conflict between the mendicant orders and the secular masters at the University of Paris in the 1250s. In his *dits* (narrative poems, spoken rather than sung) he caricatures himself, depicting his life and those of his com-

Page from a manuscript chansonnier, *or collection of songs (Paris, Bibliothèque de l'Arsenal, f. 5198, f.1,)*

panions as consisting equally of revelry and misery. Despite its serious themes his work is full of jokes, wordplay, and fantastic etymologies.

The last trouvères began compositional practices that gradually unraveled the synthesis of text and music on which courtly lyricism had been based. Adam de la Halle (or Adam le Bossu, "the Hunchback," circa 1237–1288) is considered one of the greatest musicians of his time; he was the first important trouvère to compose polyphonic music. Residing in Arras, the poetic center north of Paris, he was a prominent member of the *puy* (poetry competition) there. He joined the retinue of the count of Artois, traveling to Naples after 1282. He was much esteemed in the court of Charles of Anjou, the king of Naples and Sicily, and may have died in Italy. It is for his plays, considered monuments of French drama, that he is best known, but he also left a corpus of almost one hundred poems that include almost all the genres of his time.

From the time of Guillem de Peiteus to that of the "last troubadour," Guiraut Riquier, the troubadours and *trobairitz* engaged in a dialogue with allied and rival poets as they shaped their verse forms, artistic preoccupations, moral creeds, and stances on love and politics. To demonstrate virtuosity a poet would adapt a rival's patterns while stamping his or her own work with an idiosyncratic hallmark or creating a stage persona that distinguished him or her from the crowd. Poets congregated in castles and courts, debating questions of love and poetry and satirizing, parodying, and mimicking one another. Thus, the strong sense of self that emerges from many troubadour lyrics arose through the interplay between the singer's skill at alluding to the work of peers and his or her proclaiming of stylistic originality. This intertextual dynamic explains some of the difficulty in interpreting troubadour art: it was an insider's game.

Troubadour culture could not survive the Albigensian Crusade intact. But the tradition may have been destined to play itself out for other reasons as well. The sense of solidarity called "courtliness" had been fostered by the intimate setting, the shared values of the audience, and the purpose of class self-congratulation. Deprived of their courtly context, poets began to focus on more-universal celebrations of love and to make broader experiments with language and technique, examining the possibilities inherent in language itself.

Unlike the troubadours, whose patronage came from the courts, the trouvères belonged to the literary milieu of the rich commercial towns of northern France—especially Arras in Picardy, which became a thriving cultural center at the end of the twelfth century. The shift of poetic activity to cities pushed lyric in new directions. Literary societies that organized *puys*

appeared during the thirteenth century. The most illustrious, the *Puy* of Arras, was associated with the *Confrérie des jongleurs et bourgeois d'Arras* (Brotherhood of Performers and Burghers of Arras) and was dominated by the town's great commercial families. These urban poets, who were as likely to be clerks as burghers, continued to compose the *grand chant courtoise* but preferred racy, comic, dramatic, and more-sensational genres that formed a counterbalance to courtliness.

Troubadour song began to infiltrate areas other than northern France not long after it began. A German *minnesang* tradition indebted to the troubadours flourished. Troubadour song was a major source for Alfonso the Wise (1221–1284) in Spain, as he acknowledges in his *Cantigas* (Songs) to the Virgin Mary. In Castile, Portugal, Sicily, and Tuscany the troubadour tradition was modulated to suit local habits, and regional languages were rapidly substituted for Occitan. For these literary descendants the essential troubadour element remained: the new conception of love and the language of erotic desire.

The history of this influence is especially rich in Italy. Although the court of Boniface I of Montferrat became the Italian center of troubadour poetry, the movement also infiltrated Italy through the "Sicilian school," leading to the formation of a cadre of philosopher-poets who practiced what is known as the *dolce stil nuovo* (sweet new style). Dante and the Italian poets of his generation admired troubadour song and kept it alive by composing their own songs in Occitan. One of the earliest and most significant studies of troubadour art, Dante's *De vulgari eloquentia,* was written more than a century after the compositions it cites; Dante's observations influenced literary critics for more than seven centuries. The first linguistic analysis of the Romance languages, Dante's treatise explored the naturalness, vitality, and poetic potential of the vernacular. Dante designated the troubadours *eloquentes doctores* (masters of doctrine and language), singling out seven of them as having special merit: Thibaut de Champagne, Peire d'Alvernhe, Guiraut de Bornelh, Arnaut Daniel, Folquet de Marseille, Aimeric de Belenoi, and Aimeric de Pegulhen. Although written in Latin, *De vulgari eloquentia* not only promoted the use of the vernacular but also asserted its superiority to Latin as a primary poetic language. The troubadours served as Dante's justification for his use of Italian in his own poetry.

More than 2,500 troubadour songs survive in chansonniers. These manuscripts monumentalized the troubadours, their songs, and their compositional practices, contextualizing the poetry and creating retroactive biographies that explain the poems. As a result, the *vidas* and *razos* provide more insight into the reception of the poetry at the end of the thirteenth century than into the poetry itself. While the interest in autobiographical anecdote seems remote from the idealizing tendency of the troubadours themselves, it coincides with the thirteenth-century impulse toward organizing information and knowledge.

As the chansonniers reveal a shift of emphasis from idealization to summation, and the vidas and razos demonstrate a shift from the figurative play of poetry toward the gathering of biographical and other ancillary contexts, so, too, the proliferation of manuals of arts of composition, often called "handbooks of love," manifests the attempt on the part of poets less familiar with the courtly lyric tradition to understand, preserve, or re-create *trobar* by codifying and analyzing it and prescribing poetic techniques. The existence of such handbooks reveals that the heyday of the art itself had passed.

Biographies–Vidas and Razos:

Camille Chabaneau, *Les biographies des troubadours en langue provençale* (Toulouse: Privat, 1885; Geneva: Slatkine Reprints, 1975); Jean Boutiere and A. H. Schultz, *Biographies des troubadours: Textes provençaux des XIIIe et XIVe siècles* (Toulouse: Privat, 1950; New York: Franklin, 1972);

J. H. Marshall, ed., *The Razos de trobar of Raimon Vidal and Associated Texts* (Oxford: Oxford University Press, 1972);

Margarita Egan, *The Vidas of the Troubadours* (New York & London: Garland, 1984);

William Burgwinkle, *Razos and Troubadour Songs* (New York: Garland, 1990).

Bibliographies–Troubadours and *Trobairitz:*

Alfred Jeanroy, *Bibliographie sommaire des chansonniers provençaux (manuscrits et éditions),* Les classiques français du moyen âge no. 16 (Paris: H. Champion, 1916; reprinted, 1981);

Joseph Anglade, *Bibliographie élémentaire de l'ancien provençal* (Barcelona: Institut Estudis Catalans, 1921);

Alfred Pillet and Henry Carstens, *Bibliographie der Troubadours* (Halle: Niemeyer, 1933);

Clovis Brunel, *Bibliographie des manuscrits littéraires en ancien provençal* (Paris: Droz, 1935);

Jean Beck, *Les Chansonniers des troubadours I,* Corpus Cantilenarum Medii Aevi, Series 1, no. 1 (Philadelphia: University of Pennsylvania Press, 1938);

Robert Bossuat, *Manuel bibliographique de la littérature française du moyen âge* (Melun: Librarie d'Argences, 1951);

Robert Taylor, *La Littérature occitane du moyen âge: Bibliographie sélective et critique* (Toronto: University of Toronto Press, 1977).

Bibliographies–Trouvères:

Gaston Raynaud, *Bibliographie des chansonniers français des XIIIe et XIVe siècles,* 2 volumes (Paris: Viewig, 1884);

Alfred Jeanroy, *Bibliographie sommaire des chansonniers français du moyen âge (manuscrits et éditions),* Les classiques français du moyen âge no. 18 (Paris: H. Champion, 1918; reprinted, 1965);

Frank Gennrich, "Die beiden neuesten Bibliographien altfranzösischer und altprovenzalischer Lieder," *Zeitschrift für romanische Philologie,* 61 (1921): 289–346;

Hans Spanke, *G. Raynauds Bibliographie des altfranzösischen Liedes* (Leiden, The Netherlands: E. J. Brill, 1955);

Larry S. Crist and Roger J. Steiner, "Musica Verbis Concordet: Medieval French Lyric Poems with their Music (A Discography)," *Mediaevalia,* 1, no. 2 (1975): 35–61;

Robert White Linker, *A Bibliography of Old French Lyrics,* Romance Monographs no. 31 (University, Miss.: Romance Classics, 1979).

References:

F. R. P. Akehurst and Judith M. Davis, eds., *A Handbook of the Troubadours* (Berkeley: University of California Press, 1995);

Pierre Aubrey, *Trouvères et Troubadours* (Raphèle-les-Arles: Marcel Petit, 1980);

Aubrey and Alfred Jeanroy, *Le Chansonnier de l'Arsenal trouvères du XIIe–XIIIe siècles* (Paris: Geuthner, 1911);

Pierre Bec, ed., *La lyrique française au moyen âge (XIIe–XIIIe siècles),* 2 volumes (Paris: Picard, 1977, 1978);

Anne Callahan, "The Trobairitz," in *French Women Writers: A Bio-Bibliographical Source Book,* edited by Eva Martin Sartori and Dorothy Wynne Zimmerman (New York: Greenwood Press, 1991);

Jeanne Faure-Cousin, *Les Femmes troubadours* (Paris: Denoël/Gonthier, 1978);

Istaván Frank, *Répertoire métrique de la poésie des troubadours,* 2 volumes (Paris: H. Champion, 1953, 1957);

Frederick Goldin, ed., *Lyrics of the Troubadours and Trouvères: An Anthology and a History* (New York: Doubleday, 1973);

Alfred Jeanroy, *La Poésie lyrique des troubadours,* 2 volumes (Paris: Privat, 1934);

Guilhem Molinier, *Las Flors del Gay Saber, estiers dichas Las Leys d'Amors,* 3 volumes, edited and translated by Adolphe-Félix Gatien-Arnoult and others (1841–1843; reprinted, Geneva: Slatkine, 1977);

Ulrich Mölk and Friedrich Wolfzettel, *Repertoire métrique de la poésie lyrique française des origines à 1350* (Munich: Fink, 1972);

William D. Paden, ed., *The Medieval Pastourelle* (New York: Garland, 1987);

Linda M. Paterson, *The World of the Troubadours: Medieval Occitan Society c. 1100 – c. 1300* (Cambridge: Cambridge University Press, 1993);

Dietmar Rieger, ed., *La chanson française et son histoire* (Tübingen: Gunter Narr, 1987);

Claude Riot, *Chants et instruments: Trouvères et jongleurs au Moyen Age* (Paris: R.E.M.P.A.R.T., Desclée de Brouwer, 1995);

Samuel N. Rosenberg, ed., *Chanter M'Estuet: Songs of the Trouvères,* music edited by Hans Tischler (Bloomington: Indiana University Press, 1981);

E. Schawan, *Die altfranzösischen Liederhandschriften, ihre Verhältnis, ihre Entstehung und ihre Bestimmung* (Berlin: Weidmann, 1886);

Margaret Louise Switten, *The Cansos of Raimon de Miraval: A Study of Poems and Melodies* (Cambridge, Mass.: Medieval Academy of America, 1985);

Switten and others, *The Medieval Lyric, Anthology I: Monastic Song, Troubadour Song, German Song, Trouvère Song,* revised edition (South Hadley, Mass.: Mount Holyoke College, 1989);

Jules Veran, *Les Poétesses provençales du Moyen Age* (Paris: Quillet, 1946);

Katarina M. Wilson, ed., *Medieval Women Writers* (Athens: University of Georgia Press, 1984);

Paul Zumthor, *La Poésie et la voix dans la civilisation médiévale* (Paris: Klincksieck, 1963).

Books for Further Reading

Auerbach, Erich. *Literary Language and Its Public in Late Latin Antiquity and in the Middle Ages,* translated by Ralph Manheim. Princeton: Princeton University Press, 1993.

Auerbach. *Mimesis: The Representation of Reality in Western Literature,* translated by Willard R. Trask. Princeton: Princeton University Press, 1953.

Bec, Pierre. *La Langue occitane,* third edition. Paris: Presses Universitaires de France, 1973.

Bec. *La Lyrique française au moyen âge (XIIe-XIIIe siècles): contribution à une typologie des genres poétiques médiévaux: études et textes,* 2 volumes. Paris: Picard, 1977, 1978.

Bec. *Manuel pratique de philologie romane,* 2 volumes. Paris: Picard, 1973.

Beer, Jeanette M. A. *Early Prose in France: Contexts of Bilingualism and Authority.* Kalamazoo, Mich.: Medieval Institute Publications, 1992.

Beer, *Villehardouin: Epic historian.* Geneva: Droz, 1968.

Bezzola, Reto R. *Les Origines et la formation de la littérature courtoise en occident: (500–1200),* 5 volumes. Paris: H. Champion, 1958–1967.

Bezzola. *Le Sens de l'aventure et de l'amour Chrétien de Troyes.* Paris: La Jeune Parque, 1947.

Bloch, Marc. *Feudal Society,* 2 volumes, translated by L.A. Manyon. Chicago: University of Chicago Press, 1961.

Bloch, R. Howard. *Etymologies and Genealogies: A Literary Anthropology of the French Middle Ages.* Chicago: University of Chicago Press, 1983.

Bloch. *Medieval French Literature and Law.* Berkeley: University of California Press, 1977.

Bloch. *Medieval Misogyny and the Invention of Western Romantic Love.* Chicago: University of Chicago Press, 1991.

Bloch and Frances Ferguson, eds. *Misogyny, Misandry and Misanthropy.* Berkeley: University of California Press, 1989.

Bloch and Stephen G. Nichols, eds. *Medievalism and the Modernist Temper.* Baltimore: Johns Hopkins University Press, 1995.

Blumenfeld-Kosinski, Renate. *Reading Myth: Classical Mythology and Its Interpretations in Medieval French Literature.* Stanford, Cal.: Stanford University Press, 1997.

Bornstein, Diane, ed. *Ideals for Women in the Works of Christine de Pizan.* Detroit: Consortium for Medieval and Early Modern Studies, 1981.

Brownlee, Kevin. *Poetic Identity in Guillaume de Machaut.* Madison: University of Wisconsin Press, 1984.

Brownlee, Kevin, and Marina Scordilis Brownlee, eds. *Romance: Generic Transformation from Chrétien de Troyes to Cervantes.* Hanover, N.H.: University Press of New England, 1985.

Brownlee, Marina, Kevin Brownlee, and Stephen G. Nichols, eds. *The New Medievalism.* Baltimore & London: Johns Hopkins University Press, 1991.

Brownlee, Kevin, and Stephen G. Nichols, eds. *Images of Power: Medieval History/Discourse/Literature.* New Haven: Yale University Press, 1986.

Brownlee Kevin, and Sylvia Huot, eds. *Rethinking the Romance of the Rose: Text, Image, Reception.* Philadelphia: University of Pennsylvania Press, 1992.

Bruckner, Matilda Tomaryn. *Narrative Invention in Twelfth-Century French Romance: The Convention of Hospitality, 1160–1200.* Lexington, Ky.: French Forum, 1980.

Bruckner. *Shaping Romance: Interpretation, Truth, and Closure in Twelfth-Century French Fictions.* Philadelphia: University of Pennsylvania Press, 1993.

Bruckner, Laurie Shepard, and Sarah White, eds. *Songs of the Women Troubadours.* New York: Garland, 1995.

Burns, E. Jane. *Arthurian Fictions: Rereading the Vulgate Cycle.* Columbus: Ohio State University Press, 1985.

Burns. *Bodytalk: When Women Speak in Old French Literature.* Philadelphia: University of Pennsylvania Press, 1993.

Busby, Keith. *Gauvain in Old French Literature.* Amsterdam: Rodopi, 1980.

Calin, William. *A Poet at the Fountain: Essays on the Narrative Verse of Guillaume de Machaut.* Lexington: University Press of Kentucky, 1974.

Calin. *In Defense of Poetry: An Essay in Revaluation.* University Park, Pa.: Pennsylvania State University Press, 1987.

Calin. *The French Tradition and the Literature of Medieval England.* Toronto: University of Toronto Press, 1994.

Cazal, Yvonne. *Les voix du peuple / Verbum Dei: le bilingisme Latin / Langue vernaculaire au Moyen Age.* Geneva: Droz, 1998.

Cazelles, Brigitte. *The Unholy Grail: A Social Reading of Chrétien de Troyes Conte du Graal.* Stanford, Cal.: Stanford University Press, 1996.

Cerquiglini-Toulet, Jacqueline. *The Color of Melancholy: The Uses of Books in the Fourteenth Century,* translated by Lydia B. Cochrane. Baltimore: Johns Hopkins University Press, 1997.

Chaytor, Henry John. *From Script to Print: An Introduction to Medieval Vernacular Literature.* Cambridge: Cambridge University Press, 1945.

Cook, Thomas, ed. *The Present State of Scholarship in Fourteenth-Century Literature.* Columbia: University of Missouri Press, 1982.

Cornilliat, François, Ullrich Langer, and Douglas Kelly, eds. *What is Literature?: France, 1100–1600.* Lexington, Ky.: French Forum, 1993.

Cosman, Madeleine Pelner. *Fabulous Feasts: Medieval Cookery and Ceremony.* New York: G. Braziller, 1976.

Cosman, and Bruce Chandler, eds. *Machaut's World: Science and Art in the Fourteenth Century.* New York: New York Academy of Sciences, 1978.

Curtius, Ernst Robert. *European Literature and the Latin Middle Ages,* translated by Willard R. Trask. Princeton: Princeton University Press, 1953.

DeJean, Joan, and Nancy K. Miller, eds. *Displacements: Women, Tradition, Literatures in France.* Baltimore: Johns Hopkins University Press, 1991.

Dronke, Peter. *Medieval Latin Literature and the Rise of the European Love-Lyric,* second edition, 2 volumes. London & Oxford: Clarendon Press, 1968.

Dronke. *The Medieval Lyric.* London: Hutchison, 1968.

Dronke. *Abelard and Heloise in Medieval Testimonies.* Glasgow: University of Glasgow Press, 1976.

Duby, Georges, ed. *A History of Private Life: Revelations of the Medieval World,* translated by Arthur Goldhammer. Cambridge, Mass.: Harvard University Press, 1988.

Duby. *The Knight, the Lady, and the Priest: The Making of Modern Marriage in Medieval France,* translated by Barbara Bray. Chicago: University of Chicago Press, 1993.

Duby. *Love and Marriage in the Middle Ages,* translated by Jane Dunnett. Chicago: University of Chicago Press, 1996.

Duby. *Medieval Marriage: Two Models from Twelfth-Century France,* translated by Elborg Forster. Baltimore: Johns Hopkins University Press, 1991.

Duby. *France in the Middle Ages 987–1460: From Hugh Capet to Joan of Arc,* translated by Juliet Vale. Oxford: Blackwell, 1993.

Duby. *The Age of Cathedrals: Art and Society, 980–1420,* translated by Eleanor Levieux and Barbara Thompson. Chicago: University of Chicago Press, 1981.

Duby. *The Three Orders: Feudal Society Imagined,* translated by Arthur Goldhammer. Chicago: University of Chicago Press, 1980.

Duggan, Joseph J. *The Song of Roland: Formulaic Style and Poetic Craft.* Berkeley: University of California Press, 1973.

Economou, George. *The Goddess Natura in Medieval Literature.* Cambridge, Mass.: Harvard University Press, 1972.

Famiglietti, Richard C. *Tales of the Marriage Bed from Medieval France (1300–1500).* Providence, R.I.: Picardy, 1992.

Faral, Edmond. *Les Arts poétiques de XIIe et XIIIe siècles.* Paris: H. Champion, 1958.

Faral. *La Vie quotidienne au temps de Saint Louis.* Geneva: Famot, 1978.

Fauçon, J. Claude, Alain Labbe, and Danielle Queruel, eds. *Miscellanea Mediaevalia: Melanges offerts à Philippe Menard.* Paris: H. Champion, 1998.

Ferrante, Joan M. *The Conflict of Love and Honor: The Medieval Tristan Legend in France, Germany and Italy.* The Hague & Paris: Mouton, 1973.

Ferrante. *Woman as Image in Medieval Literature from the Twelfth Century to Dante.* New York: Columbia University Press, 1975.

Ferrante, Economou, and Frederick Goldin, eds. *In Pursuit of Perfection: Courtly Love in Medieval Literature.* Port Washington, N.Y.: Kennikat Press, 1975.

Flutre, Louis-Ferdinand. *Table des noms propres avec toutes leurs variantes, figurant dans les romans de Moyen Age écrits en français ou en provençal et actuellement publiés ou analysés.* Poiters: Centre d'Etudes Supérieurs de Civilisation Médiévale, 1962.

Galley, Michèle, and Christiane Marchello-Nizia. *Littératures de l'Europe médiévales.* Paris: Magnard, 1985.

Godefroy, Frederic, ed. *Dictionnaire de l'ancienne langue française et de tous ses dialectes du IXe au XVe siècle,* 10 volumes. Paris: Vieweg, 1881–1902.

Goldin, Frederick. *The Mirror of Narcissus in the Courtly Love Lyric.* Ithaca, N.Y.: Cornell University Press, 1967.

Gravdal, Kathryn. *Ravishing Maidens: Writing Rape in Medieval French Literature and Law.* Philadelphia: University of Pennsylvania Press, 1991.

Gravdal. *Vilain and Courtois: Transgressive Parody in French Literature of the Twelfth and Thirteenth Centuries.* Lincoln: University of Nebraska Press, 1989.

Gurevich, Aron. *Medieval Popular Culture: Problems of Belief and Perception,* translated by János M. Bak and Paul A. Hollingsworth. Cambridge & New York: Cambridge University Press, 1988.

Haidu, Peter. *The Subject of Violence: The Song of Roland and the Birth of the State.* Bloomington: Indiana University Press, 1993.

Hanning, Robert W. *The Individual in Twelfth-Century Romance.* New Haven: Yale University Press, 1977.

Hasenohr, Geneviève, and Michel Zink, eds. *Dictionnaire des lettres françaises: le moyen âge.* Paris: Livres de Poche, 1992.

Hoppin, Richard. *Medieval Music.* New York: Norton, 1978.

Huizinga, Johan. *The Autumn of the Middle Ages,* translated by Rodney J. Payton and Ulrich Mammitzsch. Chicago: University of Chicago Press, 1996.

Huizinga. *The Waning of the Middle Ages: A Study of the Forms of Life, Thought, and Art in France and the Netherlands in the XIVth and XVth Centuries.* New York: St. Martin's Press, 1985.

Huot, Sylvia. *Allegorical Play in the Old French Motet: The Sacred and the Profane in Thirteenth-Century Polyphony.* Stanford, Cal.: Stanford University Press, 1997.

Huot. *The Romance of the Rose and Its Medieval Readers: Interpretation, Reception, Manuscript Transmission.* Cambridge & New York: Cambridge University Press, 1993.

Jackson, W. T. H. *The Interpretation of Medieval Lyric Poetry.* New York: Columbia University Press, 1980.

Jackson. *The Challenge of the Medieval Text: Studies in Genre and Interpretation,* edited by Joan Ferrante and Robert W. Hanning. New York: Columbia University Press, 1985.

Jeanroy, Alfred. *Les Origines de la poésie lyrique en France au moyen âge.* Paris: H. Champion, 1965.

Kay, Sarah. *The Chansons de Geste in the Age of Romance: Political Fictions.* Oxford & New York: Clarendon Press, 1995.

Kay. *Subjectivity in Troubadour Poetry.* Cambridge & New York: Cambridge University Press, 1990.

Keene, Maurice. *Chivalry.* New Haven & London: Yale University Press, 1984.

Kelly, Douglas. *The Art of Medieval French Romance*. Madison: University of Wisconsin Press, 1992.

Kelly. *The Arts of Poetry and Prose*. Turnhout, Belgium: Brepols, 1991.

Kelly. *Internal Difference and Meanings in the Roman de la Rose*. Madison & London: University of Wisconsin Press, 1995.

Kelly. *Medieval Imagination: Rhetoric and Poetry of Courtly Love*. Madison: University of Wisconsin Press, 1978.

Kelly. *Medieval French Romance*. New York: Twayne / Toronto: Maxwell Macmillan, 1993.

Kelly. *Sens and Conjointure in the Chevalier de la Charrette*. The Hague: Mouton, 1966.

Kendrick, Laura. *The Game of Love: Troubadour Word Play*. Berkeley: University of California Press, 1988.

Kieckhefer, Richard. *Magic in the Middle Ages*. Cambridge & New York: Cambridge University Press, 1989.

Koopmans, Jelle. *Le théâtre des exclus au Moyen Age: Heretiques, sorcières, et marginaux*. Paris: Editions Imago, 1997.

Lacy, Norris J., Douglas Kelly, and Keith Busby, eds. *The Legacy of Chrétien de Troyes*. Amsterdam: Rodopi, 1987.

Lacy, ed. *The Comic Spirit in Medieval France*. Lawrence, Kans.: L'Esprit Createur, 1976.

Lacy. *The Craft of Chrétien de Troyes: An Essay on Narrative Art*. Leiden: E. J. Brill, 1980.

Lazar, Moshe, and Norris J. Lacy, eds. *Poetics of Love in the Middle Ages: Texts and Contexts*. Fairfax, Va. & London: George Mason University Press, 1989.

Le Goff, Jacques. *The Medieval Imagination,* translated by Arthur Goldhammer. Chicago: University of Chicago Press, 1992.

Leupin, Alexandre. *Barbarolexis: Medieval Writing and Sexuality,* translated by Kate M. Cooper. Cambridge, Mass.: Harvard University Press, 1989.

Lote, Georges. *Histoire du vers français. Ouvrage publié avec le concours du Centre nationale de la recherche scientifique,* 9 volumes; volumes 5–9 edited by Joelle Tamine-Gardes and Lucien Victor: Paris: Boivin, 1940–1949.

Maddox, Donald. *The Arthurian Romances of Chrétien de Troyes: Once and Future Fictions*. Cambridge & New York: Cambridge University Press, 1991.

Marrou, Henri-Irénée. *Les Troubadours,* second edition. Paris: Seuil, 1971.

Minnis, A. J. *Medieval Theory of Authorship: Scholastic Literary Attitudes in the Later Middle Ages*. London: Scolar Press, 1984.

Muir, Lynette R. *Literature and Society in Medieval France: The Mirror and the Image, 1100–1500*. New York: St. Martin's Press, 1985.

Muscatine, Charles. *Chaucer and the French Tradition: A Study in Style and Meaning*. Berkeley: University of California Press, 1957.

Nichols, Stephen G. *Fission and Fusion: Mediations of Power in Medieval History and Literature*. New Haven: Yale University Press, 1986.

Nichols. *Romanesque Signs: Early Medieval Narrative and Iconography*. New Haven: Yale University Press, 1983.

Olson, Glending. *Literature as Recreation in the Later Middle Ages*. Ithaca, N.Y.: Cornell University Press, 1982.

Owen, D. D. R. *The Vision of Hell: Infernal Journeys in Medieval French Literature*. New York: Barnes & Noble, 1970.

Patterson, Lee. *Negotiating the Past: The Historical Understanding of Medieval Literature*. Madison: University of Wisconsin Press, 1987.

Patterson, W. F. *Three Centuries of French Poetic Theory: A Critical History of the Chief Arts of Poetry in France (1328–1630)*, 3 volumes. New York: Russell & Russell, 1966.

Payen, Jean Charles. *Le Moyen âge I: des origines à 1300*. Paris: Arthaud, 1970.

Poirion, Daniel. *Ecriture poétique et composition romanesque*. Orléans: Paradigme, 1994.

Poirion. *Littérature française: le moyen âge II: 1300–1480*. Paris: Arthaud, 1971.

Poirion. *Le Merveilleux dans la littéature française du moyen âge*. Paris: Presses Universitaires de France, 1982.

Poirion. *Le Moyen âge II: 1300–1480*. Paris: Arthaud, 1971.

Poirion. *Le Poète et le prince: l'évolution du lyrisme courtois de Guillaume de Machaut à Charles d'Orléans*. Paris: Presses Universitaires de France, 1965.

Poirion and Nancy Freeman Regalado, eds. *Contexts: Style and Values in Medieval Art and Literature*. New Haven: Yale University Press, 1991.

Quilligan, Maureen. *The Allegory of Female Authority: Christine de Pizan's Cité des dames*. Ithaca, N.Y.: Cornell University Press, 1991.

Rashdall, Hastings. *The Universities of Europe in the Middle Ages*, second edition, 3 volumes, edited by F. M. Powicke and A. B. Embden. Oxford: Oxford University Press, 1936.

Regalado, Nancy Freeman. *Poetic Patterns in Rutebeuf: A Study in Noncourtly Poetic Modes of the Thirteenth Century*. New Haven: Yale University Press, 1970.

Robertson, Duncan. *The Medieval Saints' Lives: Spiritual Renewal and Old French Literature*. Lexington, Ky.: French Forum, 1995.

Rosenthal, John Thomas, ed. *Medieval Women and the Sources of Medieval History*. Athens: University of Georgia Press, 1990.

Salisbury, Joyce E. *Medieval Sexuality: A Research Guide*. New York: Garland, 1990.

Sadie, Stanley, ed. *The New Grove Dictionary of Music and Musicians*, sixth edition, 20 volumes. New York: Macmillan, 1980.

Sainte-Palaye, M. de La Curne de (Jean-Baptiste de La Curne). *Dictionnaire historique de l'ancien langage françois; ou, Glossaire de la langue françoise depuis son origine jusqu'au siècle de Louis XIV*. Paris: H. Champion, 1875–1882.

Sargent-Baur, Barbara Nelson. *Brothers of Dragons: Job Dolens and François Villon*. New York: Garland, 1990.

Sigal, Gale. *Erotic Dawn-Songs of the Middle Ages: Voicing the Lyric Lady*. Gainesville: University of Florida Press, 1996.

Simone, Franco. *The French Renaissance: Medieval Tradition and Italian Influence in Shaping the Renaissance in France,* translated by H. Gaston Hall. London: Macmillan, 1969.

Solterer, Helen. *The Master and Minerva: Disputing Women in French Medieval Culture.* Berkeley: University of California Press, 1995.

Southern, R. W. *The Making of the Middle Ages.* New Haven & London: Yale University Press, 1953.

Thorndike, Lynn. *A History of Magic and Experimental Science,* 8 volumes. New York: Macmillan, 1923–1958.

Tobler, Adolf and Erhard Lommatzsch, eds. *Altfranzösisches Wörterbuch,* 10 volumes. Berlin: Weidmann, 1925 [i.e., 1915]–1989.

Uitti, Karl D. *Story, Myth, and Celebration in Old French Narrative Poetry, 1050–1200.* Princeton: Princeton University Press, 1973.

Uitti and Michelle A. Freeman. *Chrétien de Troyes Revisited.* New York: Twayne / Toronto: Maxwell Macmillan, 1995.

Vauchez, André, ed. *Dictionnaire encyclopédique du Moyen Age.* Paris & Cambridge: Editions du Cerf, 1997.

Vitz, Evelyn Birge. *Medieval Narrative and Modern Narratology: Subjects and Objects of Desire.* New York: New York University Press, 1989.

Wagner, David L., ed. *The Seven Liberal Arts in the Middle Ages.* Bloomington: Indiana University Press, 1983.

Wilkins, Nigel E. *The Lyric Art of Medieval France,* second edition. Fulbourn, U.K.: New Press, 1988.

Wimsatt, James I. *Chaucer and His French Contemporaries: Natural Music in the Fourteenth Century.* Toronto: University of Toronto Presses, 1991.

Zink, Michel. *Littérature française du moyen âge.* Paris: Presses Universitaires de France, 1992.

Zink. *Medieval French Literature: An Introduction,* translated by Jeff Rider. Binghamton, N.Y.: Medieval & Renaissance Texts & Studies, 1995.

Zumthor, Paul. *Toward a Medieval Poetics,* translated by Philip Bennett. Minneapolis: University of Minnesota Press, 1992.

Zumthor. *Histoire littéraire de la France médiévale (VIe-XIVe siècles).* Paris: Presses Universitaires de France, 1954.

Zumthor. *Langue et techniques poétiques à l'époque romane (XIe⁻XIIIe siècles).* Paris: Klincksieck, 1963.

Zumthor. *Le Masque et la lumière: la poétique des grands rhetoriqueurs.* Paris: Seuil, 1978.

Zumthor. *Histoire littéraire de la France médiévale: VIe–XIVe siècles.* Paris: Presses Universitaires de France, 1954; reprinted, Geneva: Slatkine, 1973.

Zumthor. *Speaking of the Middle Ages,* translated by Sarah White. Lincoln: University of Nebraska Press, 1986.

Contributors

Sahar Amer . . . . *University of North Carolina, Chapel Hill*

Jeanette Beer . . . . *Purdue University*

Patricia E. Black . . . . *California State University at Chico*

Matilda Tomaryn Bruckner . . . . *Boston College*

William E. Burgwinkle . . . . *University of Hawaii*

Leslie Abend Callahan. . . . . *University of Pennsylvania*

Sally Tartline Carden . . . . *University of Missouri–Rolla*

Robert L. A. Clark . . . . *Kansas State University*

Simonetta Cochis. . . . . *Transylvania University*

Leslie Dunton-Downer . . . .

Joel N. Feimer . . . . *Mercy College*

James Hala. . . . . *Drew University*

B. Gregory Hays . . . . *University of Illinois, Urbana-Champaign*

Irving A. Kelter . . . . *University of St. Thomas, Houston*

Judy Kem . . . . *Wake Forest University*

Miren Lacassagne . . . . *Université de Paris, XVII*

Norris J. Lacy . . . . *Pennsylvania State University*

James Laidlaw . . . . *University of Edinburgh*

Edgar Laird . . . . *Southwest Texas State University*

Ian S. Laurie . . . . *Flinders University*

Yvonne LeBlanc . . . . *Culinary Institute of America*

Nadia Margolis . . . . *Christine de Pizan Society*

Diane R. Marks . . . . *Brooklyn College of the City University of New York*

Michael Meckler . . . . *Ohio State University*

Elisabeth Mitchell . . . . *Harvard University*

Don A. Monson . . . . *College of William and Mary*

R. Barton Palmer. . . . . *Clemson University*

Claudia Rattazzi Papka . . . . *Columbia University*

Sheila J. Rabin . . . . *St. Peter's College*

Earl Jeffrey Richards . . . . *University of Wuppertal*

Gerald Seaman . . . . *University of Evansville*

Gale Sigal. . . . . *Wake Forest University*

Walter Simons. . . . . *Dartmouth College*

Deborah M. Sinnreich-Levi. *Stevens Institute of Technology*

Andrew Tomasello . . . . *City University of New York*

Joan B. Williamson . . . . *Long Island University*

Cumulative Index

Dictionary of Literary Biography, Volumes 1-208
Dictionary of Literary Biography Yearbook, 1980-1998
Dictionary of Literary Biography Documentary Series, Volumes 1-19

Cumulative Index

DLB before number: *Dictionary of Literary Biography,* Volumes 1-208
Y before number: *Dictionary of Literary Biography Yearbook,* 1980-1998
DS before number: *Dictionary of Literary Biography Documentary Series,* Volumes 1-19

A

Abbey, Edwin Austin 1852-1911 . . . . DLB-188

Abbey, Maj. J. R. 1894-1969 . . . . DLB-201

Abbey Press DLB-49

The Abbey Theatre and Irish Drama,
  1900-1945 . . . . DLB-10

Abbot, Willis J. 1863-1934 . . . . DLB-29

Abbott, Jacob 1803-1879 . . . . DLB-1

Abbott, Lee K. 1947- DLB-130

Abbott, Lyman 1835-1922 . . . . DLB-79

Abbott, Robert S. 1868-1940 . . . . DLB-29, 91

Abe Kōbō 1924-1993 . . . . DLB-182

Abelard, Peter circa 1079-1142? DLB-115, 208

Abelard-Schuman DLB-46

Abell, Arunah S. 1806-1888 . . . . DLB-43

Abercrombie, Lascelles 1881-1938 . . . . DLB-19

Aberdeen University Press Limited DLB-106

Abish, Walter 1931- DLB-130

Ablesimov, Aleksandr Onisimovich
  1742-1783 . . . . DLB-150

Abraham à Sancta Clara 1644-1709 . . . . . DLB-168

Abrahams, Peter 1919- DLB-117

Abrams, M. H. 1912- DLB-67

Abrogans circa 790-800 . . . . DLB-148

Abschatz, Hans Aßmann von
  1646-1699 . . . . DLB-168

Abse, Dannie 1923- DLB-27

Abutsu-ni 1221-1283 . . . . DLB-203

Academy Chicago Publishers DLB-46

Accrocca, Elio Filippo 1923- DLB-128

Ace Books DLB-46

Achebe, Chinua 1930- DLB-117

Achtenberg, Herbert 1938- DLB-124

Ackerman, Diane 1948- DLB-120

Ackroyd, Peter 1949- DLB-155

Acorn, Milton 1923-1986 . . . . DLB-53

Acosta, Oscar Zeta 1935?- DLB-82

Actors Theatre of Louisville DLB-7

Adair, Gilbert 1944- DLB-194

Adair, James 1709?-1783? DLB-30

Adam, Graeme Mercer 1839-1912 . . . . DLB-99

Adam, Robert Borthwick II 1863-1940 . . . DLB-187

Adame, Leonard 1947- DLB-82

Adamic, Louis 1898-1951 . . . . DLB-9

Adams, Abigail 1744-1818 . . . . DLB-200

Adams, Alice 1926- Y-86

Adams, Brooks 1848-1927 . . . . DLB-47

Adams, Charles Francis, Jr. 1835-1915 . . . . DLB-47

Adams, Douglas 1952- Y-83

Adams, Franklin P. 1881-1960 . . . . DLB-29

Adams, Hannah 1755-1832 . . . . DLB-200

Adams, Henry 1838-1918 . . . . DLB-12, 47, 189

Adams, Herbert Baxter 1850-1901 . . . . DLB-47

Adams, J. S. and C. [publishing house] DLB-49

Adams, James Truslow
  1878-1949 . . . . DLB-17; DS-17

Adams, John 1735-1826 . . . . DLB-31, 183

Adams, John 1735-1826 and
  Adams, Abigail 1744-1818 . . . . DLB-183

Adams, John Quincy 1767-1848 . . . . DLB-37

Adams, Léonie 1899-1988 . . . . DLB-48

Adams, Levi 1802-1832 . . . . DLB-99

Adams, Samuel 1722-1803 . . . . DLB-31, 43

Adams, Sarah Fuller Flower
  1805-1848 . . . . DLB-199

Adams, Thomas 1582 or 1583-1652 . . . . . DLB-151

Adams, William Taylor 1822-1897 . . . . DLB-42

Adamson, Sir John 1867-1950 . . . . DLB-98

Adcock, Arthur St. John 1864-1930 . . . . . DLB-135

Adcock, Betty 1938- DLB-105

Adcock, Fleur 1934- DLB-40

Addison, Joseph 1672-1719 . . . . DLB-101

Ade, George 1866-1944 . . . . DLB-11, 25

Adeler, Max (see Clark, Charles Heber)

Adonias Filho 1915-1990 . . . . DLB-145

Advance Publishing Company DLB-49

AE 1867-1935 . . . . DLB-19

Ælfric circa 955-circa 1010 . . . . DLB-146

Aeschines circa 390 B.C.-circa 320 B.C.
  . . . . DLB-176

Aeschylus
  525-524 B.C.-456-455 B.C. DLB-176

Aesthetic Poetry (1873), by Walter Pater . . . DLB-35

After Dinner Opera Company Y-92

Afro-American Literary Critics:
  An Introduction DLB-33

Agassiz, Elizabeth Cary 1822-1907 . . . . . . DLB-189

Agassiz, Jean Louis Rodolphe
  1807-1873 . . . . DLB-1

Agee, James 1909-1955 . . . . DLB-2, 26, 152

The Agee Legacy: A Conference at the University
  of Tennessee at Knoxville Y-89

Aguilera Malta, Demetrio 1909-1981 . . . . DLB-145

Ai 1947- DLB-120

Aichinger, Ilse 1921- DLB-85

Aidoo, Ama Ata 1942- DLB-117

Aiken, Conrad 1889-1973 . . . . DLB-9, 45, 102

Aiken, Joan 1924- DLB-161

Aikin, Lucy 1781-1864 . . . . DLB-144, 163

Ainsworth, William Harrison 1805-1882 . . DLB-21

Aitken, George A. 1860-1917 . . . . DLB-149

Aitken, Robert [publishing house] DLB-49

Akenside, Mark 1721-1770 . . . . DLB-109

Akins, Zoë 1886-1958 . . . . DLB-26

Aksahov, Sergei Timofeevich
  1791-1859 . . . . DLB-198

Akutagawa, Ryūnsuke 1892-1927 . . . . . . DLB-180

Alabaster, William 1568-1640 . . . . DLB-132

Alain de Lille circa 1116-1202/1203 . . . . . DLB-208

Alain-Fournier 1886-1914 . . . . DLB-65

Alanus de Insulis (see Alain de Lille)

Alarcón, Francisco X. 1954- DLB-122

Alba, Nanina 1915-1968 . . . . DLB-41

Albee, Edward 1928- DLB-7

Albert the Great circa 1200-1280 . . . . DLB-115

Alberti, Rafael 1902- DLB-108

Albertinus, Aegidius circa 1560-1620 . . . . DLB-164

Alcaeus born circa 620 B.C. DLB-176

Alcott, Amos Bronson 1799-1888 . . . . DLB-1

Alcott, Louisa May
  1832-1888 . . . . DLB-1, 42, 79; DS-14

Alcott, William Andrus 1798-1859 . . . . DLB-1

Alcuin circa 732-804 . . . . DLB-148

Alden, Henry Mills 1836-1919 . . . . DLB-79

Alden, Isabella 1841-1930 . . . . DLB-42

Alden, John B. [publishing house] DLB-49

Alden, Beardsley and Company DLB-49

Aldington, Richard
  1892-1962 . . . . DLB-20, 36, 100, 149

Aldis, Dorothy 1896-1966 . . . . DLB-22

Aldis, H. G. 1863-1919 . . . . DLB-184

Aldiss, Brian W. 1925- DLB-14

B

N

ISBN 0-7876-3102-7

90000

9 780787 631024